Contents

Economics of Change in Less Developed Countries

DAVID COLMAN AND FREDERICK NIXSON

University of Manchester

Second Edition

Philip Allan/Barnes & Noble Books

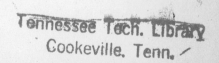

First published 1978 by

PHILIP ALLAN PUBLISHERS
MARKET PLACE
DEDDINGTON
OXFORD OX5 4SE

Reprinted 1980, 1982, 1985

Second edition published 1986 by
PHILIP ALLAN PUBLISHERS LIMITED

and in the USA by
BARNES & NOBLE BOOKS
81 Adams Drive
Totowa
New Jersey 07512

© David Colman and Frederick Nixson 1978, 1986

British Library Cataloguing in Publication Data

Colman, David, *1940–*
  Economics of change in less developed
  countries — 2nd ed.
  1. Developing countries — Economic
  conditions
  I. Title   II. Nixson, F.I.
  330.9172'4   HC59.7

ISBN 0-86003-064-4
ISBN 0-86003-166-7 Pbk

Library of Congress Cataloging in Publication Data

Colman, David.
  Economics of change in less developed
  countries

  Bibliography: p.
  1. Developing countries — Economic
  Conditions.
  2. Economic development. I. Nixson, F.I. II Title.
  HC59.7.C595 1985   330.9172'4   84-24361

  ISBN 0-389-20548-6
  ISBN 0-389-20550-8 Pbk

Typeset by MHL Typesetting Ltd, Coventry
Printed and bound in Great Britain by The Camelot Press, Southampton

Introduction

It is no exaggeration to state that development economics is at present going through a crisis. The recent spate of articles on the evolution and current state (and status) of development economics as a separate sub-discipline reflects the atmosphere of questioning and self-doubt amongst mainstream development economists (see, for example, Seers 1979; Streeten 1979; Hirschman 1981; Weisskopf 1983) and, in part, is a reflection of both the growing influence of the neoclassical revival and the increasingly penetrating critiques of radical political economists.

From a neoclassical perspective, Little (1982) has mounted an onslaught on all forms of structuralist analysis and Lal (1983, p.109) has argued that '. . . the demise of development economics is likely to be conducive to the health of both the economics and the economies of developing countries'. From a radical perspective, Weisskopf (1983, pp.895–6) relates the crisis in development economics to the 'general decline of the liberal centre in economics and politics during the last 10–15 years' and argues that 'liberal technocratic advisers are not in a position to guide a beneficent state looking after the general public interest' because they are 'prisoners of the political powers that be. Policy is ultimately shaped most by those who have the greatest economic and political resources at their disposal . . .'

Development economics, of course, has its defenders. Toye (1984) and Livingstone (1981) both see the discipline surviving and flourishing within the broad spectrum of development studies. Sen (1983, p.753) argues that 'there is still much relevance in the broad policy themes, which traditional development economics has emphasised' and Lewis (1984) concludes that 'Development Economics is not at its most spectacular, but is alive and well'.

There can surely be no doubt as to the vigour of the debate within the profession and, taken with the (seemingly exponential) rate of growth of publication of theoretical and empirical studies, this can be interpreted as a sign of health, rather than decline or demise.

This is not, of course, to deny that there are not major problems of analysis and policy prescription facing social scientists interested in development, and a number of the more important of them are discussed at some length in this book – for example, the debate over the interaction between external and internal factors in the emergence and continuation of international poverty and inequality, the choice between inward- and outward-looking development strategies and the more general confrontation between neoclassical and non-neoclassical theorising. It is our belief that the conflicts of perspective and ideology – neoclassical, structuralist, neo-Marxist, Marxist – produce greater understanding and awareness of the nature of contemporary development problems and, hopefully but less certainly, highlight possible solutions.

Since the attainment of political independence, the majority of LDCs have consciously attempted to change the structure of their economies. Many of them have achieved impressive rates of growth of national income and this has been accompanied by, and has led to, often quite significant structural changes. Change has thus been rapid and substantial, although not necessarily in a direction that everyone would consider desirable from a normative standpoint.

As we emphasised in the Introduction to the first edition of this book, one of our primary objectives is to analyse the changes that are taking place in LDCs at the present time, to examine the problems that the processes of change are generating, and to look at the agents of change themselves. Our own thinking on these issues, as reflected in the structure and contents of the book, was influenced by the observation (Szentes 1971, Part 2, Chapter 1) that there are two aspects or sides of underdevelopment: the external, international aspect which, from the historical point of view, is of primary importance; and the internal aspect which, from the point of view of future development, is of increasing importance. While not in any way wishing to minimise the need for changes in the structure of international economic and political relations (and the relationships between rich and poor countries are discussed in Chapter 5 on trade and Chapter 6 on indebtedness) we have tended to concentrate discussion on the internal aspect of the development process. Thus, we pay particular attention to the question of economic inequality within LDCs and the impact that different income distributions are likely to have on the development process. We analyse the process of agricultural and industrial development within LDCs and, although we place particular emphasis on one of the major external agents of change, the TNC (transnational corporation), we are most interested in the impact of its activities on the nature and characteristics of the development process within LDCs themselves.

The emphasis on internal socio-political and economic changes is because it is apparent that it is the structure of the LDC that determines the ultimate impact of external forces or international 'shocks' on the characteristics and direction of the development process. In the 1970s, for example, some LDCs were better able to cope with, and adjust to, massive oil price rises than were others; some LDCs have large absolute international debts but are not perceived as having a 'debt problem'; some

LDCs have managed to sustain a tough bargaining stance vis-à-vis TNCs and have enjoyed net benefits as a result. This is not to deny the existence of advice, persuasion, coercion and even destabilisation that emanates from external sources (bilateral and multilateral aid agencies, TNCs, the secret services of foreign powers). Nor is it to deny the articulation of interests between ruling elites in LDCs and external agents. But in the last analysis, it is the government of the LDC that is responsible for the economic policies implemented and the development objectives pursued.

Although it is the intention of this book to concentrate attention on the internal aspects of the development process, this should not be taken to mean that we are primarily concerned with policy issues. Obviously, we have not entirely been able to escape saying what we think LDCs should be doing. But we feel that in the development literature, as we note in Chapter 1, too much emphasis has been placed on policy prescription, without any realistic assessment made of the political acceptability of such recommendations, and with too little consideration of what we call the historico-analytic factor. There have been many impressive reports by international bodies advocating specific development policies for LDCs, but they have often had a greater effect on academic economists than on the countries at which they were aimed. All too often policy recommendations have been made without due consideration of their political acceptability to the authorities in the LDCs, or their feasibility, given international pressures. In development economics in particular, neglect of the political environment is fatal when it comes to making policy recommendations.

One other point needs to be made. We do not regard this book as a textbook on the principles of economic development, as we believe that there is no generally agreed body of theory or doctrine that is unambiguously 'development economics'. Rather, we have focused our attention upon the process of change affecting LDCs and upon those issues with which we feel that readers of the contemporary literature should have some familiarity. Nevertheless, our efforts to work within a strict word limit have required considerable selectivity in the topics covered. This is regrettable but unavoidable.

References

Hirschman, A.O. (1981) 'The rise and decline of development economics', in *Essays in Trespassing: Economics to Politics and Beyond*, Cambridge University Press.

Lal, D. (1983) *The Poverty of 'Development Economics'*, Institute of Economic Affairs.

Lewis, W.A. (1984) 'The state of development theory', *American Economic Review*, Vol. 74, No. 1, March.

Little, I.M.D. (1982) *Economic Development: Theory, Policy, and International Relations*, New York, Basic Books.

Livingstone, I. (1981) 'The development of development economics', *ODI Review*, Vol. 2.

Seers, D. (1979) 'The birth, life and death of development economics', *Development and Change*, Vol. 10.

Sen, A.K. (1983) 'Development: which way now?', *Economic Journal*, Vol. 93, No. 372, December.

Streeten, P. (1979) 'Development ideas in historical perspective', in K.Q. Hill (ed.) *Toward a New Strategy for Development: A Rothko Chapel Colloquium*, New York, Pergamon Books.

Szentes, T. (1971) *The Political Economy of Underdevelopment*, Budapest, Akademiai Kiado.

Toye, J. (1984) *A Defence of Development Economics*, Inaugural Lecture, University College of Swansea, Mimeo.

Weisskopf, T.E. (1983) 'Economic development and the development of economics: some observations from the left', *World Development*, Vol. 11, No. 10, October.

Acknowledgements

The rewriting of this book has made considerable demands on both of our families and it is out of more than a sense of obligation that we acknowledge their forebearance.

Again, Philip Leeson was unstinting in the time and effort that he put into reading and commenting on various drafts. His suggestions always led to improvements. We would also like to thank Colin Kirkpatrick for his contribution to Chapter 12. The normal disclaimer, of course, applies and we accept full responsibility for any omissions and errors.

Jennifer Vaughan has not only done much of the typing of the several drafts, but she has provided invaluable help with the additional tasks involved in preparing a book. Further typing and encouraging support has been given by Sue Massey to whom we likewise wish to express our warm appreciation. Thanks are also due to Judy Darnton, Jean Ashton and Elizabeth Lee for their assistance.

We acknowledge, with thanks, the permission of the following publishers to reprint various tables reproduced in the book: Cambridge University Press (Tables 3.3 and 5.1); Commonwealth Secretariat (Tables 6.4 and 6.5); Greenwood Press (Table 4.1); Johns Hopkins Press (Table 1.1); Methuen (Table 7.2); Oxford University Press (Tables 3.1, 4.3, 4.4, 6.2, 7.3, 8.1, 8.2, 9.6 and 9.9); Praeger Publishers (Table 1.2); Stanford University Press (Table 3.2); OECD (Tables 5.5, 6.1, 6.3, 10.2 and 10.3).

This book is dedicated to Andrew, Jonathan, Lucy, Mathew and Sophie of the younger generation.

DAVID COLMAN
FREDERICK NIXSON
University of Manchester
September 1986

List of abbreviations

BIS	Bank of International Settlements
BMR	Basal Metabolic Rate
CFF	Compensatory Finance Facility
CGFPI	Consultative Group on Food Production and Investment
CGIAR	Consultative Group on International Agricultural Research
CIMMYT	International Maize and Wheat Improvement Centre
CMEA	Council for Mutual Economic Assistance
DAC	Development Assistance Committee
DC	Developed Country
DFI	Direct Foreign Investment
EEC	European Economic Community
EOI	Export-Oriented Industrialisation
FAO	Food and Agriculture Organisation
GATT	General Agreement on Trade and Tariffs
GDP	Gross Domestic Product
GNI	Gross National Income
GNP	Gross National Product
GSP	Generalised Systems of Preference
IBRD	International Bank for Reconstruction and Development (World Bank)
ICA	International Commodity Agreement
IFAD	International Fund for Agricultural Development
ILO	International Labour Office
IMF	International Monetary Fund
IPC	Integrated Programme for Commodities
IRRI	International Rice Research Institute
ISA	International Sugar Agreement
ISI	Import Substituting Industrialisation
IWA	International Wheat Agreement
LDC	Less Developed Country
MNC	Multinational Corporation
NBTT	Net Barter Terms of Trade
NI	National Income
NIC	Newly Industrialised Country
NIEO	New International Economic Order
NNI	Net National Income
NODC	Non-Oil Developing Country
ODA	Official Development Aid
OECD	Organisation for Economic and Cultural Development
OPEC	Organisation of Petroleum Exporting Countries
PRC	People's Republic of China
RWG	Redistribution with Growth
TNC	Transnational Corporation
UN	United Nations
UNCTAD	United Nations Conference on Trade and Development
UNECAFE	United Nations Economic Commission for Asia and the Far East
UNECLA	United Nations Economic Commission for Latin America
UNIDO	United Nations Industrial Development Organisation
UNRISD	United Nations Research Institute for Social Development
USDA	United States Department of Agriculture
WHO	World Health Organisation

1

The concept and measurement of development

At the outset it is necessary to clarify the meaning of 'development'. While this is by no means a simple matter, and involves a certain amount of controversy, there is a broad measure of agreement about it (see Section 1.1). Having defined development, the problem is the way in which it should be measured. As will become clear in Section 1.2, however, this is even more problematic. In fact the direct measurement of development turns out to be unmanageable and, instead, various rather crude indicators have to be used – indicators are measurable variables which are assumed to be directly correlated with development. As will be seen, there are doubts as to whether any available indicators are particularly highly correlated with development, but there is a (rather grudging) acceptance that national income per person is as useful as any; certainly it is the most widely used. This measure of agreement is important because it provides the essential requirement for the classification of countries according to their state, or rate, of development.

In classifying countries by their state of development a strict numerical ranking could be adopted, but more usually they are arbitrarily classified into groups. A commonly used device is to classify countries, other than the centrally planned ones, into two groups: those countries with the highest per capita incomes (almost exclusively the industrialised capitalist ones) are classified as developed countries; the larger number of countries which rank lower on this scale are classified as developing, less-developed, or underdeveloped (according to the preferred terminology). While at many points in the book we shall accept this crude division of countries into two groups, it is recognised that the groups are by no means homogeneous. In particular, there are differences between the less-developed countries; thus, where it is considered appropriate, further arbitrary subdivisions can be made within the group of developing countries. This further subdivision may be made according to the per capita income criterion, as for example when employing the UN categories of low, middle, upper-middle, and high income developing countries. Alternatively, subdivision may be made according to some other characteristic,

1

such as when distinguishing the oil-exporting developing countries from those without oil, or in separating developing countries with a high proportion of industrial exports from those almost wholly dependent upon primary commodity exports. While we recognise the arbitrariness of the distinction between developed and less-developed countries, and also between different categories of less-developed countries (LDCs), we accept the conventions about the usefulness of such a distinction throughout this book.

1.1 What is Development?

Development can be considered either as a process of improvement with respect to a set of values or, when comparing the relative levels of development of different countries, as a comparative state of being with respect to such values. The values in question relate to desired conditions in society. Self-evidently, there is no universal agreement about what these desired conditions should be; individuals certainly have different preferences regarding their lifestyle and relationships with the rest of society; and through their political manifestos and the policies operated by government, nations express different collective (majority or minority) views about the desired state of society − views which change through time. Inevitably, therefore, the rate or the relative level of a country's development are normative concepts whose definition and measurement depend upon the value judgements of the analysts involved.

The assertion that development is a normative concept which will be measured differently by different people constitutes a serious charge but is one which affects all areas of the social sciences and is not unique to development studies. For as Myrdal observed (1970, p. 42), the fact is 'that value premises are needed even in the theoretical stage of establishing facts and factual relations. Answers can only be given when questions have been asked. A view is impossible except from a viewpoint'. Not only are value judgements an inevitable part of deciding what concepts and relationships should be employed to answer questions such as 'what causes development?' or 'has development occurred in any specific instance?', but value judgements are also necessary in deciding how to represent concepts empirically. For example, in defining gross domestic product, should unpaid housewives' services be included, and if so, how should they be valued? Similarly, what procedures should be used to measure the volume and value of food produced for own consumption and not exchanged in the market? These questions can only be resolved judgementally, there being no uniquely appropriate procedures.

It has thus to be recognised that value judgements are inescapable elements of factual study in the social sciences. They are, however, especially prominent elements in development economics precisely because a central aspect of the subject is to formulate criteria for development, and also because many of the commonly chosen criteria are difficult to define and measure. Consequently, there would appear to be plenty of scope for judgemental disagreements about what development is, what are its most important goals, and what are the relationships between aims. Certainly there has recently been extensive debate about these issues in the literature (see below), but this, while demonstrating the existence of disagreements about how development is caused and what weights should be assigned to specific goals, nevertheless demonstrates a broad measure of agreement about the main categories to be achieved in development.

Possibly this measure of agreement is not surprising if, as Seers has said (in Baster 1972), 'Surely the values we need are staring us in the face, as soon as we ask ourselves: what are the necessary conditions for a universally accepted aim, the realisation of the potential of human personality?' Based on this premise, that the ultimate aim and yardstick of development is that implied by the question, Seers identifies a number of objectives for development in the poorest countries. These are: (1) that family incomes should be adequate to provide a subsistence package of food, shelter, clothing and footwear; (2) that jobs should be available to all family heads, not only because this will ensure a distribution of income such that subsistence consumption levels will be generally achieved but because a job is something without which personality cannot develop; (3) that access to education should be increased and literacy ratios raised; (4) that the populace should be given an opportunity to participate in government; and (5) that national independence should be achieved in 'the sense that the views of other governments do not largely predetermine one's own government's decisions'. As progress is made towards the economic goals, that is as 'undernourishment, unemployment and inequality dwindle', Seers argues that the 'educational and political aims become increasingly important objectives of development'.

Seers's list of development criteria or objectives is similar in basic respects to those suggested by others. Myrdal, for example, adopts as 'instrumental value premises' (i.e. criteria for assessing development) certain 'modernisation ideals' which are (1) rationality, (2) development and development planning, (3) rise of productivity, (4) rise of levels of living, (5) social and economic equalisation, (6) improved institutions and attitudes, (7) national consolidation, (8) national independence, (9) democracy at the grass roots, and (10) social discipline.

Similarly, to Streeten, who participated in the preparation of Myrdal's magnum opus *Asian Drama* (1968), 'development means modernisation, and modernisation means transformation of human beings. Development as an objective and development as a process both embrace a change in fundamental attitudes to life and work, and in social, cultural and political

institutions' (Streeten 1972, p.30). More specifically (p.15), Streeten sees
the process of development in terms of progress in a number of interrelated dimensions: (1) output and incomes, (2) conditions of production,
(3) levels of living (including nutrition, housing, health and education),
(4) attitudes to work, (5) institutions, and (6) policies.[1] Streeten's concept has
evolved into what is now known as 'the basic needs' approach to development (see, for example, Streeten *et al.* 1981 and Stewart 1985). According
to this, development is to be measured or implemented with respect to the
increased satisfaction of basic needs (as defined in terms of the various
development values listed above). This automatically gives great weight to
the interests of the poorer sections of society, since it is there that basic
needs are least likely to be met. It is an influential concept which has
attempted to steer the focus of development away from growth of GNP to
the ways that the benefits of growth are distributed and to the ways that
they contribute to desirable social and political change. We return to the
question of basic needs in Chapter 3.

Little purpose would be served by presenting yet other proposed lists of
development criteria. They would inevitably include many of the components common to the lists above, and would tend to lend some support
to Seers's assertion that the criteria of development are largely self-
evident. Whether this is true or not, the lists of values presented do
indicate the extent to which there is agreement about certain key criteria,
and about development as a multidimensional process or set of objectives,
in which the dimensions are economic, social, political and cultural in the
widest sense of these terms. But the lists also indicate clearly that strong
personal values intrude into conceptions of development. This is well
borne out in Myrdal's approach; even his initial general characterisation
of development in terms of 'modernisation ideals' amounts to a strong
value judgement, namely that modern methods and attitudes (presumably
as revealed in some of the wealthier nations) are preferable to more traditional approaches (as found in the poorer countries?). While a majority of
people may agree with this value premise, there are undeniably others
who would dispute it. The personal nature of the value judgements is even
more evident in some of the individual criteria. 'Social discipline', which
for Myrdal largely involves stamping out corruption in what he calls the
'soft state', is liable to widely differing interpretations. Similarly, 'national
consolidation' and 'democracy at the grass roots' have different meanings
to different people and political systems. Indeed, there may be an innate
tendency for the development criteria proposed by private individuals,
such as development economists, to diverge considerably from those of
political authorities which make policy choices from the viewpoint of
needing to promote the continuity and development of the nation state.

It should also be reiterated that there is no agreement as to what weights
to assign to each of the individual objectives for the operational purposes

of policy formulation and measurement of development. This is partly due to the inevitable differences in personal values, but it is also due to the need for the weights to be changed with changes in the level of development. Whatever its causes, this problem of not being able readily to represent development as a single variable creates serious problems in the study of development. This emerges most clearly when we examine theories of development which, as is discussed in Chapter 2, tend to circumvent the problem by analysing only selected subsets of development objectives. The problem also poses appreciable difficulties for measuring development – an issue taken up in the next section of this chapter.

One important conclusion which emerges from the attempt to define development is that as a process it is not synonymous with economic growth. It is conceivable that, in a particular country, average GNP per capita might have risen, while at the same time income inequality increased, the poor became poorer, and negative progress been made to other development goals. Such a situation might be classed as economic growth with negative development in that, although average incomes may have risen, the economic lot of the mass of the population would have deteriorated and negative or no progress would have been made in transforming personal attitudes and institutions in the manner required by the modernisation ideals. Conversely, it is possible to envisage development with negative growth. This might occur where a major restructuring occurs in attitudes, political institutions and production relations (by such means as land reform and/or collectivisation) which creates the conditions for future development, but at a short-run cost of reduced GNP due to disruption of the previous production and distribution system. In this context Streeten (1972, p.31) has argued, 'Just as there can be economic growth without development, there can be development without economic growth'. Not everyone would agree with Streeten in this respect, however. Szentes (1971, p.14), for example, argued tellingly that:

> Any distinction between the theories of 'development' and 'growth' can at best only be accepted for practical reasons . . . however by no means, as a scientific distinction. The terminological distinction on a semantic basis is unacceptable, because development always and everywhere involves and presupposes the dialectic of quantitative and qualitative changes, of evolution and revolution. And even if a purely quantitative 'growth' can be observed in a given place and at a given time within the framework of the existing structure or system, it is not only the consequences of a previous qualitative change but it also inevitably paves the way for a new one.

Development economists were perhaps rather slow in appreciating the full implication of this remark. It is only recently that a number of writers have begun to question the generally accepted distinction between growth and development (see, for example, Palma 1978; Bernstein 1979; Warren

1980; and Nixson 1986) and to pursue to their logical conclusion the implications of the concepts of normative development outlined, as above, for example, by Seers.

The recognition that economic growth, of and by itself, did not automatically lead to the wider, normatively defined goals of development was an important step in the evolution of the study of development in the postwar period. However, the increasingly abstract and utopian definitions of development popularised in the literature pose a number of theoretical problems and force upon us the need to reconsider the concept of development. Four points in particular require brief mention (for a fuller discussion, see Nixson 1986).

Firstly, the now popular concept of development refers to an ideal world or state of affairs that is both ahistorical and apolitical – ahistorical because it postulates an idealised structure that does not and never has existed, and apolitical because development is defined in an abstract sense and is not related to any particular political/social/institutional structure. The goals of development enumerated by Seers, Streeten, Myrdal, etc., *are* of great significance and importance, but we must raise the question as to which specific socio-political framework will best permit the achievement of such objectives. The undesirable features of economic growth and structural change are not the inevitable consequence of these forces as such but are, rather, the characteristic features of the specific process of capitalist development as it is unfolding in contemporary LDCs. This is not necessarily an argument for an alternative form of socio-political organisation or development ('socialist' development is not free from its own problems) but it is an argument for emphasising the fact that 'development' does not occur in a political vacuum.

Secondly, this idealised concept of development goes some way to explaining the current state of pessimism in development economics (see Introduction). 'Development' in many LDCs has turned out to be very different from what was expected or hoped for by many development practitioners, but development economics as such can hardly be blamed for present conditions in LDCs, however misguided some of its early analyses and overoptimistic its policy pronouncements may have been (for a contrary view, see Lal 1983; Little 1982). Development theory may well have 'failed' in the sense that it gave overly simple or misleading explanations of the problems of development and underdevelopment, but it was/is *not* the cause of those problems.

Thirdly, there is a marked tendency in development economics, of both neoclassical and structuralist/dependency varieties, to confuse explanation (the historico-analytic) with policy prescription. Too often we find development specialists confusing what *ought* to be with what *is* (Lall 1976, p.182). This is not to argue against policy prescription *per se*, for as Leeson (1983, p.24) has argued: 'Certainly most development economists would reject the notion that policy advice is not a proper sphere for the involvement of the profession'. However, it is worth noting that much writing masquerading as analysis is in fact far more concerned with policy prescription, and we must avoid confusing the desire for a better world with the fuller understanding of the very imperfect reality. In this book the emphasis is firmly historico-analytic rather than policy prescriptive.

Fourthly, development economics all too often appears to assume that structural problems have somehow been 'solved' in the developed (capitalist) economies and that their problem is 'merely' one of ensuring self-sustaining and continuous growth (or, at its simplest level, that 'developed' economies have, by definition, overcome the problems of 'development'). This is clearly not the case. Problems of unemployment, inequality, deprivation and various kinds of structural disequilibria (relating to the balance of payments, deindustrialisation etc.) clearly exist in many of the developed capitalist economies. These major problems are rooted in the structure of those economies and they are not 'solved' by 'development'; indeed, they arise as a consequence of specific forms of development both within those economies and in the wider global economy.

What implications do the above arguments have for our concept of 'development'? The main point to emphasise is that development is not smooth, unidirectional and non-problematic but is rather, to quote Joseph Schumpeter (who published his theory of economic development in 1911)[2], 'lopsided, discontinuous, disharmonious'. Development is a dialectical process in that every change in the economy brings with it new problems and adjustments – to paraphrase Streeten (1983), there are always problems to every solution. It is contradictory and complex, and these aspects of the development process are best highlighted by viewing development as an historical process which is not consciously willed by anyone (Arndt 1981, p.460). The concept of economic development as an activity consciously engaged in mainly, but not solely, by governments, with the intention of approaching or reaching certain specific objectives (the normative definition of development outlined above), complements the alternative concept of development as an historical process. However, it must be recognised that once the abstract objectives of development have been defined, the concrete, specific socio-economic and socio-political structures *within which it is believed that such objectives can best be realised* must also be made explicit.

1.2 Measuring Development

Interest in measuring development is intense. Everyone who reads this book is likely to have accepted some statistical notion about the level of development of his/her own country in comparison with certain others, and will either feel satisfaction or concern about its relative position. At a national level such pride or concern has a central role in the political process and in engaging electoral support for the policies of political parties or governments. As in development studies, the focal point of concern is often the statistical evidence of a widening gap between the standards of living in the richer (so-called developed) countries and the poorer (less developed) ones (LDCs).

The fact, is, however, that it is extremely difficult to measure comparative levels of development. The statistical methods available may be thought fairly reliable for obtaining acceptable measures of rates of growth of living standards and of ordinal rankings as to whether one country is more developed than another, but they exhibit grave deficiencies when used as cardinal measures of by how much or how many times one country is more developed than any other.

The fundamental cause of the measurement difficulty lies with the definition of development. As identified in the previous section, many of the criteria or objectives by which development is to be judged or measured are qualitative ones. Such criteria as the standard of living, health levels, the educational level, and the extent of grass-roots participation in government are all qualitative ones which cannot be measured directly. They have to be measured indirectly using indicators which are directly measurable quantities. Thus among the many possible indicators of a 'nation's state of physical health' might be included the number of people per trained doctor, the rate of child mortality, or the average life expectancy; and for the standard of living one might use such indicators as average national income per person, the proportion of families with piped water to their living quarters, the proportion of households supplied with electricity, and so on.

This multiplicity of possible indicators for any given general dimension of development simply compounds the problems arising from the existence of several general dimensions.[3] Firstly, no quantitative indicator is capable of exactly measuring a qualitative criterion. Secondly, no one indicator can conceivably approximate the qualitative levels attained with respect to all the major dimensions of development, especially when it is remembered that these are economic, social, political and cultural. Thirdly, there are appreciable difficulties in deriving a method (weighting scheme) whereby various indicators for different qualities can be added together into a single index of a country's level of development.

Since the concept of development only acquires substance through a process of measurement, it is important (in the light of the foregoing statement of the problems of measurement) to examine briefly some of the major alternative proposals for development indicators, and some of the criticisms levelled at them. Most effort to date has been devoted to the development of economic indicators, and this is reflected by the fact that most of the rest of this section is devoted to economic indicators, and little to political indicators, social indicators or to combinations of these.

Economic Indicators of Development

It is natural that analysts should want to employ a single indicator of development rather than a set of separate ones. It is attractive not only because it simplifies (at least in a mechanical sense) the task of producing theoretical models of development but also because it facilitates communication and thought to consider a single series of numbers rather than several simultaneously.

In practice, one indicator has dominated all others, and that is national income or gross national product (GNP) per capita.[4] This is the name given to a series which can be calculated for any country, using a specific basic set of measurement rules which have been devised in the Western industrial countries to measure their overall level of income or production. It is important to note that the measurement rules used for adding together the values of different economic activities were not derived with any concept of development in mind, but to produce indicators of annual levels of production and income. Consequently, a love–hate relationship has developed over the use of GNP as a development indicator. In its favour (1) it is an indicator of a set of key activities, the provision of goods and services, an increase in which is almost[5] a necessary condition for development; (2) the measurement rules, which are complex, have evolved over time and are well known and understood; and (3) most member countries of the United Nations (UN) produce estimates of GNP for inclusion in UN official statistics.

Against GNP as a development indicator are the facts that (1) it is an indicator only of some economic aspects of development – it makes no allowance for changing income distribution – and it has no direct implications for the other non-economic criteria; (2) it is a heavily value-loaded indicator, and the subjective element is larger in countries with poor statistics and large subsistence sectors than in countries where a much smaller proportion of transactions bypass the market; and (3) irrespective of any deficiencies GNP may have as a measure of national economic activity, there are additional problems in using it for making international comparisons. Most of these points are perfectly obvious ones – but in view of the frequency with which GNP is encountered in international 'league tables' of development, they deserve a certain amount of amplification.

Regarding the first point, there is no way in which a simple total of the value of goods and services produced can reflect details of income distribution. It is, therefore, quite possible for any increase in average GNP per capita to be due to the increased incomes and consumption of only a relatively few richer members of society and to be accompanied by a worsening income distribution (as Chapter 3 on economic inequality reports, this relationship may even be characteristic of certain stages of development). In this case, depending upon the weight that would be assigned to income inequality as a criterion for development, it is possible for an increase in GNP per capita apparently to signal an increase in social welfare when it has in fact diminished.

The question of the value-loaded nature of GNP as a development indicator is a somewhat broader one, but basically it revolves around the appropriateness of using market prices to value social welfare. Thus, returning to the question of income distribution, it is observed that the prices and quantities of goods and services consumed depend upon the prevailing income distribution. To the extent that the distribution may be highly unequal, increases in measured GNP may give a poor indication of the extent to which social need is increasingly satisfied; certainly, at any level of GNP the pattern of consumption might be markedly changed by altering the distribution of income. This consideration is amplified by major doubts arising in relation to the possibility that, because of market imperfections, the market prices used for valuing components of GNP are appreciably different from the appropriate social valuations. Not only may prices be distorted by the existence of monopolistic forces, by policy intervention, and by the possibility that the pricing of public goods may be to some extent arbitrary, but also 'many aspects of the quality of life and the environment fall outside the market calculus' (Baster 1972, p.3) and therefore are assigned a zero price, which clearly undervalues their social worth. Thus there are a number of well-recognised sources of potential bias in GNP as a measure of the social value of national income.

In making international comparisons of development levels, the general procedure is to take each country's own estimate of GNP calculated in local currency units and then to convert these into some common currency unit, usually the US dollar, for comparative purposes. It has to be recognised that there are several sources of bias in this procedure. One of these is that the subjective elements in the measurement procedure may be resolved differently in different countries, resulting in a lack of standardisation between countries' estimates. In richer countries a high proportion of domestic services are purchased in the form of washing machines, vacuum cleaners and refrigerators; housing construction and repair costs are mainly in the form of purchased inputs; and food is largely purchased rather than home produced. Thus a high proportion of the consumption of these services is provided in the form of traded labour and consumer products which will be recorded by the normal national accounting procedures.

However, this is not so in poor countries where only a small proportion of such services will be purchased. This is particularly significant (because it constitutes a high proportion of total product) in the case of food, a high proportion of which is consumed directly by the producer and his family. But it is also true of house construction, household and other services, many of which are provided by family labour in LDCs, Hence in poor countries a high proportion of these important services is supplied without involving trade of a conventionally accountable type. If, as is often the case, due to lack of statistical evidence, national income accounts omit or inadequately allow for the consumption of such non-traded goods and services, the resultant GNP estimates will be biased in favour of the rich and against the poor countries precisely because a higher proportion of total economic activity takes a non-traded form in the latter. This is a serious problem, as Seers describes it (in Baster 1972, p.23):

> But what are all the voluminous tables of national income accounts really worth? So far as the Third World is concerned, much of what they ought to cover is virtually outside the scope of official statistics. This applies above all to output of domestic foodstuffs, even the staples, let alone subsidiary crops which come under the general heading of 'market gardening' (American 'truck farming'), not to speak of fish, forest products, etc. Extremely rough methods of estimation are often used, much of the output being assumed to rise in pro-portion to the increase in rural population, an increase which is in turn assumed to be some constant arbitrary rate in the absence of registration of births and deaths, or data on migration. Secondly, we know very little about construction in the countryside by the farming community itself; this apparently amounts to a good deal if one takes account not only of building houses but also clearing land, digging wells and ditches, constructing fences and hedges, etc. Thirdly, there are practically no basic data on domestic service and other personal ser-vices, even those which are remunerated.

Another bias arising from the use of national income accounting statistics as welfare measures is that some items which are in fact necessary and unavoidable costs of living are treated implicitly as benefits. This is true of the costs of travelling to work. To the extent that such costs may be a significant item in the accounts of rich countries and negligible in poor countries, comparison of GNP levels will exaggerate the extent of the gap between rich and poor.

There is also a major complex of biases for comparative use of national accounts statistics which arises from the choice of an exchange rate to con-vert from local currency units to (say) US dollars. In the first place, where a country operates a multiple exchange rate system it may be difficult to decide which rate to use. For example (Open University 1975, Table 2), Colombia apparently operated four separate and highly variable exchange rates for different classes of transaction, so that it may be necessary to impute an exchange rate for the sort of purpose being considered here.

More importantly, the choice of any exchange rate carries with it certain implications for the relative prices of non-traded goods and services which may be quite inappropriate and misleading. Consider, for example, an exchange rate between the pound sterling and US dollar of £1 = $1.40. A simplified interpretation of this is that (before allowing for transport costs) £1 will buy for a Briton a basket of traded American goods which would cost an American $1.40, and conversely $1.40 will buy a basket of British traded goods which would cost a Briton £1. Applying this exchange rate to an estimate of UK GNP to convert it to its dollar equivalent involves implicitly assuming that £1's worth of those British goods and services which are not traded would cost $1.40 in the USA. This is unlikely to be true. A pound's worth of car servicing in the UK may cost substantially more than $1.40 if carried out in the USA, and the same with house construction costs, electrical repairs and so forth. In that case comparing US national income per capita with the dollar equivalent (at £1 = $1.40) of UK national income per capita will overstate the margin by which the average American is better off than his British counterpart.

The magnitude of this class of bias is likely to be far larger when comparing income levels in the USA to those of the poorest countries. Indeed, the absurd results which could occur from a welfare interpretation of such comparisons are well demonstrated by Usher (1966). He reproduces UN data which indicate that for 1963 the USA had a GNP of $2,790 per capita and Ethiopia, toward the bottom of the league, only $40 per capita. As Usher asks, what conceivable meaning can be accorded to the notion that the average Ethiopian lived on 11 cents a day? A person would have starved in the USA unless he had far more than that, and yet most Ethiopians survived. The only possible conclusion is that Ethiopian prices for basic commodities were much lower relative to those in the USA than implied by the exchange rate, that the dollar cost of subsistence was much lower in Ethiopia than the USA, and that the implied ratio of American to Ethiopian living standards of 70 to 1 was a sizeable exaggeration. It is obvious that if Ethiopia's output of goods and services were valued at American prices in the first place, instead of being valued at local prices and then converted at the dollar exchange rate, then its national income would appear substantially larger than one-seventieth of the USA's. By the same token, valuing the USA's output of goods and services at Ethiopian prices would appreciably reduce the estimate of their value to Ethiopian output.

These observations are the *raison d'être* of the so-called 'binary comparison method for adjusting GNP measures. This method has been applied by Usher (1966), and more recently by Kravis *et al.* (1975 and 1978) as part of the UN International Comparison Project, to compare the value of gross domestic product (GDP) of various countries to that of the USA. It involves first obtaining what might be called the 'conventional' estimates of GDP by converting GDP in local currency (with all components of output valued at local prices) to US dollar values at the prevailing currency exchange rates. These are then compared to estimates of

GDP obtained directly in dollar terms by valuing the outputs of each country at the prices of comparable outputs in the USA.[6] While the explanation of the method by Kravis *et al.* (1975) clearly indicates that this is by no means as simple as it sounds (and many complex statistical adjustments are needed), this alternative measure does grapple with the fundamental weakness of the conventional measure, which is that it makes no correction for the fact that at any given exchange rate the relative prices (expressed in either currency) of goods and services in any pair of countries may diverge widely, especially between a DC and an LDC.[7]

From Table 1.1. it can be seen that the estimated ratio of the 1970 GDP per capita of individual countries to that of the USA under the conventional pricing rule was significantly different from that obtained by pricing all national output at US (i.e. international) prices. The measure of the difference for each country is shown by the exchange rate deviation index. For example, Kenyan GDP per capita in 1970 was conventionally estimated at only 6.9% of the USA level, whereas valuing all outputs at international prices raised this 2.32 times to 15.9%. For India the effect

Table 1.1 Comparison of National GDP per Capita at Local and International (USA) Prices, 1970

	GDP per Capita					
	Valued at local prices			Valued at international prices		
Country	National currency	$ US	% of US level	$ US	% of US level	Exchange rate deviation index
Colombia	6,113	329	6.9	763	15.9	2.32
France	16,118	2,902	60.5	3,599	75.0	1.24
Germany FR	11,272	3,080	64.2	3,585	74.7	1.16
Hungary	31,116	1,037	21.6	1,935	40.3	1.87
India	736	98	2.0	342	7.1	3.49
Italy	1,062	1,699	35.4	2,198	45.8	1.29
Japan	721	2,003	41.7	2,952	61.5	1.47
Kenya	1,027	144	3.0	275	5.7	1.91
UK	893	2,143	44.6	2,895	60.3	1.35
USA	4,801	3,984	100.0	4,801	100.0	1.00

Source: Kravis *et al.* (1976), Tables 1.1 and 1.3.

was even more marked, suggesting GDP per capita was 7.1% of the US level in 1970, rather than only 2%. Even the relative GDP of industrialised countries can be seen to be higher when valued at international prices. Thus Table 1.1 highlights one of the most important inadequacies about the conventional national income comparison, namely that it exaggerates the gap between rich and poor countries. Having said this, however, it should be emphasised that there is no way of equating a halving of the ratio between NI per capita in two countries (from, say, 20:1 to 10:1) with a halving of our degree of concern for the poorer country. There is no definable correspondence between 'units of concern' and ratios or gaps between NI per capita, although presumably most people would accept that there is some direct correlation between them. Thus it is not a matter of indifference whether the ratio is 20:1 or 10:1. One of these values will be a better indicator of relative welfare than the other, but how much better is not assessable.

What the preceding illustration and calculations show is that it is possible, by repricing methods, to adjust the conventional national income estimates so that their performance as relative welfare indicators is improved. However, these methods cannot overcome all the problems, and in any case the binary pricing approach is laborious and involves the statistician in a whole new set of subjective judgements. Naturally, therefore, consideration has been given to alternative economic indicators of development, some of which appear to represent a shortcut to the common pricing approach. Usher (1966) mentions two of these: (1) the social adequacy method; and (2) the related, direct attempt to measure levels of living. In the social adequacy method, for 'each country, income per head in local currency is divided by an estimate of the bare cost of subsistence; ratios arrived at in this way are then treated as measures of real income. The one attempt to compare incomes by this method, a comparison of Japan and the United States, raised the ratio of Japanese to American income almost 600 per cent over what it appears to be when national incomes are compared through the foreign exchange rate' (Usher 1966, p.37). The main obvious difficulty with this procedure is in defining the cost of subsistence in each country. The concept of subsistence may be defined (not without difficulty) as a purely physiological level, but is often defined to include a psychological component for consumption thought to be socially necessary, e.g. the minimum quality of housing demanded by the average European is far higher than that expected in poor African countries. But this sort of judgemental hurdle is found with all measurement procedures, including Usher's second class of method. In this, following Clark and Haswell (1964, Ch.4), an attempt might be made to 'measure' living standards in terms of a key welfare indicator such as 'grain equivalent'. In this the value of all goods and services would be divided by the local price of a standard measure of grain so that national income for countries could be expressed and compared in terms of so many grain equivalents. Interesting though this is, none of the proposed alternatives has yet supplanted national income as the main economic indicator of development.

Hicks and Streeten (1979), in their review of development indicators, also refer to a variety of other attempts and proposals to adjust the GNP measure to allow for different degrees of income inequality and to the relevance of Social Accounting Matrix Systems as providing alternative economic indicators of development.

Mixed and Non-Economic Indicators of Development

Concern about the limitations of GNP per capita as an adequate index of development has spurred experimentation in other directions. Among these have been attempts to generate single indices of development by combining together mixtures of social, political and economic indicators. One such experiment was that of Adelman and Morris (in Baster 1972) to produce an indicator of political development as measured by the degree of political participation. Another was that of Drenowski and Scott (1966) who attempted to construct a Level of Living Index based on an evaluation of certain physical and cultural basic needs. UNRISD (McGranahan *et al.* 1972) subsequently modified this approach in devising a Development Index based on the selection of 18 core indicators listed in Table 1.2. These core indicators were themselves refined out of an initial list of 73 indicators using a set of arbitrary rules of thumb. Subsequently a complex scaling and weighting procedure was applied to the 18 core indicators to enable them to be aggregated into a single 'Development Index' value for each of 58 countries for 1980. While this index did rank several countries differently from their ordering according to GNP, the differences were, in most cases, relatively small. This is perhaps not surprising when it is noted from Table 1.2 that there is a strong correlation between most individual indicators and GNP per capita.

It is true (as also confirmed by a similar exercise by Hicks and Streeten (1979)) that the correlations between indicators and GNP are lower when only developing or developed countries are considered separately, but the underlying relationships with GNP are so strong that the Development Index implies much the same ordinal ranking of countries as GNP per capita. As might have been anticipated from the earlier discussion of repricing adjustments of GNP, the Development Index implies a much lower 'development ratio' between the richest and poorest countries than does conventional GNP. In the McGranahan *et al.* comparison, the 1960 ratio of the Development Index of the US to Thailand was only 11.1 whereas in terms of GNP it was 29.1.

Thus, while the construction of a Development Index was a fascinating

Table 1.2 UNRISD Core Development Indicators: Their Correlation with
GNP per Capita 1960

	Correlation with GNP per capita		
	58 countries	27 developing countries	31 developed countries
Expectation of life at birth	0.73	0.27	0.54
% population in localities of over 20,000	0.70	0.20	0.38
Consumption of animal protein/cap./day	0.82	0.42	0.62
Combined primary and secondary enrolment ratio	0.78	0.16	0.71
Vocational enrolment ratio	0.74	0.17	0.52
Average number of persons/room	−0.75	−0.11	−0.58
Newspaper circulation/1,000 population	0.86	0.61	0.63
Telephones/100,000 population	0.93	0.73	0.88
Radio receivers/1,000 population	0.91	0.61	0.86
% EAP[1] with electricity, gas, water, etc.	0.76	0.54	0.50
Agric. production/male agricultural worker	0.93	0.61	0.87
% adult male labour in agriculture	−0.82	−0.32	−0.69
Electricity consumption, kwh/cap.	0.80	0.60	0.69
Steel consumption, kg/cap.	0.87	0.79	0.78
Energy consumption kg.coal equivalent/cap.	0.93	0.57	0.87
% GDP derived from manufacturing	0.65	0.10	0.19
Foreign trade/cap. in 1960 US dollars	0.75	0.72	0.54
% salaried and wage earners to total EAP	0.75	0.53	0.65

Source: McGranahan *et al.* (1972), Tables 13, 14 and 15.
Note: (1) EAP = Economically active population.

exercise, like other comparable exercises it does not suggest that there is
any markedly superior indicator of development than GNP per capita,
provided that allowance is made for revaluing upwards the GNP of poorer
countries to reflect that their prices are lower than implied by market
exchange rates. All the alternative indices encounter the same basic difficulties in construction. The main ones are: (1) that all components need
to be transformed to a common unit of measurement so that, for example,
such disparate indicators as expectation of life at birth, radio receivers per

1,000 of the population, and the vocational enrolment ratio can be added together with others to produce a single index; and (2) that in the absence of any natural weights, a weighting scheme has to be devised to determine what importance should be ascribed to one indicator as opposed to another.[8]

This is not the place to consider in detail the ingenious procedures which have been created to normalise and weight various lists of separate indicators and to combine them into a single measure. These are helpfully and briefly sketched out in Open University (1975), and the UNRISD method is presented in detail by McGranahan *et al.* (1972). However, as the Open University publication states (p.37), none of the alternatively proposed procedures has made much progress in supplanting GNP (or GDP) per capita which,

> ... remains the most comprehensive and widely used indicator of develop-
> ment levels. While recognising its inherent weaknesses, it is still the most con-
> venient measure of the level of development. Many studies show that
> economic and social indicators are highly correlated with the level of GDP per
> capita, and therefore a ranking based on their combination is relatively close to
> a ranking based on per capita GDP alone.

Hicks and Streeten (1979) arrive at a similar conclusion when they state (p.577):

> The search for a composite index of social welfare, analagous to GNP as an
> index of production, has been a fruitless one so far, since it has proven virtually
> impossible to translate every aspect of social progress into money values or
> some other readily accepted common denominator.

They do, however, argue, from a basic needs perspective, that information on how much is produced (GNP) should be supplemented by attention to what is produced, by what means, for whom and with what impact. To do this they advocate that 'what is required ... are some indicators of the composition and beneficiaries of GNP, which would supplement the GNP data, not replace them'.

Since it is now the practice of UN agencies, and the World Bank's annual World Development Report, to present values for a large number of indicators for all countries, the means are readily to hand to respond to this last injunction. At various points throughout this book data on alter-native indicators will be used to illuminate various qualitative aspects of the relative development of countries, while at the same time relying basically upon size of GNP per capita as the main basis for assessing stages and levels of development.

Notes

1. For those who are interested, Streeten provides a detailed breakdown of the criteria which should be considered within each of these six groups.

2. The book was entitled *Theorie der Wirtschaftlichen Entwicklung*. It was translated into English in 1934.

3. For a full discussion of proposed development indicators and of the problems associated with them, see the various contributions to Baster (ed.) (1972).

4. It should be observed that the national income measure most commonly used is in effect gross national income (GNI). This has to be distinguished from net national income (NNI), which equals GNI minus the allowance for capital depreciation. Thus, while GNI measures the income equivalent to the total value of production in society, NNI indicates the value of the product available for consumption and net new investment, and is therefore probably a better welfare indicator. These two income measures have their exact value equivalents in gross national product (GNP) and net national product (NNP). All of the four measures referred to so far include within them any net property income from abroad, the value of which does not reflect local productive activity − in the LDCs this flow is typically negative as a reflection of repatriated profits by companies and capital export by wealthy individuals. By subtracting net property income from GNP a measure is obtained of gross domestic product (GDP). If the difference between GNP and GDP is large, in so far as the latter is a measure of the total goods and services produced within the economy (before allowing for capital depreciation) it is the better indicator of the productive capacity of the economy and its employment potential.

5. As has already been said, if as GNP increases negative progress is made towards other development goals, such as equality or political participation, negative development might be judged to occur.

6. This definition of the binary method describes that applied by Kravis *et al.* in obtaining the results presented here in Table 1.1. Usher (1966) actually adopted a somewhat different version of the procedure. His method assumes that the 'true' ratio of two countries' living standards lies in between the values of the two ratios obtained by first valuing both countries' GDP at the prices of one country and then at those of the other, and that it is approximated by the geometric average of these two ratios.

7. This is well illustrated by Table 1 in Kravis *et al.* (1978) which indicates that not only do the prices of non-traded goods in 1970 vary greatly between countries, as expected, but that the prices of traded goods also differed significantly, even between DCs.

8. Note: In deriving an index for national income, all the various goods and services are measured in common units of money, and the weighting scheme is provided by their prices.

References

Arndt, H.W. (1981) 'Economic Development: A Semantic History', *Economic Development and Cultural Change*, Vol.29, No. 3, April.

Baster, N. (ed.) (1972) *Measuring Development*, Frank Cass.

Bernstein, H. (1979) 'Sociology of underdevelopment vs. sociology of development?', in D. Lehrman (ed.), *Development Theory: Four Critical Studies*, Frank Cass.

Clark, C. and Haswell, M.R. (1964) *The Economics of Subsistence Agriculture*, Macmillan.

Drenowski, J. and Scott, W. (1966) *The Level of Living Index*, UNRISD, Report No. 4, Geneva.

Hicks, N. and Streeten, P. (1979) Indicators of development: the search for a basic needs yardstick', *World Development*, Vol. 57, 567–80.

Kravis, I.B., Heston, A.W. and Summers, R. (1978) 'Real GDP per capita for more than one hundred countries', *Economic Journal*, Vol. 88, No. 350, 215–42.

Kravis, I.B., Kenessy, Z., Heston, A. and Summers, R. (1976) *A System of International Comparisons of Gross Product and Purchasing Power*, Johns Hopkins Press.

Lal, D. (1983) *The Poverty of Development Economics*, Institute of Economic Affairs.

Lall, S. (1976) 'Conflicts of concepts: welfare economics and developing countries', *World Development*, Vol. 4, No. 3, March.

Leeson, P.F. (1983) 'Development economics and its companions', *Manchester Discussion Papers in Development Studies*, 8304, Mimeo.

Little, I.M.D. (1982) *Economic Development: Theory, Policy, and International Relations*, Basic Books Inc.

McGranahan, D.V., Richard-Proust, C., Sovani, N.V. and Subramanian, M. (1972) *Contents and Measurement of Socioeconomic Development*, Praeger.

Myrdal, G. (1968) *Asian Drama: An Inquiry into the Poverty of Nations*, Allen Lane (London), Pantheon (New York).

Myrdal, G. (1970) *The Challenge of World Poverty*, Penguin Books.

Nixson, F.I. (1986) 'Economic development: a suitable case for treatment?', in B. Ingham and C. Simmons (eds.), *The Historical Dimensions of Economic Development*, Frank Cass.

Open University (1975) *International Comparisons of Levels of Development*, Statistical Sources Unit 15, Open University Press.

Palma, G. (1978) 'Dependency: a formal theory of underdevelopment or a methodology for the analysis of concrete situations of underdevelopment?', *World Development*, Vol. 6, Nos. 7/8.

Schumpeter, J.A. (1934; 1961) *The Theory of Economic Development*, Oxford University Press.

Stewart, F. (1985) *Planning to Meet Basic Needs*, Macmillan.

Streeten, P. (1972) *The Frontiers of Development Studies*, Macmillan (especially Ch. 3).

Streeten, P. *et al.* (1981) *First Things First: Meeting Basic Human Needs in Developing Countries*, Oxford University Press for World Bank.

Streeten, P. (1983) 'Development dichotomies', *World Development*, Vol. 11, No. 10, October.

Szentes, T. (1971) *The Political Economy of Underdevelopment*, Akademiai Kiado, Budapest.

Usher, D. (1966) *Rich and Poor Countries*, Eaton Paper 9, Institute of Economic Affairs.

Warren, B. (1980) *Imperialism: Pioneer of Capitalism*, Verso.

2

Economic theorising about development

(A) A METHODOLOGICAL NOTE

Where a theory purports to relate to some aspect of the real world, it is inevitably a simplified representation of the true situation. For, if it were not a simplification, it would be the real world itself, and that is not amenable to treatment in a classroom or textbook. It follows that some theories may entail a greater degree of simplification than others; that is, they may be either more partial (in the sense of only considering the main aspects of a complex system), or more general (in the sense of abstracting from a number of different situations) and less 'realistic'. However, to describe a theory as partial or general is not to denigrate it. The tests of a good (useful) theory are that the derived relationships (a) are not immediately obvious, i.e. they require the theory to generate them, (b) are verifiable, and (more strongly) are verified by observations in the real world, and (c) are non-trivial and useful to planners and policy makers. If a very simple set of hypotheses and assumptions can generate important conclusions which satisfy all of these three tests, then it is a useful theory. Furthermore, simplicity is a virtue, in the sense that there is no advantage in devising an elaborate theory when a very simple one generates essentially the same conclusions. A hypothesis is important if it 'explains' much by little, that is if it extracts the common and crucial elements from the mass of complex and detailed circumstances surrounding the phenomena to be explained and permits valid prediction on the basis of them alone.

The reason for this methodological preamble is that much of the theorising about development by economists in the post-1945 era, that is in the period when a separate literature of development economics has emerged, is now under attack. It is under attack for being both excessively simple and unreal – charges levelled at much economic theorising – and because of an alleged lack of rigour in comparison to other branches of economic theory (for a fuller critique of the theory, see Section 2.4). While this is a patently unsatisfactory state for the theory to be in, its existence can be explained at least in part by the methodological propositions stated above.

It was natural in the infancy of the subject for economists to seek simple theories and simple policy prescriptions for hastening material progress in the poorest countries. Moreover, it must have seemed plausible at that time that simple development models would provide powerful prescriptive tools, given the apparent success in the 1950s and 1960s of the industrialised countries at economic management using Keynesian macroeconomic theory. Because, also, most of the early development theorising was conducted by North American and European academics, it is quite understandable that attempts should be made to follow the Keynesian example and build a development theory using nationally defined aggregate variables such as saving and investment.

However, the theories propounded in the 1950s and early 1960s have been subjected to a rigorous test of usefulness in the last two decades by the newly independent LDCs seeking to develop national policies for economic and social betterment, and by common consent the theories have been found wanting. Not only have the predictions of the theories not been verified in a number of instances, but it has been found that variables of crucial importance to the LCDs are excluded from consideration by many of the theories, and that preoccupation with national aggregates and averages leads to the ignoring of spatial, interpersonal and intersectoral distribution problems of vital interest to LCDs.

As interest in development has grown, so it has become apparent that the dimensions of this process are numerous and that producing generalised theories to explain it requires highly complex models. This is true even if the main focus is on the economic dimensions of development and the social and political aspects are largely ignored, which is the typical characteristic of economic theorising on the subject. However, one general consequence of theoretical complexity, which can be measured in terms of the number of variables and relationships between them, is that no simple propositions may emerge to aid planners, policy makers or students of the history of change. It tends to be true that only restricted (closed) theoretical systems produce simple general conclusions. For example, for economies which are assumed to have no international sector (trade and aid), theory suggests clear relationships between domestic savings and economic growth. Where, however, an international sector is assumed to exist, no such simple relationships exist between national economic aggregates (as is discussed more fully in Chapter 5). When theories are made more complex, deduced relationships for policy purposes emerge more readily where the theory is expressed numerically rather than in general algebraic form. Since, however, the numerical information required (about such things as marginal propensities to consume and import, and the rates of population and export demand growth) differs from economy to economy, it is apparent that complex theory is more suitable as an aid to planning and policy in individual countries, and that typically few useful conclusions will emerge which are generalisable to all LDCs. However, it should be noted that the record of mathematical structural theories as a basis for planning is one of only modest achievement; given the complexity of social change, too much should not be expected.

The theories referred to in Section B below are what would now be described as 'structuralist' theories. They reflect assumptions that in LDCs there are various institutional features and weaknesses, and that markets operate imperfectly, with the consequence that uncontrolled economic change directed by market forces does not result in the pattern of development which is desired. This, as is reported in Section 2.4, is a topic of heightened debate. Critics such as Lal (1983) and Little (1982) argue strongly for rejection of the protectionist policies and attempts at economic planning which structuralist theories have supported, and for the reassertion of policies based upon the neo-classical economic principles that welfare and economic growth will be maximised by adopting free-trade policies and promoting economic competition within LDC economies. Such authors argue that there is little or no need for a separate economics of development, and Lal (p.109) even goes so far as to state his main conclusion to be that 'the demise of development economics is likely to be conducive to the health of both economics and the economies of developing countries'.

Needless to say, an entirely contrary position is maintained by development economists who firmly identify structural barriers, in both the internal systems of LDCs and in the surrounding international environment, to development of the poorest LDCs. This is reflected in the newly emerging work on structuralist macroeconomics for developing countries best epitomised by the work of Taylor (1983). A characteristic of Taylor's approach is that it recognises that different LDCs may have different 'structural deficiencies' and that macroeconomic policy needs to be adapted to the special circumstances of each. This certainly coincides with our own view that no general development theory (comparable to the contemporary post-Keynesian macroeconomic theory for industrial countries) appears appropriate, and that to try and explain 'the development process' by any simple generalisable economic theory is undesirable. Certainly we must be careful not to oversell the usefulness of development theory. Instead, it might be agreed that it is possible to identify some problems common to many poor countries and to develop partial theories to analyse these, or alternatively to identify groups of countries with essentially identical problems and to build theories for each of these groups.

In view of the preceding critical observations it may well be asked 'what purpose is served by presenting a brief survey of development theory?'. There are in fact several objectives which can be identified in response to this question. In the first place it has to be recognised that, whatever their currently perceived imperfections, the various theories to be discussed have commanded support and influenced development policy at different times and in different places. Therefore, in studying the way in which development policy has evolved in different countries and at the international level, it is necessary to have an understanding of the influence of theoretical views about development. Moreover, these theoretical views have themselves changed in response to experience and deeper understanding of development processes, and it is instructive to gain some appreciation of the progress which development theory has made.

Perhaps the most important justification for reviewing theories of development and criticisms of them is the insight this provides into the nature and dimensions of the development process. For, when particular theories were expressed or adopted, it was because it was felt that they addressed themselves to some crucial variables and relationships in the development process in a way which helped either to comprehend the process or to formulate policy to accelerate and, if necessary, initiate it. If subsequently these theories have been found wanting and have been modified, it may be because their simplifying assumptions have been too strong and the domain to which they relate has proved too limited. In other words, these theories have tended to ignore factors which have subsequently been found to be of considerable importance to developing countries. By examining both the content and some of the alleged shortcomings of the theories we can gain some idea of what domain development theory should ideally cover. To a large extent it is in these shortcomings that we identify many of the main topic areas for discussion later in the book, since it is now felt that no proper understanding or theory of the development process can ignore the special features of LDCs which have not been accounted for in most of the formal theory. Amongst these topics are such things as foreign ownership of firms, dependence upon foreign technology, barriers to international trade, problems of income distribution and nutrition, and requirements for institutional reform.

(B) THEORIES OF DEVELOPMENT

2.1 Theories of Capital Accumulation

Harrod–Domar Growth Model

An important early stimulus to economic theory about development was the Harrod–Domar growth model, so called because essentially the same theory was independently produced by the two named authors (Harrod 1939; Domar 1946). In neither case were the authors concerned with developing countries. Their prime intention was to explore the conditions for stable economic growth in developed countries. The basic assumptions were (1) that aggregate supply and demand would be balanced when investment (I_t) in any period equalled the change in national income $(Y_t - Y_{t-1})$ times the capital–output ratio (k), where k indicates the value of capital required to produce one unit of output by value in a single period, and (2) that at equilibrium in a closed economy intended investment would equal intended savings (S_t). (Note that the first assumption, of an accelerator process, involves a third which is that new capital comes into full production instantaneously.) These assumptions thus produce the equilibrium condition that:

$$I_t = S_t = k(Y_t - Y_{t-1}) \tag{2.1}$$

By dividing equation (2.1) through by Y_t to produce the saving rate, s, equal to S_t/Y_t and the growth rate, g, equal to $(Y_t - Y_{t-1})/Y_t$ we obtain the Harrod–Domar growth equation:

$$s = kg \quad \text{or} \quad g = \frac{s}{k} \tag{2.2}$$

Thus the Harrod–Domar model defines the equilibrium conditions for steady economic growth. Despite the fact that the theory was not conceived with the LDCs in mind, and that its behavioural assumptions and implications are open to question (see, for example, the critique by Ackley 1961, Ch.18), it nevertheless for a time exercised considerable influence on development economics. The immediate attraction of the model was that it relates one of the primary objectives of development, the rate of economic growth, to what is often considered its major limiting factor, investment. There is some doubt as to whether it is the level of savings which restricts investment in LDCs, as application of the Harrod–Domar formula would seem to imply, or whether, as Cairncross (1962, Ch.3) has argued, it is limited opportunities for profit that restrain the level of investment with saving levels adjusting to the scale of investment opportunities that exists. Despite this doubt, attempts have been made to employ the model, with appropriate allowances for capital depreciation, to answer such questions as: (1) what rate of savings (and hence investment) is necessary to achieve a target growth rate, given the assumed capital–output ratio of a specified economy? or (2) what saving and investment patterns will maximise consumption over time (e.g. Goodwin 1961)?

Little purpose would be served by considering in detail here all the refinements and extensions which have been proposed to make the Harrod–Domar theory more relevant for planning or expository uses. There are some obvious changes, which will not be discussed further, such as introducing capital depreciation into the model so that not all savings contribute to a net addition to capital stock, or the introduction of gestation lags so that net new investment only makes its full contribution to output after a few years. There are, however, other refinements which introduce either significant concepts or issues which feature in later chapters, and these are worthy of mention.

One simple but important extension of the model is to introduce foreign trade. This is typically done (Bruton 1955; UN ECAFE 1960, p.82) by rephrasing the model such that:

$$g = \frac{s}{k} + \frac{b}{k} \quad \text{where } b = \frac{\text{imports} - \text{exports}}{Y} \tag{2.3}$$

The significance of this is that imports can only exceed exports (and b be positive) if a country is in receipt of either aid, credit or foreign investment. Such a capital transfer enables additional investment to occur. The income-generating effects of this additional investment may, as in equation 2.3, be assumed to be the same as would occur from investment financed by domestic savings. Thus, this 'opening up' of the model indicates a strategic growth-generating role for aid and credit to poor countries. Unfortunately, however, this particular treatment of the international sector fails to portray the full importance of that sector. Equation 2.3 implies that, if trade is in balance on current account, b will equal zero and higher volumes of trade will have no beneficial effect upon economic growth. According to Bruton's own theorising, this is not adequate. It is apparent (Bruton 1955 (Ch.8); Chenery and Strout 1966) that, despite import-substituting industrialisation (see Chapter 9), poor nations need to import raw materials plus many capital and intermediate products which they cannot manufacture themselves, and that their ratio of imports to national income may well not decline as income increases. Thus it is argued that domestic savings and transfers of foreign capital are not perfect substitutes for one another and that economic growth may be constrained by a *foreign exchange gap*. What is meant by this is that the import-purchasing power conferred by the value of exports plus capital transfers may be inadequate to support the level of growth permitted via investment financed by the level of domestic savings plus those capital transfers. Conversely, a *savings gap* may be said to exist where savings are inadequate to support the level of growth which could be permitted given the import-purchasing power of an economy and the level of other resources. This *two-gap* theory, that investment and development are restricted by levels of either savings or import-purchase capacity, is clearly not adequately explained by the extended Harrod–Domar model in equation 2.3, and requires a more elaborate formulation such as that by Chenery and Bruno (1962) for the case of Israel, by Chenery and Strout (1966), or by McKinnon (1964).

If import-purchasing capacity is deemed to be the limiting constraint upon economic growth, then the two-gap theory indicates a strategic role for aid and other forms of foreign capital, namely to finance a deficit in the current account of the balance of payments to cover a higher rate of capital goods imports. This important argument has been used to justify persistent current account deficits for a large number of LDCs. However, the increasing problem of external indebtedness in many of these LDCs has led to questioning of this justification, and constitutes an issue of sufficient magnitude to warrant further examination of the two-gap model in Chapter 6 on foreign exchange flows and indebtedness.

Mahalanobis' Model

By considering simply aggregate investment, the basic Harrod–Domar model in effect assumes that all forms of investment are equally productive and also that capital is infinitely flexible as to what it can produce. Neither assumption is realistic, as is recognised by those extensions to the model which allow for different sectoral capital–output ratios, and for the level of investment in any particular sector to affect capacity in other sectors. Among the most celebrated of these extensions is the model developed by Mahalanobis (1955) which provided part of the basic rationale for the Indian Planning Commission's draft second five-year plan of India for 1956 to 1960. The multi sectoral version of this model was employed in establishing sectoral targets for the national plan, and in so far as the proposals for achieving these were implemented by the government the model may be said to have influenced economic policy, particularly with respect to the recommended emphasis on the development of heavy industry.

The Mahalanobis model shares the assumptions of the Harrod–Domar model that output is a function of capital only, that at equilibrium in the economy the output of any one sector (the i th) will equal its stock of capital times its output-capital ratio ($b_i = 1/k_i$), and that there is no international sector. The model can be applied in simplified form to two sectors only, which are defined as producing consumption and investment goods respectively. In the investment goods sector two types of machine are assumed to be made, those required to produce consumption goods and those required to make more machines. Since all savings are invested in machines it follows that:

(1) The rate of growth of consumption goods output depends in the short run upon that sector's share of the new machines produced in any period (i.e. its share of new investment).

(2) The rate of growth of consumption goods output ultimately depends upon the share of new investment in the investment goods sector – the larger this sector becomes, the greater the economy's capacity to produce machines for consumption goods manufacture.

In fact the investment goods share of investment, λ_k, is the key variable in the model, and at equilibrium $g = f(\lambda_k)$.

(3) If the marginal rate of savings (s') is raised above the average rate (s), the share of new investment in the heavy goods sector can be increased at the expense of the consumption goods sector since the marginal growth rate in consumer demand will be correspondingly reduced. Thus, if a country can raise its savings rate (which implies $s''' > s$), it is in a position to increase its rate of investment in productive capacity to permit future consumption levels to exceed what they otherwise would be.

(4) When the average and marginal rates of saving are equal $(s = s')$, an equilibrium, in which machine capacity is fully employed, is achieved when the rates of growth of national income, investment and consumption are equal to the investment goods sector's share of investment times its output–capital ratio.[1]

A particular merit of this model is that it pushes questions of inter-sectoral development choice to the forefront. In particular, it draws attention to the capital goods sector, and argues that its capacity needs to be expanded if higher growth rates are to be attempted.[2] However, it is far too partial a model to permit a full exploration of the issues of sectoral emphasis in development planning. This is partly because it does not contain any explicit mechanism relating demand for the products of the consumer goods sector to the growth and distribution of national income and also because, as always, the sectoral interdependencies, which are imposed by assuming an economy without trade, are relaxed as soon as trade is admitted. Even if demand for exports is stagnant, a range of alternative sectoral development policies becomes possible, as Raj and Sen (1961) showed in their re-examination of the Mahalanobis model. (Obviously the foreign trade possibilities of a country are of considerable significance for its sectoral development strategy, an issue which is pursued at length in the chapters on trade, Chapter 5, and industrialisation, Chapter 9.)

These limitations are in principle susceptible to treatment in full-scale planning models in which there may be a high level of sectoral disaggregation, plus systems to represent domestic and export demands as well as assumptions about the prices at which imports and foreign capital will be available. When all these features are incorporated into planning models, they yield results about sectoral interdependency which depend entirely upon the precise numerical assumptions made about demand and import supply, and are specific to a particular economy. One of the few generalisable results of such models will be that higher rates of domestic savings will lead over time to higher levels of national income and consumption.

This question of raising the savings rate of LDCs, which was brought into sharp focus by the models just discussed, became a key article of faith in the economic development literature. Thus Lewis (1954, p.155) argued:

> The central problem in the theory of economic development is to understand the process whereby a community which was previously saving and investing 4 or 5% of its national income or less, converts itself into an economy where voluntary saving is running at about 12 to 15% of national income or more.

And Rostow (1956, p.25) argued that a necessary condition for a country to launch itself into sustained economic growth is 'a rise in the rate of productive investment from (say) 5% or less to over 10% of national income (or net national product)'. Of course, the Harrod-Domar-Mahalanobis models do nothing to answer Lewis's question about the process through which this change in the savings–investment rate occurs, although they do incorporate the rationale for the target rates employed by Lewis and Rostow. If one accepts an average capital–output ratio of 4:1 (Mahalanobis 1955, p.24, accepted that for India it would lie between 3:1 and 5:1) and a population growth rate of 2.5% per annum, then investment equal to 10% of national income would be necessary to maintain average per capita output at a constant level. A higher rate of investment will be required to permit per capita output to increase – according to the theory, investment rates of 14% and 18% would lead to per capita output growth of 1% and 2% respectively. Thus the theory implies that there is a 'critical minimum effort (which) would enable the economy to escape the gravitational pull of population increase' (Myint 1964, p.103).

Theoretical Relatives of the Harrod–Domar–Mahalanobis Models: Big Push and Advanced Growth

In an early statement of the notion that poor countries need to raise their savings–investment rate sharply, Rosenstein-Rodan (1943), writing about Eastern Europe, suggested that what these poor countries needed was a 'big push' of industrial investment. The reasons for this recommendation were, however, deeper than that of simply needing to increase investment. The argument was that investment in any single industry in a poor country was unlikely to be financially attractive or successful because of the very small size of the market for its product. Expanding output in any one industry would create income for the workers in that industry, but since these workers would not spend all of this income on their own product, insufficient demand would be created to absorb the extra output. The necessary level of demand, it was argued, would only be created if several industries expanded simultaneously (i.e. by a big investment push) so that the demand for the output of one industry would be created by increasing the incomes of workers in other industries. Once the initial big push had occurred, a sufficiently broadly based market would have been created to provide the incentive for further investment. The same reasoning was used by Nurkse to put the case for balanced growth (Nurkse 1952, Ch.1). As Nurkse put it (p.12): 'An increase in production over a wide range of consumables, so proportioned as to correspond with the pattern of consumers' preferences, does create its own demand.' Thus the arguments for the 'big push' and for 'balanced growth' are essentially the same.[3]

Note that both arguments appear to advocate a strategy of developing industry rather than agriculture, a course followed by the USSR and also by India in its second five-year plan. In both these cases, however, the relative neglect of agriculture led to food supply and balance of payments problems which necessitated policy changes to increase investment in agriculture, and it seems clear that the big-push and balanced-growth theories tended to be interpreted in ways which underestimate the economic role of the agricultural sector.

Another criticism which has been levelled at these theories is that they over-emphasise the large-scale aspect of industrial investment. As Furtado (1954), for example, pointed out, large-scale output is associated with the capital-intensive production techniques employed in the industrial countries. There are other more labour-intensive technologies which are viable in small-scale production and are not constrained by the smallness of the market. The big-push and balanced-growth arguments rather took for granted the appropriateness of capital-intensive production techniques. In so doing they underplayed the problem of inelastic supplies of capital and other factors of production facing many of the LDCs. For if a particular factor is in short supply, expanding one industry, far from creating external economies to the benefit of other industries, may by bidding up the cost of the factor create external diseconomies, so disadvantaging other industries (Fleming 1955).

Another weakness of the balanced-growth argument, as naively presented, was the absence of specific recognition that not all industries produce final goods but that some are clients for the products of the others. Recognition of this fact of backward and forward linkages between industries, plus the recognition of limited decision-making capacity and resource availability, led Hirschman (1958) to propose, in diammetric opposition to the balanced-growth view, that sectoral investment strategies of unbalanced growth should be pursued. In these the State would initiate or support large-scale investment in a leading sector. Although the chosen industry might initially have excess capacity and operate at a private financial loss, the proposition is that it would create the necessary external economies to induce the development of supplying and client industries. More specifically, it was argued that expansion of the leading sector would create both new opportunities and bottlenecks elsewhere in the economy which would stimulate a secondary wave of investment and entrepreneurship. This is an argument which at first glance would appear to have particular relevance to those economic functions now generally managed by the public sector, such as railways, ports and roads, which involve large lumps of indivisible investment. However, this reveals something of the tautological character of the unbalanced-growth proposal, which is that there is always a gestation lag associated with investment and particularly so with public infrastructure investment, for clearly it would be unreasonable to expect railways or roads to begin operating instantaneously at full capacity.

The fact is that neither the unbalanced- or balanced-growth models provide adequate descriptions of the industrial development process, or operational policy prescriptions to achieve it. It hardly needs saying that the LDCs are a highly heterogeneous collection, so that the appropriate pattern of structural transformation differs for each country and depends upon its assumed national objectives, resource endowments and its prospects for trade, population growth, etc. Given suitable assumptions about these functions and parameters, programming techniques provide methods for calculating possible development plans. Exercises of this type are now numerous (see, for example, Adelman and Thorbecke 1966) and incorporate within them the basic logic of the Mahalanobis model. How influential they have been is, however, questionable, and there has been a marked diminution of emphasis on planning models in contemporary thinking about development economics.

Note also that the justification of the big-push and balanced-growth theories requires the assumption of no foreign trade, or of poor export prospects. If there *were* strong foreign demand for the product of an industry, small domestic market size would not be synonymous with lack of investment incentive. Certainly Nurkse (1952), in suggesting the need for a development policy of balanced growth, specifically assumed that export demand for the industrial products of poor countries would be low, and that industrialisation in these countries would therefore be controlled by the size of the home market. This assumption of trade pessimism underpins 'structuralist' theories and policies for development and it comes under particular attack by critics who argue for the stronger assertion of neoclassical economic principles (see Section 2.4 below).

Analysis Relating to Capital–Output Ratios (k)

The apparent prospect of using simple accelerator models of the Harrod–Domar and Mahalanobis types as crude planning aids led to extensive empirical and theoretical examination of sectoral and aggregate capital–output ratios. For planning purposes it was the incremental capital–output ratios (ICORs) relating marginal increases in capital to increases in output which were considered relevant. While naturally these were found to exhibit greater variation than the average capital–output ratios, they exhibited stability in certain ways, such as between countries with a similar level of prosperity, and in certain comparable economic sectors of different countries. Nevertheless, they varied in other dimensions and, not surprisingly, k_i was found to differ with the sector, i, of the economy (Lewis 1955, Ch.5); thus in LDCs, agriculture exhibits a lower capital requirement per unit of output than does manufacturing industry and the public sector. Also, as expected where capital becomes more abundant relative to labour as a result of economic growth, it has been observed that aggregate capital–output ratios change over time as a result of both (1) structural change within countries towards the more capital-intensive sectors, and (2) increased capital intensity within sectors. Because these two aspects of change are relatively slow, they do not of themselves preclude the possibility of identifying and employing k_i for planning purposes.

However, there is an obvious weakness for planning of treating capital–output ratios as predetermined when in fact they are adjustable through planning. Clearly, when capital is scarce, it is desirable to pursue policies which minimise the size of the aggregate k ratio for any given combination of outputs, which brings us back again to the problem of choice of production technique (which is the subject matter of Chapter 11). But it also raises the question of work organisation, for, as Reddaway (1962, Appendix C) identified, k may be reduced by, amongst other things, non-capital-using sources of productivity increase, changes due to the introduction of multiple shift working, and changes in capacity utilisation as a result of changes in demand. It is obvious that the second of these factors is amenable to deliberate adjustment in the medium and longer term, as is the first to the extent that work study and 'learning by doing' may lead to a more efficient use of resources. Of course, the influence which planners can exercise over changes in capital intensity may well be dwarfed by changes caused by unforeseen fluctuations in the economy. Sharp increases in oil prices, declines in export prices or demands, and major harvest variations may produce significant shorter-term movements in capital–output ratios. These in turn may induce longer-term changes in entrepreneurial behaviour which undermine efforts at planning.

More importantly, these three points made by Reddaway indicate the limitations of attempting to explain output changes in terms of capital only. Leaving labour out of the theory might be justified where it is assumed to be in unlimited supply, and where the labour input per unit of capital remains constant, i.e. where labour and capital are complementary. However, even with ample labour, if it is feasible to adjust the number of shifts worked or their length, labour and capital become substitutes, and variations in both labour and capital have to be studied to explain output changes. In cases where the labour supply is limited, capital growth will be constrained to the rate of labour supply growth unless, as is usually the case, capital can be substituted for labour. Where this is so, output changes again have to be explained by changes in both capital and labour. To a large extent it was because labour supply was thought not to be a limiting factor in the LDCs that in the early theorising it may have seemed adequate to omit it from consideration. This, however, ignored the facts (1) that not all the LDCs were overpopulated relative to their resources – there has been a tendency for thinking about development to be dominated by the special case of the highly populated Asian countries – and (2) that labour is not homogeneous in quality, and that there may be shortages of skilled manpower in countries with an abundance of unskilled labour.

Reddaway's first point also highlights the possibility of output changes, without any readily measurable changes in capital or labour use, through technological change. In fact it is arguable that technological change is not generally dissociated directly (disembodied) from capital and labour, but is 'embodied' in the sense that it is associated with the introduction of improved machines or with the training of, and investment in, labour (cf Solow 1962). The intense empiricism sparked off by the attempt to test hypotheses related to disembodied and embodied technical change is not of interest here. What is important is to recognise, as more recent analytical and planning models do, the contribution of technical change to economic development. The need for policies actively to steer and promote technological change is extensively pursued in the later chapters on agriculture, industry and the transfer of technology.

2.2   Theories of Economic Dualism

Theories of economic dualism – to be distinguished from the socio-political dualism of Boeke (1953) – have been ostensibly more concerned with describing certain aspects of the structural transformation which occurs within LDCs than with generating tools to assist in planning development. The influence and attractiveness of this line of theorising is due to a considerable extent to the fact that it fills an important theoretical vacuum. As Fei and Ranis (1966) explain this, neither theories of growth of a post-Keynesian type for mature industrial economies nor classical theories of growth in agrarian economies are adequate to analyse the development of contemporary underdeveloped economies. These latter countries are not agrarian in the sense that virtually their whole economy is based upon traditional agricultural and handicraft production; nor are they mature economies in which capitalist (or state-capitalist) modes of production are employed in all sectors. Rather, they are dualistic economies in which a modern dynamic capitalist sector exists alongside a (usually larger) traditional sector which is dominated by subsistence agriculture. The theories about economic dualism specifically relate to this type of economy and seek to provide an explanation of how a primarily agrarian economy is transformed via a dualistic state into a mature economy.

From a different standpoint, Szentes (1971) also considers the theories of dualism to be a step forward. As he puts it (p.83):

> That the phenomena and problems of dualism have received such a prominent treatment in the theory of development is doubtless a significant step forward towards a better understanding of the real nature and mechanism of underdevelopment. Instead of the superficial, quantitative characteristics, the idea of dualism calls attention to structural diseases, to certain peculiarities of the operation of the system, that is to say, it emphasises the need for a much more complex analysis.

At the same time Szentes feels, although this will not be pursued here, that 'Owing to the separation of the economic and social sides of dualism, sociological dualism becomes unexplainable, while economic dualism is simplified to the problem of technical coefficients and the asymmetry of production functions'.

The dual economy theory was first formally stated in a seminal article by Lewis (1954), and has been the subject of numerous extensions and modifications, most notably by Ranis and Fei (1961), Jorgenson (1961, 1967) and by Lewis himself (1968). No attempt will be made here to consider specific points of difference between these authors, but their combined work will be drawn upon in a generalised presentation of the main characteristics and propositions of the theory.

For the immediate purpose here the dual economy is assumed to be divisible into two sectors which we will designate 'industry' and 'agriculture'. This nomenclature is largely one of convenience and accords with the general structure of presentation adopted in this book. It is, however, an arbitrary nomenclature, for, as Leeson (1979) makes clear and Lewis (1979) himself restates, the concept of dualistic economic structures is capable of illuminating many aspects of development, and formal dual models have a number of alternative applications. Thus, for example, the two sectors might alternatively be labelled 'modern' and 'subsistence', 'capitalist' and 'non-capitalist', or 'export enclave' and 'domestic'. In each case the essential distinction is between (1) that small and rapidly growing sector which uses relatively large amounts of capital, with labour hired for a contractual wage or salary, and (2) the much larger sector dominated by subsistence agriculture, where little capital is used, labour productivity is low, and where payment is more in kind than in cash.

Despite the claim of Ranis and Fei that the theory explains how an agrarian economy with no modern industrial sector is transformed into a mature industrial economy, it should be pointed out that all the models of dualism require an embryo capitalist industrial sector as an initial condition. What the models in fact describe is how, and under what conditions, industry may grow from small beginnings to overtake agriculture in size, but in none of the models is there an explanation of how the industrial seed appears. Perhaps this is not truly necessary since all LDCs have at least some indigenous entrepreneurs and modern industrial plant. It is, however, interesting to note in passing that in many countries the initial injection of industrial capital often came largely from abroad, and that many indigenous industrial managers and entrepreneurs started their professional careers in foreign-owned companies (often preceded by training in foreign educational institutions); these circumstances clash somewhat with the assumptions (stated below) of a closed economy and no foreign ownership. Nevertheless, it is clear that massive structural economic change (development) does not take place without facilitating institutions – markets and legal controls – and it is likely that there is a link between the institutions favourable to the emergence of the first modern industry in a country and those needed for its further expansion. It is true that Fei and Ranis (1966) discussed the significance of the emergence of a class of capitalist entrepreneurs among agricultural landlords, and Lewis (1954) likewise discussed the role of the entrepreneur, but no attempt is made to incorporate the conditions for the growth of entrepreneurship into the formal models.

The main assumptions of the dual economy theory are:

(1) The economy is a closed one in which there is no international trade in goods and no foreign ownership of capital.[4] The principal significance of this assumption is that imports cannot be used to supplement locally produced food and agricultural raw material supplies, and sufficient resources have to be employed in agriculture to ensure an adequate marketed agricultural surplus to feed industrial workers and their families.

(2) It is assumed that land for agricultural production is in fixed supply (which is only true for some LDCs – in others, such as India, the potential to increase multiple cropping through irrigation is still considerable) and that no reproducible capital is required in agriculture. Thus labour is the one factor of production free to be adjusted in agriculture during the process of structural transformation.

(3) It is assumed that there is exogenously given technological change in both agriculture and industry which increases the productivity of all factors of production. Note that without this assumption for the agricultural sector, the maximum potential food and agricultural raw material supply would be fixed by assumption 2.

(4)   In industry, output is taken to be a function of capital and labour, and these two factors are assumed to be substitutes for one another.

(5)   It is further assumed that the whole of capital's share of industrial output is saved and reinvested in additional industrial capacity; that is, only owners of capital are assumed to save.

(6)   Two alternative sets of assumptions may be made relating to the productivity of agricultural labour. One assumption is that there is disguised unemployment in the agricultural sector such that the marginal product of a labourer is zero. Such a situation can occur where the system of land tenure grants some land use rights to every family (either directly or through a feudal system) and where each family subsists by sharing out amongst its members the product of the family holding. Under this system, agriculture forms a sink in which everybody not supported by employment in industry can find a livelihood, and it enables non-productive family members to consume at the level of the average product per person. While all family members may do some work and hence be productive at the margin, particularly in the peak agricultural labour requirement period at harvest, it is nevertheless probably true, in view of the short length of the average working day and the long periods of slack labour time, that many labourers could be withdrawn without any reduction of agricultural output because the remainder would work harder. In these circumstances it may be assumed that there is initially an infinitely elastic supply of labour from agriculture to industry at a subsistence wage (w) which has real purchasing power equivalent to a constant basket of food.

There has been an extended debate as to whether or not LDCs have disguised unemployment in agriculture in the above sense. A review of the literature on this subject by Kao, Anschel and Eicher (1964) concluded that early empirical studies pointed to its existence only on a small scale. However, the concept of 'unemployment' presents severe difficulties in poverty-stricken rural areas since, in the absence of a welfare state, survival demands that families have some income source, even if it is minimal. The evidence of the growing incidence of rural poverty as reviewed by Singh (1979) for South Asia, and in African and Latin American countries is indicative of a severe shortage of employment opportunities which, on any reasonable definition, may be taken to signify widespread rural unemployment and underemployment. (These issues are more fully explored in Ch.4 in the section on employment, 4.3.) This in turn is consistent with the existence of a very low marginal product for agricultural labour in higher populated, poor LDCs. It is, therefore, a reasonable approximation to assume that the marginal product is actually zero, although this assumption is not in reality crucial for dual economy models. Indeed, Jorgenson (1967) accepted instead, as an initial condition of the agrarian economy, that agricultural labour has a positive marginal product, but one which is less than the institutional subsistence wage (w). In this situation it can still be assumed that initially there will be an elastic supply of labour to industry at the subsistence wage (w), but it has to be accepted that any transfer of labour to industry has an opportunity cost in terms of agricultural output.

(7)   It is assumed that there is some maximum level of population growth (p) but that actual growth may be restricted below p by a Malthusian mechanism. With everyone assumed to be receiving a minimum subsistence food ration, a population growth rate higher than that of food supplies would not be possible over any length of time. Thus the population growth rate may be restricted to the rate of growth of food production if the latter is less than p. Note that, because of the assumed technological change in agriculture, even an economy with disguised agricultural unemployment could support a rate of population growth equal to that of this technological change.

(8)   It will be readily appreciated from the preceding paragraph that a critical determinant of the dynamics of population growth within the model is the assumption that the subsistence food ration is both a minimum and a maximum. Although this is usually explicitly assumed within the theory, the question naturally arises as to why, when a worker with a zero marginal product leaves agriculture, his former share of food consumption should be released to sustain him in industrial employment rather than being consumed by the remaining agricultural population to raise their living standard above the subsistence level. If the food is not released with the migrating worker, the supportable growth of the industrial labour force and of the whole population would be reduced.

Given the above assumptions, including that initially the marginal productivity of agricultural labour is zero, the theory yields a number of deductive propositions. Since there is disguised unemployment, the industrial sector is in a position to develop rapidly subject only to its rate of capital accumulation, for provided that those remaining in agriculture do not start to eat what was formerly allocated to the disguised unemployed who shift to industry, complementary quantities of food and labour can be transferred from agriculture to industry and there is no reduction in total agriculture supply. With reasonable assumptions about capital's share of industrial output and about capital depreciation rates, it can be shown that the rate of growth of industrial output and employment would be high (and accelerating because of technological change). It can also be shown that this rate will be higher than any plausible rate of population growth. Thus it follows that industry will eventually absorb all the disguised unemployed and the economy will reach a turning point, sometimes referred to as the shortage point (Ranis and Fei 1961), and pass into a second phase in which further labour transfer into industry reduces agricultural output.

Unless technological change (productivity growth) in agriculture exceeds the maximum rate of population growth, p, in this second phase, (a) the supportable rate of population growth will be reduced below that of the first phase, because agriculture supply growth due to technological change will be partially offset by a reduction in the productive labour force in agriculture, and (b) there will be a tendency for a shortage of marketed agricultural product to appear causing higher agricultural prices and a worsening of industry's terms of trade. This last effect will be due to the higher wage cost (in terms of industrial product) of maintaining the wage's purchasing power for agricultural products, and will tend to cause some substitution of capital for labour in industry. This higher wage cost will also reduce industry's profits and tend to retard its growth rate.

As more labour is sucked into industry in the second phase of the theoretically described process, another turning point – the commercialisation point – will be reached at which the marginal productivity of the remaining agricultural labour force rises to a level at which the marginal supply price of labour to industry exceeds the institutional wage (w). From this point on, in the third phase of development, continued expansion of the industrial workforce will be accompanied by a higher real wage rate. When this is combined with any worsening of industry's terms of trade as a result of growing agricultural supply shortage, industrial expansion will be further retarded. In this third phase, agriculture will be forced through competition for labour into a state of commercialisation which involves adopting modes of capitalist economic behaviour similar to those operating in the industrial sector. Thus the economy will have achieved the transition from an agrarian economy (at the beginning of phase one) to a mature economy describable by neoclassical analysis.

Despite their various shortcomings, the dual-economy models have made a notable contribution to theorising about development. In contrast to the Harrod–Domar–Mahalanobis models, they focus attention upon those structural elements in the process of change, concern with which is one of the key features distinguishing development economics from macroeconomics. In particular they focus attention upon the traditional (agricultural and informal) sector, which in most LDCs is the largest economic sector in terms of employment and contribution to GNP. They emphasise the strategic importance of a marketed surplus of agricultural output and the crucial importance of technical change in generating such a surplus in the face of an expanding population. Although, in the exposition above, this surplus has been treated simply as transfer of food, agricultural raw materials and labour to industry, it is in reality more than this. It is also a monetary flow from industry to agriculture arising out of payments for food, which (a) generates demand for the products of industry and creates the incentive for further industrial expansion, and (b) is a source of saving, both voluntary and through taxation, which may be used to finance investment in either agriculture or industry.[5]

Another distinguishing feature of the dual-economy theorising is that it places prime emphasis upon the employment of people plus the distribution of income between them. In doing this it introduces the troubling problem of population growth as a central dynamic force of structural transformation, alongside the dynamos of technological change and capital accumulation.

While there are many criticisms which can be levelled at the dual-economy models, as at any theory which makes strong simplifying assumptions, there are just one or two which should be indicated here. The models have, and this is a point which recurs throughout this book, helped to suggest a falsely optimistic picture of the ease with which poor, untrained rural dwellers can be assimilated into the industrial labour force. In fact a large number of LDCs have not yet reached the stage where the scale of growth of the industrial labour force is sufficient to require a decline in the agricultural labour force. As is indicated in Chapter 7 (Table 7.2), the number of workers in the agricultural sector has been growing rapidly in the LDCs, and may be expected to continue to grow for a fair number of years. Not only do the activities which fall under the umbrella label of 'industry' not generate as much demand for labour (in terms of numbers of people rather than value of labour) as the numerical assumptions accompanying the theorising imply, they also tend to require skilled (high valued) rather than unskilled labour. Thus a large differential emerges between the wages of unskilled urban-industrial workers and agricultural labour. This differential attracts agricultural workers to the towns on the offchance of obtaining skilled jobs and a high wage. In reality most of the migrants are not qualified for the employment they seek and they end up unemployed or in the 'informal sector' in the urban areas. (For further details see the sections of Chapter 6 on urbanisation and rural-urban migration.) The models also tend to overstate the capacity for reinvestment of the profits in industry, and to underestimate the savings potential in agriculture. Conspicuous consumption by industrial entrepreneurs and foreign ownership of industry (a topic extensively dealt with in Chapters 9 and 10) will both reduce the rate of industrial capital formation below the 100% reinvestment level of the theory.

2.3   Rostow – The Stages of Economic Growth

Rostow's stage theory of economic growth was intended as a direct counter to the Marxist stage theory of capitalist development, and his 1960 publication was entitled *The Stages of Growth: A Non-Communist*

Manifesto. Rostow's basic proposition was that all countries are located in one of a hierarchy of development stages. These were identified as (1) the traditional society, (2) the transitional stage: the preconditions for take-off, (3) the take-off, (4) the drive to maturity, and (5) the stage of high mass consumption. The currently wealthy industrial countries are identified as those which have passed through the take-off stage and are ensconced in stages 4 or 5. Since most of these countries are capitalist, the argument that in stages 4 and 5 they achieve a stable condition for self-sustaining growth and wealth presents a direct challenge to the Marxist argument of a violent end to the capitalist system.

The poor countries are required in Rostow's scheme to build a launching platform for development in the preconditions stage. In this, radical facilitating changes are required to occur in agriculture, transport and international trade, and entrepreneurial spirit and capacity has to emerge. The required changes in agriculture are towards a market-oriented economy in which food and agricultural raw materials become increasingly available to other sectors of the economy; the development of the transport sector and other social infrastructure has an obvious and vital role in economic growth; while export expansion is seen as a necessary accompaniment of increased capital imports and industrial specialisation. The critical stage is seen as the take-off, when in the space of one or two decades the rate of investment increases sharply from about 5% of GNP to over 10%. During this stage, leading economic sectors are assumed to emerge which create investment opportunities elsewhere in the economy and provide the basis for further investment and self-sustaining growth in stages 4 and 5.

Because of the widespread appeal of Rostow's theory, it also attracted a good deal of critical attention (see, for example, the contribution of Kuznets to Rostow 1963; Szentes 1971, Ch.5; and Baran and Hobsbawm 1961). The main burden of this criticism is as follows. In the absence of any clear distinction between the end of one phase and the beginning of the next, the theory becomes tautological; the rich countries have definitionally achieved the transition from an earlier condition, which may be described as traditional, to one of maturity or high mass consumption, whereas the poor countries have equally self-evidently failed to accomplish the transition or achieve take-off. Furthermore, even for the rich countries, it is by no means certain that they have achieved a self-sustained growth and thus escaped the fate predicted by the Marxists, for as Kuznets observes (in Rostow 1963, p.41), 'no growth is purely self-sustaining or self-limiting'.

Yet another important line of criticism is that Rostow's theory in effect assumes that the still underdeveloped countries are in a traditional (or, more probably, preconditions) stage, essentially the same as that from which the now-rich countries started their development. This is an implication which is widely disputed, as will be made more fully clear in Section C below. For instance, it may be argued that in the traditional stage countries are not totally stagnant but change, albeit slowly, in response to historic forces which differ from one country to another. But more importantly, it is argued that the condition of the now-poor countries has been shaped by markedly different forces from those which had prevailed in rich countries before their industrial revolution (take-off). The history of colonialism, and the transmission of various influences from the rich countries, make the condition of the now underdeveloped countries markedly different from that of the rich countries when they were at a comparable stage of GNP per capita, and raise obvious doubts about whether they can follow the same development path.

2.4 Critique

Using Chenery's (1965) classification of development theories, those presented to this point may be characterised as structuralist, and they come under attack from the proponents of two alternative schools of thought, namely neo-Marxist and neoclassical economics. The neo-Marxist label is attached, with more or less appropriateness, to some members of the dependency school. From this perspective underdevelopment is seen as being caused by the dominant influence exercised by developed capitalist countries as a result of certain political and economic institutions which lock poor LDCs into a dependent relationship. In actuality, this is also a school of structuralist thought, emphasising dislocations and biases in institutions governing the allocative processes of the economy, but one which has a totally different perspective from the post-Keynesian structuralism of Nurkse, Hirschman, Lewis and Myrdal. A lengthier exposition of dependency theory and criticisms of it is presented in Section C below. In this section attention is briefly confined to the criticisms of the structuralist theories made by those urging re-emphasis of neoclassical economics, and by others who are of a structural persuasion but who feel that development economics has not yet succeeded in assembling the appropriate elements of the economics discipline which are appropriate for the study of development.

A fundamental weakness of much development theorising is seen by some to stem from the fact that its intellectual origins are remote from LDCs. Streeten (1972, especially in Ch.5), Myrdal (1970, Ch. 1) and Szentes (1971, Part 1) have argued that economists of all persuasions have in their development theories tended to misapply concepts and categories carried over from, for example, Keynesian macroeconomics or Marxist doctrine. As one illustration of this, Streeten points out that in Western orthodox models the conventional distinctions between what are variables and what are parameters (constants) are based upon (among other things such as ideological factors, vested interests, and covenience of measurement) the assumption that certain institutions and attitudes are given and adapted. In LDCs such institutions and attitudinal behaviour may not exist — indeed, Chapter 1 mentions the possibility that underdevelopment may be identified by the very absence of certain institutions and attitudes — and they may need to be classified as variables to be acted upon rather than as parameters. Thus, for example, in considering the role of capital formation on economic growth, it may be feasible in Western economies to assume that adequate supplies of skilled manpower are or will be available, and that ready markets exist for the product. In LDCs, however, it is probable that the capacity to absorb (utilise) capital is limited by shortages of trained manpower, lack of complementary facilities, and limited market size. In such situations the level of capital formation has to be planned in conjunction with many complementary factors such as, for example, the provision of skilled manpower. While this latter point is generally recognised in the development literature, there are no development models which integrate educational, institutional, and more conventional economic variables together.

As a further illustration of the necessity to adopt different definitions of concepts and rules of measurement in considering LDCs, Streeten made a telling point in relation to food. In DCs food is defined as an element in consumption, but in countries where malnutrition inhibits the working capacity of labour it could appropriately be classed as investment.

The neoclassical critics of development economics present different arguments against the application of conventional macroeconomic categories to the management of LDC economies. In the first place they are opposed to macroeconomic management and planning of the neo-Keynesian type which stems from acceptance and application of the models referred to in Sections 2.1 to 2.3. Lal (1983, p.8) posits an interesting relationship between Keynesian and development economics. Whereas Keynes had been addressing the problem of there being insufficient aggregate demand to stimulate full utilisation of the capital stock, with consequent unemployment, LDCs' problems were seen by development economists as arising from there being too few 'machines' adequately to employ the existing 'men'. Thus:

> The allocation of resources, a major concern of orthodox economics, was considered of minor importance compared to the problems of increasing resources — subsumed in the portmanteau term 'capital' — and of ensuring their fullest utilisation. The Keynesian modes of thought also led to an implicit or explicit rejection of the primary role assigned by orthodox economics to changes in relative prices in mediating imbalances in the supply and demand for different 'commodities' . . . (Lal 1983, p.8)

Exactly the same point is made by Little (1982, p.20) who attributes structuralist mistrust of the price mechanism to the perception that 'Change is
inhibited by obstacles, bottlenecks, and constraints. People find it hard to
move or adapt, and resources tend to be stuck. In economic terms the supply of most things is inelastic'.

A related belief attributed to the structuralists, and much criticised by
Little and Lal, was their underlying pessimism about the capacities of
international trade to act as an 'engine of growth', and/or their perception
that export possibilities were poor and LDCs' terms-of-trade were
inevitably disadvantageous. Hence Little (pp.51–2) describes the intellec-
tually important position of India in the 1950s and 1960s as:

> Thus, export pessimism, India's lack of many minerals, the idea that she must
> become independent of aid (and pay her debts) showed structurally that *all*
> manufactures must be made in India. There seemed to be no possibility of
> choice, and so world prices were irrelevant. So far as industry was concerned
> the pattern would be determined almost entirely by domestic demand. Thus,
> 'balanced' growth was also taken for granted and no allowance was made for
> the role of total inelasticity.

In practice this entailed that India, under the influence of Prime Minister
Nehru and of Mahalanobis, set up a machinery for development planning
using input–output analysis techniques in which price changes were of
minimal importance,[6] with the objective of achieving rapid, self-reliant,
industrially-based development. Little and Lal, who were both involved in
Indian planning, observe that the planning process ignored international
price signals as a guide to resource allocation and as indicators of potential
gains from trade. As a consequence they argue that India's development
was adversely affected when compared to the performance of East Asian
countries which emphasised export-led growth and free-trade,[7] and that
forced industrialisation entailed considerable sacrifices in terms of growth
of income. Their rejection of planning is not, however, on the grounds
that market forces approximate perfect competition – they accept that
institutional structures are imperfect so that market induced solutions
may be second-best – rather they argue (Lal 1973, p.75) 'The strongest
argument against planning of the Soviet or Marxist variety is that, whilst
omniscient planners might forecast the future more accurately than
myopic private agents, there is no reason to believe that flesh-and-blood
bureaucrats can do any better – and some reason to believe they may do
much worse.' Recent liberalisation of the Chinese economy to decentralise
decision making and allow room for the profit motive suggests that
China's current leaders sympathise with this statement.

Clearly there is a fundamental gulf between the structuralists and those
who emphasise neoclassical economic management of LDCs. The structuralists believe that, while unrestricted market forces have a role to play

in many areas of the economy, these have to be supplemented by state direction of resources and planning in others to overcome institutional weaknesses and lack of market dynamism in others. The neoclassical economists, while agreeing that there are market imperfections, believe that attempts to accelerate investment in activities which are uneconomic at world prices and require import-tariff (or, even worse, import-quota[8]) protection lead to even poorer results in terms of GNP than if free trade had prevailed even with market imperfections.

This in turn introduces a further source of disagreement between those advocating neoclassical economic policies and some of the structuralists. While neoclassical economists and structuralists such as Hirschman, Nurkse, Rostow, and Lewis incline towards the position that social welfare and development will be maximised if the growth of GNP is maximised, this is not agreed by all. As has become clear from Chapter 1 on the meaning of development, there are others who may be classed as structuralists, as well as the dependency theorists, who choose to define development in terms other than simply increasing national income. Fundamental differences of view are inevitable in the face of this lack of consensus by development economists about what development is. It is, however, natural that those working in the tradition of positive economics should have concentrated their attention upon measurable variables such as gross domestic product and capital formation. They could hardly have done otherwise, and the inclusion of qualitative variables might in any event expose the analysis to even more serious sources of subjective bias. While attempts to improve the relevance of existing models are necessary, it seems unlikely that all of the criticisms of development theory can possibly be met.

(C) ALTERNATIVE VIEWS OF DEVELOPMENT: UNDERDEVELOPMENT AND DEPENDENCE

2.5 Introduction

In this section we present a brief survey and critique of alternative views of the problems of development and underdevelopment. These views have developed largely within the structuralist/neo-Marxist/Marxist framework of analysis and have given rise to various theories of 'dependency'. These theories have in turn been subject to increasingly severe criticism in recent years which has called into question the validity and usefulness of the dependency perspective.[9]

The terms 'underdevelopment' and 'dependency' tend to be used interchangeably in the literature and for many writers 'underdevelopment' and 'dependent development' are identical. In so far as there is a conceptual distinction, underdevelopment theory implies an extremely negative view regarding the possibility of development within the existing international economic system, whereas dependency theory acknowledges that some development and industrialisation is occurring but stresses that it is a 'distorted' or 'dependent' process of development. These issues will be further discussed below.

In the late 1960s and early 1970s it became commonplace in much of the literature on economic development to describe or characterise LDCs as dependent economies. The condition of dependency, it was argued, encompassed all or most of the following features:

(1) From their common historical background (colonialism), LDCs inherited particular structures of production and trade, notable among which was the production of primary commodities (raw materials and foodstuffs) for export to the developed capitalist economies.
(2) They were initially dependent on imports for their manufactured goods requirements. With the gradual establishment of import-substituting consumer goods industries, they became dependent on imports of intermediate and capital goods.
(3) Partly as a result of industrial development, they became heavily dependent on imports of foreign technology, although this form of dependency covered many other spheres of activity – agriculture, communications, education, medicine, and so on.
(4) The LDCs were in general deeply penetrated by foreign capital, largely in the guise of the transnational corporation (TNC), with its associated patterns of production, technology transfer, marketing, expertise, etc.
(5) Because of their inherited structures of production and trade and their penetration by foreign capital, LDCs experienced a drain of surplus, the result of unequal exchange (see Chapter 5) and profit repatriation by TNCs.
(6) At a very general level, there existed a condition of cultural, psychological, social and political dependence. Nominal political independence had been gained by all but a few LDCs, but this had not been matched by economic independence, a situation which was first generally recognised in the early 1960s (at least in independent Africa) and which gave rise to the concept of 'neo-colonialism' (see, for example, Nkrumah 1965).[10]

Dependency theory itself largely originated in Latin America and the

Caribbean (for an example of the latter, see Girvan 1973) and contains two
basic strands of thought (O'Brien 1975; Palma 1978):

(1) The first is the 'structuralist' tradition of the UN Economic Commission for Latin America (ECLA). This emphasised the failure of
exports to stimulate growth because of the alleged long-run secular
decline in the terms of trade between primary products and
manufactured goods and the consequent need for industrialisation
behind protective barriers (the move from an outward-orientated to
an inward-orientated development path). The subsequent 'failure'
of this import-substituting industrialisation strategy –
industrialisation did not bring with it the expected developmental
and modernisation benefits – led to the realisation that the forms
of dependency may have changed but that the essential condition
had not been eliminated. The structuralist analysis of these problems is discussed in the chapters on trade, income distribution,
industrialisation and the TNC and will not be further examined in
this section.[11]

(2) The second is a 'Marxist or neo-Marxist' ('neo' implying that it
diverged from orthodox Marxism in a number of respects) perspective deriving from the work of Baran (1957), Frank (1967, 1969,
1972), Dos Santos (1973) and others. It is to a discussion of this latter influence that we devote the rest of this chapter. It should be
pointed out that there is considerable overlap in the views of structuralist and Marxist writers, and particular writers are not always
easy to categorise. Indeed, the question of who is, or is not, a 'Marxist' has generated much controversy, but these problems will not be
pursued in this chapter.

2.6   The Concept of Underdevelopment

The basic starting point of the analysis of underdevelopment and
dependence is the recognition that underdevelopment is not a condition
that all countries experience, or a stage that all countries pass through,
before development. Rather, development and underdevelopment are
regarded as opposite sides of the same coin (Frank 1967, p.9). It is held
that the development of some countries actively led to the underdevelopment (or distorted development) of others, and that underdevelopment is a
'normal' part of the development of the world capitalist system. Szentes
(1971, p.132) argues that:

The socio-economic state of the developing countries is not merely 'economic
underdevelopment', not just a sign of not having participated in development,

of their having fallen behind in progress, but it is the product of a specific development, which is most closely connected with, moreover derived from, the development of capitalist world economy.

The development gap between developed and less-developed countries (that is, the difference in the levels of productive forces) was held to widen as a result of colonialism and the interaction of the two groups of countries. In the LDCs themselves, the establishment of 'alien' forms of economic and social/political organisation and the external orientation of their economies led to a pattern of development very different from that which would have occurred if their development had been based mainly on internal socio-economic forces.

A complete understanding of the present position of LDCs must thus begin with an analysis of colonialism, seen as the objective consequence of the emergence and development on a world scale of the capitalist mode of production (Szentes 1971, Part 2, Ch.1).[12] Colonialism is seen as essentially an economic phenomenon, the earliest period of which was associated with piracy, the plunder of treasure from foreign lands, and the slave trade (the period of so-called primitive capital accumulation). As industrial capitalism developed in western Europe, the nature of its impact on the rest of the world changed. An international division of labour was established in which colonial possessions were formally incorporated into the spheres of interest of the metropolitan powers and functioned as suppliers of minerals and agricultural raw materials to the metropolitan powers, as markets for industrial products, as areas of expanded investment opportunities (and thus as a regular source of income to the metropolitan powers), as well as fulfilling strategic and political functions.

Large areas of the world were thus incorporated into the expanding world economy through the vigorous outward thrust of the rapidly growing societies of western Europe. New patterns of production and trade were introduced along with more advanced technical, scientific and infrastructural facilities. New cultural and religious values were also introduced. But in this process, old societies, institutions, cultures and values were partially, if not completely, destroyed and the processes of change (albeit slow) that were taking place in these societies were retarded and distorted.[13]

Marx on India

Marx wrote several articles analysing the impact of British rule on India (Marx 1853, 1973; see also Kiernan 1974). Marx regarded Asian society as stagnant, based on a village system described as 'undignified, stagnatory and vegetative'.[14] He argued that Britain's conquest of India had a twofold mission:

(a) destructive – the plunder and annihilation of the old Asiatic society (including the destruction of native communities and the elimination of Indian industries); and

(b) constructive – the laying of the material foundations of Western society in Asia. This regeneration consisted of, *inter alia*, (i) the political unification of the country, (ii) the establishment of private property in land, (iii) the creation of a class of Indians 'endowed with the requirements for government and imbued with European science', and (iv) the establishment of a communication network, especially the development of a railway system, leading to the creation of 'fresh productive powers'.

The latter was considered to be most important. Industrial interests in the UK (the so-called millocracy) recognised the need to pursue policies expanding the Indian market for UK manufactured goods (especially textiles) and to ensure guaranteed and regular supplies of raw cotton to the UK mills. Railways were needed to develop the production and export of cotton and other raw materials but, Marx argued:

> You cannot maintain a net of railways over an immense country without introducing all those industrial processes necessary to meet the immediate and current want of railway locomotion, and out of which there must grow the application of machinery to those branches of industry not immediately connected with railways. The railway system will therefore become, in India, truly the forerunner of modern industry. (Marx 1973 edition, p.323)

In turn, industrialisation would dissolve the caste system and other impediments to social change.

But as Kiernan (1974, pp. 189–91) notes, emancipation from the past proceeded more slowly than Marx expected. Indian religion and social habits retarded social change; since there was no Indian State there was no tariff policy to protect Indian industry; capital flowed into land rather than into industry, and the countryside was able to absorb surplus labour power.

Baran (1957, Ch.5) has stressed the point that capitalist penetration developed some of the prerequisites of capitalist development but blocked others, mainly through (i) the removal of the previously accumulated and currently generated economic surplus which retarded capital accumulation, and (ii) the destruction of indigenous industries. Capitalist development was 'distorted' to suit the purposes of Western imperialism (Baran 1957, p.144).[15] Of major importance for Baran was the nature of the wealthy class, either surviving from pre-colonial times or created under colonial rule. This was a class that either could not or would not develop into an autonomous bourgeoisie, and was thus incapable of establishing the capitalist mode of production in its own country. Rather, it was a 'comprador bourgeoisie' whose position was dependent on, and allied to, foreign interests.

Baran has been classified by some as a 'neo-Marxist' and controversy has arisen over the relationship between 'neo-Marxism' and 'classical' Marxism. Foster-Carter (1974, p.69) has argued that:

> The rise of a neo-Marxist school centred on the problem of underdevelopment (albeit conceived very differently from its original bourgeois meaning) ... must be seen against a backcloth of the perceived inadequacy, not only of bourgeois descriptions and prescriptions, but also of traditional Marxist ideas about 'backward' countries.[16]

Leys (1975, Ch.1), however, has maintained that there is no necessary conflict between Marx's views on India and the 'neo-Marxists'' views of the non-development of contemporary LDCs. From Marx's writings on Ireland, Leys argued that, had he lived long enough, Marx would have produced a theory of underdevelopment along the lines of today's 'neo-Marxists' and that thus there was no real inconsistency between Marx and Baran regarding the latter's insistence on the part played in the process of underdevelopment by surplus transfer:

> Underdevelopment theory is thus partly a correction and partly an expansion of Marx's interpretation of history, an extension of his method and central ideas which, in a world scale, was still in embryo at his death. (Leys 1975, p.7)

Underdevelopment theory should thus be the history of LDCs viewed in their own right, rather than merely seen as sources of primitive capital accumulation for the Western economies.[17]

Dos Santos (1973) made a similar point when he argued that theories of imperialism were essentially eurocentric, that is, imperialism was analysed from the standpoint of the problems of the advanced capitalist country. Until recently, little attention had been devoted to its impact on LDCs, but Dos Santos believed that the study of the development of LDCs had to give rise to a theory of dependence. It is within this context that we must briefly discuss the work of Andre Gunder Frank.

Andre Gunder Frank

In his work on Latin America, Frank coined the now famous expression, 'the development of underdevelopment' (used by many others – for example, Rodney 1972) to refer to the continuous process by which capitalist contradictions and capitalist development generate underdevelopment in the peripheral satellite countries whose economic surplus is expropriated, whilst generating development in the metropolitan centres that appropriate the surplus. The 'contradictions' that Frank refers to are:

The expropriation/appropriation of the surplus. Using Baran's (1957) concept of 'potential' or potentially investible economic surplus (an economic surplus that is not available to society because its monopoly structure prevents its production, or if it is produced, it is appropriated and wasted through luxury consumption), Frank argued that the non-realisation and unavailability for investment of 'potential' economic surplus was due essentially to the monopoly structure of capitalism (Frank 1969, pp. 6–7). Chile (the country Frank was analysing) was always subject to a high degree of monopoly, both external and internal, and the external monopoly resulted in the expropriation of a considerable part of the economic surplus produced in Chile and its appropriation by another part of the world capitalist system. Furthermore:

> The monopoly capitalist structure and the surplus expropriation/appropriation contradiction run through the entire Chilean economy, past and present. Indeed, it is this exploitative relation which in chain-like fashion extends the capitalist link between the capitalist world and national metropolises to the regional centres (part of whose surplus they appropriate), and from these to local centres and so on to large landowners or merchants who expropriate surplus from small peasants or tenants and sometimes even from these latter to landless labourers exploited by them in turn ... at each point the international, national and local capitalist system generates economic development for the few and underdevelopment for the many. (Frank 1969 edition, pp. 7–8)

Metropolis – satellite polarisation. The metropolis expropriates the economic surplus from its satellites and appropriates it for its own economic development, leading to polarisation in which there is development at the centre and underdevelopment at the periphery. One important corollary of this thesis is that, if it is in fact the case that satellite status generates underdevelopment, then it follows that the weaker are metropolis–satellite relationships (for example, at times of war and economic depression), the greater are the possibilities for the local development of the satellite.

The contradiction of continuity in change. The structural essentials of economic development and underdevelopment are continuous and ubiquitous throughout the expansion and development of the capitalist system. Even though important historical changes have taken place in specific parts of the system, the basic condition of underdevelopment is constant and has been so for centuries, ever since the capitalist system expanded across the world.

Two major implications of Frank's analysis require brief mention. At the political level, the conclusion is drawn that the Latin American bourgeoisie is incapable of undertaking its 'historical task', that is, it cannot adopt independent, nationalist policies leading to a democratic political system and independent national development. This is because of its origins and economic connections. What exists, Frank argued in a later work (Frank 1972), is a lumpenbourgeoisie, a class which is a passive or active tool of foreign industry and commerce, and whose interests are thus identical.

The second major point is that, according to Frank, most of Latin America was incorporated into the world capitalist system during the very first phase of its colonial history, and thus it does not make sense to speak of feudal, semi-feudal or archaic elements in Latin American society. This is an attack on both orthodox notions of dualism, with their concept of an untouched, traditional society coexisting with, but independent of, a modern capitalist sector, and on the parallel orthodox Marxist notion of pre-capitalist modes of production (feudalism, Asiatic mode, etc.) which give way to capitalism.

Frank's work has been extensively criticised from many different quarters (the extensive bibliography given in Frank 1977 illustrates the reaction his work has provoked; Booth 1975 provides a good survey of the work of both Frank and his critics; see also Palma 1978; Brewer 1980; Booth 1985). In his later work (1972, 1977) Frank has answered some attacks from the left by stressing that underdevelopment must be understood and defined in terms of social classes and that dependence 'should not and cannot be considered a purely "external" relationship imposed on Latin America from abroad and against their wishes. Dependence is also, and in equal measure, an "internal" integral element of Latin American society' (Frank 1972, p.3). We return to this point below.

A significant criticism has been made by Laclau (1971) who argues that Frank confuses the concept of the capitalist mode of production with participation in a world capitalist economic system. The pre-capitalist character of the dominant relations of production in Latin America:

> ... was not only *not* incompatible with production for the world market, but was actually intensified by the expansion of the latter. The feudal regime of the haciendas tended to increase the servile exactions on the peasantry as the growing demands of the world market stimulated maximisation of their surplus. (Laclau 1971, p.30)

Furthermore, Laclau maintains that to affirm the feudal character of relations of production does not necessarily involve maintaining a dualistic thesis (in which dualism is taken to imply that no connections exist between the 'modern' and 'traditional' sectors of the economy). As the above quote shows, the connections between the two sectors ('feudal' and 'modern') were strong and it is necessary to examine the system as a whole and show the 'indissoluble unity that exists between the maintenance of feudal backwardness at one extreme and the apparent progress of a bourgeois dynamism at the other' (p.31). Booth (1975) argues that a major gap in Frank's analysis is a discussion of the interconnections between different modes of production combined in a single, national or international, economic system.

From another viewpoint Cardoso (1972) has argued that dependency, monopoly capitalism and development are not contradictory terms and that there is occurring a kind of dependent capitalist development in some LDCs. Taking into account the characteristics of contemporary industrial development and the operations of TNCs in LDCs in countries such as Argentina, Brazil, Mexico and India, there is an 'internal structural fragmentation', linking the most advanced parts of these economies to the international capitalist system. Separate from, although subordinate to, these advanced sectors, the backward economic and social sectors become 'internal colonies' and a new kind of dualism is created (Cardoso 1972, p.90). We return to the work of Cardoso below.

Frank's analysis may be relevant to agro-mineral societies, but his pursuit of a general explanation of underdevelopment obscures the diversity of economic structure and experience. Both open, export-orientated economies and 'inward-looking' semi-industrialised economies are in some sense dependent, but the nature of the 'dependency' differs markedly in the two cases. In view of these problems, it would perhaps be better to abandon the idea of underdevelopment as an active process in the contemporary world and concentrate instead on the varied processes of change that are actually taking place.[18]

2.7 Dependency Theory and Dependent Capitalist Development

What clearly emerges from the above discussion is that dependency cannot be viewed as a purely external phenomenon and this is a point that is stressed by a leading dependency theorist, Dos Santos (1973). Dos Santos defines dependence as a 'conditioning situation, in which the economies of one group of countries are conditioned by the development and expansion of others' (p.76). That is, dependence is based on an international division of labour which allows industrial development to take place in some countries while restricting it in others, 'whose growth is conditioned by and subjected to the power centres of the world' (p.77). The concept of dependence must take into account the articulation of dominant interests in both the metropolitan centres and the dependent societies – domination is only possible when it is supported by local groups which profit from it ('External domination, in a pure sense, is in principle impracticable') (p.78).[19]

From this analysis follows a most important conclusion:

> . . . if dependence defines the internal situation and is structurally linked to it,
> a country cannot break out of it simply by isolating herself from external
> influences; such action would simply provoke chaos in a society which is of its
> essence dependent. The only solution therefore would be to change its internal
> structure – a course which necessarily leads to confrontation with the existing
> international structure. (Dos Santos 1973, p.79)

The definition of dependence given by Dos Santos has been widely
quoted and as Palma (1978, p.901) has argued, it represents 'the beginnings of an interesting attempt to break with the concept of a mechanical
determination of internal by external structures which dominated the
traditional analysis of the left in Latin America and which particularly
characterised Frank's work'. Nevertheless, Palma criticises the definition
as being both static and unhistorical (1978, p.901) and Warren (1980,
p.165) too argues that:

> The characterisation of dependency as a 'conditioning situation' . . . is mean-
> ingless as it stands, since *all* phases of the development of any society in the
> modern period are conditioned by external areas in various ways (and condi-
> tioning operates both ways). The formulation can have meaning only if it
> specifies the mechanism or effects (or direction of effects) of the conditioning,
> or both. Otherwise the definition becomes either tautological or says simply
> that some economies have a more powerful effect on other economies than
> those do on them. Dos Santos' definition qualifies as both tautology and
> truism.

Lall (1975) is another critic of the concept of dependence who argues
that it is defined in a circular manner – 'LDCs are poor because they are
dependent and any characteristics that they display signify dependence'
(p.800). For Lall, any concept of dependence which is to serve a useful
analytical purpose must satisfy two criteria:

(1) It must identify certain characteristics of dependent economies
    which are not found in non-dependent ones.
(2) These characteristics must be shown to exert an adverse influence
    on the process and pattern of growth and development in the
    dependent economy.

After discussing so-called static and dynamic characteristics of
dependence, Lall concludes that the concept as applied to LDCs is
impossible to define and cannot be shown to be related causally to the continuation of underdevelopment. He argues that it makes more sense to
think in terms of a pyramidal structure of socio-political dominance in the
capitalist world, 'with the top (hegemonic) position held by the most
powerful capitalist country and the bottom by the smallest and poorest
ones, and a more or less continuous range occupied by various developed
and less developed countries, with relative positions changing between the
two' (Lall 1975, p.803).

Lall's critique is a powerful one, but it could be argued that it treats dependency as a purely economic phenomenon, rather than as a concept with its roots in political economy. Dependence is a concept empty of meaning if it fails to analyse emerging or existing patterns of class structure and conflict in the LDCs and the relationships that exist between indigenous ruling classes, groups or elites and foreign interests.[20] It is indeed a strong point of much dependency writing that it does attempt to incorporate non-economic factors, that is, it is multi- (or inter-) disciplinary in intent.

The most influential and sophisticated presentation of this approach is to be found in the work of Cardoso and Faletto, first published in English in 1979 (see also Palma 1978). Their theoretical approach is 'structural and historical':

> ... social structures are the product of man's collective behaviour ... although enduring, social structures can be, and in fact are, continuously transformed by social movements ... our approach emphasises not just the structural conditioning of social life, but also the historical transformation of structures by conflict, social movements and class struggles. (Cardoso and Faletto 1979, p.x)

Situations of dependency are not stable and permanent and do not necessarily generate further underdevelopment and dependency. Cardoso and Faletto argue that we need to analyse both the mechanisms that perpetuate these situations *and* the mechanisms within the system that bring about change. Furthermore, dependency and imperialism are not simply viewed as the 'external and internal sides of a single coin, with the internal aspects reduced to the condition of "epiphenomenal"' (p.xv). The impact of imperialism depends, *inter alia*, on the forms of local societies colonised or otherwise incorporated into the global capitalist economy, the reaction of those societies against their incorporation, their political dynamic and their attempts at alternative strategies. Most importantly, they argue:

> We conceive the relationship between external and internal forces as forming a complex whole whose structural links are not based on mere external forms of exploitation and coercion, but are rooted in coincidences of interests between local dominant classes and international ones, and, on the other side, are challenged by local dominated groups and classes .... External domination in situations of national dependency (opposed to purely colonial situations where the oppression by external agents is more direct) implies the possibility of the 'internalization of external interests'. (Cardoso and Faletto, p.xvi)

The expansion of capitalism in different countries in the periphery thus had varying consequences, even though all countries were subject to the same global system.[21] Cardoso and Faletto analyse two basic historical situations of dependency in some detail (dependency in enclave situations, and dependency where the productive system was nationally controlled) and emphasise the specificity of 'situations of dependency'. They *do not* attempt to develop a general 'theory' of dependency or 'dependent capitalist development', applicable to all circumstances at all times, but, in Palma's (1978) terminology, they are concerned with the elaboration of a methodology for the analysis of 'concrete situations of under-development'.

What, then, are the essential characteristics of contemporary 'situations of dependency'? According to Cardoso and Faletto (1979, p.xx), a system is dependent when 'the accumulation and expansion of capital cannot find its essential dynamic component inside the system'. The dominant centres of world capitalism possess, by definition, the technological and financial sectors essential to production and capital accumulation. Even the semi-industrial LDCs, however, remain dependent as their capital goods sectors are not strong enough to ensure the 'continuous advance of the system, in financial as well as in technological and organizational terms' (p.xxi). The development of industrial capitalism in the LDCs thus creates 'concrete situations of dependency with features distinct from those of advanced capitalist societies' (p.xxii), in particular, a reliance on the manufacture of products which in the centre are mass consumed but which in the periphery are typically luxurious consumption.[22]

Cardoso and Faletto argue that dependent capitalist development is taking place in some Latin American economies but it is development that produces '. . . as it evolves, in a cyclical way, wealth and poverty, accumulation and shortage of capital, employment for some and unemployment for others' (Cardoso and Faletto 1979, p.xxiii). 'Development' in reality is thus very different from the various normative conceptions outlined (and criticised) in Chapter 1.

2.8 Dependency Theory: A Critique

As noted above, from the early 1970s onwards, dependency theory was increasingly criticised by a number of writers, most effectively by those writing from an explicitly Marxist perspective. Leys (1977), in an abrupt reversal of his earlier views, condemned underdevelopment and dependency theory for its theoretical repetition and stagnation, the existence of fundamental problems of analysis which it would not solve (for example, the meaning of development, the concept of 'exploitation') and its co-option by 'developmentalists allied to international capital' (Leys 1977, p.92). In particular, Leys was influenced by evidence suggesting that indigenous capitalism was emerging in a number of LDCs (a point further discussed in Chapter 9), evidence which was usually unacknowledged or underplayed by dependency theorists.

Warren (1980, Chapter 7) presented a powerful, general critique. Referring to dependency theory as 'nationalist mythology', he argued, *inter alia*, that:

(1) Dependency theory was static in that, although in some versions it recognised the possibility of dynamic development (in the work of Cardoso, for example), only the forms of dependency changed, not the situation or condition of dependency itself.

(2) The centre–periphery model was taken as given – political independence, nationalism and industrialisation in a number of key LDCs (see Chapter 9 for further discussion) were not given their due weight.

(3) Direct foreign investment (DFI) via transnational corporations could not be assumed to command political (or even economic) power in host LDC countries – the dependency perspective seriously underestimated the bargaining power of the LDC state, and a strong state could increasingly integrate transnational investments into its national priorities (see Chapter 10 for further discussion).

(4) Most dependency theorists incorrectly assumed imperialism to be monolithic, thus failing to recognise the possibilities for LDCs exploiting intra-imperialist rivalries.

(5) LDCs did not respond in an identical manner to stimuli emanating from developed capitalist economies – the capacity to respond varied between countries and illustrated the role of policy choice in determining *actual* development (for example, the apparent ability of some of the newly industrialising countries (NICs) to adjust to and overcome shocks originating in the international economy in the mid- to late-1970s – see Chapter 9).

(6) Dependency theory assumed that there was a 'latent, suppressed historical alternative to the development that actually took place' (p.166), that the failure of this alternative to materialise was the result of external forces, but that *if* it had materialised, it would have proved to be a more autonomous (and by implication, superior) 'model' of development. It could not be assumed, however, that the 'social forces capable of embodying the allegedly suppressed alternative actually exist' (p.167) or that any alternative development model would of necessity be superior to the development that actually took place.

In this work, Warren emphasised the importance of the achievement of *political* independence by LDCs and the relative freedom that this gave them in terms of the economic policies they could pursue. He concluded that:

The concept of dependence has always been imprecise; such significance as it has relates almost entirely to *political* control of one society by another. Since national economies are becoming increasingly *interdependent*, the meaning of dependence is even more elusive, not to say mystical. (Warren 1980, p.182)

Warren's work was a powerful assertion of the classical Marxist position that LDCs would develop from pre-capitalist agrarian societies to industrial capitalist economies, as did the now-developed countries before them. It has attracted much attention, most of it hostile (see, for example, Lipietz 1982), and has in part generated much Marxist writing which has tried to elaborate what the relationships are between the capitalist and pre-capitalist modes of production in LDCs (see Foster-Carter 1978). Booth (1985) has produced a more sympathetic critique of Warren's work, in the context of a general critique of dependency theory which he accuses of being guilty of 'circular reasoning, fallacious inferences from empirical observation and a weak base in deductive theory' (p.762).

With respect specifically to Warren, Booth argues that his 'method of argument takes us from the indiscriminate pessimism of the dependency view of the world to a barely less misleading generalized optimism' (p.766). He maintains that Warren fails to give full recognition to important systematic variations within the general pattern of LDC development, and that specific national policy regimes and institutional arrangements are not properly considered in the analysis of the variations in economic performance between countries.

Booth concludes that:

While the need to move on from the type of generalised controversy represented by Warren vs dependency is now obvious and widely accepted, there is as yet little real understanding of what this might entail. (p.767)

2.9   Conclusions

Godfrey (1980, p.4) has suggested that the questions raised by the dependency school can be reduced to two, *viz*: what are the limits of capitalist development in the LDCs, and, in the determination of the limits, what is the relative importance of internal and external variables and in what way do they interact with one another?

Most dependency theorists would tend to the view that capitalist development in LDCs is either impossible or of a 'distorted', 'dependent' nature. Emphasis is placed on the primacy of external forces, and such views are often accompanied by a 'Third Worldist' ideology which sees the poor LDCs as being exploited by the rich developed capitalist economies. The prime contradiction or conflict is thus between countries rather than between classes.

On the other hand, Warren and those sympathetic to his theoretical perspective argue that capitalism has taken root in a significant number of LDCs and that the prospects for its expansion are good. Emphasis is placed on the primacy of internal factors in the emergence and growth of capitalism in LDCs, with the state playing a strategic role. Those close to, but critical of, Warren's analysis argue that the diversity and specificity of LDC experience must be explicitly recognised and that, without retreating from theory, the need is for more detailed case studies of LDC development. The need is for a 'theory of the articulation of external and internal variables in determining limits on capitalist development' (Godfrey 1980, p.4).

It is undoubtedly the case that dependency theory has provided many important insights into the characteristics of LDCs and the interaction between them and developed capitalist economies. But its Marxist critics argue that it is necessary to move forward to a different kind of theory and to a more clearly defined relation between theory and practice which will permit the drawing of conclusions relevant to contemporary struggles within these countries (Leys 1977, pp.100–1). One of those conclusions, in marked contrast to the 'Third Worldist' ideology briefly referred to above, has been well stated by Brewer (1980, p.293):

> ... opposition to the dominance of the major imperial powers is not necessarily genuine anti-imperialism and may represent no more than a desire by a newly formed bourgeoisie to establish itself within a world system that it does not wish to change. Socialists have frequently been deceived by anti-imperialist rhetoric into supporting viciously reactionary regimes. In any Marxist analysis the fundamental division must be that between classes, between capitalists and workers and not between nations.

Notes

1. In the Mahalanobis planning exercise the output–capital ratios are adjusted for capital depreciation. This adjustment involves adding replacement requirements to the capital side of the ratios. For example, if a machine which does not depreciate produces annual output equivalent to one third of its cost, the output–capital ratio is 1:3, but if the machine depreciates and has to be replaced every third year, the adjusted ratio will be 1:4.
2. It is easier to accept this emphasis in the Indian context in which Mahalanobis wrote. Despite low average per capita incomes in India, its huge population creates a sizeable market for heavy industrial products and steel which, given the availability of coal and iron ore, justified the development of heavy industry. In LDCs with much smaller populations, and without the required raw materials, heavy industry is difficult to justify and does not receive the same emphasis, although, as Frances Stewart (1976) has argued,

the capital goods industry is an important force for technical progress. (Issues relating to heavy industry are more fully discussed in Ch. 11.)

3. Although, as Myint (1964) states, the big-push theory results from logic relating the investment rate through the output–capital ratio to the rate of population growth, whereas the balanced growth theory evolved from wider concerns about the vicious circle between poverty, small markets and lack of investment incentives.

4. It is true that Lewis (1954) did discuss an open dualistic economy model. However, as previously noted, most of the generalisations which emerge about relationships in a closed economy disappear when trade is permitted. It is also true that the model can be adapted to consider the relationships between an export-orientated primary product enclave and an agricultural hinterland in which goods are all produced locally but for which modern capital goods are all imported.

5. Note that without such savings from agriculture out of this surplus the average consumption levels in agriculture would exceed the subsistence level by the amount of industrial product consumed; and unless, as it most certainly the case, the industrial wage were actually higher than the subsistence level, agricultural workers would have higher consumption levels than those in industry.

6. Basic input-analysis problems are solved with prices fixed. It is possible in principle to develop programming models around input output accounts in which an iterative problem is solved with input and output prices revalued after each round of the solution process.

7. In view of the extensive central direction and intervention which has been applied to the South Korean, Taiwanese and Singaporean economies, an immediate reaction might be that it is hard to accept these countries as adopting truly free-trade policies. However, Lal (1983, p.46) forcefully makes the subtle argument that *laissez-faire* must be distinguished from free trade. The distinction made is far from clear, but it is important in the context of Lal and Little's arguments in so far as it enables them to oppose impediments to free trade without opposing all forms of government intervention and direction. It would appear, from Lal, that giving employment or other direct subsidies for production is seen as an acceptable form of economic intervention, not inconsistent with free trade, but that border taxes and subsidies on goods and commodities, which clearly infringe free trade, are unacceptable.

8. At least with tariffs it is seen that some relationship is maintained between international and domestic prices, whereas with quotas the link can be almost completely severed, subject to the efficiency of the inevitable black markets.

9. Much has been written on dependency theory in recent years. Among the better articles, books and collections of articles are: Palma 1978; Booth 1985; Roxborough 1979; Brewer 1980; Blomstrom and Hettne 1984; Seers (ed.) 1981; Limqueco and McFarlane (eds) 1983.

10. Neo-colonialism was defined, in a resolution at the All-African People's Conference, Cairo, 1961, as 'the survival of the colonial system in spite of the formal recognition of political independence in emerging countries which become the victims of an indirect and subtle form of domination by political, economic, social, military or technical means'. Quoted in Leys (1975, p.26).

11. Leys (1977) re-emphasises the point that dependency theory has largely emerged from a continually revised interpretation of the process and characteristics of the development experience (largely of Latin America), mainly from an orthodox (i.e. non-Marxist) viewpoint. He concludes: 'The main stream of UDT (underdevelopment and dependency theory) can thus be seen as eventuating in radical structuralism – i.e. as a structuralist analysis of the obstacles to capitalist development in the Third World in which progressively more and more of what were originally seen as means to structural change – international manufacturing companies, Third World governments and the interests they mostly represent, etc. – come to be seen as yet further structures which themselves need to be changed' (p.97).

12. Barratt Brown (1974, Ch. 1) uses the concept of imperialism to 'encompass the outward drive of certain peoples (generally, since 1600, nation states) to build empires – both formal colonies and privileged positions in markets, protected sources of materials and extended opportunities for profitable employment of labour' (p.22). The term 'imperialism' is more commonly used (by Marxists) to describe the outward expansion of monopoly capitalism over the past 100 years (Lenin, *Imperialism – The Highest Stage of Capitalism*).

13. It would be wrong to regard all pre-colonial societies as stagnant, backward, primitive, etc. Hodgkin (1972) notes that 'technological advance and social change, in a centralising, modernising direction were ... taking place in a number of African societies in the late eighteenth and nineteenth centuries, as a result both of internal forces and external stimuli' (p.106).

14. Fernbach in his Introduction to Marx (1973 edition, pp. 26–7) notes that Marx was later to revise his views on the stagnant character of Indian society and to deny that the west European path of historical development was a necessary model for all societies.

15. India is usually quoted as the classic example of this process. It has been estimated that in the early decades of the twentieth century, Britain annually appropriated over 10% of India's GNP and this figure would have been higher in the eighteenth and nineteenth centuries. For a different view, see Mukerjee (1972).

16. For a criticism of Foster-Carter, see Taylor (1974).

17. Leys presents a broad outline of what he considers to be the main elements of underdevelopment theory: plunder and extortion – the slave trade – the period of primitive capital accumulation; the extraction of the investible surplus; the development of new social strata; the replacement of primitive by capitalist accumulation; replacement of direct rule by independent governments; external orientation of LDC economies; monopoly elements – force, trading companies, commodity markets, technology; import-substituting industrialisation and the TNC.

18. A further point deserves brief mention. Frank (1977, p.362) states that he has never had the temerity to claim to be a Marxist nor the desire to deny it, and thus we must avoid the mistake 'which Laclau makes – of reading Frank as a theoretically naive Marxist' (Leaver 1977, p.114). Leaver also suggests that 'the almost universally accepted conflation of Baran and Frank' must be challenged, but he does not develop this argument.

19. The situation is not static; there is interaction between the conditioned situation and the conditioning situation, and changes in either can affect the other; the situation of dependence itself alters with changes in the centre and changes in the dependent structures, redirecting the dependency relationship (Dos Santos 1973, p.78).

20. Given that the concept of dependency is not encompassed by a list of the characteristics of LDCs, or the processes of change taking place within them, it also follows that the theory of dependency does not fall within the positivist-deductive methodology discussed in Section A of this chapter. We cannot appeal to empirical evidence to prove or disprove the existence of dependency. In O'Brien's words (1975, pp. 11–12), the concept of dependence is a 'higher level or general hypothesis', the objective of which is 'to define the problem or area of interest and to try and show how lower level, more specific *ad hoc* hypotheses fit within this framework . . . The theory of dependency therefore represents a framework of reference within which various heterogeneous phenomena are analysed to see how they link and interact with each other to form a total system'.

21. In an influential, but demanding, article, Brenner (1977) has forcibly argued that the impact of capitalism on 'backward' areas was mediated through the class structures in those areas. It was not incorporation into the world economy *as such* that was the cause of underdevelopment, but rather it was the nature and characteristics of the class structure through which export production was carried out that determined whether export production would lead to underdevelopment or development. The production and export of sugar from the Caribbean is contrasted by Brenner with the production and export of tobacco from Colonial Virginia (in the southern USA) – the former leading to 'underdevelopment', the latter, eventually, to 'development'.

22. It is of interest to note the similarity of this conception of dependent development and Samir Amin's model of peripheral industrialisation, as outlined in Amin (1974b) for example. According to Amin, in LDCs exports and the consumption of luxury goods constitute the main peripheral-dependent relationship, whereas in the developed capitalist economy, so-called 'self-centred' development consists of the production of 'mass' consumption and capital goods. For a critique of Amin, see Schiffer 1981; Smith 1980, 1982.

References

Ackley, G. (1961) *Macroeconomic Theory*, Macmillan.

Adelman, I. and Thorbecke, E. (eds) (1966) *The Theory and Design of Economic Development*, The Johns Hopkins Press.

Agarwala, A.N. and Singh, S.P. (eds) (1958) *The Economics of Under-Development*, Oxford University Press.

Amin, S. (1974a) *Accumulation on a World Scale: a Critique of the Theory of Underdevelopment* (2 vols), Monthly Review Press, New York.

Amin, S. (1974b) 'Accumulation and development: a theoretical model, *Review of African Political Economy*, No. 1, August–November.

Baran, P. (1957) *The Political Economy of Growth*, Monthly Review Press, New York.

Baran, P.A. and Hobsbawn, E.J. (1966) 'The stages of economic growth: a review', *Kyklos*, Vol. 14, Reprinted in Wilber (1973).

Barber, W.J. (1967) *A History of Economic Thought*, Penguin Books.

Barratt Brown, M. (1974) *The Economics of Imperialism*, Penguin Books.

Beckford, G. (1972) *Persistent Poverty: Underdevelopment In Plantation Economies of the Third World*, Oxford University Press.

Blomstrom, M. and Hettne, B. (1984) *Development Theory in Transition*, Zed Books Limited.

Boeke, J.H. (1953) *Economics and Economic Policy of Dual Societies*, Institute of Pacific Relations, New York.

Booth, D. (1975) 'Andre Gunder Frank: an introduction and appreciation', in I. Oxaal, T. Barnett and D. Booth (eds), *Beyond the Sociology of Development*, Routledge and Kegan Paul.

Booth, D. (1985) 'Marxism and development sociology: interpreting the impasse', *World Development*, Vol. 13, No. 7, July.

Brenner, R. (1977) 'The origins of capitalist development: a critique of neo-Smithian Marxism', *New Left Review*, No. 104, July/August.

Brewer, A. (1980) *Marxist Theories of Imperialism: a Critical Survey*, Routledge and Kegan Paul.

Brookfield, H. (1975) *Interdependent Development*, Methuen.

Bruton, J. (1955) 'Growth models and underdevelopment economies', *Journal of Political Economy*, Vol. 63, reprinted in Agarwala and Singh (1958).

Cairncross, A.K. (1962) *Factors in Economic Development*, George Allen and Unwin.

Cardoso, F.H. (1972) 'Dependent capitalist development in Latin America', *New Left Review*, No. 74, July–August.

Cardoso, F.H. (1973) 'Associated-dependent development: theoretical and practical implications', in A. Stepan (ed.) (1973), *Authoritarian Brazil*, Yale University Press.

Cardoso, F.H. and Faletto, E. (1979) *Dependency and Development in Latin America*, University of California Press.

Chenery, H. (1965) 'The structuralist approach to economic development', *American Economic Review*.

Chenery, H.B. and Bruno, M. (1962) 'Development alternatives in an open economy: the case of Israel', *Economic Journal*, Vol. 72.

Chenery, H.B. and Strout, A.M. (1966) 'Foreign assistance and economic development', *American Economic Review*, Vol. 61, No. 4, Pt. I.

Domar, D. (1946) 'Capital expansion, rate of growth and employment', *Econometrica*, Vol. 14.

Dos Santos, T. (1973) 'The crisis of development theory and the problem of dependence in Latin America', in H. Bernstein (ed), *Underdevelopment and Development*, Penguin Books.

Fei, J.C. and Ranis, G. (1966) 'Agrarianism, dualism and economic development', Ch. 1 of Adelman and Thorbecke (eds) (1966).

Fleming, J.M. (1955) 'External economies and the doctrine of balanced growth', *Economic Journal*, Vol. 65, Reprinted in Agarwala and Singh (eds) (1958).

Foster-Carter, A. (1974) 'Neo-Marxist approaches to development and under-development', in E. de Kadt and G. Williams (eds) (1974), *Sociology and Development*, Tavistock.

Foster-Carter, A. (1978) 'The modes of production controversy', *New Left Review*, No. 107, January–February.

Frank, A.G. (1967) *Capitalism and Underdevelopment in Latin America*, Monthly Review Press, New York; Modern Reader Paperback Edition 1969.

Frank, A.G. (1969) *Latin America: Underdevelopment or Revolution*, Monthly Review Press, New York.

Frank, A.G. (1972) *Lumpenbourgeoisie: Lumpendevelopment: Dependence, Class and Politics in Latin America*, Monthly Review Press, New York.

Frank, A.G. (1977) 'Dependence is dead, long live dependence and the class struggle: an answer to critics', *World Development*, Vol. 5, No. 4.

Furtado, C. (1954) 'Capital formation and economic development', in Agarwala and Singh (eds) (1958).

Girvan, N. (1973) 'The development of dependency economics in the Caribbean and Latin America: review and comparison', *Social and Economic Studies*, Vol. 22, No. 1, March.

Godfrey, E.M. (1980) 'Is dependency dead?', *IDS Bulletin*, Vol. 12, No. 1, December.

Goodwin, R.M. (1961) 'The optimal growth path for an underdeveloped economy', *Economic Journal*, Vol. LXXI, No. 283.

Harrod, R.F. (1939) 'An essay in dynamic theory', *Economic Journal*, Vol. 49, No. 1.

Hirschman, A.O. (1958) *The Strategy of Economic Development*, Yale University Press.

Hodgkin, T. (1972) 'Some African and Third World theories of imperialism', in R. Owen and R.B. Sutcliffe (eds) (1972), *Studies in the Theory of Imperialism*, Longman.

Jorgenson, D. (1961) 'The development of a dual economy', *Economic Journal*, Vol. 71.

Jorgenson, D. (1967) 'Surplus agricultural labour and the development of a dual economy', *Oxford Economic Papers*, Vol. 19.

Kao, C.H.C., Anschel, K.R. and Eicher, C.K. (1964) 'Disguised unemployment in agriculture: a survey', Ch. 7 in C.K. Eicher and L.W. Witt (eds) (1964), *Agriculture in Economic Development*, McGraw-Hill.

Kay, G. (1975) *Development and Underdevelopment: A Marxist Analysis*, Macmillan.

Kiernan, V.G. (1974) 'Marx and India', in *Marxism and Imperialism*, Edward Arnold.

Laclau, E. (1971) 'Feudalism and capitalism in Latin America', *New Left Review*, No. 67, May–June.

Lal, D. (1983) *The Poverty of Development Economics*, Hobart Paper 16, Institute of Economic Affairs.

Lall, S. (1975) 'Is "dependence" a useful concept in analysing underdevelopment?', *World Development*, Vol. 3, Nos. 11 and 12.

Leaver, R. (1977) 'The debate on underdevelopment: "On situating Gunder Frank"', *Journal of Contemporary Asia*, Vol. 7, No. 1.

Leeson, P.F. (1979) 'The Lewis model and development theory', *The Manchester School*, No. 3, 1979, 196–200.

Lewis, W.A. (1954) 'Economic development with unlimited supplies of labour', *Manchester School*, Vol. 22, Reprinted in Agarwala and Singh (eds) (1958).

Lewis, W.A. (1955) *The Theory of Economic Growth*, George Allen and Unwin.

Lewis, W.A. (1968) 'Reflections on unlimited labour', Princeton Special Paper.

Lewis, W.A. (1979) 'The dual economy revisited', *The Manchester School*, No. 3, 1979, 211–229.

Leys, C. (1975) *Underdevelopment in Kenya: The Political Economy of Neo-Colonialism*, Heinemann.

Leys, C. (1977) 'Underdevelopment and dependency: critical notes', *Journal of Contemporary Asia*, Vol. 7, No. 1.

Limqueco, P. and McFarlane, B. (eds.) (1983) *Neo-Marxist Theories of Development*, Croom Helm.

Lipietz, A. (1982) 'Marx or Rostow?', *New Left Review*, No. 132, March/April.

Little, I.M.D. (1982) *Economic Development, Theory, Policy, and International Relations*, Twentieth Century Fund.

McKinnon, H.B. and Strout, A.M. (1966) 'Foreign assistance constraints in economic development and efficient aid allocation', *Economic Journal*, Vol. 54.

McKinnon, R.I. (1964) 'Foreign exchange constraints in economic development', *Economic Journal*, Vol. 74.

Mahalanobis, P.C. (1955) 'The approach of operational research to planning in India', *Sankhya: The Indian Journal of Statistics*, Vol. 16, Parts 1 and 2.

Marx, K. (1853) 'The East India Company – its history and results' and 'The results of the British rule of India', Reprinted in D. Fernbach (ed.) (1973), Karl Marx, *Surveys from Exile*, Political Writings, Vol. 2, Penguin Books.

Marx, K. and Engels, F. (1971 edition) *Ireland and the Irish Question*, Progress Publishers, Moscow.

Meier, G.M. (ed.) (1970) *Leading Issues in Economic Development* (2nd edn), Oxford University Press.

Mukerjee, T.G. (1972) 'Theory of economic drain: impact of British rule in the Indian economy 1840–1900', in D.E. Boulding and T. Mukerjee (eds) (1972), *Economic Imperialism*, University of Michigan Press.

Myint, H. (1964) *The Economics of the Developing Countries*, Hutchinson University Library.

Myrdal, G. (1970) *The Challenge of World Poverty*, Penguin Books.

Nkrumah, K. (1965) *Neo-Colonialism: The Last Stage of Imperialism*, Heinemann.

Nurkse, R. (1952) *Problems of Capital Formation in Underdeveloped Countries*, Basil Blackwell.

O'Brien, P.J. (1975) 'A critique of Latin American theories of dependency', in I. Oxaal, T. Barnett and D. Booth (eds) (1975), *Beyond the Sociology of Development*, Routledge and Kegan Paul.

Palma, C. (1978) 'Dependency: a formal theory of underdevelopment or a methodology for the analysis of concrete situations of underdevelopment?', *World Development*, Vol. 6, No. 7/8, July/August.

Raj, K.N. and Sen, A.K. (1961) 'Alternative patterns of growth under conditions of stagnant export earnings', *Oxford Economic Papers*, Vol. 13.

Ranis, G. and Fei, J.C. (1961) 'A theory of economic development', *American Economic Review*, Vol. 51, Reprinted in Eicher and Wit (eds) (1964).

Reddaway, W.B. (1962) *The Development of the Indian Economy*, George Allen and Unwin.

Rodney, W. (1972) *How Europe Underdeveloped Africa*, Bogle-L'Ouverture Publications London, and Tanzania Publishing House, Dar es Salaam.

Rosenstein-Rodan, P.N. (1943) 'Problems of industrialisation of Eastern and South-Eastern Europe', *Economic Journal*, Vol. 53, Reprinted in Meier (1970).

Rostow, W.W. (1956) 'The take-off into self-sustained growth', *Economic Journal*, Vol. 66, Reprinted in Agarwala and Singh (1958).

Rostow, W.W. (1960) *The Stages of Growth: A Non-Communist Manifesto*, Cambridge University Press.

Rostow, W.W. (ed.) (1963) *The Economics of Take-Off into Sustained Growth*, Macmillan.

Roxborough, I. (1979) *Theories of Underdevelopment*, Macmillan.

Schiffer, J. (1981) 'The changing post-war pattern of development: the accumulated wisdom of Samir Amin', *World Development*, Vol. 9, No. 6, June.

Seers, D. (1963) 'The limitations of the special case', *Bulletin of Oxford Institute of Economics and Statistics*, Vol. 25, No. 2.

Seers, D. (ed.) (1981) *Dependency Theory: A Critical Reassessment*, Frances Pinter.

Smith, S. (1980) 'The ideas of Samir Amin', *Journal of Development Studies*, Vol. 17, No. 1, October.

Smith, S. (1982) 'Class analysis versus world systems: critique of Samir Amin's typology of underdevelopment', *Journal of Contemporary Asia*, Vol. 12, No. 1.

Solow, R.M. (1962) 'Technical progress, capital formation and economic growth', *American Economic Review*, Vol. 25.

Stewart, F. (1976) 'Capital goods in developing countries', in A. Cairncross and M. Puri (eds) (1976), *Employment, Income Distribution and Growth*, Macmillan.

Streeten, P. (1972) *The Frontiers of Development Studies*, Macmillan.

Sunkel, O. (1969) 'National development policy and external dependence in Latin America', *Journal of Development Studies*, Vol. 6, No. 1.

Sunkel, O. (1973) 'The pattern of Latin American dependence', in V. Urquidi and R. Thorp (eds), *Latin America in the International Economy*, Macmillan.

Szentes, T. (1971) *The Political Economy of Underdevelopment*, Akademiai Kiado, Budapest.

Taylor, J. (1974) 'Neo-Marxism and underdevelopment – a sociological phantasy', *Journal of Contemporary Asia*, Vol. 4, No. 1.

Taylor, L. (1983) *Structuralist Macroeconomics: Applicable Models for the Third World*, Basic Books.

UN Economic Commission for Asia and the Far East (ECAFE) (1960) *Programming Techniques for Economic Development*.

Warren, B. (1980) *Imperialism: Pioneer of Capitalism*, NLB and Verso.

Wilber, C.K. (1973) *The Political Economy of Development and Underdevelopment*, Random House.

3

Economic equality and economic development

3.1 Introduction

We noted in Chapter 1 the distinction that is commonly made between the concepts of economic growth and economic development. The concept of economic development raises a number of normative issues, one of the most important of which concerns the degree of economic equality throught to be necessary or desirable, both as a means of stimulating, or as a trade-off against, economic growth, and as a development objective.

Although many LDCs have experienced rapid rates of growth of GDP over the past two decades, it has become increasingly obvious that this process has often brought little, if any, benefit to a substantial minority, or perhaps even a majority, of the population of these countries. Economists, planners and international agencies have expressed concern over the fact that perhaps one-third (the World Bank's estimate) of the population of LDCs has received no net benefit from growth. In some countries, the proportion of the population excluded from receiving the benefits of growth will be even higher and, in certain cases, large sections of the population may have sunk into even greater poverty as the result of the specific processes of change taking place within these societies.

Economic and social inequalities exist in many related and overlapping forms in LDCs. Inequalities in the distribution of personal income and wealth (especially land) are perhaps the most obvious, but inequalities between rural and urban areas, different regions and different religious and ethnic groups are all important and raise difficult policy issues. In the case of regional inequalities, tension can arise which may ultimately lead to armed conflict if not solved. Differential access to modern sector facilities (education, health, housing, employment) is both a cause and a consequence of economic and social inequalities in general. Many see unemployment as the prime cause of inequality and thus stress the need to create widespread employment opportunities within the LDC as a step towards the elimination of poverty and inequality. The International Labour Office in Geneva is a strong supporter of this argument, although it also focuses attention on the problem of the 'working poor', that is, those whose income falls below some specified minimum, even though they have a full-time job (see ILO 1972, Ch. 3). Unemployment is also, of course, a symptom of inequality.

In this chapter, we are concerned with the distribution of income and specifically with (1) the impact of economic growth on the pattern of income distribution over time and (2) the influence of the distribution of income on economic growth. We will argue that greater equality is a necessary condition if economic growth and development are to occur which will beneficially affect the lives of the mass of the population.

We do not propose to define the concept of economic equality in a formal manner (for a rigorous discussion of the welfare economic analysis of the distributional consequences of growth, see Fields 1980, Ch. 3; see also Bigsten 1983, Ch. 4). The concept of economic equality ecompasses, in Tawney's (1964, pp. 48–9) words, equality of 'circumstances, institutions, and manner of life'. As such, it refers to more than merely the distribution of income, but we shall assume that a society that aims at a lower degree of inequality in its income distribution will also be concerned with the reduction of those other economic and social inequalities referred to above.[1] Mehmet (1978, Ch. 8) makes a similar point when discussing economic planning and social justice:

> Our concept of egalitarian development in LDCs does not call for perfect equality for everyone in consumption or living standards ... We rather focus attention on the elimination of *excessively large disparities* between different individuals, groups and regions ... we are proposing a planning strategy that would *tend* to equalise living standards without necessarily leading to perfect equality as the final result. (Mehmet 1978, p.176)

3.2   The Distribution of Income in LDCs

Measurement of the degree of income inequality in LDCs is by no means straightforward, and there is no ideal way of empirically comparing differences in income distributions between countries. In the first place the necessary data are frequently unobtainable for LDCs, and even when available, they are not always reliable. Secondly, conceptual problems exist as to the basic unit for which the data should be analysed (whether it should be the individual, the nuclear family, or the household), the period over which income should be measured, and the definition of income that should be used (a problem of particular importance in LDCs). Thirdly, there are various alternative measures of inequality, and countries are liable to rank differently according to the measure chosen.

Fields (1980, Ch. 2) discussed four classes of measures:

(1) The relative inequality approach which considers the income changes of various groups relative to others. This approach is discussed in further detail below.

(2) The absolute income approach which looks at changes in various groups' incomes, the best-known example of which is perhaps the work of Ahluwalia and Chenery (in Chenery *et al*. 1974, Ch. II). It is proposed that society is divided into a number of socio-economic groups, defined by assets, income levels and economic functions. For policy purposes, certain poverty groups (small farmers, landless labourers, urban underemployed) may be identified, but to illustrate the problem, the population is divided into quintile groups and the rate of growth of income of each group, g_i, is assumed to measure the increase of its social welfare over the specified period. The rate of increase in welfare of the society as a whole is thus taken as the weighted sum of the growth of income of all groups:

$$G = w_1g_1 + w_2g_2 + w_3g_3 + w_4g_4 + w_5g_5$$

where G is the index of growth of total social welfare and w_i is the weight assigned to group i. As Ahluwalia and Chenery (1974, p.39) note:

> A summary measure of this type enables us to set development targets and monitor development performance not simply in terms of growth of GNP but in terms of the distributed pattern of income growth. The weights for each income class reflect the social premium on generating growth at each income level.

For example, an increase in income of $1 for a group with an annual income of $100 could be given the same weight as an increase of $100 for a group with an annual income of $10,000 and 'The use of such a weighted measure of growth would adjust the growth rate of countries with an inequitable pattern of development downwards, while countries pursuing income equalization will show a higher rate of growth' (Bigsten 1983, p.141).

(3) The absolute poverty approach which examines the proportion of the population which is poor and the incomes received by those who remain poor; that is, the focus of attention is on changes in the economic well-being of the poor, ignoring the remainder of the income distribution.

(4) The relative poverty approach which considers the absolute income received by the poorest 40% (or some other predetermined percentage) of the population.

The choice of measure is important in that, as Fields (1980, p.30) argues, 'How income distribution is studied . . . may lead to fundamentally different judgements about the success or failure of economic growth, even to the point of questioning whether there was any development at all'. Changes in inequality and poverty may go in different directions in a given country and, in particular, poverty may decrease while inequality increases. Knight (1976, p.169) too points out that 'There is no "right" index. Different indices have different properties and different value judgements implicit in them'.

In practice, most studies of income distribution in LDCs have used the relative inequality approach and two types of measure of inequality have been most frequently used. There are measures which express the whole frequency distribution of the population by income level, and there are single-valued measures which summarise such distributions. Since, in ranking countries according to their degree of income inequality, it is simpler to use a single-valued index, this type of measure is often used.

Of the single-valued measures of inequality the Gini coefficient is perhaps the most frequently used. This measure is calculated as the ratio of the areas under two different Lorenz curves. A Lorenz curve (see Figure 3.1) shows, in this case, the proportion of total income received by the bottom $x\%$ of income receivers (for all values of x up to and including 100%). The Gini coefficient is the ratio of the area between the line of equality and the Lorenz curve, (A), and the total area $(A+B)$ under the line of equality. The coefficient aways has a value of less than or equal to one, where one indicates perfect inequality.

For simple expository purposes it is probably more revealing to examine simplified distributions of income rather than single-valued summary

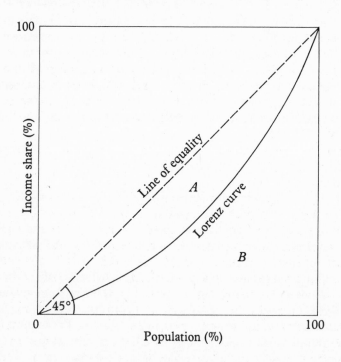

Figure 3.1   A Lorenz Curve

measures. Accordingly, Table 3.1 presents data which the World Bank has compiled for 66 countries according to (1) their level of overall inequality, and (2) their level of per capita income. It should be stressed that the classifications used are arbitrary and the 'moderate' and 'low' inequality categories should not be interpreted as meaning that the distribution of income is in some sense acceptable or poses no particular problems.

Keeping in mind the various qualifications, the data in Table 3.1 clearly show a higher degree of inequality in less-developed than in developed countries. Approximately half of the LDCs fall in the high-inequality category and a further one-third display moderate inequality. These same proportions apply also to the middle-income category of countries, and contrast markedly with those for the high-income countries which, with the exception of Finland, France and Venezuela, are equally distributed between the moderate- and low-inequality categories. More specifically, the relatively high-income inequality of the poorer countries is revealed by the large number of them in which the richest 20% of the population receive over 60% of the GNP, and in which the poorest 40% of the population receive less than 10% (or slightly more) of GNP. By contrast in the developed countries, in only two cases (France and the Federal Republic of Germany) do the richest 20% of the population receive more than 50% of GNP, although the percentage of GNP received by the poorest 40% is below 15% in a number of cases. Thus, without allowing for the countries omitted from Table 3.1, there is strong evidence that income is distributed more unequally in poor than in rich countries. This has in turn been interpreted as meaning that the level of inequality in the size distribution of income diminishes with development, a point that we return to in Section 3.3.

Various theories have been advanced in an attempt to explain the determinants of income distribution (those theories are summarised in Cline 1975; Bigsten 1983, Ch. 2).

They have in general emphasised explanations of functional income shares. It has usually been assumed that individuals possess various quantities of the factors of production (land, labour, capital and enterprise) which determine their income shares and hence the size distribution of personal incomes (Adelman and Morris 1973, p.142). Knight (1976) points to the need for an explanation of the distribution of the ownership of factors among households, and argues that the distribution of assets is determined primarily by historical, institutional and political forces, although economic forces and government policies are important. The distribution of political power in most LDCs is very uneven and is probably correlated with the distribution of income and wealth, with causation running both ways (from wealth to political power and vice versa). Knight concludes that:

Table 3.1 The Distribution of Income: Cross-Classification of Countries by Income Level and Equality

Income up to US $300

High inequality (Share of lowest 40% less than 12%)

Country/Year	Per capita GNP (US $)	Lowest 40%	Middle 40%	Top 20%
Kenya (1969)	136	10.0	22.0	68.0
Sierra Leone (1968)	159	9.6	22.4	68.0
Philippines (1971)	239	11.6	34.6	53.8
Iraq (1956)	200	6.8	25.2	68.0
Senegal (1960)	245	10.0	26.0	64.0
Ivory Coast (1970)	247	10.8	32.1	57.1
Rhodesia (1968)	252	8.2	22.8	69.0
Tunisia (1970)	255	11.4	53.6	55.0
Honduras (1968)	265	6.5	28.5	65.0
Ecuador (1970)	277	6.5	20.0	73.5
El Salvador (1969)	295	11.2	36.4	52.4
Turkey (1968)	282	9.3	29.9	60.8
Malaysia (1970)	330	11.6	32.4	56.0

Moderate inequality (Share of lowest 40% between 12% and 17%)

Country/Year	Per capita GNP (US $)	Lowest 40%	Middle 40%	Top 20%
Burma (1958)	82	16.5	38.7	44.8
Dahomey (1959)	87	15.5	34.5	50.0
Tanzania (1967)	89	13.0	26.0	61.0
India (1964)	99	16.0	32.0	52.0
Madagascar (1960)	120	13.5	25.5	61.0
Zambia (1959)	230	14.5	28.5	57.0
Dominican Republic (1969)	323	12.2	30.3	57.5

Low inequality (Share of lowest 40%, 17% and above)

Country/Year	Per capita GNP (US $)	Lowest 40%	Middle 40%	Top 20%
Chad (1958)	78	18.0	39.0	43.0
Sri Lanka (1969)	95	17.0	37.0	46.0
Niger (1960)	97	18.0	40.0	42.0
Pakistan (1964)	100	17.5	37.5	30.0
Uganda (1970)	126	17.1	35.8	47.1
Thailand (1970)	180	17.0	37.5	45.5
Korea (1970)	235	18.0	37.0	45.0
Taiwan (1964)	241	20.4	39.5	40.1
Surinam (1962)	394	21.7	35.7	42.6

Income US $300–750

Country (year)	GNP			
Colombia (1970)	358	9.0	30.0	61.0
Brazil (1970)	390	10.0	28.4	61.5
Peru (1971)	480	6.5	33.5	60.0
Gabon (1968)	497	8.8	23.7	67.5
Jamaica (1958)	510	8.2	30.3	61.5
Costa Rica (1971)	521	11.5	30.0	58.5
Mexico (1969)	645	10.5	25.5	64.0
South Africa (1965)	669	6.2	35.8	58.0
Panama (1969)	692	9.4	31.2	59.4
Iran (1968)	332	12.5	33.0	54.5
Guyana (1956)	550	14.0	40.3	45.7
Lebanon (1960)	508	13.0	26.0	61.0
Uruguay (1968)	618	16.5	35.5	48.0
Chile (1968)	744	13.0	30.2	56.8
Greece (1957)	500	21.0	29.5	49.5
Yugoslavia (1968)	529	18.5	40.0	41.5
Bulgaria (1962)	530	26.8	40.0	33.2
Spain (1965)	750	17.6	36.7	45.7

Income above US $750

Country (year)	GNP			
Venezuela (1970)	1004	7.9	27.1	65.0
Finland (1962)	1599	11.1	39.6	49.3
France (1962)	1913	9.5	36.8	53.7
Argentina (1970)	1079	16.5	36.1	47.4
Puerto Rico (1968)	1100	13.7	35.7	50.6
Netherlands (1967)	1990	13.6	37.9	48.5
Norway (1968)	2010	16.6	42.9	40.5
Germany, Fed. Rep. (1964)	2144	15.4	31.7	52.9
Denmark (1968)	2563	13.6	38.8	47.6
New Zealand (1969)	2859	15.5	42.5	42.0
Sweden (1963)	2929	14.0	42.0	44.0
Poland (1964)	850	23.4	40.6	36.0
Japan (1963)	950	20.7	39.3	40.0
United Kingdom (1968)	2015	18.8	42.2	39.0
Hungary (1969)	1140	24.0	42.5	33.5
Czechoslovakia (1964)	1150	27.6	41.4	31.0
Australia (1968)	2509	20.0	41.2	38.8
Canada (1965)	2920	20.0	39.8	40.2
United States (1970)	4850	19.7	41.5	38.8

Source: Chenery *et al.* (1974), Chapter 1, pp. 8–9.
Note: The income shares of each percentile group were read off a freehand Lorenz curve fitted to observed points in the cumulative distribution. The distributions are for pretax income. Per capita GNP figures are taken from the World Bank data files and refer to GNP at factor cost for the year indicated in constant 1971 US dollars.

Economists should be prepared to enter more explicitly into the realm of political economy. There is need for a more realistic theory of government than is normally assumed, and for a study of the relationships between the distribution of political power and the distribution of income. By examining the economic interests of the different groups in society, and the extent to which government policies are consistent with these interests, it may be possible to throw light on the role, the sources and the effects of political power. (Knight 1976, p.174)

Given the present state of our knowledge, any attempt at explaining the distribution of income has to be eclectic. For the purposes of this chapter, it is sufficient to state that the economic structure, the system of property ownership and social relations, market forces constrained by the economic and socio-political environment within which they operate, the structure of the labour market, government fiscal and social policies, and political, legal and social institutions are all factors which, acting together, determine the distribution of income and wealth in any country.[2]

In an attempt to investigate empirically the interactions between economic growth, political participation and the distribution of income in LDCs, Adelman and Morris (1973) constructed 35 indicators (taken from the 48 indicators listed in Table 3.2) of economic, social and political influences which could be expected, on theoretical grounds, to affect the distribution of income. Analysing data for 43 countries (for the 1950s and early 1960s), Adelman and Morris found that, on average, the poorest 60% of the population received 26% of total income. Their share was inversely related to the extent of socio-economic dualism and positively related to the level of social and economic modernisation and the expansion of secondary and higher education. The income share of the poorest 60% was smallest where 'a sharply dualistic development process had been initiated by well-entrenched expatriate or military elites ideologically oriented to receive most of the benefits of economic development' (p.160) and the authors found no support for the hypothesis that economic growth raised the share of income of the poorest groups of the population.[3]

The average share of income received by the top 5% of the population was 30%. Their share was higher in resource-rich countries, but in all countries the extent of the direct economic role of the government had an important moderating influence. The average share of the top 5% was significantly smaller in countries with large public sectors and important government net investments than in predominantly private enterprise economies.

The average share of the middle 20% of the population (the two deciles clustered around the median income) was 12%. This was the only share that appeared to vary systematically with the level of development, although the relationship was non-linear. The major influence differentiating between countries with respect to the share of this income group was the extent of socio-economic dualism.

Table 3.2 Adelman and Morris: 48 Qualitative Measures of Social, Economic and Political Characteristics of LDCs

Political indicators	Economic indicators	Socio-cultural indicators
Degree of national integration and sense of national unity	Per capita GNP in 1961	Size of the traditional agricultural sector
Degree of centralisation of political power	Growth rate of real per capita GNP, 1950/51–1963/64	Extent of dualism
Extent of political participation	Abundance of natural resources	Extent of urbanisation
Degree of freedom of political opposition and the press	Gross investment rate	Importance of the indigenous middle class
Degree of competitiveness of political parties	Modernisation of industry	Extent of social mobility
Predominant basis of the political party system	Industrialisation, 1950–63	Extent of literacy
Strength of the labour movement	Character of agricultural organisation	Extent of mass communication
Political strength of the traditional elite	Modernisation of techniques in agriculture	Degree of cultural and ethnic homogeneity
Political strength of the military	Improvement in agricultural productivity, 1950–63	Degree of social tension
Political and social influence of religious organisation	Adequacy of physical overhead capital	Crude fertility rate
Degree of administrative efficiency	Effectiveness of the tax system	Degree of modernisation of outlook
Extent of leadership commitment to economic development	Improvement in the tax system, 1950–63	Predominant type of religion
Extent of direct government economic activity	Effectiveness of financial institutions	Level of socio-economic development
Length of colonial experience	Improvement in financial institutions, 1950–63	
Type of colonial experience	Improvement in human resources	
Recency of self-government	Structure of foreign trade	
Extent of political stability	Rate of population growth	
	Country size and orientation of development strategy	

Source: Adelman and Morris 1973, pp. 15–16.

Adelman and Morris concluded thus:

> ... our analysis supports the Marxian view that economic structure, not level of income or rate of economic growth, is the basic determinant of patterns of income distribution. (Adelman and Morris 1973, p.186)

The methodology used by Adelman and Morris, their manipulation of data and their interpretation of the results have all been criticised (see, for example, Lal 1976; Cline 1975). Knight (1976) has pointed out that their results may indicate symptoms or non-casual associations, or that the direction of causation may be the opposite to that suggested. Equally important are the criticisms that can be made of the authors' attempts to quantify essentially non-quantifiable factors (especially political and socio-cultural variables) and their classification of countries on this basis. The dependence on cross-section data is also open to criticism, although, in inferring dynamic relationships from cross-section data, the authors (pp.187–8) make explicit their assumption that average country traits associated with successive development levels represent the path of change of a typical LDC undergoing economic growth.

3.3 Economic Growth and Income Distribution Over Time

A number of empirical studies (Adelman and Morris 1973; Paukert 1973; Chenery *et al.* 1974; Chenery and Syrquin 1975, Ch. 3; Ahluwalia 1976) have broadly supported the hypothesis first advanced by Kuznets of a 'long swing in the inequality characterising the secular income structure: widening in the early phases of economic growth when the transition from the pre-industrial to the industrial civilisation was most rapid; becoming stabilised for a while; and then narrowing in the later phases' (Kuznets 1955, p.18).

Kuznets argued that the relationship between inequality and per capita income took the form of an inverted U-shaped curve. Inequality was low in an unchanging, 'traditional' society, but it increased as the shift from agricultural to industrial activities and the move of population from rural to urban locations occurred. He suggested (pp.7–8) that inequality within the urban sector was greater than in other sectors, and this overall ine-quality increased as the urban sector grew more than proportionately to the rest of the economy. In addition, the concentration of savings in the upper income groups led to the concentration of an increasing proportion of income-yielding assets in the hands of this group, which in turn led to larger income shares in the future. At more mature levels of development, inequality began to decrease. Thus we find that both extreme economic underdevelopment and high levels of economic development are associated with greater income equality (Adelman and Morris 1973, p.188).

Kuznets's analysis was largely based on the historical experience of developed Western economies (the USA, the UK and Germany) and he was at pains to point out that it was dangerous to draw conclusions from historical experience and apply them to contemporary LDCs. But this warning was rarely heeded and the notion of a conflict between equity and economic growth was generally accepted.[4] One of the most influential models of development, the 'Lewis model' (Lewis 1954; discussed in Chapter 2), postulated that the level of savings in a society depended on the functional distribution of income rather than on the level of income. His model suggested that income must be redistributed in favour of the class that saves and invests (the capitalist class) in order to ensure capital accumulation and growth (although this did not necessarily imply that, overall, the distribution of income would become less equal). Following this line of argument, however, in Pakistan (to take one example) the concept of 'functional inequality' was promoted. That is, inequality was regarded as a positive virtue, and whenever there was a conflict between growth and equity, the latter was usually sacrificed without hesitation (Maddison 1971, p.85).

Lewis (1976, p.26) has re-emphasised the link between growth and inequality, stating that 'Development must be inegalitarian because it does not start in every part of an economy at the same time'. He argues that growth takes place in enclaves within the LDC and that this process can generate inequalities both between the enclave and the 'traditional sector' and within the enclave itself. Distribution will depend on the pattern of growth, the main ingredients of which are the original distribution of property, the economic structure and dependence on foreign resources.

The orthodox view that inequality was essential for growth was vigorously challenged by Myrdal (1968, Ch. 12; 1971), who argued that quite the opposite was the case and that greater equality was in fact a necessary pre-condition for more rapid economic development:

> ... inequality and the trend towards rising inequality stand as a complex of inhibitions and obstacles to development and that, consequently, there is an urgent need for reversing the trend and creating greater equality as a condition for speeding up development. (Myrdal 1971, pp.63–4)

He argued that the consequences of an unequal distribution of income were malnutrition, poor housing, poor education, etc., for the vast majority of the population, which in turn led to low levels of productivity. A redistribution of income to these groups would lead to an increase in production through increasing the consumption, and hence the health and productivity, of the poor. On the other hand, the 'middle classes' indulged in conspicuous consumption and wasteful expenditures (including the export of capital), instead of living frugally and saving and investing a substantial part of their income. Myrdal argued that social inequalities resulted from economic inequalities and in turn reinforced them, and both were a cause, and a consequence, of poverty.

Myrdal (1971) noted the apparently paradoxical situation that, although the policy declarations of most LDC governments favoured greater equality (in many cases, some form of 'socialism' was the development objective), inequality was increasing in most LDCs. The paradox was resolved by reference to the distribution of political power in LDCs. The classes that held power were unlikely to implement measures that would produce a distribution of income less favourable to them and their supporters. But as the masses were thought to be 'passive, apathetic and inarticulate', political changes could not be expected to occur as a result of pressure from below and would thus ultimately have to come about as a result of changes within the ruling classes themselves. We return to this point below.

Empirical Evidence

Cross-Country Data   Paukert (1973) presents information (*circa* 1965) on income distribution by size for 56 countries, both less developed and developed. Using the Gini coefficient as a measure of overall income inequality, Paukert found a sharp increase in inequality as one moved from countries in the lowest income group to those in the $101–200 *per capita* income group, and a further but less pronounced increase as one moved on to the $201–300 group. This group and the next ($301–500) represented the peak of inequality. There was a substantial reduction in inequality in the $501–1,000 group, and further reductions in inequality as one moved to even higher income groups.

With respect to the share of income accruing to the top 5% of income recipients, Paukert found that it was highest in countries in the $201–300 and $301–500 groups. In countries with a *per capita* income greater than $500, the share of the top 5% diminished significantly. A similar pattern of change was found with respect to the top 20% of income recipients.

With respect to the share of income occurring to the bottom 20% of income recipients, Paukert found that it was highest in the poorest countries and lowest for those countries in the $301–500 group. Above the $200 level, however, there was no clear pattern, and Paukert concluded that although the share of the poorest classes in the least developed countries was higher than elsewhere, it could not be generally assumed that their share was always higher in developing than in developed countries (Paukert 1973, p.117).

Overall Paukert concluded that the data supported the view that there was a clear long-term trend towards greater equality as *per capita* incomes rose. The greater inequality in LDCs was largely due to the high share of income received by the richest 5% of the population. The highest levels of inequality was to be found in the $200–500 *per capita* income range, and countries in the $501–1,000 range, with the exception of the Republic of South Africa, had a significantly lower degree of inequality.

Ahluwalia's (1976) analysis appeared to give further support to the basic pattern outlined above. His results were based on a sample of 60 countries, including 40 LDCs, 14 developed and 6 socialist countries, and he found 'clear evidence of a non-monotonic relationship between inequality and the level of development' (Ahluwalia 1976, p.309). The income shares of all percentile groups except the top 20% first declined and then increased as *per capita* GNP rose. The income shares of the top 20% displayed a 'corresponding opposite pattern'. Ahluwalia further showed that the 'turning point' (that is, the point at which the share of income of different groups began to change) occurred at different levels of *per capita* income for different income groups. For example, the share of the top 20% began to decline at a *per capita* income of $364 (in 1965–71 prices) but the income share of the bottom 60% only began to improve at a *per capita* income level of $412 and the figure for the bottom 20% was $593 (Ahluwalia 1976, Table 1, p.311). Ahluwalia remarked that '. . . the cross-section evidence suggests that the reversal of the "deteriorating phase" of relative inequality begins fairly early, first for the middle income groups and much later for the lower income groups. It appears that if there is a "trickle down" process, then it takes substantially longer to reach the bottom!' (p.310).

Ahluwalia was careful to qualify his analysis. He noted (p.307) that 'The use of cross-country data for what are essentially dynamic processes raises a number of familiar problems. Ideally, such processes should be examined in an explicitly historical context for particular countries'. Notwithstanding his own reservations, however, he concluded that there was 'strong support for the proposition that relative inequality increases substantially in the early stages of development, with a reversal of this tendency in the later stages' (p.338).

The attempts to test Kuznets's hypothesis by the use of cross-country data, and the work of Ahluwalia in particular, have recently been criticised with great force by Saith (1983). He criticises Ahluwalia on three grounds: (1) 'methodological doubts deriving from lapses in the use of regression techniques on cross-sectional data' (p.373), i.e. (i) the assumption made that the income share of any group varies systematically with the level of GNP *per capita* only, whereas the structural features of the economies concerned are also of major importance (a point also emphasised by Fields 1980, p.71), and (ii) the 'implicit homogeneity assumption' that every LDC will move along the inverted U-curve, its pace being determined by the rate of growth of GNP *per capita*, an assumption which ignores differences in both the internal and international conditions facing contemporary LDCs as compared to the developed countries at an earlier period; (2) doubts relating to the sensitivity of the estimates to variations in the size of the country-sample used, in particular the inclusion of both socialist and developed economies in the sample; and (3) doubts relating to the weakness of the data base and to the sensitivity of the results to isolated data variations. Saith concludes that 'As a paradigm, the cross-country

U-hypothesis is arguably more of a hindrance than an aid to our comprehension of the relationship between economic growth and income distribution. It obfuscates more than it clarifies' (Saith 1983, p.382).

Time-Series Data   Care must thus be taken when using cross-section data and, ideally, dynamic relationships should be inferred from time-series data. In his study of Puerto Rico, Argentina and Mexico, Weiskoff (1970) examined the relationship between economic growth and income distribution over time, although the data used were limited and thus they did not permit a systematic study of secular trends. In all three countries different measures of inequality gave different results.

During the period 1953–63, Puerto Rico experienced a rapid growth of real incomes accompanied by an increase in inequality in the distribution of income (as measured by the Gini ratio). The bottom 60% and the top 5% of the population lost, relatively, and the middle strata gained. In Mexico during the period 1950 to 1963, economic growth was again rapid but, according to the Gini coefficient, inequality increased from 1957 to 1963, following a period of greater equality between 1950 and 1957. The income shares of the bottom 30% of families declined throughout the entire period, and again it was the middle-income groups that gained at the expense of other groups. In Argentina, the period 1953 to 1961 was marked by political revolution, recession and a slight real growth of incomes. All the measures showed an increase in inequality between 1953 and 1959 (a year of severe recession) with a movement to equality in the 1959–61 period (although income distribution was still more unequal in 1961 than it had been in 1953). During the entire period only the top 5% of families increased their income share.

The time-series data thus gave limited support to the notion that growth and equality were inversely related at least at low levels of economic development. Fields (1980, Ch. 4), however, has surveyed the experience of a number of LDCs, for which data on relative inequality have been published for two or more points in time. He fails to find a pronounced pattern and concludes that:

> Growth itself does not determine a country's inequality course. Rather, the decisive factor is the *type* of economic growth as determined by the environment in which growth occurs and the political decisions taken. (Fields 1980, p.94)

Conclusions

Although cross-section data appear to indicate an inverted U-shaped relationship between inequality and *per capita* income, there is no necessary fixed relationship between equity and growth. It is not necessarily the case that high growth rates require an unequal distribution of income, nor that high growth rates are responsible for an unequal distribution of income. China's economic growth record has been more impressive than that of India and yet it is generally agreed that it is a more egalitarian society (Weisskopf 1975). Recent work on Cuba (Brundenius 1981) finds that the equity strategy of the 1960s induced growth in the 1970s. Other things being equal, we would expect to find a less unequal distribution of income in a country effectively pursuing explicitly socialist objectives than in a country following a free enterprise development path. Thus a great deal depends on the economic and social–political structure of the economy in question and its broad development objectives.

The argument that there is an inevitable conflict between equity and growth is not valid either on theoretical or empirical grounds. Cline (1975, p.374) stresses the point that there is 'no inexorable theoretical basis justifying a worsening of the distribution (of income) in the course of development', and Ahluwalia concludes that 'there is little firm empirical basis for the view that higher rates of growth inevitably generate greater inequality' (in Chenery et al. 1974, Ch. 1, p.13), even though his data seem to support the inverted U-shaped relationship. A conflict may exist in particular cases, but the explanation must be sought in the specific circumstances of each individual case and not in terms of a generalised relationship.[5] (Growth with equity in the agricultural sector is discussed in Chapter 7.)

3.4   The Distribution of Income and its Effects on Economic Growth

Income Distribution, Savings and Growth

We have already noted above the widely held view that an unequal distribution of income (distributed in favour of profits) is necessary to ensure a high rate of savings and hence growth, as profit receivers are assumed to save a higher fraction of their incomes than wage earners.

This view is dependent upon both a particular view of the growth process (conceived of most simply in terms of the Harrod–Domar model – see Chapter 2), and a particular interpretation of the development experience of the capitalist economies of the West. It is argued that the lessons of that experience are of significance to LDCs. Economic development was partly due to, and accompanied by, the rise to power of an indigenous capitalist class which allegedly saved and invested, in a productive manner, a substantial proportion of its income. The capitalist class abstained from lavish consumption, worked hard and in general lived a life according to a rigorous religious code, the 'Protestant Ethic'.

The argument that this experience (or more accurately, this particular interpretation of history which not everyone would accept) is of relevance to today's LDCs must presuppose the existence of a capitalist class in LDCs similar to that which existed in nineteenth century Europe and North America. Whether or not such a class exists is a key question in the political economy of development, and is referred to in several places in this book (see particularly Part C of Chapter 2). Kuznets (1955, p.22) noted the absence of a substantial 'middle class' in LDCs, that is, there was a sharp contrast between the vast majority of the population whose average income was well below the low countrywide average and a small top group with a very large relative income excess. Weiskoff's (1970) data discussed above, however, suggest that this class might have been growing in certain countries in recent years.

Other writers, for example Fanon (1967) and Baran (1957), have argued that an independent capitalist class, devoted to the national development of the LDC economy, does not, and cannot, exist. Baran in particular argued that a comprador class would develop (see Part C of Chapter 2).[6] A distribution of income in favour of this class would not therefore lead to a high rate of savings and hence economic growth.

The middle- and upper-income groups in LDCs are in any case subject to economic and social pressures very different from those faced by their nineteenth-century counterparts in Western Europe and North America: savings are likely to flow into 'safe' investments − either abroad (capital flight) or domestically into real estate and other non-productive forms; expenditure on foreign travel and conspicuous consumption is likely to be greater; the hoarding of gold, jewellery, etc., may be a prevalent social trait. The government too may be unable or unwilling to promote rapid capital accumulation − much public expenditure may be wasteful and contribute nothing to the development effort.

The empirical work that has been carried out on the determinants of savings in LDCs (reviewed in Snyder 1974) suggests that, *inter alia*, current income, wealth holdings and the distribution of income are of importance. Thirlwall (1983, Ch. 12) has also surveyed the literature and concludes that, on the basis of both time-series and cross-country evidence, the level of savings *per capita* and the savings ratio are primarily a function of *per capita* income and, to a lesser extent, a function of the rate of growth of income and its distribution between wages and profits. Much work remains to be done, though, on the determinants of savings in LDCs.

It is possible, however, to provide a qualified answer to an alternative question: what would be the effect of income redistribution on savings and growth? Cline (1972), who attempts to quantify this effect, argues that the impact of income redistribution on savings depends on the nature of the consumption function. Only a non-linear Keynesian consumption function unambiguously leads to a decline in aggregate savings when income is redistributed from high-income to low-income recipients. Cline (1972, Ch. 4) applies such a consumption function (estimated from family budget studies) to the new or simulated levels of income for the new income distributions, and aggregates the implied savings to determine new aggregate personal savings for comparison with the original personal savings. Assuming an income redistribution to the degree of equity in the UK and using a log-linear form of the consumption function, he finds that there would be little decline in personal savings in Argentina, a decline of 5.5% in Brazil, 7.6% in Mexico and no change in Venezuela (where a linear consumption function is used). The impact on savings of a radical income redistribution would thus vary but would not be as drastic as is usually assumed, given that other major sources of savings (government savings, the retained earnings of incorporated enterprises and foreign savings) would not be adversely affected.

Cline next calculates the impact on growth of the hypothesised income redistribution, using a Harrod–Domar-type relationship. Depending on the assumptions made, the redistribution would entail a sacrifice of annual growth of approximately 1% in Brazil and Mexico, 0.65% in Argentina and zero in Venezuela (with the linear function) or a maximum of 1.0% with an alternative specification of the consumption function. Cline stresses that these calculations are over-estimates (because of the consumption function assumed) and they assume an income redistribution unlikely to be realised in practice. Nonetheless, the vast majority of the populations of Argentina, Brazil and Mexico would benefit if the strategy of redistribution with slower growth was selected.

Income Distribution, Consumption and Employment

Different income groups consume different bundles of goods and thus the distribution of income is an important determinant of the pattern or composition of aggregate consumption. A highly unequal income distribution is likely to increase the demand for sophisticated durable consumer goods, luxuries, etc., and depress the demand for basic, essential mass-consumption items, for example textiles.[7] The composition of imports is also affected in so far as upper- and middle-income groups are more likely to consume imported goods or import-intensive domestically produced goods (although, as we note in Chapter 11, the poor may also consume such goods). This in turn has important consequences for those countries attempting to industrialise on the basis of import-substituting industrialisation (ISI). Industries established will often be producing non-essentials consumed by the wealthier classes and the needs of the poor may be neglected (these issues are discussed in greater detail in Chapter 9).

In principle, income redistribution in favour of the poor would increase the demand for essential goods (in the production of which there are greater possibilities for the utilisation of labour-intensive methods of production, thus stimulating employment) and reduce the demand for non-essentials, thus easing the balance of payments constraint. Taking an optimistic view of the course of events, greater equality could stimulate the demand for foodstuffs, thus increasing agricultural output, incomes and employment, and act as a check on rural–urban migration and rapid urbanisation.

On the other hand, a very different scenario can be imagined. The additional demand for foodstuffs might have to be met by increased imports, worsening the balance of payments constraint, and other sectors also may not be sufficiently flexible to respond to increased demands, thus generating inflationary pressures. What has been referred to as the problem of 'structural-lock' emerges. The structure of industry which developed with a particular (or only slowly changing) distribution of income may be unable to respond rapidly to the new pattern of demand in the post-redistribution situation. In other words, there is an imbalance between the country's production and demand structures. Excess capacity in some sectors and shortages in others, inflationary pressures, a worsening balance of payments position and perhaps social tension and political unrest are the likely outcomes of attempts at effective income redistribution in many LDCs (especially the more 'developed' Latin American economies).

Recent years have seen the publication of the results of a large number of simulation exercises which have attempted to test the hypotheses discussed above (the earlier ones are summarised in Cline 1975; see also Bigsten 1983, Ch. 5). In general, the results have been disappointing for those who believe that a redistribution of income would have a positive effect on consumption and employment. Variations in consumption patterns by income class were perhaps not as great as originally supposed and the range of factor proportions across industries not as wide as had been expected (Thirsk 1979, pp.50–1). When correction is made for possible aggregation bias, however, the results are more encouraging (Thirsk 1979; James 1980), and it has become increasingly obvious that the simulation results must be treated with great caution. The remainder of this section briefly summarises some of the more important and interesting simulation exercises, draws together the lessons that can be learnt from them and discusses redistribution within a broader socio-economic analytical framework.

A number of studies have reached negative or agnostic conclusions with respect to the impact of income redistribution on consumption and employment:

Figueroa (1975): this study is based on data from the mid-1960s for Peru. It finds that although an income transfer from the rich to the poor would increase industrial employment, the increase would at best be marginal.

There is no trade-off, therefore, between a more equal income distribution and industrial employment, that is, income redistribution would not reduce industrial employment.

Ballentine and Soligo (1978): this study uses data from a 1968 closed input–output model of the Colombian economy. Data are available both on the factor source of income of households (that is, it is known how households earn their incomes) and on household expenditure, for each income class. Assuming the imposition of a tax-subsidy scheme that transfers income from the rich to the poor, redistribution causes the composition of final consumption demand to reflect more closely the consumption bundles of the poor. However, there is no substantial shift in factor earnings towards the poor reinforcing the shift in disposable income and, indeed, the factor earnings of the rich rise more than those of the poor. The authors find no evidence to support the hypothesis that the poor consume a bundle of goods which generates more earnings for the poor than does the bundle consumed by the rich, largely because of the fall in the consumption of personal services by the rich: 'The fall in the earnings and employment of service workers is the cause of the decline of factor earnings of the poor' (p.704). The authors are careful to point to the shortcomings of their data and the limitations of their model. In particular, the assumptions that consumer expenditure patterns, factor input coefficients (technology) and the distribution of wealth remain constant must be open to question, a point that we return to below.

Berry (1981): a dynamic input–output model is developed to estimate the employment effects of a redistribution of expenditure, using Indian data for 1963, with 1968 as the terminal year for the dynamic analysis. Two redistributions are simulated: (i) the rural and urban shares of total private consumption expenditure remain constant, but there is a 'radical' intra-rural and intra-urban redistribution; (ii) each rural group's share of total rural consumption and each urban group's share of total urban consumption remains constant, but there is a 'radical' redistribution from urban groups as a whole. Both redistributions increase labour requirements, as compared to a situation of constant inequality, but the increase is not great. In the first case an increase in labour requirements in agriculture is only partially offset by a fall in the services and construction sectors, but import requirements rise because of the increase in agricultural output. In the second case, the increase in labour requirements is negligible, as compared to the constant inequality case, as is the effect on imports, which rise marginally. Even though he is careful to point to the limitations of his analysis, Berry concludes that there is little support for the notion that an expenditure redistribution could be an important instrument for employment promotion.

Paukert et al. (1981): a semi-closed input–output model was developed and applied to four countries – the Republic of Korea, the Philippines, Iran and Malayasia – in order to ascertain the effects on output and employment of hypothetical redistributions of household income. The application of the model to Korea (the country with the least unequal distribution of income) resulted in almost no changes in the structure of the economy and the level of employment. In the case of the other three countries, there was a certain and positive, although not always strong, impact of income redistribution on employment. Redistribution would contribute, to a limited extent, to economic growth and employment but, contrary to expectation, would not result in a significant reduction in imports, the latter being a reflection of 'the important and often overlooked fact that in many developing countries a substantial share of imports for private consumption is food for the poor and not luxury goods for the rich' (p.105). From evidence from the Philippines, it was concluded that the ability of the domestic agricultural sector to meet the higher demand for foodstuffs was one of the main preconditions for the redistribution of income to increase employment. If the higher demand for foodstuffs was met by imports, the redistribution of income would not bring about the expected increase in employment but would instead cause a deterioration in the balance of payments.

Sinha et al. (1979): based on a standard macroeconomic model of the Indian economy, this study concluded that income redistribution would have a limited effect on employment creation. It noted that the marginal employment intensity of the consumer's basket of goods did not vary monotonically with the level of disposable income *per capita*, and, indeed, the marginal effect was greater for the middle-income groups, suggesting that they were the most favourable target group with respect to securing the maximum impact on employment through income redistribution Ch. 5). Income transfers to the lowest income groups thus have a minimal impact on employment and it was concluded that, apart from the direct effect of the transfer itself, an income transfer could bring little, if any, substantial benefit to the poor (p.137): 'If the increase in incomes is to be maintained ... the income transfer must ... be placed on a permanent basis'.

Other studies reach more positive conclusions than those summarised above, or so qualify the methodologies used as to add a greater degree of realism to the simulation exercises:

Cheema and Malik (1984): based on 1979 data for Pakistan, this study supports the hypothesis that income transfers from the rich to the poor will change both the composition and level of consumption demand. In all cases, the income transfer increases the demand for income-inelastic, basic necessities (e.g. wheat, pulses, edible oils, clothing and footwear) and decreases the demand for income-elastic luxury goods (personal effects, meat, fish and poultry, furniture and fixtures). The overall effect on aggregate consumption would be positive, and the employment effects would also be positive and significant in all cases. The authors conclude that 'any income transfer favourable to the poor will have positive effects on consumption, social welfare, and employment' (p.356).

Tokman (1976; 1975): in his 1976 article on Venezuela, Tokman made projections for 1985 for aggregate consumption, assuming that consumption expanded more rapidly for lower- than for upper-income groups. He concluded that the structure of consumption did not change significantly in the event of changes in income distribution benefitting lower-income groups, the main variations being a fall in expenditure on services and an increase for processed and non-processed foods. The effect on employment was insignificant *if* no account was taken of the possibilities of using alternative technologies. However, when income redistribution is combined with the adoption of a technological policy that emphasises the utilisation of more labour-intensive techniques of production, the situation changes, an argument more fully developed in Tokman (1975).

In this article, an inter-industry model is developed to analyse the relationships between the distribution of income, technology and employment in the industrial sector in Ecuador. Contrary to what might be expected, Tokman finds no support for the assertion that non-durable consumer goods are more likely to be produced by relatively labour-intensive techniques of production, although when that group is disaggregated, significant variations in factor intensity are found. For example, beverages and tobacco use highly capital-intensive techniques; food processing, textiles and printing use 'intermediate' technologies; while shoes, clothing and furniture use typically labour-intensive technologies.

The empirical evidence also casts doubt on the assertion that small-scale establishments are likely to be more labour-intensive. Under those circumstances, it is not surprising that a redistribution of income in favour of lower income groups leads to an insignificant increase in employment. Two implications of this are: (i) the consumption preferences of those groups benefitting from the income redistribution will need to be 'directed' towards those goods considered essential for subsistence and in the production of which labour-intensive methods are feasible; and (ii) more labour-intensive techniques will in general need to be promoted where feasible. Under those conditions, the impact of a redistribution on employment is quite significant (an increase of approximately 18% compared to the situation with unchanged policies). Tokman concludes (p.68) that:

> ... technological policy has a significant effect on the employment level. Hence, together with the requirement of influencing the consumption pattern, policy makers must also adopt a strategy which directs demand increases towards those establishments which use more labour-intensive techniques.

Undoubtedly, a redistribution of income can result in higher levels of employment in the industrial sector, which in turn can generate an improvement in the present distribution of income.

Thirsk (1979): this study suggests that the apparently limited impact of income redistribution on total employment may be the result of an aggregation bias. While inter-industry variations in factor demands are recognised, little attention is given to the diversity of factor proportions *within* each industry. If, however, firms in a particular size class cater for the needs of distinct income groups, and the main determinant of factor proportions is firm size, then the composition of firm size in each activity would be directly affected by an income redistribution. Extending the model of Ballentine and Soligo (1978), it is shown that, if the poor buy largely from small (and hence relatively labour-intensive) firms in each sector, a fiscal redistribution will raise the income of the poor by an amount larger than that initially transferred (perhaps between $2-3 for each dollar redistributed). Thirsk concludes (p.65): 'Knowing *who* supplies the goods and services may turn out to be just as important as knowledge of *what* goods and services are brought (*sic*) by different income groups'.

House (1981): this analysis develops the ideas advanced by Thirsk (1979) and applies them to the Kenyan furniture-making industry. An expenditure survey found that poor households in Nairobi (and by inference, in other urban and rural areas) buy low quality, relatively inexpensive furniture from the very labour-intensive informal sector. As incomes rose, preferences moved in favour of more expensive, middle-quality furniture, and at the top of the income scale were found the purchasers of luxury items of furniture, which were highly skill- and import-intensive, produced by larger-scale enterprises. A policy of income redistribution would create employment in the low-income sector of the industry, mainly in the rural and urban informal sectors, and alleviate existing deficiencies in the stocks of basic furniture of the poorest households (p.353).

James (1980): this study is also concerned with the possible aggregation bias arising out of the classification of products into broad categories. In the Indian sugar-processing industry, there are two similar but distinct products which serve different ends of the market – the traditional product gur, which is essentially sugar cane in concentrated form and serves low-income consumers, and refined white sugar which serves upper-income consumers. When the product is thus disaggregated, simulated income redistributions favouring lower-income groups result in a significant increase in demand for gur, especially in urban areas, a decline in the consumption of sugar in rural areas and an increase in its consumption in urban areas. With respect to the employment effects, James found that the disaggregative approach implied an increase in employment over 50% greater than that resulting from the aggregative approach.

What conclusions can be drawn from the simulation exercises? Clearly, it would be unwise to generalise on the basis of the often conflicting and ambiguous results obtained from the simulation exercises discussed above. Nevertheless, it is of value to attempt to draw the threads of the discussion together and present a number of tentative conclusions:

(1)   The relationships between income distribution/redistribution, consumption, employment and technology are not as straightforward as is sometimes suggested. Lower-income groups do not necessarily consume more labour-intensive products, and the fall in the consumption of labour-intensive services (servants, security guards, chauffeurs, etc.) by upper-income groups as a result of income redistribution may largely offset gains in employment elsewhere in the economy.

(2)   The balance of payments effects of an income redistribution are not necessarily positive. Cline (1972), for example, has calculated the change in final demand resulting for each product sector from an income redistribution and uses input–output analysis to determine the change in imports. He finds that the final import effect is very small and that income redistribution has little effect on growth through its import repercussions. The basic reason for this is that the higher import coefficients applied to smaller absolute production changes of the declining group (transport equipment, rubber, metallurgy and electrical machinery) yield a fall in imports approximately equal to the rise in imports from the smaller import coefficients applied to much larger absolute production increases in agriculture and processed foodstuffs.

(3)   The results of the aggregative simulation exercises thus do not provide strong support for the hypothesised effects of income redistribution. Cline (1972, p.179) concludes that while the effects are in the theoretically correct direction, they are of minor importance and thus there is little empirical evidence to support the view that income redistribution would be a powerful stimulus to economic growth although, conversely, even radical redistribution would not do irreparable damage to growth prospects.

It is perhaps not surprising that the simulation exercises do not provide more positive results, given the problems relating to data availability and reliability, and the nature and characteristics of the economic models/methodologies used. In particular, two kinds of aggregation bias have been identified – the failure to distinguish between large and small firms (Thirsk 1979) and the failure to identify product characteristics (James 1980) – and when those are corrected for, the simulation exercises provide more direct support for the positive effects of income redistribution.

(4)   Perhaps the most important point to emphasise is that it is highly unlikely that a radical income redistribution will occur whilst 'all other

things remain equal'. Social, political and institutional changes are likely to accompany, and be complementary to, income redistribution policies. Indeed, the simulation exercises discussed above can be used to support the argument that income redistribution is likely to be ineffective in the absence of radical reforms in other areas, a point that we return to in Section 3.6 below.

3.5   Income Distribution in the Newly Industrialising Countries (NICs): Are They a Special Case?

The recent experience of a small number of mainly East Asian economies (and in particular the so-called 'Gang of Four' – Singapore, Hong Kong, Taiwan and the Republic of Korea) has led a number of (largely neoclassical) economists to question the general validity of the inverted U-curve hypothesis, and to resurrect the concept of 'trickle-down' effect. Fields (1984), for example, has argued that rapid economic growth in these economies has been accompanied by marked improvements in employment and income distribution conditions and the reduction of levels of absolute poverty.

The four East Asian economies have low to moderate levels of inequality

Table 3.3   Inequality in Hong Kong, the Republic of Korea, Singapore and Taiwan, 1950s–80s

Year	Hong Kong	Korea	Singapore	Taiwan
Early 1950s				0.5
1964		0.34		
1966	0.487		0.499	
1968–72				0.3
1970		0.33		
1971	0.411			
1975			0.452	
1976	0.435	0.38		
1976–78				0.27
1980			0.455	
1981	0.447			

Source: Taken from Fields 1984, Table 3, pp. 76–7.
Note: For Hong Kong, Korea and Taiwan, inequality is measured by the Gini coefficient among households; for Singapore the Gini coefficient is among individuals.

with respect to the size distribution of income, although various estimates conflict with one another and there is disagreement with respect to the extent and direction of changes in inequality over time. Table 3.3. summarises various estimates of the Gini coefficient for the four economies:

Taiwan: Taiwan has the lowest Gini coefficient of any LDC (Fields 1984, p.79) and inequality fell dramatically throughout the 1960s and 1970s. For writers such as Ranis (1978; 1983), Taiwan's success is based on both initial conditions and government policies. The initial conditions relate to its 'unique advantages, in terms of its initial geographic and cultural homogeneity, its high quality human infrastructure and the "good luck" to have had a rurally-oriented colonial master [Japan]' (Ranis 1978, p.408). Government policies included an emphasis on rural development and an export-oriented, decentralised and labour-intensive industrialisation strategy.

Singapore: the Gini coefficient fell between 1966 and 1975 but rose slightly between 1975 and 1980. As in the other 'Gang of Four' member countries, rapid economic growth has been associated with export-oriented industrialisation (EOI) policies. The government has deliberately restricted the rate of growth of real wages and has placed great emphasis on education and upgrading the labour force.

Hong Kong: the Gini coefficient fell between 1966 and 1971 but rose thereafter. Both Hsia and Chau (1978) and Chow and Papanek (1981) characterise Hong Kong as an inegalitarian society (cf. the view of Fields above), although both sets of authors see much to admire in Hong Kong's combination of rapid growth, unchanged (or slightly improving) income distribution and 'dramatic improvement in the absolute income of the poor (as well as elegant (*sic*!) profits for the rich)' (Chow and Papanek 1981, p.473). The general conclusion drawn by Chow and Papanek (1981, p.481) is that:

> ... over the past two decades Hong Kong has made remarkable strides in improving the absolute income of all groups in the population by relying on the classical private enterprise formula of rapid growth based on inexpensive labour ... the poor majority had to accept continuing great inequality in income ... and sharp setbacks every few years when the vagaries of the world market reduced the demand for Hong Kong's exports.

Republic of Korea: along with Taiwan, the Republic of Korea has one of the lowest levels of income inequality amongst LDCs, and throughout the 1960s and early 1970s appeared to combine rapid economic growth with a stable, or slightly improving, income distribution (Rao 1978). Land reform, an emphasis on agrarian development, improved education and labour-intensive export-oriented industrialisation are generally advanced as the main economic explanations of this record of successful growth and development. Recent evidence, however, suggests that income inequality increased noticeably in the 1970s and that the question of social inequality has become a serious social problem (Koo 1984). Two explanations are suggested: (i) by the early 1970s, the reduction of unemployment had reached its maximum level and, as a result, the equity-promoting efforts of export-oriented industrialisation were weakened; (ii) there was a shift in the industrial structure during the process of industrialisation, with the movement of labour from agriculture to the non-agricultural sector where, in general, income inequality is greater (Koo 1984, p.1031). Of greater significance, however, is the role that the state plays in shaping the distributive process during industrialisation. Koo (1984) argues that through (i) 'favourist' policies towards big business, (ii) corporatist control of labour organisations, (iii) inflationary financing, and (iv) generally regressive tax policies, the pattern of income inequality in South Korea is directly related to its political economy and the role of the state in the process of export-oriented industrialisation, issues to which we return in Chapter 9.

Clearly, the experience of the 'Gang of Four' is open to various interpretations. On the one side are sympathetic observers and energetic advocates (and ideologues) of free enterprise, export-oriented industrialisation who emphasise the importance of economic policy (for example, Fields 1984) and the transferability of that particular 'model' of development to other LDCs (Chow and Papenek 1981). For Fields, the major factor underlying the economic success of the 'Gang of Four' is not merely the adoption of EOI as such, but the functioning of labour markets and, in particular, the wage-setting mechanism in those countries. The absence or relative weakness of minimum wage legislation and trades unions, and government and transnational corporation pay policies which 'follow the private sector, not lead it as other developing regions' (Fields 1984, p.81) are seen as positive features to be emulated elsewhere. For others, however, such policies are the opposite of what economic development *should* be about (see Chapter 1) and they focus attention on the coercive and repressive role of the state in the development process (Bienefeld 1981; Koo 1984).

3.6   The Policy Implications: Is Egalitarian Development Possible?

Before considering the variety of policy instruments that can in principle be used by governments to pursue the objective of a more equal distribution of income ('egalitarian development'), it is useful to outline the conditions that must be satisfied if the strategy is to succeed. They are identified by Griffin and James (1979; 1981) as:

(1) The supply condition − the quantity produced of basic needs goods and services (for a brief discussion of basic needs, see Chapters 1 and 9) supplemented by net imports if necessary, must be sufficient to ensure the achievement of minimum consumption standards.

(2) The demand condition − in so far as goods and services are allocated by the market, the effective demand of the poorest groups must be sufficient to allow them to meet those minimum standards.

(3) The delivery condition − available supplies of wage goods must actually reach the poor.

(4) The strategy of egalitarian development must be sustainable over time.

Alternative policy measures to redistribute income and raise the effective demand of the poor can be categorised thus:

(1) *Pricing policy*: discriminatory pricing policies can be used to reduce the price of certain goods and services which account for a large proportion of the total expenditure of the poor or, alternatively, such goods can be distributed directly to recipients. Price controls can, however, harm some poverty groups whilst helping others. Policies which lower the price of basic foodstuffs benefit those who rely on the market for supplies, leave unaffected those who are self-sufficient, and harm poor peasants whose livelihood depends on the sale of foodstuffs in the market (Griffin and James 1981, Ch. 3).

(2) *Employment creation and minimum wages*: public works programmes can be used to create extensive employment opportunities in labour-intensive sectors, for example construction. The implementation of a minimum wages policy will help those previously employed at below the minimum, but may well discourage labour-intensive activities if the policy is effectively implemented. Neoclassical economists in particular are opposed to minimum-wage legislation, seeing it as a factor market 'distortion' with harmful consequences for employment creation (see Selowsky 1981).

(3) *Income transfers*: the scope for direct income transfers is limited in LDCs and unless such transfers are continuous and sustained, they are not likely to be effective (see Sinha *et al.* 1979, Ch. 7). Incomes policies can be used to control (or prevent) income increases for middle- and upper-income groups whilst permitting the incomes of poorer groups to rise relative to all other groups.

(4) *Public goods*: the provision of goods and services on a collective basis − education and health facilities, water supplies and sanitation, etc. − should in principle be effective, but in practice is only of limited benefit to

the poorest groups. This also appears to be true of the public distribution of foods grains – the poor lack the political power to ensure their full access to the benefits arising from such policies (Griffin and James 1981, Ch. 3).

(5) *Measures to raise the productivity of the poor*: such measures will benefit small farmers and artisans who own productive assets, and wage workers who may gain from higher productivity, but the impact on inequality and poverty is not unambiguous – labour may be displaced, land values and rents may rise.

(6) *Asset redistribution*: the most radical and, in principle, the most effective policies relate to the redistribution of the ownership of the means of production. Gross inequalities in the ownership of property give rise to similar inequalities in the distribution of income. Thus many would argue that a more equal structure of property ownership (or state ownership of productive assets) is an essential precondition for a more equal income distribution. In the majority of LDCs, the ownership of land is highly unequal and emphasis is therefore placed on the need for effective land reform in order to promote agricultural growth, rural development, greater employment and greater equality.

A number of general points can be drawn from the discussion of policy alternatives:

(1) Single policy instruments are unlikely to be effective. Income redistribution and the eradication of poverty will require at the very least a combination of policies pursued vigorously and on a long-term basis. Furthermore, '. . . a relatively egalitarian distribution of income has to be "built into" the structure of the economy and cannot be imposed by income redistribution measures' (Paukert *et al*. 1981, p.104).

(2) Asset redistribution is generally regarded as the most effective policy option (see, for example, Sinha *et al*. 1979, p.139), coupled with more general, radical agrarian reform, ensuring a more egalitarian distribution of income among rural households, greater rural employment creation and a reduction in rural–urban migration (Paukert *et al*. 1981, pp.106–7).

(3) Policies aimed at raising or maintaining the rate of economic growth remain important – redistribution *and* growth must be combined, and a number of economists (for example, Foxley and Munoz 1974) have suggested that an income redistribution policy, to be effective, requires the achievement of some minimum rate of economic growth. What matters, however, as we have noted already, is the *character* of economic growth.

Although an abundance of policy instruments exists, and both LDC governments and international organisations emphasise the necessity and/or desirability of greater equality, few LDCs apart from those that have experienced revolutionary changes and/or have deliberately pursued egalitarian (socialist) policies and some of the NICs referred to in Section 3.5 above are moving towards greater equality. Economists are at present devoting much effort and ingenuity to the problem of evolving redistributive strategies but are paying little attention to political questions and the likelihood of such policies being actively implemented. As in other areas of development economics, too much attention is paid to policy prescription while the analysis of socio-economic structures (if considered at all) is relegated to second place.[8]

There are no overwhelming reasons why the ruling groups in LDCs should pursue egalitarian policies, especially if such policies are harmful to their own economic and political interest. As Myrdal notes:

> It has never occurred in recorded history that a privileged group, on its own initiative and simply to give reality to its ideals, has climbed down from its privileges and opened its monopolies to the unprivileged. The unprivileged have to become conscious of their demands for greater equality and fight for their realisation ... But when that pressure from below is almost totally absent, as in most underdeveloped countries, we should not be surprised that the inegalitarian social and economic stratification from colonial times is preserved and that development moves in the direction of greater inequality. (Myrdal 1971, pp.88–9)

It is possible that enlightened self-interest plus popular pressure may lead the ruling groups to attempt to bring about a less unequal distribution of the benefits of growth, if only to strengthen their own position. But in the contemporary world, the repression of such popular movements is a more likely outcome. As Leys (1975, p.6) argues:

> ... in Africa, Latin America and South-East Asia most governments closely control political activity and harass or suppress 'radical' parties, where political organisation is not banned altogether.

These problems are of particular relevance to strategies of redistribution with (or from) growth (RWG) which were promoted by a number of influential organisations in the 1970s (for example, the International Labour Office – ILO 1972; the World Bank – Chenery et al. 1974).

The ILO (1972) in its report on Kenya advocated the maintenance of rapid growth, the stabilisation of the incomes of the top 10% of the population for a number of years, and the channelling of the income and resources which growth would have brought to this group into various forms of investment which would benefit the poorest 40% of the population (Jolly 1976). The policy proposals involved a wide range of government initiatives aimed at expanding the resources available to the poor. The strategy was not to be based on direct income transfers from rich to poor but on investment which would provide the unemployed and the working poor with the basis for earning a reasonable minimum level of income.

In a further development of this approach by Chenery *et al.* (1974), the target growth rate was so defined as to give a higher weight to the growth of incomes of the poorer groups, and 'target' poverty groups (in both rural and urban areas) were identified (see discussion in Section 3.2) and public investment redirected to raise the productive capacity and incomes of these groups.[9] The conclusion was reached that:

> ... there is considerable potential for raising income in low-income groups through a policy of 'investment transfers'. Such a strategy, although operating at the margin, can achieve substantial improvements in patterns of asset concentration over time. If income in the poorer groups is constrained by lack of physical and human capital and access to infrastructure, the reallocation of public resources can provide a powerful mechanism for removing these constraints. The extent of resource transfer involved – 2 per cent of GNP per year for 25 years – is not small, but it should be feasible in many countries. (Chenery and Ahluwalia in Chenery *et al.* 1974, Ch. XI, pp. 234–5)

The RWG strategy was explicitly reformist and evolutionary and it was argued that such a policy was less likely to face opposition from vested interests than more radical proposals for asset or income redistribution. Although presented as a politically neutral and technical document ('a framework for analysing the interconnections between economic growth and redistribution' – Jolly 1976, p.48), one of its major critics, Colin Leys (1975), argued that the Chenery *et al.* publication was, in fact, a 'highly political document' (p.4) and must be viewed as such. Leys maintained that the authors of the Report assumed that the LDCs would continue to be predominantly capitalist economies in which income distribution was determined mainly by the distribution of ownership of productive capital, and that political power in these societies would continue to be based primarily on the private ownership of capital. Social revolution ought to be avoided and the status quo maintained. In other words, capitalist development in LDCs had to be given a more 'human' and 'acceptable' face, leaving intact the social, political and economic structures within which poverty and inequality had their roots.

Stewart and Streeten (1976) have argued that economic growth is by definition vital if effective redistribution is to occur with a RWG strategy, but redistribution may adversely affect the growth rate in so far as it involves a switch from the consumption and production of high-technology goods to the consumption and production of goods for the poorer groups. Technological advance has neglected the latter and,

> ... a policy which switched a substantial amount of resources to them would thus almost certainly reduce the rate of growth measured in conventional terms, at least for a time ... To the extent that the switch in resources was successful, the source of redistribution – the extra incomes generated by advanced technology among the elite – would dry up. (p.396)

But the basic problem remains one of political feasibility. There are no obvious reasons why ruling groups should adopt even mildly reformist RWG strategies. Advocates of RWG argue that in the absence in the foreseeable future of radical political changes in LDCs, a reformist strategy is, in effect, better than nothing and the only chance that exists to alleviate the lot of the poor. As Leys (1975, p.8) shows, this position allows RWG to be presented as 'a realistic and humane response to the improbability that radical changes will bring about radical improvements in the lot of the poor'. But given the uncertainty surrounding future developments in LDCs and, at the same time, the role of foreign interests and international organisations in influencing the extent and direction of change, Leys feels that the Report's judgement that radical social changes are 'unlikely' takes the form of a programme rather than a prognosis. This approach enables the advocates of RWG to promote it as an alternative approach to development, to be preferred to the advocacy or pursuit of revolutionary change.

3.7   The Case Against Egalitarian Development

Not everyone, of course, will accept the argument for egalitarian development. Bauer (1972; 1981), for example, has long been a critic of egalitarian ideologies and Lal (1976; 1983) and Little (1982) have more recently joined the debate.

For Bauer (1981), economic differences result largely from differences in people's capacities and motivations. The pursuit of economic equality will do more harm than good 'by politicizing life, by restricting the accumulation and effective deployment of capital, by obstructing social and economic mobility at all levels, and by inhibiting enterprise in many different ways' (p.24). Furthermore, 'Politicians and intellectuals have supplied articulation and a veneer of intellectual respectability to envy and resentment' (p.24). Lal (1983) points to the lack of a consensus about the ethical system for judging the desirability or otherwise of particular income distributions and argues that 'There is . . . likely to be little agreement about either the content of "distributive justice" or whether we should seek to achieve it through some form of coercive redistribution of incomes and assets when this would infringe other moral ends, such as "liberty"' (p.89). In addition, both those authors (quite rightly) point to the confusion in much of the literature that equates poverty alleviation with reduction in income inequality.

Toye (1983, p.103) in a wide-ranging review of Bauer's work, accuses him of partiality and inconsistency and of being guilty of both mistakes of logic and of reliance on unscientific generalisations. In addition, the simulation exercises discussed in Section 3.4 do not, as a matter of course, support Bauer's assertions as to the likely negative consequences of income redistribution. Perhaps of greater importance, however, are the arguments advanced in Section 3.2 — just as economists must enter the realm of political economy to begin to explain the underlying causes of the distribution of income, so too must a political economy approach be used to explain changes in the distribution of income and what different groups or classes regard as the 'right', 'justifiable' or 'acceptable' distribution of income. Lal (1983) is quite right in pointing to the lack of an ethical consensus on these matters — an individual's ethical notions will be at least in part determined by his or her class position, education, status, income, wealth and so on, and the opportunities for change will be largely determined by the balance of political forces within the country concerned. As Schaffer and Lamb (1981, p.2) have argued:

> Equity as a concept and practice is above all a political fact. It is an *ideological construct* about distribution, about the apportionment of resources in society, and therefore political in the sense of an intervention in the struggle of political ideas.

3.8 Conclusions

The gap between rhetoric and reality is perhaps greatest in the field of development and equality. Some governments proclaim political and economic objectives of an egalitarian, even socialist, nature but pursue policies that have the opposite effect. Other governments deliberately create greater economic and social inequalities, creating demand profiles favourable to TNCs and channelling resources to already engorged ruling groups.

Greater economic and social equality should be regarded both as a goal of development and as a means by which growth and development can be accelerated. The objective of redistribution is not merely to take from the rich to give to the poor, nor merely to redistribute poverty, but to create the conditions within which the development effort can be maximised. Income redistribution must thus be viewed in a dynamic context and cannot be separated from complementary social, political and institutional changes. Redistribution cannot take place in a political vacuum and the most radical redistributions in LDCs have occurred during, and as part of, social and political upheavals of a fundamental kind. The objective of greater equality can only be achieved by the elimination of the political, social and economic structures within which inequality is located, and we do not hold out much hope for RWG-type solutions.

We would argue that radical changes, that is changes in the distribution of the ownership of productive assets, are a necessary but not a sufficient condition for economic development. Land reform, for example, must be accompanied by measures aimed at the promotion of agrarian reform. It may in fact be the case that income redistribution has little overall effect on employment if steps are not taken at the same time to design and produce goods which are 'appropriate' in terms of the needs they meet and the production technologies that they utilise. The characteristics of the goods produced in the post-redistribution environment are thus of importance in this context.

The short-run costs (in terms of economic growth foregone) of radical changes may be high and in any case are likely to be increased by both domestic and foreign opposition (sabotage, 'destabilisation', etc.) to such measures. The difficulties involved in the specification of 'basic needs' and development objectives, the redirection of resources towards the creation of 'desirable' products and technologies, the re-orientation of the productive structure to meet the needs of the mass of the population, the mobilisation of the population to work on community-based development projects, the balance of material and moral incentives, the re-evaluation of the role of the market and the creation of effective and efficient development planning structures are all problems that remain to be solved. But the existence of such problems cannot be used as an argument against radical changes as they are problems that ultimately must be faced and tackled by all LDCs.

Notes

1. Tawney argues that '. . . in spite of their varying characters and capacities, men possess in their common humanity a quality which is worth cultivating, and that a community is most likely to make the most of that quality if it takes it into account in planning its economic organisation and social institutions − if it stresses lightly differences of wealth and birth and social position, and establishes on firm foundations institutions which meet common needs and are a source of common enlightenment and common enjoyment. The individual differences of which so much is made . . . will always survive, and they are to be welcomed, not regretted. But their existence is no reason for not seeking to establish the largest possible measure of equality of environment, and circumstance, and opportunity. On the contrary, it is a reason for redoubling our efforts to establish it, in order to ensure that these diversities of gifts may come to fruition' (Tawney 1964, pp.55−6).
2. Bigsten (1983, Ch. 2, p.18) notes the two major directions in income distribution theory (the human capital-oriented group which considers inequalities to be individually made, and the environmentalists who consider them to be society-made) and concludes that 'A comprehensive theory certainly would have to incorporate traits from both these sides, but an analysis designed for LDCs would have to lean more in the environmentalists' direction than would a corresponding analysis for DCs'.

3. Indeed, Adelman and Morris (1973) advance the hypothesis that the poorest 60% of the population may experience an absolute as well as a relative decline in their average income, and they conclude that 'The frightening implication of the present work is that hundreds of millions of desperately poor people throughout the world have been hurt rather than helped by economic development' (p.192).

4. Johnson (1958) stated the orthodox view thus: '... the cost of economic equality may be great to any economy at a low level of economic development that wishes to grow rapidly, particularly as it is evident that historically the great bursts of economic growth have been associated with the prospect and the result of big windfall gains; it would therefore seem unwise for a country anxious to enjoy rapid growth to insist too strongly on policies aimed at ensuring economic equality and a just income distribution' (p.159). Implicit in this and similar arguments is the view that more rapid growth in the present means greater equality in the future through the higher income 'trickling down' to the poor. The creation of more and better-paid jobs and government redistributive policies (progressive taxation, free education, etc.) made possible by the higher level and rate of growth of income are essential elements in this process. Even accepting the existence of these redistributive mechanisms in contemporary LDCs, it can still be argued that expectations are such that the length of time required for such 'trickling down' to be effective is politically unacceptable.

5. An alternative approach to this question is developed by Bornschier (1983). He argues that, from a 'world economy' perspective, the integration of the LDC into the world economy (as measured by the extent of 'MNC penetration' of its economy) is an important determinant of the degree of inequality within the LDC. Utilising the concept of the inverted U-shaped curve relationship, he argues that the greater is the degree of MNC penetration, the higher is the maximum level of inequality experienced by the LDC and the higher is the level of *per capita* income at which the 'turning point' occurs. He concludes: '... less developed countries do not automatically decrease their inequality in development .... A substantial change in income distribution towards lower inequality is only expected if the power structure and the world economic position of a country change or if the integration into the world economy is reduced ... world economic integration puts considerable constraints on autonomous internal changes in the distribution of power' (Bornschier 1983, p.19). While many would find the conclusion unexceptional, its theoretical and empirical underpinnings are highly contentious.

6. Fanon (1967, p.141) directed his invective against the bourgeoisie in LDCs: 'A bourgeoisie similar to that which developed in Europe is able to elaborate an ideology and at the same time strengthen its own power. Such a bourgeoisie, dynamic, educated and secular, has fully succeeded in its undertaking of the accumulation of capital and has given to the nation a minimum of prosperity. In underdeveloped countries, we have seen that no true bourgeoisie exists; there is only a sort of little greedy caste, avid and voracious, with the mind of a huckster, only too glad to accept the dividends that the former colonial power hands out to it. This get-rich-quick middle class shows itself incapable of great ideas or inventiveness. It remembers what it has read in European textbooks and imperceptibly it becomes not even the replica of Europe, but its

caricature'. Such views have been challenged by, among others, Warren (1973; 1980).

7. The classification of goods and services into 'essentials' and 'luxuries' is in practice difficult and the terms 'essential consumption' and 'luxury consumption' are imprecise in content. Nevertheless, the attempt must be made by any country that wishes to pursue an effective redistributive policy. An essential item in one country may be considered a luxury in another and thus 'Factors to be considered in the definition of consumption categories include the historical and political framework, the level of *per capita* income, and national habits and traditions' (Ffrench-Davies 1976, p.114).

8. '. . . it seems difficult to avoid the conclusion that much wasted ingenuity has been put into devising *forms* of redistribution, when it is not lack of ingenious schemes but a basic political contradiction between the schemes and the real as opposed to nominal objectives of decision makers, that is critical' (Stewart and Streeten 1976, p.396).

9. It is argued that RWG also involves (i) accelerated GNP growth by raising savings and allocating resources more efficiently with benefits to all groups in society; (ii) redistribution of existing assets; and (iii) transfer of income to support the consumption of the poorest groups. But the redirection of public investment is the dominant element (Ahluwalia and Chenery in Chenery *et al.* 1974, Ch. 2; Jolly 1976, pp. 46–7.)

References

Adelman, I. and Morris, C.T. (1973) *Economic Growth and Social Equity in Developing Countries,* Stanford University Press.

Ahluwalia, M.S. (1976) 'Inequality, poverty and development', *Journal of Development Economics,* Vol. 3, December.

Ballentine, J.G. and Soligo, R. (1978) 'Consumption and earnings patterns and income distribution', *Economic Development and Cultural Change,* Vol. 26, No. 4, July.

Baran, P. (1957) *The Political Economy of Growth,* Monthly Review Press, New York.

Bauer, P.T. (1972) *Dissent on Development,* Weidenfeld and Nicolson.

Bauer, P.T. (1981) *Equality, The Third World and Economic Delusion,* Weidenfeld and Nicolson.

Berry, R. (1981) 'Redistribution, demand structure and factor requirements: the case of India', *World Development,* Vol. 9, No. 7, July.

Bienefeld, M. (1981) 'Dependency and the newly industrialising countries (NICs): towards a reappraisal', in D. Sees (ed.), *Dependency Theory: A Critical Reassessment,* Frances Pinter.

Bigsten, A. (1983) *Income Distribution and Development,* Heinemann.

Bornschier, V. (1983) 'World economy, level development and income distribution: an integration of different approaches to the explanation of income inequality', *World Development,* Vol. 11, No. 1, January.

Brundenius, C. (1981) 'Growth with equity: the Cuban experience (1959–1980)', *World Development,* Vol. 9, Nos. 11/12, November/December.

Cairncross, A. and Puri, M. (eds.) (1976) *Employment, Income Distribution and Development Strategy*, Macmillan.

Cheema, A.A. and Malik, M.H. (1984) 'Consumption and employment effects of income redistribution in Pakistan', *Pakistan Development Review*, Vol. XXIII, Nos 2 and 3, summer–autumn.

Cheenery, H.B., Ahluwalia, M.S., Bell, C.L.G., Duloy, J.H. and Jolly, R. (1974) *Redistribution With Growth*, Oxford University Press.

Chenery, H.B. and Syrquin, M. (1975) *Patterns of Development 1950–1970*, Oxford University Press.

Chinn, D. (1977) 'Distributional equality and economic growth: the case of Taiwan', *Economic Development and Cultural Change*, Vol. 26, No. 1, October.

Chow, S.C. and Papenek, G. (1981) 'Laissez-faire, growth and equity – Hong Kong', *Economic Journal*, Vol. 91, No. 362, June.

Cline, W.R. (1972) *Potential Effects of Income Redistribution on Economic Growth: Latin American Cases*, Praeger, New York.

Cline, W.R. (1975) 'Distribution and development: a survey of literature', *Journal of Development Economics*, Vol. 1.

Denslow, D. Jr. and Tyler, W. (1984) 'Perspectives on poverty and income inequality in Brazil', *World Development*, Vol. 12, No. 10, October.

Elliott, C. (1975) *Patterns of Poverty in the Third World*, Praeger, New York.

Fanon, F. (1967) *The Wretched of the Earth*, Penguin Books.

Ffrench-Davies, R. (1976) 'Policy tools and objectives of redistribution', in Foxley (ed.) (1976b).

Fields, G.S. (1980) *Poverty, Inequality and Development*, Cambridge University Press.

Fields, G.S. (1984) 'Employment, income distribution and economic growth in seven small open economies', *Economic Journal*, Vol. 94, No. 373, March.

Figueroa, A. (1975) 'Income distribution, demand structure and employment: the case of Peru', *Journal of Development Studies*, Vol. 11, No. 2, January; Reprinted in Stewart, F. (ed.) (1975), *Employment, Income Distribution and Development*, Frank Cass.

Foxley, A. (1976a) 'Redistribution of consumption: effects on production and employment', in Foxley (ed.) (1976b).

Foxley, A. (ed.) (1976b) *Income Distribution in Latin America*, Cambridge University Press.

Foxley, A. and Munoz, O. (1974) 'Income redistribution, economic growth and social structure: the case of Chile', *Oxford Bulletin of Economics and Statistics*, Vol. 36, No. 1, February.

Frank, C.R. Jr. and Webb, R.C. (eds.) (1977) *Income Distribution and Growth in the Less-Developed Countries*, The Brookings Institution.

Ginneken, W. van, (1980) *Socio-Economic Groups and Income Distribution in Mexico*, Croom Helm for the ILO.

Griffin, K. and James, J. (1979) 'Problems of transition to egalitarian development', *The Manchester School*, Vol. XLVII, No. 3, September.

Griffin, K. and James, J. (1981) *The Transition to Egalitarian Development: Economic Policies for Structural Change in the Third World*, Macmillan.

House, W.J. (1981) 'Redistribution, consumer demand and employment in

Kenyan furniture-making', *Journal of Development Studies*, Vol. 17, No. 4, July.

Hsia, R. and Chau, L. (1978) 'Industrialisation and income distribution in Hong Kong', *International Labour Review*, Vol. 117, No. 4, July/August.

International Labour Office (1972) *Employment, Income and Equality: A Strategy for Increasing Productive Employment in Kenya*, Geneva.

James, J. (1980) 'The employment effects of an income redistribution: a test for aggregation bias in the Indian sugar processing industry', *Journal of Development Economics*, Vol. 7.

Johnson, H.G. (1958) 'Planning and the market in economic development', *Pakistan Development Review*, Vol. VIII, No. 2, June; Reprinted in *Money, Trade and Economic Growth*, George Allen and Unwin, 1962.

Jolly, R. (1976) 'Redistribution with growth', in Cairncross and Puri (eds.) (1976).

Knight, J.B. (1976) 'Explaining income distribution in less developed countries: a framework and an agenda', *Oxford Bulletin of Economics and Statistics*, Vol. 38, No. 3, August.

Koo, H. (1984) 'The political economy of income distribution in South Korea: the impact of the state's industrialisation policies', *World Development*, Vol. 12, No. 10, October.

Kuznets, S. (1955) 'Economic growth and income inequality', *American Economic Review*, Vol. 45, No. 1, March.

Lal, D. (1976) 'Distribution and development: a review article', *World Development*, Vol. 4, No. 9.

Lal, D. (1983) *The Poverty of 'Development Economics'*, Hobart Paperback 16, Institute of Economic Affairs.

Lewis, W.A. (1954) 'Economic development with unlimited supplies of labour', *Manchester School*, Vol. 22, May.

Lewis, W.A. (1976) 'Development and distribution', in Cairncross and Puri (eds.) (1976).

Leys, C. (1975) 'The politics of redistribution with growth', *Institute of Development Studies Bulletin*, Vol. 7, No. 2, August.

Little, I.M.D. (1982) *Economic Development: Theory, Policy, and International Relations*, Basic Books.

Maddison, A. (1971) *Class Structure and Economic Growth: India and Pakistan Since the Moghuls*, George Allen and Unwin.

Mehmet, O. (1978) *Economic Planning and Social Justice in Developing Countries*, Croom Helm.

Morley, S.A. and Williamson, J.G. (1974) 'Demand distribution and employment: the case of Brazil', *Economic Development and Cultural Change*, Vol. 23, No. 1, October.

Myrdal, G. (1968) *Asian Drama*, Penguin Books.

Myrdal, G. (1971) *The Challenge of World Poverty*, Penguin Books.

Paukert, F. (1973) 'Income distribution at different levels of development: a survey of evidence', *International Labour Review*, September.

Paukert, F., Skolka, J. and Maton, J. (1981) *Income Distribution, Structure of Economy and Employment*, Croom Helm for the ILO.

Ranis, G. (1978) 'Equity with growth in Taiwan: How "special" is the "special case"?', *World Development*, Vol. 6, No. 3, March.

Ranis, G. (1983) 'Alternative patterns of distribution and growth in the mixed economy: the Philippines and Taiwan', in F. Stewart (ed.), *Work, Income and Inequality*, Macmillan.

Rao, D.C. (1978) 'Economic growth and equity in the Republic of Korea', *World Development*, Vol. 6, No. 3, March.

Saith, A. (1983) 'Development and distribution: a critique of the cross-country U-hypothesis', *Journal of Development Economics*, Vol. 13, No. 3, December.

Schaffer, B. and Lamb, G. (1981) *Can Equity Be Organized?* UNESCO and Gower.

Selowsky, M. (1981) 'Income distributon, basic needs and trade-offs with growth: the case of semi-industrialised Latin American contries', *World Development*, Vol. 9, No. 1, January.

Sinha, R., Pearson, P., Kadekodi, G. and Gregory, M. (1979) *Income Distribution, Growth and Basic Needs in India*, Croom Helm.

Snyder, D.W. (1974) 'Econometric studies of household saving behaviour in developing countries: a survey', *Journal of Development Studies*, Vol. 10, No. 2, January.

Stewart, F. (ed.) (1975) *Employment, Income Distribution and Development*, Frank Cass.

Stewart, F. (ed.) (1983) *Work, Income and Inequality: Payment Systems in the Third World*, Macmillan.

Stewart, F. and Streeten, P. (1976) 'New strategies for development: poverty, income distribution and growth', *Oxford Economic Papers*, Vol. 28, No. 3, November.

Tawney, R.H. (1964) *Equality*, George Allen and Unwin (first published 1931).

Thirlwall, A.P. (1983) *Growth and Development, with special reference to Developing Economics*, 3rd Edn, Macmillan.

Thirsk, W.R. (1979) 'Aggregation bias and the sensitivity of income distribution to changes in the composition of demand: the case of Colombia', *Journal of Development Studies*, Vol. 16, No. 1, October.

Tokman, V. (1975) 'Income distribution, technology and employment in developing countries: an application to Ecuador', *Journal of Development Economics*, Vol. 2.

Tokman, V. (1976) 'Income distribution, technology and employment in the Venezuelan industrial sector', in Foxley (ed.) (1976b).

Toye, J. (1983) 'The disparaging of development economics', *The Journal of Development Studies*, Vol. 20, No. 1, October.

Warren, B. (1973) 'Imperialism and capitalist industrialisation', *New Left Review*, No. 81, September–October.

Weiskoff, R. (1970) 'Income distribution and economic growth in Puerto Rico, Argentina and Mexico', *Review of Income and Wealth*, December. Reprinted in Foxley (ed.) (1976b).

Weisskopf, T.E. (1975) 'China and India: contrasting experiences in economic development', *American Economic Review Papers and Proceedings*, Vol. LXV, No. 2, May.

4

Population, employment and urbanisation

4.1 World Population Growth

The second half of the twentieth century has witnessed what can reasonably be called a population explosion. In the first half of the century, from 1900 to 1950, the world's human population is estimated to have grown from 1.6 to 2.5 billion people,[1] but by the year 2000 it will probably have exceeded 6 billion. Hence this century will have witnessed very close to a fourfold increase in the human population, and the post-1950 period will witness a remarkable increase of approximately 2.4 times. The main factor responsible for this is the rapid surge in population growth in LDCs since 1950, which (as can be seen from Table 4.1) peaked at approximately 2.4% per annum around 1970, but which has subsequently declined slowly. To a much lesser extent the postwar 'baby-boom' in the industrialised countries has been a contributory factor, but annual population growth in those countries had fallen to around 0.7% by 1985 and is likely to fall further.

Further growth in the global population is built into the present structure of the human race, and arises in particular because such a high proportion of the population of LDCs has not yet reached reproductive age. Something approaching 44% of the population of low-income LDCs is below the age of 15, and for middle-income LDCs the figure is 40%. These proportions contrast markedly with the corresponding figure of 23% aged less than 15 in industrialised countries, and they ensure that whatever happens to female fertility rates (see below), the necessary adjustment to a mature age-structure in the population of LDCs will produce huge further increases in their populations. This explains why Table 4.1 projects such a significant increase in the ratio of the populations of the less to the more developed areas. From a level of 2.03 this ratio may well rise to 4.95 in the year 2025, a development graphically illustrated in Figure 4.1.

Self-evidently, population growth is caused by birth rates exceeding death rates. Globally both of these parameters have been declining rapidly in recent years. But, as Table 4.2 records, in the less-developed areas death rates have been declining more rapidly than birth rates, while the converse

Table 4.1 Population Size and Rate of Increase for the World, the More Developed Regions, and the Less Developed Regions, Medium Variant, 1950–2025 (as assessed in 1980)

Year	World Population (millions)	World Rate of increase (percentage)^c	More developed regions Population (millions)	More developed regions Rate of increase (percentage)	Less developed regions Population (millions)	Less developed regions Rate of increase (percentage)
1950	2,525	–	832	–	1,693	–
1955	2,757	1.76	887	1.28	1,870	1.99
1960	3,037	1.94	945	1.27	2,092	2.25
1965	3,354	1.99	1,003	1.19	2,351	2.33
1970	3,695	1.94	1,047	0.87	2,648	2.38
1975	4,067	1.91	1,092	0.84	2,975	2.32
1980	4,432	1.72	1,131	0.71	3,301	2.08
1985	4,826	1.70	1,170	0.68	3,656	2.04
1990	5,242	1.65	1,206	0.61	4,036	1.98
1995	5,677	1.60	1,242	0.58	4,435	1.89
2000	6,119	1.50	1,272	0.48	4,847	1.77
2005	6,558	1.39	1,298	0.40	5,261	1.64
2010	6,988	1.27	1,321	0.35	5,667	1.49
2015	7,407	1.17	1,342	0.31	6,066	1.36
2020	7,813	1.07	1,360	0.27	6,453	1.24
2025	8,195	0.96	1,377	0.24	6,818	1.10

Source: Ghosh (1984), p.412.

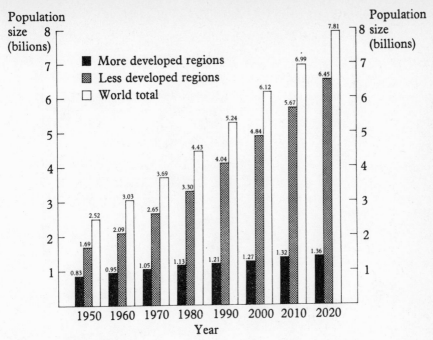

Source: Based on Table 4.1.

Figure 4.1 Population Size for More Developed Regions, Less Developed Regions, and World Total, Medium Variant, 1950–2020 (as assessed in 1980)

has occurred in the developed countries. Consequently, while population growth rates declined in many LDCs (and has almost ceased in the UK, Switzerland, Austria, West Germany and Belgium), it increased in most LDCs until 1975/80. The dramatic postwar declines in death rates were due substantially to the spread of medical knowledge and treatment which accompanied economic growth and modernisation in LDCs. Both reduced infant mortality and increased longevity for those who survive childhood have contributed to the declining death rate and are reflected in higher life-expectancy (see Table 4.2). These in turn have been factors contributing (with a lag) to the decline in birth rates, for, as Birdsall (1977) records, almost all studies of the determinants of fertility (the average number of lifetime births per woman) indicate a positive effect of infant mortality on fertility; that is, reduced infant mortality leads to a fall in the birth rate. It is, of course, only one determinant of fertility, but it is a major one, others being female education and labour force participation, family planning services and the effects of improved economic well-being.

Table 4.2 Crude Birth and Death Rates (per 1000), and Life Expectancy at Birth, 1950/55 and 1975/80

	Crude birth rate			Crude death rate			Life expectancy at birth		
	1950/55	1975/80	% change	1950/55	1975/80	% change	1950/55	1975/80	% change
World total	36.3	28.5	-11.5	18.9	11.4	-39.7	47.0	57.5	22.3
More developed	22.7	15.8	-30.4	10.1	9.4	-7.3	65.2	71.9	10.3
Less developed	42.9	33.0	-23.1	23.2	12.1	-47.8	42.4	55.1	30.0
Africa	47.9	46.0	-4.0	27.4	17.2	-37.2	37.3	48.6	30.3
Latin America	42.4	33.6	-20.8	15.4	8.9	-42.2	51.2	62.5	22.1
North America	25.1	16.3	-35.1	9.4	9.1	-3.2	69.0	73.0	5.8
East Asia	37.7	21.0	-44.3	19.2	7.3	-62.0	47.5	67.6	42.3
South Asia	44.2	37.1	-17.1	25.8	14.8	-42.6	39.4	50.6	28.4
Europe	19.8	14.4	-27.3	10.9	10.5	-3.7	65.4	72.0	10.1
Oceania	27.6	21.8	-21.0	12.4	9.0	-17.4	60.7	65.6	8.1
USSR	26.3	18.3	-30.4	9.2	9.0	-2.2	61.7	69.6	12.8

Source: UN Statistical Tables – reproduced in Ghosh (1984), p. 438.

The future growth of the world population depends crucially upon what happens to fertility and death rates, and to the birth rate which is a function of these two. To illustrate this, consider the following grossly simplified example. Hypothesise a population in which everyone born survives exactly to their 50th birthday and where the females and males comprise exactly half the population. An idealised stable size of population will have exactly the same number of people in each annual age cohort. Thus, suppose there are n females in each age cohort of $2n$, with a total population of $100n$. $2n$ people die each year and need to be replaced by new births to maintain the population. This birth rate of 2 per 100 of the population (or 20 per 1,000) can just be achieved if the average number of births equals two for each woman during her lifetime. This rate of 2 per woman is the so-called replacement fertility rate – in practice, to allow for male to female ratios of greater than 1, and other structural features, the replacement fertility rate may slightly exceed two, but it is always close to it. If the longevity of each person born were 60 years, the total population would be $120n$, but $2n$ births only would would still be needed to offset deaths per year, giving a birth rate of 2/120 or 1.66 per 100. At longevity of 70 years per person the birth rate consistent with the replacement fertility rates in the population with the idealised structure drops to 2/140 or 1.43 per 100 (14.3 per 1,000).

However, the actual age cohort structure of LDCs departs quite radically at this point in time from the idealised rectangular one hypothesised above. If cohorts were of equal size, then in a population with life expectancy of 55 years (LDCs in Table 4.2), 27.3% of the population would be less than 15 years old, while the comparable figure for a population with 72 years life expectancy (DCs in Table 4.2) would be 20.8%. The actual figure for the industrialised countries, of 23% in 1980, conforms well to the idealised one, indicating that at replacement fertility rates, birth rates will not greatly exceed those required to balance deaths. But for the developing countries as a whole in 1980 over 40% of the population were less than 15 years old, while in Africa and South Asia the figure exceeds 44%. This means that even if the female fertility rate in LDCs falls to the replacement level of 2 per woman, the rate of recruitment of women to childbearing age cohorts greatly exceeds the number required to balance the rate of deaths. Hence LDC population growth is assured well into the twenty-first century until the age structure of the population stabilises along with the fertility rate.

Perhaps the most important determinant of when, and at what level, the human population eventually stabilises will be the path of change in fertility rates. Underlying the large decline in birth rates shown in Table 4.2 have been significant reductions in fertility. The most dramatic decline has been in East Asia where the Republic of Korea, Taiwan, Singapore and Hong Kong have all sharply reduced fertility rates as a result of strong family planning programmes (which incorporate fiscal disincentives for large families) and of what Maudlin and Berelson (1977) call their 'high social setting'.[2] In East Asia, Indonesia and the Philippines have also achieved significant fertility declines (see Table 4.3). In South Asia, despite the progress India and Sri Lanka have achieved with family planning programmes, high fertility rates in Bangladesh and Pakistan have restricted the decline in the overall regional birth rate. In Latin America the birth rate decline has been slightly faster than in South Asia; Maudlin and Berelson attribute the fertility decline in this region more to the 'high social setting' than to official family planning programmes. The one developing region which stands out from Table 4.2, as making minimal headway in reducing fertility, birth rates and population growth, is Africa. Many African countries remain opposed to birth control policies, and in several countries birth rates are still increasing. Kenya is the outstanding country (see Table 4.3) with population growth expected to rise to 4.5% per annum and a projected population vastly larger than the present one. For Africa as a whole the projections are for a doubling of population between 1980 and 2000 to reach around 820 million, and projections for the end of the twenty-first century are as high as 2,676 million (Tabah 1972).

Table 4.3 Total Fertility Rates in Selected Countries

	1983 population[1] (million)	Total fertility rates		
		1978[2]	1981[3]	1983[4]
China	1,019.1	2.3	2.3	2.3
India	733.2	5.0	4.8	4.8
Bangladesh	95.5	6.4	6.4	6.0
Pakistan	89.7	6.7	6.4	5.8
Sri Lanka	15.8	3.6	3.5	3.4
Indonesia	155.7	4.9	4.4	4.3
Philippines	52.1	5.0	4.6	4.2
Republic of Korea	40.0	2.8	3.0	2.7
Singapore	2.5	2.1	1.7	1.7
Vietnam	58.5	5.5	5.1	4.9
Brazil	129.7	4.9	4.0	3.8
Mexico	75.0	5.7	5.0	4.6
Egypt	45.2	5.0	4.8	4.6
Kenya	18.9	7.8	8.0	8.0
Nigeria	93.6	6.9	6.9	6.9

Sources: World Bank, World Development Report, 1985, Annex Table 1; 1980, Annex Table 18; 1983, Annex Table 20; 1985, Annex Table 20.

The actual ultimate size of the global population in the next century is very sensitive to the changes in fertility and death rates which occur in future, and there are wide confidence intervals associated with any long-term projections. However, as Frejka (writing in 1981) notes, those confidence intervals have narrowed appreciably as the relevant birth and death rates decline asymptotically to their limits; 'previous projections set upper and lower boundaries for the world population in the year 2000 of 5.1 billion and 6.7 billion; the present calculations indicate a lower boundary of about 5.3 billion and an upper boundary of 6.4 billion. The earlier calculations indicated the world population would eventually stabilise between 6.4 billion and 15.1 billion; the present projections indicate stability between 7.0 billion and 13.5 billion'. It can therefore be seen that the long-run uncertainties are considerable, but there is a relatively high probability that in the year 2000, world population will reach and exceed the level of 6.1 billion (projected using the UN medium variant as assessed in 1980 – see Table 4.3), and a lesser probability that it will stabilise around 10.6 billion in the middle of the next century.

4.2 Some Economic Consequences

Rapid population growth in the last few decades has, as already noted, led to very high proportions (in most cases over 40%) of LDC populations being in the under-15 age category. As Birdsall (1977) notes, this entails a large proportion of available resources being tied up in looking after the health and well-being of children, and also high costs for education and schooling. To achieve comparable school and higher education enrolment rates to those found in industrialised countries, LDCs would need to spend a much higher proportion of GNP on education than that spent by DCs. This is well illustrated by Zymelman (1976) who estimated that East African countries spent an average of 3.76% of GNP on education to achieve enrolment ratios of 46% in primary, 5.9% in secondary and 0.5% in higher education; whereas, by comparison, OECD countries only allocated 4.18% of their GNP to achieve enrolment ratios of 98% in primary, 70% in secondary, and 11.8% in higher education. Moreover, according to Zymelman, the relative unit costs of education, calculated as a percentage of GNP per capita, are higher in LDCs, and very considerably so at secondary and higher education levels.

Such high proportions of young people do not only pose problems of costs at the macro-level for LDCs, they also constitute a problem at the micro-level for families. Inevitably the average number of children per family and per adult worker tends to be high, the incidence of large families is considerable, and so-called dependency ratios (the number of non-earning family members per earner) is high. Not only does the frequency of child-bearing and the time spent looking after small children limit female participation in the labour force, but there is often pressure in older children to be kept out of school either to look after children or to undertake simple work tasks in order to supplement family earning capacity. Thus, large poor families can be pressurised by short-term economic pressures into foregoing the opportunities which education might provide for breaking the cycle of deprivation, and the incidence of poverty is greatest in large families.

Rapid population growth also has well-defined implications for the growth in numbers of working age and hence the number of jobs which need to be created. Those born in the last year will, subject to infant and childhood mortality rates, be entering the potential workforce in, say, 15 years time – the age group 15 to 64 is sometimes defined as the economically active population.[3] Not everyone within this age range is a member of the labour force. Female participation rates in the labour force are lower than those for males, and they differ widely between societies depending upon variations in religion, tradition and economic well-being. Also for males allowance has to be made for those in full-time education and for those who become disabled or chronically ill and unable to work. Nevertheless, nearly all males in the 25–55 age group are in the labour force (Durand 1975), and age/sex participation rates in individual countries exhibit a degree of predictability.[4] Given, therefore, that those who will be of 'working age' in 15 years time are already born, it is possible using the latest census data, plus projected age/sex mortality and national age/sex participation rates, to estimate the number of net likely additions to the labour force and hence the number of jobs which may be required for a number of years ahead. And, since one of the features of rapid population growth is that numbers recruited to the labour force exceed retirements in any year, it follows that LDCs need to continually expand job opportunities; the faster the rate of population growth the greater the lagged demand for new jobs. Thus at the present time LDCs are being called upon to create jobs in unprecedented numbers to match the recent exceptional population growth rates, and will need to continue to do so for several decades to come. This is indicated by Table 4.4 which presents World Bank estimates of labour force growth up to the year 2000. As can be seen, it is estimated that the numbers joining the labour force in the LDCs will have increased in each of the last five decades of this century. Whereas it is estimated that 83 million joined the labour force of the countries represented in the decade 1950 to 1960, by the decade 1990–2000 the comparable estimate approximately trebles to the enormous total of 238 million. If this is taken as a target (a topic more fully explored in the next section), it entails creating between 1990 and 2000 approximately half as many jobs in total as there were in these LDCs in 1950!

Before examining the problems and contemporary position of LDC job creation and employment in more detail in the next section, it should be

Table 4.4 Labour Force by Region, 1950–2000

	Estimated labour force (million)[5]						Change in labour force (million)				
	1950	1960	1970	1980	1990	2000	1950–60	1960–70	1970–80	1980–90	1990–2000
Low-income Asia[1]	259 (44)	298 (42)	351 (39)	429 (38)	524 (37)	623 (37)	39	53	78	95	99
Sub-Saharan Africa[2]	79 (46)	94 (44)	115 (42)	143 (40)	183 (38)	235 (38)	15	21	28	40	52
Middle East and North Africa[3]	23 (31)	27 (29)	33 (27)	42 (27)	56 (27)	70 (27)	4	6	9	14	14
East Asia and Pacific[4]	36 (44)	44 (41)	56 (40)	72 (41)	90 (42)	109 (44)	8	12	16	18	19
Latin America and Caribbean	54 (35)	67 (32)	85 (31)	110 (31)	148 (33)	193 (35)	13	18	25	38	45
Southern Europe	38 (45)	42 (43)	45 (41)	52 (40)	59 (40)	66 (41)	4	3	7	7	7
All developing countries	488	571	685	848	1058	1296	83	114	163	210	238

Source: Squire (1977) Table 10, p.45.

Notes: (1) Includes Afghanistan, Bangladesh, Bhutan, Burma, India, Indonesia, Cambodia, Laos, Maldives, Nepal, Pakistan, Sri Lanka and Vietnam.
(2) Excludes the Republic of South Africa.
(3) Excludes capital-surplus oil exporters.
(4) Excludes Japan.
(5) Figures in brackets are labour-force participation rates for the whole population.

observed that it is inappropriate simply to see population growth as a problem. All readers will be familiar with the hypothesis that poor families in some societies have large families because this serves the long-term interests of the parents. But as societal conditions change, and the relative costs to benefits ratio of extra children deteriorates, adults increasingly opt to limit family size; this in some complex way lies behind the fertility declines observed in most countries. At a more macro-level, the political leaders of some countries oppose family planning programmes because they believe that nation status and international political influence is positively linked to population size. Small African countries, in particular, appear to have believed that larger populations have been desireable to consolidate their nationhood. In a different context concern in industrialised countries is occasionally expressed about the prospects of population decline, for the obverse of high proportions of young people accompanying rapid population growth is that population decline is marked by an increasing proportion of old people and a rise in the burden of health care and maintenance for the aged. A continual flow of newly trained, energetic young people is seen as essential for continued innovation and economic growth, and to support retired workers in the style to which they are accustomed. Thus some industrialised countries pursue 'pro-natalist' policies, using fiscal incentives to encourage families to produce and support children.

The simple fact that a number of LDCs have been able to achieve high per capita increases in GDP in conjunction with high population growth rates (e.g. Brazil, Malaysia, Kenya) alone indicates that it cannot simply be asserted that rapid population growth impedes growth and development.[5] Rather, as Todaro (1977, Ch. 6) concludes, the causes of low levels of living and gross inequalities found in many LDCs are to be found in the dualistic nature of the national and international social order rather than in population growth. Nevertheless, rapid population growth does intensify problems of underdevelopment and makes it more difficult to resolve problems of poverty and inequality.

4.3 Employment, Unemployment, and Underemployment

In examining labour force figures such as those presented in Table 4.4, great care has to be taken not to adopt an inappropriate concept of the form of employment assumed for the labour force, or to interpret participation in it as signifying full-time, salaried and pensionable employment, for the reality is considerably different and there has been extensive debate about precisely how to define employment and unemployment in LDCs. One thing agreed by all commentators is that 'Western' notions of these concepts are invalid, and many alternative proposals have been preferred for their measurement.[6]

According to Squire (1981, p.61) most countries follow ILO recommendations in compiling statistics on employment and unemployment. Samples of the population are recorded, and employment details are collected for a reference period, usually of a week. Typically, part-time workers are included in the total of those employed, and the unemployed include those who did not work or worked for less than one day during the reference period (week) and were actively seeking work. While providing valuable data on trends, the limitations of this approach are transparently clear.

There may be significant numbers of potential workers who judge that the probabilities of finding acceptable employment are so low that they do not actively seek employment. That is, the statistics record the visibly unemployed (those actively seeking but not finding work), but exclude those *'invisibly unemployed'*, 'discouraged workers' who do not feel that an active search is worthwhile. Attempts to quantify these suggests that the numbers of invisibly unemployed are significant, but not as numerous as the visibly unemployed. For example, in West Malaysia allowing for discouraged workers boosted the estimated unemployment rate from 6.8 to 8.8% (Turnham 1971).

Characteristically, recorded rates of visible unemployment in LDCs are relatively low when compared to rates in DCs. For example, Morawetz (1974) in a survey paper on LDC unemployment in the early 1970s cites estimated visible unemployment rates of less than 4% for Brazil, Egypt, India, Indonesia, Pakistan and Mexico.[7] These rates tend to be low because, in the absence of state supported unemployment benefits, poor people cannot afford to be unemployed. Visible unemployment is more associated with formal sector higher remuneration opportunities, and urban areas. Hence there is some tendency for unemployment rates to be higher among more educated people, who have more incentive to spend time seeking employment because the potential reward from a successful search is high, and because they are more likely to have the means to finance a period of unemployment. Robinson (1983, p.5) records that in India some 700,000 university graduates were estimated to be unemployed, or 10% of all graduates. For associated reasons open employment is typically higher in urban than in rural areas. One reason for this is that better qualified, younger workers are drawn to urban areas from rural ones to seek higher paid employment. (The issue of rural–urban migration is dealt with more fully in Section 4.5.) According to Deshpande (1983), who examined employment in Bombay, such was the magnetism of big city rewards that, for every additional job created in the organised sector in Bombay in the 1970s, three migrants over 15 years old were drawn to the city, with the consequence that visible unemployment rates for both males and females in the 15–19 age group were around 20%.

By far the largest problem area with the statistics is that so much of what is recorded as employment is only partial employment. That is, many of those classed as employed are in fact underemployed. It should be remembered that in many LDCs a majority of workers are self-employed, rather than in the organised sector, and that there are no standard hours of work for self-employment. Many of the self-employed are engaged in marginal economic activities with relatively short working hours at low rates of remuneration, and would like to increase their incomes through work if suitable opportunities existed. Again, Indian data may be used to indicate the structure of employment for one particular case. According to Robinson (1983), only 39% of the Indian labour force is employed in the organised sector. Of these, 29% are wage labourers in the rural sector, primarily dependent upon agricultural work, 6% are in public sector employment and only 4% are in private organised sector employment. This leaves a massive 61% of self-employed, of whom 49% are in agriculture and 12% in other activities. Cursory consideration of these figures illuminates the large potential for underemployment. Large numbers of the (29%) wage labourers in the rural sector may only be able to find part-time work at some seasons of the year; many of those (49%) classed as self-employed in agriculture farm very small holdings (see Chapter 6) and may well be classed as underemployed; and a substantial proportion of the self-employed, including those with very small holdings classed as agriculturalists, may be quite appropriately classified as being in the informal sector. The informal sector, which will be discussed in more detail in a following section, is the sink in which people without adequate land or opportunities to join the organised sector are forced to devise some, usually minimal, means of survival.

In terms of employment structure, the Indian data above are by no means atypical of the situation found in LDCs, although structures do vary considerably and the data are not wholly reliable. Using a different classification, ILO (1977) estimates that the percentage of the Indian labour force in wage employment around 1970 was 17%. This compares with figures of 22% for Pakistan, 33% for Indonesia, 15% for Thailand and 9% for Tanzania.

It is one thing to accept that underemployment of workers is widespread and another to measure it. Various approaches to measurement have been suggested, including application of productivity, time, income and willingness criteria (Krishna 1973; Rath 1983). The full details of these alternatives will not be reviewed here, but all have their merits. Under the willingness criterion workers are classified as underemployed if they wish to work longer hours at the wage rates and conditions prevailing but are unable to do so because of market imperfections. Applying the time criterion involves establishing a norm of full-time working days for full-employment, and classifying as underemployed those who do not succeed in reaching the norm; this in principle permits calculation of the amount of underemployment. Application of the productivity criterion relates to

Lewis's (1954) notion of disguised unemployment – see Chapter 6 for further discussion. Here underemployment is diagnosed where marginal and average labour productivity falls below the subsistence wage level; in these conditions some labour is defined as disguisedly unemployed since it could be diverted to other jobs (if they existed) with no or minimal loss of output in the sectors they currently work. Finally, application of an income criterion has been advocated by those (e.g. ILO 1971) whose principal concern is with the alleviation of poverty. Under this criterion those unable to find employment which is capable of generating a poverty income level might be defined as underemployed. None of these criteria is easy to apply, but that cannot obscure that the underlying magnitude of underemployment may be presumed to be large, and that the majority of the underemployed live in poverty. One heroic estimate of underemployment is that for agriculture and rural industry by Robinson (1983) on the basis of micro-data collected by Rath (1983). According to this assessment, the unutilised work potential of the 160 million or so people employed in agriculture and the rural sector might amount to the equivalent of as many as 35–40 million workers, or 20–25% of the labour force. Such are the measurement problems that this should in no way be taken as an accurate estimate; rather, it is referred to simply as a crude indication of the scale of underemployment.

Given the scale of underemployment, and the problems of measuring employment and the labour force, considerable qualification has to be attached to data on labour force and employment growth in LDCs such as those in Table 4.4, and to those presented by Squire (1981) in his comparative analysis of employment growth in LDCs in the 1960s with that of the DCs in the 1880s. The basic argument deployed by Squire in relation to the data in Table 4.4 is that by historic standards the rate of employment growth achieved by the LDCs in the 1960s is superior in all sectors to that achieved by the DCs at a comparable stage in their development. Of course many factors, such as population pressure and technological availabilities, differentiate the situations; nevertheless, the basic argument that the LDCs are creating jobs at relatively rapid rates to assimilate the expanding labour force seems well justified. However, the precise magnitudes of job creation, especially in the agricultural and service sectors, must be heavily qualified given the extent of underemployment in the labour force.

4.4 Urbanisation in LDCs

The combination of population growth and changes in economic structure has produced rapid growth in the degree of urbanisation in LDCs, where this is measured by the percentage of total population living in urban areas. Not only does urban population growth reflect the underlying population growth of LDCs, but it is also substantially augmented by migration from rural to urban areas. In fact, between 1950 and 1980 rural–urban migration accounted for around half of urban population growth in LDCs which grew at 4% per annum, approximately twice as fast as population growth. Over the longer period 1920 to 1970 it is estimated (World Bank 1979, Ch. 6) that the proportion of the world's population living in urban areas rose from 19 to 37%. It is further estimated that by the year 2000 the urban areas of LDCs will have to absorb an additional billion people, and that by that date over half of the world population will live in urban areas.

Against this background the number of very large cities in the less developed world has grown rapidly. In 1950, only one city in the Third World, Greater Buenos Aires, had a population of over 5 million people, as compared to five cities in the industrialised countries that had reached or exceeded that size. By the year 2000, it is estimated that there will be 40 cities of or above this size, compared with only 12 in the industrialised countries. Twenty cities in LDCs (including two in the People's Republic of China) are expected to have populations of more than 10 million people, and Mexico City may well reach 30 million (World Bank 1979, Ch. 6).

Urbanisation patterns vary markedly between different regions of the Third World. Latin America is the most urbanised region, with about two-thirds of its inhabitants urban dwellers. The World Bank (1979, p.73), describes the pattern of urbanisation in Latin American countries as being characterised by:

> Heavy concentration of economic activities and wealth in a few very large urban centres, providing a stark contrast to the economic stagnation and much lower average incomes in many of the peripheral regions. Although average urban incomes are relatively high, poverty remains a serious problem in many cities.

Low-income Africa and Asia, on the other hand, are still largely rural, with only about one-quarter of their population living in urban areas. For low-income Africa, urban growth is a more recent phenomenon but is very rapid because of high natural population growth and massive rural–urban migration. According to the World Bank (1979, p.75), urban poverty is a relatively minor problem when compared to the rural poverty experienced by these countries. In low-income Asia, the level and rate of urbanisation are expected to remain low, even though this area contains some of the world's largest cities. The World Bank argues that the cities here do not, in general, offer better working and living conditions than do rural areas and that the incidence of poverty is equally severe in both urban and rural areas.

Between the two extremes outlined above lie the countries of East Asia, the Middle East and North Africa. Of these, East Asia is less urbanised (less than 40% of the population lived in urban areas in 1975) than the other two regions (approximately 50% urbanised in 1975), and in all three areas the rate of growth of urban population is decreasing. Nevertheless, by the year 2000, most of the countries in these areas will be predominantly urban, with rural–urban migration playing a significant role in the transformation process.

The rapid urbanisation of the LDCs poses a number of problems for policy makers in those countries. Urbanisation is costly, in that it entails the provision of urban transport facilities, housing, health, educational and recreational facilities, etc., and the concentration of economic activity in urban areas exacerbates both inter- and intra-regional income differentials. Congestion and pollution are also becoming problems of increasing severity in a number of Third World cities, such as Lagos, Bangkok and Mexico City.

Rapid urbanisation also requires the creation of large-scale employment opportunities. A major feature of the economic development of the now-developed Western industrialised countries was the large-scale movement of labour from the land and its increasing concentration in expanding urban areas. In general, the creation of urban employment opportunities in these countries matched the growth of the urban labour force. In contrast to this historical experience, contemporary LDCs, as noted above, are faced with problems of rapid urban population growth, largely resulting from rural–urban migration, but formal sector urban activities increasingly appear unable to expand employment opportunities sufficiently rapidly to absorb, in a productive manner, the growing urban labour force. Todaro (1976, p.14) notes the important relationships between migration, high levels of urban unemployment and underemployment, widespread poverty and unequal distribution of income, and he argues that employment creation, especially in rural areas, and the narrowing of the rural–urban income differential are essential components of any development policy aimed at reducing poverty, both urban and rural (see below). Within a broader theoretical framework that emphasises the diversity of the historical origins and contemporary experience of urbanisation in LDCs, Gilbert (1982, p.4) argues that:

> The process of urbanisation cannot be understood in isolation from social differentiation, political conflict, the operation of governments, and the nature of the dominant economic system. The future of the Third World city cannot be understood without questioning the basis of the world division of labour and the interests of governments ostensibly managing cities.

4.5 Rural–Urban Migration in LDCs

A high degree of labour mobility is both necessary and desirable in an expanding economy, but contemporary rural–urban migration (one aspect of labour mobility) is more likely to have a negative impact on economic development. The rapidly expanding urban areas are characterised by many writers as 'parasitic' development in so far as they absorb a large volume of resources, financial, physical and human but make only a limited contribution to the development effort (their 'generative' capacity). The rural areas are adversely affected in that, contrary to the popular misconception of teeming, overcrowded areas, they often suffer from a general labour shortage. Godfrey (1969) cites West Africa as an area with a labour deficiency in agriculture. Furthermore, migration is often selective with respect to age and educational levels so that many of the more productive rural dwellers migrate. The stagnation of the rural areas and rapid expansion of shanty towns surrounding the urban centres, plus the growth of employment in the so-called 'informal sector' (see Section 4.6), attest to the detrimental impact of rural–urban migration in contemporary LDCs.

Amin (1974, p.66) has noted that modern migrations are of labour rather than peoples, that is of individual workers, rather than whole families, and the migrant moves into a receiving society that is already organised and structured and which often accords the migrant an inferior status. We are concentrating in this section on net rural–urban migration, but it should be remembered that migration can also be rural–rural or urban–urban and, less frequently, urban–rural. In the more developed urbanised LDCs, urban–urban migration (from smaller urban centres to the metropolitan area) may be significant (as, for example, in Chile (Herrick 1965)), although inter-urban migration is often merely a relay point in the rural–urban chain; that is, the migrant moves to a smaller urban centre before moving to a larger one. In West Africa Amin (1974, p.69) notes the importance of rural–rural migration, the migrant leaving one rural area and moving to another because of greater possibilities of producing for the export market. Although we have dismissed (net) urban–rural migration as insignificant, sociologists have noted that the pattern of migration (especially in Africa) is circulatory, that is, migrants return to the rural areas at the end of their working life (Garbett and Kapferer 1970). Finally, for the sake of completeness, we may note the phenomenon of international migration, the most important aspect of which is, from the viewpoint of the LDCs, the loss of educated and skilled manpower to the developed, Western economies (the so-called 'brain drain').

The Theoretical Framework

Traditionally, migration studies emphasised the importance of 'push–pull' factors. Poverty and the lack of economic opportunities would 'push' labour from the rural areas while the attractions of the urban areas (job opportunities and opportunities for education, marriage, the attraction of the 'bright lights', etc.) 'pulled' labour to the towns. Obviously, migration in the real world must be the result of some combination of these two set of forces and thus it can be hypothesised that net rural–urban migration is some function of rural–urban income differentials, taking into account the probability of getting a job in the urban area. This approach implies that the predominant cause of rural–urban migration is economic, a conclusion non-economists accept (Gugler 1969, p.137; Gugler 1982), although social and psychological factors must also be taken into account.

The best-known model of economic development (Lewis 1954; extended and refined by Ranis and Fei 1961; see Chapter 2) is based on the assumption that the existing real-wage differential between the rural and urban areas is the sole determinant of rural–urban migration and migration will continue as long as this differential exists. The reinvestment of the surplus by capitalists leads to the expansion of the capitalist sector and the creation of more jobs, until surplus labour is absorbed and the labour supply schedule ceases to be perfectly elastic. The possibility of large-scale open employment in urban areas is not explicitly considered by the model.

Reality has not matched this interpretation of the development process. As we have already noted, large-scale net rural–urban migration has continued in the face of growing urban unemployment. Todaro (1969) has argued that the large pool of unemployed and underemployed in the urban sector must affect the potential migrant's 'probability' of finding a job in that sector. Consequently, when analysing the determinants of urban labour supplies, he argues that we must examine not only prevailing real-income differentials but also the rural–urban 'expected' income differential, that is, the income differential adjusted for the probability of finding an urban job (Todaro 1969, p.138). Provided, therefore, that expected urban incomes exceed those in rural areas, migrants may continue to flock to urban areas despite high and even increasing levels of unemployment.

Migration is seen as a two-stage process. The unskilled worker migrates to the urban areas and initially spends some time in the 'informal' urban sector from which he moves, in the second stage, to a more permanent modern sector job. An important aspect of this model is thus the length of time spent looking for a formal sector job, and it follows that the urban wage premium must be high enough to offset the potential income loss involved in being unemployed for a considerable length of time. The migrant must thus balance the probabilities and risks of being unemployed in the city (or employed in the informal sector at a much reduced income) for a certain period of time against the favourable urban wage differential (Todaro 1969, p.140) and must perceive the urban wage as being sufficiently high to compensate for the loss.

Todaro (1976, pp.35–6) summarises the four essential features of his model thus:

(1) Migration is stimulated primarily by rational economic considerations of relative benefits and costs, mostly financial but also psychological.

(2) The decision to migrate depends on 'expected' rather than actual urban–rural real-wage differentials where the 'expected' differential is determined by the interaction of two variables – the actual urban–rural wage differential *and* the probability of successfully obtaining employment in the urban modern sector.

(3) The probability of obtaining an urban job is inversely related to the urban unemployment rate.

(4) Migration rates in excess of urban job opportunity growth rates are not only possible but also rational and probable in the face of continued positive urban–rural *expected* income differentials. High rates of urban unemployment are therefore inevitable outcomes of the serious imbalances of economic opportunities between urban and rural areas in most underdeveloped countries.

Todaro's model of rural–urban migration is set out formally as follows. It is assumed that the percentage change in the urban labour force as a result of migration during any period is a function (F) of the difference between the discounted streams of expected urban and rural real income, expressed as a percentage of the discounted stream of expected rural real income:

$$\left(\frac{\dot{S}}{S}\right)_t = F \frac{V_u(t) - V_r(t)}{V_r(t)}$$

where:

$\dot{S}$ = net rural–urban migration

S = existing urban labour force

$V_u(t)$ = discounted present value for expected urban real-income stream over unskilled workers planning horizon

$V_r(t)$ = discounted present value of expected rural real-income stream over same planning horizon

It is further assumed that the planning horizon is identical for each worker, the fixed costs of migration are identical for all workers and that the discount rate factor is constant over the planning horizon and identical for all potential migrants.

Permanent rural income (that is, the present value of the expected income stream over n period) is expressed thus:

$$V_r(0) = \int_{t=0}^{n} Y_r(t)e^{-rt} \, dt$$

where:

$Y_r(t)$ = net expected rural real income in period t based on average real income in x previous periods

r = discount factor reflecting the degree of consumption time preference of the typical unskilled rural worker

Permanent urban income is represented thus:

$$V_u(0) = \int_{t=0}^{n} p(t)\, Y_u(t) e^{-rt}\, dt - C(0)$$

where:

$Y_u(t)$ = net urban real income in period t

$C(0)$ = initial fixed costs of migration and relocation in the urban sector

$p(t)$ = probability of finding a modern sector job in time period t

The inclusion of $p(t)$ means that even if $Y_u(t) - Y_r(t)$ was positive, the 'expected' differential, $p(t) Y_u(t) - Y_r(t)$ could be negative. $p(t)$ depends on the probability of being selected from the pool of urban 'traditional sector' workers in the current or previous time periods. The length of time spent in the urban 'traditional sector' is thus of importance. The probability of being selected is equal to the ratio of new modern sector employment openings in period t relative to the number of accumulated job seekers in the urban 'traditional sector' at that time.

The Todaro model has been modified and extended by a number of authors (surveyed by Todaro 1976, Ch. 3; see also Squire 1981, Ch. 7), but Todaro (1976, p.45) believes that its 'fundamental contribution' remains widely accepted as 'the "received theory" in the literature on migration and economic development'. Before taking a critical look at the Todaro model, however, we must briefly consider the policy implications that flow from it. Migration and urban unemployment are positively related in so far as any attempt to increase urban employment opportunities without reducing the rural–urban income differential will eventually lead to even greater unemployment.[8] Rising labour productivity in the urban sector will, if it is permitted to increase the rural–urban income differential, lead to increased migration and even greater unemployment. Likewise, the introduction of labour-intensive technologies in the urban sector, while leaving the differential unchanged, may lead to both higher employment and unemployment in that sector.

All these points lead to the conclusion that rural life must be made more attractive. Agricultural productivity and incomes must be raised, thus reducing the differential; rural employment opportunities expanded, both farm and non-farm; and physical and social infra-structural facilities (roads, schools, health facilities, etc.) introduced or improved. The

regeneration of the rural areas and the narrowing of rural–urban inequalities are the necessary preconditions for preventing further over-
urbanisation, reducing the level of urban unemployment and stemming
the emigration from the land.

The Todaro model of rural–urban migration has been extremely
influential, in part because the migrant can be conceived of as acting in a
rational, income-maximising manner, rather than responding irrationally
to the lure of the bright lights of the city. In principle, Todaro's urban
real-income variable $Y_u(t)$ includes all the elements that constitute urban
real income – money wages, urban amenities and the other attractions of
urban life. Likewise, rural real income $Y_r(t)$ includes, in principle, all factors which affect the migrant's rural income and must incorporate such
variables as the system of land tenure, inheritance laws, social structures,
and so on. In principle, the Todaro model encompasses all these elements.
The landless labourer and the small farmers, the displaced share cropper
and the educated youth all migrate in response to economic incentives in a
perfectly rational consistent manner. In a sense, therefore, the model is
able (or at least, should be able) to incorporate and 'explain' all observed
patterns of migratory behaviour, but a closer inspection reveals that it does
not provide a necessary understanding of the real factors and forces
involved in any given situation. Thus what appears to be the major
strength of the model (its generality) is in fact its major weakness.

Todaro's theory of migration falls within the general framework that
treats migration as a form of investment in human capital. The migration
decision is viewed in a costs and returns framework, such that the decision
to migrate will not be taken unless expectations are that the costs of migration (money and non-money) are less than or equal to the present discounted values of the expected amounts by which the urban benefit
stream exceeds that for rural areas. The decision to migrate is portrayed as
being taken by an autonomous individual, unconstrained by considerations of sex, class, age or race, abstracting from the economic and social
structures of which in reality the migrant is a part. But individual actions
and decisions are not made independently of society. As Gugler (1982,
p.54) notes:

> Migration is rarely a solitary affair. Potential migrants do not weigh their deci-
> sion in isolation, rather, they are members of groups, such as family, local com-
> munity, classmates, which evolve patterns of behaviour which are modified
> over time as experience dictates. Even where individuals migrate alone, others
> are involved in implementing the move, in adapting to the urban environment,
> and in securing a foothold in the urban economy. Frequently migrants have to
> make arrangements so that parents are taken care of, that wife and children
> who stay behind are assisted.

We thus need to examine the economic and social structures together
and analyse the behaviour of individuals within that structure.[9] The

rural–urban real-income differential is one aspect of a particular socio-economic system and one manifestation of the development path being pursued at that particular time and place. The differential arises as a result of the policies being pursued (with respect, for example, to urban development, industrialisation, rural development, etc.) and migration must thus be viewed within this broader analytical framework.[10]

The logical corollary of this argument is that Todaro-type models of migration are tautological (if it is assumed that the migrant is an income maximising individual, he/she will obviously move to that area where the chances of success seem greatest). Such models only have an explanatory value if the real-income differential, adjusted to take into account the probability of getting a job in the modern sector, was the *basic* cause of migration (Amin 1974, p.90). Furthermore, there is evidence that migrants do not necessarily come primarily from 'poor regions' or from among the poorest people. In Tanzania, for example, the 'poor' Masai do not migrate, whereas a large number of farmers from the richer region of Kilimanjaro do, a phenomenon only 'explained' by the Todaro model if the expected income differential is greater for the latter than for the former.

As we have already noted above, although economic factors are the prime determinants of the decision to migrate, non-economic factors are of importance. It has been argued by some sociologists (for example, Garbett and Kapferer 1970) that migration must be viewed as a process, rather than as a static, once-only phenomenon,[11] which takes account of the total context within which migration occurs and the factors related to this overall context which influence the decisions of the migrants at various points in their migratory careers. The choice is made with reference to both economic and sociological alternatives in that the individual may attempt to maximise gains in terms of a number of alternatives, for example, maximisation of the migrant's income, the educational opportunities for his/her children, the migrant's political position and influence, and so on. Various factors act as constraints on one another and in the process of making a choice, individuals generate constraints which affect the pattern of future choice. Specific choices are open to an individual at a certain time in life or at a certain point in his/her career, but not at others; for example, marriage and children alter the range of options open. Various social attributes (skill, education, etc.) affect the range of alternatives open to the migrant, thus affecting the pattern of migration, and access to information is also an important consideration.

We must also examine the choices faced by individual migrants as they are affected by the structure of social relationships. Relatives and friends play a crucial role in the migratory process, providing information on job opportunities, accommodation and food while the migrant is looking for a job, and so on.[12] Migration must thus be understood in terms of the total array of economic and social relationships, including both urban and rural relationships. Within this context, the individual has his/her decisions constrained by his/her position in a particular structure of social relationships, and the individual's choices are contingent on, and constrained by, the choices of others. Todaro-type models present, to say the least, an incomplete picture in so far as they over-emphasise monetary rewards and in practice exclude social relationships.[13]

Two further points must be briefly discussed before we consider some empirical studies. The first concerns the role of the informal sector. The Todaro model ignores this sector (apart from acknowledging the fact that the migrant may spend some time there before finding modern sector employment), but we have already argued that it is incorrect to assume a person is unemployed merely because he/she is unable to find a wage job in the modern sector of the urban economy. The migrant may even actively seek to earn his/her living in the informal sector and it is thus both inaccurate and derogatory to assume that all those outside the formal sector are unemployed, especially given the relatively small size of the formal sector in LDCs. A three-sector model at the very least is required to analyse the migratory decision (rural sector, modern urban sector, 'traditional' or informal urban sector) and we also need to analyse the historical evolution of urbanisation in each particular LDC. We discuss the informal sector in Section 4.6 below.

The second point concerns the rural–urban income gap. There has been a marked tendency to exaggerate the size of this gap (the term 'labour aristocracy' is often loosely and inaccurately used to refer to certain parts of the 'modern sector' urban labour force). Amin (1974, p.108) has argued that a loose comparison between urban wages and rural incomes is dangerous, given (i) the differences in types of consumption in urban and rural areas; that is the high rents and food prices in urban areas, expenditure on transport, entertainment, etc., and what Lewis (1954) refers to as the difference in 'conventional standards', with workers in the capitalist sector acquiring tastes and a social prestige which conventionally are recognised by higher real wages, and (ii) the often considerable differences in the amount of work needed to earn a reasonable income – the urban worker is likely to have to work harder. The distribution of income is also likely to be more unequal in the urban area. Amin concludes:

> ... we express serious doubt concerning the thesis of a widening difference between the income of the farmer and those of unskilled urban workers ... on the whole, the most significant difference is not the divergence between the income of the peasant and the wage of the unskilled urban worker, but the gap which separates both the peasantry and the lowest class of urban workers from the new social classes which developed during the last decades of colonisation and after independence (notably administrative bureaucracies) ... The migrants are an impoverished proletariat. On the urban labour market as well

as on the plantations they occupy the lowest positions and are the worst paid
... In a very general way migration serves to provide cheap labour to the host
areas. (Amin 1974, p.109)

Empirical Evidence

Rather than attempting to give a detailed summary of the various
empirical analyses of rural–urban migration, we will first summarise
some of the major conclusions to emerge and then look at one study in
greater detail.

(1) It is generally found that there is an inverse relationship between
the propensity to migrate and the distance from the nearest large
urban centre, although distance is closely related to cultural and
social differences between regions and to the flow of information
(Beals *et al.* 1967; Caldwell 1967, 1968, 1969; Sahota 1968).

(2) Migrants move in response to income differentials; the study of
Beals *et al.* (1967), although it is concerned with inter-regional
rather than rural–urban migration, clearly showed that migrants
moved to regions with high wage levels.

(3) There is a positive relationship between the size of the rural centre
and rural–urban migration (Caldwell 1967, 1968, 1969); greater
urbanisation or population density in either the origin or destination region increases migration (Beals *et al.* 1967).

(4) Caldwell found that a disproportionate fraction of the wealthier
households of a village were 'migrant households', that is they were
linked by absentees or returnees to the town. The explanation
given was that 'many migrants send remittances back home and
many returnees bring back money and possessions, while, at the
same time, better off households are more likely to send their
children to school and so intentionally or unintentionally equip
them for town jobs' (Caldwell 1968, p.367).

(5) There is a strong association between the presence of friends or
relatives in the urban area and migration; they provide temporary
accommodation and information and thus 'chain migration' is an
important phenomenon (the term is used by Caldwell but the
phenomenon is also noted by Sahota (1968)).

(6) There is some dispute over the relationship between education and
migration. Beals *et al.* (1967) conclude that the direct effect of
education is to reduce migration, arguing that this disproves the
hypothesis that educated people migrate because they are
dissatisfied with rural life. But Knight (1972) maintains that the
effect of education is to raise the expected rural–urban income differential and increase the probability of getting a job in the modern

sector. Caldwell finds a strong positive association between education and rural–urban migration – 'schooling itself turns people towards town life' (Caldwell 1969, p.60) – arguing that the content of school courses is an important influence alienating children from rural life (but Godfrey (1973) regards this as an oversimplification). However, a more recent study (Barnum and Sabot 1976, p.77) concludes that the more formal education a rural resident has, the greater is his propensity to migrate. Both the rural–urban income differential and the net return to migration increase with education.

(7) There are marked concentrations of migrants within certain population subgroups (Squire 1981, p.101). Migrants are usually under 30 years of age, they are usually unmarried and 'clear patterns of sex selectivity can be discerned within major regions' (Gugler 1982, p.59). In Latin America, for example, women outnumber men in the cities and are predominant in rural–urban migration. In Africa, on the other hand, migrants are usually male and men outnumber women in the cities.

(8) The majority of migrants believe that they have improved their economic well-being via migration (Gugler, 1982, p.55) and that after a time, migrants enjoy employment and income opportunities similar to those experienced by the resident urban population (Squire, 1981, p.105).

Godfrey's (1973) study, which we will look at in greater detail, incorporates and develops much of the material of the earlier empirical works already referred to. He attempts to test the Todaro hypothesis, although he argues that it is difficult to translate into testable terms as, strictly speaking, it deals with the migrant's subjective expectations and is thus not refutable. In a reformulation of the hypothesis, net rural–urban migration is predicted to vary directly with the differential between the urban wage rate and average rural income, and inversely with the degree of difficulty of getting a job in the modern sector (approximated by the total supply of labour to urban areas minus the number employed in the modern sector, expressed as a proportion of the change in the number employed in the modern sector in the same period).

The country studied is Ghana over the period 1955–65. The period 1960–65 was marked by a tough wages policy, and as the urban–rural income differential fell, and the difficulty of getting a modern sector job increased, the Todaro model would predict a lower rate of rural–urban migration for this period. But even taking into account data deficiencies, the evidence suggests a higher rate of migration in 1960–65 than in 1955–60. Data inaccuracies are unlikely to be responsible for this seemingly perverse result and thus Godfrey first attempts to respecify the model. He argues that the informal sector must be incorporated into the model and that other variables should also be included in the migration function – the gap in social and infrastructural assets (health facilities, water supplies, etc.), the number of kinsmen already resident in urban areas (the influence of chain migration), changes in attitudes explainable solely in sociological and/or political terms and an educational variable.

With respect to the latter, Godfrey rejects the so-called 'white-collar hypothesis' (educated people migrate because they have been taught to despise the rural environment and to aspire to urban, white-collar employment) and argues that:

> ... having acquired a certain level of education, a school-leaver may feel it necessary to leave the village, irrespective of the state of the urban labour market, because the acquisition of that level of education differentiates him from his age-group to the extent that he feels himself to be in the 'migrant' category. As enrolment ratios rise, so, of course, does the level of education that performs this function. (Godfrey 1973, p.71)

Education is in principle incorporated into the Todaro model because it can be argued that the expected urban income and the probability of getting a modern sector job are positively related to the migrant's educational level. Godfrey argues that education also has an effect on migration quite separate from the effect on expected income. The Ghanaian data show a continuous increase in the number of people leaving schools in rural areas with a certain minimum primary education and a first-level rural enrolment ratio that only began to rise significantly after 1961. His argument is that the higher the enrolment ratio, the less is the school-leaver differentiated from the rest of his age group, and this to a certain extent offsets the increase in the number of school-leavers on the migrant flow. In other words, when education is felt to confer a distinction between the educated and the rest, migration is stimulated, but as more children receive education up to any given level, the less the distinction is felt and the less it operates only at a higher educational level. Thus Godfrey is saying that education and migration are positively related to one another, both in terms of increasing the economic incentive to migrate (as in Todaro) and in altering the school-leaver's perception of himself/herself. But as the proportion of children entering school rises, the level of education required to fulfil the latter function also rises.

However, even with the educational variable included, Godfrey still feels that additional explanatory variables need to be included in the migration function, in particular the number of kinsmen already in the urban area. If this was in fact an important variable, it would give a built-in dynamic to the migration process and would make the control or diminution of rural–urban migration more difficult. Godfrey concludes that in order to better understand the migratory process:

The most promising alternative to an aggregative, probabilistic approach may be that of micro-studies of particular villages or particular groups within villages over time, with the aim not so much of statistically 'explaining' as of understanding what is going on.[14] (Godfrey 1973, pp.74–5)

Conclusions

The experience of rapid urbanisation and rural–urban migration is not necessarily negative. The World Bank (1979, p.75) argues that urbanisation creates opportunities for increases in productivity and incomes and for reductions in the incidence of poverty. Squire (1981, Ch. 7) argues that migration is not a cause of urban unemployment and that attempts at restricting migration are misdirected. Labour-market imperfections, along with inappropriate government investment and pricing policies, are seen as the main factors underlying most urban problems.

With respect to rural–urban migration, the empirical studies clearly show the dominance of economic motives in the migratory decision, but even taking into account the concessions that some economists have made towards the inclusion of sociological variables, the methodological framework used is still that of the autonomous, income-maximising individual. There is, on the other hand, general agreement that the necessary policy measures required to achieve an appropriately balanced distribution of population need to be wide-ranging. There is stress on the need for radical changes of a structuralist nature in government policies – integrated rural development programmes, the development of labour-intensive techniques in the rural sector to create extensive employment opportunities, the redirection of the educational system towards the needs of rural development and the creation of an appropriate balance between urban and rural areas. However, whether such radical structural changes can be expected in the absence of prior political and social change must remain an open question at the present time.

4.6   The Urban Informal Sector

We noted in Section 4.3 above the multi-dimensional nature of the employment problem in LDCs and the difficulties associated with the definition and measurement of 'employment', 'unemployment' and 'underemployment'. As Moser (1978) has noted, there has been a shift in emphasis in development studies away from a preoccupation with *unemployment* to the identification of *employment* as the most important problem in LDCs. Clearly, in the absence of unemployment benefit or other social security payments, and assuming that family support will not continue indefinitely, those without jobs in the modern or formal sector of the urban economy must find alternative means of survival, legal or illegal, within the so-called 'informal sector' of the economy.

The concept of the informal sector was introduced by Hart in 1971 (see also Hart 1973; for further work from a sociological perspective see Roberts 1978; Lloyd 1979; Worsley 1984). Based on empirical work undertaken amongst the low-income section of the urban labour force in Accra, Hart drew the distinction between formal, that is wage-earning, activities (the organised sector of the economy) and informal, that is self-employment, activities (the unorganised sector). Informal sector activities were in turn divided into two categories – legitimate and illegitimate. Examples of the former included in Hart's typology are: primary and secondary activities (market gardening, building contractors, self-employed artisans, manufacturers of beers and spirits); tertiary enterprises with relatively large capital inputs (housing, transport, commodity speculation); small-scale distribution (petty traders, street hawkers); other services (shoeshiners, barbers); private transfer payments (gifts, borrowing, begging). Illegitimate activities included receiving stolen goods, drug pushing, prostitution, smuggling, petty theft, larceny, gambling, etc.

Obviously, the activities Hart included in the informal sector were extremely heterogeneous and, as Moser (1978) noted, it is not clear if it was people or their activities that were being classified. Nevertheless, Hart's ideas were taken up by the ILO and more fully developed in their Report on Kenya (ILO 1972). Informal sector activities were characterised by:

Ease of entry
Reliance on indigenous resources
Family ownership of operation
Small scale of operation
Labour-intensive and adapted technology
Skills acquired outside the formal school system
Unregulated and competitive markets

Formal sector characteristics were the obverse of the above:

Difficult entry
Frequent reliance on overseas resources
Corporate ownership
Large-scale of operation
Capital intensive and often imported technology
Formally acquired skills, often expatriate
Protected markets (through tariffs, quotas, trade licences)
(ILO 1972, p.6)

The ILO noted the apparent neglect of, or actual discrimination against, the informal sector by governments and argued instead for its active promotion. It was this sector that provided a wide range of low-cost goods and services using labour-intensive technologies for their production and stimulating the development of indigenous entrepreneurial abilities. Linkages between the formal and informal sectors needed to be recognised and encouraged to develop, and efforts should be put into the identification and development of products for production or use in the informal sector.

An alternative approach to the informal sector, based on the concept of a fragmented labour market, is presented by Mazumder (1976). He argues that employment in the formal sector is protected, '. . . so that the wage-level and working conditions in the sector are not available, in general, to the job-seekers in the market unless they manage to cross the barrier of entry somehow' (Mazumder 1976, p.656). This 'protection' arises as a result of trade-union action, or government intervention, or both, and ensures that workers in the protected formal sector enjoy better working conditions, fringe benefits, social security provisions and job security than those in the unprotected, informal sector. Contrary to the conventional wisdom, Mazumder argues that: (1) there is a pronounced selectivity of workers found in the informal sector, a disproportionate number of whom are very young or very old, female, and with lower levels of education; (2) earnings are low in this sector partly because of the selective factors which influence the type of labour found in the sector; (3) there is no evidence to suggest that this sector is an important point of entry in the formal labour market for new migrants to urban areas; and (4) there is a wide diversity of earnings within the informal sector, and within important components of it (the self-employed, for example).

Mazumder remarks that the 'free play of market forces' can by themselves create a 'protected' sector. The general tenor of his argument, however, is that 'distortions' in the labour market should be removed in order to improve short-run allocational efficiency, but more importantly, there must be an outward shift in the demand curve for unskilled labour, arising from an increase in the output of the commodities and services that unskilled labour produces (Squire 1981, Part III).

The final approach to the formal/informal sector dichotomy that deserves brief consideration is that of Weeks (1975). For Weeks, the distinction between a formal and informal sector is based on 'the organisational characteristics of exchange relationships and the position of economic activity *vis-à-vis* the State' (pp.2–3). Formal sector enterprises are 'officially recognised, fostered, nurtured and regulated by the State', whereas operations in the informal sector are characterised by the absence of such benefits – 'Enterprises and individuals operate outside the system of benefits and regulations of government and thus without access to the formal credit institutions and sources of transfer of foreign technology' (p.3).

Weeks argues that neither sector is inherently dynamic or static, and that what requires investigation are the conditions under which change in the informal sector will be involutionary (that is exhibiting a process of internal adaptation leading to static or only slowly growing output per head and capital accumulation and hence labour absorption) or evolutionary (rapid output growth and capital accumulation). He asserts that there are considerable advantages in having a 'dynamic, evolving low-wage sector in less developed countries' (p.8) in that the informal sector: (i) will produce an important proportion of consumer goods purchased, especially by low-income groups; (ii) will possibly provide a source of indigenous capital goods as well as training ground for indigenous entrepreneurs; and (iii) will lead increasingly to the use of more labour-intensive technologies. He recommends that linkages between the two sectors should be strengthened and suggests a number of policy measures that could stimulate evolutionary growth, especially government policies that will redirect final demand towards the informal sector.

Although the concept of the 'informal sector' is intuitively appealing and theoretically useful, it is not without problems. Nine deficiencies of the formal/informal sector dichotomy have been listed by Bromley (1978). They are:

(1) The division of all economic activities into two categories is crude and simplistic.

(2) No adequate guidelines exist to classify all economic activities as unambiguously belonging to one sector or the other.

(3) Many investigations assume that the two sectors are separate and independent of one another, when this is clearly not the case (cf. Weeks, above).

(4) It is often mistakenly believed that a single policy prescription can be applied to the informal sector as a whole.

(5) There is a tendency to view the informal sector as exclusively urban.

(6) There is some ambiguity as to which other sectors are also consistent parts of the total national system (should there be a 'state sector', for example?)

(7) The informal sector is often viewed as having a present but no future, i.e. many of the policy recommendations (e.g. government recognition and support), if adopted, would in effect convert the informal into a formal sector.

(8) There is a tendency to confuse neighbourhoods, households, people and activities, with enterprises. 'Only enterprises can usually be conveniently classified into one or other of the two sectors, and extrapolations from classification of enterprises to descriptions of activities, people, households and neighbourhoods frequently lead to confusion and error' (Bromley 1978, p. 1935).

(9) There is a tendency to regard as synonymous 'the urban informal sector' and 'the urban poor'.

To overcome some of these theoretical difficulties, Moser (1978) and a number of other authors have proposed the use of the concept of 'petty commodity production'. It is explicitly recognised that economic activities are spread over a continuum, rather than fitting neatly into a two-sector model. Workers are employed in a variety of different categories outside the well-defined wage sector of large-scale enterprises (wage and salaried employees of small-scale enterprises, self-employed owners, unpaid family labourers, casual workers in wage-sector employment, quasi-wage-earning journeymen) and the linkages between these enterprises and the 'formal' sector are numerous and diverse (Moser 1978, p. 1056).

This alternative theoretical approach can also more easily incorporate the analysis of social relations of production (defined in terms of the ownership and control of the means of production) as well as the forces of production (technology, resources, labour power) and can lead to an elaboration of the articulation of different modes of production within the Marxist tradition (Bienefeld 1975). The recognition that enterprises within the informal sector are articulated as part of the capitalist mode of production, and that their development is linked to the development of the whole economic system, provides a number of important insights:

> ... petty commodity production performs a number of important functions within the capitalist mode of production. At the same time, because of its dependent position, there are constraints and limitations on the level of capital accumulation possible within it. Hence, the urban petty commodity sector, which includes artisan production and trading, is concerned with the provision of goods and services considered unprofitable by foreign or large-scale capital. However, this does not necessarily imply that it is a static form of production using traditional techniques making only poor quality goods, non-competitive with factory production, or low-income families ... [it] ... has developed with modern capitalism, with new skills and means of production continually introduced following technological development. (Moser 1978, p.1058)

By focusing on the structural relationships and linkages between the two sectors, Moser (1978) argues that we can go beyond the debate over whether the relationship between the formal and informal sectors is 'benign' (as would be assumed by the ILO, for example) or 'exploitative' (as would be asserted by Marxist critics, for example Leys 1973):

> The importance of the petty commodity approach is not that it condemns the informal sector concept, or state and international agency measures to promote informal sector development, but that it puts them in their correct perspective by showing that in themselves they cannot really provide solutions to the problems of unemployment and poverty. (Moser 1978, p.1062)

4.7 Conclusions

In this chapter we have, *inter alia*, highlighted the complex interrelationships between the development process, population growth, employment creation, urbanisation and migration. The analysis of these relationships cannot be separated from issues concerning the balance between agricultural and non-agricultural development, macroeconomic policy or the choice of techniques of production (which are discussed in later chapters). Policy choices taken under these headings act upon individuals in society and largely determine the nature of their relationship to the general economic system (*i.e.* jobs, sources of income) as well as where they are located, both geographically and in the socio-economic hierarchy. This is true not only in the short run where changes in job availability and wage levels are seen to affect migration rates and directions, but also in the long run where population growth is itself found to be dependent upon the nature of the economic development which occurs. Changes in the pattern of employment, the degree of income inequality, levels of income, and the extent of provision of public services in family planning, health and education which accompnay development will all have some influence upon the growth of population and therefore upon the extent of the long-run employment creation problem.

Rapid population growth and accelerating urbanisation, coupled with growing unemployment and underemployment, are both causes and consequences of economic backwardness and poverty in LDCs. Isolating employment creation as a key variable at the centre of this nexus of interrelationships, it is clear that there is no simple policy solution to reducing underemployment rates. Nevertheless, the 'employment problem' reflects many of the key issues in development, embodying within it shortages of opportunities, growing inequality, and differences in attitudes and expectations between young and old, educated and non-educated. It is natural, therefore, that employment issues should be made a central focus of development economics, a focus reflected in this text.

Notes

1. See Todaro (1981), p. 159.
2. In this context 'social setting' is defined to be a function of adult literacy, primary and secondary school enrolment, life expectancy, infant mortality, the share of the male labour force in non-agricultural activities, GDP per capita, the degree of urbanisation, the position of women in society, and the dominant religious–cultural tradition.
3. Criticisms of this concept are stated by ILO (1971), not only on the grounds

that not everyone in this age group works, but also because in the absence of universal schooling many children work, and in the absence of compulsory retirement so may older people.

4. Participation rates do vary with changes in both supply and demand for labour. To this extent they are not exogenous constants, but are variables which are functions of economic changes.

5. For a fuller account of this debate see Todaro (1977), Chapter 6.

6. See, for example, ILO (1966), ILO (1977), Krishna (1973), Squire (1981, Ch.4), and Brahmananda (1983). Godfrey (1986) presents an extensive exploration of the concepts of employment, unemployment, and underemployment in Chapter 1.

7. Higher rates were recorded for several smaller countries.

8. A factual example can be given. In 1964 and 1970, the Government of Kenya concluded two 'Tripartite Agreements', between itself, the employers' federation and the trade unions. The major provisions of the 1970 agreement were:

(i) The Government and employers agreed to expand employment by 10% of their regular establishment.
(ii) Employees agreed to a 12 month wage standstill.
(iii) There were to be no strikes or lockouts during the period of the agreement.

The registration of those seeking employment under the agreement totalled 290,911. Only 46,680 jobs were created by the scheme, 30,203 in the private sector and 15,477 in the public sector (an increase of 7.3% for the two sectors combined, although this was not necessarily a net addition to employment). The ILO Report (1972) concluded that 'Both agreements succeeded in generating a certain amount of additional employment in the short run. Yet they probably contributed more to raising expectations than to realising them . . . The additional employment generated almost certainly has had no lasting effect . . .'

9. Developing this point, Godfrey (1973, p. 73) argues that we should perhaps discard the Todaro approach with its 'implicit definition of the decision maker as an economic man who will act consistently at different points in time. It may make more sense to distinguish between at least two decisions made at different points in time – the initial decision whether or not to migrate and the later decision, faced after a period of unemployment whether or not to return to traditional farming . . . these two decisions, although made by one individual, are made by two different people'. Apathy, frustration and fatalism may become the dominant personality traits of a migrant unemployed for a long period of time – the experience makes the migrant a 'different' person.

10. Amin (1974, pp. 88–9) makes a similar point when he argues that the distribution of the factors of production is not given a priori and distributed geographically unequally but rather is the result of the development strategy being followed: 'Economic (so-called 'rational') choice and notably the decision of the migrant to leave his region of origin, is then completely predetermined by the overall strategy determining the allocation of factors'.

11. In Central and Southern Africa, for example, the pattern of migration is circulatory in that many migrants return to the rural areas at the end of their working life. Circular migration constitutes a response to family separation, but as Gugler (1982, p. 62) notes, this strategy fails with the appearance of urban unemployment.

12. Mayer's (1961) study of Red Xhosa and School Xhosa in East London (South Africa) illustrates how individuals are constrained in their actions by a particular structure of social relationships. The School Xhosa adapt well to urban life and stay for long periods, the loose-knit social network permitting a cleaner break to be made with the village and greater independence in the town. The Red Xhosa, on the other hand, adapt badly to urban life, staying for short periods only. They have a close-knit social network, maintain close ties with their homelands and rely on contacts in the town to help them.

13. Two points deserve brief mention, although lack of space prevents fuller discussion: (1) economic, cultural and social factors are not independent of one another. The economic structure of society both influences and is influenced by values, attitudes and institutions. The distinction between 'economic', and 'non-economic' or 'personal' factors must thus be used with care; (2) the concept of rationality is used in a normative or ideological manner. The migrant is 'rational' if his/her objective is the maximisation of income, but other forms of behaviour may be perfectly rational, given a different system of economic organisation, social structure, cultural values and so on. What is considered rational in one society would be considered highly irrational in another. Economic rationality is neither timeless nor universal.

14. Godfrey develops this point further in a subsequent paper (Godfrey 1979) when he argues that the emphasis should be on the impact of structural change, both rural and urban, on migration. 'In both cases, what matters is not so much the motives of individuals involved as the interaction between the processes of structural change and of migration' (p. 244).

References

Amin, S. (1974) 'Modern migrations in Western Africa', in S. Amin (ed.) (1974), *Modern Migration in West Africa*, Oxford University Press.

Bairoch, P. (1975) *The Economic Development of the Third World since 1900*, Methuen.

Barnum, H.N. and Sabot, R.H. (1976) *Migration, Education and Urban Surplus Labour: The Case of Tanzania*, Development Centre, OECD, Paris.

Beals, R.E., Levy, M.B. and Moses, L.N. (1967) 'Rationality and migration in Ghana', *Review of Economics and Statistics*, November.

Bienefeld, M. (1975) 'The informal sector and peripheral capitalism: the case of Tanzania', *Institute of Development Studies Bulletin*, Vol. 6, No. 3.

Birdsall, N. (1977) 'Analytical approaches to the relationship of population growth and development', *Population and Development Review*, 3(1), pp. 63–96; reprinted in Ghosh (1984) *op. cit.*

Brahmananda, P.R. (1983) 'The dimensions of the problems of unemployment in India', in Robinson *et al.* (1983), pp. 33–45.

Bromley, R. (1978) 'Introduction – the urban informal sector: why is it worth discussing?', *World Development*, 6(9/10).

Caldwell, J.C. (1967) 'Migration and urbanisation', in W. Birmingham, I. Neustadt and E.N. Omaboe (eds) *A Study of Contemporary Ghana*, Vol. II, *Some Aspects of Social Structure*, George Allen and Unwin.

Caldwell, J.C. (1968) 'Determinants of rural–urban migration in Ghana', *Population Studies*, Vol. XXII, No. 3.

Caldwell, J.C. (1969) *African Rural–Urban Migration*, Hurst.

Deshpande, L.K. (1983) 'Urban labour markets: problems and policies', in Robinson *et al.* (1983), pp. 83–92.

Durand, J.D. (1975) *The Labour Force in Economic Development*, Princeton University Press.

Frejka, T. (1981) 'Long-term prospects for world population growth', *Population and Development Review*, 7(3), pp. 489–511; reprinted in Ghosh (1984).

Garbett, G.K. and Kapferer, B. (1970) 'Theoretical orientations in the study of labour migration', *The New Atlantis*, 2(1).

Ghosh, P.K. (ed.) (1984) *Population, Environment and Resources, and Third World Development*, Greenwood Press.

Gilbert, A. (1982) 'Urban development in a world system', in Gilbert and Gugler (1982).

Gilbert, A. and Gugler, J. (eds) (1982) *Cities, Poverty and Development: Urbanisation in the Third World*, Oxford University Press.

Godfrey, E.M. (1969) 'Labour-surplus models and labour-deficit economies: the West African case', *Economic Development and Cultural Change*, 17(3).

Godfrey, E.M. (1973) 'Economic variables and rural–urban migration: some thoughts on the Todaro hypothesis', *Journal of Development Studies*, X(1).

Godfrey, E.M. (1979) 'Rural–urban migration in a "Lewis-model" context', *The Manchester School*, 47(3).

Godfrey, E.M. (1986) *Global Unemployment*, Wheatsheaf Books.

Gugler, J. (1969) 'On the theory of rural–urban migration', in J.A. Jackson (ed.) *Sociological Studies 2*, Cambridge University Press.

Gugler, J. (1982) 'The rural–urban interface and migration', in Gilbert and Gugler (1982).

Harbison, F.H. (1967) 'The generation of employment in newly developing countries', in J.R. Sheffield (ed.), *Education, Employment and Rural Development*, East African Publishing House, Nairobi.

Hart, K. (1971) 'Informal income opportunities and urban employment in Ghana', paper delivered to Conference on Urban Unemployment in Africa, Institute of Development Studies, University of Sussex; extracts published in Jolly *et al.* (1973); revised version in *Journal of Modern African Studies*, Vol. 11, No. 1, 1973.

Herrick, B.H. (1965) *Urban Migration and Economic Development in Chile*, MIT Press.

ILO (1966) *Measurement of Underemployment: Concepts and Methods*, Geneva.

ILO (1971) *Concepts of Labour Force Underutilisation*, Geneva.

ILO (1972) *Employment, Incomes and Equality: a strategy for increasing productive employment in Kenya*, Geneva.

ILO (1977) *Yearbook of Labour Statistics*, Geneva.

Jolly, R. (1970) 'Rural–urban migration: dimensions, causes, issues and policies', paper for *Cambridge Overseas Studies Committee Conference*.

Jolly, R., DeKadt, E., Singer, H. and Wilson, F. (eds) (1973) *Third World Employment: Problems and Strategy*, Penguin Books.

Knight, J.B. (1972) 'Rural–urban income comparisons and migration in Ghana', *Bulletin of Oxford University Institute of Economics and Statistics*, May.

Krishna, R. (1973) 'Unemployment in India – Presidential Address', *Indian Journal of Agricultural Economics*, Vol. 28, pp. 1–23.

Lewis, W.A. (1954) 'Economic development with unlimited supplies of labour', *The Manchester School*, 22, pp. 130–90, May.

Leys, C. (1973) 'Interpreting African underdevelopment: reflections on the ILO Report on employment, incomes and equality in Kenya', *African Affairs*, Vol. 72, No. 289.

Lloyd, P. (1979) *Slums of Hope? Shanty Towns of the Third World*, Penguin Books.

Maudlin, W. and Berelson, B. (1977) *Conditions of Fertility Decline in Developing Countries 1965–75*, Population Council, New York.

Mayer, P. (1961) *Townsmen or Tribesmen: Conservatism and the Process of Urbanisation in a South African City*, Oxford University Press.

Mazumder, D. (1976) 'The urban informal sector', *World Development*, 4(8).

Morawetz, David (1974) 'Employment implications of industrialisation in developing countries', *Economic Journal*, 84(335).

Moser, C.O. (1978) 'Informal sector or petty commodity production: dualism or dependence in urban development?', *World Development*, Vol. 6, No. 9/10, September/October.

Ranis, G. and Fei, J.C.H. (1961) 'A theory of economic development', *American Economic Review*, Vol. 51.

Rath, N. (1983) 'Measuring rural unemployment in India', in Robinson *et al.* (1983), pp. 46–58.

Roberts, B. (1978) *Cities of Peasants*, Edward Arnold.

Robinson, A. (1983) 'Introduction', in Robinson *et al.* (1983), *op. cit.*, pp. 1–29.

Robinson, A., Brahmananda, R.P. and Deshpande, L.K. (eds) (1983) *Employment Policy in a Developing Country*, Macmillan.

Sabot, R.H. (ed.) (1982) *Migration and the Labour Market in Developing Countries*, Westview Press.

Sahota, G.S. (1968) 'An economic analysis of internal migration in Brazil', *Journal of Political Economy*, March/April.

Sinclair, S. (1978) *Urbanisation and Labour Markets in Developing Countries*, Croom Helm.

Squire, L. (1981) *Employment Policy in Developing Countries: A Survey of Issues and Evidence*, Oxford University Press for the World Bank.

Streeten, P. (1972) *The Frontiers of Development Studies*, Macmillan.

Tabah, Leon (1972) 'World population trends: a stocktaking', *Population and Development Review*, 6(3), pp. 355–89; reprinted in Ghosh (1984).

Todaro, M. (1968) 'The urban employment problem in less developed countries: and analysis of demand and supply', *Yale Economic Essays*, 8.

Todaro, M. (1969) 'A model of labour migration and urban employment in less developed countries', *American Economic Review*, March.

Todaro, M.P. (1976) *International Migration in Developing Countries. A Review of Theory, Evidence, Methodology and Research Priorities*, International Labour Office, Geneva.

Todaro, M.P. (1977) *Economic Development in the Third World*, Longman.

Todaro, M.P. (1981) *Economic Development in the Third World*, Longman.

Turnham, D. (1971) *The Employment Problem in Less-Developed Countries*, OECD Development Centre, Paris.

Ward, B. (1976) *The Home of Man*, Penguin Books.

Weeks, J. (1975) 'Policies for expanding employment in the informal urban sector of developing countries', *International Labour Review*, 11.

World Bank (1979) *World Development Report, 1979*, World Bank.

Worsley, P. (1984) *The Three Worlds: Culture and World Development*, Weidenfeld and Nicolson.

Zymelman, M. (1976) *Patterns of Educational Expenditures*, World Bank Staff Working Paper No. 246.

5

The international setting: trade

It is hardly surprising that problems of trade between the LDCs and developed countries should dominate the agendas of international agencies concerned with economic affairs, for economic relationships between countries are largely definable in terms of the patterns of trade and exchange between them. Certainly the pattern of trade between DC and LDC countries yields a fairly clear picture of the economic relationship between them, the predominant features of which still reflect a past in which, under colonial domination, the trade of LDCs was subservient to the needs of the metropolitan countries. In that era the colonies provided a captive market for the manufactured products of the colonising countries while in return supplying them with raw materials and tropical foodstuffs. Although, as will be seen in the next section, trade patterns between more and less developed countries have exhibited certain modifications in the last two decades, topical questions still revolve around whether the basic relationships of the colonial period have changed. Does trade contribute to the growth and development of poorer nations, or does it serve to reinforce the hierarchy of rich and poor nations? Is the pattern of trade preserved by protective policy actions of the richer countries designed to maintain their economic advantage over poorer countries? Do the institutions controlling international trade hinder economic development by passing on most of the gains from trade to the richer nations? In other words, is the system of international trade inherently unfair to the poorer nations? These are essentially long-term questions about the capacity of international trade to promote economic development. In addition there are shorter-run issues concerning the possible disadvantages of reliance upon primary products for the bulk of export earnings. For example, do prices and revenues of primary commodities exhibit greater short-run instability than those for manufactured goods, and, if so, does such instability hamper development?

5.1   Pattern of Trade Between LDCs and MDCs

The stereotypical picture of trade is of the LDCs exporting primary agricultural and mineral commodities to the industrialised countries in exchange for manufactured goods. While still broadly true, there have been major changes in the composition of trade flows since 1950 and hence in the appropriateness of this simple picture.[1] The most dramatic change can be seen (from Table 5.1) to be the doubling of the share of fuel in the value of LDC exports between 1955 and 1978, from around one-quarter to one-half of the total. Of course this increase reflects the success, at raising oil prices, of the OPEC countries, which constitute only a small proportion of all LDCs and a smaller proportion of the total population of such countries.

More insight into the changed export composition of poorer (oil-importing) LDCs is obtained by considering what has happened to non-fuel exports. Here it can be seen that there has been a substantial expansion in the share of manufactured exports, from 10% of LDC non-fuel exports in 1955 to 44% in 1978 (plus a further increase to 53% by 1982 – see Chapter 9), with a corresponding decline in the share of primary

Table 5.1   The Structure of LDC Exports: Selected Years 1955–78 (%)

	1955	1960	1970	1978
Total exports	100	100	100	100
Food	36.5	33.6	26.5	16.4
Agricultural raw materials	20.5	18.3	10.0	4.8
Minerals, ores	9.9	10.6	12.3	4.6
Fuels	25.2	27.9	32.9	52.8
Manufactures[a]	7.7	9.2	17.7	20.9
Total non-fuel exports	100	100	100	100
Food	48.9	46.7	39.5	34.8
Agricultural raw materials	27.4	25.3	14.9	10.1
Minerals, ores	13.3	14.6	18.3	9.7
Manufactures[a]	10.4	12.8	26.4	44.4
Share of DCs in exports of LDCs				
Total non-fuel exports	76.3	74.3	71.9	65.4
Food	79.0	77.7	74.0	65.6
Agricultural raw materials	74.3	67.8	64.4	61.8
Minerals, ores	94.5	92.0	89.2	78.0
Manufactures[a]	45.9	54.0	61.2	63.3

Source: Riedel 1984, p.60.
Note: (a) Manufactures = SITC 5 to 8, less 68.

commodity exports. The category of primary exports which has declined most in importance is agricultural raw materials, down from 27% of non-fuel exports in 1955 to only 10% in 1978. Doubtless a major factor contributing to the loss of share in this category is the expansion of capacity to process agricultural raw materials in the LDCs themselves, both to cater for the expanded demand in home markets and as a result of deliberate policies to increase exports of raw materials in manufactured form. In the case of the food category, volume growth of exports has been restrained by the increasing dependence of many LDCs on imports of staple foods (see Chapter 8 for more details). Nevertheless, the continued dominance of LDCs as world exporters of coffee, tea, cocoa, sugar and tropical fruits and spices ensures that food continues to account for a large proportion of non-fuel exports.

As Riedel clearly illustrates, it is not only the OPEC group of countries whose trade pattern needs to be distinguished from that of the other non-industrial countries; there are major differences discernible between other groups of LDCs. Among non-oil exporting countries a sharply distinct group is the 'Four political entities in East Asia (South Korea, Taiwan, Hong Kong and Singapore) (which) alone in 1978 accounted for more than 60% of total LDC manufactured exports, but alas only about 3% of the total population of developing countries (excluding the People's Republic of China). These four entities together with Lebanon and Macao, are the only LDCs in which manufactures account for as much as 75% of exports'. (Riedel 1984, p.61). This leaves the primary commodity exporting countries which Riedel in turn subdivides into three groups: (1) the 'balanced exporters'; (2) African primary exporters; and (3) non-African primary exporters.

The balanced exporters, including such countries as Brazil, Egypt, Mexico and Pakistan, are a group in which the share of manufactured exports has more than doubled since 1960 to reach an average of 39% of exports in 1976–78, and where this increase in share was almost wholly at the expense of the share of the largest single primary export. The non-African primary exporters constitute an intermediate case between these and the African primary exporters in which there has been remarkably little change in export composition over the period 1960–78. In these African countries manufactures had only captured a 7% share of exports by 1976–78, and on average the single largest primary commodity accounted for 46% and the second largest for 16% of the value of total exports. Thus only this group of countries corresponds particularly closely to the stereotype of LDCs highly dependent for export earnings upon a very small number of primary commodities. The NICs have clearly broken out of the mould, the non-African primary exporters are progressively doing so and the richer OPEC countries are clearly a special case.

A further dimension of change in trading patterns is displayed in the reduction in the degree to which LDC trade is dominated by exchanges with the industrialised countries (ICs). This has been occurring steadily (see Table 5.2), with the proportion of developing country exports which go to ICs having fallen from around 75% in 1960 to 60% in 1982, and with the proportion of developing country imports from ICs having fallen in a similar manner. Accompanying this reorientation has been an expansion of trade between the LDCs themselves, to the extent that the share of developing country imports originating within that group of countries has risen from an average of 19.4% in 1962 to 30.3% in 1983. Thus here again the conventional picture of LDCs being dependent upon the ICs as outlets for their exports and suppliers of their imports is becoming less clear as LDCs increasingly trade among themselves along the lines urged by Lewis (1980) in his Nobel Prize acceptance speech.

Table 5.2 Percentage of Developing Country Exports and Imports, by Country Group (3 year moving average percentage)

	1962	1965	1968	1971	1974	1977	1980	1983
Exports to:								
Industrial countries	70.1	73.1	69.7	68.3	69.2	64.9	65.9	60.1
Oil-exporting developing countries	4.1	3.7	3.7	2.7	2.4	3.7	3.7	5.1
Non-oil-exporting developing countries	15.5	15.5	16.8	17.9	19.8	21.5	22.4	26.1
USSR/E.Europe	3.9	4.4	4.0	3.9	4.4	4.6	4.0	4.1
Other	6.4	3.2	5.8	7.2	4.3	3.7	4.0	4.6
Imports from:								
Industrial countries	72.0	74.2	69.7	68.9	67.2	66.3	65.2	61.9
Oil-exporting developing countries	6.9	6.4	6.1	6.0	8.6	10.5	7.8	11.6
Non-oil-exporting developing countries	12.5	13.5	13.9	13.8	15.1	15.8	16.5	18.7
USSR/E.Europe	4.5	5.6	5.7	5.1	5.5	4.8	4.6	4.0
Other	4.1	0.3	4.7	6.2	3.7	2.4	3.2	3.9

Source: IMF, Direction of Trade, Statistics Yearbook 1983 and 1985.

5.2 Can Trade Lead to Development?

As far as international trade theory is concerned, the answer to this question is undoubtedly affirmative. But, as Smith and Toye (1979) set out in their review of trade theory and development, the main lines of orthodox reasoning rest on incompatible and challengeable assumptions.

The theory of comparative advantage is based upon assumptions of full employment, complete factor mobility and the existence of different techniques of production in different countries. From this latter assumption it follows that relative production costs differ between countries, and that all countries, including the LDCs, can increase their consumption of goods (and value of production) above the levels achieveable by autarkic production with no trade by specialising in the production and trade of those commodities for which they have the relative lowest production costs.

The Hecksher–Ohlin–Samuelson (HOS) theory argues that the opportunity for mutually beneficial trade derives from inter-country differences in factor endowments. In this theory, comparative advantage arises from the different factor intensities in producing different products rather than from differences in production techniques. It leads to the conclusion that poor countries (those with abundant labour) should specialise in producing and trading labour-intensive goods while the richer countries (with relatively scarce labour and abundant capital) should specialise in capital-intensive ones. This theory also implies that free trade and specialisation in production will tend to bring about factor price equalisation, and thus pull the returns to labour in LDCs up towards the levels in DCs. This theoretical outcome hinges very much upon the strong (and arguable) assumption that at least some factors of production are internationally perfectly mobile. Edwards (1985, pp.29–44) presents an extensive and readable critique of the HOS theory under the heading 'The fall of the Hecksher–Ohlin theory'.

> [In] the third variant of the story of mutually beneficial trade, the idea of trade as a 'vent for surplus', again rests on different assumptions from those underlying the comparative advantage or the factor endowment theory. This time we revert to the assumption of differences in technology between the rich and poor country, but combine this with the assumption that before trade takes place some resources in the poor country are unemployed. Trade is said to benefit the poor country because incomes are created thereby for the previously unemployed resources. (Smith and Toye 1979, p.4)

Thus the elementary theory of trade argues not only that trade can promote development (in the form of higher consumption and production), but that it will do so. In the HOS version the theory also argues that trade will help reduce the income gap between poor and rich countries.

These arguments have had a pervasive influence since the theory of comparative advantage was first published by Ricardo in 1817, and have led policy makers to emphasise trade expansion as a means of promoting development. However, the persistence of large international differences in per capita incomes has led to doubts about the relevance of the assumptions of neoclassical trade theory and about the capacity of the existing system of trade to improve the relative incomes of underdeveloped countries. While theory demonstrates that trade *can* increase welfare, developments of the theory make it clear that this is not a necessary outcome. This is clearly shown by Steedman (1979) who begins his analysis by considering the implications of specialisation and trade in economies which may produce (or specialise in) some subset of three alternative products: (1) a consumption good, C; (2) machines, M_1, used in the production of C; and (3) machines, M_2, used in the production of both M_1 and M_2. If growth of consumption per unit of labour is taken as being equivalent to development, then it transpires that there exist well-defined situations in which the free-trade specialisation chosen by entrepreneurs may not be optimal and may actually reduce development when compared to a situation of no trade.[2] Unsurprisingly, it is shown that the possibility of specialisation causing losses from trade survives the introduction of more realistic and complex elements into the theory, such as non-tradeable goods and choices of alternative techniques of production. This is because, as Steedman observes (p.49), 'Under free trade, decisions are made by individual capitalists under the pressures of competition, and the resultant effects on the "country", whether beneficial or harmful, are unforeseen and unintended consequences of these decisions. Thus the question whether countries gain from trade is left open'.

While Steedman's theoretical analysis merely argues that specialisation by producers in LDCs may, but will not necessarily, lead to losses through trade, others argue more strongly that such losses will inevitably tend to occur. Such critics argue that the standard theory of trade, which leads to propositions that trade will (or may) stimulate development, is based on oversimplified assumptions, and that in practice the current international trade system (or a freer version of it) can only serve to reinforce the differential status of developed and less well-developed countries. Some writers focus upon theoretical inadequacies in dealing with the dynamics of economic behaviour in relation to investment, production and trade. For example, Kitamura (1968) argued 'that in a changing world of capital accumulation and technical progress, free trade does not tend to maximise the welfare of the less-developed countries nor to ensure their balance of trade . . .' and that 'international trade if not assisted by the consciously guided transfer of factors of production, has no inherent tendency to equalise income and productivity levels. Indeed, the trade mechanism works the other way round – in favour of the progressive countries and against stagnant ones'.

Underlying this viewpoint is the important argument that, although some developed countries may well have high wage rates relative to those in underdeveloped countries, because of traditionally high rates of productivity growth and technological change the ratio of labour productivity to wage rates may still be higher in the richer countries. In this situation, as accepted by some Marxist economists (Brown 1974, Ch. 10), capital will be attracted to these rather than the poorer nations, thus extending the technology gap and increasing the international difference in wage levels. It follows that if free trade is unlikely to increase the relative capital endowment of the underdeveloped countries, international income disparities are only likely to be reduced if conscious decisions are taken to direct capital to the LDCs in the form of aid, technical assistance and preferential trade arrangements.

Another fundamental set of criticisms of free trade as a mechanism for promoting development is directed at standard theory's implicit assumptions that there are no basic institutional differences between nations in the way their production and trade are managed. One very influential criticism is that in many developing countries the main exporting industries have been and continue to be dominated by foreign ownership. In the colonial heyday of the eighteenth and nineteenth centuries LDC export production in mining and plantation agriculture was initiated and controlled by European-based companies, whose main function was to serve the markets of the metropolitan countries and to provide cheap, secure supplies of raw materials to their processing industries (*e.g.* in textiles, rubber products, copper and sugar refining). This, it can be argued, assisted the competitive advantage of many industries in the wealthy countries so that it is now difficult for poorer countries with weak domestic markets (particularly those in Africa) to establish viable industries since so many industries exhibit economies of size. However, the growth of the textile industry in Asia, the nationalisation of foreign oil interests by the Middle Eastern countries in the 1950s and 1960s, and the acquisition by Malaysian owners of former British-owned rubber plantations in Malaysia are all indicators of ways in which the colonial heritage of foreign ownership of LDC primary commodity production has been diminished in some of the more dynamic LDCs. It is again in sub-Saharan Africa that this legacy persists more clearly than elsewhere.

In recent discussion the focus of attention has switched from the old colonial structures of foreign dominance to the role of modern transnational corporations (TNCs) in production, trade and development. In some cases these TNCs are also engaged in the production of primary commodities (such as soyabeans, beef and strawberries) for export, where their role has attracted heavy criticism (*e.g.* Feder 1979; George 1978), but more significantly they are involved in industrial production employing modern technology. Their role in the development of LDCs is complex and is discussed extensively in Chapters 10 and 11; but here again the simple stereotype of foreign-owned companies dominating the primary commodity exports of LDCs is of reduced validity.

One of the main criticisms voiced against the role of established foreign firms engaged in exporting primary products from LDCs is that they have often found that the safest and most remunerative investments for their profits have been in the already industrialised countries, with the result that there has been a massive repatriation of profits from the poorer to the richer countries. (See, for example, de Janvry (1981, p.51) for estimates of net repatriation of capital to US firms from Latin American countries.) Although it is not only foreign firms which are responsible for exporting capital, this does lend substance to the charge that foreign capital operates in an exploitative manner within the developing countries. Further support for this is found in the enclave nature of much foreign-owned primary industry. This is clearly noticeable in both plantation agriculture and mining (Beckford 1972), which tend (a) to export virtually all of their output; (b) to be capital intensive relative to much of the rest of the economy and to import most of their capital equipment; (c) to be demanding of the provision of roads, railways, ports and other forms of social capital; and (d) to promote few backward linkages into input-supplying industries or forward linkages into secondary industry. These features do much to account for the main charge made against foreign ownership of industry, which is that it has not tended to reinvest its profits in the expansion of the local developing economies but has used them 'exploitatively' for the benefit of the richer nations. They may also cause there to be a weak relationship between export and GNP growth in LDCs.

However, these criticisms of the institution of foreign ownership have to be set against evidence of the more positive role which foreign capital has played in LDCs. The NICs are frequently held out as an example of how development may best be achieved. These countries have successfully pursued export-led growth policies in which foreign firms, TNCs, have played a major role through the establishment of new industries with direct marketing links to the DCs, and through the introduction of new technology. TNC involvement in these and other LDC countries has entailed substantial new investment, which helps offset the notion that foreign firms are principally concerned to repatriate profits. Where there are profitable investment opportunities, new foreign capital is attracted to LDCs, and of course the attractions are greater in the more dynamic and successful LDCs.[3] Some critics would still argue that this is a form of exploitation since foreign firms are attracted by the availability of cheap labour, less stringent planning and environmental controls, and (for agricultural TNCs) cheap land. It does, however, seem unreasonable to criticise TNCs for taking advantage of such opportunities as these, and the relevant question to pose is to what extent, and under what conditions, LDCs benefit from the participation of foreign capital. Although there may be circumstances in which the existence of benefits is doubtful, it is equally apparent (Colman 1984) that there are other instances where LDCs do gain from the activities of TNCs.

A somewhat different argument, popularly associated with the names of Prebisch and Singer, also pointed to institutional factors which cause the industrialised nations (the Centre) to 'exploit' the less-developed primary-producing ones (the Periphery) through international trade (Prebisch 1950, 1967; Singer 1950; Baer 1961). The main challenge was directed at the validity of the assumption in trade theory of classically competitive factor and product markets in both the Centre and the Periphery. Neoclassical economic theory suggests that, where competition exists, technological changes which result in increased total factor productivity will lead to reduced product prices. Prebisch argued that this process operates at the Periphery, competing down export prices to the benefit of consumers at the Centre. However, at the Centre more monopolistic forces are believed to operate, particularly in the labour market where union power is seen as extracting the gains from increased productivity in the form of higher wages, and in the product market where firms are seen as having sufficient market power to pass on higher wage costs in the form of higher prices to consumers at the Periphery and at the Centre. Thus it was argued that as a result of differences in competitive structure, the prices of primary exports from the Periphery are depressed relative to those of imported manufactured items, and trade will act as an 'exploitative' force on behalf of the Centre.

However, as Spraos (1983) notes, such competitive differences in labour markets between the Periphery and Centre are neither necessary nor sufficient to cause a decline in the net barter terms of trade of primary for manufactured goods. He indicates (p.42) that Prebisch himself did not long adhere to this simple version of the argument, and came to accept more 'empirically plausible arguments' for the declining terms of trade. Spraos identifies two major sustainable arguments for this position, neither of which can be classed as institutional. These are that, 'first, primary commodities suffer from a downward demand bias, the measure of which is their lower income elasticity compared with manufactures; second, they suffer from an upward supply bias because they draw on the pool of excess labour in the less progressive sectors of the developing countries' economies'. But, again, Spraos notes that these are not conclusive arguments for declining primary commodity terms of trade since there are developmental factors which offset them, such as the progressive exhaustion of mineral reserves, the move away from specialisation by

LDCs on primary sector production, and the possibility of slower technical progress in non-manufacturing than in manufacturing. The third acceptable argument he identifies is an institutional one. This, associated with the names of Prebisch and Emmanuel, is 'that primary commodities of developing countries have had to contend with the continuously increasing power of labour unions in developed countries'.[4]

Emmanuel's name is closely linked to a more extreme neo-Marxian view of the adverse effects of trade upon development. This is the proposition that trade is a form of unequal exchange through which the advanced countries exploit poorer ones by obtaining more labour for less through trade. Emmanuel puts forward a number of explanations about the institutional and behavioural causes of this. However, as Brown (1974, Ch. 10) clearly argues, most of these explanations are questionable. A key problem centres on Emmanuel's view that real wages are exogenously given, and that wage differences between rich and poor countries are the cause of inequality which is preserved by mechanisms which lead trade to be exploitative of low-wage economies. More appropriately, wages must be seen as reflecting economic performance plus the bargaining power of workers. The answer to the question of why differences in the economic performance of countries persist despite international trade is a complex one and centres round the behaviour of capital accumulation and productivity growth; it cannot lie with exogenously given differences in wage rates. There is in addition the problem of non-homogeneity of labour in different countries; in other words, because the inherent productivity (due to higher investment in training, nutrition, etc.) of the average West German worker is higher than that of the average Indian worker, it is difficult to evaluate clearly the meaning of unequal exchange. Despite these question marks, the concept of unequal exchange has had a significant impact upon thinking about trade and development.

Trade theory also directs comparatively little attention to the influence of transport, handling and insurance charges upon the patterns of and rewards from trade. The fact is, however, that the major share of the transport charges in international trade accrue to richer nations such as Japan, Norway, and the USA which own substantial merchant fleets. Since on bulky cargoes such as ores, oil and grains, ocean transport charges may account for a significant percentage of the landed price of the commodity, it is clear that the maritime nations derive substantial freight revenues from trade and that little accrues to the poorest LDCs, as in general these do not own major shipping lines.

Let us summarise the theoretical arguments. Following Adam Smith and Ricardo, the theory of specialisation according to comparative advantage and the Hecksher–Ohlin–Samuelson theory argue that trade is mutually beneficial, which may be interpreted as suggesting that trade leads to development. However, these theories leave open the issue of the distribution of the gains from trade between trading partners, which opens the gates for the argument that the main benefits accrue to the DCs and for arguments about unequal exchange. However, while it is clear that there is no theoretical basis for stating how any welfare gains that arise from trade will be distributed between countries, this is not equivalent to asserting that exchange is unequal.

5.3   Does Trade Lead to Development?

While theoreticians have been exploring the question of whether trade can cause development, others have been undertaking statistical analysis on the data about LDC exports and GNP growth to assess whether trade does cause development. In statistical terms the analyses conducted are mostly rather simple, but nevertheless they are widely held to support the view that faster growth of exports is associated[5] with higher GNP growth.

These analyses, which include those by Kravis (1970), Michaely (1977) and Balassa (1978), represent a continuum in sophistication as to how the two main variables, GNP and exports, should be measured in the analysis, but they all identify a positive relationship between the variables for the different samples of countries considered. However, as always when a large cross-section of countries is considered, the overall statistical result may be dominated by the behaviour of a subset of those countries. It is thus perhaps significant that Michaely obtained different results when he subdivided his sample of LDCs into (i) a group of 23 with a 1972 per capita income of above 300 dollars, and (ii) another group of 18 with a per capita income of 300 dollars or less. For the first group the relationship between the annual growth of export's share of GNP[6] and the annual growth of per capita GNP[7] was significantly positive (at around 0.5), while for the second group he found virtually no relationship. He concludes (p.52): 'That this seems to indicate that growth is affected by export performance only once countries achieve some minimum level of development'.

The distinction noted by Michaely between the behaviour of the richer and poorest LDCs is an important one which reflects the picture referred to above about the marked differences in the changing composition of exports between, what Riedel calls, the balanced exporters and the poorer primary exporters. In the more successful LDCs (NICs and balanced exporters) the changing composition of exports, to include a higher proportion of manufactures, is linked to a positive relationship between the rate of growth of exports (as a share of GNP) and the growth of GNP. By contrast in the poorer LDCs, particularly the African primary exporters, which remain overwhelmingly dependent upon primary commodity exports, exports do not appear to provide a strong stimulus for growth.

5.4   Trade Policy for Development

Despite the obvious importance of identifying and examining different
approaches by LDCs to trade policy, only a brief discussion will be
presented here to avoid duplication of material elsewhere in the book. As
Haq asserts (in Streeten 1973, p.101):

> Trade should not be regarded as a pacesetter in any relevant development . . .
> but as a derivative. The LDCs should first define a strategy for attacking their
> problems of unemployment and mass poverty. Trade possibilities should be
> geared to meeting the objectives of such a strategy.

Thus formulation of trade policy strategy constitutes a part of a development planning process which simultaneously establishes policies for
industrial and agricultural expansion. The links with industrial development policy are particularly strong, since decisions relating to which
industries are to be developed, whether these are to be primarily orientated to domestic or international markets, and whether they are to be
fostered through the imposition of import tariffs or through other forms of
subsidisation, all manifest themselves directly in the volume and pattern
of trade. The same applies to policies of expanding agricultural production. It is this simultaneous relationship between the physical economic
flows, *i.e.* between trade, production, investment and consumption, which
leads to policy aspects bearing on trade also being extensively discussed in
the chapters on industrial development (Chapter 9), agricultural development (Chapter 7) and theories of development (Chapter 3).

In the broadest terms trade and production strategies pursued by LDCs
have ranged from policies of near self-sufficiency (autarchy), through
Import Substituting Industrialisation (ISI) designed to limit reliance upon
certain classes of imports, to export-led growth at the other extreme.
Examples of autarchic policies are few and the clearest examples are those
of Burma and the People's Republic of China (PRC), which until after the
death of Chairman Mao pursued a policy of very restricted trade, based on
a highly critical philosophical view of the capitalist economies and of the
deleterious effects of consumerism. Since 1978 deliberate steps have been
taken to open up the PRC to international trade and private enterprise.
True, the steps in this direction have been cautious, but the views of the
present political leadership are clearly that faster development and greater
economic efficiency in the PRC require more open competition internationally and internally.

The pursuit of ISI, and the trade restrictions that accompany it, has
been widespread in LDCs and has reflected a complex of objectives. In
some cases policies of ISI have been influenced by notions of trade as unequal exchange, about the exploitative nature of trade, or by sheer export
pessimism. In others it has reflected well-articulated policies of

industrialisation in which a sequence of industries is developed in turn to replace specific imports.[8] In many cases this has required the imposition of extreme measures of trade protection (tariffs, import quotas, embargoes) to overcome the limitations inherent in producing for what is often a small market. Such policies, as we shall consider elsewhere (Chapter 7), have in many cases led to under-emphasis on the agricultural sector, the neglect of which has led to serious development bottlenecks in several countries. They have also tended to reduce incentives to exporting industries, since these have to pay higher prices for some domestically-produced inputs than their overseas competitors, and they have also resulted in overvalued exchange rates with respect to 'free trade' levels. Nevertheless, inward-looking trade and development strategies held an important place in the developing countries during the 1960s and 1970s. And as Haq opines:

> Import substitution strategy carries fewer risks for the harassed policy makers because high-cost goods produced under protective walls can still be shoved down the throats of the local populations by closing down any decent alternative ... as far as the LDC policy makers are concerned (the) high element of risk is fairly decisive in their attitude towards outward-looking strategies.

In recent years the tide of opinion has moved against ISI in favour of export-led growth. Partly this reflects the difficulties experienced with ISI, particularly in Latin American countries,[9] but it also reflects the influence which the NICs have had upon thinking about development, plus the statistical evidence mentioned above of a positive relationship between export growth and GNP growth. Certainly the main international agencies involved in development – The World Bank and International Monetary Fund (IMF) – are strongly committed to opening up LDCs to trade and reducing import barriers. When countries (both DC and LDC) with international debt problems approach the IMF for loans and other assistance in rescheduling debt repayments, support is usually conditional upon undertakings about changes in economic policy. In DCs, the requirements are typically that public expenditure (including that on subsidising nationalised industries) be reduced, while in LDCs conditionality may entail *inter alia* both cuts in public expenditure and removal of import restrictions. That is, the standard medicine of the IMF is to expand the role of private enterprise in production and trade. Justification for this policy lies in the gross distortions and inefficiencies which frequently arise when political and bureaucratic controls impede the normal working of market mechanisms, examples of which are readily found in industries operating at very low capacity utilisation, in ever-increasing price differentials of domestic goods over their imported equivalent, and in uncompetitive industries. Despite widespread evidence that efforts by central bureaucracy to control and integrate the many complex processes of an economy are often seriously deficient, there are vociferous critics of the monotheistic views of international bodies which favour free enterprise.[10] They see these open-economy policies as denying LDCs the opportunity to pursue independent and different policies of development, and more critically as forcing them to submit to the unwelcome embrace of (and control by) TNCs and foreign capital.

In the debate about export-led as opposed to ISI trade strategies, much clearly hinges upon expectations about export prospects. Thus there are many economists who are optimistic about the prospects for LDC trade and critical of the results of ISI. Myint (1971, pp.31,32), for example, in his review of the prospects of the South East Asian economy, envisaged (correctly) a rapidly expanding and healthy demand for the area's exports, and advocated a dismantling or reduction of many of the measures of protection for domestic industries. Similarly, Kravis (1970) argued that the rate of increase of demand for the primary exports of LDCs is currently at least as great as it was for the now-developed countries during their period of rapid industrialisation in the nineteenth century, while the rate of increase in demand for their manufactured products is substantially greater. If correct, this rather undermines any arguments that currently underdeveloped countries are disadvantaged by markedly worse export demand prospects than those facing the industrialised countries at a comparable stage in their development. Of course, not all LDCs have promising export prospects, but, as Kravis argues, this may be due to deficiencies in supply conditions within countries rather than to any deficiency in export demand.

Deficiencies in supply conditions may arise from geographical factors – small landlocked countries such as Rwanda, Malawi or Zambia suffer from high transport costs in trade, the absence of strong domestic and complementary markets in neighbouring countries, and weaknesses in their (educational, transport, communication, and general institutional) infrastructure. Such factors as these may go a long way to explaining the already observed distinction between the NICs plus balanced exporters, which have developed relatively successfully through outward-looking trade and industrialisation policies, and the primary commodity exporting countries which have had disappointing growth records (in many cases negative ones in the recent years of global recession from 1974 to 1983). The performance of countries in the latter group cannot necessarily be attributed to the failure of export-led policies of development, given the progress of the first group. But at the same time it is apparent that no truly satisfactory general development and trade policy has been devised which meets their needs. To get new industry moving in these countries will demand special measures of aid and protection which will inevitably include elements of ISI. Infant industries generally need protection; the skill in national economic management is to know when to wean infants from the breast of state support and to switch attention to younger infants.

5.5 Barriers to Manufacturing Export Growth

Despite the fact that a number of comparatively small developing countries – which are not among the poorest of that group – have succeeded in creating the necessary industrial supply conditions to rapidly expand their manufactured exports, the developing countries as a whole are experiencing difficulties and obstacles in penetrating industrial export markets. As Table 5.3 shows, the export shares which LDCs hold of the manufactured goods markets of DCs are substantially smaller than those for primary products. Fuel (principally oil) is of course a special case, and in this category the DC market share held by the LDCs had actually risen between 1960 and 1980 to reach almost 78%. However, the market share of both agricultural and mineral products (SITC, classes 3 + 4), the principle exports of the poorest LDCs, declined steadily over the last two decades so that in 1980 both stood at around 28%. While exports of manufactures from LDCs rose rapidly during the same period and their share in DC imports steadily increased, the degree of market penetration achieved by 1980 was still comparatively low, only 4.6% in machinery and 14.8% in the other manufactured category. Earlier data, from 1964 to 1972 (Fels and Glisman 1975), indicated that developing countries were having difficulties expanding and even holding onto their share of what were classified as raw-material-intensive manufacturing and labour-intensive manufacturing markets. These are precisely the categories of manufactures in which LDCs might be expected to have a comparative advantage since they supply a substantial proportion of the DCs' raw materials and have large quantities of cheap unskilled labour.

The failure of the developing nations to achieve greater shares of the manufactured imports of industrialised countries has been assessed by many to be a demand problem arising from policies by the latter countries to restrict the growth of certain classes of imports. Such policies have been pursued for a variety of reasons, including the prevention of rapid rundown of domestic industries such as textiles and the provision of short-run support for the balance of payments.

The policy measures employed to control imports can be broadly classified into tariff and non-tariff barriers, and it is argued that the industrial countries have used these in such a way that they discriminate most heavily against the exports of developing countries. For example, it is observed that many developed countries employ a 'cascading' or 'escalating' system of import tariffs in which the rate of tariff increases with the degree of processing an item has undergone. This is clearly revealed in the UNCTAD (1981a) estimates of nominal and effective tariffs erected by DCs against imports from LDCs, a characteristic sample of which is presented in Table 5.4. In each of the four cases presented the raw material can enter the DCs with a zero or very low tariff. The combination of this plus progressively higher nominal tariff rates for more

Table 5.3 Exports of Developing Market Economies (LDCs) to Developed Market Economies (DCs), and Their Share of DC Import Markets, by Commodity Group

SITC Class	All products 0–9	Agricultural products 0+1	Raw materials excl. fuel 2+4	Fuels and combustibles 3	Chemicals 5	Machinery 7	Other manufactured 6+8
			LDC exports to DCs (billion dollars US)				
1960	19.9	6.3	5.81	5.17	0.17	0.1	2.31
1965	26.1	7.4	6.23	8.38	0.23	0.1	3.71
1970	40.1	9.8	7.33	13.81	0.44	0.8	7.73
1975	148.1	18.3	13.41	94.23	1.38	3.5	16.91
1980	392.5	34.1	25.77	262.98	4.47	14.1	48.22
			Share of LDC exports in DC imports (%)				
1960	24.8	42.9	37.5	66.0	3.9	0.4	10.8
1965	21.4	36.2	34.9	69.8	3.1	0.4	10.6
1970	18.8	34.3	30.5	66.1	3.1	1.3	12.0
1975	26.9	28.1	29.7	78.9	3.8	2.5	12.2
1980	30.5	28.3	28.4	77.8	4.9	4.6	14.8

Source: UN Statistical Yearbook 1981, Table 15.

Table 5.4 Nominal and Effective Tariff Protection in DCs on Selected Primary and Processed Goods Imported from LDCs (Post-Kennedy Round Ad Valorem or Equivalent)

	United States		EEC		Japan	
	Nominal	Effective	Nominal	Effective	Nominal	Effective
Hides and skins	1.1	1.1	0	0	0	0
Leather	4.7	12.0	4.8	12.3	11.6	34.7
Leather goods other than shoes	7.7	11.4	7.3	10.4	11.8	15.0
Shoes	16.6	25.3	11.9	19.3	22.9	36.5
Wood in the rough	0	0	1.0	1.1	2.3	2.3
Wood simply worked	0.3	0	1.6	4.0	2.9	8.5
Plywood	8.5	13.8	11.3	19.6	14.0	25.4
Wood manufactures	6.7	13.6	8.7	16.3	11.5	23.2
Cotton, raw	6.2	6.2	0	0	0	0
Cotton yarn and thread	10.5	25.0	10.0	32.9	2.8	6.8
Cotton fabric, woven	13.8	24.6	12.0	19.1	7.9	17.8
Cotton clothing	20.0	35.4	14.0	20.8	14.7	27.5
Bauxite	0	0	0	0	0	0
Alumina	0	0	5.6	11.1	0	0
Aluminium, unwrought	4.0	6.0	5.8	5.6	10.4	11.4
Aluminium, wrought	5.9	11.5	12.8	29.3	13.6	29.0

Source: UNCTAD (1981a) p.113.

highly processed forms of the product provides an encouragement for the processing industries of DCs by offering them cheap raw materials, combined with protection from competition from processors with comparable production costs in LDCs. Thus EEC shoe producers can import hides and skins at international prices, and could charge 11.9% more for their shoes than an LDC shoe producer would receive for comparable shoes with the same EEC wholesale market price – the LDC exporter receives the market price less the 11.9% tariff. This represents effective protection of 19.3% for the EEC shoe producers' production margins, where the degree of 'effective protection' is defined to be the percentage by which the value added in domestic production of, say, shoes is increased as a result of import barriers and other forms of support.

Admittedly the levels of tariff presented in Table 5.4 were lower than they had been before the, so-called, Kennedy Round of negotiations of the General Agreement on Trade and Tariffs (GATT), and have been reduced further as a result of the subsequent Tokyo Round. Nevertheless, recognition during the 1960s of the significance of the discrimination by DCs against processed and manufactured imports from LDCs led to pressure (orchestrated within UNCTAD) for the granting of certain tariff exemptions for such imports. As a consequence 19 developed market-economy countries and 6 socialist Eastern European countries introduced Generalised Systems of Preference (GSPs) to grant preferential access, through abolition or reduction of tariffs, to certain classes of imports from designated LDCs. The USSR is in fact credited with the first GSP in 1965, followed by Australia in 1966, with the majority of the remaining schemes being started in 1971 and 1972.

Most of the schemes were originally scheduled to run until 1981, and they have now been extended. While the restrictions written into the schemes have been progressively relaxed somewhat, many have criticised the limited value of the concessions made by the DCs (Murray 1973a and 1973b; Baldwin and Murray 1977; and Morton and Tulloch 1977, pp.169–75). Most minerals and industrial raw materials enter the DCs with zero or low tariffs and therefore offer no scope for preferential tariffs to LDCs. Many agricultural products, particularly those produced by the northern industrial countries with high levels of subsidy or tariff protection, are also excluded or admit only small margins of preference under the GSP. It is true that the majority of industrial products are included in the GSP schemes, but the small number of 'sensitive' products subject to a range of trade restrictions include some very important items. These include footwear, and also textiles, trade in which is restricted by the Multifibre Agreement and also by the ceiling restrictions and tariff quotas of the various GSP schemes. An indication of the scope of the GSP schemes for the 19 OECD preference-giving countries is given by UNCTAD (1981b):

Of these countries' $157.9 billion imports from beneficiary countries in 1976, about 50% were non-dutiable leaving $78.1 billion potentially available for concessions under GSP. However, only $26.3 billion, or one-third, of these dutiable imports consisted of products covered by the schemes, and [only] $10.5 billion or 40% of these imports are estimated to have received preferential treatment in 1976. (UNCTAD 1981b, p.33)

That is to say, only 6.6% of the OECD countries' 1976 imports from beneficiary LDCs received any margin of preference. And, of course, here it should be noted that the margin of preference may be small rather than duty free.

Nevertheless, the GSP schemes do have positive trade creation effects as far as LDCs are concerned. A study by Murray of the USA's scheme indicates that as much as 10% of the USA's $3.5 billion of GSP category imports in 1977 may have been attributable to the scheme (UNCTAD 1981b). Although relatively small in terms of total imports, this is a significant amount, and the trade creation effects of GSP schemes have been increased since 1977 by their progressive extension to new products. Subsequently also the tariff reductions for a whole range of products negotiated at the Tokyo Round of GATT have affected the position of the GSPs. The reduced tariffs have meant an erosion of the benefits of GSPs, but their own trade-creating influence will have more than outweighed this and reduced the need for GSPs.

Not only is the total impact of the GSP schemes limited, but it is spread unevenly between the LDCs. Because the schemes are directed towards industrial products, the immediate benefits tend to accrue mainly to that small group of better-off LDCs which dominate the LDCs' exports of manufactured products; Baldwin and Murray (1977) identify Taiwan, Mexico, Yugoslavia, South Korea, Hong Kong, Brazil, Singapore, India, Peru, Chile, Argentina and Iran as the countries which gain most. It is, however, precisely because of the strong competitive position of some of these countries in certain markets that some products are excluded from the schemes, and ceilings are placed upon the eligibility of others. In particular, the country ceilings on preferential access are designed to limit the extent to which these economically strong LDCs can benefit from the trade-creating effects of the GSP schemes. In so far as such country quotas are not effective for the poorest countries with a low proportion of manufactured exports, the poorest LDCs should tend to benefit in time from the trade diversion effect. This is that trade will tend to be switched to cheaper sources, from suppliers without preferential access on their marginal exports (because they have exceeded their quota) to those which are eligible for preferential treatment. However, the difficulty here is that the most weakly industrialised LDCs may be unable to capitalise on any tariff advantages they possess because of lower capacity to cope with non-tariff barriers to trade. Non-tariff barriers are of various types and include packaging and marketing regulations, health regulations for foodstuffs, safety regulations, import quotas, production subsidies in importing countries, and policies whereby government departments purchase primarily domestically produced goods. Walter (1971) has presented empirical evidence that these barriers discriminate against the manufactured exports of the least industrialised LDCs. He proposes, as arguments to explain the evidence, that the LDCs are less able to cope with the frequent changes and many details of the legislative barriers, that these barriers principally operate against the class of products exported by LDCs, and that these countries are hampered by shortages of credit in financing the long delivery delays incurred for border inspections.

It thus appears that trade restrictions by rich countries do limit the opportunities of LDCs to profit by outward-looking trade strategies. At the same time, however, it seems (and is logical) that the main beneficiaries of any general dismantling of tariff barriers to trade will be the better-off, more industrialised LDCs, and that it might do little to assist many of the poorest countries to increase their exports of manufactured products. This may explain why so many poor countries have rejected outward-looking policies in favour of an inward-looking policy of import substituting industrialisation.

5.6 Issues Relating to Export Dependency on Primary Commodities

Terms of Trade

When reference is made to the 'terms of trade' what is meant is the value (price) of one commodity bundle in terms of another. A decline in the terms of trade for a specified bundle of goods means that a given quantity of it can only buy a smaller quantity of some other bundle than was formerly the case. To calculate a terms of trade series therefore requires the construction of two indices of value. At this level we may value (price) one commodity in terms of some (or all) others to obtain a measure of the *commodity terms of trade* (CTT), or we may compare the price of a standard bundle of exports (PX) to that of a standard bundle of imports (PM) to obtain the *net barter terms of trade* (NBTT), such that NBTT = *PX/PM*.

In general debate about development issues there is, however, a tendency to draw inferences from terms of trade measures about the welfare implications of trade for LDCs. Unfortunately neither the commodity nor the net barter terms of trade are directly suitable as trade welfare measures. Hence a number of modified measures have been proposed which have a greater welfare content. For example, a decline in a country's

NBTT may be caused by a rapid expansion of export supply pushing down prices; if export volume increases more rapidly than the NBTT declines, the country's import purchasing capacity will have increased, which may be loosely interpreted as an increase in that country's welfare through trade. The net barter terms of trade, multiplied by a volume index of exports, Qx, yields the *income terms of trade* (ITT), where $ITT = NBTT.Qx$.

Any growth of export volume may result from productivity growth in the exporting economy and such increases in productivity would be expected typically to result in a decline in export prices. Using the so-called *single factoral terms of trade*, defined as $SFTT = NBTT.\pi x$, where πx is the labour productivity in export production, the terms of trade may be said to improve provided that SFTT changes positively. This indicates that the import purchasing power of the exports produced by one unit of labour have increased, which again may be taken to indicate an improvement in welfare. If it is appropriate to adjust the terms of trade for productivity in export production, it is equally right to adjust for changes in labour productivity abroad in the production of imports, πm. Thus the *double factoral terms of trade* (DFTT) are defined as:

$$DFTT = NBTT. \frac{\pi x}{\pi m}$$

An increase in the DFTT would signify that a unit of labour employed in producing exports can purchase, through trade, more units of labour in the form of imports. Yet further modifications are possible (Spraos 1983) to allow for the implications of reduced unemployment, and to obtain employment adjusted measures of the terms of trade.

Another reason for rejecting a simplistic welfare interpretation of terms of trade indices relates to the quality factor. A ton of wheat or bauxite remains of much the same quality in terms of productive services irrespective of its year of production. The same is not true of manufactured items such as vehicles, textile machines or refrigerators. These have changed markedly over time in the sense of providing improved services per unit cost. If, therefore, the commodity terms of trade between, say, wheat and motor cars remained constant over time, wheat producers would become progressively better off in terms of motor car services. In this situation even declining wheat-to-car prices would not necessarily rule out a welfare gain to wheat exporters.

Despite the need for sophistication if terms of trade measures are to be used in debates about trade-induced welfare effects, the standard practice is to present only the NBTT and CTT measures. Very few attempts have been made to measure the factoral terms of trade, the most notable exception being Spraos (1983), and some of the difficulties encountered in his analysis illustrate why this is so. Nor is it usual to adjust the indices for changes in product quality; given the huge number of products traded that is a Herculean task.

In addition to the arguments particularly associated with Prebisch, about how labour union monopoly power at the Centre causes the terms of trade for primary commodities and hence LDCs to decline, other reasons have been proffered. In particular it is noted that income elasticities of demand for agricultural commodities fall as income rises so that demand for them increases more slowly than for manufactured goods. It follows that any tendency for the ratio of productivity to demand growth to rise more rapidly in agriculture than in industry will cause a relative decline in agricultural product prices. Any global tendency for decline in agriculture's terms of trade has been magnified for the underdeveloped countries by the industrial countries' pursuance of policies of paying their farmers more than world prices. The output expansion effects of these policies have increased the industrial countries' exportable surpluses of some agricultural commodities and reduced their import demand for others. It is also noted that, as a result of technological advances, synthetic substitutes are being continuously developed to compete with those agricultural commodities which are industrial raw materials, e.g. nylon and polyester for natural fibres, and plastics for rubber. Continuous reductions in real production costs for these synthetic substitutes, coupled with the ability to control their quantity and quality, has placed a powerful constraint upon the prices of natural raw materials. In addition there is a tendency for technological advance to reduce the weight of metal and other minerals required to produce a unit of manufactured goods; hence the rate of growth of demand for the minerals tends to be slower than that for the end product. Then there is also the tendency for structural change away from such industries as textiles, shipbuilding and iron casting towards those like electronics and aircraft manufacture, which are much less dependent upon raw materials. Thus there are several hypotheses to explain a decline in the terms of trade for primary commodities and conse-quently for those of developing countries. It is therefore clear that any general evidence of this effect cannot be interpreted as confirming the validity of any one hypothesis, but will be consistent with all of them.

Turning to the empirical evidence, the relationship between primary and manufactured goods prices appears to be characterised by short periods in which the terms of trade move sharply in favour of the former; the evidence in Table 5.5 indicates that such short periods occurred from 1950–54 and 1973–74, and less markedly in 1962–63 and 1979–81. Typically these short periods seem to be interspersed by longer ones in which prices for manufactures rise relative to those of primary com-modities. It is on the basis of the evidence of these longer periods that most commentators tend to argue that the primary commodity terms of trade show a secular tendency to decline. Certainly examination of the data from 1950 up until 1983 lends some support for this view if the effects of oil price rises are discounted. The effects of real increases in oil prices since 1972 can be seen from Table 5.5 to have resulted in large improvements in the commodity terms of trade for minerals and hence all primary products. The CTT for food and, in particular, agricultural non-food commodities have fared less well, and in 1983 they stood below their 1950 level. Note, however, that in both these cases they had in 1973–74 been above their 1950 levels, and that 1950 was a year of historically high prices.

The cyclical nature of commodity terms of trade makes an unambiguous assessment of their long-term trend difficult. After all, stocks of many non-reproducible minerals (and slow-to-reproduce timber) are being steadily

Table 5.5   Changes in the Terms of Trade

	Commodity terms of trade for primary[a] products (1963=100)				Net barter terms of trade for developing countries		
	All primary ÷ manufactured	Food ÷ manufactured	Agricultural non-food ÷ manufactured	Minerals ÷ manufactured	All developing (1963=100)	Major oil[b] exporters (1969=100)	Non-oil[b] exporters (1969=100)
1950	133	—	—	113	112	—	—
1952	122	—	—	109	106	—	—
1954	120	127	119	109	112	—	—
1956	114	109	118	112	107	—	—
1958	106	106	101	110	104	—	—
1960	101	96	107	99	104	110	90
1961	98	93	103	102	102	—	—
1962	107	104	108	93	98	—	—
1963	100	100	100	100	100	—	—
1964	102	104	101	101	101	—	—
1965	100	100	100	101	99	—	—
1966	98	99	98	98	101	—	—
1967	94	97	90	110	100	—	—
1968	94	95	91	109	101	—	—
1969	94	95	92	95	101	100	100
1970	92	95	86	95	100	98	99
1971	97	96	85	107	101	114	93
1972	104	102	93	110	101	117	94
1973	126	124	127	123	111	137	100
1974	175	134	119	276	156	331	96
1975	154	114	93	257	147	321	86
1976	160	117	102	265	157	340	90
1977	165	124	105	267	158	321	98
1978	146	109	98	236	151	305	93
1979	163	107	102	285	170	382	91
1980	219	114	98	430	203	523	86
1981	242	107	96	517	209	616	79
1982	234	98	86	504	207	607	76
1983	223	100	97	468	—	—	—
1984	228	99	106	475	—	—	—

Notes: (a) Calculated using data in the UN Monthly Bulletin of Statistics, September and December issues.
(b) *Source*: OECD, 1974 Review, *Development Cooperation*, Table II-3, Paris, November 1974, and International Financial Statistics.

depleted and may be expected to impart increasing scarcity value. This is what happened with oil (prior to 1986), and applies equally to some other non-reproducible commodities. Further caution about long-term CTT movements is justified in the light of Bairoch's (1975, pp.112,113) careful examination of data for the period 1870–1938. Bairoch concluded that during this period 'in fact a real secular improvement occurred in the terms of trade of primary products *vis-à-vis* manufactures'.[11] This underlines the sensitivity of the message conveyed by terms of trade statistics to the choice of dates covered. The fluctuating property of such statistical series means that it is feasible to choose high valued starting and low valued terminal dates, thus giving an impression of decline, or vice versa. Equally critical are the commodity and country coverage of the measures presented, since conditions vary greatly between one market and another.

If attention is switched from the commodity terms of trade to the net barter terms of trade the picture becomes somewhat clearer. As the series in Table 5.5 indicate, a clear distinction must be drawn between the oil-exporting developing countries and the non-oil exporters. Such has been the rise in oil prices since 1972, and the rise in the NBTT of the oil exporters has been so large, that the NBTT for the developing countries as a whole have doubled in the last decade. Underlying this, however, has been a decline in the NBTT of the non-oil exporting nations, a significant contributory cause of which has been the increased cost of their oil imports. This group of nations includes the least developed countries, and just how difficult their plight has been is indicated by the various trade indicators in Table 5.6 for the period 1970 to 1978. Here it can be seen, taking all the years together, that the least developed[12] among the low-income developing countries fared worst in all four dimensions of trade performance. Their NBTT declined by a greater amount (even allowing for the increase in 1976), their volume of exports declined over the whole period, and the actual purchasing power of their exports declined. Neither of the last two of these statements is true for the high and medium-income developing countries or for the low-income countries as a whole. This underlines yet again the importance of disaggregating the developing countries into subgroups when analysing development problems.

If it is accepted that the terms of trade for non-oil primary products have shown a tendency to decline in the post-1950 era, the question naturally arises as to whether this in itself is evidence that export dependence upon primary products creates economic vulnerability. Answers to this question are difficult in so far as some countries which are heavily dependent upon primary commodity exports have achieved high growth rates and development performance while others have not. The successful primary commodity exporting LDCs are generally those which Riedel (1984) classifies as balanced exporters and which have managed to diversify into

Table 5.6   Trade Experience of Developing Countries, 1970–78 (%)

	Average annual change 1970–73	Change over previous year				
		1974	1975	1976	1977	1978
Volume of exports						
High-income countries	8.9	−17.1	−9.3	15.5	1.8	4.4
Medium-income countries	12.4	−3.5	−3.6	12.9	9.4	6.1
Low-income countries	3.5	−7.2	−1.9	11.9	6.2	0.0
of which: least developed countries	−4.2	−6.8	−4.9	7.7	8.3	−2.2
All developing countries	8.9	−10.1	−6.9	14.8	4.8	3.8
Purchasing power of exports						
High-income countries	13.4	58.2	−10.0	19.7	2.4	−7.8
Medium-income countries	10.0	20.3	−11.9	17.7	8.4	−4.4
Low-income countries	2.9	8.3	−10.2	17.9	10.4	−5.8
of which: least developed countries	−5.3	−10.6	−7.9	24.3	11.5	−13.4
All developing countries	11.1	45.3	−11.6	19.9	4.3	−7.3
Volume of imports						
High-income countries	9.7	19.7	8.9	12.2	10.9	5.6
Medium-income countries	4.5	16.7	15.8	5.2	14.2	3.2
Low-income countries	1.0	6.8	11.8	−1.6	11.6	5.9
of which: least developed countries	−3.1	1.1	13.0	−1.9	24.5	3.1
All developing countries	6.9	17.2	10.5	8.2	11.7	5.2
Net barter terms of trade						
High-income countries	3.8	92.9	−0.9	3.3	1.4	−12.1
Medium-income countries	−2.0	24.5	−8.5	3.7	−0.9	−10.0
Low-income countries	−0.7	16.3	−7.0	4.7	3.6	−6.1
of which: least developed countries	−1.1	−4.1	−4.3	16.9	1.9	−10.4
All developing countries	1.6	63.8	−4.7	3.7	0.0	−11.2

Source: UNCTAD (1979) *Handbook of International Trade and Developing Statistics* (UN Publication, Sales No. E/F.79.II.D.2).
Note: High-income countries are those with incomes > $800 in 1976, and middle-income countries are those with incomes between $400 and $800.

manufactured exports while maintaining a significant share of primary exports. Some of these countries also tend to export those primary commodities which have exhibited firm terms of trade. For it has to be recognised that there are some non-oil primary commodities, the prices of which have fared well in international trade over long periods of time. These include cocoa, coffee, palm and other oils, fishmeal, timber, bauxite and nickel, all of which offer LDCs opportunities for future exploitation.

Indeed, it is important to note that the terms of trade of primary commodities exported by LDCs have been improving relative to those exported by DCs. Since 1975 LDC commodity terms of trade for exports of food, agricultural non-food, and minerals have all increased more rapidly than those for DCs. This may reflect a relative shortage, due to supply difficulties or restraints, of LDC commodity exports to those of DCs. The fact is that world commodity markets are increasingly dominated by the developed market countries which have progressively increased their share of the market economies' exports of primary commodities excluding oil (SITC classes 1, 2 and 4) from 60% in 1960, 67% in 1970, to 70% in 1980. Thus the difficulties which some LDCs experience in exporting primary commodity exports may well lie with their own supply performance. This certainly seems to be true of the least developed LDCs which have not only found it very difficult to diversify exports away from traditional lines, but have at the same time (see Table 5.6) experienced great difficulty in increasing export volume, even though world markets could have readily absorbed additional supplies from what are usually quite small economies. (An exception here is Bangladesh, which has a population of around 90 million, and obtains 65% of its export earnings from jute.) Indeed, the purchasing power of the exports of this group of countries as a whole has shown an alarming decline of around 2% per year over the period 1970 to 1982 (UNCTAD 1971c, pp.14 and 15). Given their need to import essential supplies (in particular oil), capital items and in some cases food, this contraction of import purchasing power is profoundly serious. To the extent, however, that it is due to a complex of factors such as failure to increase supply of primary commodity export supply, inability to diversify exports, and general failure to improve productive efficiency in all sectors, as well as to weak export prices for some primary commodities, the blame for the situation cannot be solely attributed to either any exploitative tendencies inherent in trade or to the problem of dependency upon primary exports. After all, successful competition in manufactured export markets is even more demanding of a wide range of skills. The essential problem is that for several different reasons these countries are economically inefficient, *i.e.* underdeveloped.

Short-Term Instability of Export Earnings

A widely accepted hypothesis which has exercised an important influence on international trade policy is that, because of their reliance upon primary commodities, the export earnings of underdeveloped countries exhibit a high degree of short-run instability. As an ancillary proposition it is argued that such instability is damaging to the growth and development prospects of these countries. This follows because it is assumed that fluctuating export receipts will cause fluctuations in the capacity to import the capital goods on which growth and development depend. Here it should be noted that what is being considered is fluctuations in earnings about an underlying trend. If this underlying trend is downward, that is of course an unambiguously detrimental factor, but it is not what is meant by a fluctuation.

With regard to variations in the value of commodity trade at the world market level it is popularly argued that, because of price-inelastic demand, short-term shifts in aggregate demand or supply of primary products lead to price changes of greater proportionate magnitude than those in the volume of trade. It should, however, be observed that a given proportionate reduction of demand will tend to have a greater adverse effect upon total export earnings for a commodity than an equivalent proportionate supply increase. From the standpoint of international trade policy this is an important distinction, since demand shifts are beyond the control of the exporters but are mainly dependent upon fluctuations in the level of economic activity in the industrial countries. It is evident that such fluctuations have been large − witness the world economic boom of 1972−74 and the subsequent recession of 1975−83 − and precisely because they have not originated in the economic conditions of the underdeveloped countries there is a basis for arguing that the rich countries should compensate poorer ones for any damage caused to their economies by such fluctuations.

Of course, the export earnings of an individual country for a particular commodity need not move in line with total world export earnings from that commodity. Exports from a particular country may increase at a time of world supply shortage and high prices (and vice versa), so that they may fluctuate more than world export earnings of that commodity. Few countries, however, are dependent solely upon one export product, and export concentration ratios have declined indicating a steady process of export diversification by the majority of developing countries. It is therefore probable that there are offsetting movements in the earnings from different products which will damp down fluctuations in total export earnings, except at times of extreme world economic recession or boom when all commodity prices will tend to move together.

Empirical evidence about export-earning instability has not substantiated the view that it represents a grave problem for the less-developed countries; although most of the analysis has been conducted on pre-1970 data, it suffers from a number of measurement disputes, and has been confused by the choice of different samples of countries for which to test the various hypotheses. MacBean (1966), in his much cited analysis for the period 1946−58, even went so far as to conclude that although the export revenues of developing countries were more unstable than those of developed countries, the difference was not marked. MacBean's analysis also failed to discover much empirical support for the hypotheses that export instability tends to increase if (a) primary commodities constitute a higher proportion of total exports; (b) a smaller number of commodities dominate the primary export fraction; or (c) if exports are mainly destined for one geographic market, e.g. the former colonising nation. Various writers have, however, been critical of MacBean's work. Ady (1969), for example, argues that his methods of analysis have systematic biases which play down the extent of instability in the underdeveloped countries. And, in contradiction of MacBean, Erb and Schiavo-Campo (1969) found evidence that export-earning instability in the underdeveloped countries during 1954–66 was significantly higher than in developed countries, as did Glezakos (1973) for a slightly later period. However, the evidence available does not suggest that the LDCs as a group suffer extreme instability as a consequence of their reliance on primary products.[13] This does not rule out the possibility of exceptional variability for some commodities and countries. Certainly some commodities such as cocoa, copper and cotton have experienced greater export-earnings stability than others, e.g. bananas, coffee and rubber. However, it does not appear that the more volatile commodities are responsible for the higher levels of instability in those countries where this is greatest. Rather, exceptional export-earning instability is mainly due to special internal factors, often political, which influence the volume of exports.

The concern with short-term export instability is due to the hypothesis that it hampers development. Since instability is defined in such a way that on average downswings equal upswings, 'the hypothesis is equivalent to stating that the damaging effects of downward export fluctuations are greater than the beneficial effects of upward deviations' (Schiavo-Campo and Singer 1970, p.167). Support for this form of the hypothesis is along the lines that unanticipated increases in foreign exchange earnings cannot be exploited readily for investment because of shortages of complementary local factors of production (particularly skilled human capacity) and thus tend to be dissipated on consumer goods, whereas unexpected shortfalls in earnings lead to cutbacks in capital equipment and delays in investment projects.

Again, the empirical analysis which has been conducted, largely by MacBean, fails to support the hypothesis that export-earnings instability reduces economic growth in the poorer countries. Indeed, analysis by Knudsen and Parnes (1975), echoed by Yotopoulos and Nugent (1976), turns this whole argument on its head. Their analysis, based on the permanent income hypothesis, incorporates the idea that instability of export-earned income leads to higher savings and hence investment, because consumers base their spending decisions more on the stable, reliable component of income rather than its transitory, unstable element. According to their results (p.123), 'investment is not deterred by instability in income but is, in fact, stimulated by it. The lower propensities to consume measured under higher levels of instability have resulted in increased aggregate savings, which, in turn, have increased aggregate investment. Instability has not adversely affected savings or investment, but it has had a positive effect on these parameters necessary for economic growth'.

The indeterminate quality of the empirical analysis need not be, and clearly has not been, accepted as indicating that export-earning instability is not a problem for developing countries. The analysis does not preclude the possibilities that (a) certain countries are severely handicapped by export fluctuations; (b) in periods other than that for which the analysis has been conducted a widespread problem has existed; and (c) that although differences in economic growth rates between countries cannot be adequately explained by differences in export instability, such rates might have been higher in all countries given greater stability. In view of these possibilities it is perhaps not surprising that in international trade negotiations many participants adhere to their *a priori* views about the harmful effects of export variability upon development, and of the need for stabilisation policies to be implemented. This pressure has led to the introduction of a variety of policies to help offset export-earning instability for some underdeveloped countries. The exact measures are discussed below, but it is worth noting that because stabilisation can be interpreted as simply the smoothing out of payments over time without any need for continuous long-term transfers from one group of countries to another, it is much easier to reach international agreement on stabilisation policies than for policies to counteract any long-run tendencies for decline in the terms of trade of particular nations, since these latter require a net secular transfer of funds to disadvantaged nations.

5.7 Policies to Increase the LDCs' Share of the Benefits from Trade

The preceding discussion has highlighted a number of issues relating to international trade which cause concern to developing countries. Most significantly, there is the feeling that the LDCs are not receiving a fair share of the expansion of world trade, and that they are not being paid adequately for the share that they do have. This amounts to concern that the export earnings of the LDCs are not rising fast enough. Added to this is concern that too high a proportion of the export revenues which 'do accrue' to the developing countries are subsequently exported as profits by transnational companies. In addition, there is wide acceptance, despite the absence of clear empirical support, of the view that heavy reliance upon primary commodities leads to fluctuations in export earnings which disrupt the development plans of poorer countries.

Increasing awareness of these problems, coupled with more sophisticated and extensive political representation of LDCs in international bodies, led, in the wake of the 1973 oil price shock, to mounting pressure for changes in the conduct of international trade. Manifestations of this pressure included the creation and convening, in 1974 and 1975, of the World Food Council under the aegis of the UN Food and Agriculture Organisation, to help deal with malnutrition and financing of food imports in the LDCs. Pressure was also exerted at the International

Monetary Fund for changes in its lending criteria; these are discussed below. The most dramatic efforts stemmed from the adoption, at the sixth special session of the UN General Assembly in 1974, of a resolution calling for a Programme of Action on the Establishment of a New International Economic Order (NIEO). This resolution has been the basis for a series of negotiating rounds including those of the Fourth and Fifth meetings of the UN Conference on Trade and Development (UNCTAD) in 1976 at Nairobi and 1979 at Manila. The resolution embodies:

> ... a six-point plan covering buffer stock arrangements, a common financing facility for the management of commodity markets, a network of supply and purchase agreements (multilateral commodity schemes), transfer of primary processing activities from rich to poor countries, index linking of prices of primary commodity exports from poor countries to the price of their imports, and ... as a residual measure, a system of compensatory financing to stabilise and guarantee poor countries' export earnings from commodity exports. (Wall 1976, pp.17, 18)

At UNCTAD IV the proposals were shaped into an 'Intregrated Programme for Commodities', the central core of which was proposals for the setting up of a 'common fund' to finance the holding of international buffer stocks of primary commodities (UNCTAD 1974). It was suggested that as much as $6,000 million would eventually be required to finance buffer stocks of up to ten key commodities (cocoa, coffee, copper, cotton, jute, rubber, sisal, sugar, tea and tin), and that up to eight other commodities (bananas, bauxite, iron ore, meat, rice, wheat, wool and tropical timber) should be included in the integrated programme. Subsequent negotiations have failed to realise the full grandeur of this vision and progress has been very slow. Only the most faltering of steps have been taken against the emergence of a new consensus among producers at UNCTAD 'that it may be more fruitful to concentrate on developing co-operation on research, marketing, technical information etc., rather than on the adoption of buffer stock arrangements' (Joekes and Kirkpatrick 1979).

Agreement at UNCTAD was reached in 1979 to open for ratification a much reduced Common Fund. This was to consist of $470 million of directly contributed capital available for buffer-stock arrangements (at the so-called 'first window') and $350 million to finance research, development and marketing at the 'second window' (of which $70 million was to be directly contributed and the rest voluntarily). However, by 31 March 1982 the Common Fund had only been ratified by 21 states representing a mere 21.5% of its capital; to come into force it needed ratification by 90 states representing two-thirds of its capital.

In a similar vein very little progress has been achieved in setting up new commodity agreements with buffer stocks. New agreements were negotiated for olive oil in 1980, jute in 1982, and tropical timber in 1983, but none of these incorporated market control mechanisms, and all are confined to research, development and promotional activities. The only really new ICA incorporating a buffer stock is that inaugurated for natural rubber (INRA) in 1980, and this has operated fairly successfully.[14] Other commodities had agreements which were in force in 1974, but in many cases they have had a chequered history in the last decade. The International Cocoa Agreement was abrogated in 1980 and a new one started in 1981 in rather difficult circumstances.[15] The International Tin Agreement was replaced in 1982, after considerable upheaval of the market, by a producers' cartel, only to run into dramatic liquidity difficulties in 1985 which (at the time of writing) threaten its continued existence and the basic credibility of ICAs. It was undoubtedly naive of the architects of the NIEO to place so much faith in international buffer-stock agreements, given the inherent problems of such agreements as discussed below.

International Commodity Agreements

Failure to make more progress with the Integrated Programme for Commodities (IPC) stems from two principal causes. The first of these, as already referred to, is the intrinsic difficulty of managing markets through ICAs. The second has been the fundamental difference between DCs and LDCs about the objectives of the IPC. LDCs have tended to interpret the commodity price objectives of the Programme as being not only to stabilise prices but to increase them, and in this way help to create a new international economic order. DCs, while content in principle to countenance self-financing price stabilisation, were not willing to accept general measures to raise commodity prices or to shoulder the burden of the financial transfers to commodity producers which such measures would entail.

A key requirement for successful market management by an ICA is a strong political commitment by major signatories to bear any costs which may be involved. Where such a commitment exists, as with the International Wheat Agreements (IWA) between 1949 and 1971, international market control can be achieved without buffer stocks or the restrictive application of export quotas. During the 1950s and 1960s the domestic wheat policy of the USA, the world's main wheat exporter, supported by Canada, was based on accepting export subsidies for surplus wheat which stabilised wheat prices within the agreed international price band. Thus the USA bore most of the cost of managing the international wheat market. When in 1971, during the Nixon Administration, the USA cut support to wheat farmers and sharply reduced wheat and other grain stocks, a more commercial approach to wheat exports was adopted and willingness to underwrite the IWA disappeared. Since that date it has not been possible to achieve agreement between wheat importers and exporters on price stabilisation measures, and the IWA has withered to an

International Wheat Convention for food aid plus a secretariat collating market information.

Even where there are buffer-stock arrangements, political commitment is required for them to operate successfully. This is exemplified by the current (1983–92) International Coffee Agreement which is actually working, because of strong commitment by the USA to support the coffee exporting regimes. This support is critical, for the ingredients for breakdown of the agreement are certainly present. The agreement sanctions the efforts of coffee exporters to raise prices to the signatory importing countries by restricting coffee exports. However, these high prices do not apply to non-signatories and a parallel market emerged in 1983–84 whereby non-signatory Eastern-bloc countries could buy coffee at roughly half the price paid by signatory importers. Under other political circumstances this could be a recipe for breakdown in the agreement, but in this case steps were inaugurated in 1984 to strengthen the agreement by raising prices in the parallel market. This problem of non-signatories is a characteristic one in ICAs, and is an invariable source of tension since non-members carry none of the costs of executing the agreement. A classic example of this is the EEC's non-membership of the International Sugar Agreement (ISA). As a result of its extensive price support policies for sugar-beet production, the EEC has with the aid of export subsidies raised its share of the world export market from 4.9% in 1972 to over 20% in the early 1980s. That this has been achieved against a background of supply restraint by the exporting members of the ISA merely underlines the benefits which non-members may reap as free-riders.[16]

A closely related problem is that at any point in time at which an ICA is effective (i.e. is stopping prices from rising above the negotiated price ceiling or from falling below the floor price), there is a temptation for member countries to renege on their commitments and obtain a better price in free international markets. Thus, for example, the UK as a major wheat importer decided not to rejoin the IWA between 1956 and 1959, in the expectation of lower prices on the free market. The fact is that whenever an ICA is effective in the above sense, either importers are paying higher prices or exporters are receiving lower prices than they otherwise would. If the costs involved are high, pressure builds up to break or renegotiate the agreement. Tension is therefore an automatic consequence of effective action.

Buffer-stock schemes are difficult things to set up and manage. The key to success lies in fixing upper and lower price levels which can be successfully defended with the funds available to the manager of the stock. All too frequently buffer-stock managers have run out of funds before succeeding in preventing prices falling below the 'floor'. This, for example, happened with the 1981 International Cocoa Agreement, which exhausted $220 million dollars of its funds within a few months of its launch, with prices still languishing at c85 per pound, well below the agreed floor price of c104. Similarly, the dramatic collapse of the International Tin Agreement in 1985, with debts of $300m, arose because all its liquid resources had been exhausted without it being able to stem the fall in tin prices. If it had not been for the application of restrictive export quotas at various times between 1956 and 1985, this liquidity crisis would have occurred earlier. In contrast 'at the other end of the range unless a buffer stock is very large, it will become exhausted in the effort to check the upswing of prices, and beyond a certain point a buffer-stock manager is unable to prevent further upswing of price' (Commonwealth Secretariat 1975). This was precisely the situation encountered by the International Coffee Agreement in 1986, when, in the face of a Brazilian crop failure, the suspension of all export restrictions failed to prevent coffee prices rising well above the ceiling which had been agreed. Thus, the fixing of price limits to defend by means of a buffer stock plus supply controls, in addition to being a politically contentious matter between the signatories, also raises serious technical, forecasting difficulties.

In view of all these difficulties it is unfortunate that the flag of the NIEO should have been attached so firmly at the outset to the creation of commodity buffer stocks. Undoubtedly one of the main inspirations for this from the LDC viewpoint was OPEC's success in cartelising the supply of crude oil. The LDCs clearly hoped to link the creation of new ICAs to measures to restrict supplies and force up prices. However, such restrictions, by means of production and export quotas, generate a situation where particular producers or countries could profitably produce more than their quota allotment. Collective supply restraint will, when (as is typical of most primary products) total demand is price inelastic, raise prices, revenue and profitability, and so produce the signals to encourage more supply. This creates pressures for suppliers to manoeuvre for extra quotas and to evade supply control. Such pressures have been apparent between OPEC members, and between exporting members of the International Coffee Agreement. Examples of successful actions to push up prices by international supply restriction have been few, and there appear to be distinct limitations on the scope for extending this type of action to other commodities. Favourable conditions for successful agreement to restrict supply exist when:

(1) There are no close substitutes for the commodity so that the price elasticity of demand is low even in the medium and long run; following the oil price rises there has been a marked upsurge of investment in substitutes such as nuclear power and coal production (and non-OPEC oil production) which has weakened OPEC's ability to maintain high oil prices.

(2) There are few producing countries, so that potential conflicts of

interest in reaching agreement are reduced; or there is a small group of countries dominating export sales which can undermine the position of the other exporters if they fail to comply with any agreement, e.g. Brazil has sufficient market power to manipulate the international coffee market idependently.

(3) The production and distribution systems within countries are oligopolistic (as in metals) rather than atomistic (as in agriculture). Where atomistic structures exist, it is very difficult to control non-quota sales.

(4) The commodity is storable so that the sale of surplus product can be deferred.

(5) It is also helpful if storage is cheap, as with oil and phosphate rock which can be stored in the ground at zero financial cost.

There are very few commodities which satisfy even most of these favourable conditions for the implementation of output restriction and buffer-stock types of ICA, and it is doubtful if many more of such schemes will emerge to assist the level of stability of the commodity export earnings of developing countries.

International Compensatory Finance

It is questionable whether a commodity-by-commodity approach is appropriate to the trade problems of the developing countries. A more fundamental approach would be to try and increase the level and stability of earnings from total commodity and product exports. One proposal which recognises this calls for the index linking of commodity export prices to the import prices paid by developing countries. It is, however, unlikely that much progress will be made in this direction in view of the formidable technical problems of producing the indices and of the potential for conflicts of interest even among developing countries. For example, the interests of the oil- and non-oil-exporting developing countries conflict sharply, and the non-oil-exporting developing countries have suffered more than any others from the changes in relative commodity and product prices since 1972.

There has, however, been progress on another proposal, that of providing compensatory finance to offset unanticipated falls in the export earnings of developing countries. One scheme with a compensatory finance element is the Lomé Convention, an agreement between the European Economic Community and a number of African, Caribbean and Pacific (ACP) countries. The First Lomé Convention ran for five years from 1975 with 46 ACP countries, and the Second from 1980 with 63 LDCs. The main export-earning stabilisation element of the Convention, called STABEX, applies only to exports to the EEC of a number of

selected tropical agricultural commodities, plus iron ore and simple processed items.

In Lomé II, STABEX made available 550 million European currency
units over five years − 1 ecu = US$1 in August 1984 − which could be
drawn upon by any signatory country in the rather stringent event that its
earnings from exports to the EEC of one or more of the covered products,
taken separately, had (1) fallen by at least 7.5% below the average of earnings in the preceding four years and (2) that the commodity(ies) in question amounted to more than 7.5% of the country's total export earnings
(reduced to 2.5% for the poorest countries). Although some of the
signatory LDCs may be required to repay without interest any stabilising
finance received from STABEX, no repayments are required from the
poorest. The funds, however, have not always been adequate for
STABEX's limited aims, and 'For the first time STABEX resources for
1980 were insufficient to meet justified transfer requests in full. 20% of
the STABEX funds for 1981 were advanced, but transfers had to be reduced by 40.49% for least developed and 52.54% for other ACP states for all
requests over one million ecu' (Lister 1982, p.438). Thus the total of ecu
138m transferred in 1981 (for 1980 claims), while a negligible sum,
represented only about 2% of the export value of the items covered by
STABEX. The distribution of these transfers was, furthermore,
somewhat uneven with more going to richer nations, such as Senegal
which received 17% of the total. Some of this unevenness should have
been reduced by the introduction in Lomé II of a comparable stabilisation
fund, SYSMIN with ecu 280m, to stabilise mineral export earnings.
Given the dominance of transfers over advances, the Lomé Convention
can be seen as giving genuinely stabilising aid, although, as Wall noted in
1978, in so far as these transfers may be a substitute for other forms of aid
paid by EEC member countries, it may not represent additional aid.

A second more general compensatory finance system for developing
countries is that operated by the IMF. This started life as a scheme of compensatory lending to any signatory country to the IMF of funds which
could be used to compensate for uncontrollable reductions in countries'
overall export earnings below their estimated medium-term trend. It was,
however, extended in 1981 to cover particular balance of payments problems relating to food imports; that is, it now includes a specific food-
financing facility to allow for uncontrollable increases in cereal import
costs above the trend in such costs. In addition, borrowing allowances
under the Compensatory Finance Facility (CFF) as a whole have been
increased so that countries may borrow annually up to 125% of their IMF
quota. As a stabilising device the generality of the IMF scheme makes it
far more attractive than the individual commodity agreements which have
been discussed. In contrast to them, there is no need to negotiate trade
quotas, to agree upon price ranges for specific qualities of produce or to

consider a wide range of other technical details. From the poorer developing countries' point of view, however, the repayment of IMF loans, despite the provision of allowable repayment periods of three to five years, may be difficult even in periods of high export earnings.[17] The CFF scheme is not as attractive as STABEX in which transfers dominate over loans, and it is not a substitute for the net transfer of resources to LDCs as envisaged in the resolution proposing a New International Economic Order.

Other Policies

While the slow progress with International Commodity Agreements and the introduction of compensatory finance schemes have clearly not brought about dramatic changes in the international economic order, the LDCs have made steady if unspectacular and inadequate progress in the international organisations where major decisions are taken affecting international trade. The 1974 resolution calling for an NIEO was an important flexing of political muscle by the so-called group of 77 developing countries. It signified the increasingly cohesive voice with which LDCs approach negotiations in GATT and UNCTAD, and their dealings with the World Bank and IMF. In the Tokyo Round of GATT this relative togetherness achieved significant progress in obtaining Most-Favoured Nation (MFN) tariff reductions from the DCs for LDC exports, without in turn having to make major reciprocal concessions. It is true that these MFN tariff reductions (which are estimated to be of the order of 26% for industrial products exported by LDCs) have reduced the benefit to LDCs of the Generalised Systems of Preferences, but Balassa (1980) firmly rebuts arguments that this loss of preference outweighs benefits to LDCs from the trade-creating impact of the tariff reductions.

Similarly, LDC pressure has driven UNCTAD, however slowly, to strive for the objectives of the NIEO, as evidenced by the eventual creation of a Common Fund (albeit one much smaller than originally demanded) and the emergence of a steady trickle of ICAs. The (limited) progress in increasing the flexibility in IMF lending and certain changes in World Bank policy can in part also be seen as reactions to the pressure from LDCs. LDCs do, however, persistently voice dissatisfaction at the continued domination of the policies of these two organisations by the industrialised countries. They feel that they should have a larger say in shaping the policies of these powerful organisations. This pressure has, nevertheless, been largely resisted by the DCs which take the line that since they are the main suppliers of funds along with some of the OPEC countries, they should be able to control IMF and World Bank policy.

Conscious of the resistance of DCs to their demands for trade reform and dissatisfied with their conditions of exchange, LDCs have on various occasions sought to join forces in regional customs unions. Examples of such unions are the East African Community (which broke up in 1977), the Central American Common Market, and the Economic Community of West Africa set up in 1979. It was hoped that the setting up of such communities would, through the creation of larger regional market units, enable local industries to take advantage of economies of size in production, lead to increased industrial activity within each Community, and generate a rapidly increasing volume of intraregional trade. The outcome of these experiments has fallen somewhat short of expectations, and there is no evidence that this type of policy provides for a radical improvement in individual countries' benefits from trade. There are various reasons for this, but prominent among these is the fact that neighbouring LDCs often have similar resource endowments, structured economies and industrialisation plans. Also their transport and communications infrastructure is often better developed for trade with countries outside the customs union. Thus their main opportunities for trade are not with neighbouring countries but with countries with completely different resource endowments.

LDCs should not, and do not, rely upon agreements with other countries to expand their exports. The primary responsibility lies with the development policies of the LDCs themselves. The whole of commercial and industrial policy has implications for trade in that changes in industrial structure and activity influence import demand and export content. Some authors (Little *et al.* 1970, Ch.4) have argued that in many cases developing countries appear to have pursued policies of industrialisation which have reduced the potential benefits from trade and international specialisation, and to the extent that this is true they have some scope to improve their own position. This issue is dealt with more fully in Chapter 8, but it is evident from the discussion there that the least developed countries experience great difficulty in devising policies which greatly increase their rates of development and export growth.

5.8 Conclusion

Although the NICs have succeeded in increasing their share of world trade in the last two decades, the share of the LDCs as a whole in non-fuel trade has been declining as the value of world trade expands. Many commentators (e.g. Kravis 1970) have suggested that this failure of the poorest LDCs to reap greater benefits from expanding world trade is substantially due to deficiencies in the economic policies and internal structures of these countries, and that it cannot be attributed to deficient demand for their products. It can also be argued that the LDCs' declining share of trade is not as serious as it first appears, for a large and rapidly increasing component of the exports by developed countries is accounted for by reciprocal trade in similar manufactured products, e.g. motor cars exchanged for motor cars. Nevertheless, there is widespread acceptance of the view that international trade has not worked to the advantage of the poorer nations in the manner anticipated by neoclassical economic theory. This feeling has been compounded by the increasing volume of literature which asserts that the institutions organising international trade operate to 'exploit' the LDCs. The widespread acceptance of this, in spite of the strong and growing evidence which exists of a positive relationship between growing exports and GNP in the LDCs, has fuelled demands by the developing countries for measures to reform international trade and open up markets for their products.

The efforts of LDCs to achieve more rapid economic growth and trade have been overshadowed by the global economic recession which began in 1974. While there is widespread recognition of the mutual interdependence between economies and that acceleration of LDC growth (or its resumption in some of the poorest countries) depends upon acceleration of the industrial economies, the dominant concern to contain inflation, and the policies to achieve this, have both restrained economic (and hence trade) growth and affected DC attitudes to the North–South negotiations. The dramatic economic boom of the late 1960s early 1970s was accompanied by rapid inflation, and was fuelled by high levels of public spending in the DCs plus a substantial expansion of lending to LDCs to finance trade expansion. Reaction to this inflation in the industrial countries has generally been to cut back public expenditure,[18] to reduce protection for declining industries, to look less favourably upon subsidies and transfers to productive activities, and to rely more on private and less on public enterprise. These attitudes have spilled over into the arena of international negotiations. They have (1) hardened DC resistance to the incorporation of transfers of funds into the IPC and Common Fund; (2) militated against using ICAs to raise commodity prices; (3) led to tougher terms for credit and loans to LDCs, coupled with tighter attitudes to repayment of outstanding debt; (4) led the USA to reduce its contributions to the World Bank (and other UN organisations), thus restricting the Bank's ability to increase its aid programmes; (5) led to greater insistence by the DCs that the LDCs reduce their own barriers to trade; and (6) led to emphasis of the virtues of trade rather than aid. This switch of emphasis in DC policy from willingness to use public funds for priming investment pumps (both national and international) to increased reliance upon unsubsidised free enterprise, has undoubtedly conflicted with the aspirations and expectations of LDCs. Those least developed LDCs which lack the depth of entrepreneurial talent or the general infrastructure needed for successful broadly-based commercial competition have found this regime exceptionally abrasive and many have recorded negative growth rates. For them, at least, specifically tailored programmes involving special trade concessions and aid are essential to their progress; adherence to the slogan 'trade not aid' is seen by them as unsatisfactory.

Notes

1. Moore (1985, Ch.4) presents a detailed examination of changes in the structure of international trade.
2. In particular, losses from trade 'are "more likely" the greater is the divergence between rates of profit and growth, *i.e.* the smaller is the capitalists' savings ratio, *s*' (Steedman 1979, p.56).
3. Complementarily, the likelihood of withdrawal of capital is greater from weaker economies.
4. Spraos draws a strong distinction between *increasing* union power and simply the existence of a given degree of labour power, arguing that 'a continuous deterioration of the net barter terms of trade of commodities requires a continuously increasing degree of monopoly in manufacturing' (Spraos 1983, p.26).
5. Note the use of the word *associated*. It is not possible to state that more rapid export growth *causes* higher GNP growth (development) or vice versa. The interaction between the two variables is complex and there is a mutual interdependence.
6. Note that it is not the share of exports in GNP which matters but its rate of growth. Countries differ greatly in the actual shares of exports in GNP for a whole variety of reasons.
7. Balassa (1978) argues that in this test the variable which should be used is simply the annual growth in GNP, and not the per capita figure. He does, however, state that this modification does not greatly affect the results.
8. As Meier (1980, p.305) indicates, in many cases ISI policies were far from well-articulated, but 'were adopted in an *ad hoc* and indiscriminate fashion in a number of developing countries'.
9. These are discussed in detail in Chapter 9, and by Meier (1980), Chapter 12.
10. Payer (1975, 1982) has written trenchant criticisms of the IMF and World Bank for fostering a particular capitalist form of development on LDCs, and for stifling alternative processes of development.
11. The data presented by Brown (1974, Table 26, pp.246, 247) confirm Bairoch's conclusions but also, most interestingly, indicate that from 1796 to 1870 the net barter terms of trade of primary for manufactured goods almost doubled.
12. The least-developed countries are: Afghanistan, Bangladesh, Benin, Bhutan, Botswana, Burundi, Cape Verde, Central African Republic, Chad, Comoros, Democratic Yemen, Ethiopia, Gambia, Guinea, Haiti, Lao People's Democratic Republic, Lesotho, Malawi, Maldives, Mali, Nepal, Niger, Rwanda, Samoa, Somalia, Sudan, Uganda, Tanzania, Upper Volta, Yemen and Democratic Yemen.
13. One factor generally ignored is the fact that the reactions to economic recession by agriculture (and to a lesser extent mining) are different to those of

manufacturing industry. In times of recession industry cuts output by eliminating overtime and laying off workers, rather than reducing prices to maintain volume throughput. In agriculture, output does not tend to fall in recession, hence prices fall. Thus it might be expected that agricultural commodity prices will be more unstable than industrial ones. This is not to say that industry is not just as seriously affected by recession; rather, it is that the pain is absorbed in different ways.

14. For a detailed description of the INRA agreement, see Stubbs (1984).
15. Within months of its commencement in October 1981, the $220m fund had been exhausted trying unsuccessfully to defend the floor price.
16. It is true that at the same time as increasing its sugar exports to 4 million tons, the EEC has continued to guarantee favourable prices to the ACP countries for the 1.3 million tons of sugar imported by the EEC under the Lomé Convention.
17. For detailed criticism of IMF lending in general, see Pirzio-Biroli (1983), and of CFF see Green and Kirkpatrick (1982).
18. With the notable exception of the USA from 1982 to the time of writing.

References

Ady, P. (1969) 'International commodity policy', in I.G. Stewart (ed.), *Economic Development and Structural Change*, Edinburgh University Press.

Baer, W. (1961) 'The economics of Prebisch and the ECLA', *Economic Development and Cultural Change*, Vol. 10, No. 2; reprinted in I. Livingstone (ed.) (1971), *Economic Policy for Development*, Penguin Books.

Bairoch, P. (1975) *The Economic Development of the Third World since 1900*, Methuen.

Balassa, B. (1978) 'Exports and economic growth: further evidence', *Journal of Development Studies*, 5, pp. 818–19.

Balassa, B. (1980) *The Tokyo Round and the Developing Countries*, World Bank Staff Working Paper, No. 370.

Baldwin, R.E. and Murray, T. (1977) 'MFN tariff reductions and LDC benefits under the GSP', *Economic Journal*, Vol. 87, No. 345.

Beckford, G.L. (1972) *Persistent Poverty: Underdevelopment in Plantation Economies of the Third World*, Oxford University Press.

Brown, M.B. (1974) *The Economics of Imperialism*, Penguin Books.

Clement, M.O., Pfister, R.L. and Rothwell, K.J. (1967) *Theoretical Issues in International Economics*, Houghton Mifflin.

Colman, D.R. (1984) 'Food and agricultural exports from less-developed countries – exploitation by transnational firms', *Manchester Papers on Development*, No. 9.

Commonwealth Secretariat (1975) *Terms of Trade for Primary Commodities*, Commonwealth Economic Papers No. 4.

de Janvry, A. (1981) *The Agrarian Question and Reformism in Latin America*, Johns Hopkins University Press.

Edwards, C. (1985) *The Fragmented World: Competing Perspectives on Trade, Money and Crisis*, Methuen.

Emmanuel, A. (1972) *Unequal Exchange*, New Left Books.

Erb, G.F. and Schiavo-Campo, S. (1969) 'Export instability, level of development, and economic size of less developed countries', *Bulletin Oxford University Institute of Economics and Statistics*, Vol. 131.

Feder, E. (1979) *Strawberry Imperialism: An Enquiry into the Mechanisms of Dependency in Mexican Agriculture*, Institute of Social Sciences, The Hague.

Fels, G. and Glisman, H.H. (1975) 'Adjustment policy in the German manufacturing sector', *Adjustment for Trade*, OECD Development Centre.

George, S. (1978) *Feeding the Few: Corporate Control of Food*, Institute of Policy Studies, Washington.

Glezakos, C. (1973) 'Export instability and economic growth: a statistical verification', *Economic Development and Cultural Change*, 21(4), pp. 670–8.

Green, C. and Kirkpatrick, C. (1982) 'The IMF's food financing facility', *Journal of World Trade Law*, 16(3), pp. 265–73.

Haq, M. ul (1973) 'Industrialisation and trade policies in the 1970s', in P. Streeten (ed.), *Trade Strategies for Development*, Macmillan.

Joekes, S. and Kirkpatrick, C. (1979) 'UNCTAD V: the results', *Journal of World Trade Law*, 13(6).

Kitamura, H. (1968) 'Capital accumulation and the theory of international trade', *Malayan Economic Review*, Vol. 3, No. 1; Reprinted in I. Livingstone (ed.) (1971) *Economic Policy for Development*, Penguin Books.

Knudsen, O. and Parnes, A. (1975) *Trade Instability and Economic Development*, Lexington Books.

Kravis, I.B. (1970) 'Trade as a handmaiden of growth: similarities between the nineteenth and twentieth centuries', *Economic Journal*, Vol. 80, pp. 850–72.

Lewis, W.A. (1980) 'The slowing down of the engine of growth', *American Economic Review*, 70(4), pp. 555–64.

Lister, M. (1982) 'The functioning of Lome II'. *Journal of World Trade Law*, 16(4), pp. 434–40.

Little, I., Scitovsky, T. and Scott, M. (1970) *Industry and Trade in Some Developing Countries*, Oxford University Press.

MacBean, A.L. (1966) *Export Instability and Economic Development*, George Allen and Unwin.

Meier, G.M. (1980) *International Economics: The Theory of Policy*, Oxford University Press.

Michaely, M. (1977) 'Exports and growth: an empirical investigation', *Journal of Development Studies*, 4, pp. 49–53.

Moore, L. (1985) *The Growth and Structure of International Trade since the Second World War*, Wheatsheaf Books.

Morton, K. and Tulloch, P. (1977) *Trade and Development*, Croom Helm.

Murray, T. (1973a) 'How helpful is the generalised system of preferences to developing countries?', *Economic Journal*, Vol. 83, No. 330.

Murray, T. (1973b) 'EEC enlargement and preferences for the developing countries', *Economic Journal*, Vol. 83, No. 331.

Myint, H. (ed.) (1971) *South East Asia's Economy in the 1970s*, Asian Development Bank/Longman.

Payer, C. (1975) *The Debt Trap: The IMF and the Third World*, Monthly Review Press.

Payer, C. (1982) *The World Bank*, Monthly Review Press.

Pirzio-Biroli, C. (1983) 'Making sense of the IMF conditionality debate', *Journal of World Trade Law*, 17(2), pp. 115–53.

Prebisch, R. (1950) *The Economic Development of Latin America and its Principal Problems*, UN Economic Committee for Latin America.

Prebisch, R. (1967) 'Commercial policy in the underdeveloped countries', *American Economic Review Papers and Proceedings*.

Riedel, J. (1984) 'Trade as the engine of growth in developing countries, revisited', *Economic Journal*, 94, pp. 56–63.

Schiavo-Campo, S. and Singer, H.W. (1970) *Perspectives of Economic Development*, Houghton Mifflin.

Singer, H. (1950) 'The distribution of gains between investing and borrowing countries', Paper and Proceedings, *American Economic Review*, 40(2), pp. 473–85.

Smith, S. and Toye, J. (1979) 'Three stories about trade and poor countries', *Journal of Development Studies*, 15(3), pp. 1–18.

Spraos, J. (1983) *Inequalising Trade?: A Study of Traditional North/South Specialisation in the Context of Terms of Trade Concepts*, Oxford University Press.

Steedman, I. (1979) *Trade Amongst Growing Economies*, Cambridge University Press.

Streeten, P. (ed.) (1973) *Trade Strategies for Development*, Macmillan.

Stubbs, R. (1984) 'The International Natural Rubber Agreement: its negotiation and operation', *Journal of World Trade Law*, 18(1), pp. 16–31.

UNCTAD (1974) *An Integrated Programme for Commodities*, TD/B/C/1/166.

UNCTAD (1981a) *Proceedings of the United Nations Conference on Trade and Development*, Fifth Session, Manila, Vol. III, Basic Documents.

UNCTAD (1981b) *Operation and Effects of the Generalised System of Preferences*, TD/B/C.5/71.

UNCTAD (1981c) *Trade and Development Report 1981*.

Wall, D. (1976) 'The European Communities Lome Convention, "STABEX" and the Third World's aspirations', *Guest Paper* No. 4, Trade Policy Research Centre.

Walter, I. (1971) 'Non-tariff barriers and the export performance of developing economies', Plans and Proceedings, *American Economic Review*, 61(2), pp. 195–205.

Yotopoulos, Pan A. and Nugent, J.B. (1976) *Economics of Development: Empirical Investigation*, Harper and Row.

6

The international setting: foreign exchange flows and indebtedness

It will be recalled from Chapter 2 that according to the 'two-gap' theory, investment and hence growth may be restricted by the shortage of either domestic savings or foreign exchange. This argument rests on the assumption that some proportion of the capital items and intermediate inputs required for economic expansion has to be purchased from abroad using foreign exchange, and cannot be produced domestically. If domestic savings are not sufficient to enable acquisition of sufficient domestic resources to utilise fully the available foreign exchange for investment, a savings gap is assumed to exist. Alternatively, if foreign exchange availability is insufficient to permit all the available domestic savings to be invested, then a foreign exchange gap is said to exist. If either of these gaps were to exist, one of the two factors would be restricting investment and growth below the potential level permitted by the other factor.

Note that either gap can only exist *ex ante* with respect to what might be achieved in terms of desired or planned higher growth rates if more domestic savings or foreign exchange were available. There can be no gaps in an *ex post* sense, in that the necessary savings and foreign exchange flows must by definition have been available to permit whatever actual level of investment (and hence growth) occurred. Thus the gaps can only be envisaged in terms of what could have been rather than what has been the case. It is generally accepted (see, for example, Chenery and Bruno 1962; McKinnon 1964; and Chenery and Strout 1966) that in the early stages of development a foreign exchange gap will typically exist, because the capacity to profitably invest imported products and materials will exceed available foreign exchange earned from exports – available, that is, after deducting the value of imported consumption items and repayment of debt to foreigners. This assumption that foreign exchange is almost inevitably a limiting factor in development is the major factor underpinning arguments of international bodies, such as the World Bank, that official aid and other exchange flows from developed countries are necessary for development in most LDCs; such flows are also justified on the grounds that they augment domestic savings. In the light of this argument this chapter is devoted to examining some of the doubts which have emerged about the value of aid and foreign exchange flows to underdeveloped countries, and to the related issue of the external indebtedness of some countries in the wake of these flows. While inevitably this involves some reference to the role of official aid, as opposed to other types of foreign exchange flow, it must be emphasised that this is not a chapter about aid as such. Indeed, reasons of emphasis and space have dictated omission of detailed consideration of the efficacy and impact of specific forms of aid − only brief reference is made to them here.

6.1   Alternative Sources of Foreign Exchange

In examining the productivity to the underdeveloped countries of foreign exchange flows which are additional to export earnings, and which are therefore on the capital account of the balance of payments, a distinction needs to be made between (1) economic aid (which excludes military assistance), and (2) commercial loans and transfers. What distinguishes aid from commercial flows is that the former has a concessional element, either because it is given in the form of grants which are not required to be repaid, or because it is lent at below market interest rates, with long repayment periods, and often with a so-called 'grace period' which waives interest payments in the first few years after the loan. Flows in both categories may emanate from the governments of the donor countries and be of an 'official' nature, or they may arise from the commercial activities of banks and firms and may be 'private'. In fact, however, only a small proportion of private flows can be classed as aid, and this is the proportion made up of the grants of voluntary organisations (see Table 6.1, row C.2). After discounting grants, private flows can be classed as falling into two clear categories: (1) commercial loans and export credits by private banks and firms, to be repaid over typically short repayment periods at market rates of interest − often at variable interest rates in the current situation of fluctuating commercial rates; and (2) direct investment by firms. As can be seen from Table 6.1, private direct investment in LDCs grew only slowly in real terms between 1970 and 1982, and exhibited sharp annual fluctuations. It is the category of export credits and commercial lending which has risen most over this period, private commercial lending having grown from 42% of private flows in 1970 to 63% in 1982.[1]

Both the major classes of private flow have to be paid for by recipient countries. Loans have to be serviced by payment of interest and by repayment (amortisation) of the principal. Direct investment, while not necessarily involving any contractual repayments, usually entails repatriation of profits and management fees. Thus both of the major private

Table 6.1 Composition of Net Resource Receipts by Developing Countries from All Sources in Constant Prices

| | $ billion (1981 prices) | | | | | | |
	1970	1972	1974	1976	1978	1980	1982[4]
A. Official flows							
A.1 Concessional	21.30	21.48	29.10	30.19	33.53	36.21	34.97
A.2 Non-concessional	10.20	8.19	13.47	18.78	22.92	21.81	23.12
B. Private flows	20.30	23.13	23.61	34.98	48.15	35.14	37.09
Total[5] = A+B = C+D	51.73	52.80	66.18	83.95	104.60	93.16	95.18
C. Bilateral flows							
C.1. Total official	18.45	18.47	24.13	24.45	26.36	28.65	27.37
C.1.a DAC[1]	(14.58)	(14.43)	(14.51)	(14.09)	(15.66)	(17.56)	(18.93)
C.1.b OPEC	(1.00)	(1.44)	(7.32)	(7.67)	(8.23)	(8.47)	(5.63)
C.1.c CMEA[2]	(2.86)	(2.60)	(2.29)	(2.69)	(2.47)	(2.62)	(2.81)
C.2 Private grants[3]	2.22	2.27	2.15	2.00	1.97	2.24	2.36
C.3 Direct investment	9.51	9.24	3.33	12.33	13.83	10.22	11.24
C.4 Export credits and other lending[6]	16.86	17.60	28.41	35.66	51.59	39.79	39.78
D. Multilateral flows[7]	4.69	5.22	8.16	9.51	10.85	12.26	14.43

Source: OECD (1984), Table D, p.28.
(1) DAC = Development Assistance Committee.
(2) CMEA = Council for Mutual Economic Assitance (COMECON).
(3) Grants by voluntary agencies.
(4) Certain figures are preliminary.
(5) Total have been adjusted slightly so that numbers exactly add up.
(6) A high proportion of export credits are guaranteed by governments and are therefore official flows – however, most of C.4 is private bank lending.
(7) Nearly all the multilateral flows are official and can be classed as aid.

sources of foreign exchange tend, with a time lag, to have offsetting negative effects on the balance of payments of LDCs, and loans and credits are the source of their indebtedness.

Of course, the concessionary loans which form part of official resource flows also add to indebtedness but, because of the concessionary element and the significant proportion of grants, such official flows have a smaller impact upon indebtedness and have a lower cost to the recipient countries. Also the debt which they comprise is more easily rescheduled when repayment difficulties arise. For this reason, considerable importance attaches to the growth in these official flows relative to private and non-concessional public flows. It is therefore significant that the growth in concessional official flows has been substantially slower than those of non-concessional official and private flows (see Table 6.1). It is true that the real value of concessional aid did grow between 1970 and 1982, and also that total (concessional and non-concessional) official development flows grew slightly more quickly than the rate of growth of GNP in the main industrial economies. This latter development was, however, largely due to the fact that the OPEC and CMEA countries became increasingly important sources of official funds during this period; their combined share of bilateral Official Development Aid (ODA) rose from 21% in 1970 to 31% in 1982. In contrast the main industrial countries, which are members of the Development Assistance Committee (DAC), increased the absolute value of official flows more slowly, and only managed to maintain these at the same low rate (0.34 to 0.35 of their GNP) during this period; since 1977/78 they have channelled a higher proportion of this through bilateral concessional loans rather than multilateral loans and grants. Thus because of tight fiscal and monetary policies in donor countries which have restricted grant-aid supply, and because of burgeoning demand for additional foreign exchange by LDCs trying to cope with high oil prices and increased food imports as well as their capital investment plans, LDCs have as a group increasingly had to satisfy their additional foreign exchange requirements through commercial borrowings. But, irrespective of whether borrowings are commercial or concessionary, unless such funds cause the receiving economy as a whole to generate additional foreign earnings plus savings (through import substitution) at a rate sufficient to leave a surplus after servicing the debt incurred, they will have a negative effect upon its balance of payments which can lead to debt repayment problems. Precisely because a number of LDCs have encountered serious debt repayment problems and have had to reschedule payments under threat of default, the doubts which are the subject of this chapter have been raised about the effectiveness to LDCs of foreign aid and borrowings, and about the whole rationale of the two-gap theory that foreign exchange availability may be the critical constraint upon development.

Self-evidently, most private lending (and the export credit element of official flows) is advanced for specific uses and is negotiated with firms or institutions to facilitate particular investment projects or to finance nominated import contracts. Similarly, much official aid is advanced for specific uses, and the recipient country has little flexibility in its use. This is obviously true of aid in kind, which may take the forms of food aid (free or concessionary deliveries of products such as grain, flour or milk powder), items of machinery such as tractors, or of technical assistance personnel such as agronomists, engineers, teachers and so on. It is also true of grants and concessional loans which are donated or advanced against agreed projects for road building, harbour improvement, irrigation schemes and the like. In these latter cases the degree of flexibility the receiving country has for using the aid may be further restricted by contract clauses requiring that any import requirements for the assisted project must be purchased from the donor country. This sort of 'tying' is especially common with bilateral aid, that is aid given directly from one country to another, for every donor country has an understandable wish to see that any export orders which may arise are placed with its own industries rather than with competitors, even though this may diminish the spirit of beneficence in giving the aid. By its very nature, aid given multilaterally is less restricted by such nationalistic considerations.

Multilateral aid is that channelled through international organisations such as the World Bank, the Food and Agriculture Organisation, or the World Health Organisation, all of which operate under the umbrella of the United Nations, and also through the EEC. When aid is received through any of these institutions, it originates from all the countries which contribute to them and hence it is a multilateral contribution from many countries to the recipient. Because this eliminates the particular nationalistic pressures from the donors which are associated with bilateral aid, it has often been suggested (e.g. Pearson 1969, p.215) that donor countries should switch more official aid from bilateral to multilateral channels. While apparently the proportion of DAC country aid which was transferred multilaterally increased until 1977/78, according to Garcia-Thoumi (1983) it has subsequently declined, as donor countries have exhibited an increasing preference for retaining control in their own hands. In principle this may be no bad thing, for, in so far as different countries have different priorities and attitudes towards the disbursement of aid, it allows for a greater range of experiments with forms of aid than would probably occur if most aid were channelled multilaterally through a few very large international organisations. Nevertheless, a major limitation of the effectiveness of bilateral aid is the tendency of donors to use it as an arm of trade policy rather than as a straightforward aided transfer of resources.

From the recipient countries' point of view there can be no doubt that their preference is for aid with as few strings as possible, and on the cheapest possible terms. Thus their ideal is for financial grants in aid, which are not tied to specific imports or projects but which are available to support general development programmes, i.e. the preference is for *programme* rather than *project* aid. But the desire of donor governments and international agencies to ensure that aid is used productively, and in an accountable way, means that most aid is given in project form. There is only a limited amount of aid which is not tied in some way. One example was the general budgetary aid which was given by Britain to some former colonies after their independence as a form of revenue support to the new governments; there is a limited amount of non-project aid advanced by the World Bank; and any concessionary elements in the compensatory finance schemes operated by the IMF and STABEX (see Chapter 5) may also be viewed as programme aid. But these do not amount to a very significant proportion of total aid, which consequently must be considered as being largely tied in varying degrees.

6.2   The Contribution of Aid and Foreign Exchange Flows to Development

As a starting point, general support might be expected to exist for one of the conclusions of the previous chapter, namely that economic grant aid can be expected to make a positive contribution to the development of poor nations. For grant aid would seen to represent an unambiguous addition of resources to the recipient country in the form of additional import-purchasing capacity, and might therefore be expected to increase GDP per capita. There are those, however, for example Bauer (1971, Ch.2) and Griffin (1970, 1971, whose views are examined more fully below), who argue that the case for aid in general (including grant aid) is by no means axiomatic and that aid will not automatically lead to greater development. Specifically, Bauer argues that aid may be inimical to greater self-reliance and to desirable structural reorganisation in recipient nations, that it feeds bureaucracy and the expansion of state controls, and thus that aid as charity may be bad for the recipient. However, Bauer does concede that there are situations (not usually found in the least developed countries) in which the right entrepreneurial and institutional setting exists for aid to play a positive role in development and stimulating the economy of the recipient country. Nevertheless, we cannot agree with Bauer's general assessment, and instead accept that aid, and more particularly grant aid, has a positive role. Undoubtedly there are tales (not all apocryphal) which have passed into the folklore of development studies, of grant-aid dispatched in the form of snowploughs to desert countries, and of tractors sent without implements and spare parts to countries with virtually no mechanics in rural areas. Such gross mistakes are, however, not characteristic, and there seems to be no strong reason to doubt that well thought out grant aid can promote development.

Given the last assertion it is of interest to refer very briefly to the debate about the contribution of what is possibly the most important form of grant aid (given that we have excluded military 'aid' from consideration), namely food aid. Food aid is used for two distinctly different purposes. One is to alleviate the localised effects on food supplies of natural disasters such as floods, droughts or earthquakes. In such circumstances there can be few reservations about the desirability of donations of food to save life, diminish human suffering, and to preserve human strength and health which is the very basis of continued self-reliance. It is vital that such humanitarian aid should arrive speedily, in useful forms and in appropriate amounts. Sadly, as reported more fully in Chapter 8, despite good intentions there are generally substantial delays in food aid deliveries which significantly diminish their capacity to serve as emergency relief. There are also difficulties in deciding when genuine emergencies have occurred, and of ensuring that the food reaches those most in need rather than being corruptly handled by those already adequately provided for. Timeliness is less critical for the other major role for food aid which is to provide free or (more usually) cheap food, on a longer-term basis to countries with a chronic malnutrition/food-supply problem.[2] The main bilateral supplier of food on this basis has been the USA through its Public Law 480 programmes, although Canada has been a steady source of food aid; since 1963 the World Food Programme has also provided food aid multilaterally, and in recent years the EEC has emerged as a major supplier. Most of this food aid has been in the form of wheat and wheat flour, and also of surplus dairy products in the form of skimmed-milk and some butter-oil.

The efficacy of these programmes is controversial and has been challenged by many writers (e.g. Schultz 1960; Stevens 1979; and Cathie 1982). The controversy centres around four issues: (1) whether supplies of food aid depress market prices for food crops in LDCs, reduce incentives to farmers and cause long-term reductions in LDC food production; (2) whether the forms of food supplied as aid are appropriate to the needs of recipient countries; supplying wheat to countries whose indigenous grains are rice, maize or millet can cause permanent changes in food consumption habits towards commercially imported wheat and away from domestically producible grains; also supplying skimmed-milk powder through nutrition programmes to mothers with very young children can lead to a variety of health problems by inducing a reduced incidence of breast feeding; (3) because much food aid is sold, through 'fair price shops' or their equivalent, the food may not reach the poorest people with the

most serious nutrition problems; and (4) the spending by recipient governments of counterpart funds accumulated from sales of food aid may cause
price inflation. In principle there are ways of avoiding most of these problems, the foremost of which is to ensure that food-aid supplies are strictly
'additional'; that is, food aid should not displace any commercial demand,
should increase consumption in any period by exactly the amount of the
food aid, should augment the diets of people who could not otherwise consume that food, and furthermore should be converted into a form of
investment (in human capital, or as public capital through food-for-work
programmes which create additional employment). These are demanding
conditions to achieve and in practice most food-aid schemes fail to attain
them. Nevertheless, lessons have been learnt, and there are those such as
Singer (1978) who remain confident that food aid can play a positive role
in development.

As has already been stated, food aid (as with all aid in-kind) falls into the
more general category of 'tied' aid. The tying clauses in aid contracts
involve the receiving country agreeing to place certain business orders in
the donor country – obviously, nothing is more completely tied in this
sense than that the recipient agrees to accept the aid in the form of a
shipload of food from the donor. All forms of tying clearly render aid an
official arm of the donor country's trade (and, in certain instances, foreign)
policy, and diminish its status as a gift. It may also be an adjunct of
domestic policies in donor countries; there is no doubt, for example, that
USA grain shipments of food aid, sent since 1954 under Public Law 480,
have been primarily inspired by the existence of large publicly owned
stocks which accumulated because of the USA's policies of price support
for her farmers. Similarly, EEC food-aid programmes have been more
influenced by the existence of surplus grain and dairy products than by a
spirit of simple beneficence, although there is a powerful public sentiment
in EEC countries against destroying food when it could be dispatched as
aid to LDCs – that sentiment is not well informed on questions of the
effectiveness of such aid. Furthermore, there is little doubt that electorates
in donor countries are more willing to support aid policies if they can see
that any export orders which arise are passed to them rather than to competitors in other countries. From the recipient's point of view, however,
the tying of aid will diminish its effectiveness if it results in the necessity to
buy more expensive and less efficient products and services than could be
obtained from sources other than the donor. The question which therefore
arises is this: by how much does the tying of aid reduce its value to the recipient? For reasons well and fully spelt out by Bhagwati (1967), there is no
straightforward empirical answer to this question. But, within wide
margins for error, attempts have been made to estimate the costs to the
receiver of tying aid. For example, analysis by UNCTAD (1967) of some
subset of tied credits led to estimates that as a proportion of the nominal

value of the aid, the cost of tying was 12.4% to Chile between 1964 and 1967, 15% to Iran in 1966–67, and 20% to Tunisia in 1965. These were considered to be conservative underestimates in each case, and this limited evidence suggests a cost for the types of project-tied aid studied of, on average, at least 10% to 20%.

A more fundamental set of questions, attacking the efficacy of both aid and commercial exchange flows, has been raised by Griffin (1970) who has gone as far as to assert (p.100) that 'capital imports, rather than accelerating development, have in some cases retarded it'. While Griffin's position provoked a highly critical response (in a collection of three papers in 1971 by Kennedy and Thirlwall, Stewart and Eshag), particularly with respect to the empirical support for his arguments, some of the points he raises command attention, although some of his conclusions should be viewed with caution.

Perhaps the most important observations relate to the effects of foreign exchange inflows on domestic savings and consumption. Certainly the main point of dispute between Griffin and his critics revolves around Griffin's statements (reiterated in 1971, p.158) that (1) 'given the level of income, the larger the capital inflow the lower the level of domestic savings', and (2) 'the higher is the ratio of aid to income the smaller will be the rate of domestic savings'.

The logic of Griffin's major argument for the first of these conclusions is not wholly sound and must be seriously questioned.[3] As is shown in note 3, there is certainly a basic algebraic flaw in a critical restatement of his views (in 1971) in his use of comparative static equilibrium analysis. This led to the erroneous conclusion that there is in theory a negative relationship between the levels of capital inflow and domestic saving when in fact, according to his own stated assumptions and definitions, the relationship is positive. Thus his attempts to prove his first point axiomatically with the conventional elementary assumptions of macroeconomic theory seems to be misconceived, and its formal justification requires a more complex model embodying assumptions, such as (one considered at length in his 1970 paper) that the marginal propensity to consume increases by more than a certain (calculable) amount when foreign capital becomes regularly available to a country. That is, the first statement depends upon the second one holding in a particularly strong form, namely that the savings rate falls by more than a specified proportion of the increase in the capital inflow rate. Whether the evidence supports this strong version of the second hypothesis is debatable.

Certainly the evidence reviewed by Griffin, showing an inverse relationship between the saving and capital inflow ratios, has attracted much criticism. With some justification it has been argued that there are inherent biases in the cross-country form of analysis upon which most of the evidence is based. But Kennedy and Thirlwall (1971) and Papenek

(1972) have gone further and argued that the causal mechanism may well be the reverse of that claimed by Griffin. Papenek put forward the fairly convincing argument that in years of low export prices or crop failures, the tendency is for consumption rates to be maintained and for the domestic savings rate to fall, which can only be accomplished if foreign capital inflows increase; thus it is low savings rates which necessitate high capital inflow rates. This argument, however, does not appear sufficiently general to prevent us from concluding that the evidence is consistent with the hypothesis that the savings ratio declines as capital inflows increase. This is perfectly plausible in poor societies with a high marginal propensity to consume, so that the savings *rate* can decline simultaneously with an increase in the *level* of savings.

This behaviour can also be interpreted slightly differently, as indicating that some proportion of the foreign exchange inflow is used to raise domestic consumption and that not all of it is directly invested. That the evidence suggests this happens should engender no surpirse, for not only do all societies tend to consume some proportion of the extra resources made available to them, but some types of aid, like food aid, health and emergency aid, are deliberately designed to permit consumption and are not directly intended to promote investment. Clearly this cannot be deplored and, as Frances Stewart (1971) pointed out, in developing countries some forms of what are typically classed as consumption expenditure, such as nutrition, health and education, represent investment in human capital and may well raise growth rates. However, the essential point is, and this does not seem to be in dispute, that not all foreign capital flows can be treated as net additions to domestic saving and investment in the manner suggested by equation 2.3 in Chapter 2. Consequently, instead of such flows contributing to growth (g) at a rate ($A/Y)(1/k)$, they will only contribute $(1-c)(A/Y)(1/k)$, where A = foreign capital inflow, Y = national income, k = the capital–output ratio, and c = the proportion of A which is consumed. Furthermore, capital inflows may, as already discussed, influence the savings rate which may change from s to s'. Thus the equation 2.3 may need to be restated as:

$$g = \frac{s'}{k} + (1-c)\frac{A}{Y} \cdot \frac{1}{k} \tag{6.1}$$

and the contribution of capital inflows to growth will be:

$$g_A = \frac{s'-s}{k} + (1-c)\frac{A}{Y} \cdot \frac{1}{k} \tag{6.2}$$

In Griffin's view, even this may overstate the contribution to growth of aid/foreign capital in so far as it may be used to finance projects and production techniques which have a higher capital–output ratio (k') than those financed by domestic savings.[4] This possibility is envisaged as a consequence of transnational companies importing capital in connection with relatively capital-intensive processes, and because in the public sector aid is often channelled into capital-intensive rural development projects or infrastructure such as roads and railways which show a low direct rate of return but have a long productive life. However, as Chapter 11 makes clear, capital-intensive industrial processes in LDCs are not necessarily 'inappropriate' and may well have low capital–output ratios overall; also, infrastructure and other forms of public investment may well generate sizeable external economies in the form of benefits to private enterprises and individuals, so that the total rate of return to the economy may be higher than it immediately appears to be. Thus, arguably it is not relevant to query the contribution of foreign capital to development simply on the grounds that it is used to promote capital-intensive private and public projects. What is probably of more concern to critics who raise this point is the effects of capital inflows upon the economic and political structure of the recipient countries.

As regards the political effects, it has already been observed in Chapter 2 that the relationship which has emerged in many LDCs between the local power elite and both transnational corporations and major aid-giving bodies has frequently led to projects and actions which have not seemed to be in the best interests of development in its broader sense. Thus it has sometimes suited local elites, in terms of enhanced electoral appeal, to support the channelling of aid into prestige projects such as the building of large airports, super-highways and large irrigation projects. This has also been acceptable to the donors, who have often in the past (but to a decreasing extent) wished to have something to show for their money. But often the show-piece projects have had low or negative returns, and the maintenance of the capital and services associated with them has been a major burden to the budgets of LDCs. Similarly, local elites have frequently found association with the activities of foreign companies to be personally rewarding, and so they have encouraged investment by such companies despite the issues relating to the developmental impact of penetration by foreign companies. These issues are more fully aired in Chapter 2, section C and Chapter 10, but there is one aspect of them which deserves comment here. This is a matter which has been raised forcibly by Griffin (1970), and introduces a broader one about the rationale for the *ex ante* existence of a foreign exchange gap.

The specific issue relates to the impact of foreign exchange flows (other than those arising directly from exports) upon the import requirements for the growth of LDCs. Large aid projects and investment by foreign firms may act to raise import requirements in two ways. Firstly, they may, through the employment of predominantly skilled and expatriate labour, cause the distribution of income to be tilted towards those with a high propensity to consume imported foodstuffs and luxury goods. Secondly, they may result in investment and production processes which have a high initial imported capital content and a continuing dependence upon imported intermediate goods and replacement capital. Thus foreign exchange flows on capital account may increase the propensity to import and create a long-term dependence of the economy upon imports. How does all this relate to the existence or non-existence of a foreign exchange gap? Well, if an *ex ante* foreign exchange gap is assumed to exist, it rests, among other things, upon assumptions about the imports required to achieve target rates of growth. In effect these assumptions reduce to another, which is that domestic resources cannot be substituted for imported ones beyond a certain level. But it is clear that this assumption implies others about the future scale and types of foreign enterprises and aid projects, and about income distribution. Griffin's point (1970, p.102) is that in the long run all of these are variables which can be adjusted by policy so as to reduce the ratio of imports to GDP. That is, (1) capital goods and import-substituting industries can be developed to reduce import dependence; (2) only projects which are orientated primarily to the use of domestically available inputs need be encouraged; (3) the income distribution can be adjusted in favour of those with a low marginal propensity to consume imports; and (4) imports of luxury goods could be severely restricted. Thus, in the long run at least, in Griffin's view an *ex ante* foreign exchange gap has little meaning in that it involves assuming to be fixed things which are variable. This at once raises doubts about the appropriateness of using the concept of an exchange gap to justify increasing foreign exchange flows to LDCs on capital account, and it raises the question of whether the real issues are not about the ways in which such flows are employed in the LDCs to create import dependence, and about their effects upon income distribution and the structures of political power.

From all that has been said it will be evident that some of the doubts raised about the contribution of aid/foreign exchange to the LDCs have a genuine basis. Certain tying restrictions in the giving of aid undoubtedly diminish its value to the recipient. The long-run consequences of aid and commercial transfers may well be associated with changes in economic and political structures, which may be held to have adverse consequences on certain of the dimensions of development (see Chapter 1) such as income distribution and national independence. There is no doubt also, as discussed in the next section, that many LDCs have encountered serious debt service problems as a result of borrowings made on capital account. But these reservations do not add up to a conclusion that aid and other exchange flows have made a negative contribution to development in a general sense. In any case a clear distinction must be made between alternative types of exchange flow. Most of the major queries must be held to relate to commercial loans and direct investment. But, despite unease about long-term consequences of penetration by foreign firms and organisations – and in some cases, such as the extreme one of the British Phosphate Commission's exploitation up to 1970 of Ocean Island, the results have been disastrous for development – it would be foolish to deny that in many cases these have made an important contribution to growth and development of poor countries. Certainly foreign firms are much in evidence in the newly industrialised countries, whose economic success must in part be attributed to their ability to harness the energies of transnational firms to serve local development goals. Much depends upon the sector of the economy in which the foreign organisation operates, and on local controls over its operation.

In the case of grants and concessional aid there is much less doubt about their positive effects. There is no obvious reason why these should be employed in such ways that a significant proportion is consumed rather than invested, or that serious debt problems should arise. It is, however, true that aid has frequently been used for political ends by donor and recipient countries' governments – for a full discussion of this see the book by Judith Hart (1973) – and that the full economic implications of many aid projects have not been correctly anticipated, so that the economic returns to some projects have been low and in some cases negative. Such distortions are not inevitable concomitants of aid schemes, and there is no intrinsic reason why aid in most of its various forms should have anything other than a beneficial impact upon recipient countries.

6.3   The Problem of the LDCs' External Indebtedness

During 1983 and 1984 the term 'Debt Crisis' was used with increasing frequency to describe the problems many LDCs (and their creditors) were experiencing in servicing the volume of debt they had amassed in the preceding decade. Such were the difficulties that an unprecedented number of countries had to reschedule their debts in these two years; they were unable to meet the interest and amortisation payments required by their original loan agreements with foreign governments, international institutions and banks, and were forced to conclude new arrangements. From the creditors' standpoint there was considerable anxiety that major LDC debtors might refuse to accept the rescheduling terms, but instead would simply default (refuse to pay the costs of loans) which might have completely disrupted the international monetary system and have bankrupted commercial banks in DCs which had loaned substantial funds. While a number of smaller banks came near to collapse (e.g. Continental Illinois in the USA), breakdown of the system was avoided, but at substantial cost. This section explores some aspects of the nature and size of LDCs' indebtedness problems, plus the implications for the future financing of LDCs.

Even accepting that LDCs typically have a foreign exchange gap, and that they should therefore be provided with the external finance to run current account trade deficits, the rate of growth of LDC indebtedness between 1974 and 1982 was remarkable and, as events have demonstrated, in many cases unsound. Underlying the accumulation of indebtedness has been a persistent over-optimism by borrowers and lenders alike. In the early 1970s, when price inflation was especially rapid everywhere, real interest rates were low or even negative, export markets for LDCs were expanding rapidly and commodity prices were rising quickly – the conditions were right for borrowing funds. Commercial banks in the industrialised countries became increasingly active in making international loans based on the recycling of petrodollars from the OPEC countries and the lending of the increasing volume of Eurodollars caused by persistent US trade deficits. With hindsight it is acknowledged that in many instances money was borrowed and lent on the basis of inadequate project appraisals and exaggeratedly optimistic forecasts of the time needed to construct capital projects, their efficiency when operating, and the marketability of their products. For their part, the Western commercial banks involved in these loans possibly took an over-relaxed attitude to the productivity of their loans; it was reasonable for them to assume that at the end of the day the IMF and Western governments would do their best to prevent LDCs having to default on loans and to effectively guarantee the integrity of the system of financing international trade. On the other hand, in some LDCs economic mismanagement and widespread corruption led to both poor investment decisions and a diminution of the cost effectiveness of good projects.

Some of the main features of the debt problem from the point of view of non-oil developing countries (NODCs) are revealed by Table 6.2.[5] From this it can be seen that each of the three indicators presented deteriorated between 1973 and 1978. Long-term debt of the NODCs rose during these years as a proportion of both export value and GDP, and annual debt service payments rose from 14 to 17.3% of the value of exports. The latter indicates the proportion of total export receipts required simply to pay off existing debts, and it was of course much higher for some individual countries. This proportion rose further in 1979, but at the same time the volume of long-term debt diminished relatively, and all three indicators showed an improvement in 1980. Thereafter, however, the situation deteriorated sharply again. In 1979–80 the second large increase in oil prices engineered by OPEC had severe deleterious effects on the current account trade deficits of oil-importing countries. At the same time interest rates began to rise sharply as tighter money supply policies were instituted in major industrial countries; 'the six-month Eurodollar rate payable on

Table 6.2 Long-Term Debt Ratios for Non-Oil Developing Countries

	1973	1975	1976	1977	1978	1979	1980	1981	1982
Ratio of external long-term debt to exports of goods and services[1]	88.7	97.7	102.6	104.9	111.2	101.9	92.9	103.2	109.1
Ratio of external long-term debt to GDP[1]	16.6	18.3	20.5	22.1	23.7	22.7	21.8	24.3	25.2
Debt service ratio[2]	14.0	14.0	13.9	14.0	17.3	18.1	16.3	21.0	22.3

Source: Finance and Development (1983), p.23.
Notes: (1) Ratio for year-end debt to exports or GDP for the year indicated.
(2) Payments of interest and amortisation as percentages of exports of goods and services, both for long- and short-term debt.

variable debt rose from an average of 8.3% in 1972–78 to 17.2% in 1981, descending again to 9.8% in 1983 . . .', and subsequently rose again (Commonwealth Secretariat 1984, p.20). The sharp increase in interest rates caused serious problems to those LDCs with substantial amounts of variable interest debt. At the same time, however, the anti-inflationary economic policies of the industrial countries caused the growth of world trade to slow down and prices for LDC commodity exports to fall. This combination of forces exerted a formidable squeeze on the capacity of non-oil-exporting LDCs to service their debt. This is illustrated by the calculation:

> If rates of interest are adjusted for changes in the export unit values of developing countries it becomes clear that the real interest rate, which remained negative in the 1970s, rose to over 20% in 1981–82 in respect of the non-oil countries, and has not fallen significantly since. (Commonwealth Secretariat 1984, p.20)

Increasing numbers of small- and medium-sized countries (in terms of indebtedness) were forced to seek debt rescheduling agreements with the international commercial banks and the IMF after 1978. But in 1982 the situation became critical when those major Latin American countries, which are the most heavily indebted developing countries of all, ran into foreign exchange crises. Mexico was the first of these to seek loan rescheduling, and the acute nervousness in banking circles which accompanied this was compounded by similar problems with Brazil and then by the alarm caused by the threat of suspension of payments by Argentina in the wake of the 'Falklands War' with Britain.

The rapidity with which the indebtedness of these three big borrowing nations had grown is revealed in Table 6.3 which presents data for the largest 20 borrowers. What is equally striking about the debt structure of Brazil, Mexico, Argentina, and a number of other upper- and middle-income developing countries, is the extent to which they have had to rely upon commercial bank loans rather than Official Development Aid. Well over 50% of their debt was in the commercial category and a significant proportion was in short-term loans at high rates of interest. This is reflected in the rapid increase in interest and other debt service payments of these countries between 1980 and 1982. The real value of their outstanding debt steadily increased and by 1982 had risen to approximately 420% of the annual value of exports. The costs of servicing this in 1982 were equivalent to 28.8% of exports for Argentina, 39.1% for Brazil and a staggering 55.8% for Mexico. With strains such as these it was not surprising that something had to give. Commercial banks were increasingly nervous about extending further short-term loans at even very high interest rates. Under the threat of default they were anxious to call in debts and to reduce their exposure in LDCs. They were therefore reluctant to carry on

Table 6.3 The 20 Largest Developing Country Borrowers[a]: Disbursed Long-Term Debt, Year-end 1979–82 ($ billion)

Borrower	Year-end disbursed debt					Debt service paid[d]				Interest paid			
	1979	1980	1981	1982	of which to banks 1982	1980	1981	1982	1983	1980	1981	1982	1983
1. Brazil	50.8	57.1	64.7	72.6	43.9	13.3	15.3	18.1	13.1	6.0	7.6	9.1	8.7
2. Mexico[c]	37.7	43.5	53.5	60.4	38.9	9.6	10.7	11.8	10.6	5.0	6.3	6.1	8.3
3. Argentina	12.6	16.0	23.7	27.1	15.5	2.8	4.4	6.3	7.0	1.3	1.8	3.4	3.1
4. Venezuela[b]	12.3	13.8	14.9	16.5	12.9	4.7	5.0	5.2	4.0	1.5	2.0	2.2	2.0
5. Algeria[b]	17.0	17.3	16.9	16.8	3.2	4.1	4.2	4.6	4.8	1.5	1.7	1.8	1.8
6. Korea Rep.	15.5	17.6	20.0	22.0	8.7	3.3	3.9	4.5	4.3	1.4	1.8	2.1	2.0
7. Iran[b]	10.1	10.0	6.9	5.0	0.2	2.0	5.3	2.9	2.2	0.8	0.9	0.7	0.5
8. Yugoslavia	13.5	15.1	15.1	14.4	4.1	3.3	3.4	3.6	2.4	1.2	1.6	1.5	1.3
9. Chile	7.1	8.9	11.9	13.4	8.5	2.2	3.0	2.4	2.4	0.8	1.1	1.7	1.6
10. Indonesia[b]	15.1	16.6	17.5	20.4	3.8	2.1	2.5	2.8	3.1	1.0	1.2	1.3	1.4
11. Egypt[c]	12.2	13.8	15.2	16.6	0.5	1.5	2.1	2.5	2.3	0.3	0.6	0.6	0.7
12. Saudi Arabia[b]	2.7	2.9	2.4	2.7	0.8	2.0	2.2	2.1	1.8	0.2	0.2	0.2	0.3
13. Nigeria	4.2	5.2	6.0	7.9	3.5	1.2	1.8	2.0	2.0	0.5	0.6	0.9	0.9
14. Iraq[b]	2.3	2.5	3.0	2.2	0.1	1.1	1.8	1.9	0.4	0.2	0.2	0.2	0.2
15. Peru[c]	6.5	7.1	7.4	8.4	2.9	1.6	2.0	1.6	2.0	0.6	0.7	0.9	1.0
16. Philippines	7.5	8.7	10.2	11.9	3.9	1.2	1.7	1.8	1.9	0.6	0.7	1.0	1.1
17. Greece	5.6	7.0	8.2	8.8	5.4	1.3	1.7	1.7	1.9	0.6	1.0	1.0	0.9
18. Turkey	11.8	13.9	14.5	15.0	3.6	1.1	1.3	2.1	3.3	0.6	0.7	1.2	1.1
19. Portugal	5.2	6.0	7.1	9.1	5.2	1.2	1.6	1.8	2.0	0.5	0.7	0.9	1.0
20. India	16.5	18.2	18.9	20.7	0.5	1.4	1.4	1.7	1.9	0.3	0.4	0.6	0.7
Total 20 countries	266.2	301.2	388.1	372.0	165.6	61.2	75.4	81.4	73.4	24.8	31.8	37.5	38.4
(% of grand total LDCs)	(68.1)	(67.7)	(67.5)	(67.4)	(82.6)	(74.3)	(75.7)	(75.7)	(76.4)	(70.5)	(73.6)	(74.6)	(79.8)

Source: OECD (1984), pp. 77 and 78.

Notes: (a) Borrowers are ranked by average debt-service payments in 1981–82. Next-ranking countries include Israel (not including official military debt), Morocco, Thailand, Taiwan, Ivory Coast.

(b) OPEC Member.

(c) Net oil exporter.

(d) Debt-service payments are interest payments plus amortisation (repayment of loan principal).

rolling over loans and extend further credit simply to enable LDCs to appear to be paying off their previously accumulated debts, and the rate at which new credit was extended to LDCs slowed down markedly in 1982 and 1983.

Balance of payments crises are a product of a sudden or final loss of confidence by international bankers in a country's ability to cover a trade deficit. A sudden loss of confidence may occur when, after a period of increasing trade deficits, there is a sharp and unforeseen deterioration in a country's trade prospects due to, say, a decline in its terms of trade − a crop failure leading to a sharp cutback in export volume and earnings is less likely to affect banking confidence since it will usually be discounted as a temporary setback. When export prices fall or import prices rise, this may be seen in the present context as being equivalent to an unanticipated fall in the rate of return to borrowed capital, a fall which may make the initial borrowing uneconomic and its servicing difficult. Conversely, any improvement in the Net Barter terms of trade makes loan servicing easier and reduces the real value of the outstanding debt. A balance of payments crisis may also arise when a country's repeated and prolonged failure to meet expected and target levels of performance on its trading account finally (and fairly suddenly) results in a loss of creditworthiness. Such a situation is likely to occur if there are chronic weaknesses in a country's economic structure of the type discussed in Chapter 12.

Clearly all the underlying conditions were there in 1982–83 for a debt crisis, and ensuring the capacity of LDCs to meet the costs of their outstanding debts plus their continuing participation in world trade called for major debt-rescheduling arragements. The IMF, the Paris Club of Western commercial banks and the Bank of International Settlements all played large roles in these agreements which had two broad aims. On the one hand, there was the need to create confidence among the commercial banks to ensure that they would continue to finance LDCs and, on the other, there was a need to bring about substantial changes in the economic policies of certain LDCs in order to reduce their trade deficits and enable them to finance their debt.

The policy changes required by an LDC to correct a balance of payments crisis have the basic objective of reducing imports and increasing exports; they include the orthodox macroeconomic prescriptions of devaluation and deflation. Devaluation has been the main mechanism argued and insisted upon by the IMF. 'Between 1981 and mid-1983 the real exchange rate of Mexico depreciated by one-third; of Brazil by one-sixth; of Argentina by two-fifths; of Yugoslavia by three-fifths; of Ecuador by two-fifths' (Commonwealth Secretariat 1984, p.60). Its effects in increasing exports are, however, typically slow and may well be meagre. In the case of undifferentiated primary commodity exports and unsophisticated manufactured products there should be little difficulty in finding markets for any available supplies without having to devalue. Devaluation may well stimulate additional exports where there is underutilised production capacity or (in association with deflationary measures) by reducing domestic consumption and thereby releasing additional supplies for export; in the case of agriculture, devaluation may stimulate a switch out of food production into cash crops for export, thus intensifying any underlying problems of malnutrition. In general, however, the effect of devaluation on exports will be delayed and will await the completion of investment projects stimulated by the higher export prices in terms of local currency.

The main impact of devaluation (again combined with deflation) in the short term is upon imports. In the absence of deflationary measures, devaluation alone may have a relatively small impact, given the limited capacity of local industry to produce substitutes for imports. But when accompanied by deflationary measures to cut back public investment and spending, and when supported by special controls to make it harder to import luxury (and even basic essential) items, the effect can be substantial. As a result of this combination of measures, forced upon them by the crisis, the developing countries as a whole managed to reduce imports by $60 billion between 1981 and 1983, with much of this attributable to the main Latin American country borrowers. This had the overall effect, as shown in Table 6.4, of swinging the balance of payments account for goods and services of the NODCs into surplus in 1983 and 1984 from what had been large deficits. The significance of this balance of payments surplus is profound in that it denotes a net transfer of resources from the developing countries to the richer creditor nations. More goods and services were exported for consumption elsewhere than were imported. This is of course precisely the way in which debts are repaid, but there can be little doubt that it entails a major disruption of the investment and development plans of the LDCs concerned. Moreover, the deflationary pressures involved in squeezing trade deficits are often felt most heavily by the poorest classes of society. Higher prices for basic necessities caused by devaluation, reduced employment and reductions in public spending on social services, transport, education and health are all bound to worsen the lot of the poor. In Latin America the middle classes, whose salaries are no longer indexed, have also been hard hit. Thus the effects of the severe deflation in LDC economies have inevitably included the diminution of what are in many cases already low living standards, and a reduction in their rates of economic growth.

Because the adjustments called for in the debtor countries have been so painful, there has been considerable resistance to the orthodox deflationary and devaluation medicine prescribed by the IMF and international bankers, and there have been demands for alternative policies. What are these alternatives? As already discussed, one option would be for the DCs

Table 6.4   Non-Oil Developing Countries: Balance on Current Account and
Interest Payments, 1973–84 ($ billion)

Year	Balance on current account excluding interest payments on external debt and official transfers (1)	Interest payments on external debt (2)
1973	−4.4	6.9
1974	−27.7	9.3
1975	−35.8	10.5
1976	−21.7	10.9
1977	−17.7	12.7
1978	−24.2	18.1
1979	−36.1	25.9
1980	−48.7	39.0
1981	−54.4	54.7
1982	−19.2	63.0
1983	+2.8	59.2
1984[a]	+13.7	63.7

Source: Commonwealth Secretariat (1984).
Notes: China is not included in the years up to 1977.
             (a) Projections.

to increase concessional programme aid, but this they have proved unwilling to do. Another option is for the DCs to support a debt moratorium and write off existing debts. This makes sense precisely because so much of additional LDC debt is extended in the form of credit simply to pay off existing debts. Since it seems manifestly impossible for the LDCs to pay off all their debt in even the medium term, and since it is in the interests of the DCs to maintain a high volume of exports to LDCs, there seems to be an obvious realism to cancelling old debts and wiping some slates clean. This has in fact happened to a limited extent; the UNCTAD Secretariat estimates that some $5.7 billion of debt relief has been granted of which $3.3 billion was in the form of debt cancellation, much of it for the least developed countries. This is of course a minute amount in relation to the end-1983 total debt of the developing countries, which was around $800 billion. Another area in which it is argued that the DCs could take positive action to assist the LDCs would be through trade liberalisation although, as already noted, the impact of this is unlikely to be as large as its supporters urge. It would be of much greater value to LDCs if the DCs were to reduce interest rates and accelerate growth and world trade. This would undoubtedly reduce the cost of their debt and make it easier for LDCs to improve their trade balance in goods and services. Unfortunately, these measures would also lead to accelerating price inflation in the DCs which is precisely what current policies aim to prevent.

There are also policies which the LDCs can pursue, although these may have only limited impact. In Latin America concern has been focused upon the repatriation of profits from the TNCs to headquarters in other countries. In the last decade LDCs have reacted by channelling considerable efforts into devising contracts and regulations which try to control and monitor excess profits, transfer prices and management charges. But it is not only TNCs which have been responsible for capital transfers from LDCs. In Latin America in particular, rich citizens and local firms transferred enormous sums to North America and Europe to protect their funds against correctly anticipated currency devaluations. The Bank of International Settlements reported (1984) that an estimated $55 billion had been exported in this way from Latin America between 1978 and 1983. Control of such capital exodus is a question for LDC policy, and indicates that a sizeable responsibility rests with the LDCs.

The debt crises of the early 1980s were not confined to Latin America, and the fact that international actions between 1982 and 1984 focused upon containment of the problem in the major debtor countries should not be allowed to obscure the high indebtedness of some of the East Asian NICs, or the deteriorating situation of many low-income countries, particularly those in Africa. The latter is something clearly emphasised by the Commonwealth Secretariat Report and illustrated by one of its tables, presented here as Table 6.5. Comparing these data with those in Table 6.2 indicates that the indebtedness position of the low-income developing countries as a whole did not deteriorate as rapidly as that of all NODCs. They were of course helped by a lower reliance upon commercial borrowings than the upper- and middle-income NODCs, and by the fact that some larger low-income countries such as India and Pakistan managed to contain their borrowing relatively well. However, in contrast, the position of the low-income African countries can be seen to have deteriorated very rapidly in the decade 1973–83; the debt to export and debt service ratios of these countries more than trebled in this period. The combination of higher debt-service payments and weak export growth combined to produce a sharp decline in net transfers to African countries, as well as a smaller decline for low-income Asia: 'In Africa, 16 countries registered negative transfers at some time in the period 1971–81' (Commonwealth Secretariat 1984, p.41). The profound significance of this reduction in resource transfers can be assessed by contrasting it with FAO's (1981) projections of the level of external assistance required for LDC agriculture in order to tackle the problem of malnutrition. FAO's estimates call for a three to fourfold increase in real external assistance for LDC agriculture alone.

Table 6.5 Features of Low-Income Developing Country, and African External
Public Debt[a]

	1973	1980	1981	1982	1983
1. *Total outstanding debt* ($bn)					
Low-income countries	25.4	71.4	75.2	81.8	87.8
Africa	14.2	50.9	55.5	62.5	66.3
2. *Ratio of external debt to exports*					
Low-income countries	227.9	134.8	133.3	146.5	148.9
Africa	71.5	143.2	168.6	204.5	223.5
3. *Share of official creditors in long-term total debt*					
Low-income countries	84.5	76.0	79.0	81.1	82.3
Africa	47.8	45.2	46.5	46.8	48.7
4. *Share of short-term debt in total debt*					
Low-income countries	2.3	5.9	4.3	3.3	2.6
Africa	2.7	8.4	11.1	12.6	11.0
5. *Debt service ratio*[b]					
Low-income countries	14.6	19.3	12.6	14.6	13.3
Africa	8.8	17.4	19.7	23.7	25.1
6. *Interest payments ratio*					
Low-income countries	6.1	4.4	5.1	5.4	5.4
Africa	5.9	8.1	9.2	11.0	10.8

Source: Commonwealth Secretariat (1984), Table 3.2.
Notes: (a) Low-income countries exclude China for 1973. Africa includes some
middle-income countries and excludes South Africa for years 1980
onwards. All ratios are given in percentages.
(b) Payments (interest, amortisation or both) as percentages of exports of
goods and services.

This underlines that the debt crisis is far from over. Simply financing
existing debt is going to pre-empt a substantial proportion of LDC exports
in the foreseeable future. Even satisfying a minimum of LDCs' extra
needs is bound to entail additional transfers, extra indebtedness and great
problems of debt servicing. For the resumption of even moderate
economic growth, many LDCs are going to require additional transfers
and loans from DCs, and this is going to place great strains upon the aid
and international finance systems.

Notes

1. This percentage is calculated from Table 6.1 in terms of row numbers as:

   $[B-(C.2 + C.3)]/B$.

2. Countries in this situation are also typically short of foreign exchange, hence the rationale for food aid rather than commercial imports.
3. The form of consumption function used by Griffin (1971, p.158) is:

   $$C = d + a(Y + A)$$

   where C = consumption, Y = a measure of national income (it is not precisely clear what measure, since the consumption is also assumed to be possible out of A), A = capital inflows, a = the marginal propensity to consume, and d is an intercept constant. If one accepts this, then the savings identity would seem logically to be:

   $$S = (Y + A) - C$$

   rather than

   $$S = Y - C$$

   as suggested by Griffin. Using the correct savings identity, the savings function becomes:

   $$S = -d + (1-a)Y + (1-a)A$$

   and not, as Griffin obtains,

   $$S = -d + (1-a)Y - aA$$

   This is a very significant difference. In contrast to Griffin's result which indicates that capital inflows are associated with a reduction in domestic savings, the correct result shows them to be positively associated with domestic savings.
4. In this case aid/foreign capital's contribution to growth should be formally restated as:

   $$g_A = \frac{s'-s}{k} + (1-c) \cdot \frac{A}{Y} \cdot \frac{1}{k'}$$

5. The 'Evolution of the Debt Problem' between 1978 and 1984 is well reviewed in OECD (1984), pp. 9–14.

References

Bank of International Settlements (1984) *Annual Report 1984*, Geneva.

Bauer, P.T. (1971) *Dissent on Development*, Weidenfeld and Nicolson.

Bhagwati, J. (1967) 'The tying of aid', *UNCTAD Secretariat: Progress Report*, TD/7/Supp 4, United Nations. Reprinted as Ch.10 of Bhagwati and Eckaus (1970).

Bhagwati, J. and Eckaus, R.S. (1970) (eds) *Foreign Aid*, Penguin Books.
BOUIES (1971) 'Foreign capital, domestic savings and economic development: three comments and a reply', *Bulletin of Oxford Institute of Economics and Statistics*, 33(2).
Cathie, J. (1982) *The Political Economy of Food Aid*, Gower.
Chenery, H.B. and Bruno, M. (1962) 'Development alternatives in an open economy: the case of Israel', *Economic Journal*, 72.
Chenery, H.B. and Strout, A.M. (1966) 'Foreign assistance and economic development', *American Economic Review*, 61(4).
Commonwealth Secretariat (1984) *The Debt Crisis and the World Economy*, Report by a Commonwealth Group of Experts, London.
Eshag, E. (1971) 'Comment', in BOUIES (1971).
FAO (1981) *Agriculture Toward 2000*, Rome.
Garcia-Thoumi, I. (1983) 'ODA from developed countries', *Finance and Development*, 20(2), IMF and World Bank, Washington.
Griffin, K. (1970) 'Foreign capital, domestic savings and economic development', *Bulletin of Oxford Institute of Economics and Statistics*, 32(2).
Griffin, K. (1971) 'Reply' in BOUIES (1971).
Hart, J. (1973) *Aid in Liberation*, Gollancz.
Hayter, T. (1971) *Aid as Imperialism*, Penguin Books.
Isenman, P.J. and Singer, H.W. (1977) 'Food aid: disincentive effects and policy implications', *Economic Development and Cultural Change*, 25(2).
Kennedy, C. and Thirlwall, A.P. (1971) 'Comment', in BOUIES (1971).
McKinnon, R.I. (1964) 'Foreign exchange constraints in economic development and efficient aid allocation', *Economic Journal*, 54.
OECD (1984) *External Debt of Developing Countries: 1983 Survey*, Paris.
Papanek, G.F. (1972) 'The effect of aid and other resource transfers on savings and growth in less developed countries', *Economic Journal*, 82(327).
Payer, C. (1974) *The Debt Trap*, Penguin Books.
Pearson, L.B. (Chairman) (1969) *Partners in Development: Report of the Commission on International Development*, Pall Mall Press.
Schultz, T.W. (1960) 'Value of US farm surpluses to underdeveloped countries', *Journal of Farm Economics*, 42. Reprinted as Ch.12 of Bhagwati and Eckaus (1970).
Singer, H. (1978) *Food Aid Policies and Programmes: A Survey of Studies of Food Aid*, WFP/CFA, 5/5c.
Stevens, C. (1979) *Food Aid and the Developing World – Four African Case Studies*, Croom Helm.
Stewart, F. (1971) 'Comment', in BOUIES (1971).
UNCTAD (1967) *UNCTAD Secretariat: Progress Report*, TD/7/Supp 8, United Nations.

7

Agricultural transformation and economic development

During the process of economic development the agricultural sector is transformed, both internally and in its relationship with other economic sectors. The dimensions of this transformation are not only economic but also include formal and informal institutional changes which are sociological or political in character.

Examination of these changes can be pursued from a predominantly historical standpoint by analysing in detail the actual processes of transformation in different societies in the past (Ohkawa and Rosovsky 1960; Boserup 1965; Myrdal 1971). Alternatively, the process may be examined in a potentially more prescriptive way by developing simplified models of change to use in posing questions about what should occur for economic development to achieve specified goals, or what might occur in specified circumstances (Lewis 1954; Ranis and Fei 1961; Nicholls 1963; Jorgenson 1970). In fact there is a degree of complementarity between the two approaches, the historical study serving to isolate apparent key changes and their nature as a basis for the specification of the theoretical models. It is apparent, however, that this complementarity cannot be complete as there is no obvious reason why the pattern of historical development of any currently rich countries should be closely followed by any of the currently poor nations in their quest for material advance. Not only does an international pool of technology and experience exist which might enable the poor countries to short-cut some of the steps taken by the now rich nations, but the environment facing the poor countries is substantially different in largely adverse ways from that faced by the rich nations before their industrial development; population growth rates are far higher in poor nations today than they were in Europe in the eighteenth and nineteenth centuries; commercial competition for export markets is now more intense; the material expectations of people are higher because of external contacts through different media; the rate of technological advance in the rich countries gives them a remarkable and seemingly ineradicable edge in economic competition; and history, of colonialism in particular, has created a legacy of institutions and commercial structures which shape current options for development. Nevertheless, it is accepted that there are some general characteristics of the development process which on historical evidence will feature in the transformation of currently poor countries as and when their development intensifies. For the agricultural sector, certainly, there is a consensus about the basic pattern of change, and this will be briefly considered below.

~ The main reason for attempting to identify characteristic transformation patterns is to assist in the formulation of policies to accelerate development. If a clear view can be formed in advance of the required structural change in a national economy, particularly with respect to the changing relationship between sectors, then it should be possible to frame more effective policies to speed up development and to avoid potential bottlenecks and blockages to change. Thus, after considering some general aspects of structural transformation in development, in particular those concerned with agriculture, it is logical to proceed to discussion of the policy choices poor countries face in expediting development. Ideally the links between agriculture and other sectors of the economy require that policy strategies start with an integrated approach in which the choice of agricultural policy is conditioned by the choices made for the public and various industrial sectors of the economy. That such integration is necessary is clearly indicated by the discussion of theories of development (Chapter 2), and from the observation (e.g. Balassa *et al.* 1971; Ranis 1983) that commercial policies pursued by poor countries to foster industrialisation have often had effects which might inhibit agricultural expansion. Nevertheless, for expository purposes agricultural development policies will have to be considered principally from a narrowly agricultural standpoint, with the primary emphasis being placed upon technology policy.

7.1 Key Features of Agriculture's Transformation

One universally recognised feature of structural economic change is that as countries develop, the proportions of GDP and employment accounted for by agriculture must decline. This stands to reason, for improved living standards entail an increasing personal consumption of goods and services other than food, and this necessitates a concomitant rise in the proportion of human and other resources allocated to non-agricultural production. It has escaped few people's attention that in the rich countries of Western Europe and the USA, agriculture accounts for less than 10% of the labour force, while by contrast in many of the poorest countries less than 20% of the active population are supported by employment outside the agricultural sector (see Table 7.1). This observation has been central to the perception of how development should occur, and of the role the agricultural sector should play in this. Industry is perceived to be the leading sector in development while agriculture is accorded a declining

Table 7.1 Population Engaged in Agriculture and Income Levels Per Capita in Selected Countries, 1960 and 1970

	Percentage of economically active population in agriculture			GDP per capita (US $)		
	1960	*1970*	*1982*	*1960*	*1970*	*1982*
Central African Republic	94.1	87.2	86.3	n.a.	113	n.a.
Kenya	85.8	80.4	76.5	84	143	344
Ghana	61.5	54.8	49.2	198	263	668
Malawi	92.5	87.5	82.3	39	70	213
Nigeria	70.8	67.0	51.4	80	138	825
Tanzania	89.4	85.9	79.8	53	95	253
Burma	68.3	63.7	50.4	61	80	167
India	74.1	67.7	61.7	73	96	242
Indonesia	74.8	70.0	57.3	73	74	575
Malaysia	63.6	56.5	46.2	73	333	1,781
Nepal	94.4	91.6	92.3	n.a.	76	150
Pakistan	76.0	70.5	53.5	81	175	355
South Korea	66.4	58.0	38.6	150	266	1,734
Thailand	83.8	76.5	74.4	96	182	759
Turkey	78.2	69.1	51.5	190	362	1,143
Egypt	58.5	54.8	49.6	129	232	711
Iran	53.9	46.3	37.0	204	355	2,378[1]
Iraq	53.2	46.6	39.0	245	371	n.a.
Libya	55.8	42.6	13.0	143	1,871	10,017[1]
Saudi Arabia	71.5	60.5	58.9	352	886	12,094
Brazil	51.9	43.7	36.6	247	461	2,232
Chile	29.8	25.4	17.5	274	872	1,456
Colombia	51.5	45.2	25.7	252	370	1,424
Mexico	55.1	46.6	34.3	331	710	2,346
Peru	52.5	45.6	35.9	242	523	1,204
Australia	11.4	8.4	5.4	1,580	3,020	10.988
Canada	13.1	8.0	4.6	2,229	3,888	12,098
German Federal Republic	14.3	9.3	3.5	1,301	3,039	10,689
Japan	32.9	20.7	9.7	462	1,969	8,973
UK	4.0	2.8	1.9	1,360	2,214	8,495
USA	6.6	4.0	2.0	2,797	4,826	13,152
USSR	42.1	31.9	15.1	n.a.	1,327	2,674

Source: UN, FAO (1973 and 1983) *Production Yearbook*, and UN (1980 and 1982) *National Account Statistics*.
Note: (1) 1981 data.

role. This has led many countries to adopt negative policies towards agriculture in which emphasis has been placed on accelerating the transfer of investible resources away from agriculture into industry and the public sector.

Underlying this strategy was the anticipation that, in line with the historic precedents of the USA, Western Europe and Japan, rapid expansion of industry would create demand for labour on a scale that would require a transfer of labour from the agricultural and handicraft sectors. This in turn would raise rural living standards and would reduce population pressure on the land in the most populous countries, thus paving the way for the reorganisation of agriculture into larger sized holdings. It would also require an increase in agricultural efficiency for a sufficiently large marketable food surplus to be transferred to the burgeoning urbanised industrial labour force and their families. Also, because of the dominance of the agricultural sector in poor countries, it was evident that the capital to finance industrial expansion, at least in the early stages of development, would have to be largely raised from agriculture by taxation, voluntary transfer (savings) or by encouraging the terms of trade to move against agriculture and in favour of industrial goods; apparently in Japan at the end of the nineteenth century over 80% of the central government tax revenue was contributed by the land tax (Ohkawa and Rosovsky 1960).[1]

Reflecting the dominant theoretical views of the early 1960s, Kuznets (1961) succinctly summarised these changing relationships between agriculture and the rest of the economy in terms of three 'contributions' to development. Firstly, there is the 'product contribution' whereby an increasing amount of food is supplied to the expanding non-agricultural population, and industrial crops are produced as a basis for processing industry. Secondly, there is the 'factor contribution' through which agriculture supplies the rest of the economy with labour and a net outflow of capital; it is perhaps emphasis on these aspects of change which led to some of the more negative aspects of agricultural policy, i.e. those of squeezing as much as possible out of agriculture. Thirdly, there is the 'market contribution whereby agricultural revenue from cash sales (domestically and for export) creates a demand for products of the industrial sector; agricultural exports also create a flow of foreign exchange which can be used to purchase capital items from abroad. Inadequate allowance for this third factor may partially account for the under-utilisation of the industrial capacity created by India in the 1950s.

7.2 Conflicting Policy Objectives

As already noted, in the 1950s and 1960s, development policies emphasised extracting a surplus out of agriculture to invest in the other expanding sectors of the economy. This fitted in with the thrust of development theory, as reflected by dual-sector models, in which an emergent agricultural surplus was seen as a necessary condition of general development (see, in particular, Nicholls (1963) and Jorgenson (1970)). Kuznets's list of agriculture's contributions to development can be reinterpreted as identifying the various means and forms through which this surplus could be transferred. The surplus could be extracted through (1) a marketed food surplus transferred at low prices; (2) export and cash crop production promoted both as a source of foreign exchange and to provide a base for taxing agriculture;[2] (3) savings and taxes of farmers which could be channelled into non-agricultural investment; (4) surplus labour which would be siphoned off as wage differentials grew; and (5) by turning the terms of trade against agriculture, thus forcing farmers to pay more for domestically produced manufactured inputs and to receive less for their produce than would otherwise be the case. The latter results from import tariff and restriction policies for protecting domestic industry from foreign competition, which simultaneously raise agricultural input prices and produce an overvalued exchange rate which depresses local currency receipts from agricultural exports. Modes of extraction (1) and (2) correspond to the product contribution, (3) and (4) to the factor contribution, and (5) relates to a stronger form of the market contribution whereby the agricultural sector is encouraged to buy more domestically produced manufactured goods, but on disadvantageous terms which aid the transfer of farming profits to industry.

From a forward-looking rather than an historical perspective, the 'contributions' of agriculture may be reinterpreted as policy objectives. Examining these through the modes of extraction listed above reveals a number of self-evident contradictions between policy objectives. Amongst the most readily apparent of these are those between (1) increasing the marketed food surplus and keeping food prices low; (2) increasing foreign exchange earnings through export crop production and expanding food production; and (3) taxing agriculture heavily (either through direct taxation or overvalued exchange rates) and increasing production of either food or export/industrial crops.

Clearly, however, these are not simply conflicts bounded within the restricted sphere of agricultural policy, to be resolved inside Ministries of Agriculture; they also reflect problems of achieving balance between agriculture and other sectors. Low food prices are desirable from the standpoint of keeping down wages in the non-agricultural sector, but they reduce the welfare and capacity to invest of those farmers with a marketed surplus, and they may diminish the welfare of agricultural labourers whose money wage income may be reduced, causing their real income to be lower despite lower food prices. The greater the priority given to accelerating industrialisation, or to public sector growth, the greater the pressure to squeeze agriculture hard, to extract the maximum surplus, and to sacrifice the welfare of agriculturalists. The same conflict of objectives is mirrored in the trade-off between food and export crop production. To meet industry's import requirements for capital and intermediate goods, priority has to be assigned to increasing exports and foreign exchange earnings. In the absence of oil or other large-scale forms of exploitable mineral resources, agricultural policy is directed to emphasise export crop production. This entails drawing resources away from food production and heightens problems of stimulating an adequate marketed food surplus at 'reasonable' prices. One controversial way of resolving this conflict is to encourage the growth of large commercial grain-producing farms which market nearly all their output, but to simultaneously play down the allocation of resources to the traditional small-peasant farm sector. This is controversial and, as will be explored more fully below, it may be interpreted as representing (in Lipton's (1968) terms) the assertion of 'urban bias' in policy formulations, or in de Janvry's (1981) terms, as creating a dominated, exploitable sub-economy of the rural peasantry.

In the frictionless world of equilibrium models of the dual-economy class, gross conflicts such as those above are glossed over by exploring only solutions which have balance and harmony imposed upon them. Through closed-economy assumptions domestic food production and total food demand are forced to be equal, as are the marketed food surplus and the food requirement of the non-agricultural population. Also, by assuming away or fixing real income differentials, model solutions are explored in which there are no divergences between agricultural and industrial wages or prices. Balance between all these sets of factors does not necessarily accompany economic development in reality. Food imports can be used to bridge the gap between total domestic food supply and demand, or more specifically between the marketed food surplus and food requirements of the non-agricultural sector. Likewise, subject to the operation of labour and other markets, there is nothing to prevent divergence between the living standards of different groups in society. Because, in the poorest countries there is a close association between poverty and the agricultural sector, these conflicts of interest assume great importance in debates about agricultural policy.

Another factor which has greatly complicated the formulation of agricultural policy in the poorest countries is that workforce growth continues to outstrip the rate of job creation in the non-agricultural sectors. Thus, far from there being a need for agriculture to release labour to the rest of the economy, there is pressure for it, and the rural economy generally, to absorb more labour. A major factor behind this is the high population growth rates in many LDCs. As indicated in Table 8.3 in Chapter 8, the annual rate of population growth over the last two decades has varied from 2.5% in the Far East to a high of 2.8% in Africa. This compares most unfavourably with the comparable rates of population growth in Western European countries in the years preceding the start of their

Table 7.2 Changes in the Structure of the Active Population of the Less Developed Countries between 1900 and 1979, According to Type of Employment[1]

Percentages	1900	1920	1930	1950	1960	1970	1980
Agriculture	77.9	77.6	76.6	73.3	70.7	66.0	60.1
Extractive industries		0.4	0.4	0.6	0.6		
Manufacturing industries	9.8	8.5	8.5	7.6	8.9	13.0	15.9
Construction		1.0	1.1	1.8	2.0		
Trade, banking		5.4	5.4	5.8	5.9		
Transport communication	12.3	1.6	1.8	2.0	2.2	21.0	24.0
Services		5.5	6.1	8.9	9.6		
Total	100	100	100	100	100	100	100
Absolute figures (millions)							
Agriculture	213.0	238.0	249.0	304.0	366.0	435.0	489.2
Extractive industries		1.1	1.3	2.5	3.2		
Manufacturing industries	26.5	26.0	27.7	31.5	46.0	85.0	129.5
Construction		2.9	3.6	7.2	10.6		
Trade, banking		16.4	17.6	24.2	30.8		
Transport communication	33.5	4.9	6.0	8.3	11.4	140.0	195.6
Services		16.9	19.9	17.0	49.9		
Total	273.0	306.0	325.0	415.0	518.0	660.0	814.3

Sources: 1900 to 1970 from Bairoch (1975, p.160).
1980 calculated using the data for Economically Active Population (FAO 1984) and percentage shares of labour by sector (World Development Report 1984).
Note: (1) Excludes the People's Republic of China.

industrial development; in the eighteenth and nineteenth centuries Western European population growth was 0.5 to 0.7% per annum (Bairoch 1975, p.8).

In the poorest countries industrial, public sector and service job creation has not been adequate to counteract these high population growth rates. Although rates of industrial output growth in LDCs have been high by the historical standards of the now rich countries (see Table 9.2, Chapter 9, for details), this has not in many countries been matched by comparable industrial job creation. Consequently, for the LDCs as a whole, the workforce attributed to the agricultural sector is continuing to increase. This is revealed by the updated version of Bairoch's interesting table, presented here as Table 7.2. As can be seen, between 1950 and 1980 agriculture absorbed 185 million, or almost half, of the estimated 399 million increase in the economically active population of LDCs. True, over the same period the overall proportion of the active population in agriculture is estimated to have fallen from 73.3% to 60.1% of the total, which conforms to the broadly expected pattern of transformation.[3] Nevertheless, the recent large increase in numbers primarily dependent upon agriculture presages yet a further increase at least until the end of the century for the LDCs taken all together.

Many middle-income LDCs have already passed the peak of their agricultural labour force and are on the paths of decline and consolidation of holdings. Some of these, such as Nigeria, Malaysia, South Korea, the oil-rich Middle-East countries, and the bigger Latin American countries, already stand out from Table 7.1 as having passed the peak. But many of the poorer African and South Asian countries still have to plan to absorb more people into agriculture (or at least into the rural and informal sectors) for many years to come. It is a simple matter to use Dovring's (1959) formula to calculate approximately when the agricultural labour force of individual countries will reach its maximum, or to calculate what rate of non-agricultural job creation is required to halt its expansion.[4] For instance, a country such as Tanzania, with a 2.5% population growth rate and around 80% of its workforce in agriculture, would need a net expansion in industrial jobs of 12.5% per year to bring about a decline in the agricultural labour force. Since currently industrial and service sector jobs are being created in Tanzania at much below this rate, the agricultural labour turning point may not even be achieved in the next century.[5] Other very poor countries such as Bangladesh, Ethiopia and Nepal are even further away from this goal.

The preceding discussion reveals certain other conflicts relating to agricultural policy, and it underscores certain obstacles to rational debate which arise from use of the broad conventional categories which have been created for the purposes of theoretical analysis and statistical description. Consider what is meant by the statement that 80% of the economically active population are involved in agriculture. Does this mean that 80% of all workers are engaged full-time in crop and livestock production, and derive little of their income from non-farming activities? It is clear that it does not. Agriculture in such a context is something of a residual category into which people are classified by default. Thus, in two-sector theoretical models, large-scale commercial agriculture has been classed as part of the capitalist,[6] industrial sector, and the term 'agricultural' is applied to the whole non-capitalist, subsistence sector (Ranis and Fei 1961; Jorgenson 1970). Using this definition all people in domestic service, or in the urban informal sector (shoe-shine 'boys', street beggars, etc.) are lumped together with peasant farmers, rural labourers, village craftsmen and the openly unemployed, as belonging to the agricultural sector. In fact, the number 'employed' in the urban informal sector plus the number of urban unemployed is typically large in the major cities of developing countries and constitutes one of the most serious modern social and political problems in these countries. It is highly arbitrary to classify agricultural employment in a way which includes such people. It is often the case, however, that these fringe urban dwellers retain close links with their rural origins, and are supported by relatives in rural areas while seeking to establish an urban economic base. Given their skills and rural contacts they could, if the opportunity were created, probably be drawn back into agricultural (or rural) employment more readily than they could be assimilated into industrial occupations.

In a different set of contexts the terms 'agricultural' and 'rural' are often used interchangeably, while a similar tendency is followed in equating 'industrial' with 'urban'. In fact the rural sector contains much more economic activity even in poor countries than just primary agriculture, i.e. farming. In addition to service activities for farming at both the input supply and product marketing ends, the rural areas provide a wide range of employment activities serving basic human needs, e.g. weaving, pottery, house construction, etc. Thus if rural development is defined as improved living standards for the non-urban population, it must be recognised that success in agricultural development may not be synonymous with that in rural development. Furthermore, it would entail placing an extraordinary burden upon agricultural policy in the poorest countries to ask it to resolve simultaneously all the conflicts between expanding food output, increasing export earnings, achieving high technical and economic efficiency, and absorbing ever more workers in order to prevent them drifting, unwanted, to overcrowded urban areas. Most agriculturalists and agricultural development economists have, at least implicitly, rejected the notion that all these policy conflicts can be satisfactorily resolved through the medium of agricultural policy, and the principal emphasis has been upon 'productivist' policies emphasising output expansion and rapid technological change. In emphasising these goals they have sought to establish the need for a positive role for agriculture and to overcome the negative, extractive mentality engendered by the early theorising.

7.3   Some Issues of Agricultural Technology

Faced by the pressures of rapid population growth and even more rapid food demand growth it is inevitable that a high policy priority in LDCs is accorded to increasing food production. As a result of severe indebtedness and balance of payments difficulties this pressure extends to increased agricultural production for export. The scope for LDCs to achieve the desired output increase (of the order of 3% per annum) by bringing more arable land under cultivation has progressively diminished. If China is included, about 70% of the population of LDCs live in countries which are land scarce, i.e. in countries already cultivating more than 70% of the potential arable land.[7] Countries which have a relative abundance of land to be cultivated are mainly in Latin America and Africa, but as the current agricultural crisis in Africa demonstrates, the availability of additional land with arable potential does not necessarily imply easy solutions. Rather, the main way of achieving agricultural output growth will have to be through increasing yields per hectare. This in turn will be achieved through the further uptake and more intensive use of new technology in LDC agriculture. The new technology will take many forms, such as improved seeds, increased application of chemicals, use of new forms of tree crop management, mechanisation or investment in improved irrigation and drainage; but its essential characteristic is that it is technology based upon modern methods of agricultural science.

Following upon the work of Hayami and Ruttan (1971) there is clear evidence that the type and direction of technological change are influenced by market forces. Their hypothesis of 'induced innovation' is that relative factor scarcities (as reflected in relative factor prices) cause changes in factor use which tend to save (increase the productivity of) the scarcer factors. Thus in countries with land shortage, and high land – labour price ratios, such as Japan and Taiwan, technological change in the 1950s and 1960s greatly increased land productivity (i.e. yields) but had a relatively small effect upon labour productivity; whereas in land-abundant but relatively scarce-labour countries, such as Venezuela, Argentina or the United States, the main impact of technological change was upon output per worker rather than yields.[8] Underlying this process of induced technical innovation are the responses of various classes of entrepreneurs and of public institutions:

(1) The dominant behaviour of rationally motivated farmers involves expanding production by increasing, mainly, the use of those new inputs which reduce the need for additional units of the relatively most expensive traditional inputs. Thus in land-scarce, labour-abundant areas farmers will tend to increase the use of fertiliser, improved seeds, and insecticides (the so-called 'biological' technology inputs) more rapidly than tractors and other forms of 'mechanical' technology. In other words, their emphasis will be on land- rather than labour-saving technology.

(2) Input manufacturing, importing and marketing firms in the private sector will identify the opportunities for profitably increasing the supply of those inputs in demand by farmers, and will respond accordingly.

(3) It is also argued that in public research institutions, research programmes will tend to respond to market forces and will be induced to concentrate on increasing returns to the scarcest factors of production.

(4) At an even higher level it is argued by Binswanger and Ruttan (1978) that market forces also induce institutional innovation, so that new institutions are created and old ones modified to increase the responsiveness of research and technology supply to market opportunities.

While the evidence for induced technological innovation is strong, it cannot be inferred that market forces will necessarily lead to rapid or optimal rates of technological change. Of course, if induced institutional change is defined to include all public-sector changes which affect technological change then, tautologically, all technological change is market induced. But that is grossly oversimplistic; for, although the public sector plays a central role in LDCs in mobilising resources for technological change, and governments also exert considerable influence on market signals through price and tax instruments, policy is aimed at a broad set of not necessarily consistent objectives. The impact of particular institutional changes can easily be nullified by negative price policies. Many instances have been observed where major public campaigns of exhortation of farmers to adopt a new technology have failed because product prices were depressed under policies pursued by state marketing boards.

Schultz (1964), in his influential book *Transforming Traditional Agriculture*, propounded the view that traditional agriculture was characterised by zero or very low productivity growth, and that the potential of existing technology had been exhausted by poor farmers who had already achieved high levels of economic efficiency. Traditional farmers in LDCs were perceived as being 'poor but efficient' and as being caught in a low-equilibrium trap. The key to springing this trap was seen by Schultz[9] to require the supply of new productivity-increasing technology, or of 'sources of permanent income streams', which was how he characterised investment. If new inputs and methods of production were made available, he argued, traditional peasant farmers would react by saving to invest in the new technology, thus leading to increased production.

While this view of peasant farmers as 'poor but efficient' is open to criticism (see next section, and Ghatak and Ingersent 1984, pp.127–42), there is general acceptance of the implication that market forces may be too weak to induce adequate technological change. Hence it is accepted that publicly funded research, at both national and international levels, is an essential element in agricultural development policy. A considerable body of empirical analysis has now been amassed which indicates that the social returns to agricultural research tend to be very high. This is revealed in Evenson's (1981) summary of a large number of such studies; of the sixty or so estimates of annual rates of return reported, only three are less than 10%, the majority exceed 40% and some research projects are estimated to have yielded returns of over 100% per year. However, inevitably the distribution of the benefits from research is uneven, but in many instances it is uneven in a particularly noteworthy way. In an analysis of the social returns to modern rice varieties in Colombia, Scobie and Posada (1978) estimated the annual rate of return to the country as a whole to lie between 79 and 96%, but they also estimated that producers (both those who adopted the technology and those who did not) actually suffered a loss of welfare and that it was only consumers who gained. Put at its simplest, the reason for this is that technological change causes the supply curve to shift to the right more quickly than demand, which causes product prices to fall. The more inelastic is demand the greater the price reduction. This is of course precisely the basis for general economic development; technological change leads to real price reductions enabling consumers to spend an increasing proportion of their income on non-basic goods. Technical innovation is beneficial to society, but competitive market forces mean that innovating producers may be unable to increase their profits and indeed may even (in the Colombian rice case) suffer a diminution of profits. It is because of this that Schultz (1979) argues, 'The only meaningful approach to modern agricultural research is to conceptualise most of its contributions as *public goods*. As such that must be paid for on public account'.

As Hillman and Monke (1983) argue, the institutional structures and information processing systems required for vigorously responsive (induced) research programmes are often lacking in LDCs. Only 4% of world agricultural research and development (R&D) expenditures are made by LDCs. The overwhelming proportion of agricultural R&D expenditure is accounted for by the industrialsed countries. It is hardly surprising, therefore, that much attention in the last two decades has been devoted to the issue of international technology transfer from DCs to LDCs. This is seen as a way of short-cutting and cheapening the costs of agricultural R&D in the LDCs and of speeding up and supporting local research programmes.

A powerful stimulus to investment in international technology transfer was the success in the 1950s of the Rockerfeller Foundation's support from 1943 of what was later to become CIMMYT (*Centro Internacional de Mejoramiento de Maiz y Trigo*) in Mexico, and of the research programme at the Philippines College of Agriculture (started in 1956 with Rockerfeller Foundation support) which was the basis for the foundation of IRRI (the International Rice Research Institute). These institutes, by applying the then latest methods in plant-breeding and agricultural science, and by bringing together large international teams of scientists, produced the dwarf high-yielding varieties of wheat (at CIMMYT) and rice (at IRRI) along with improved husbandry recommendations which formed the basis of what has come to be popularly known as the Green

Revolution. The perceived success of this combination of modern scientific methods with international capital and scientists was adopted as a model, when in 1971 CGIAR (the Consultative Group on International Agricultural Research) was set up to take over the funding of CIMMYT and IRRI (plus two other centres, CIAT and IITA) to tackle other technology transfer problems – since 1964 nine new centres have been either absorbed into the CGIAR system or newly created.[10]

That there is international support for the IARCs does not in any way diminish the importance which must attach to local research programmes. Internationally orientated research programmes are best suited to technologies which are widely adaptable to the environmental conditions in a large number of countries. Evenson (1981) identifies as the outstanding examples of wide adaptability the dwarf wheat and rice varieties produced at CIMMYT and IRRI and the 'interspecific' sugar-cane hybrids developed in Java and India in the 1920s. Even in these cases local adaptive research programmes have significantly enhanced the value of the international varieties to particular locations. There are, however, crops, such as maize, where environmental tolerance is low and for which local adaptive research is of prime importance.

The significance of local LDC research and knowledge is underlined by critics who argue that the international technology transfer process incorporates within it systematic biases, which devalue local ideas and methods, and emphasise the superiority of Western (and particularly midwestern USA) technological solutions to agricultural problems. Chambers (1983), and Biggs and Clay (1983) highlight instances where important local production systems (e.g. relating to goats, donkeys and local trees) have been largely ignored in framing research and production plans, or where sophisticated local knowledge of agricultural conditions was overlooked until plans were well advanced. In the past, inadequate research attention has been given to drought resistant food crops in Africa, to pulses, or to tree management (for fuel and erosion control); while the bulk of attention has been given to export crops and a few major food crops. Among the arguments of these critics are that if agricultural development is to benefit the rural poor, research programmes should be more closely geared to the perception which the poor have of their problems, to the resources they work with, and to their own ranking of agricultural priorities and ideas for solutions. What is wanted is a 'bottom-up' rather than a 'top-down' approach to agricultural development policy or, in the terms of the subtitle to Chambers's book, 'putting the last first'.

Arguments for more 'bottom-up' emphasis in agricultural development planning can be illuminated by reference to the issue of conflicting policy objectives. Such arguments represent a plea for more emphasis to be placed upon equalising the distribution of development benefits and upon the rural poor, and for less emphasis on 'first-world' values, 'urban-bias' and the extraction of agricultural surplus for non-agricultural development. Chambers, however, does not explicitly argue that 'putting the last first' will increase national economic growth or that there is no trade off between growth and equity; for him, as for de Janvry (1981), it is more a question of placing elimination of the poverty trap at the top of the development agenda.

Undoubtedly there have been many examples where agricultural development schemes based on experience with projects previously executed in other countries have failed because, with hindsight, they have taken insufficient account of local conditions. These, and other projects which have been successful, were promoted in an attempt to accelerate development, to modernise agriculture and to short-cut the local learning process. It was because of the paucity of local research and institutional capacity that so many early agricultural development projects have been based on imported models. Inevitably these shortcomings have been rectified to some extent over the last two decades, and the very fact that many local agricultural systems are now seen to be rationally based upon a sophisticated local understanding of conditions reflects an increase in research into traditional farming systems. There is now widespread support for what is now called farming systems research.[11] To some extent this has originated with CIMMYT and IRRI, which have developed new methods for testing agricultural technology in farmers' own fields (as opposed to only in experiment stations), and for efficiently assessing local conditions. Increasingly these, and other IARCs, are involved in collaborative research with local institutions in many LDCs. For Chambers and other critics, this may not be sufficient to eliminate 'first-world biases', but it does reflect an increasing orientation of research to local requirements. Nevertheless, the fact remains that underlying this particular issue is the question of which agricultural policy objectives should receive most emphasis. Should it be growth, increased marketed output and exports, equity, or is it feasible to combine growth with equity? Essentially the same questions underlie the issue of appropriate technology.

Observers may attach the adjective 'inappropriate' to a whole range of technological and production changes in LDCs. To some, the promotion of export crops rather than food crops, or the encouragement of large-scale estate and company agriculture in preference to peasant farming, is seen as unambiguously inappropriate. Criticism (e.g. Pearse 1980; Griffin 1974) has also attached to the 'Green Revolution' technology as applied in Asia on account of its uneven impact upon different regions and groups of farmers; this has happened despite the fact that the components of the biological technology (improved seeds, fertiliser, insecticides, fungicides, new husbandry, and water management) which are the central feature of the 'Green Revolution' are easily divisible for application by small farmers, and are generally perceived to be scale-neutral.[12] Most commonly, however, the notion of inappropriateness attaches to the introduction of tractors, combine harvesters, threshers or other forms of labour-saving technology into labour-abundant economies.

In what sense may this be said to be inappropriate? From the standpoint of the farmer buying a tractor (possibly with subsidised credit), its adoption may well prove highly appropriate. In addition to increasing his profits, employing tractor power may reduce the hidden managerial costs of handling a large labour force, it may provide a form of personal transport and the basis for non-farming enterprise, and it may also confer prestige. These private gains to the tractor-owning farmers may, however, be accompanied by adverse effects on others. For example, in the Punjab area of Pakistan, McInerney and Donaldson (1975) estimated that the introduction of each large tractor in irrigated rice- and wheat-growing areas caused the loss of over eight jobs. Thus there were social (or external) costs of unemployment and poverty to set against the private gains of innovating farmers. From the standpoint of tenants who lost their farms, or of the unskilled labourers who lost their jobs, the adoption of tractors was clearly inappropriate. But what is the balanced judgement for society as a whole, and indeed can such a judgement be produced given the range of conflicting interests in society?

If markets could be adjudged to operate 'perfectly' and to generate prices (values) for all goods and services which accurately reflect their social worth, then the private benefits from technological innovation would accurately reflect its social value. However, it is generally accepted by economists (and this is the whole basis of social cost–benefit analysis) that market prices do not necessarily fully reflect values to society as a whole. Even if markets do work efficiently, it has to be accepted that the prices formed reflect the expenditure pattern arising from the prevailing income distribution, and that that distribution will not be universally accepted as ideal. Then there is the question of the external effects of economic activity for which there are no markets; these may take the form of non-market benefits such as improved public amenity, but more significantly they include the various forms of pollution which are a burden to society but are not borne as costs to producers.

Of more direct significance to the issue of inappropriate technology is that product and input prices may be distorted by overvalued exchange rates or by subsidy and tax policies; wage rates also may be subject to arbitrarily imposed minima which do not reflect the opportunity cost of the least skilled categories of labour. Still other prices may be distorted by the exercise of monopsony or monopoly power and by the existence of other market imperfections. Griffin (1974), for example, observes that credit availability and interest rates are often much less favourable for small farmers than for large landlords. While a number of studies (e.g. Bottomley 1975; and Adams and Graham 1981) show that there are good reasons for the high cost of small loans to peasant farmers, i.e. that the cost of making such loans is high in terms of administration and the probability of default, it remains true that many subsidised loan schemes are specially targeted at better-off farmers and largely exclude small producers who have to rely on the higher cost informal loan market.

Griffin also argues that large landlords in India use their power as monopsonists in the local labour market to force down wage rates for hired labour. This is more controversial, but it ties in with the more general theme explored by de Janvry (1981), that in Latin America there are self-reinforcing systems of interest between large landowners, industrialists and politicians which result in the benefits of development accruing mainly to the already better-off. His is a complex thesis which attempts to explain the whole nexus of choices (1) between export and food crop research programmes, (2) of subsidy, tax and price policies, (3) of land reform programmes and (4) of technology policies, in terms of the politics of power. What he may be interpreted as arguing is that there is a causal relationship in which the economically and politically powerful promote fiscal and institutional policies which cause technological changes that accord with their own self-interest and view of society's objectives. He further argues that the successful achievement of these aims necessitates the existence of an exploited sub-economy of poor subsistence farmers and landless workers to provide the surplus necessary for growth of the dynamic sectors of the economy. This is an issue taken up in the final section of the chapter, but the point to note here is that it underlines the relationship between policy objectives, price signals, and the type of technological change which occurs.

If technological change occurs which is considered inappropriate by some group, it is because the relevant price signals are inconsistent with the objectives of that group. This may be because these price signals could have been designed with other policy objectives in mind (including the promotion of narrow self-interest by powerful groups), or it may be the unintentional outcome of trying to formulate intervention policies with imperfect knowledge and foresight. In any event there is a close link between price and technology policy so that, as Krishna (1982) observes, 'a good technology policy is equivalent to a good price policy'. In arriving at this conclusion Krishna argues that the main impetus for agricultural growth will come from new technology rather than higher prices, but that negative price policies or inappropriate (output-to-output, and output-to-input) price ratios may frustrate technology policy and bias its effects.

7.4   A Brief Note on Pricing Policies

In making his point Krishna may have been thinking about the subsidy and credit scheme for large landowners which encouraged the spread of large tractors in the Punjab of Pakistan in the early 1970s. Alternatively, he may have been thinking of the complex agricultural pricing policies which are associated with the food price subsidies which are prevalent in LDCs. Both these types of price policy, plus that involved in taxing export crops, have the capacity to arbitrarily adjust output-to-output and output-to-input price ratios. Inevitably some groups in society will lose as a result of such changes and will consider the outcome inappropriate.

Many LDCs, as well as countries such as Poland and Portugal, operate extensive consumer food price subsidies. One requirement for such policies is the creation of large state food trading organisations, which are often invested with monopsony–monopoly rights in international trade in food. The necessity for such bodies arises from the fact that subsidy is injected by the State in the form of compensation to such bodies for the fact that the price at which they sell food (i.e. basic grains, cooking oil, sugar, salt) to wholesale or retail outlets is less than the price at which such produce is procured. The procurement of food for such policies is from two sources, imports and domestic producers. Imports for such schemes may be of two types, commercial and concessionary. Budgetary costs become a major constraint upon the operation of such schemes and frequently become the focus of continuous political attention. Budgetary costs may clearly be reduced in a number of ways: (1) the most obvious way is to limit the subsidy, and to ensure that the subsidised price maintains a reasonable link with the procurement price; (2) another way is to restrict the entitlement to subsidised food, by making a subsidised ration available to certain groups only, as in the fair food price shops of India and Pakistan; (3) a further way is to procure the maximum proportion of supplies from domestic producers, using legal compulsion if necessary (as in China, India and Sri Lanka and the USSR at various times), at prices which are fixed to control the subsidy cost of domestic procurements; and (4) political attempts may be used to maximise access to concessional imports, even though this may entail encouraging a dietary switch from domestic grains to those produced by the major donors.

Option (1) of keeping the subsidised price in step with the procurement price would undoubtedly be favoured by economic advisers, but the frequency of food riots attests to the extreme political difficulties faced in times of rising international prices by governments impaled on the budgetary hook. In recent years there have been serious food riots in Morocco, Sudan, the Dominican Republic, Peru and Egypt, and recent Polish political history is intimately intertwined with abortive attempts by governments to raise food prices. Resistance to attempts to cut food subsidies is perhaps inevitable when unskilled wage rates are closely related to the price of food, and when food subsidies represent, in effect, 15–25% of the income of the poor in countries such as Bangladesh, Sri Lanka and Egypt.[13] While reducing entitlements under option (2) may face less resistance than raising food prices, it too may prove politically difficult.

This leaves option (3) as one which is attempted despite the depressant effect it has on farmers' returns and upon agricultural output.

The extensive documentation available on the Egyptian pricing policy enables something of the nature of the issue to be briefly revealed (see Scobie 1983; and von Braun and de Haen 1983). In Egypt in the 1970s fixed consumer prices for rice varied from a low in 1974 of 12% only of the c.i.f. import price to 60% in 1971, but for most of the decade were in the 30 to 40% range. At the same time the procurement price for domestically produced rice was only slightly above the fixed consumer price, at 13.7% of the c.i.f. import price in 1974 and 61% in 1971. The situation for wheat was very similar to that for rice, and the picture which emerges is one of large consumer subsidies and low incentives to producers to supply to the authorities. Typically, the Egyptian procurement prices for domestic grains were below the open market prices, since the authorities cannot fully control grain sales and hence cannot prevent the emergence of domestic markets at prices above the procurement level. Nevertheless, the open market prices for wheat, maize, and rice in Egypt were substantially below their import price equivalent. Clearly in these circumstances most Egyptian grain producers sold produce on the open market, and the General Authority for the Supply of Commodities had to rely mainly on imports for its requirements of wheat and maize. It was these large-scale imports themselves combined with the subsidised retail price which helped to keep open market prices down and acted to reduce the incentives to domestic supply. That domestic supply was restrained by this price policy is reflected in the decline in Egypt's self-sufficiency in basic foodstuffs over the last two decades – self-sufficiency in wheat declined from 0.35 in 1965 to 0.24 in 1980, that in maize from 0.93 to 0.77, and that in sugar from 0.99 to 0.65. The foreign exchange costs of the policy inevitably grew, and the cost of the food subsidies grew from 0.1% of Egyptian GDP to a remarkable 8.1% in 1979.

What this illustrates is the extent to which in some countries agricultural pricing policy comes to be dominated by objectives other than promoting production. In the process, not only may output prices be significantly depressed but they may be arbitrarily adjusted relative to other output prices and to the prices of inputs. This leads to adjustment of the patterns of production and technological change which in themselves may not be thought desirable but which are the accidental outcome of the conflict between policy objectives. Where governments have embarked upon extensive policies of food subsidies, they may well be trapped into policies which control agricultural prices in ways which diminish agriculture's contribution to development, and into policies which in themselves are socially suboptimal.

In countries poorer than Egypt, where foreign exchange is more of a constraint, the policy conflict has often been resolved in favour of price policies which, while promoting agricultural exports simultaneously tax such exports to generate government revenues,[14] rather than in favour of consumer subsidies. This also leads to the holding back of agriculture and has been one of the concerns of the World Bank (1981, p.56) Report on Sub-Saharan Africa, which indicates that there has been a widespread practice of paying producers of export crops prices very much less than the State trading authorities obtained from their sale onto world markets.[15] Again this represents a major distortion of pricing incentives to farmers, which concerns economists because of its impact upon technological change, the welfare of producers and farm labour, and upon the vitality of the agricultural sector.

7.5   Peasant Farm and Rural Landless Households

A key to understanding the concern about distributional issues, and also the scope (or lack of it) for solving them through agricultural policy, lies in knowledge of the behaviour of peasant farm, landless and near landless rural households. Such households account for the majority of the world's poor, and hence programmes aimed at reducing the numbers living in absolute poverty will have to be directed at them.

Table 7.3 gives an indication of the numbers of farming and landless households in South Asia and of how these have changed since 1961. Unsurprisingly, in view of population growth in the region, it can be seen that numbers of both cultivating and landless households have increased substantially.[16] One inevitable consequence of the former increase has been declining average holding sizes, more fragmentation of holdings, and increased numbers of submarginal holdings which are unable to provide for the subsistence needs of their operation. This emphasises the arbitrariness of the distinction between landless and cultivating households, for the majority of the latter also rely on off-farm income for a substantial proportion of their income. In India according to Bhalla and Chadha (1982), households with between 0.10 and 2.49 acres of land obtained 69% of their income in 1974/75 from non-farm activities while those with 2.50 to 4.99 acres earned 37% of their income in the same ways. Despite their off-farm earnings, 31% of households in the smaller holding class were estimated to be living below the poverty line, along with 24% in the larger farm group. Even in the top size group – those with more than 25 acres – 4% had 1974/75 incomes below the poverty level.

However, not only has population pressure reduced the average amount of land available to cultivating households, there has also been a tendency for real agricultural wage rates to decline as labour supply growth has outstripped demand – this relationship has been influenced by the impact of new technology. This has intensified the difficulties that landless and

Table 7.3 Rural Population: Cultivators and Others in South Asia (million)[1]

	India			Pakistan			Bangladesh		
	1961	*1971*	*1977*	*1961*	*1972*	*1976*	*1961*	*1967*	*1977*
Rural population	360.1	438.9	503.0	35.8	47.4	52.5	52.4	61.6	69.0
Rural households	72.5	78.4	89.8	6.2	8.9	9.9	8.8	9.9	11.8
Cultivating households	65.2	70.5	80.8	3.6	5.2	4.4	6.0	6.9	6.1
Of which (%):									
Wholly owned	74	76	76[2]	41	42	57[2]	61	66	66
Partly owned-rented	22	20 }	24[2]	17	24 }	43[2]	37	30 }	34
Wholly rented	4	4 }		42	34 }		2	4 }	
Others	7.3	7.9	9.0[2]	2.6	3.7	5.5[2]	2.8	3.0	5.7[2]
Of which:									
Landless	6.8	7.6	8.6	n.a	n.a.	1.0	n.a	n.a	5.7
Others	0.5	0.3	0.4[2]	n.a	n.a	4.5	n.a	n.a	0[2]

Source: Singh, World Bank (1979), Tables 1.2 and 1.3.
Notes: (1) As Singh notes, the statistical basis for some of these estimates are shaky, and hence one or two apparent inconsistencies arise in comparing the last two years' data, particularly for Pakistan.
(2) These data are deduced from the remaining values in Singh's Table 1.3.

submarginal farming households have experienced in securing adequate living standards through wage employment in rural areas. Certainly the evidence for South Asia reviewed by Singh (1979, pp.135–47) indicates considerable growth in rural poverty in the last two decades, a tendency certainly mirrored in other LDCs in other regions.

One thing which is obvious is that for the majority of rural households in LDCs, economic decisions about farming activities are integrated into a household economic strategy which involves decisions (among others) about whether children should work or go to school, what involvement family members should have in off-farm employment, or whether the labour of some family members should be exported to the cities or even abroad. It is recognition of this which has imparted momentum to the support for farming systems research, as a means of examining agricultural decisions within the context of complex resource allocation systems. Nevertheless, many economic studies have focused upon the farming enterprises of peasant farmers in isolation from other household income-earning activities. These studies, and particularly those which were interpreted as indicating that peasant farmers were economically efficient (in the sense of allocating resources in ways apparently consistent with profit maximisation), have greatly influenced attitudes towards agricultural development policy.

One noteworthy study was that conducted by Hopper in 1961 and published in 1965. It was this which provided the empirical basis for Schultz's (1964) assessment that peasant farmers were 'economically efficient' although poor. Hopper statistically analysed data for the farms in an Indian village and concluded that the hypothesis was sustainable, and that inputs were allocated so their marginal value products were equal to one another, and such that marginal costs equalled marginal revenues. This type of evidence of Pareto optimality was confirmed by later studies (e.g. Sahota 1968; Yotopoulos 1967; and Chennareddy 1967) and had the effect of creating the impression that peasant farmers were entrepreneurially efficient and thus able to respond vigorously and rapidly to new opportunities. It also provided a basis for optimism that if new technological options could be introduced, supported by positive price signals, agricultural output growth would be favourable. Although questions of equity were not to the fore in the early 1960s, these notions of peasant economic efficiency may have encouraged the view that poor peasant farm households would be capable of looking after their own interests in the developing environment, and that policies need not be specially orientated towards those with small holdings.

The strong version of the hypothesis that peasant farmers are efficient but poor, encounters several legitimate criticisms and needs to be qualified. In the first place the theoretical requirement is that to be economically efficient, production must be both allocatively efficient (as discussed above) and technically efficient, in the sense of being on the outer bound production frontier. Farmers can be efficient allocatively without being so technically; thus it is a mistake to confuse economic with allocative efficiency. This is especially true since, almost by definition, most producers are less technically efficient than one or two leaders, and hence it is only possible to assess relative (and not absolute) technical and economic efficiency.[17] Secondly, there is in any case a fundamental weakness in the method used to test the hypothesis. The so-called null hypothesis for the test is that producers are allocatively efficient (that is, that they choose input levels so that the marginal productivity of each factor is equal), and standard statistical procedures are employed to estimate the probability that the hypothesis is false. If the probability is high that the null hypothesis is false, it is rejected in favour of (in this case) the alternative hypothesis that the marginal products are different. Rejection of the null hypothesis is generally accepted to be a strong result, carrying a high degree of conviction that the alternative hypothesis may be true. Thus the standard procedures are fairly strong where they indicate that differences in sample behaviour exist, but they are weak where they fail to reject a null hypothesis of sameness since in this case there is a high probability that the hypothesis which has not been rejected is nevertheless false, i.e. the probability of a Type II error is high.

Even allowing for the weak statistical test, a further problem arises in that the form of efficiency in resource allocation which is hypothesised is consistent with most (if not all) conceivable forms of rational economic behaviour, and not just with profit maximisation. Allocative efficiency is, for example, certainly consistent with the concept that peasant farm households maximise their utility rather than their farming profit. The theory of utility-maximising peasant farmers owes much to the work of the Russian economist Chayanov,[18] whose approach has been refined by subsequent economists, with notable contributions by Mellor (1966, Ch.9) and Nakajima (in Wharton 1970, Ch.6). In this theory peasant farm households are assumed to allocate family labour and other resources to farm production in order to maximise household utility, subject to the constraint of available land (or of land rent conditions), and influenced directly by the family's desire for consumption goods (retained and marketed output) and for leisure. Where the peasant family does not hire or supply labour in the local labour market, or where there are imperfections in the labour market, this theory implies different resource allocations from those which would satisfy the profit-maximisation rule. However, these differences are ones of degree rather than being basic in character. Resources will still be allocated so as to equate marginal value products, and responses to relative price changes should not qualitatively differ from those under profit maximisation, although resource use will be pushed to the point where the marginal costs of inputs are equated not to marginal revenue but to the marginal utility of the output.[19] The utility-maximising theory of behaviour does provide a highly acceptable explanation of why subsistence households with large families and little land are likely to employ their labour at higher levels per hectare, and at lower marginal productivity per hectare, than would 'capitalistic' farms maximising profit and hiring labour at the going wage rate. It also explains why output per hectare on such subsistence holdings is likely to exceed that of larger farmers using the same *basic technology*, and why smaller farmers place a higher valuation upon land and are prepared to pay high prices to rent or buy land where they can. Moreover, the utility-maximising theory of household production and consumption can be expanded to explain the allocation of household labour between on- and off-farm uses.

There is ample evidence that the utility-maximising model has good explanatory power for traditional farming systems, and that farmers with small subsistence holdings achieve higher land productivity yields at the expense of lower labour productivity than do large farmers. That is, smaller farm households allocate their abundant labour more intensively and operate with higher labour-to-land ratios. Evidence of this type has been forcefully used by, among others, Griffin (1974) and Berry and Cline (1979) to argue that because small farmers achieve higher land productivity, redistributing large landholdings to smallholders will raise total agricultural output while at the same time improving equity.

Some of the data employed to underpin this argument has unfortunately been of dubious validity. Clearly, in comparing the land productivity of different farm sizes, it is important to ensure not only that all farms employ essentially the same technology but also that the inherent quality of the land is the same. However, in the case of some of the Latin American data cited by Berry and Cline there must be grave suspicions that, in comparing the productivity of farms of over 1,000 hectares with those less than two, inherent fertility differences may exist. What is needed is to compare land productivity within a contiguous area of agricultural quality. One set of data which approaches this ideal is that collected by Hart (1978) for the 200 hectares of rice paddies farmed by the inhabitants of a Javanese village.[20] This data presented as Table 7.4 does reveal both the higher pre-harvest labour inputs and yields of the smaller holdings, and it supports arguments, such as Griffin's, in favour of distributive land reform.

Another criticism of the poor but efficient hypothesis, one fully explored by Ghatak and Ingersent (1984, Ch.6), is that allocative efficiency is not synonymous with economic efficiency. While the latter necessitates the former, it also requires production to be operated at the maximum level of technical efficiency consistent with profit maximisation. Not only is there evidence that producers generally operate at levels of resource use which fall short of profit-maximising levels, there is also evidence that

Table 7.4 Pre-Harvest Labour Input and Wet Season Rice Yield, by Holding Size in a Javanese Village, 1975/76

Holding size (ha)	<0.19	0.19–0.29	0.30–0.49	0.50–0.99	>1
Average size (ha)	0.118	0.271	0.377	0.676	3.147
Labour input per hectare (hours)					
Female: Family	455	354	143	66	20
Hired	233	266	306	306	360
Total	688	620	449	372	380
Male: Family	619	456	383	133	70
Hired	147	180	223	296	374
Total	766	636	606	429	444
Total labour input/ha.	1454	1256	1055	801	824
Yield per hectare (tons of wet paddy)	3.12	2.55	2.22	2.32	1.97

Source: Hart (1978), p.143.

producers do not necessarily adopt cost-minimising (outer-bound production function) technology. There are strong subjective and objective factors which give rise to these types of economic inefficiency (as narrowly perceived). The most widely accepted subjective factor[21] is that poor farming households surviving on the margin of subsistence have every reason to be risk averse. They cannot afford to risk failure, and hence are likely to adopt low-risk survival strategies, which may involve (1) delaying the adoption of new technologies until they are better understood and proved to be superior to existing ones; (2) concentrating on low-risk food crops, even though there may be other higher-risk crops which have higher expected value of output levels; and (3) seeking low-paid, but secure, off-farm work to provide a steady income flow, even though that may entail sacrificing higher valued, but higher risk, crop or livestock output. Of course, such cautious behaviour probably applies in some measure across all farm sizes.

Reinforcing the subjective checks to economic efficiency are usually objective ones relating to market failure. Instances of this are well illustrated by IRRI (1977) studies of the reasons why Asian rice producers failed to achieve economic optimum rice yields. Among the reasons recorded were that inputs such as fertiliser and insecticide were often not available at the time required, credit was not available, and there was inadequate information available about the appropriate input combination to use. Tenant farmers may also be inhibited from achieving socially optimal levels of output or technical change by the forms of tenancy under which they operate. While this is still a controversial issue among economists,[22] the standard view is that where share-tenancy prevails, as in parts of Asia and Latin America, there are losses in economic efficiency. However, probably the most critical set of objective constraints to the productive efficiency of the smallest farmers, in the sense of constraints amenable to alleviation by policy initiatives, remains (as discussed in Section 7.3 above) their limited access to low-cost credit and hence to various physical factors of production. This is a particular handicap to small farmers' ability to innovate rapidly, and, although there is ample evidence that small farmers are innovative, other evidence suggests that larger farmers have responded with more dynamic efficiency to new technological opportunities. Pearse (1980, p.111), for example, reports that following the release of new high-yielding wheat varieties in North India in the mid-1960s,

> ... there was a steady increase in expenditure on production costs per land unit from year to year amongst the larger cultivators, reversing the initial situation, in which the smallest cultivators had highest production costs, due to the intensity of their use of inputs. The economic performance on a per hectare basis of the large cultivators is seen rapidly to surpass that of the small in the four years during which the technology spread through the area, though the situation of the small cultivator has also improved.

Pearse also cites other studies indicating the existence of a 'reversal' pattern, whereby smaller producers are unable to benefit from the new technology to the same extent as large operators, and hence they progressively lose their traditional lead in terms of resource-use intensity.

It is not solely deficiencies in factor markets which explain the unequal response of Asian farmers to the new biological technology of the Green Revolution. At least in Asia, farmers (including submarginal ones) have been fortunate that a suitable technology has emerged to raise productivity to land and labour in grain production, that progress is also being made in livestock production, and that this has been backed by infrastructural investment, particularly in irrigation. In Africa (and parts of Latin America), the absence of comparable new technologies for widespread intensification of food production is itself the principal objective obstacle to overcoming rural poverty. There is, however, a whole complex of factors which interact with the available technology to trap the poor. Myrdal (1970) discussed these in terms of 'the vicious circle of poverty'; Lipton (1977) has written about 'why poor people stay poor'; and Chambers (1983) has written about 'integrated rural poverty' and the 'deprivation trap'.

Chambers characterises the situation in terms of five mutually reinforcing sets of factors: these are poverty, physical weakness, vulnerability, powerlessness and isolation. It is not possible to dwell upon the detailed relationships between these factors here, for the dynamic interactions are highly complex and are variable in nature from country to country. However, those with some familiarity with rural poverty in LDCs will not only recognise the significance of these or similarly categoriesed conditions but they will be able to identify some key relationships from their own experience. No-one who has observed hungry and ill peasant farming people can doubt that their productive energies are impaired, or that many of their decisions are based on short-run criteria rather than upon the longer-term ones needed to increase efficiency. Not only are they forced by weakness to reduce time devoted to short-term investment, such as weeding crops, but the drudgery of their condition leads to children being withheld from school to assist with daily tasks. This impairs the accumulation of human capital. Such may be the extremity of their condition, that they mortgage their assets and future on highly unfavourable terms to ensure short-run survival. Paradoxically, the very poor are often forced to take exceptional risks, and this frequently leads to their losing what land or other productive assets they possess. The catalogue of such choices for poor people is capable of lengthy extension. Nevertheless, they are rational choices, dictated by pressing immediate need, despite the fact that they ultimately intensify the poverty trap. There can be no doubt that the condition of what Chambers calls 'integrated rural poverty' does represent a profound objective obstacle to agricultural efficiency and development.

7.6 Agricultural Development Strategies

In addressing the issue of agricultural development strategies there is a grave danger of committing what Seers (1963) called the fallacy of 'generalising from the special case'. The special case which tends to dominate the literature on this issue is that of the 'Green Revolution' in South Asia and its precursors in East Asia. As will be discussed, there may be (are) severe limitations for the immediate applicability of this experience to sub-Saharan Africa and also parts of Latin America. Nevertheless, many agricultural development economists have devoted considerable attention to the articulation of over-arching, general strategies for agricultural development in the now poorest LDCs, and the topic remains a focus of wide interest.

As noted earlier, agricultural development strategies cannot be examined in isolation, and have to be integrated with the plans for other sectors of the economy. This dictates a need for balance; balance between flows of goods, capital, and labour between the various sectors and regions of the economy, and balance in flows between the national economy and the rest of the world. For Ranis (1983) the ideal balance is that achieved by Taiwan and other East Asian NICs during the course of their post-1945 development. Ranis characterises them as having followed a two-bladed development strategy in which 'One blade is represented by balanced growth of the labour intensive variety, encouraged by the allocation of a substantial volume of infrastructure to the rural areas, both in the pre- and post-independence periods: the second blade is represented by the rapid deployment of a labour intensive technology embedded in output mixes directed towards external markets'. Ranis sees the key to the success of Taiwanese development and that of other East Asian NICs as residing in (1) the heavy investment in labour-intensive employment in the rural areas in the early stages of development; (2) the fact that this investment was directed not only at agriculture but also at rural small-scale industrialisation;[23] (3) that industry was not protected by excessive import tariffs but was export orientated and aimed at being internationally competitive from the outset;[24] and (4) that there was a strong commitment to both physical and human capital development and to investment in agricultural research and development. In this context agriculture played a dynamic early role in expanding food supplies, creating employment, and in providing a rapidly growing market for industrial products. The emphasis on rural industrialisation smoothed the path for rapid transformation, by facilitating the ready transfer of full- and part-time workers from agriculture to industry.

It might well have been with East Asia in mind that Mellor (1983), in reviewing his earlier views on agricultural development strategies, accepted that he had previously tended to understate both the capital requirements essential to accelerating agricultural output growth and also the key role of agriculture as a market for non-agricultural capital goods and services. He also re-emphasised the importance of consumer goods both of the food and non-food varieties. This is worthy of note, particularly in the context of the current debate (below) about agriculture in sub-Saharan Africa. The fact that it was food production, and in particular rice, that was the focus of investment and research in East Asia meant that there were potential benefits for all members of society, while the complementary stress on industrial consumer goods created new wants which stimulated farmers to intensify their efforts, thereby supporting industrialisation. As Lewis has stated (1978, p.75):

> The most important item on the agenda of development is to transform the food sector, create agricultural surpluses to feed the urban population, and thereby create the domestic basis for industry and modern services. If we can make this domestic change, we shall automatically have a new international economic order.

This emphasis on food rather than export crops is also reflected in the rural development strategy proposed by Johnston and Clark (1982). They argue for a three-pronged strategy comprising simultaneous programmes aimed at production, consumption and organisations. In advocating organisational programmes Johnston and Clark are reflecting the concerns of Griffin, Lipton, Chambers, de Janvry and others that the institutional structures and managerial methods often found in LDCs are biased towards elites and militate against the type of development which they wish to promote. Similarly, the emphasis on consumption programmes reflects recognition of the integrated poverty of the rural poor, and of the need to pursue nutritional, educational and family planning programmes if the rural poor are to develop the capacities to participate fully in agriculture-led rural development.

As regards the agricultural production programme, Johnston and Clark opt strongly, along with other writers, for the so-called unimodal strategy. This is contrasted to the alternative strategies in Thorbecke's (1979, p.198) classification, which are (1) the bimodal or dualistic strategy, (2) the industrialisation first strategy, which takes a very negative approach to agriculture, and (3) a strategy for collectivisation, or socialisation of rural areas. The unimodal strategy is closely identified with the agricultural development patterns of Japan, Taiwan and South Korea.

These countries pursued unimodal strategies involving the promotion of labour-using, capital-saving technologies which rely heavily on readily divisible biological technology such as the high-yield, fertiliser-responsive food crops which have been central to the 'Green Revolution'. Because of the nature of supporting policies and institutional structures, small farms in these East Asian countries, and in the Punjab, were able to participate in the large productivity and income gains to which the package of biological technology plus investment in irrigation and rural infrastructure gave rise.

This success, in devising institutional policies which enabled wide diffusion of the benefits of technological change in agriculture, is held up by some proponents of the East Asian approach (e.g. Ranis 1983; Hayami 1983) as a model because it holds out more general promise of achieving growth with equity through what Hayami calls an appropriate 'dialectic between technological and institutional innovations'. However, Johnston and Clark (1982, pp.252–53) and Mellor (1983, p.223) argue that undue emphasis on equity considerations should not be allowed to impede policies to push forward unimodal type 'Green Revolution' policies. The important thing is seen as being to raise food output, employment and productivity growth across the whole spectrum of farm sizes. While it is important to pursue unimodal strategies which avoid deliberately channelling the benefits of change to elite groups, their argument is that the main development gains arise from broad participation, rapid modernisation and expansion of agriculture. To these authors it is then clear that there is a potential trade-off between growth and equity, and that there should be only limited reductions of agricultural growth to achieve equity beyond the limits obtainable through a unimodal strategy centred on promoting biological technology and on ensuring adequate access to new inputs by small farmers through special credit, advisory and cooperative systems. Johnston and Clark are particularly clear about this in their statement (p.87) that 'We believe that land tenure reform promises benefits for the rural poor which are largely illusory and which in practice will usually have the effect of restricting income-earning opportunities in the agricultural sector'.

However, where access to the land is biased towards larger producers it is clear that there are marked limits to the rural equity-generating potential of agricultural growth. In this connection the East Asian NICs stand out as distinctly 'special cases'. In Taiwan, for instance, the distribution of operational rights (tenancies plus owner-occupied farms) in the land was already relatively egalitarian in the pre-World War Two period because large landlords found it more profitable to rent out their land to tenants (Thorbecke 1979, p.137). The postwar land reforms which transferred ownership to tenants consolidated the user rights of small farmers, and ensured equitable participation in the rapid agricultural development of the 1950s and 1960s.

The prospects for agricultural growth with equity elsewhere are distinctly more restricted than in East Asia unless the unimodal strategy is supplemented by land tenure reform. Vyas (1983) strongly makes the point that despite rapid deployment of the new scale-neutral agricultural technology in South Asia (India and Pakistan), there has been little or no impact on rural poverty. According to Vyas (p.54), the poorest 30% of households in South Asia, the near-landless and landless, have holdings which are so small that deployment of the new technologies is insufficient to significantly affect their degree of poverty. Above this 30% is a class of small farmers 'which can be termed potentially viable farmers, who with the application of modern technology can raise productivity to a level which will permit them to cross the poverty line. The new technology can presumably help this group'. But help will be needed, if it is to do so, in the form of those institutional components of the unimodal strategy designed to overcome the problems small farmers experience in obtaining access to modern inputs. Clearly, therefore, unimodal strategies which confine their institutional components to promoting agricultural research, credit and input delivery systems, and to expanding agricultural extension services, will largely bypass the rural poor and will promote the emergence of commercial farmers from among, perhaps, the upper 70% of those in the land operation distribution. Certainly Khan agrees with this when he states (1983, p.236):

> The hope that an appropriate institutional reorganisation would automatically promote egalitarian growth is unrealistic. Much of the hope of a non-revolutionary solution of the institutional problem of agriculture is based on the experience of East Asia. This hope is unlikely to be realised in contemporary developing Asia. Historical difference between East Asia and the contemporary developing Asia makes the cost of such reform in the latter a great deal higher...

This quote taken from Khan highlights the dilemma of land reform's role in any agricultural development strategy. In South Asia the productivity case for large-scale further distribution of land ownership is now weaker than it was. In India average holding size declined from 2.84 to 2.00 hectares and holdings of over 10 hectares declined in number from 3.4 to 2.4 million between 1953/54 and 1976/77, trends which have subsequently continued. This has resulted from population pressure acting via inheritance and land purchase, and from the land reform already enacted to impose upper size limits to holdings. Furthermore, according to the data previously cited by Pearse (1980), the standard assumption that large farms have lower land productivity than small ones may no longer hold following the 'Green Revolution' in parts of South Asia. It should also be remembered that in the much-quoted Taiwanese case the key post-1945 land reform was not one of breaking up large holdings but entailed conferring ownership on tenants. A similar reform was enacted in the Philippines in 1972. This type of tenancy reform, which does not increase the number of operating units, does not, of course, directly benefit the landless, and hence its equity effects are limited. Nevertheless, the case for such a reform in Asia and elsewhere rests upon the perception that tenants are at a disadvantage by comparison with owners in securing credit for inputs, and are vulnerable to displacement by landowners encouraged to take advantage of new technical possibilities by farming the land themselves. Reforming the system to give more protection to the rights of tenants will provoke resistance and evasion by landlords, but if pushed through should release the high productive potential of small tenant farmers in Asia. Such granting of improved security of tenure or ownership to existing tenants has the virtue of avoiding the short- and medium-run costs of disrupted production which have often attended more comprehensive reshaping of rights in land. Where more radical reforms have taken place and land rights are extended to previously landless people with no local roots, the lack of managerial ability and capital by the incoming settlers has, when combined with the costs of public support (in the form of set-up grants, credit for inputs and new extension services), often entailed high social cost with reduced agricultural output.

The higher disruption costs of a more radical reform, which breaks up large holdings to create either a large increase in the number of operational holdings or a number of collective or cooperative units, are more supportable where potential productivity gains are higher than they appear to be in South Asia. Such higher gains are likely where land ownership is highly skewed, and where farming intensity is markedly lower on the larger holdings. Such conditions appear more prevalent in Latin America than in the other less developed continents, something supported by Berry and Cline's analysis of potential productivity gains from farm-size equalisation in a number of Latin American and Asian countries.

Not surprisingly, perhaps Berry and Cline's study does not consider the role of land reform in Africa. This may partly reflect the weakness of the data base, but it also, no doubt, reflects the prevalence of communal land tenure throughout much of sub-Saharan Africa, accompanied by the absence of private land ownership in some areas and hence markets for agricultural land and tenancies. This is one of several factors which differentiate the problems of African agricultural development from those of other developing regions, and which contribute to the fact that devising generalised agricultural development strategies for Africa (which simultaneously reconcile food output growth, equity, and foreign exchange saving) are more difficult to devise. This is clearly revealed in the attempts to propose strategies for agriculture in sub-Saharan Africa in reports published by the World Bank (1981) and USDA (1980). Both reports (but particularly the USDA report, pp.145–60) recognise the acute deficiencies of the region in infrastructure, skilled manpower, appropriate technological packages, research and extension, and in the marketing systems for inputs and outputs. Note that these deficiencies still exist some two decades after most of the sub-Saharan African countries became independent, during which time major infusions of external aid and advice have been injected. In many African countries these efforts have failed to build an adequate base for sustained advance of agriculture on the appropriate scale, and many of the projects begun, and much of the advice given, during this period have been subsequently judged to be misconceived because, as short-cuts, they failed to adequately allow for the inherent limitations of the complex situation.

The USDA report admits that there will be no magic solution and that laying the foundations for success will take a long time. The World Bank, because of its political position, is probably obliged to sound more optimisic. It proposes a general four point plan, backed by substantial external aid, which appears on the surface to be of the unimodal variety. Specifically (on p.50) it proposed emphasis on (1) smallholder production; (2) changing incentive structures − in particular by raising agricultural output prices; (3) expanding agricultural research; and (4) undertaking quick yielding activities in irrigated agriculture. However, more detailed examination of the proposed Agenda for agriculture reveals it to have a more bimodal character; there is acceptance (1) that the 'smallholder strategy' may have to be based on the leading role of larger than average farmers; (2) that there should be concentration of resources on regions of high potential; (3) that it was a mistake in early post-independence to target efforts to more marginal areas; (4) that development projects should be based around commercial lead crops such as cotton (rather than around food crops for which adequate technological packages may not exist); and (5) that projects based entirely on food crops should be of a smaller, pilot scale. These 'biases' have attracted a fair amount of criticism; by Lipton (1983) and Loxley (1983)[25] for putting insufficient emphasis on food production and nutrition; by Guyer (1983)[25] for failing to take account of the implications of the key role of women in African food production (another aspect of striking difference from Asia) and for overemphasising 'northern' cereal crops at the expense of roots and tubers such as cassava and yams; and by Williams (1983)[25] for continued emphasis on a large-farm, project-based approach. Such criticisms highlight once again the difficulties of agreeing how the inherent conflicts of agricultural policy are to be resolved. The critics attach more weight to equity and the painstaking construction of a firm broad base of human development, while the Bank's chosen strategy for agriculture places more emphasis on growth, on foreign exchange saving, and upon the need for rapid results with proven technologies, despite the limited success of such an approach to date.

7.7 Chinese Agricultural Development

As a footnote to consideration of agricultural development strategies, and to issues of agricultural development in general, this chapter is rounded off by a brief account of some of the effects of recent changes in Chinese agricultural policy.

Prior to 1978 Chinese agricultural production was directed from the political centre with output targets and quotas transmitted through the state level to individual communes. The latter had been established following the end of the Civil War in 1949. An Agrarian Reform Law was published in 1950, and policy was directed towards 'the elimination of landlords, land distribution and the creation of mutual aid teams as the operational units in agriculture, and of peasants' associations as the political and social channels for rural money-lending and took a firm grip on the trade and the rural credit systems' (Henle 1974, p.127). After a period of reorganisation and experimentation 76,000 communes were established as the main organisational units in agriculture, and ownership of land was transferred to the village level, except for up to 5% of the land which was allowed to remain in small private plots. Free markets in products were restricted and a system of delivery targets enforced. Output, mainly of grain, was purchased by a state monopoly which distributed it at subsidised prices to urban dwellers. These urban dwellers obtained food more cheaply and were often better fed than those in rural areas. A most interesting aspect of Chinese agricultural development is the extent to which the communes were required to provide the labour and materials for the construction of roads, irrigation projects, reafforestation schemes and other public works. In this way considerable capital investment was created at small cost to the central government without the need for much expensive equipment, and the infrastructural foundation was laid for the acceleration of agricultural production after 1978.

The command economy which operated from 1950 to 1978, while reasonably well suited to grain production, stifled the potential gains to be obtained from regional specialisation and diversification of production (Yan Ruizhen 1985). Rural incomes were depressed with a consequent loss of morale (Tang 1980), and intraregional agricultural trade was exceptionally limited, as it still largely remains according to Lewis (1984); essentially the command system gave priority to near self-sufficiency in regional grain production and minimised the demands placed upon an inadequate transport system. Although basic grains production during this period is estimated to have grown at rates at least as large as population growth, it is apparent with hindsight that the full potential of Chinese agriculture was not realised.

Since 1978 the degree of centralised control has been greatly diminished and much more responsibility has been transferred to individual households within communes. While collective ownership of the means of production (including land) still exists, production is managed on the basis of separate households, each assuming sole responsibility for their own profits or losses. Up until 1984 households still had to fulfil production contracts with the collective and pay taxes to it to meet the costs of public capital. But, having met these requirements, rural households became free to exploit their resources to the best economic advantage. The rural economy has become more specialised. According to Yan Ruizhen (1985, p.4):

> This is characterised by two opposing trends: large numbers of peasants, having left farmland, are engaged in other undertakings such as forestry, animal husbandry, fishery, sideline occupations, rural industries, and service trades; on the other hand, the land is being concentrated in the households that are more skilled in crop cultivation.

This specialisation has extended to the more rapid development of a wide range of rural service activities which have supported the newly released impetus for agricultural growth.

The extent to which market forces have been given a freer rein since 1978 is particularly noteworthy. Accompanying the relaxation of procurement controls, procurement prices were, according to Lewis (1984, p.39), raised by more than 40% between 1977 and 1981. This, with the freeing of other prices, must have provided a considerable increase in incentives to production. (It is worth noting in parenthesis that prices charged to urban dwellers for grain do not appear to have been increased to a comparable extent, and Lewis (p.30) reports that by 1981 the cost of urban food subsidies reached $10 billion – the equivalent of 25% of Chinese fiscal resources and perhaps 30% of urban income.) Controls have apparently been released further since 1985 according to Yan Ruizhen (1985, pp.9,10). From that date 'the system for purchasing farm products is to be reformed. The state does not issue any mandatory quotas to peasants.

Table 7.5 Average Annual Growth Rates of Selected Crops in China (%)

Crops	1953–78	1979–83
Grain	2.4	4.9
Oilseeds	0.8	15.1
Sugarbeet	6.9	27.7
Timber	5.6	7.1
Fruits	3.9	7.6
Tea	4.6	8.4
Meat	3.6	10.4
Aquatic products	4.0	3.2
Silkworm cocoons	4.0	9.1

Source: Yan Ruizhen (1985).

While offering fixed prices for grains and cotton by contract purchasing, other products are allowed to float at free prices and are handled by the open market'.

It clearly appears that the combination of freeing agricultural markets and of allocating rights in output away from collectives and to individual cultivators has produced a rapid upsurge in agricultural output growth. The data presented by Yan Ruizhen (1985) (here Table 7.5) show that between 1979 and 1983 output growth for several major commodities was over double the rate of the preceding 15 years. Assuming these estimates to be a reasonable reflection of the outcome of recent developments, it is apparent that a key factor enabling this upsurge of agricultural growth was the infrastructural investment, particularly in irrigation and crop research, which had taken place in earlier years. Without the potential capacities this enhanced capital stock provided, the gains to increased specialisation in agricultural production in China could not have been realised so quickly.

Notes

1. As has been discussed already in Chapter 6, not all saving need be from domestic sources, and development aid can provide an additional source of funds for investment in industry and the public sector. Aid cannot, however, entirely or even largely supplant domestic saving and the need for the agricultural sector initially to contribute much of it.
2. There has been and still is widespread use of monopsonist marketing boards which pay LDC producers of cash crops prices less than the price obtained by selling produce for export or to local industry.
3. One feature of the pattern of employment in less developed countries which is perhaps surprising is the high proportion of the active population engaged in the trade, transport and service (including government) sectors. This highlights the weakness of classifying any employment which is non-agricultural as being industrial. Also, as Bairoch points out, the proportion employed in the trade, transport and service sectors is far higher than in the rich countries at a comparable stage of development and it may be excessive for the needs of poor countries.
4. If one assumed a country to have a workforce of 1 million of whom 20% were employed in industry, a 2.5% population growth rate would imply an addition of 25,000 people to the workforce. If all these were to be absorbed into industry, employment in that sector would have to grow from 200,000 to 225,000, that is by 12.5%.
5. According to the World Bank's Development Report (1980), annual output growth in the Tanzanian industrial and service sectors between 1970 and 1978 only averaged 2.3 and 6.4% respectively. Employment growth rates may reasonably be assumed to have been less than for output growth.
6. Lewis (1954) certainly accepted sectoral definitions in which the capitalist sector produces its own food.

7. For more detail, see FAO (1983). Note that the proportion uncultivated will include grazing land, and that its arable potential will typically be less than that of land already under cultivation.

8. Another important study which has contributed support to the notion that market forces induce innovation to save the relatively scarce factors is Binswanger and Ruttan (1978).

9. Schultz has made these points forcefully and elegantly in a 1979 paper reprinted in Eicher and Staatz (1984).

10. Among these are centres dealing with potatoes (CIP in Peru), livestock (ILCA in Ethiopia), dry land agriculture (ICARDA in the Lebanon), semi-arid areas (ICRISAT in India), and with food policy (IFPRI in Washington DC). CIAT in Colombia has a mandate covering cassava and field beans. IITA in Nigeria deals with farming systems, maize, rice, roots and tubers, and field legumes.

11. Clayton (1984, Ch.7) strongly espouses farming system analysis and provides a fairly detailed account of its history and methodology.

12. A new input is defined to be scale-neutral if it has equi-proportional production potential for both small and large farms. Scale neutrality is seen as a key property of 'appropriate technology'.

13. Pinstrup-Anderson (1984) reports the results of several studies which have attempted to estimate the income equivalence of food subsidies by income groups.

14. In this apparently contradictory policy considerable non-price support is given to export crops in terms of research expenditures and infrastructural provision (including irrigation and road works where appropriate). This helps maintain the profitability of export over domestic crops at relatively attractive levels, particularly for large commercial farmers who can take advantage of economies of size, despite any taxes on exports.

15. For example, the IBRD report (1980, p.56) reports that for four major cocoa-exporting countries – Cameroon, Ghana, Ivory Coast and Togo – the *highest* proportion of cocoa receipts paid to producers during the 1970s was the 56% paid by the Ivory Coast between 1971 and 1975. In Togo between 1976 and 1980 producers received only 26% of the price.

16. This reflects the earlier observation (Table 7.2) that the numbers employed in agriculture are continuing to grow.

17. See, for example, Sidhu (1974); Russell and Young (1983).

18. Chayanov's main work was published in 1925 in Russian under a title which translates into Peasant Farm Organisation. An English translation of this work forms the core of Throner, Kerblay and Smith (eds) (1965) *A.V. Chayanov: The Theory of Peasant Economy*, Irwin for the American Economics Association.

19. The theory does admit the possibility that higher output prices (or off-farm income) will lead to a negative supply response, but for various reasons this is most unlikely in the aggregate.

20. In this case, if there is any bias it would appear to arise from the possibility that the most fertile, best irrigated land tends to be operated and owned by the larger farmers with official positions in the village (*i.e.* those with *bengkok* land).

21. See, for example, Lipton (1968).
22. See Ghatak and Ingersent (1984, pp.86–95) for a discussion of some of the issues relating to forms of tenancy.
23. The choice of a small-scale technology promoted the maximum linkages and mutual stimulus between agriculture and industry (particularly rural industry), an aspect of agricultural development strategy strongly urged by Johnston and Kilby (1975, Ch.7).
24. This signifies that appropriate pricing policies were adopted for agricultural outputs and inputs.
25. These are all contributions to a review of 'The World Bank's prescription for rural Africa', published in *Review of African Political Economy*, 27/28, 1983, pp.186–204.

References

Adams, D.W. and Graham, D.H. (1981) 'A critique of traditional credit projects and policies', *Journal of Development Studies*, 8(3), pp.347–66.

Bairoch, P. (1975) *The Economic Development of the Third World since 1900*, Methuen.

Balassa, B. *et al.* (1971) *The Structure of Protection in Developing Countries*, Johns Hopkins Press.

Berry, A.R. and Cline, W.R. (1979) *Agrarian Structure and Productivity in Developing Countries*, Johns Hopkins Press.

Bhalla, G.S. and Chadha, G.K. (1982) 'Green Revolution and the small peasant', *Econ. and Pol. Weekly*, 15, May.

Biggs, S.D. and Clay, E.J. (1983) *Generation and Diffusion of Agricultural Technology: A Review of Theories and Experience*, ILO, World Employment Programme Research, Working Paper, Geneva.

Binswanger, H.P. and Ruttan, V.W. (1978) *Induced Innovation – Technology Institutions and Development*, Johns Hopkins Press.

Boserup, E. (1965) *The Conditions of Agricultural Growth*, George Allen and Unwin.

Bottomley, A. (1975) 'Interest rate determination in underdeveloped rural areas', *American Journal of Agricultural Economics*, 57(2), pp.279–91.

Chambers, R. (1983) *Rural Development: Putting the Last First*, Longman.

Chayanov, A.V. (1966), edited by Thorner, D., Kerblay B. and Smith, R.E.F. *The Theory of Peasant Economy*, Irwin.

Chennareddy, V. (1967) 'Production efficiency in South Indian agriculture', *Journal of Farm Economics*, 49(4), pp.816–20.

Clayton, E. (1983) *Agriculture, Poverty and Freedom in Developing Countries*, Macmillan.

de Janvry, A. (1981) *The Agrarian Question and Reformism in Latin America*, Johns Hopkins Press.

Dovring, F. (1959) 'The share of agriculture in a growing population', *Monthly Bulletin of Agricultural Economics and Statistics*, FAO, Vol. 8. Reprinted in Eicher and Witt (1964).

Eicher, C.K. and Staatz, J.M. (eds) (1984) *Agricultural Development in the Third World*, Johns Hopkins Press.

Eicher, C.K. and Witt, L.W. (eds) (1964) *Agriculture in Economic Development*, McGraw-Hill.

Evenson, R.E. (1981) 'Benefits and obstacles in developing appropriate technology', *Annals of American Academy of Politics and Social Sciences*, 458, pp.54–67. Reprinted in Eicher and Staatz (1984), pp.348–61.

FAO (1983), *The State of Food and Agriculture*.

Ghatak, S. and Ingersent, K. (1984) *Agriculture and Economic Development*, Wheatsheaf.

Griffin, K. (1974) *The Political Economy of Agrarian Change*, Macmillan.

Hart, G. (1978) *Labour Allocation Strategies in Rural Javanese Households*, PhD, Cornell University, University Microfilms International.

Hayami, Y. (1983) 'Growth and equity – is there a trade-off?', in *Maunder and Ohkawa* (eds), pp.109–16.

Hayami, Y. and Ruttan, V.W. (1971 and 1985) *Agricultural Development: An International Perspective*, Johns Hopkins Press.

Henle, H.V. (1974) *Report on China's Agriculture*, UN Food and Agriculture Organisation.

Hillman, J.S. and Monke, E.A. (1983) 'International transfer of agricultural technology', in *Growth and Equity in Agricultural Development*, Proceedings of 18th International Conference of Agricultural Economists, Gower, pp.519–28.

Hopper, D.W. (1965) 'Allocation efficiency in traditional Indian agriculture', *Journal of Farm Economics*, Vol.47, No.3.

IRRI (1977) *Constraints to High Yields on Asian Rice Farms*, Los Banos.

Johnston, B.F. and Clark, W.C. (1982) *Redesigning Rural Development: A Strategic Perspective*, Johns Hopkins Press.

Johnston, B.F. and Kilby, P. (1975) *Agriculture and Structural Transformation*, Oxford University Press.

Jorgenson, D.W. (1970) 'The role of agriculture in economic development: classical versus neoclassical models of growth', in Whaton (1970), Ch.11.

Khan, A.R. (1983) 'Institutional and organisational framework for egalitarian agricultural growth', in *Maunder and Ohkawa* (eds), pp.229–37.

Krishna, R. (1982) *Some Aspects of Agricultural Growth, Price Policy and Equity*, Food Research Studies in Agricultural Economics, Trade and Development 18(3), Stanford; excerpts reprinted in C.K. Eicher and J.M. Staatz (eds), (1984), *op. cit.*

Kuznets, S. (1961) 'Economic growth and the contribution of agriculture: notes on measurement', *International Journal of Agrarian Affairs*, Vol.3. Reprinted in Eicher and Witt (1964).

Lewis, W.A. (1954) 'Economic development with unlimited supplies of labour', *The Manchester School*, 22, pp.130–90.

Lewis, W.A. (1978) *The Evolution of the International Economic Order*, Princeton University Press.

Lewis, C.M. (1984) *Emerging Issues in China's Food Trade and Distribution System*, World Bank AGREP Division Working Paper 91.

Lipton, M. (1968) 'Strategy for agriculture: urban bias and rural planning', in P. Streeton and M. Lipton (eds) (1968), *The Crisis of Indian Planning*, Oxford University Press.

Lipton, M. (1968) 'The theory of the optimising peasant', *Journal of Development Studies*.

Lipton, M. (1977) *Why Poor People Stay Poor*, Temple Smith.

Lipton, M. (1983) 'African agricultural development: the EEC's new role', *Development Policy Review*, 1, pp.1–21.

McInerney, J.P. and Donaldson, G.F. (1975) *The Consequences of Farm Tractors in Pakistan*, World Bank Staff Working Paper, No. 210.

Maunder, A. and Ohkawa, K. (eds) (1983) *Growth and Equity in Agricultural Development*, Proceedings of 18th International Conference of Agricultural Economists, Gower.

Mellor, J. (1966) *The Economics of Agricultural Development*, Cornell University Press.

Mellor, J. (1983) 'Agricultural growth – structures and patterns', in *Maunder and Ohkawa* (eds), pp.216–26.

Myrdal, G. (1970) *The Challenge of World Poverty*, Penguin Books.

Myrdal, G. (abridged by Seth King) (1971) *Asian Drama: An Inquiry into the Poverty of Nations*, Pantheon Books.

Nakajima, C. (1970) 'Subsistence and commercial family farms: some theoretical models of subjective equilibrium', in Wharton (1970).

Nicholls, W.H. (1963) 'Development in agrarian economics: the role of agricultural surplus, population pressure, and systems of land tenure', *Journal of Political Economy*, Vol.71. Reprinted in Wharton (1970).

Ohkawa, K. and Rosovsky, H. (1960) 'The role of agriculture in modern Japanese economic development', *Economic Development and Cultural Change*, Vol. 9, Pt.2. Reprinted in Eicher and Witt (1964).

Pearse, A. (1980) *Seeds of Plenty, Seeds of Want: Social and Economic Implications of the Green Revolution*, Oxford University Press.

Pinstrup-Anderson, P. (1984) *Food Prices and the Poor in Developing Countries*, Paper presented to the IVth European Congress of Agricultural Economics.

Ranis, G. (1983) 'Growth and equity in development: an overview', in Maunder and Ohkawa (eds) 1983, pp.31–47.

Ranis, G. and Fei, J.C. (1961) 'A theory of economic development', *American Economic Review*, Vol. 51. Reprinted in Eicher and Witt (1964).

Russell, N.P. and Young, T. (1983) 'Frontier production functions and the measurement of technical efficiency', *Journal of Agricultural Economics*, 34(2), pp.139–50.

Sahota, G.S. (1968) 'Resource allocation in Indian Agriculture', *American Journal of Agricultural Economics*, Vol.50, No.3.

Schultz, T.W. (1964) *Transforming Traditional Agriculture*, Yale University Press.

Schultz, T.W. (1979) 'The economics of agricultural research', an *IADS Occasional Paper*. Reprinted in Eicher and Staatz (1984), pp.335–47.

Scobie, G.M. (1983) *Food Subsidies in Egypt: The Impact on Foreign Exchange and Trade*, IFPRI Research Report No.40.

Scobie, G.M. and Posada, R. (1978) 'The impact of technical change on income distribution: the case of rice in Columbia', *American Journal of Agricultural Economics*, 60(1), pp.85–92. Reprinted in Eicher and Staatz (1984), pp.378–88.

Seers, D. (1963) 'The limitations of the special case', *Oxford Bulletin of Economics and Statistics*, 25(2), pp.77–98.

Sidhu, S. (1974) 'Relative efficiency in wheat production in the Indian Punjab', *American Economic Review*, 64, pp.742–751.

Singh, I. (1979) *Small Farmers and the Landless in South Asia*, World Bank Staff Working Paper 320.

Streeten, P. and Lipton, M. (eds) (1968) *The Crisis in Indian Planning*, Oxford University Press.

Tang, A.M. (1980) 'Food and agriculture in China: trends and projections, 1952–77 and 2000', in A.M. Tang and J.B. Stone (1980).

Tang, A.M. and Stone, B. (1980) *Food Production in the People's Republic of China*, IFFRI Research Report 15.

Thorbecke, E. (1979) 'Agricultural development', in W. Galenson, *Economic Growth and Structural Change in Taiwan*, Cornell University Press.

USDA (1980) *Food Problems and Prospects in Sub-Saharan Africa*, International Economics Division, ESCS.

von Braun, J. and de Haen, H. (1983) *The Effects of Food Price and Subsidy Policies on Egyptian Agriculture*, IFPRI Research Report No. 42.

Vyas, V.S. (1983) 'Growth and equity in Asian agriculture: a synoptic view', in Maunder and Ohkawa (eds), pp.52–59.

Wharton, C.R. Jr. (ed.) (1970) *Subsistence Agriculture and Economic Development*, Frank Cass.

World Bank (1981) *Accelerated Development in Sub-Saharan Africa: An Agenda for Action*, The World Bank.

Yan Ruizhen (1985) *Economic Reform in Rural China*, Paper presented to 19th Conference of International Association of Agricultural Economists.

Yotopoulos, P.A. (1967) *Allocative Efficiency in Economic Development*, Centre of Planning and Economic Research, Athens, Research Monograph 18.

8

Malnutrition: a classic syndrome of underdevelopment

The significance of a low level of development is only partially expressed in national aggregate statistics about growth rates of GDP, average per capita incomes and so forth. Its more profound implications are revealed in the poor quality of life of many individuals, and in particular in their extreme poverty. While poverty has many dimensions (see Table 1.2 and Chapter 3), and is reflected in the low level of satisfaction of all basic needs, probably its most serious manifestation is in the form of malnutrition plus the complex of conditions that follow from this, such as low life expectancy, high infant mortality, low resistance to disease and various forms of physical or mental damage. Certainly many definitions of poverty are in terms of a level of income below that required to purchase the necessary food requirement. Thus, for example, Lipton (1982, p.2) assesses the income below which poverty can be said to exist as that household income which if 80% is spent on food will meet 80% of 1983 FAO/WHO estimates of the household's caloric requirements; similarly, but with a higher cut-off point, Knudsen and Scandizzo (World Bank 1979, p.22) adopt as the poverty line 'the minimum income level at which existing expenditure patterns would satisfy nutritional requirements'. Because such a high proportion of the income of poor people is of necessity spent on food, it is possible to identify food as the most important of all basic needs, and malnutrition as the characteristic outcome of poverty and underdevelopment.

In the past many writers have argued that food shortages and inadequate supply were the principal causes of malnutrition. This view echoes those put forward as long ago as 1800 by Malthus, a political economist and cleric. Malthus argued that the capacity of the human race to reproduce itself at a geometric rate was much greater than the capacity of the economic system to expand food production, which he imagined to be limited to an arithmetic growth rate by the fixed availability of land. From this he concluded that the size of the human population would be restrained

by the positive checks of malnutrition and starvation, unless it was voluntarily restrained by the preventive checks of late marriage and various
forms of bith control – as a churchman, Malthus himself considered
'artificial' types of birth control as vice. Malthus saw clearly that the more
affluent societies were more likely to employ preventive checks to population growth and that it was poorer countries and people who were more
likely to reproduce rapidly and suffer the positive checks from hunger.

In formulating his theories Malthus failed to anticipate the extent to
which technology could expand the capacity for food production, and to
which new types of agricultural inputs could substitute for land; nor did
he foresee the capacity of modern medicine to limit the force of the
natural, positive checks to population growth. Despite these and other
legitimate criticisms of the relevance of his theories,[1] Malthus's vision in
many basic respects proved to be an accurate one. Certainly preventive
measures (of birth control) have been effective in the richest countries and
have helped reduce population growth to very level levels. Also, as noted
in Chapter 4, birth and population growth rates have been significantly
reduced in certain middle-income LDCs. However, in many of the
poorest LDCs these rates remain high and are a continuing cause for concern. It is also in the poorest countries that the operation of the positive
checks are most clearly evident, their main expression being the appallingly
high rate of child mortality – in the poorest areas of LDCs as much as
40% of live-born children typically die before the age of five – and in the
relatively low life expectancy of the survivors from childhood. Malthus,
then, was basically correct in foreseeing that the burden of any limitations
on the capacity of food supplies to grow at the same rate as food demand
would fall mainly upon the poor, who comprise a high proportion of the
populations of LDCs.

8.1   Extent of Malnutrition in LDCs

In this discussion the term malnutrition will be used to describe any
dietary shortage. However, as Berg (1981, p.5) indicates, a distinction can
be drawn between undernutrition and malnutrition. According to Berg,
undernutrition relates to inadequate quantities of food and hence to inadequate intake of calories or food energy, while *malnutrition* is the
pathological condition brought about by inadequacy of one or more
nutrients. These are not exactly the same; and although undernourished
people are almost certainly malnourished, malnourishment is the term
popularly applied to all nutrient deficiencies. Further justification for this
form of usage arises from recognition that the main cause of malnutrition
is inadequate calorie intake. It is now accepted that although symptoms of
protein deficiency may be common, in many cases they arise from an

insufficiency of calories, the calorie shortfall causing protein to be burnt as energy. As a consequence (as noted by Poleman 1981, p.12) FAO's estimates of average daily protein requirements were sharply reduced in 1971 from 61 to 40 grams, with a consequent dramatic reduction of the extent to which diets were assumed to be deficient in protein. Because of the interaction between protein and caloric energy in human metabolism, the latter is accepted as a more reliable indicator of the state of nutrition.

As it is not possible to measure directly the nutritional status of all those living in LDCs, the extent of malnourishment can only be derived indirectly with the help of assumptions. The critical assumptions in this calculation relate (i) to the physiological nutrient requirements of different types of individuals (by age, sex and environment/country), (ii) to the available food supplies, and (iii) to the distribution of those supplies within populations. Widely different assumptions about these factors, and in particular about the nutrient intake cut-off point below which malnutrition is defined to exist, have led to substantially different estimates of the extent of the problem.

In early attempts to quantify global malnutrition, the required nutrient standards applied were high, and were more attuned to the heavier bodyweights of citizens of richer countries in temperate (cool) climates. Thus FAO in its 1948 World Food Survey adopted an average daily standard of 2,600 calories per person. Clearly the danger of setting too high a standard is that it will lead to exaggeration by counting, as malnourished, people whose needs and wants are below the standard; and early estimates of the extent of malnutrition were very high. In its Second World Food Survey in 1952 FAO adopted a more sophisticated basis which took account of regional differences in nutritional requirements and led to lower standards.[2] These 1952 standards were revised in 1973 in concert with the World Health Organisation (FAO 1973). A subsequent more radical revision in FAO's approach was taken in 1974 in connection with the Fourth World Food Survey (FWFS). For this exercise FAO adopted conservative standards based upon the concept of the Basal Metabolic Rate (BMR), where a BMR is in essence the amount of energy used up per day by a resting individual. Because the energy requirements for a minimally active life exceed the BMR, FAO estimated that the average energy requirement for bodily maintenance be set at 1.5 BMR. Nevertheless, individuals' maintenance requirements vary considerably due to different metabolic efficiencies, and in order to minimise the extent to which those with low requirements are classified as malnourished, a standard of 1.2 BMRs (or 80% of 1.5 BMR) was adopted for nutritional requirements.

However, as Poleman (1981, p.12) notes in relation to this standard, 'If anything, it errs on the side of being too low', and, for example, for an Indian adult male it is equivalent to an intake of only 1,770 calories per

Table 8.1 Two Alternative Estimates of the Malnourished Population in LDCs[1] (millions)

Region	Calorie requirement (cals/day)	Reutlinger and Selowsky – estimates for 1965[2]			FAO 4th World Food Survey estimates for 1972–74	
		Total population	Population with calorie deficit	Population with calorie deficit > 250 cals	Total population	Population consuming < 1.2 BMR
Far East	2,210	869	736 (87)	563 (65)	1,042	297 (29)
Latin America	2,390	244	113 (46)	55 (23)	302	46 (15)
Africa	2,350	247	190 (77)	151 (61)	301	83 (28)
Middle East	2,450	144	91 (63)	75 (52)	182	29 (16)
Total		1,504	1,130 (75)	844 (56)	1,827	455 (25)

Notes: (1) Figures in brackets are percentages.
(2) The estimates presented are those in which a calorie to income demand elasticity of 0.15 was imposed. With an elasticity of 0.3, Reutlinger and Selowsky obtained estimates of 900 million malnourished, of whom 849 million had deficits of more than 250 calories.

day. Certainly the effect of adopting this low standard rather than the revised version of the 1952 standards (FAO 1973) leads to a substantially lower estimate of the extent of malnutrition. This is revealed in Table 8.1 which compares the estimates of the Fourth World Food Survey with those obtained for a slightly earlier period using a different (econometrically-based) methodology by Reutlinger and Selowsky (1976). The FAO estimates for 1972–74, using the 1.2 BMR standard, put the number of malnourished at 25% of the population of LDCs, while the Reutlinger/Selowsky estimates based on the earlier standard put the figures for 1965 at 56% having a deficit of more than 250 calories per day and 75% having a deficit of some degree. This is an exceptionally high degree of divergence, and opinion is that the 1.2 BMR standard is too low while that of the earlier FAO/WHO recommendations is too high for the purposes of defining serious malnutrition. Hence Knudsen and Scandizzo (World Bank 1979, p.4) adopt the pre-1974 FAO/WHO standards minus 200 calories 'to take account of individual variations in basic energy needs and variations in social standards'; and Lipton (1982) similarly proposes that for the purpose of defining 'ultra poverty' the standards be set at 80% of the 1973 FAO/WHO levels.

Adopting these lower nutritional standards, and employing essentially the same methodology as Reutlinger and Selowsky, Knudsen and Scandizzo still obtain high estimates of the extent of malnourishment in five major Asian countries and in Morocco. Their estimates, reproduced in Table 8.2, are that with the exception of Sri Lanka, which operates an extensive policy of subsidised food rations, from 30 to 55% of people on average consumed less than 2,000 calories per day and a significant proportion consumed below 1,600 in four of the six countries. Magnitudes of this order signify widespread serious malnutrition in LDCs. There are critics, however, such as Poleman and Lipton, who argue that the estimates in Tables 8.1 and 8.2 substantially overstate the case. After reviewing at length the evidence about the effects of malnutrition on mortality by age, work performance, and upon physical and mental damage, they conclude that the numbers seriously at risk from malnutrition are much lower than are usually estimated. Such a position is founded upon the view that human beings are highly resilient and adaptable, and that this includes ability to adjust to low nutrient diets. In particular, the data suggest that most children above the age of four, adolescents and adults are able to withstand and recover from quite severe malnutrition, and that those principally at risk are young children and unborn infants. Risk is in fact highest in the first year of life when the occurrence of Marasmus – a severe wasting caused by lack of food energy – results in smaller brains with fewer cells and in mental damage. However, 'severe short-term energy-protein malnutrition in the second year of life generally does not retard intellectual function permanently' but nevertheless does cause

Table 8.2   Cross-Country Comparison of Degrees of Malnourishment

Country	Base year	Calorie requirement	% of population consuming below			
			110% calorie requirement	*100% calorie requirement*	*90% calorie requirement*	*80% calorie requirement*
Bangladesh	1974	2020	85	64	32	9
India	1974	1910	41	26	14	6
Indonesia	1976	1920	59	44	30	16
Morocco	1971	2276	51	40	28	18
Pakistan	1972	2058	91	58	0	0
Sri Lanka	1970	2000	46	0	0	0

Source: World Bank (1979).

reduced brain weight (Berg 1981, p.11). Hence Poleman, rather than estimating the number of malnourished, argues that for policy purposes concern should be focused on those children under four plus nursing and pregnant women who are at risk from malnutrition where the risk arises from their belonging to families with inadequate incomes. On this basis, even if 50% of families were adjudged to have inadequate incomes, only 238 million (12.6%) of the population of LDCs (excluding China) were assessed to be at risk in 1975, and only 48 million (2.5%) if only 10% of families had inadequate incomes (Poleman 1981, p.53).

Lipton (1982) also accepts that young children and nursing mothers are most at risk, but that policy measures should be focused on whole families of the 'ultra-poor', where the ultra-poor are those forced into under-nourishment (p.49). He argues (p.62) that in low-income countries on a particular day, 2–3% of people (perhaps 3–5% of under-fives) are severely malnourished due to poverty, and that during a typical five-year period 10–15% of 'ultra-poor' people may have a substantial risk of falling into this 2–3% group. He concedes that a further 25–35% of people may often be forced into serious hunger, but without being at nutritional risk. He therefore suggests that only 10–20% of people in LDCs, rather than the 40–70% often claimed, should be seen as being too poor to avoid under-nutrition.[3]

A nutrition-related measure of poverty-line income probably provides the most reliable basis for measuring the progress in development. This is true irrespective of which of the nutritional standards discussed above is chosen as the basis for the measure, since all of them are closely related by definition. Using any particular poverty line, it should be possible to answer the key questions 'what is happening to the proportions of LDC populations which are malnourished, and what is likely to happen to them in the future?'. Unfortunately, attempts to quantify development progress in this way are scanty. In the FAO Fourth World Food Survey a comparative estimate of numbers consuming less than 1.2 BMR suggested that the extent of the LDC population which was malnourished may have risen from 401 million (24%) to 455 (25%) in the short interval from 1969–71 to 1972–74. Reutlinger and Selowsky, comparing base-line 1965 estimates (see Table 8.1) with projections for 1975 and 1990, also projected rising numbers of those with some degree of food deficit because of population growth (but a significantly reduced percentage); however, their projections entail a significant decline in those with deficits of more than 250 calories.[4] Given the rates of economic growth in LDCs since the mid-1960s, this is what might have been expected, granted that some of the benefits of growth have percolated down to the poorer and poorest members of society. Of course there are some 'crisis' countries where low (even negative) income and food supply growth coupled with rapid population growth have combined to cause increased malnutrition. But on a global basis it seems probable that some progress has been made towards reducing malnutrition and other related symptoms of underdevelopment. This view is substantiated by data presented at a recent conference (FAO 1983) which indicates (1) declining rates of infant and child mortality in all LDC continents between 1968 and 1980, and (2) a diminution between 1970–72 and 1978–80 in the number of countries with a high risk of calorie shortfall. However, many countries remain in the high-risk category, especially in sub-Saharan Africa.

As the same FAO (1983) report points out, however, in a significant number of LDCs improvements in the nutritional balance have been due in substantial measure to increased cereal imports. During the period 1970–80 cereal imports grew at an annual rate of 6.4% in 46 high-food-risk LDCs, 2.6% in the 32 medium-risk countries and 4.3% in the 18 at low-risk countries. In fact net cereal imports by the largest 90 LDCs (excluding China) rose from 10.1 million tonnes per year in 1961–65 to 33.2 million tonnes in 1975–79. Without this contribution to supplies from trade and aid the extent of malnutrition would have been greater in many countries. The fact is that food production growth in many LDC countries did not manage to keep pace with growth in demand. As Table 8.3 indicates, food production in developing market economies is calculated to have grown at 2.8% per annum or 0.4% per capita, per annum during 1961/65–80. Given that per capita food demand has grown as a result of income growth, and because of the effect of increased demand for livestock products upon use of cereals for animal feed, this rate of growth of per capita production was less than that in food demand – hence the increase in cereal imports. The shortfall can be seen to have been particularly critical in Africa where per capita food production declined at around 1.0% a year during the last two decades, and to a lesser extent in the Far East where output growth slowed down in the second

Table 8.3   Rates of Growth in Agricultural Production and Demand in LDCs
(% per year)

	Population growth 1961/65–80	Demand growth 1961/65–79	Production growth 1961/65–80	
			Total	Per caput
90 LDCs	2.6	3.0	2.8	0.2
Africa	2.8	2.9	1.8	−1.0
Far East	2.5	2.8	2.9	0.4
Latin America	2.7	3.2	3.0	0.3
Near East	2.6	4.1	3.0	0.4
Low-income	2.4	2.5	2.3	−0.1
Middle-income	2.8	3.7	3.2	0.4

Source: FAO (1981), Table 2.2.

half of the 1970s. Indeed, in Africa even availability of imports was inadequate in many cases to overcome deficiencies in domestic supply; of 36 African countries, FAO (1983) estimates that no less than 14 had negative growth in per capita calorie supplies during 1970–80, while in other regions 7 countries including India, Bangladesh and Sri Lanka also recorded negative supply growth.

Thus there are a number of countries with large populations, mainly in Africa, but also in Asia, where population growth does appear to be pressing against the capacity for food supply growth; and Bangladesh, China and India all have extensive programmes to introduce methods of birth control. But for those worried that this confirms the more pessimistic assessments of the world's maximum sustainable population, it should be emphasised that the general condition has been one of increasing per capita food supplies; as the first row of Table 8.3 reveals, for 90 LDCs taken together per capita food production grew by 0.2% a year in the 1960s and 1970s. Thus, to the extent that food supplies have not generally exerted a tight constraint on global population growth in the recent past, there is no compelling reason to believe that they will do so in the near future. As Sinha (1976, p.5) states, 'the unprecedented rate of population growth which has been experienced by the developing world is itself partly a sign of the success of developmental efforts and not of failure'. However, as already stated, a large number of the additional population are undernourished, and there is likewise no reason for optimism that this condition will disappear.

While the most important dimensions of the 'World Food Problem' (WFP) are to be observed in the long-run underlying persistence of widespread chronic malnutrition, it appears to be the periodic worsening of the problem arising from the inevitable fluctuations around the trend which does most to focus attention upon it. In particular, the food shortages of 1972–75 caused a sharp upsurge of concern about present and future food supplies, and led to questioning as to whether sufficient priority has been attached to agricultural expansion by both developing and developed countries. (Similarly, the famines in Ethiopia, the Sudan and many other African countries in 1984 and 1985 prompted a sharp upsurge in public awareness of the problems.) In periods such as this, increases in food prices, which are the natural indicators of shortages, seriously affect people in the richer nations and cause them to have heightened awareness of the scarce economic nature of food. More critically, an undoubted consequence of this period of global high prices must have been an increase in the number of poor people, predominantly in developing countries, whose nutritional intake fell below the prescribed standards. Such periods of aggravation of the food problem are rightly a matter of deep concern, but they should not be allowed to obscure the fact that the true nature of the WFP is the chronic, deep-seated one that at any time a substantial proportion of the world population is too poor to purchase sufficient nutrients to feed itself adequately at prevailing prices. For the most part these hungry people will be the families of landless-workless men, families with farm holdings too small to generate even subsistence needs, or families of the working poor. Inevtiably, most of these people live in poor countries which cannot afford and do not provide welfare benefits so that, by definition, the malnutrition problem can be seen to be directly attributable to, and the most serious consequence of, underdevelopment.

8.2   Some Elementary Analysis

In analysing the link between poverty and malnutrition it is of critical importance to distinguish between the concepts of biological shortage (discussed in Section 8.1) and economic shortage. The notion of biological shortage is conceptually straightforward – it is that there are insufficient nutrients to supply the physiological needs of some person or group of persons. The economic notions of demand and shortages are entirely different and can be readily illustrated with the aid of two simple diagrams, Figures 8.1 and 8.2.

The market demand curve for a commodity is conventionally defined as the amounts of that commodity which would be purchased during a specified time interval at alternative prices of the commodity by a group of people with fixed disposable incomes, the prices of all other commodities being held constant. It is generally assumed that such a curve will be negatively sloping so that at lower prices more will be consumed, as in Figure 8.1. The rise in food purchases from Q_1 to Q_2 as price falls reflects

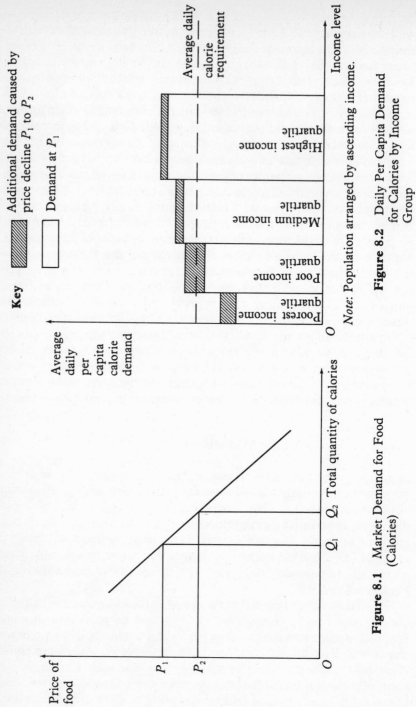

Key

▨ Additional demand caused by price decline P_1 to P_2

▢ Demand at P_1

Figure 8.2 Daily Per Capita Demand for Calories by Income Group

Note: Population arranged by ascending income.

Figure 8.1 Market Demand for Food (Calories)

that people would always like to consume more than they do, but that their ability to satisfy these wants is restricted by their purchasing power, or income. In economic terms the fact that goods have prices is taken to reflect that desired consumption exceeds available supplies, which are therefore in this economic sense always scarce or short. Markets balance people's desire to satisfy their wants and needs by purchasing goods, with the availability of such goods. In achieving this balance there is no necessity that any one individual's needs will be met. This is made clear in Figure 8.2 which depicts the distribution of individual's behaviour underlying the effect of the price change on demand in Figure 8.1.[5] Because of an unequal distribution of income, the average amount of food acquired by the poorest 50% of the population is shown as falling below the recommended level. As prices fall from P_1 to P_2, the real value of fixed money incomes rises, so that all income groups are able to increase their food purchases. Despite this, the poorest quartile (25%) of the population is shown as still unable on average to satisfy its nutrient needs even with a large proportionate demand increase, but the next quartile up the income distribution is shown as now achieving its recommended needs. The richer two quartiles, which had been able to satisfy their needs at price P_1, would (as shown in Figure 8.2) typically increase their intake further as prices fall to P_2, but by relatively small proportions reflecting the decline of income and price elasticities of food demand at higher income levels.

What all this underlines is that even at very low food prices there can be no guarantee that hunger and malnutrition among the poor will be eliminated. It is in the nature of the market system that nearly everybody has less than they want, and that some people have less than they need, whatever the prevailing price. Provided that income continues to be unequally distributed, it seems inevitable that hunger and malnutrition will continue as long as we rely upon the competitive market system to allocate available food supplies.

While the basic relationship between poverty and nutritional intake presented in Figure 8.2 is quite adequate, it is simplified in some noteworthy respects. One of these relates to the importance of own-production (or subsistence) in providing for the nutritional needs of the poor in LDCs. Many of the poorest people live in rural areas and farm on a small scale as their principal means of support. However, their resources are often inadequate and they are reliant upon purchases in the market for the balance of their needs; and, with the growth in the numbers of rural and urban landless poor, the reliance of the poor upon purchased supplies (or payment in kind) has increased. Nevertheless, own-production represents a very important form of what Sen (1981) calls entitlements to food (and other goods). Sen identifies as sources of entitlement (1) own-labour power, which can be hired to someone else for payment or used to produce for oneself in conjunction with other resources, and (2) inherited and transfer entitlement, which derives from resources given by others and which can be sold to augment income or bartered directly for food and other goods. The point here is that inherited or accumulated wealth is not typically counted as income but can nevertheless be exchanged for food, and as with own-production it modifies the relationship between income and food consumption. Of course, it is true that the poorest people do not have much accumulated wealth, but, as Sen indicates, there are occasions when a sudden drop in the value of accumulated wealth causes people normally considered to have wealth to join the ranks of the very poor. In particular, Sen cites cases when, as a result of drought, the livestock of pastoralists have become valueless, as a consequence of which the pastoralists have been the most vulnerable group to famine. Broadly, what this adds up to is that in seeking to use income as the explanatory variable of food consumption of individuals or families, the income measure used should make full allowance for own-production and all other entitlements which are exercised.

Turning briefly to the economics of supply, theory suggests that the higher the price the greater will be supply. But at higher prices the poor are increasingly unable to feed themselves adequately. Of course, technological change does shift the food supply curve to the right over time. The future of the world food problem depends greatly upon the rate of such shifts in relation to corresponding shifts in the demand curve (arising from population and income growth). If, as in the past, technological change shifts agricultural supply curves to the right more rapidly than the demand curves, the real price of food will fall and an increasing proportion of productive resources can be deployed for non-food production. If, however, supply shifts exactly match demand shifts, then food prices will remain constant. Any tendency of supply shifts to lag behind those in demand will cause prices to rise, and it is this condition which can be defined as a situation of increasing economic shortage.

The theory also provides a basis for assessing the prospects for future growth of food supplies in the face of ever-increasing demand. Supply curves slope upwards because, it is recognised, higher prices will make it profitable to allocate new resources to production. With this principle in mind it seems feasible to argue that the world economic *potential* for supply growth is more than adequate to cope with the expected doubling of the world population to eight and a half billion by AD 2025. This is based on the reasoning that, even making no allowance for new technological innovations, if prices were sufficiently high, it would be possible to switch a massive amount of resources from industrial production into intensive agriculture. Such a process would represent a reversal of the historic process of development, whereby food expenditure and agricultural employment have fallen as proportions of the relevant totals. Control of the ecological consequences of such an intensification of agricultural production would itself demand substantial resources, thereby increasing production costs and agriculture-related employment still further.[6]

This extreme scenario highlights several important aspects of the world food problem and of underdevelopment. It is not limitation on the technical capacity to produce food which is the prime cause for concern about hunger and malnutrition in poor countries. It is lack of income by the poor in underdeveloped countries, which is a necessity for them to convert their biological food demand into effective economic demand, and for them to pay the higher prices needed to stimulate food production or encourage importation of food. The question of how such incomes are to be obtained by the poor is the key issue of development. Another highlighted aspect is the central role of agricultural technology, in that large-scale mobilisation of resources and changes in farming technique are required in some, mainly developing countries, if the massive technical potential for increasing world food production is to be realised. Unless cost-reducing, yield-increasing technological change in agriculture continues at a rapid rate, it is inevitable that world food prices will rise and cause the development problem to be more intractable than it is now.[7] High priority for agricultural development is essential in the economic plans of poor countries and in international policies to assist these countries, to ensure that rates of technological changes do not fall below the levels which have been achieved historically.

Simple economic analysis also illuminates the existing and prospective pattern of world trade in foodstuffs. A direct implication of the conclusion that the rich will always be able to purchase as much food as they need (and often more) is that the wealthier nations are always likely to be able to acquire food supplies on an adequate scale for their population, whereas the poorer ones may not find themselves in such a favourable position.[8] In fact the action of commodity exporters and brokers may well result in food (as opposed to tropical fruit and beverage crops) being exported from poor countries with a chronic malnutrition problem to countries which on average are overfed. Such exports will occur if the export price obtainable by traders exceeds the price which food commodities command in domestic markets − such action will of course bid domestic prices up to the international level. This situation is most likely to occur with concentrated protein sources, for which transport costs to the final destination are a smaller percentage of export (fob) value, than for bulky starchy foods. In some cases it may be commercially profitable for poor countries to export high-quality protein foods and to import cheaper, low-quality (in terms of protein) foods such as grains and, in some of these, the nutritional position may be improved by such trade; but in some instances it may even pay private traders to export basic grains from countries with serious malnutrition problems. Typical examples of the sort of trade that arises in foodstuffs are the export to developed countries of beef from Kenya and Brazil, manioc from Thailand and oilseeds from a number of tropical countries (Abbott 1972). At the same time there has been a major trade in wheat and other grains from the USA, Canada and Australia to various developing countries, particularly to India.

Food exports from poor countries are, of course, more likely to occur in periods of global food shortage and high prices, such as that occurring from 1973–75, which is when the capacity of the rich to outbid the poor for food supplies becomes most evident. That this capacity has been heightened by economic development is one of the paradoxes of development. As rail, road, telephone and port facilities in poorer countries have been improved, and as their professional expertise in organising international trade has grown, so increasingly have separate regional markets in agricultural products coalesced into a single global market in which price signals emanating from North America, Europe and Japan directly influence food prices in Central Africa, Asia and South America, and can induce the export of food from these countries.

8.3   Future Prospects and Policy Options

From the analytical framework sketched in the previous section, four main factors can be identified which will determine the extent to which the domestic agriculture of LDCs meets the nutritional needs of their citizens. The actual nutritional outcome of these will be modified by the availability of food imports and aid, the ability to purchase imports, and by the extent to which LDCs are prepared to subsidise food consumption by the poor (matters which are discussed briefly later). The four principal factors are: (1) the rate of population growth – although this is expected to fall below 2.5% annually in the remainder of this century, it is expected to remain above 2% into the early part of the next, with the most rapid growth occurring in Africa followed by South Asia; (2) the annual rate of growth of GNP and hence income per capita, which in the decade 1971–80 averaged approximately 2.5% in the LDCs; (3) changes in the distribution of income, and of available food supplies – any increase in inequality will, given the link between poverty and malnutrition, increase the number of malnourished; and (4) the rate of cost-reducing technical change in agriculture; in order to improve the nutritional condition of LDCs, food supply at constant real prices needs to expand as rapidly as possible. (The constant-real price qualification is important because if the stimulus to output growth was higher real prices, the poor could become more seriously disadvantaged.) Moreover, the main source of increased supply will have to be yield increases resulting from technological change, rather than expansion of the cultivated area in LDCs, since the scope for the latter is now severely limited in most LDCs.

Using projected values of variables 1, 2^9 and 4 above, FAO (1981) has constructed alternative estimates for the LDC food economy in the year 2000. In the basic 'continuation-of-trends' scenario it is assumed that for 90 LDCs population growth will slow down to average 2.4% between 1980 and 2000, food demand growth will fall slightly to 2.9%, and production growth will be maintained at 2.8% to give per caput food output growth of 0.4% annually. Even this scenario is based on some optimistic assumptions, such as that there will be no further declines in production of any commodity/country which previously experienced a declining trend, and that countries which have been exhibiting a declining per capita consumption will no longer do so. This last assumption is equivalent to assuming that low-income LDCs with output growth rates lower than demand growth will be able to import the balance of requirements needed to prevent declining consumption. Even with these assumptions the situation is projected to worsen, with an increase in the number of seriously malnourished from a 1974–76 estimate of 435 million people to 590 million in the year 2000. Such an achievement is estimated to involve rates of increase in cereal imports by low-income countries in Africa and the Far East higher than those occurring in recent years. If realistic restrictions are placed upon cereal import growth by these countries, then the number of malnourished could rise by 685 million in 2000.

FAO (1981) has used the 'continuation-of-trend' scenario as a basis for identifying the inputs and investments which would be required to raise agricultural output growth to a higher rate and hence create a more favourable nutritional outcome. This approach therefore places the emphasis upon agricultural technology as the principal means of ameliorating malnutrition. The projections indicate the need for substantially increased investment in such things as land development, irrigation, machinery and food storage, as well as for continued rapid growth in the use of fertiliser and other current inputs. Raising annual output growth in the rest of this century from 2.8 to 3.8% in the LDCs is estimated to require a more than doubling of current annual investment and a tripling of current input use. Commitment of additional resources on this scale in market economies will depend primarily upon the extent to which strong demand generates the necessary (high price) incentives to invest. It will also be determined by the willingness of international donors and LDC governments to subsidise and promote technological change. In view of the slow (and, in some LDCs, negative) GDP growth rates in 1981–83, and of cutbacks in international aid, it cannot be said that the prospects are good for increasing agricultural output growth rates above 2.8% through greatly increased investment – especially since agricultural growth in the early 1980s has failed to reach even this level. While it is nevertheless vitally important that a firm commitment to increasing LDC agricultural output be maintained, both internationally and nationally, it is important to recognise that there are alternative policies which might be pursued to reduce the incidence of malnutrition.

Although no attempt is made here to classify policies for tackling the food problem of the poor countries according to whether they originate within these countries, rather than at an international level with the support of the rich countries, it has to be recognised that the distinction between policies at the two levels is significant. International-level policies reflect not purely humanitarian or imperialistic considerations but also acceptance that some major irritants of the problem arise from demand-supply conditions in world markets which are outside the control of the poor countries. It is considered appropriate that the rich countries should at least partially compensate the poorer ones for certain adverse external effects of the fluctuations in economic activity in the industrial nations. Nevertheless, the main attack on the nutrition problem of poor countries must be managed directly through the policies of the countries themselves. This is especially true in relation to expanding domestic food supplies and the taking of steps to adjust income distributions. Individual countries may wish, and be able, to enlist international support for their domestic policies, but while considering the policy options discussed below it should be remembered that the initiative lies primarily with the developing countries.

The types of policy which might be pursued to reduce the incidence of malnutrition are characteristic of the policy options for promoting economic development generally. Broadly, there are three groups of policies: (1) those which aim to accelerate change without modifying institutional structure or materially interfering with the 'free' operation of markets; (2) those which require the introduction of new major institutions to modify either the operations or outcomes of existing market systems; and (3) policies which aim to bypass normal market operations. The majority of the commonly applied policies of agricultural development fall within the first two of these groups. Since the first of these is extensively discussed in Chapter 7, little further consideration is given here.

There are aspects of the second and third policy categories, however, which are not discussed elsewhere, and which merit a brief mention here. The third category of policies recognises the inherent weaknesses of market systems (particularly in developing countries), and represents the most direct means of tackling the food problem. It should, therefore, in principle be both the cheapest and most effective approach to the problem. Basically, it entails making direct transfers of food to those unable to purchase their needs in open markets − direct transfers of income would represent the same direct type of policy – but this has not been widely employed by developing countries for obvious fiscal reasons. Such policies are, however, as Reutlinger and Selowsky (1976) showed, the most cost-effective policies for dealing with malnutrition, since they are targeted directly at the poor. Concessional sales policies through 'fair-price' shops, such as are extensively applied in South Asia, are much blunter and therefore less effective policy instruments, since inevitably many benefit who are quite capable of meeting their needs from their own resources, and in any case in several countries (e.g. India) fair-price shops are restricted to urban centres, thus excluding the rural poor and providing an additional incentive for migration to urban areas.[10]

The main source of food supplies for free distribution in LDCs is international food aid. This food aid is transferred partly (around 25%) through the multilateral World Food Programme (WFP), but mainly through the bilateral schemes of the principal donor countries, which are the USA, the EEC, Canada and Japan. Whereas all multilateral food transfers are a form of grant aid, over 70% of bilateral 'donations' are on a concessional basis, that is they are bought on concessional terms rather than being free. Most food aid, whether given to or bought by the (112 in 1980/81) recipient countries, is sold under special schemes rather than given to the needy. In fact, according to Maxwell and Singer (1979) 66% of food aid is sold by recipients, 16% is distributed through food-for-work schemes, 11% goes to supplementary feeding programmes and 7% only is distributed as emergency food relief.

In principle, emergency food relief programmes are relatively uncontroversial. They constitute responses to localised man made or natural disturbances to food supplies which can have disastrous consequences for poor countries lacking the resources to replace capital destroyed. In such cases it is appropriate that food should be distributed free to people within the designated disaster area. There are, of course, sometimes difficulties in assessing when a disaster has occurred and what its geographical extent may be. Such difficulties contribute to the delays which typically occur in delivering food aid, and which do much to nullify the effectiveness of such programmes. Frequently aid arrives too late. Analysis of 84 emergency operations by the WFP indicated that the average delay from the date of receipt of an aid request to the first delivery of food was 172 days and the arrival of the main consignment took 196 days. In the extreme case of general food aid from Europe, Stevens (1977) reported that the *average* time from request for food aid to its date of shipment was 431 days when destined for Egypt, 479 days for Bangladesh and 503 days to Sri Lanka. Doubtless delays have been reduced since the mid-1970s, but the fact remains that bureaucratic aid mechanisms are much slower to respond than commercial supplies and do much to undermine the effectiveness of food aid in dealing with emergencies.

With more general food aid, which can be directed at the chronic, persis-tent aspect of malnutrition in LDCs, the problem of delays in individual requests is less crucial. Nevertheless, many other objections have been raised about the effectiveness of these programmes – for a fuller review, see Maxwell and Singer (1979) or Cathie (1982). Many criticisms arise from the fact that much food aid is sold. Even at concessional prices in fair-price shops the seriously malnourished may be too poor to derive much benefit. Lappe, Collins and Fowler (1979) cite studies indicating that in Bangladesh 90% of food aid may have been sold to the middle class, and that in Upper Volta 75% of food aid was distributed to the better-off urban dwellers, rather than to the rural poor. Another heavily researched criticism is that sale of food aid (as opposed to distribution to those unable to buy in the market place) inevitably means that food prices and incen-tives to local production are reduced. Further objections relate to the way food aid is distributed between recipient countries, and in particular to the apparent direction of USA aid more towards politically sensitive coun-tries, such as Egypt, Israel, Jordan and formerly South Vietnam, than to the poorest countries. Concern has also been expressed by developing countries about the use, by donors, of concessional food aid as a means of creating new commercial markets at the expense of other exporters. This concern was reflected in the setting up in 1954 by the FAO Committee on Commodity Problems (CCP) of a Consultative Subcommittee on Surplus Disposal. This could be interpreted as acknowledgement of the fact the the donors' primary aim for food aid is to dispose of surplus food. Never-theless, the existence of grain and skimmed milk powder surpluses in developed countries is what has provided the basis for internationally sponsored emergency food relief, food-for-work schemes, and supplemen-tary feeding of children and pregnant and nursing mothers in LDCs. Despite the criticisms, benefits do accrue to the malnourished from these programmes and, in regions such as sub-Saharan Africa in particular, food aid plays and will continue to play a vital role. (Cereal food aid to sub-Saharan Africa rose from 958 to 2,289 thousand tonnes between 1974/5 and 1980/1 or from 11.2 to 27.3% of total food aid, and much more will be needed in future according to FAO (1981) projections.) There is no doubt, however, that food aid programme administration could be improved and directed more effectively to tackle the problem of malnutrition if the political will existed to change the emphasis of objectives and the rules of policy.

Turning briefly to policies in the second category – new institutions to moderate the impact of market forces upon the malnourished – there have been disappointments and some developments in the decade follow-ing the upheaval of 1973–75 when there was a sharp deterioration in available cereal stocks combined with increased import demand and high prices. These events gave rise to a new sense of concern about future food supplies to LDCs and a whole set of new internationally supported institutions was created to help overcome the impending problems. Among these organisations are the World Food Council (WFC), the International Fund for Agricultural Development (IFAD) and the Consultative Group on Food Production and Investment (CGFPI).

Much discussion arising from these initiatives was directed towards creating a new food reserve system – additional, that is, to the one embodied in the commercial grain and food products trading system. The focus of discussion was on the creation of buffer fund (and commodity) stocks either at the international or national level. At the national level such schemes may greatly augment food storage capacity and reduce food losses from on-farm storage, thus creating both long- and short-term benefits. In the short term such schemes help ensure that food supplies last from one harvest to the next,[11] while in the longer run they should help eliminate the extreme high prices in years of poor harvest and can provide emergency food reserves. This thinking was one of the factors underlying the UNCTAD negotiations started in 1976 relating to the establishment of a multilateral, multicommodity scheme embracing buffer stocks for a possible 18 commodities as part of the creation of a New International Economic Order (NIEO). It must be stated, however, that buffer stock schemes, except in so far as they include provision for emergency food relief, do not frontally attack the malnutrition problem. To the extent that they help poor consumers in some years by holding down prices, and poor peasant producers in others by supporting prices, such schemes may alleviate the food problem at the margin; but their effectiveness in this is constrained by the fact that price stabilisation rather than solving the food problem is their main objective. This narrow role was not what was envisaged by the LDC and middle-income countries involved in the NIEO negotiations. They had in mind broader objectives (of higher export commodity prices and additional food aid) which would have involved the new system being turned into a new channel for aid from the developed countries (DCs). Failure by the DCs to accept this interpretation, perhaps inevitably, has meant that after many rounds of negotiation, little progress has been made towards implementing the proposals for a system of integrated buffer stocks. (See Chapter 5 for more detailed discussion of the NIEO proposals, and of the relative ineffectiveness of buffer stock schemes.) More positive, but hardly decisive, developments have been the extension of the IMF Compensatory Finance Facility to enable countries to borrow funds to cover increased cereal import costs at times of reduced export earnings, and the EEC's STABEX Convention for helping stabilise the export earnings of a large number of poorer LDCs (STABEX also is more fully discussed in Chapter 5).

One policy of institutional change which must be mentioned in this context is redistributive land reform. As is more fully discussed in Chapter 7, one of the most critical issues in agricultural development strategy is whether it is more efficient to distribute land in small parcels to peasants, or to create larger holdings on which there is a tendency to substitute machinery and other inputs for labour. There can be little doubt that where the latter strategy increases the number of landless-workless people, it exacerbates the food problems of the rural poor, whereas distributive land reform, although it may reduce the rate of growth of marketed surplus, puts either food or income directly into the hands of some of the poorest families. This highlights once again the links between unequal income distribution and the food problem.

As to the other set of policies which may exert beneficial influence upon the food problem – those which neither create new institutions nor explicitly interfere with the operation of markets – it includes all those aspects of policy which improve efficiency in the production and distribution of foodstuffs and exert a downward influence on prices. Its principal component is the set of national policies typically operated by Ministries of Agriculture via existing institutions such as extension services, parastatal marketing organisations, rural development agencies and research organisations. These are discussed extensively in Chapter 7 and it would be superfluous to consider them further in detail here. But what should be re-emphasised is that these policies, which form the core of agricultural policy, are not specifically intended to tackle the food problem as we have defined it. Their main objectives are in increasing agricultural supply rather than in reducing the gap between the biological need for food and the expressed economic demand for food in the market place. Such general measures cannot therefore be expected to have a dramatic impact upon the food problem, and will only help alleviate it to the extent that the development benefits they produce trickle down to the poorest (unemployed and underemployed) members of society. This observation also extends to general (non-radical) development policies directed at sectors other than agriculture. Their contribution to solving the food problem (as a key symptom of the deprivation associated with underdevelopment) rests more upon the extent to which the benefits are distributed to the poor than upon simply increasing the rate of economic growth. However, because general development policies by definition are not specifically aimed at the poorest people, it is doubtful whether, except in the very long run, they can have a major impact upon the problem of malnutrition. It is for this reason that we have argued that specifically designed food distribution policies or radical redistributive measures are best suited to overcoming this 'malnutrition' syndrome of underdevelopment.

Notes

1. For a helpful appreciation of Malthus and his critics, see T.H. Hollingworth's introduction to the edition of Malthus's work published in 1973 (Malthus 1973).
2. According to Poleman (1981, p.4), the specific allowances adopted were 2,230–2,300 cals per day for the far East, 2,400–2,430 cals for Africa and 2,440–2,600 for Latin America.
3. The key to this phrase 'too poor to avoid undernutrition', is the evidence collated by Lipton that families consuming less than FAO/WHO-recommended diets frequently opt not to increase calorie consumption, but choose instead to diversify their diet and consume more expensive forms of calories. This is seen as indicating that they do not perceive their priority to be more calories, and that even if they had more income it could not be assumed that it would be used to eliminate their calorie deficit.
4. Reutlinger and Selowsky in fact generated three sets of projections for each of 1975 and 1990 under three alternative sets of assumptions, so that this statement represents an average position.
5. Figure 8.2 reflects the Reutlinger and Selowsky (1976)/Knudsen and Scandizzo (World Bank 1979) approach to estimating the number of people malnourished. Using an estimated caloric demand function with respect to income, they calculate the average caloric demand for the different income groups, and thereby estimate the number of people in income groups which consume less than nutrient need.
6. For a more than usually balanced account of the ecological and resource implications of substantially increasing world agricultural output, see Borgstrom (1969).
7. Of course it is true that high food prices may increase the GDP per capita in poor countries. But the benefits of this will primarily go to those with land, and the poor will be further disadvantaged.
8. Referring to countries as if they were indivisible consumer units is a useful form of shorthand. It is not used to imply that the food balance is not the outcome of independent decisions taken by producers, middlemen and consumers.
9. In fact FAO presents estimates of food demand growth which depend on both income and population growth, rather than presenting the assumed rate of income growth.
10. There are exceptions such as Sri Lanka which has effectively, but expensively, pursued a subsidised rationing policy for all, and among middle-income countries Portugal, which subsidises consumption of all major temperate foods.
11. It should be recognised that, for many, hunger and malnutrition may be a seasonal phenomenon. Supplies are plentiful and cheap immediately after harvest but scarce and expensive immediately before harvest. Evidence of such a pattern is presented by Haswell (1975, Ch.4).

References

Abbott, J.C. (1972) 'The efficient use of world protein supplies', FAO, *Monthly Bulletin of Agricultural Economics and Statistics*, 21(6).

Berg, A. (1971) *The Nutrition Factor*, The Brookings Institution.

Berg, A. (1981) *Malnourished People: A Policy View*, World Bank, Poverty and Basic Needs Series, Washington, DC.

Bhagwati, J. and Eckaus, R. (eds) *Foreign Aid*, Penguin Books.

Boerma, A.H. (1975) *Political Will and the World Food Problem*, UN Food and Agricultural Organisation, Rome.

Borgstrom, G. (1969) *Too Many: A Study of Earth's Biological Limitations*, Macmillan.

Cathie, J. (1982) *The Political Economy of Food Aid*, Gower Press.

FAO (1973) *Energy and Protein Requirements*, Nutrition Meetings Report Series, 52, Rome.

FAO (1977) *The Fourth World Food Survey*, Rome.

FAO (1981) *Agriculture: Toward 2000*, Rome.

FAO (1983) *Progress Report on WCARRD Programme of Action*, Rome.

Haswell, M. (1975) *The Nature of Poverty*, Macmillan.

Isenman, P.J. and Singer, H.W. (1977) 'Food aid: disincentive effects and their policy implications', *Economic Development and Cultural Change*, 25(2).

Lappe, F.M., Collins, J. and Fowler, C. (1979) *Food First: Beyond the Myth of Scarcity*, Ballatine.

Lipton, M. (1982) *Poverty, Undernutrition and Hunger*, World Bank Staff Working Paper.

Malthus, T.R. (1973) *An Essay on the Principle of Population*, Dent.

Maxwell, S.J. and Singer, H.W. (1979) 'Food-aid to developing countries: a survey', *World Development*, 7(3).

Poleman, T.T. (1981) 'Quantifying the nutrition situation in developing countries', *Food Research Institute Studies*, XVIII(1), Stanford.

Reutlinger, S. and Selowsky, M. (1976) *Malnutrition and Poverty: Magnitude and Policy Options*, World Bank Staff Occasional Papers, No. 23, Washington, DC.

Rogers, K.D., Srivastava, U.K. and Heady, E.O. (1972) 'Modified price, production and income impacts of food-aid under differentiated distribution', *American Journal of Agricultural Economics*, 54(2).

Sen, A.K. (1981) *Poverty and Famines: An Essay on Entitlement and Deprivation*, Oxford University Press.

Sinha, R.P. (1976) *Food and Poverty*, Croom-Helm.

Stevens, C. (1979) 'Food-aid – More Sinned Against than Sinning', *ODI Review*, No. 2.

World Bank (1979) *Nutrition and Food Needs in Developing Countries*, World Bank Staff Working Paper No. 328, prepared by O. Knudsen and P. Scandizzo, Washington, DC.

9

Industrial development in LDCs

9.1 The Desire for Industrialisation

In its broadest sense, the term 'industrialisation' denotes the organisation of production in business enterprises, characterised by specialisation and the division of labour, and involving the application of technology and mechanical and electrical power to supplement and replace human labour. Conceived of in this way, all sectors of the economy (the production of consumer goods and capital equipment, agriculture and service activities) can be 'industrialised' and thus it is the rational approach to the production process itself that is of significance, not merely the production of commodities considered to be 'industrial'.

In this chapter, however, we are concerned with a much narrower concept of industrialisation – the development of manufacturing enterprises, producing what are commonly accepted as industrial goods, within the so-called 'modern' sector of the economy. A number of poor countries have focused attention on the importance of stimulating the development of small-scale, rural industries, but few LDCs, with the possible exceptions of India, Taiwan and the People's Republic of China, have made real progress in this area. Similarly, the recent emergence from obscurity of the so-called urban 'informal sector' (discussed in Chapter 4), with emphasis placed on the encouragement of small-scale, labour-intensive activities within that sector, has not altered the fact that for most politicians and policy makers in LDCs, industrialisation remains synonymous with the establishment of large-scale, capital-intensive enterprises in the 'modern' sector of the urban economy.

Indeed, for many people in positions of power in LDCs, industrialisation and development are seen as being synonymous with one another. The industrialisation of a basically agricultural, primary export-oriented economy was seen as the means by which the chains of dependence forged during the colonial period could be broken, matching the newly acquired political independence with economic independence. Industry would create extensive employment opportunities, absorbing excess labour leaving the rural sector, it would raise output per head and living standards

267

throughout the economy and, significantly, it would induce necessary and desirable changes in social and cultural attitudes and institutions through the 'modernising' impact of imported organisational methods and technologies. In some LDCs, industrialisation was seen as the means by which specific socialist objectives could be achieved (with the experience of the Soviet Union very much in mind); in others, economic planners were more concerned with the role of industry in alleviating the balance of payments constraint, diversifying the economy and reducing excessive dependence on the export of a few primary commodities, the prices of which were allegedly subject to a long-run secular deterioration and which, in the short run, exhibited substantial year-to-year fluctuations around the trend.

9.2   Industry versus Agriculture

Industrial development and agricultural development have too often been viewed as conflicting objectives and a largely unproductive debate has flourished over the relative priority to be afforded to the expansion of the two sectors. Sutcliffe (1971, Ch.3) has argued that conflict is not inevitable and that the concept of 'priority', as used in the debate, is a misleading one:

> To give priority to something does not necessarily involve the expenditure of more than a very small amount of time or money. Matters of priority can be small or large. To give 'priority' to agriculture does not imply that investment, employment, output or productivity in agriculture should grow *faster* than in industry or that public investment in agriculture should be greater than that in industry ... It is quite possible that if the aim of a government was to encourage the maximum growth of industry within ten years, then for the first five years most attention would be devoted to agriculture, which could thereby more effectively provide raw materials for industry and demand for its products ... 'Priority' to industry here appears to imply 'priority' for agriculture; 'priority' is thus robbed of any operational meaning. (Sutcliffe 1971, p.72, emphasis in original)

It is now generally accepted that for the majority of LDCs, industrial and agricultural development should, as far as possible, proceed simultaneously. Agriculture provides the market for manufactured goods, satisfies the food requirements of the urban population, releases labour and capital for the industrial sector and earns the foreign exchange required for the importation of machinery and raw materials. Industry in turn supplies the inputs (tractors, fertilisers, etc.) required for the modernisation of the agricultural sector and the consumer goods demanded by the rural population and provides a market for a part of agricultural output through the processing and manufacture of foodstuffs for both domestic consumption and export.

These are essentially arguments for 'balanced growth' between the two sectors, but not all the arguments are equally valid for all LDCs. An over-populated country with a poor agricultural resource endowment may have no alternative but to attempt to industrialise and export manufactured goods with which to import essential foodstuffs. In open economies, the concept of 'balanced growth' loses a great deal of its meaning, and in any case it does not indicate which sector should be made the 'spearhead' of the development effort.

Paul Baran (1957), with the experience of the Soviet Union in mind, argued that under conditions of socialist planning,

> ... there can be no question as to whether development should proceed through industrialisation or through improvements of agriculture. It can take place only by a *simultaneous* effort in both directions ... the investment policy has to place its main accent on the development of industry – lifting agriculture at the same time high enough to support the industrialisation process – so as to be able eventually to turn around and give agriculture a major boost with the help of the expanded resources of industrial production. (Baran 1957, pp.282–3)

Baran's recommendation partly reflected the Soviet Union's decision that agriculture was to serve industry even though, as already indicated, the development of the two sectors was closely interrelated. The other important characteristic of the Soviet Union's industrialisation experience was the emphasis placed on the establishment of producer goods industries (especially producer goods that manufactured other producer goods). In contrast to this, the Maoist 'model' of development attempted to develop heavy industry, light industry and agriculture simultaneously. Heavy industry remained the focus of the development effort but was not to be promoted at the expense of the other two sectors. Light industry was to be expanded in order to raise the living standards of the mass of the population and to permit a reduction in the contribution of the agricultural sector to state revenues – the source of finance for industrial expansion (Magdoff 1975).

The above discussion should make it clear that the categories that are conventionally used for the classification of activities must be treated with caution. Some activities, for example the processing of foodstuffs, are an integral part of both the industrial and agricultural sectors, thus under-mining the 'industry–agriculture' dichotomy. In the industrial sector itself, we must clearly distinguish between producer (or capital) goods industries and consumer goods industries. (The Marxist tradition in particular has always made a sharp distinction between capital goods (Department I) and consumer goods (Department II).) The more common distinction between heavy and light industries is less satisfactory as it gives no indication of the destination of the output of those industries. Capital goods industries (machines that make machines) need not, of necessity, be 'heavy'. Intermediate goods (iron and steel) could fall into either category and so presumably could consumer goods. Although, therefore, definitional problems exist, we assume, with Stewart (1976, p.121), that the distinction between capital and consumer goods is 'unproblematic'. The importance of different types of industries will be made clearer in later sections of this chapter.

9.3 The Growth of Industry in LDCs

Table 9.1 presents data on changes in the distribution of manufacturing value added (MVA) between different economic groupings over the period 1963–84. The share of the LDCs in global MVA rose from 7.8% in 1963 to an estimated 11.6% in 1984. Over the same period, the share of the developed market economies fell from 77.0% to 63.5%, largely as a result of the rapid growth of the centrally planned economies whose share of global MVA had risen to 24.9% by 1984. China's share in global MVA at constant 1975 prices was estimated by UNIDO (1985, p.35) to have risen from 3.45% in 1979 to 3.94% in 1982. The overall growth performance of the LDCs, although impressive in many respects, would, if maintained for the rest of the twentieth century, not be sufficient for those countries to achieve the so-called 'Lima Target' of accounting for 25% of global MVA by the year 2000. (For a discussion of the Lima Declaration and Plan of Action, see Singer 1979.)

Table 9.1 Estimated Shares in Manufacturing Value Added (MVA), by Economic Grouping, Selected Years, at Constant (1975) Prices (%)

Economic grouping	Year				
	1963	1970	1975	1980	1984
Developed market economies	77.0	73.3	67.9	65.5	63.5
Centrally planned economies	15.2	18.3	22.5	23.8	24.9
Less developed economies	7.8	8.4	9.6	10.7	11.6

Source: UNIDO (1985), Figure 1, p.16.
Notes: (i) China is excluded from these data.
        (ii) Figures for 1984 are estimates.

Table 9.2 Average Annual MVA Growth Rates in 95 LDCs, by Income Group, 1963–73 and 1973–81

Income group	GNP per capita, 1978 (current dollars)	MVA growth rate for income group (%)		Group share in population of LDCs, 1980 (%)	Number of countries in group
		1963–1973	1973–1981		
Low	295	4.6	4.7	50.7	28
Lower-middle	295–600	7.1	8.1	18.2	21
Intermediate	600–1,320	8.8	6.8	15.7	24
Upper-middle	1,320–2,415	9.1	6.1	12.3	11
High	2,415	7.5	3.7	3.1	11

Source: UNIDO (1985), Table 11.1, p. 17.

Table 9.2 presents data on growth rates of MVA for five income groups of LDCs for the periods 1963–73 and 1973–81. For the first period there was a strong, positive relationship between per capita GNP and rate of growth of MVA (with the exception of the high-income group). The relationship was less marked in the second period, when there was a marked deceleration in growth of MVA for those economies with a per capita GNP greater than $600. For the period as a whole, the low-income group achieved only a modest rate of growth of MVA, and given that this group accounted for approximately 50% of the total population of LDCs, the implications of this relatively poor performance are of far-reaching significance.

When the data presented in these two tables are disaggregated, a number of interesting points emerge. The share of the larger LDCs (with a population of more than 20 million towards the mid-1970s) rose from 5.6% of global MVA in 1963 to 8.0% in 1981 (UNIDO 1985, p.18). The share of the least developed countries remained unchanged at 0.2% over the entire period, and their position relative to other LDCs deteriorated quite significantly (in terms of their share of MVA of all LDCs).

There were also important regional changes which are highlighted in Table 9.3. LDCs in West Asia and South and East Asia have experienced a significant increase in their share of global MVA, whereas the increases for Africa and Latin America have been more modest. Latin America remains, however, the most industrialised region.

Table 9.4 identifies the ten LDCs which made the largest contributions to total LDC MVA at various times. In 1963, six of the largest contributors to LDC MVA were Latin American and together they accounted

Table 9.3   Shares of LDCs, by Region, in World MVA
(at constant 1975 prices), 1963−81 (%)

Region	Year			
	1963	1973	1979	1981
Africa	0.8	0.8	0.9	1.0
West Asia	0.5	0.6	0.9	1.0
South and East Asia	2.1	2.6	3.1	3.2
Latin America	4.7	5.5	5.7	5.9

Source: Taken from UNIDO (1985), Table 11.2, p.19.

for over 48% of LDC MVA (Brazil and Mexico alone accounted for just over 30%). By 1981, however, only four Latin American countries featured in the 'top ten', together accounting for less than 44% of LDC MVA. The fall in the relative share of LDC MVA of India over this period is also noteworthy.

What is clearly illustrated by Table 9.4 is the emergence of the Republic of Korea, Indonesia and Hong Kong as increasingly important LDC producers of manufactured goods. This point is further emphasised by the data in Table 9.5. Five countries − Brazil, Hong Kong, India, Mexico and the Republic of Korea − have made important contributions to the *increase* in LDC MVA. The large Latin American economies, and Brazil and Mexico in particular, dominate the overall picture presented in Tables 9.4 and 9.5, but the shift in the focus of LDC industrialisation to South and East Asia is very apparent.

What emerges clearly from the above discussion is that although there have been important changes in the structure of the world economy and the global distribution of MVA, the participation of most LDCs in the industrialisation process has been relatively limited. As UNIDO (1985, pp.20−2) notes:

> Industrial progress in the developing countries is dominated by the performance of a few countries and, to a lesser extent, by sporadic bursts of growth in a limited number of other countries. While such a pattern can provide instances of encouraging industrial performance, these instances are often isolated. They have little impact on the bulk of the population in the developing countries and, perhaps, only limited applicability to industrial conditions in those countries. Such a wide disparity in industrial capabilities is a poor substitute for the more broadly based effort that is required to alleviate poverty and better integrate the industrial efforts of individual developing countries.

Table 9.4 The 10 LDCs with the Largest Share of Total LDC MVA (at constant 1975 prices), 1963, 1973 and 1981 (%)[a]

1963		1973		1981	
Country	Share of LDC MVA	Country	Share of LDC MVA	Country	Share of LDC MVA
Brazil	19.64	Brazil	22.74	Brazil	22.71
India	13.48	Mexico	12.36	Mexico	13.88
Mexico	10.71	India	9.06	India	8.61
Argentina	9.02	Argentina	8.40	Republic of Korea	4.86
Venezuela	3.81	Turkey	4.21	Argentina	4.85
Turkey	3.43	Venezuela	3.08	Turkey	3.69
Philippines	2.82	Republic of Korea	2.85	Indonesia	2.77
Peru	2.76	Philippines	2.48	Philippines	2.62
Chile	2.40	Peru	2.30	Venezuela	2.46
Egypt	2.10	Iran (Islamic Republic of)	2.06	Hong Kong	2.27
Total	70.17	Total	69.54	Total	68.72

Source: UNIDO (1985), Table 11.3, p. 21.
Note: (a) Data were available for 97 LDCs.

Table 9.5 Contribution of Selected LDCs to the Increase in MVA of Total LDC MVA (at constant 1975 prices) (%)[a]

1963–73		1973–75		1975–77		1977–79		1979–81	
Brazil	25.4	Brazil	27.8	Brazil	25.2	Brazil	25.7	Mexico	35.0
Mexico	13.8	Mexico	15.4	Republic of Korea	8.7	Mexico	19.1	Indonesia	14.6
Argentina	7.9	Iran (Islamic Republic of)	9.7	India	8.5	Republic of Korea	10.0	India	13.5
India	5.2	Republic of Korea	9.0	Mexico	7.0	India	6.3	Hong Kong	8.7
Turkey	4.9	Turkey	5.9	Turkey	4.8	Indonesia	4.5	Pakistan	6.9
Republic of Korea	4.5	Indonesia	4.7	Thailand	4.1	Hong Kong	3.7	Republic of Korea	5.9
Iran (Islamic Republic of)	2.6	India	4.1	Hong Kong	3.7	Iraq	3.6	Egypt	5.5
Venezuela	2.4	Peru	3.4	Iran (Islamic Republic of)	3.4	Nigeria	3.2	Singapore	5.0
Philippines	2.2	Thailand	2.9	Philippines	3.2	Thailand	2.7	Philippines	5.0
Hong Kong	1.9	Egypt	2.5	Argentina	3.0	Saudi Arabia	2.2	Nigeria	4.9
Total	70.8	Total	85.4	Total	71.6	Total	81.0	Total	105.0

Source: UNIDO (1985), Table 11.5, p. 22.
Note: (a) Data were available for 97 LDCs.

Table 9.6 Distribution of GDP by Sector[a] in LDCs, 1965 and 1983 (%)[b]

Income groups	Agriculture		Industry		(Manufacturing)		Services	
	1965	1983	1965	1983	1965	1983	1965	1983
Low-income economies[c] (excluding India and China)	43	37	29	34	14	14	28	29
	44	38	16	19	11	12	40	43
Middle-income[d] Lower	31	22	24	33	15	16	45	45
Middle-income Upper	17	11	35	37	22	24	49	52
Industrial market economies	5	3	39	35	29	24	56	62

Source: World Bank (1985), Annex, Table 3.

Notes: (a) The agricultural sector comprises agriculture, forestry, hunting and fishing. The industrial sector comprises mining, manufacturing, construction and electricity, gas and water. All other branches of economic activity are categorised as services.

(b) All figures are weighted averages.

(c) LDCs with per capita GNP of less than $400 in 1983.

(d) LDCs with per capita GNP of $400 or more.

9.4 Industrialisation and Structural Change

Economists have long been interested in the identification and measurement of patterns of structural change as per capita income grows. As noted in Chapter 7, economic growth is associated with a consistent decline in the share of agriculture in national product, and a consistent increase in the share of the industrial sector, with no clear pattern emerging for the share of services.

Table 9.6 gives data on the sectoral division of GDP for three groups of LDCs, classified according to per capita income, and for the industrial market economies. It is clear that there are significant variations between different groups of countries, with the share of agriculture in GDP in 1983 varying between 11% for the upper middle-income group to 38% for the low-income economies (excluding India and China). The share of the industrial sector varies less widely and it is of interest to note that the share of industry in GDP was greater in the upper middle-income LDCs than in the industrial market economies in 1983.

In addition to changes in the *intersectoral* distribution of GDP, there have been important *intrasectoral* changes, that is, changes in the composition of MVA. The data in Table 9.7 show that the proportion of MVA accounted for by heavy industry has increased in all economic groupings, and for the world as a whole, the heavy industry subsector accounted for two-thirds of global MVA in 1980. When the data are rearranged to conform to an end-use classification, a similar pattern emerges (see Table 9.8). Focusing attention on the LDCs, it is clear that consumer non-durables remain the dominant grouping, even though there has been a dramatic fall in their share of manufacturing output over the period covered. The capital goods sector is relatively less developed in the LDCs, as compared to the other two economic groupings, and the implications of this characteristic of the LDCs are more fully discussed in Chapter 11.

The sectoral distribution of the labour force (Table 9.9) has changed less dramatically during this period. For all groups of LDCs, the industrial sector's share of the total labour force was less than its share of GDP, often by a significant amount (as in the low-income LDCs, for example). This is a reflection of the concentration of underemployed low-productivity labour within the agricultural sector, and the general use of capital-intensive methods of production in the 'modern' industrial sector, indicating rising labour productivity within that sector.

Data on employment growth in the industrial and/or manufacturing sectors of LDCs are usually incomplete and often unreliable (see Chapter 4). The LDCs exhibit great diversity with respect to rates of growth of employment and productivity within the industrial/manufacturing sector, as the countries included in Table 9.10 clearly show.

Employment data are available for a number of other LDCs not included

Table 9.7 Shares of Light and Heavy Industry in Manufacturing Output, by Economic Grouping and Developing Region, Selected Years (%)

Economic grouping or region	1963		1973		1980	
	Light industry	Heavy industry	Light industry	Heavy industry	Light industry	Heavy industry
World	40.5	59.5	35.2	64.8	33.5	66.5
Developed market economies	37.9	62.1	33.1	66.9	32.3	67.7
Developing countries[a]	56.9	43.1	46.3	53.7	42.9	57.1
Asia	59.5	40.5	48.3	51.7	46.2	53.8
Latin America	53.9	46.1	42.6	57.4	38.8	61.2
Centrally planned economies	44.3	55.7	37.2	62.8	33.0	67.0

Source: UNIDO (1983), Table 111.1, p.62.
Note: (a) Although the totals for developing countries include those for certain African countries, precise figures for the African region cannot be derived.

Table 9.8 Composition of Manufacturing Output, by Economic Grouping, 1963, 1973 and 1979 (%)

Classification	Developed market economies			Developing countries			Centrally planned economies		
	1963	1973	1979	1963	1973	1979	1963	1973	1979
By end use:									
Consumer non-durables	37.0	31.4	30.8	51.9	40.1	37.6	48.1	41.6	38.4
Industrial intermediates	19.4	22.7	23.7	27.3	31.5	31.2	16.3	18.4	17.8
Capital goods (including consumer durables)	43.6	45.9	45.5	20.8	28.4	31.2	35.6	40.0	43.8

Source: UNIDO (1983), Table 111.2, p.63.

Table 9.9 Distribution of Labour Force[a] by Sector in LDCs, 1965 and
1981 (%)

	Agriculture		Industry		Services	
	1965	1981	1965	1981	1965	1981
Low-income economies	77	73	9	13	14	15
(excluding India and China)	81	72	7	11	12	16
Middle-income						
Lower middle-income	66	54	13	17	22	29
Upper middle-income	45	30	21	28	34	42
Industrial market economies	14	6	39	38	48	56

Source: World Bank (1985), Annex, Table 21.
Notes: (a) The labour force comprises economically active persons aged 10 years and over,
including the armed forces and the unemployed, but excludes housewives,
students and other economically inactive groups.

in Table 9.10. South Korea experienced an average annual rate of growth
of employment in the manufacturing sector of approximately 12% over
the period 1963–76 (Hong 1981, p.377). Indonesia achieved an average
annual rate of growth of manufacturing sector employment of 3.7% over
the period 1965–71 (Pitt 1981, p.192). In the case of Pakistan, during the
period 1961–72, the large-scale manufacturing sector was estimated to
have achieved an average annual rate of growth of employment of 3.2%,
but this was more than offset by the decline in employment in the small-
scale manufacturing sector and overall, therefore, Pakistan experienced a
fall in employment in manufacturing (Guisinger 1981, p.307).

During the early 1970s, a number of LDCs experienced rises in productivity, although growth rates were usually below those for employment. In
the latter half of the 1970s, productivity growth in many LDCs was
adversely affected by external economic conditions (Chile, India and
Kenya being obvious exceptions) (UNIDO 1985, p.126). In general,
employment in heavy manufacturing activities grew more rapidly than
employment in light manufacturing, but the major part of manufacturing
sector employment was still provided in the more labour-intensive, light

Table 9.10 Growth of Labour Productivity in Manufacturing (%)

Country	Period	Value added	Employment	Productivity
			Growth rates	
Argentina	1970–74	4.5	3.5	1.0
	1974–81	−1.8	−5.7	4.1
	1970–81	0.3	−1.9	2.3
Chile	1971–74	−0.3	1.0	−1.3
	1974–79	2.8	−2.6	5.6
	1971–79	−1.2	−2.4	1.2
Cyprus	1974–80	12.5	8.6	3.6
Ghana	1970–74	8.7	6.4	2.1
	1974–75	−3.6	4.8	−8.1
	1970–75	7.1	6.5	0.6
Guatemala	1971–74	6.8	3.9	2.8
	1974–75	0.7	3.5	−2.7
	1971–75	5.4	4.0	1.3
Honduras	1971–74	4.6	7.1	−2.3
	1974–75	0.4	7.8	−6.9
	1971–75	3.5	7.7	−3.9
India	1970–74	2.3	2.9	−0.6
	1974–78	6.4	4.3	2.0
	1970–78	4.1	3.8	0.3
Iraq	1970–74	8.9	8.5	0.4
	1974–75	14.3	8.7	5.2
	1970–75	9.4	7.8	1.5
Kenya	1970–74	8.9	10.6	−1.5
	1974–80	14.6	5.2	8.9
	1970–80	11.3	6.6	4.4
Nicaragua	1973–74	10.9	14.7	−3.3
	1974–77	6.9	6.1	0.8
	1973–77	7.6	7.5	0.1
Nigeria	1970–74	6.9	9.2	−2.1
	1974–75	20.6	31.2	−8.1
	1970–75	7.8	12.0	−3.7
Panama	1970–74	5.5	5.1	0.3
	1974–79	3.4	2.0	1.4
	1970–79	3.0	2.2	0.8
Turkey	1970–74	10.6	7.3	3.1
	1974–79	5.7	3.9	1.7
	1970–79	7.9	5.3	2.4
Zambia	1970–74	7.3	6.2	1.1
	1974–75	−4.4	3.2	−7.3
	1970–75	5.6	6.2	−0.5
Zimbabwe	1970–74	9.7	7.9	1.7
	1974–80	0.2	0.3	−0.1
	1970–80	2.5	2.6	−0.1

Source: UNIDO (1985), Table VII.2, p.128.

manufacturing sector. Over the period 1968–75, food, textiles and wearing apparel together accounted for almost half of the total increase in manufacturing sector employment (Kirkpatrick *et al.* 1984, p.18).

9.5 Strategies of Industrial Development: Import-Substituting Industrialisation (ISI)

The pursuit of industrial development essentially involves a choice between producing goods for overseas markets (export-oriented growth – EOI) or for the domestic market (import substitution). Obviously the two strategies are not mutually exclusive, and in reality the question of strategy relates to the degree of emphasis attached to serving one set of markets rather than another. Even if the LDC decides to pursue a policy of ISI, however, it still has a number of options open to it:

(a) it can use its foreign exchange to import investment goods (for example, looms), raw materials, fuels, etc., to manufacture consumer goods (cloth);

(b) it can use its foreign exchange to import capital goods (machine tools) to make both investment goods (looms) which in turn produce consumer goods (cloth), and to make intermediate goods and develop domestic raw material supplies;

(c) it can use its foreign exchange to import capital goods (machine tools) to make capital goods. (This classification is based on Raj and Sen 1961.)

The Raj and Sen classification is useful in that it allows us to view ISI either as involving a choice between different 'options' (variations (a), (b), or (c)) or as a sequence, beginning with the first stage (a) and moving on to stage (b), and eventually to stage (c).

The great majority of LDCs, almost irrespective of their economic size or natural resource endowment, have pursued variation (a) of the ISI strategy, that is, the importation of investment goods to produce consumer goods, previously imported, for the domestic market. We will refer to this as 'market-based' ISI to indicate that, in general, it has taken the existing distribution of income and its associated features (high demand for non-essential consumer durables and personal services by middle- and upper-income groups; depressed demand for essential mass-consumption goods) as given, and has depended heavily on a variety of foreign inputs (technology, expertise of all kinds). The more advanced, semi-industrialised LDCs have moved on to variation (b), and a limited number of LDCs (Brazil, India, Mexico, South Korea) have made significant progress in the establishment of capital goods industries. The transition from one stage of ISI to the next has been difficult to achieve in practice, however, an issue that we will discuss in greater detail below.

A number of LDCs (usually referred to as 'newly industrialising countries' – NICs) have pursued so-called outward-looking, export-oriented industrialisation strategies. Hong Kong, Singapore, Taiwan and the Republic of Korea (the 'Gang of Four') are the best-known examples, but a number of other semi-industrial LDCs – Brazil, Mexico, Argentina, Malaysia, India and Pakistan – remain, or have become, important exporters of manufactured goods. In some cases they are pursuing a transitional, 'post-ISI' model of development (see below) but, as we shall see, ISI remains of importance in intermediate and capital goods sectors in those economies.

The Origins of ISI

The impulses underlying the process of ISI are diverse. ISI was initiated in many Latin American countries as a response to the disruption caused by World War I, the economic depression of the 1930s and World War II, when either imports were not generally available, or there was insufficient foreign exchange to pay for them and thus domestically produced goods had to be substituted for those previously imported.[1] But ISI became more widespread in the post-1945 world. In some cases it was stimulated by balance of payments difficulties (import substitution was seen as being 'easier' than export promotion); in other cases, newly independent governments wishing to stimulate industrial development would impose protective tariffs on imports of manufactured goods and force international corporations (or local enterprises previously engaged in the import of the goods) to establish domestic production facilities if they wished to protect their market position. Kilby's (1969) study of Nigeria's industrialisation provided support for this 'market protection' hypothesis. In Latin America, the UN Economic Commission for Latin America (ECLA) early on gave greater intellectual respectability to the pressures from various social groups for accelerated industrialisation (Felix 1968) by stressing the need for ISI based on protection, to stimulate employment, alleviate the balance of payments constraint and secure the benefits of technical progress. In other words, ISI was pursued as a conscious national development strategy.[2] In addition, Hirschman (1968) has pointed to the process of 'import swallowing' that occurred as an economy grew along an export-propelled path. As the domestic market expanded as the result of export-led growth, certain industries with locational characteristics that gave them a high degree of natural protection against imports (industries producing heavy, bulky final products which are costly to transport — for example, cement and brewing) became economically viable and could be established without deliberate government protection or intervention.

We must note here the importance of foreign private investment in the ISI process in most LDCs. Indeed, private direct foreign investment can be said to be part cause and part effect of the ISI process. An important feature of the postwar period has been large-scale direct investment (that is, the establishment of productive facilities) in manufacturing industries by transnational corporations (TNCs), and Barratt Brown (1974, Ch.9) presents data which suggest that by 1966 approximately one-third of all manufactured output in LDCs, and nearly one-half of the growth of the previous decade, came from foreign firms. (Data for more recent periods, although not exactly comparable, give a rather different picture — see Chapter 10, Section 10.4 below.) Many would agree, however, that the emphasis on the quantitative aspects of direct foreign investment hides its qualitative significance. Within manufacturing, direct investment has tended to concentrate in industries characterised by rapidly changing, advanced technology, a high degree of product differentiation and capital intensity. The concentration of foreign investment in the modern, rapidly growing sectors of the LCD economy has permitted it to exert an influence greater than that to be expected judged only by its quantitative measure. We return to this issue in Chapter 10.

The Concept and Measurement of ISI

Attention has been focused on the problems of measuring the amount of ISI that has actually taken place within any one country or group of countries, but relatively little attention has been devoted to the critical examination of the concept of ISI itself. In particular, the distinction between ISI as an historical phenomenon (an *ex post* concept) and as a development strategy (an *ex ante* concept) has not always been clearly made and this confusion has had an adverse impact on the planning of industrialisation strategies.

For Chenery (1960) and others, ISI was a 'cause' of economic growth, and it thus recommended itself as a development strategy. Historically, import substitution had always accompanied economic growth (Maizels 1963 showed that the import content of supplies declined with the progress of industrialisation, at least up to the point where a fairly mature level had been reached), but it could equally be a cause or a concomitant of that growth. Studies based on historical data do not tell us whether a deliberate ISI strategy is of relevance to today's LDCs and will provide the basis of a long-run development strategy.

Chenery's influential study published in 1960 seemed to indicate that ISI was responsible for perhaps 50% of industrial growth in a large number of countries. His analysis was based on a cross-section regression equation in which per capita value added in each industrial sector was regressed on per capita income and population of the economy concerned. He found that as income grew, the industrial sector grew more rapidly than the rest of the economy and he established the existence of a fairly uniform pattern of change in the production and import of industrial products. For each industry the positive deviation from proportional (or 'normal') growth was calculated.

Non-proportional growth could be attributed to:

(a) the substitution of domestic production for imports (that is, import substitution, defined by Chenery as the difference between growth in output with no change in the import ratio and the growth that actually took place);

(b) the growth in the final use of industrial products;

(c) the growth in intermediate demand arising from both import substitution and final demand changes.

Chenery concluded that:

> ... the effect of income growth on final demand accounts directly for only 22% of industrialisation. To this should be added the intermediate demand deriving from the growth of final demand, which increases the pure demand effects to 32% of the total deviation from proportionality.
>
> The increased share of domestic production in total supply, defined here as import substitution, is more important than the pure demand effects, since it accounts for 50% of industrialisation. (Chenery 1960, p.641)

For Chenery, import substitution arose largely out of changes in supply conditions, that is, changes in comparative advantage, rather than from changes in demand.

Chenery's attempt to identify a 'normal' pattern of industrialisation and his concept of import substitution have been subject to many criticisms. (For a further discussuion of Chenery's later work in which the importance of ISI is downgraded, and for the criticisms made of 'patterns' analysis, see Kirkpatrick *et al.* (1984), Chapter 2, Section 2.4.) The results are obtained from cross-section data which represent the relative position of a large number of countries at one point in time, but not necessarily the trend that will be followed by any one country over a long period of time. Indeed, a study by Steuer and Voivodas (1965) re-ran Chenery's model using time series data and obtained results inconsistent with the 'normal' pattern. Chenery's definition and measure of import substitution is very sensitive to the levels of income between which it is measured and the time periods chosen.

Furthermore, Sutcliffe (1971) maintained that the phenomenon actually measured by Chenery should be referred to as 'the reduction in the import content of manufactured supplies' and suggests that the term 'import substitution' should be used to cover '. . . only the direct substitution of domestic production for the import of the same product' (p.255). This definition appears to be of greatest relevance to policy issues since it relates to the identification of import substitution opportunities (see following section), but it is still open to criticism.[3] There is no one generally accepted and consistent measure of import substitution; different measures can produce different and often conflicting estimates of the quantitative importance of ISI[4] and thus great care must be taken when interpreting and using the results.

The Estimation of the ISI Potential

Under a regime of ISI, the development planner will usually consider a product suitable for domestic production if the domestic market, as given by the value or volume of imports of that product, is equal to or greater than the minimum economic output of a manufacturing unit. Protection will be given to the domestic producer so that the price of the imported product is equal to or greater than the price of the domestic product (assuming that imports are permitted after domestic production has commenced). Examples of this approach to the estimation of ISI potential can be found in the work of Maitra (1967) and Van Arkadie (1964), both of whom are concerned with estimating the potential for ISI in East Africa.

A number of criticisms must be made of this approach. Trade data may not be sufficiently disaggregated to permit the identification of specific products, especially in the case of consumer goods where product differentiation is important. Furthermore, if tariff protection is required, there will be a reduction in market demand as a result of raising prices to protect the domestic product, unless the price elasticity of demand is zero (Helleiner 1972). But at a more general level, it is not necessarily the case that products that do not enter the country (or enter in only small amounts) do not merit investment and, conversely, because certain products are imported in large amounts, this does not mean that domestic production is desirable.

Under the ISI strategy, given the typical structure of tariff protection (high for consumer goods, low or zero for capital and intermediate goods), the production of consumer goods (often of a luxury or non-essential character) is likely to take priority and this may lead to a timid and conservative, not to say perverse, industrialisation policy. In general, criteria based on import data say nothing about the suitability of the product for domestic production and there is the need for full project appraisal, taking into account the factor endowments and development objectives of the LDC and the engineering and technological characteristics and demands of the project in question. But once we admit the importance of these other variables, we no longer have a policy of ISI in any meaningful sense.

Another important point is that the market for imported goods is unlikely to be representative of the demands of the population as a whole. ISI is more likely to cater for the demands of urban dwellers in general and middle- and upper-income groups in particular, rather than cater for the great mass of the population in rural or semi-urban areas. Market-based ISI accepts the pattern of demand, and the underlying pattern of income distribution, as given, whereas it may be both necessary and desirable to change both consumption patterns and distribution structures, which are aspects of a social and economic structure which industrialisation should radically change. This is more than an attack on ISI *per se*, but that does not destroy the validity of the criticism.

We return to the question of ISI and the distribution of income below.

Alternative Critiques of ISI

In this section we attempt to outline two alternative ways of analysing the ISI process, the neoclassical critique and the structuralist/dependency/ neo-Marxist critique. The neoclassical approach can be referred to as a school of thought in that it presents a coherent and consistent theoretical critique of the ISI process. This is not the case with the structuralist/dependency/neo-Marxist 'school', which embraces a wide variety of non-neoclassical perspectives, and we use that term simply for convenience. This will be elaborated below.

At a purely descriptive level both 'schools' exhibit some similarities. It would be generally agreed that the majority of LDCs have relatively small, inefficient industrial sectors, highly protected and unable to withstand foreign competition, monopolistic in structure, overdiversified and with substantial excess capacity, utilising complex capital-intensive technologies, with low levels of productivity and low employment-creation potential. Furthermore, the incentives for the establishment of, and government preoccupation with, the manufacturing sector have led to the serious neglect of other areas of the economy, especially agriculture. It might even be agreed that industrialisation has given rise to an excessive dependence on foreign capital and technology, with a consequent diminution of domestic ownership and control; that such development has hampered the emergence of export industries; that it has produced a rigid, inelastic import structure and that the bottlenecks and distortions that have arisen as a result of ISI have aggravated already existing inflationary pressures. Most critiques of ISI would agree that it has not alleviated the balance of payments constraint on development.

The Neoclassical School

A growing body of literature in recent years has attempted to explain the persistence of underdevelopment as the result largely of distorted and inefficient factor and goods markets in the LDCs. The major source of these alleged imperfections is government intervention in the economy aimed especially at the rapid promotion of industrialisation (usually ISI) via the imposition of tariff barriers and other protective devices. The central problem of economic development is seen as the promotion of efficient resource allocation through the elimination of divergencies between market and social prices.

The apotheosis of this approach is to be found in the study of Little, Scitovsky and Scott (1970). The burden of their message is that excessive protection, permitting or encouraging the overdevelopment of ISI, violates the principle of comparative advantage and gives rise to distortions in domestic product markets. In domestic factor markets, labour is overvalued, capital is undervalued and the domestic currency is overvalued in terms of foreign currencies. Industrial development has been based on capital-intensive technologies because of factor market imperfections and this has exacerbated employment problems, added to the rapid growth of urban centres and has accelerated rural–urban migration. ISI has aggravated existing inequalities in the distribution of income and, in particular, the high protection given to industry has turned the domestic terms of trade against the agricultural sector, thus discouraging agricultural output and exports. Excess capacity within the industrial sector is a general problem and the ISI process generates inflationary pressures throughout the economy.

Little et al. (1970) argue the case for the promotion (that is, the subsidisation of labour costs, provision of training facilities, etc.) rather than the protection of industry, and in general for policies designed to eliminate the disadvantages under which industry suffers rather than offsetting them by policies with allegedly undesirable side-effects. Protection should be lowered and rationalised, import controls removed, the exchange rate devalued and the free play of market forces encouraged. As a result, domestic industries would either have to face foreign competition or perish, exports (especially of manufactured goods) would be encouraged, industry would not be overencouraged at the expense of other sectors and more extensive employment opportunities would be generated through the use of labour-intensive (or appropriate) technologies. In a critique of the neoclassical perspective, Sutcliffe (1973) has noted that '... the neoclassical approach, emphasises – indeed is often obsessed by – the question of the efficient allocation of resources in the short run, while it pays little attention to the economic determinants of long-run growth and none at all to the socio-political aspects' (p.60). Specifically, it is an over-simplification to assume that a total structural transformation can be brought about by the free play of market forces while underestimating, misinterpreting or ignoring the role of the state, the problems associated with foreign penetration of the economy, economic and political dependence and the disintegrated nature of the LDC economy.

The Structuralist/Dependency/Neo-Marxist Critique

Writers within this broad analytical framework focus attention to differing degrees on the question of the ownership and control of the means of production and the social relations arising out of differing ownership patterns. They are concerned with the problems that arise from the distorted structure of production inherited from the colonial period, the contemporary foreign penetration of the economy, the importation of an 'alien' technology, the operations of transnational corporations (TNCs) (discussed in greater detail in Chapter 10), the distribution of income and the balance of social forces within the economy. Many structuralist critiques of the industrialisation process are avowedly non-Marxist, but they have little in common with the neoclassical position.

At a more general level, dependency, neo-Marxist and Marxist analyses have focused attention on the nature and characteristics of the development process, and have raised the question as to whether capitalism can be regarded in the contemporary developing world as a progressive force and can thus be expected to lead to independent capitalist industrialisation (see below). With regard to policy prescriptions, structuralists, as the name implies, place great emphasis on the need for radical changes in the economic structure of the economy (land redistribution, agrarian reform, a more equal distribution of income) while neo-Marxist and Marxists emphasise the necessary, radical political changes that must take place before genuine economic restructuring is possible.

The Impact of ISI on Imports and the Balance of Payments

Attention has been focused in the past on the behaviour of the import co-efficient (the ratio of total imports to GDP) during ISI. In general, the import coefficient falls as ISI proceeds, although this does not imply either a reduction in absolute value or quantity of imports. It is also likely that some minimum limit on imports will exist, determined, *inter alia*, by the country's resource endowment, technological trends affecting the utilisation of resources, the size of the country and its level of development and rate of growth (Robock 1970).

Of greater importance is the change in the composition of imports that occurs as ISI proceeds. Typically, ISI begins with the domestic manufacture of consumer goods (the highest tariffs are imposed on consumer goods imports and so we get the perverse result that the 'least' essential imports are given the greatest incentive for domestic production). Thus as domestic consumer goods production increases, the commodity composition of imports changes, with consumer goods imports becoming less important and imports of machinery, equipment, raw materials and other imports and fuels becoming of greater significance. In other words, 'nonessential' consumer goods imports are replaced by 'essential' imports needed to maintain domestic output and employment. ISI increases the proportion of domestic value added supported by imports, and in these circumstances any decline in export proceeds not counterbalanced by a net inflow of foreign capital will lead to forced import curtailments and industrial recession. In general, therefore, the economy becomes more dependent on foreign trade and more vulnerable to fluctuations in foreign exchange receipts. ISI, originally conceived of as lessening external dependence, is more likely to have the opposite effect, and Baer notes that:[5]

> ... the net result of ISI has been to place Latin American countries in a new and more dangerous dependency relationship with the more advanced industrial countries than ever before. (Baer 1972, p.106)

The inflexibility or rigidity of the post-ISI structure is not total, however. There is always likely to be some margin of 'non' or 'less essential' imports of finished goods which can be varied with little impact on income or employment, although this margin does become narrower over time.

Turning to the wider problem of the impact of ISI on the balance of payments, there is no evidence that convincingly shows that foreign exchange savings result from ISI policies. Analytically, we can separate out a number of different aspects of the relationship between ISI and the balance of payments although, in reality, such effects will interact with one another in a complex way and are unlikely to be individually identifiable.

Leff and Netto (1966) constructed a sequential model to show the national income and balance of payments effects of an ISI programme. Applying the model to Brazil, they found that massive ISI policies and foreign capital inflows did not eliminate the balance of payments deficit. On the contrary, the deficit was larger at the end of the sequence than it was at the beginning, largely because of the dynamic income-creating effects of ISI; that is, the generation of additional income through investment in ISI activities and the consequent creation of additional demand for new imports.

They concluded:

> ... the conditions of many underdeveloped countries approximate those of our model, and its conclusions have a validity going beyond the Brazilian experience: import substitution cannot be relied upon to end the international disequilibrium of most underdeveloped countries. (Leff and Netto 1966, p.229)

In this case, therefore, imports stimulated by growing national income are greater than the foreign exchange saved by the domestic production of the goods formerly imported.[6]

A second aspect of the relationship between ISI and the balance of payments is the import intensity (or import content) of ISI industries. This feature in itself does not explain the apparent worsening of the external deficit, except perhaps in the short run, but it does aggravate the problem. Different domestically produced commodities will have different import contents. In Colombia, for example, the ILO (1970) estimated that basic industrial consumer goods (clothing, footwear, furniture, beverages, etc.) had an import content of less than 5% while other goods (for example, electrical consumer durables, bought very largely by the rich) had an import content of about 30%. The choice of industries in an ISI programme, itself partially determined by the distribution of income within the ISI economy, will thus influence the balance of payments impact of the industrialisation programme.

In the Leff and Netto model, profit remittances arising from private foreign investment have only a negligible effect on the balance of payments deficit, but it is unlikely that this conclusion could be generalised (even assuming that it is valid for Brazil). Where TNCs have been heavily involved in the ISI process, profit remittances, royalty payments, the effects of transfer pricing, etc., are likely to have a significant balance of payments effect and should not be neglected. We return to these issues in Chapter 10 on TNCs.

Two further related effects on the balance of payments must be mentioned. Little et al. (1970), among others, argue that ISI leads to a redistribution of income, from agriculture to manufacturing (because of agriculture's deteriorating terms of trade vis-à-vis industry) and that within manufacturing itself there is a redistribution from wages to profits (because of the capital-intensity of techniques employed). Income is thus redistributed in favour of those groups (the urban sector and middle- and upper-income groups) which are likely to have a higher marginal propensity to consume imported goods (and services) or domestically produced import-intensive products, thus further aggravating the balance of payments problem. We discuss in greater detail the relationship between income distribution and development in Chapter 3.

The second effect involves the concept of the effective rate of protection, defined as the percentage excess of domestic value added, obtained through the imposition of tariffs and other protective devices on the product and its inputs, over what value added would be at world prices. In other words, the effective rate of protection shows the percentage by which value added at a stage of fabrication in domestic industry can exceed what this would be in the absence of protection (Little *et al.* 1970). In certain cases, protection is so high that domestic value added, measured at world prices, is negative; that is, the value of the domestic industry's output at world prices is less than the cost of its inputs and hence the activity is fundamentally inefficient.

In a study of 48 manufacturing industries in Pakistan, Soligo and Stern (1965) found that in 23 industries, value added measured at world prices was negative. Fourteen of these industries were in the consumer goods sector. The authors concluded that investment had either been premature or overextended, primarily in consumer goods industries (although some of these industries may have been genuine 'infant' industries), and that, in general, investment made on the basis of ISI potential too often ignored comparative advantage considerations. The use of world prices in this type of calculation is not without controversy, but Soligo and Stern's and similar studies highlight the extreme inefficiency that exists in the manufacturing sectors of many LDCs which have pursued the ISI strategy.

The actual experience of ISI thus seems to suggest that the economy will not experience a lessening of the balance of payments constraint. It will become increasingly dependent on inflows of foreign capital (private and public) to maintain the real capacity to import if export earnings cannot be significantly increased. ISI may successfully create income and employment, but the redistribution of income towards sectors and groups with high marginal propensities to import and the establishment of highly import-intensive industries will have a detrimental effect on the balance of payments position.

ISI and the Rate of Saving

Many authors have argued that ISI will reduce the rate of saving. The establishment of a domestic consumer goods sector and the development of an ISI-based business community will lead to pressures to minimise constraints on consumption, especially if excess capacity exists (which is likely to be the case), thus reducing the rate of saving below that which could have been achieved. This phenomenon would not be present, of course, if industrialisation concentrated on the establishment of capital goods rather than consumer goods industries.

Khan (1963) introduced the concept of 'consumption liberalisation'. When ISI occurred, domestic absorption often exceeded what would have been absorbed or demanded if the good had continued to be imported, and when the good concerned was a consumption good, the effect was to liberalise consumption and reduce aggregate savings and the development effort. Khan calculated that for cotton cloth, for example, during the period 1955/56 to 1959/60, 46% of increased production (in Pakistan) was due to consumption liberalisation; for sugar during the same period, consumption liberalisation accounted for 49–51% of increased production.

Actual consumption exceeded 'normal' consumption (determined by the aggregate consumption constraint necessary to achieve the planned rate of saving and consumer preference as to the distribution of expenditure between different commodities within the overall constraint) for three main reasons: (1) high levels of protection led to excessive investment in ISI industries which in turn led to attempts to utilise capacity through sales campaigns, etc., aimed at raising consumption; (2) if the only control over consumption consisted of import licences, then the 'decontrol' of consumption would automatically occur as ISI took place; (3) the shift in the distribution of income in favour of the urban sector would create upward pressures on the consumption function. Khan's general conclusion was that the liberalisation of consumption of import substitutes meant the liberalisation of consumption in general and hence a reduction in savings.

ISI and Long-Run Growth and Development

Perhaps the most crucial problem of the ISI process is its apparent inability in the long run to continue to reduce the import ratio and thus to sustain a growth rate of GNP in excess of the growth in the capacity to import. In other words, ISI generates a high rate of growth in its initial stages but such growth is short lived (perhaps 10 to 15 years) and the economy experiences stagnation at a low level of development once ISI opportunities appear to have been exhausted and the foreign exchange constraint once again becomes dominant. Broadly, we can distinguish between those writers who believe that stagnationist tendencies are inherent within the ISI process itself and those who believe that poor planning and implementation of the ISI strategy, rather than the strategy itself, is at the root of the problem.

The latter school has already been referred to above in our discussion of the neoclassical critique. Bruton (1970) lists three general features arising from ISI: the distortion of the economy; the creation of activities alien to the economic and social environment of the community; and the creation of conditions which dampen productivity growth. He argues that government policies should concentrate on these issues and, like Little *et al.* (1970), recommends promotion rather than protection – uniform tariffs, currency realignments, subsidies to firms doing research, tax advantages or subsidies aimed at correcting market imperfections, provision of market information, etc.

There are a number of important structuralist/dependency models of stagnation which must be briefly considered, but before doing so we must again look at the ISI 'model' itself. Hirschman, as noted above, described the ISI process as 'industrialisation by tightly separated stages' and as a 'highly sequential' affair (Hirschman 1968). ISI typically began with the establishment of consumer goods industries (the technology required may be less complicated and the cost differential lower than for capital goods) and then, in principle, moved on to intermediate and finally to capital goods. The influential UNECLA (1964) study of Brazil asserted that in practice this was virtually impossible to achieve. Rather, the substitution process 'might be regarded as a building of which every storey must be erected simultaneously, although the degree of concentration on each varies from one period to another' (pp.6–7).

The transition from consumer to intermediate goods is difficult to achieve (greater capital requirements, more complex technologies, lack of TNC cooperation, etc.) and thus the first stage of the process may be pushed to the maximum possible extent – what Felix (1964) has referred to as the 'premature widening' of the productive structure. The problems associated with the tendency of ISI to get 'stuck' at the stage of consumer goods substitution are not, of course, insuperable and to a certain extent are related to the particular kinds of consumer goods industries established. For example, modern sophisticated luxury consumer goods industries are likely to require equally sophisticated capital goods which, to say the least, will prove very difficult to produce locally.

Determined government action in some of the larger LDCs (for example, Brazil and India) has led to the establishment of intermediate (iron and steel) and capital goods (machine-making) industries. But it could be argued with some validity that these industries would not have been established in the absence of specific government intervention, that is, if the ISI process had been purely unplanned and spontaneous, completely determined by the free play of market forces.

The UNECLA (1964) study of Brazil focused attention on the economic and social characteristics of the ISI model of development and argued that stagnation arose from a number of specific imbalances or disequilibria that arose during ISI. These took the form of sectoral imbalances (between industry and other sectors of the economy and, within the industrial sector itself, between consumer and capital goods); regional imbalances (a large part of the population lived in very underdeveloped areas which had not benefited from the economic transformation taking place within the Centro-Sur region); social imbalances (unequal distribution of income and increasing social inequalities) and financial imbalances (the generation of inflationary pressures).[7]

The authors of the report argued that Brazil had to move from the ISI model to a self-sustaining growth model, by means of the reduction in the duality of the system and the expansion of the market. Government action would be required to improve infrastructure facilities, encourage investment to intermediate industries, the primary sector and underdeveloped areas, and to achieve a better distribution of income. We shall see below that the 'Brazilian model of development' turned out to be rather different from that envisaged by ECLA.[8]

Felix (1968) accepted the view that for many Latin American countries ISI had lost its capacity to lower the import coefficient and that ISI became progressively harder to sustain with the attempt to establish intermediate and capital goods industries. He argued that insufficient attention had been paid to the changing composition of final demand under ISI and he maintained that only by postulating a persistent import bias to changes in the final demand mix could a levelling-off of the import ratio be adequately explained. Rising incomes shifted demand towards products with high income elasticities of demand and higher import intensities (than products with slow-growing demand). But he further argued that import-biased demand shifts occurred independently of income changes, through the international demonstration effect:

> ... the import bias of consumer demand is positively related not merely to rising income but also to the rate of product innovation in advanced countries, to factors reducing information lags concerning such products in borrowing countries, and to the trend towards greater technological complexity of these products and their components. (Felix 1968, p.67)

Felix tested his model with data for Argentina and found that the intermediate import requirements per composite unit of Argentine output were higher in 1960 than in 1953, even though there had been considerable ISI in the intervening years. The reason for this was attributed to the shift in demand to 'dynamic' industries (income elasticity of demand greater than one) with above-average import coefficients.

The final stagnationist model we consider is that of Merhav (1969). He argued that the importation of technology developed in industrialised countries made monopoly (used in a broad, generic sense) inevitable at a very low level of development in LDCs. The application of monopoly theory to the problem of development led to the conclusion that monopoly, after the initial spurt of growth in which it establishes itself, was likely to halt, or seriously retard, further growth. The monopolistic structure was likely to be strongly resistant to change and would be characterised by relatively inefficient techniques, smaller plants, lower output and higher prices as compared to the industrialised economies. In the latter, Merhav argued that monopolies grow via diversification, but in LDCs:

> ... the investment opportunities presented by diversification are not only narrow from the outset, but tend to shrink rapidly in consequence of the market restrictions engendered by oligopoly and monopoly, and as a result of the dependence upon imports of capital goods. (Merhav 1969, p.82)

Thus in LDCs, monopolistic industries diversified into increasingly suboptimal products (suboptimal relative to the size of the domestic market for these products), but this could not assure sustained growth because of the lack of a domestic capital goods sector, resulting in import leakages reducing the size of the domestic income multiplier. Furthermore, the very process itself created a bias against the establishment of a capital goods industry.

Two possible exits from the impasse were examined by Merhav – government intervention and foreign trade – but it was concluded that neither was likely to rescue the underdeveloped private enterprise system from its predicament.

9.6   An Evaluation of Import-Substituting Industrialisation and the 'Post-ISI' Model

It was noted in Section 9.5 that both neoclassical and dependency/neo-Marxist writers have, in various ways and to varying degrees, expressed disappointment over, and disillusion with, the experience of 'market-based' ISI in the post-World War Two period. Market-based ISI was seen as essentially a self-terminating process, unable to sustain growth in the longer run, either because of the massive misallocation of resources associated with its incorrect implementation (the neoclassical case) or because the strategy contained within itself conflicts and contradictions which, in the context of a 'distorted' LDC economy, aggravated existing structural disequilibria and resulted in stagnation.

In particular, the latter interpretation of the ISI experience has been increasingly challenged over the past few years. Warren (1980, p.243) argued that the 'really unusual feature of postwar industrialisation in the Third World' was its 'sustained momentum over a longer period than any previously recorded'. In addition, it became clear that much of the work appearing in the 1960s and 1970s, both structuralist and dependency/neo-Marxist, was too mechanistic in that it implied that stagnation and collapse were inevitable, that structural constraints were rigid and unchanging and that sustained growth and structural change were unlikely to be achieved. We return to these issues in Section 9.9 below.

Two further points require specific mention: firstly, as Schmitz (1984) has argued, most evaluations of ISI, and in particular those from a neoclassical perspective, have focused on indicators of *static* inefficiency, and very little attempt has been made to investigate industrial performance from a dynamic perspective. As Schmitz (1984, p.6) notes:

> Most accounts remind us of the importance of learning by doing and external economies to industrial growth; but in the actual evaluation these considerations simply evaporate.

There are both conceptual and measurement problems associated with the assessment of dynamic effects. Are dynamic factors to be evaluated at the firm, industry or national level? With respect to firms or industries, the available empirical evidence suggests that 'the more successful learners tend to come from LDCs with a relatively long industrialisation experience stretching back to at least the 1920s (e.g. Argentina, Brazil or India)' (Schmitz 1984, p.6). At the macro-level, there may well be a conflict between micro-economically inefficient activities (considered individually) which, taken together, produce a macro-economically efficient result through developing linkages and externalities.

The second point relates to the relationship between ISI and export-oriented industrialisation (EOI). Should ISI be seen as a necessary precondition for the creation of a manufacturing base from which an EOI strategy could be launched? If the answer to this question is generally positive, ISI and EOI are not necessarily mutually exclusive and attention thus needs to be focused on the transition from ISI to EOI which in turn has implications for the form ISI should take and the appropriate timing of the transition (Bienefeld 1981, p.89). The neoclassical school would, in general, argue that the less 'locked-in' to an ISI strategy an LDC becomes, the easier and less costly it is to move to an EOI strategy. Schmitz (1984, p.14), on the other hand, after reviewing the experience of several of the Far-Eastern economies, points to 'the importance of accumulating industrial experience for success in export manufacturing' but concludes that the available evidence is not sufficient 'to make the case for ISI as a precondition for EOI'.

The 'Post-ISI' Model

The attempt has been made to identify a 'post-ISI' model of industrialisation (see *World Development*, Vol. 5, Nos. 1/2, 1977) as a kind of transitional stage between ISI and full-EOI.

The late 1960s − early 1970s saw the major Latin American economies attempting to reorientate the direction of their development effort, from the so-called inward-looking model of ISI to outward-looking EOI (for a critique of these concepts, see Section 9.10 below). In Mexico, for example, as early as the 1960s efforts to promote manufacturing exports were initiated (Aspra 1977). Financial assistance to exporters was made available, export duties were reduced and other tax concessions granted and the attempt was made to promote re-exports of raw materials and intermediate goods. In the border area with the USA, attempts were made to attract assembly activities for re-export back to the USA.

In Brazil from the mid-1960s onwards, efforts were made to expand and diversify exports, the tax system was modernised to stimulate investment in priority sectors, the financial system was reformed (including the indexing of key prices to the rate of inflation), direct foreign investment (DFI) was encouraged, and massive government investment programmes were implemented to eliminate structural bottlenecks in the economy (in the power, transport and communication sectors, for example).

The 'post-ISI' model has a number of characteristics, although they are not unique to that model or strategy of industrialisation, and indeed, whether the 'post-ISI' model can best be seen as essentially a continuation of ISI rather than as a different strategy of industrialisation must remain an open question. With that qualification, therefore, the main features of the 'post-ISI' model are:

(1) The state continues to play a key role in the development process, not to supplant but to encourage and sustain the process of capitalist development.

(2) Direct foreign investment continues to be of crucial importance, especially in the manufacturing sector.

(3) Efforts are made to expand and diversify exports (this does distinguish the 'post-ISI' phase from the preceding market-based ISI).

(4) Greater reliance is placed on the market as the main allocator of resources, with emphasis placed on growth and efficiency, rather than on equity (with the exception of Chile, 1970–73 and Peru for a brief period after 1968).

(5) The reform and modernisation of the tax system, capital markets and, most importantly, the exchange rate system, in order to eliminate overvalued exchange rates and to prevent their reoccurrence in the future.

Neoclassical economists place great emphasis on the latter set of policies. Devaluation is seen as the 'first step' to a new industrialisation strategy. In the longer run, exchange rate policies must be complemented by export-promotion policies which will make the growth of exports profitable and secure. (For a further discussion, see Kirkpatrick and Nixson 1983, pp.31–4.)

The 'post-ISI' model poses a number of questions for which, as yet, there are few satisfactory answers. Does the 'post-ISI' model have features which clearly distinguish it from earlier phases of ISI (and, indeed, how different is it from EOI)? Is there a common 'post-ISI' model? What determines the success of this model – why do some LDCs seem to have been able to implement this model with some degree of success (Brazil, for example) while others have failed (Argentina)? What is the relative importance of external and internal factors in determining the success or otherwise of the 'post-ISI' model and how do they interact with one another? What is the role of the state in the 'post-ISI' model? Some of these issues will be taken up in the following sections.

9.7   The Export of Manufactured Goods

Statistical Overview

Since 1960, manufactures have consistently accounted for between 50–60% of total world trade. For the developed market economies, manufactures accounted for an estimated 73% of their total exports in 1983. For the LDCs, the figure was 25.2% (UNIDO 1985, Table III.1, p.38).

If, however, mineral fuels and related materials are excluded, the differences between these two groups of countries are less marked. Manufactures accounted for almost 79% of the exports of non-oil products of the developed economies in 1982, and 53% of the LDCs' exports of non-oil products in the same year. Given that such exports only accounted for less than 13% of LDC non-oil trade in 1960, there has quite clearly been a significant change in the commodity composition of LDC exports, a reflection of their 'costly and arduous efforts to industrialise' (UNIDO 1985, p.38).

The developed market economies still accounted for over 80% of world exports of manufactures in the early 1980s while the share of the LDCs stood at approximately 11%. Exports of manufactures grew rapidly during the late 1960s – early 1970s, and continued to grow at a moderate pace during the remainder of the 1970s. The fall in exports during the early 1980s was thus a significant departure from recent trends, although the relative shares of the main economic groupings were not affected. The relevant data are given in Table 9.11.

The direction of trade in manufactures is outlined in Table 9.12. The developed market economies and the centrally planned economies largely trade with other members of their respective 'blocs'. In the case of the LDCs, however, 59% of their exports of manufactures went to the developed market economies in 1982, and 37.6% went to other LDCs. Although the overall value of intra-LDC ('South–South') trade has increased, the share of manufactures has not and UNIDO (1985, p.40) asserts that it was probably less in the early 1980s than it was in 1963. (For

Table 9.11 World Exports of Manufactures (SITC 5–8 less 68) and the Shares of the Major Economic Groupings

Year	Total (billions of dollars)[a]	Increase over preceding year (%)	Developing countries (%)	Centrally planned economies (%)	Developed market economies (%)
1969	165.0	17.4	4.6	10.4	85.0
1970	189.9	15.2	5.0	10.0	85.0
1971	216.0	13.7	5.2	9.6	85.2
1972	258.9	19.9	5.7	9.9	84.4
1973	346.9	34.0	6.7	9.4	83.9
1974	458.4	32.2	6.8	8.5	84.7
1975	500.1	9.1	6.3	9.3	84.4
1976	564.4	12.8	7.5	8.9	83.6
1977	647.3	14.7	7.8	8.9	83.3
1978	784.0	21.1	8.1	8.7	83.2
1979	941.0	20.0	8.7	8.4	82.9
1980	1,090.2	15.9	9.1	8.1	82.8
1981	1,087.0	−0.3	10.5	8.0	81.5
1982	1,042.1	−4.1	10.7	8.7	80.6
1983[b]	1,051.0	0.9	10.9	8.8	80.3

Source: UNIDO (1985), Table III.2, p.39.
Notes: (a) At current prices.
      (b) Estimate.

Table 9.12 World Trade in Manufactures (SITC 5–8 less 68), by Origin, Destination and Economic Grouping at Current Prices, Selected Years

Origin of exports	Year	Exports to developing countries		Exports to centrally planned economies[a]		Exports to developed market economies	
		Value (millions of dollars)	Share (%)	Value (millions of dollars)	Share (%)	Value (millions of dollars)	Share (%)
Developing countries	1963	1,404	41.2	102	3.0	1,902	55.8
	1970	3,231	33.7	559	5.8	5,808	60.5
	1975	11,935	37.9	1,172	3.7	18,352	58.3
	1980	37,560	38.1	3,222	3.3	57,764	58.6
	1982	41,520	37.6	3,760	3.4	65,046	59.0
Centrally planned economies	1963	1,635	15.1	8,043	74.3	1,147	10.6
	1970	2,899	15.2	13,381	70.2	2,804	14.7
	1975	6,790	14.6	31,835	68.6	7,756	16.7
	1980	15,784	18.0	54,692	62.3	17,268	19.7
	1982	19,807	21.9	53,651	59.3	17,062	18.8
Developed market economies	1963	16,950	25.7	2,168	3.3	46,470	71.0
	1970	32,462	20.2	6,634	4.1	121,256	75.6
	1975	111,298	26.5	26,518	6.3	282,155	67.2
	1980	233,721	26.0	42,430	4.7	622,646	69.3
	1982	234,088	28.1	36,346	4.4	563,642	67.6

Source: UNIDO (1985), Table III.3, p.39.
Note: (a) Excluding trade among the centrally planned economies of Asia.

a discussion of 'South–South' trade, see Lall (1985), Ch.11.) The data in Table 9.12 also illustrate the large imbalance in trade in manufactured goods between developed and less developed economies, with exports of manufactures from the developed market economies to the LDCs totalling roughly 3.6 times greater than manufactured exports from the latter grouping to the former.

An important characteristic of LDC exports of manufactures is the large proportion of the total accounted for by relatively few major LDC exporters. The data in Table 9.13 show that in 1970, 12 LDCs accounted for almost 55% of total LDC manufactured exports and it was estimated that this share would have risen by the early 1980s (note that Taiwan – an important NIC – is not included in the table). Especially noteworthy is the rapid increase in the share of the Republic of Korea and, to a lesser extent, the share of Singapore and Brazil, and the fall in the relative share of Hong Kong and India. The data in Table 9.13 also show the sharp

Table 9.13   Exports of Manufactures (SITC 5–8 less 68) by Selected Developing Countries and Areas, 1970–82 (%)

Country or area[a]	Average annual growth rate[b]		Share in total			
	1970. –80	1980–82	1970	1980	1981	1982
Republic of Korea	37.8	22.1[c]	6.0	14.4	15.2	...
Hong Kong	21.0	0.3	18.5	12.0	11.0	10.6
Singapore	35.7	5.6	4.0	8.3	8.0	8.1
Brazil	35.4	1.5	3.4	6.9	7.3	6.2
India	15.5	...	9.8	4.0	...	...
Malaysia	36.2	6.4	1.0	2.2	1.8	2.2
Kuwait	37.2	15.5[c]	0.9	2.0	2.0	...
Argentina	22.4	−0.3	2.3	1.7	1.4	1.5
Mexico	16.1	−5.7[c]	3.7	1.6	1.3	...
Thailand	47.8	5.6	0.3	1.5	1.4	1.4
Pakistan	12.1	4.4	3.8	1.1	1.1	1.1
Philippines	31.4	−1.9	0.7	1.1	1.1	0.9
Sub-totals			54.4	56.8	51.6	...
Other countries	25.6	...	45.6	43.2	...	...
All developing countries	26.3	6.8	100.0	100.0	100.0	100.0

Source: UNIDO (1985), Table III.5, p.42.
Notes: (a) Ranked by value of exports in 1980.
        (b) Compound growth rates.
        (c) Annual growth rate in 1981 over 1980.
        ... Data not available.

Table 9.14   Growth and Composition of Trade by the Developed Market Economies and the Developing Countries and Areas in Industrially Processed Goods and Intermediates, 1970–81 (%)

Economic grouping	Year	Consumer non-durable goods	Intermediates	Capital goods and consumer durables	Other industrially processed goods	All industrially processed goods and intermediates
Average annual growth rate of exports, 1970–81[a]						
Developed market economies		16.9	15.3	17.1	18.3	16.7
Developing countries and areas (major exporters)[b]		22.6	24.4	35.3	23.3	25.7
Other developing countries[c]		27.8	13.1	26.0	14.2	15.0
Average annual growth rate of imports, 1970–81[a]						
Developed market economies		18.1	14.1	16.3	17.9	16.0
Developing countries and areas (major exporters)[b]		23.3	18.5	22.4	20.6	20.8
Other developing countries[c]		17.9	18.5	19.7	23.0	19.7

Share in total exports of industrially processed goods and intermediates					
Developed market economies	1970	8.9	34.2	47.1	9.8	100.0
	1981	9.2	30.1	49.2	11.5	100.0
Developing countries and areas (major exporters)[b]	1970	28.1	25.9	12.9	33.0	100.0
	1981	21.3	23.1	28.8	26.7	100.0
Other developing countries[c]	1970	3.4	44.8	2.3	49.4	100.0
	1981	10.8	37.1	6.4	45.7	100.0
Share in total imports of industrially processed goods and intermediates					
Developed market economies	1970	10.2	36.3	39.8	13.7	100.0
	1981	12.5	30.3	40.9	16.3	100.0
Developing countries and areas (major exporters)[b]	1970	6.7	39.3	40.8	13.2	100.0
	1981	8.4	31.8	46.9	12.9	100.0
Other developing countries[c]	1970	7.3	34.2	45.4	13.1	100.0
	1981	6.2	30.6	45.4	17.8	100.0

Source: UNIDO (1985), Table III.7, p.44.

Notes: (a) Compound growth rates.

(b) Argentina, Brazil, Hong Kong, Kuwait, Malaysia, Republic of Korea and Singapore. Excluding India and Mexico, for which comparable data for 1981 were not available.

(c) Forty-seven, for which comparable data were available for 1970 and 1981.

deceleration in rates of growth of exports of manufactures from LDCs in the early 1980s, affecting both major and marginal exporters of manufactures.

Data on the functional composition of trade are given in Table 9.14 for the developed market economies, several of the major LDC exporters and a residual group of 47 LDCs. Comparing rates of growth of exports and imports for all industrially processed goods and intermediates (the right-hand column), it will be noted that for both developed market economies and major LDC exporters, exports have consistently grown faster than imports. In the other group of LDCs, however, the rate of growth of imports has been significantly above the rate of growth of exports, especially for intermediate and other industrially processed goods. Between 1978 and 1981, the rate of growth of exports of all industrially processed goods and intermediates fell to an annual average of 0.4%, while imports continued to grow at 16.7% per annum (UNIDO 1985, Table III.7, p.44).

With respect to the composition of trade, the import figures show only minor variations between the three groups of countries but the export composition reveals a different pattern. The share of capital goods and consumer durables is smaller for both groups of LDCs than for the developed

Table 9.15 Manufactures Imported by Developed Market Economies from LDCs, 1975 and 1982

Manufactures	1975 ($m[b])	1982 ($m[b])	Growth rate[a] 1975–82 (%)	LDC share in imports from world (%) 1975	LDC share in imports from world (%) 1982
Non-ferrous metals	3,746	6,659	8.6	25.3	24.2
Steel	705	2,743	21.4	2.9	7.1
Chemicals	1,570	4,464	16.1	3.8	4.6
Other semi-manufactures	1,879	5,068	15.2	6.5	8.9
Engineering products	4,649	19,861	23.1	2.9	5.7
Textiles	2,681	5,906	11.9	15.5	19.7
Clothing	4,438	14,132	18.0	31.1	42.4
Other consumer goods	2,601	9,816	20.9	9.5	14.2
Total	22,269	68,649	17.4	6.8	9.8

Source: UNIDO (1985), Table III.8, p.45.
Notes: (a) Compound growth rate.
      (b) At current prices.

market economies. For the major LDC exporters, the share of consumer non-durable goods and capital goods and consumer durables is very much higher (50.1% in 1981) than in the other LDC groups (17.2% in 1981).

The importance of the developed market economies as importers of manufactures from LDCs is further illustrated in Table 9.15. The LDCs are clearly important suppliers of clothing, non-ferrous metals and textiles. The LDCs have made less progress with respect to exports of

Table 9.16 Exports of Industrially Processed Goods[a] as Share of Gross Manufacturing Output, 1970–80 for Selected LDCs

Country	Exports – gross output (unweighted average)	
	1970–74	*1974–80*
Brazil	5.9	6.0
Chile	22.7	28.0
Colombia	7.0	8.1
Ecuador	6.9	14.0
Egypt	24.9	19.1
Ghana	19.3	13.0
Hong Kong	62.3	64.1
India	7.9	8.8
Indonesia	24.2	25.5
Kenya	19.7	19.4
Malaysia	44.9	45.2
Mexico	5.8	5.5
Nigeria	9.6	3.8
Pakistan	32.5	32.4
Peru	16.0	13.7
Philippines	17.2	19.0
Republic of Korea	23.8	27.4
Singapore	61.6	69.8
Thailand	13.7	16.3
Turkey	6.9	4.9
Venezuela	22.0	21.4
Average	13.7	14.7

Source: Taken from UNIDO (1985), Table II.14, p.55.

Note: (a) This categorisation is used to include several 'processing' industries which are regarded as manufacturing activities in production statistics but are often omitted from statistics covering trade in manufactures.

engineering products and chemicals (which constitute the bulk of developed economy imports of manufactures), but they have achieved high rates of growth over the period 1975–82 for these two categories and this suggests that LDC competitiveness has improved since 1975 (UNIDO 1985, p.46).

One further point deserves brief mention. For very few LDCs do exports of manufactures account for more than one-third of gross manufacturing output (see Table 9.16). Hong Kong and Singapore are obviously exceptional in this respect. The larger LDCs, with the exception of Pakistan, exported a relatively modest proportion of total output – less than 10% for such important semi-industrial LDCs as Brazil, India and Mexico. As UNIDO (1985, p.54) notes, this fact 'underlines the importance of domestic demand and the need to expand the domestic markets'.

9.8 Export-Oriented Industrialisation (EOI)

In principle, as noted in Section 9.5, ISI and EOI are not mutually exclusive and their separation has been referred to as a 'false dichotomy' (Robock 1970). Industries that were initially established to serve the domestic market should, once the period of 'infant' development is past, be able to break into export markets and thus at least partially alleviate the much publicised foreign exchange constraint. In this sense, ISI could be regarded as merely a prelude to entry into foreign markets (see above).

In practice, however, these two strategies have generally been regarded as alternatives, with ISI assumed to be an 'easier' alternative to export promotion. In particular, it was difficult to see how exports could be promoted efficiently, cheaply and acceptably in a manner analogous to the protection of domestic industries under ISI. But the apparent 'failure' of ISI as a development (or industrialisation) strategy and the success of those economies vigorously promoting exports, has led to a reappraisal of the possibilities of EOI. Indeed, it would be no exaggeration to say that EOI has become an article of faith amongst some neoclassical development economists and international organisations.

EOI is characterised as an 'outward-looking' development strategy and its advocates emphasise the beneficial learning effects that competition in overseas markets engenders (Keesing 1967). More specifically it is argued that EOI leads to, or is associated with, economic development by:

(i) the use of labour-intensive technologies, consistent with the LDCs' factor endowments and comparative advantage, to produce competitive exports;

(ii) greater direct employment creation associated with the use of labour-intensive technologies;

(iii) a more equitable size distribution of income, in part resulting from the creation of greater employment opportunities;

(iv) a more efficient allocation of scarce resources, resulting from the stimulus of international competition, with beneficial effects on growth and development.

Overall, advocates of EOI such as Balassa (1978, p.181) argue that EOI leads to a better growth performance than ISI because export-oriented policies:

> ... lead to resource allocation according to comparative advantage, allow for greater capacity utilisation, permit the exploitation of economies of scale, generate technological improvements in response to competition abroad and, in labour-surplus economies, contribute to increased employment.

Various attempts have been made to test empirically the relationship between EOI and economic growth. Balassa (1978) investigated the relationship between export expansion and economic growth in an 11-country sample for the period 1960–73. He obtained positive, statistically significant results (especially for the sub-period 1966–73) and he concluded that:

> ... trade orientation has been an important factor contributing to inter-country differences in the growth of incomes ... the estimates presented ... provide evidence on the benefits of export-orientation as compared to policies oriented to import substitution. (Balassa 1978, p.188)

Tyler (1981) analysed a sample of 55 middle-income LDCs for the period 1960–77. He found a positive and highly significant relationship between economic growth and manufacturing output growth and a similar relationship between growth of GDP and export growth. Those LDCs enjoying the fastest rates of growth had also experienced the fastest rates of growth of manufacturing exports. Tyler concluded that:

> ... countries which neglect their export sectors through discriminatory economic policies are likely to have to settle for lower rates of economic growth as a result ... economic policies entailing appropriate price incentives for exports appear to take on a central importance in the economic growth of developing countries. (Tyler 1981, p.129)

These types of analyses have several limitations. Using export performance as an index of the commitment to export promotion excludes those countries which have attempted to pursue EOI and have failed. Including only middle-income LDCs in the sample may well imply that LDCs may have to reach some minimum level of per capita income or industrialisation before successful EOI becomes possible. The statistical problems associated in these exercises are also relevant. Exports are a part of output and we would expect to see a positive association between their rates of growth. In addition, correlation does not indicate the direction of causation, and it is possible that higher rates of growth of domestic output lead to higher rates of growth of exports, rather than *vice versa*.

More generally, such studies do not provide insights into the pattern and characteristics of growth in LDCs pursuing EOI. Specifically, we are interested in the relationship between EOI and the rate of growth of employment, EOI and the distribution of income, and EOI and external vulnerability to events or 'shocks' in the international economy beyond the control of the individual LDC.

With respect to EOI and the growth of employment, the general presumption would be that rapid economic growth resulting from the adoption of policies conducive to EOI would in turn lead to higher rates of growth of employment. But as Krueger (1978) notes, the relationship between trade strategies and employment is a complex one, depending on:

(i) the effect of the choice of trade strategy on the overall rate of growth, and hence on the rate of growth of employment;
(ii) the effect on the demand for labour via the influence of the trade strategy on the composition of output;
(iii) the effect of the trade strategy on factor prices.

Krueger's empirical work relating to point (ii) indicates greater labour intensity in export-oriented than in import-competing industries (except for intra-LDC trade). She concludes that 'the labour-abundant developing countries probably would be well-advised to specialise in the export of labour-intensive products' and that 'altering trade strategies toward a greater export orientation will certainly be consistent with the objective of finding more employment opportunities' (Krueger 1978, p.274).[9]

Other evidence is more ambiguous, however (surveyed in Kirkpatrick and Nixson 1983, p.38). Given that in most LDCs manufactured exports account for a limited proportion of manufactured output and that the latter in turn represents a small part of GNP, employment created by the growth of manufactured exports will not prove to be a panacea for the labour absorption problems of LDCs.

With respect to the relationship between EOI and the distribution of income, even though the available empirical evidence (see Chapter 3, Section 3.4) indicates a relatively low degree of inequality in some NICs, it cannot be unambiguously asserted that EOI is the *cause* of the lower degree of inequality. In a labour-abundant LDC, EOI may well be associated (indeed, may well depend upon) the employment of large numbers of workers at very low wages and it cannot be hypothesised *a priori* what the distributional implications of that particular strategy of industrialisation will be.

Finally, we must consider the relationship between EOI and external vulnerability. This aspect is complex and with a number of dimensions. It cannot simply be assumed that the EOI strategy creates greater dependence on, and greater vulnerability to, fluctuations within international markets, as compared to ISI as many critics allege. Indeed, the reverse might well be the case. If EOI is accompanied by significant export diversification, export earnings may become more stable. EOI need not automatically be associated with greater 'openness' (as measured by the share of exports and imports in GNP), but even if it is, the ultimate impact of EOI on development will depend in large part on the ability of the LDC to use international exchange relationships to further development objectives, and this cannot be predicted *a priori*. The role of foreign capital in EOI is clearly of importance in this respect, a point to which we will return below.

An Evaluation of EOI

Clearly, it is too early to be able to evaluate fully the impact of EOI on longer-term processes of growth and development. Nevertheless, a number of important issues are raised by the experience of EOI, issues which have serious implications for both the neoclassical and dependency/neo-Marxist perspectives.

(1) There is not a single 'model' of EOI, and the various NICs differ from one another quite significantly. Even with respect to the 'Gang of Four' (Hong Kong, South Korea, Singapore and Taiwan), there are major differences with respect to the role of the state, the importance of foreign capital, the level of external indebtedness and socio-economic and sociopolitical structures. As Lall (1978) has pointed out, we can distinguish between different categories of manufactured exports,[10] every one of which will have different implications for the overall balance of payments effect, domestic linkage creation, the role of TNCs and dependence on foreign capital, points which are discussed in further detail in Chapters 10 and 11.

(2) The neoclassical case for the more efficient allocation of resources associated with EOI rests largely on the assertion that incentive structures are such that they give equal weight to production for the domestic and export markets (that is, there is no bias in favour of either market which will lead to 'distortions' in resource allocation). A bias in favour of exports can only be justified if it can be shown that export-oriented industries are genuine infant industries and that there are significant dynamic external economies and 'learning-by-doing' benefits. However, the neoclassical interpretation of EOI is being increasingly challenged with respect to South Korea. The attempt by the Korean Government in the late 1970s both to maintain the high rate of growth of manufactured exports and to change the structure of Korean industry in favour of heavy and chemical industries, involved a heavy reliance on subsidised credit, but it has been argued that:

> Investment in heavy and chemical industries exceeded what was permitted by market size, financing capacity and technical and engineering capacity. Excess capacity resulting from overinvestment is most evident in the machinery and plant manufacturing industry. (Kim 1985, p.175)

In other words, the 'distortions' and 'inefficiencies' in resource allocation may be as great under EOI as under ISI if it cannot be shown that the industries established under either regime have a long-run comparative advantage. This is not to argue that EOI does not have beneficial development effects, but it is a challenge to the neoclassical interpretation of EOI.

(3) EOI, and the NIC phenomenon in general, is often interpreted as a 'free-market' model of development (with perhaps Hong Kong approaching most closely the neoclassical ideal of minimum government intervention in the development process). As Bienefeld (1981, pp.88–9) has argued, however:

> '... the experience of the majority of NICs ... (leaves) ... no doubt about the extent to which power was generally centralised within monolithic states, nor about the extent to which that power was exercised directly in the economic sphere. Such intervention has included wide-spread intimidation and repression practised in the labour market; direct state involvement in production to establish and support major projects considered to be of particular national significance; heavy state involvement in international financial markets spreading many risks to the national economic level; an extensive and continuing use of tariff protection and export subsidy....'

(4) The extent and nature of foreign involvement in EOI, especially direct foreign investment (DFI) by TNCs, varies widely between the different NICs, and these differences have important implications for the development process. What proportion of manufactured goods exports is accounted for by TNCs (see Chapter 10)? What technologies does the TNC utilise in export-oriented manufacturing sectors? How important is foreign technology to a successful EOI strategy? (Stewart (1977), Chapter 7, suggests that it is crucial, and that EOI is unlikely to be compatible with successful local innovation, a point discussed further in Chapter 11.) What is the likely distribution of the gains arising from EOI between foreign and national capital and between capital and labour? Existing theory and the available empirical evidence are such that, as yet, neither satisfactory nor unambiguous answers can be given to such questions, thus illustrating the limitations inherent in any attempt to evaluate comprehensively the experience of EOI.

(5) The NIC phenomenon poses a number of problems for dependency theory. Browett (1985) suggests that the approaches of neither neo-Marxists such as Frank and Amin nor 'classical' Marxists such as Warren are adequate to provide a comprehensive interpretation of uneven

development within the capitalist world economy in general, or the NIC phenomenon in particular. With respect to South Korea, Luedde-Neurath (1980) points to the rapid development of indigenous Korean manufacturing enterprises, the emergence of Korean TNCs (see Chapter 10), Korea's increased sophistication in the procurement and absorption of foreign technology and its attempts to expand local research and development activities. He argues that '. . . the benefits to Korea from the strategy of export orientation have been understated by dependency analysis while the problems have been exaggerated' (p.51) but that '. . . dependency thinking can be extremely useful . . . when it is perceived as a body of theories which expose potentially problematic types of interaction between internal and external factors of LDCs, as well as possible adverse implications for their development' (p.53). Bienefeld (1981, pp.90–1), too, argues that the 'NIC phenomenon strengthens the basic premises of dependency' but Koo (1984) on South Korea, and Amsden (1979) on Taiwan, are rather more critical, both in effect arguing that the primacy of 'endogenous productive and social relations' (Amsden 1979, p.342) and the role of the state in promoting a particular pattern of capital accumulation must be recognised.

(6) What are the possibilities for the generalisability of EOI amongst all, or a significant number, of LDCs? In a revealing simulation exercise, Cline (1982) demonstrated that if all LDCs achieved the same intensity of exports of manufactured goods as the 'Gang of Four' (G-4), LDC manufactured goods exports would rise sevenfold and their share of developed economy manufactured imports would rise from approximately 16% to 60%. If only seven major NICs achieved the G-4 export intensity, the rise in LDC manufactured exports would still be fourfold. Assuming that developed economies would react defensively once LDC import penetration ratios rose beyond 15%, Cline calculates that approximately 80% of the prospective value of LDC export markets in developed economies would be vulnerable to protectionist responses, and that 'the bulk of the market would be vulnerable to closure of access because of high import penetration' (p.85). Cline accuses the advocates of the G-4 model of being guilty of the fallacy of composition – what can be achieved by a small group of LDCs is not possible for the great majority of LDCs. Cline concludes:

> It is seriously misleading to hold up the East Asian G-4 as a model for development because that model almost certainly cannot be generalised without provoking protectionist response ruling out its implementation. (Cline 1982, p.89)

Cline's analysis, as he himself recognises, clearly requires qualification. The prospects for intra-LDC (South–South) trade need to be taken into account, and it is obviously unrealistic to expect all LDCs to be able to adopt successfully the EOI model. Ranis (1985) argues that those who advocate EOI do not mean that LDCs should export as much as possible but rather that LDCs should move in the direction of market liberalisation as soon as possible, although, as noted above, 'liberalisation' does not appear to be a relevant factor in explaining successful EOI in Korea and Taiwan (and see also Evans and Alizadeh 1984).

The broad implications of Cline's analysis have not been undermined, however, and if other factors are also taken into account (identified by Kaplinski (1984) as increasingly restricted market access combined with major changes in manufacturing technology which together might lead to the movement of certain manufacturing processes back to the developed economies), the prospects for future EOI strategies do not look promising. This is not to argue that there will be no EOI in the future, but rather that there is no justification for the unbounded export optimism of many of the advocates of EOI.

(7) A final point relates to some apparent similarities between EOI and ISI. Both are highly import-intensive strategies of industrialisation, and the net balance of payments effect of EOI may in reality be limited. Foreign capital (either in the form of DFI or borrowing in international capital markets) plays an important role in both 'models' and both successful export-oriented industrialisers (Korea) and 'post-ISI' industrialisers (Brazil and Mexico) top the list of LDC debtors (see Chapter 6). We have argued that the state plays a crucial role in both EOI and ISI. Furthermore, even under the full EOI regime, ISI continues to be of importance in certain intermediate and capital goods sectors, actively promoted by direct government intervention.[11] The attempt to find similarities between these two strategies of industrialisation should not be pushed too far, but the comparison is suggestive and comparative analysis could prove to be very useful in increasing our understanding of the industrialisation process in contemporary LDCs.

9.9 Dependent or Independent Capitalist Industrialisation?

An important controversy emerged during the 1970s within the dependency/neo-Marxist/Marxist schools of thought concerning the nature of the industrialisation process. Dependency theorists argued that a process of dependent development was taking place within the LDCs, dominated by foreign corporations and interests through their control of capital, technology and markets. The concept of dependence presupposed that there was an equivalent concept of independence, and Sutcliffe (1972) attempted to clarify the idea of independent industrialisation.

Independent industrialisation should originate with and be maintained by social and economic forces within the industrialising country. Its four main characteristics, Sutcliffe argued, were that the domestic market should be paramount; the industrial sector should contain a wide range of industries (including capital goods industries); the industrial effort should be domestically financed (although actual control was more important than ownership); and there should be independent technological development, consisting of the ability and opportunity to copy, develop and adapt, or at least to choose, technology suitable to the country's resources (historically a condition of development). The social and political counterpart to these factors was the existence of a class (an industrial bourgeoisie) which was both willing and able to invest in a productive manner the economic surplus that it appropriated. This class required the powers of the state to defend and support it, which in turn had to be independent both of domestic interests opposed to industrialisation (for example, landowners or commercial interests) and independent of foreign interests.

For a variety of reasons, capitalist development in LDCs had not led to independent industrialisation and Sutcliffe concluded that, in recent decades, 'rapid industrial growth seems to have taken place only, or at least mainly, in those capitalist countries most obviously satellised by the advanced countries', although 'this is not necessarily a permanent situation' (p.192). For Sutcliffe, the basis of metropolitan dominance was the monopoly of technology (embodied in certain capital goods) that prevented LDCs from establishing complete industrial structures because of their inability to establish industries possessing the most advanced and complex technology of that period of time.

Within his overall attack on dependency theory, Warren (1973) challenged the concept of dependent industrialisation. His main points were that the prospects for successful capitalist economic development for a significant number of LDCs were good and that substantial progress in capitalist industrialisation had already been achieved; any obstacles to this development originated within the LDCs themselves and that ties of dependence were being loosened; and that the distribution of power within the capitalist world was becoming less uneven (see also Chapter 2, Section C).

The attainment of political independence by many LDCs in the post-World War Two period permitted their industrial development but, even more importantly, industrialisation was encouraged by rivalry between capitalist economies, between the Western and Eastern blocs and by the rise of new ruling groups within the LDCs themselves. Since independence, LDCs had increasingly improved their bargaining position and their ability to control resource-based TNCs, and although they had yet to achieve similar results with manufacturing TNCs, Warren argued that conflicts over foreign manufacturing investment occurred within a long-term framework of eventual accommodation, mutually acceptable and mutually advantageous. Furthermore, Warren maintained that the establishment of capital goods industries in LDCs led to 'automatic' technological progress and obstacles to technology transfer lay in the ability or inability of the LDCs themselves to assimilate technology, rather than in imperialist monopoly or domination. Western technological superiority was based on conditions that were losing their force and the technology that was actually transferred was more important than that which was 'blocked'. Independent industrialisation, based on Sutcliffe's four criteria, was in fact taking place rapidly within LDCs.

In general, private investment in LDCs was creating the conditions for the disappearance of imperialism as a system of economic inequality between nations: 'imperialism declines as capitalism grows' (Warren 1973, p.41). Furthermore, it was no longer necessary to associate industrialisation with a particular ruling class (and specifically not with the national bourgeoisie) and in most LDCs the role of the state was of particular importance as it assumed the role of a bourgeois ruling class before the full emergence of that class.

Warren's views clearly contradicted the then dominant structuralist/ dependency/neo-Marxist interpretation of ISI, and his critics (for example, McMichael et al. 1974; Emmanuel 1974) were quick in restating the 'orthodox' 'radical critique', emphasising the limited nature of industrialisation in LDCs, its domination by foreign capital and its differences as compared to the industrialisation experience of the advanced capitalist economies.

Warren, however, in his 1973 article and in his later book (1980), forced economists and other social scientists to look more critically at the experience of industrialisation in general and ISI in particular, to recognise the importance of the NIC phenomenon and to re-examine the dependency paradigm.

Two examples of this kind of re-evaluation can be given in the industrialisation of Brazil in the 'post-ISI' phase, and the emergence and consolidation of indigenous capitalism in Kenya.

The general interpretation of Brazilian development was that opportunities for further ISI were 'exhausted' by the early 1960s, the economy had lost its dynamism and inflation had got out of hand. A military coup occurred in 1964, the economic objectives of which were the control of inflation, the elimination of price distortions, the modernisation of capital markets, the introduction of incentives to direct resources to areas and sectors considered by the government to be of high priority, the attraction of foreign capital inflows and the use of public funds in infrastructure projects and certain government-owned heavy industries (especially steel, mining and petrochemicals) (Baer 1973). After a period of stabilisation between 1964 and 1967, the economy began to grow rapidly in 1968, with industry as the 'leading sector'. Brazilian growth averaged 10% per annum in real terms between 1968–73 and was hailed as an 'economic miracle'.

The essential characteristics of the 'Brazilian model' were as follows: a redistribution of income in favour of the top 5% of income receivers[12] and functionally in favour of profits and rents, to create what Furtado (1973) referred to as a demand profile most attractive to TNCs – income had to be redistributed towards those classes providing a demand for the output of domestic consumer goods industries (although this view tended to ignore the availability of credit and hire purchase facilities which permitted lower-income groups to purchase consumer durables – see Wells 1974); massive government investment in physical and social infrastructure facilities, power generation and the directly productive activities mentioned above; increased foreign capital inflow and a corresponding increase in both real and financial indebtedness (the increased importance of TNCs in certain sectors of the economy was referred to as 'denationalisation' of Brazilian industry), and the promotion of exports of manufactured goods, often through the use of subsidies. This was the 'post-ISI' model referred to in Section 9.6 above.

From 1974 onwards, the Brazilian economy continued to grow in real terms at approximately 7.0% per annum (Andrade 1982). Of significance to our argument is the way in which the Brazilian experience was reinterpreted. 'Stagnationist' interpretations were questioned and the slowing down in the growth of the economy in the early 1960s, previously characterised as the breakdown of the model of ISI, was instead seen merely as a 'crisis' prior to a new stage of capitalist development (Tavares and Serra 1973). Bacha (1977) interpreted the Brazilian 'miracle' as merely conforming to the cyclical pattern of growth of the Brazilian economy and Palma (1978) too argued that dependency theorists, when considering Brazil, failed to take into account the cyclical pattern of capitalist development.

This interpretation of Brazilian development relied heavily on purely empirical observations and no convincing theory of the Brazilian economic cycle is advanced. Neither is it clear whether other LDCs, pursuing ISI, would also be prone to such cyclical phenomena. However, there is no real inconsistency between the views of the Brazilian economists referred to above and some versions of the stagnationist theories. Cyclical fluctuations around the longer-run trend line of economic growth are not separate from the policies pursued by the government, and cyclical and stagnationist factors may well interact with one another in a manner which could both deepen the cyclical downswing and lengthen the period of stagnation. What is of importance to the present discussion is to note that continued Brazilian growth and industrialisation in the 'post-ISI' period disproved the pessimistic prognostications of many structualist/dependency theorists about the possibilities for development in LDCs and forced the reappraisal of the experience of post-World War Two development referred to above.

Our second example relates to the emergence of indigenous capitalism in Kenya, a country that has been at the centre of the debate over the nature and characteristics of the development process in the post-colonial period (for a summary of that debate, see Godfrey 1982). The work of Swainson (1980) is of particular importance. She examined the origins of an African trading class in the 1940s and 1950s and noted that even before political independence was gained in 1963, the larger African traders were beginning to move into small-scale manufacturing (saw mills, bakeries, motor mechanics). In the 1950s, foreign capital was active in encouraging the creation of an African trading class (for example, in the wholesaling and retailing of tobacco and cigarettes), but in the post-independence period it was the state that acted on behalf of the indigenous capitalist class, providing it with the advantages denied to it during the colonial period.

Swainson's central thesis was that the emerging African entrepreneurial class (bourgeoisie) was not subservient to or dependent on foreign capital, but was in fact consolidating its position both politically and economically and was capable of challenging foreign capital. As evidence to support this view she referred to legislation that enabled African traders to gain footholds in the commercial sector (including the procurement of businesses from both non-citizen- and citizen-Asians); the significant extension of credit facilities to African enterprises (the most powerful elements of which had been able to capture the largest proportion of state finance); the expansion in the number of African joint stock companies and the movement of African enterprises into the manufacturing sector since the mid-1970s; moves by the state to Africanise positions within TNC subsidiaries located in Kenya and to localise the ownership of these companies; the marked pattern of African managers using TNC subsidies to acquire their own capital for investment; the large numbers of Kenyan directors who developed their own enterprises at the same time as holding down professional or executive occupations; and the state control of certain productive sectors (for example, oil refining, power supply) and the state regulation of DFI in Kenya.

Swainson emphasised the high degree of interlinkage between foreign and domestic capital in Kenya and between positions within the state bureaucracy and private enterprise. A number of Kenyan capitalists had, however, developed independently of foreign capital and had developed links with foreign capital only once it was advantageous for them to do so.

Swainson concluded her analysis thus:

> Two parallel and contradicting tendencies have been exhibited in post-colonial Kenya: the development of a domestic bouregoisie and a rapid internationalisation of the global economy. In comparison with large multinational firms in Kenya, indigenous capital is small and insignficant. Nevertheless, at the *present stage* of accumulation in Kenya it is still the case that value formation is *nationally* based and the state is able to support the interests of the internal bourgeoisie. During the independence period, within the limits set by Kenya's position in the global economy, the indigenous bourgeoisie have extended their control over the means of production. (Swainson 1980, pp.289–90)

For a fuller discussion of indigenous manufacturing enterprises in LDCs, see Kirkpatrick *et al.* (1984), Chapter 4, Section 4.16.

9.10   Conclusions

In this final section we will briefly consider some of the issues that arise from the industrialisation experience of the LDCs in the post-World War Two period.

The dominant industrial strategy in this period has been market-based ISI and we noted the widespread disillusion over the outcome of that process. ISI was seen by most economists as a 'inward-looking' strategy of industrialisation and development, and given its apparent 'failure', the 'outward-looking' strategy of EOI was recommended in its place.

But is ISI in any meaningful sense 'inward-looking'? It has been heavily dependent on foreign capital, technology and expertise of all kinds; it has assimilated the consumption patterns, tastes, marketing strategies (the consumption technology) of the advanced capitalist countries; changes in the structure of imports and the failure of ISI to save foreign exchange have arguably tightened the external constraint on development and made the ISI economy more vulnerable to external shocks. This is indeed a strange kind of 'inward-looking' development and, as we note below, we can conceive of alternative 'inward-looking' strategies very different from market-based ISI and which may offer a real alternative to EOI.

The neoclassical critics of ISI also ascribe its failure in large part to excessive, irrational and harmful government intervention in the industrialisation process (see, for example, Little 1982; Lal 1983). Without doubt, government intervention has been widespread and most LDCs have at one time or another attempted various kinds of planning. But given that the industrial sector in most LDCs is largely in private hands (even though state enterprises are of importance in many countries, for example, Brazil, Turkey, South Korea), planning has been at most indicative in nature. Planning ministries have produced plans with targets set for the private sector and governments have implemented policies with which to influence private-sector behaviour in a manner consistent with the achievement of such targets. Very few LDCs have attempted to go beyond this.

Without doubt, the record of planning in general, and industrial planning in particular, in LDCs is disappointing (for a further discussion see Kirkpatrick *et al.* (1984), Chapter 6, Section 6.3). But it cannot be concluded that all attempts at planning will inevitably result in failure, and we must reject the neoclassical assertion that most government intervention in LDCs is irrational. The attempt must be made to understand why governments behave as they do in the economic sphere, recognising that most government policies serve specific group or class interests and/or are directed at the achievement of certain objectives, even though those interests and objectives may not be made explicit or public and, indeed, might not be in the general public interest. Of course, governments do make mistakes (in the sense that they pursue policies inconsistent with their real objectives), but this is a different argument from that made by the neoclassical school.

What, then, might our proposed planned 'inward-looking' strategy of industrialisation and development look like? It would presumably first of all have to define economic, social and political objectives consistent with the resources, aspirations and commitment to development of the LDCs themselves. Such a programme would not imply autarkic development but it would require that the presumed relationship between trade and development be reversed, with trade policies designed to meet development objectives (ul Haq 1973). In addition, as Singh (1979) has argued, there would be no inevitable conflict between meeting the basic needs of the population of the LDCs (for food, clothing, shelter, household requirements, etc.) and the transformation of productive structures via industrialisation. Indeed, industrialisation, including the establishment of strategic capital goods industries, is essential to meet basic needs.[13]

The main components of the redefined 'inward-looking' industrialisation strategy would include:

(1) a balance between industrial and agricultural development (see Section 9.2);

(2) the exploitation of existing and the development of new export opportunities – all the available evidence supports the view that the availability of foreign exchange is crucial to the success of any conceivable industrialisation strategy;

(3) the continuation of ISI in strategic sectors of the economy (intermediate, investment and capital goods sectors) on a national and/or regional basis;

(4) the reappraisal of the role of foreign capital in the industrialisation process (Chapter 10) and the recognition of the need to achieve a

balance between the importation of technology and the development of an indigenous technological capability (Chapter 11);

(5) a planned and rational allocation of resources by the government in order to achieve development objectives as rapidly and efficiently as possible, with greater attention placed on effective plan implementation and on the relationship between planning and markets in LDCs.

Clearly, the formulation and implementation of such an 'inward-looking' industrialisation programme in most LDCs would require quite radical political changes within those countries (a necessary but not sufficient condition for the success of such a programme) and important changes in the relationships between developed countries and LDCs. Whether such changes are likely to be forthcoming remains a key question in the political economy of development.

Notes

1. It is interesting to compare this point (emphasised by, among others, Hirschman 1968) with Andre Gunder Frank's Centre–Periphery analysis: 'If it is satellite status which generates underdevelopment, then a weaker or lesser degree of metropolis–satellite relations may generate less deep structural under-development and/or allow for more possibility of local development... It is also significant for the confirmation of our thesis that the satellites have typically managed such temporary spurts in development as they have had, during wars or depressions in the metropolis, which momentarily weakened or lessened its domination over the life of the satellites' (Frank 1967, pp.11–12). For a critique of this argument, see the papers by Miller and Albert and Henderson in the Special Issue of *World Development*, 'The two world wars and economic development,' Vol. 9, No. 8, August 1981.

2. Raul Prebisch, the first Secretary General of UNCTAD and an early advocate of ISI, became an early critic of the type of development resulting from ISI, and stressed the need for changes in the social and economic structures of the LDCs, changes which were complementary to the process of industrialisation (see his Report to the first UNCTAD 1964).

3. Morley and Smith argue that the exclusion of intermediate demands, generated by import substitution itself, will underestimate the amount of ISI that is actually taking place:

   If an import is to be replaced without induced rises in imported inputs or reductions in the supplies available for final demand in other sectors, production must be increased not only in the industry finally processing the good, but also in its supplier industries and so forth. In effect, the newly required intermediate output was previously 'supplied' by the import of the final product. An accurate assessment of the total supply of each sectors' products should therefore include such 'implicit' imports. (Morley and Smith 1970, p.279)

Their results from Brazilian data show approximately one-third more import substitution than Chenery for manufacturing and 53% more for the economy as a whole. Thus a Chenery-type definition of import substitution will lead to underestimation, to an extent depending on the development of intermediate goods industries.

4. For a further discussion of these and other issues, see Fane (1973) and Winston (1967).

5. Bruton (1970) also notes that '... the economic structure that the ISI approach to development spawns is no more flexible and adaptable than the one that is sought to be replaced ... (it) ... is so incompatible with the rest of the system that adjustments to changes in demands, in technology, in any part of the routine are accomplished painfully, if at all' (pp.136–7). Furthermore the ISI economy becomes very vulnerable to import price increases as the increase in oil prices in the 1970s demonstrated.

6. Doherty (1970) also tentatively concludes that the balance of payments position may deteriorate as a result of ISI, depending on the sectoral composition of the ISI programme and various import propensities.

7. The ECLA study characterised Brazil as 'one of the most perfect examples of dual economy to be found in all Latin America' (p.54) and maintained that the various aspects of duality had been aggravated by development.

8. Baer and Maneschi (1971) build a short-run income determination model in which, in the absence of government countermeasures, stagnation is inevitable: '... import-substitutive industrialization, which occurs in a setting where there are no other basic structural changes, results in the establishment of an industrial productive capacity for which eventually there is no adequate demand ... the process is self-terminating since it neither generates sufficient income nor distributes it adequately enough to occupy the new capacity fully and keep it expanding' (p.183). Leff (1967) argues that Brazilian stagnation resulted from constraints imposed by lagging supplies of imports, but this view has not gone unchallenged.

9. For a fuller discussion, see Krueger et al. (1981), and Krueger (1982 and 1983).

10. Lall (1978) identifies four categories of manufactured exports: (i) IS industries which have turned to exporting; (ii) traditional LDC exports (footwear, textiles, processed foods, etc.); (iii) TNC investment in 'modern' industries undertaken specifically for export (the Philips and General Electric complexes in Singapore); and (iv) TNC 'sourcing' investments (see Chapter 10).

11. In the case of Brazil, for example, Weisskoff (1980) presents a fascinating analysis of continued ISI and the more recent 'importation of substitutes', arising from the development and popularisation of new processes and products in the developed capitalist economies which are then introduced into LDCs.

12. Between 1960 and 1970, the share of the top 5% increased from 27.4% to 36.3% of total income; the share of the bottom 40% of income receivers fell from 11.2% to 9.0% (Baer 1973).

13. Surprisingly little attention appears to have been devoted to the elaboration of 'alternative' industrialisation strategies. Thomas's (1974) 'basic industries' strategy is an obvious exception. See also the discussion in Roemer (1981).

References

Amsden, A. (1979) 'Taiwan's economic history: a case of Etatisme and a challenge to dependency theory', *Modern China*, Vol. 5, No. 3, July.

Andrade, R. de Castro (1982) 'Brazil: the economics of savage capitalism', in M. Bienefeld and E.M. Godfrey (eds), *The Struggle for Development: National Strategies in an International Context*, John Wiley.

Aspra, L.A. (1977) 'Import substitution in Mexico: past and present', *World Development*, Vol. 5, Nos. 1/2.

Bacha, E. (1977) 'Issues and evidence on recent Brazilian economic growth', *World Development*, Vol. 5, Nos. 1/2.

Baer, W. (1972) 'Import substitution and industrialization in Latin America: experiences and interpretations', *Latin America Research Review*, Spring.

Baer, W. (1973) 'The Brazilian boom 1968–1972: an explanation and interpretation', *World Development*, Vol. 1, No. 8, August.

Baer, W. and Maneschi, A. (1971) 'Import substitution, stagnation and structural change: an interpretation of the Brazilian case', *The Journal of Developing Areas*, Vol. 5, No. 2, January.

Balassa, B. (1978) 'Exports and economic growth', *Journal of Development Economics*, Vol. 5, No. 2, June.

Baran, P.A. (1957) *The Political Economy of Growth*, Monthly Review Press, New York.

Barratt Brown, M. (1974) *The Economics of Imperialism*, Penguin Books.

Bienefeld, M. (1981) 'Dependency and the newly industrialising countries (NICs): towards a reappraisal', in D. Seers (ed.), *Dependency Theory: A Critical Reassessment*, Frances Pinter.

Browett, J. (1985) 'The newly industrialising countries and radical theories of development', *World Development*, Vol. 13, No. 7, July.

Bruton, H.J. (1970) 'The import-substitution strategy of economic development: a survey', *Pakistan Development Review*, Vol. 10.

Chenery, H.B. (1960) 'Patterns of industrial growth', *American Economic Review*, Vol. 50, No. 4, September.

Cline, W.R. (1982) 'Can the East Asian model of development be generalised?', *World Development*, Vol. 10, No. 2, February.

Doherty, N. (1970) 'Import substitution and the balance of payments', *Eastern African Economic Review*, Vol. 2, No. 2, December.

Emmanuel, A. (1974) 'Myths of development versus myths of underdevelopment', *New Left Review*, No. 85, May–June.

Evans, D. and Alizadeh, P. (1984) 'Trade, industrialisation and the visible hand', *The Journal of Development Studies*, Vol. 21, No. 1, October.

Fane, G. (1973) 'Consistent measures of import substitution', *Oxford Economic Papers*, Vol. 25, No. 2, July.

Felix, D. (1964) 'Monetarists, structuralists and import-substituting industrialisation: a critical appraisal', in W. Baer and I. Kerstenetzky (eds), *Inflation and Growth in Latin America*, Irwin.

Felix, D. (1968) 'The dilemma of import substitution – Argentina', in G.F. Papanek (ed.), *Development Policy – Theory and Practice*, Harvard University Press.

Frank, A.G. (1967) *Capitalism and Underdevelopment in Latin America*, Monthly Review Press, New York.

Furtado, C. (1973) 'The post-1964 Brazilian "model" of development', *Studies in Comparative International Development*, Summer.

Godfrey, E.M. (1982) 'Kenya: African capitalism or simple dependency?' in M. Bienefeld and E.M. Godfrey (eds), *The Struggle for Development: National Strategies in an International Context*, John Wiley.

Guisinger, S. (1981) 'Trade policies and employment: the case of Pakistan', in Krueger *et al.* (eds) (1981).

Helleiner, G.K. (1972) *International Trade and Economic Development*, Penguin Books.

Hirschman, A.O. (1968) 'The political economy of import-substituting industrialisation in Latin America', *Quarterly Journal of Economics*, Vol. LXXXII, No. 1, February.

Hong, W. (1981) 'Export promotion and employment growth in South Korea', in Krueger *et al.* (eds) (1981).

International Labour Office (1970) *Towards Full Employment: A Programme for Colombia*, Geneva.

Kaplinsky, R. (1984) 'The international context for industrialisation in the coming decade', *The Journal of Development Studies*, Vol. 21, No. 1, October.

Keesing, D.B. (1967) 'Outward-looking policies and economic development', *Economic Journal*, Vol. LXXVII, No. 306, June.

Khan, A.R. (1963) 'Import substitution, export expansion and consumption liberalisation: a preliminary report', *Pakistan Development Review*, Vol. 3.

Kilby, P. (1969) *Industrialisation in an Open Economy: Nigeria 1945–1966*, Cambridge University Press.

Kim, I.J. (1985) 'Imported inflation and the development of the Korean economy', in S. Griffith-Jones and J. Harvey (eds), *World Prices and Development*, Gower.

Kirkpatrick, C.H., Lee, N. and Nixson, F.I. (1984) *Industrial Structure and Policy in Less Developed Countries*, George Allen and Unwin.

Kirkpatrick, C.H. and Nixson, F.I. (eds) (1983) *The Industrialisation of Less Developed Countries*, Manchester University Press.

Koo. H. (1984) 'The political economy of income distribution in South Korea: the impact of the state's industrialisation policies', *World Development*, Vol. 12, No. 10, October.

Krueger, A.O. (1978) 'Alternative trade strategies and employment in LDCs', *American Economic Review Papers and Proceedings*, Vol. 68, No. 2, May.

Krueger, A.O., Lary, H.B., Monson, T. and Akrasanee, N. (eds) (1981) *Trade and Employment in Developing Countries*, University of Chicago Press for National Bureau of Economic Research.

Krueger, A.O. (ed.) (1982) *Factor Supply and Substitution*, The University of Chicago Press for National Bureau of Economic Research.

Krueger, A.O. (1983) *Synthesis and Conclusions*, The University of Chicago Press for National Bureau of Economic Research.

Lal, D. (1983) *The Poverty of Development Economics*, Institute of Economic Affairs.

Lall, S. (1978) 'Transnationals, domestic enterprises and industrial structure in host LDCs: a survey', *Oxford Economic Papers*, Vol. 30, No. 2, July.

Lall, S. (1985) *Multinationals, Technology and Exports: Selected Papers*, Macmillan.

Leff, N.H. (1967) 'Import constraints and development: causes of the recent decline in Brazilian economic growth', *Review of Economics and Statistics*, November.

Leff, N.H. and Netto, A.D. (1966) 'Import substitution, foreign investment and international disequilibrium in Brazil', *Journal of Development Studies*, Vol. 2, No. 3, April.

Little, I. (1982) *Economic Development: Theory, Policy, and International Relations*, Basic Books Inc.

Little, I., Scitovsky, T. and Scott, M. (1970) *Industry and Trade in Some Developing Countries*, Oxford University Press.

Luedde-Neurath, R. (1980) 'Export-orientation in South Korea: how helpful is dependency thinking to its analysis?', *IDS Bulletin*, Vol. 12, No. 1, December.

Magdoff, H. (1975) 'China: contrasts with the USSR', in *China's Economic Strategy, Monthly Review*, Vol. 27, No. 3, July–August.

Maitra, P. (1967) *Import Substitution in East Africa*, Oxford University Press.

Maizels, A. (1963) *Industrial Growth and World Trade*, Cambridge University Press.

McMichael, P., Petras, J. and Rhodes, R. (1974) 'Imperialism and the contradictions of development', *New Left Review*, No. 85, May–June.

Merhav, M. (1969) *Technological Dependence, Monopoly and Growth*, Pergamon.

Morawetz, D. (1974) 'Employment implications of industrialisation in developing countries: a survey', *Economic Journal*, Vol. 84, No. 335, September.

Morley, S.A. and Smith, G.W. (1970) 'On the measurement of import substitution', *American Economic Review*, Vol. LX, No. 4, September.

Morley, S.A. and Smith, G.W. (1971) 'Import substitution and foreign investment in Brazil', *Oxford Economic Papers*, Vol. 23, No. 1, March.

Nixson, F.I. (1981) 'State Intervention, Economic Planning and Import-Substituting Industrialisation: The Experience of the Less Developed Countries', *METU Studies in Development*, Special Issue, Ankara, Turkey.

Nixson, F.I. (1982) 'Import-substituting industrialisation', in M. Fransman (ed.), *Industry and Accumulation in Africa*, Heinemann.

Palma, G. (1978) 'Dependency: a formal theory of underdevelopment or a methodology for the analysis of concrete situations of underdevelopment?', *World Development*, Vol. 6, No. 7/8, July/August.

Pitt, M.M. (1981) 'Alternative trade strategies and employment in Indonesia', in Krueger *et al.* (eds) (1981).

Raj, K.N. and Sen, A.K. (1961) 'Alternative patterns of growth under conditions of stagnant export earnings', *Oxford Economic Papers*, Vol. 13, No. 1, February.

Ranis, G. (1985) 'Can the East Asian model of development be generalised? A comment', *World Development*, Vol. 13, No. 4, April.

Robock, S.H. (1970) 'Industrialisation through import-substitution or export industries: a false dichotomy', in J.W. Markham and G.F. Papanek (eds), *Industrial Organisation and Economic Growth*, Houghton Mifflin.

Roemer, M. (1981) 'Dependence and industrialisation strategies', *World Development*, Vol. 9, No. 5, May.

Schiffer, J. (1981) 'The changing post-war pattern of development: the accumulated wisdom of Samir Amin', *World Development*, Vol. 9, No. 6, June.

Schmitz, H. (1984) 'Industrialisation strategies in less developed countries: some lessons of historical experience', *The Journal of Development Studies*, Vol. 21, No. 1, October.

Singer, H.W. (1979) 'Policy implications of the Lima target', *Industry and Development*, No. 3.

Singh, A. (1979) 'The "basic needs" approach to development vs. the new international economic order: the significance of Third World industrialisation', *World Development*, Vol. 7, No. 6, June.

Soligo, R. and Stern, J.J. (1965) 'Tariff protection, import substitution and investment efficiency', *Pakistan Development Review*, Vol. 5, Summer.

Steuer, M.D. and Voivodas, C. (1965) 'Import substitution and Chenery's patterns of industrial growth – a further study', *Economia Internazionale*, Vol. 18, No. 1, February.

Stewart, F. (1973) 'Trade and technology', in Streeten (1973).

Stewart, F. (1976) 'Capital goods in developing countries', in A. Cairncross and M. Puri (eds), *Employment, Income Distribution and Development Strategy: Problems of the Developing Countries*, Macmillan.

Stewart, F. (1977) *Technology and Underdevelopment*, Macmillan.

Streeten, P. (ed.) (1973) *Trade Strategies for Development*, Macmillan.

Sutcliffe, R.B. (1971) *Industry and Underdevelopment*, Addison-Wesley.

Sutcliffe, R.B. (1972) 'Imperialism and industrialisation in the Third World', in R.B. Sutcliffe and R. Owen (eds.) (1972), *Studies in the Theory of Imperialism*, Longman.

Swainson, N. (1980) *The Development of Corporate Capitalism in Kenya, 1918–1977*, Heinemann.

Tavares, M.C. and Serra, J. (1973) 'Beyond stagnation: a discussion on the nature of recent development in Brazil', in J. Petras (ed.), *Latin America: From Dependence to Revolution*, John Wiley.

Thomas, C.Y. (1974) *Dependence and Transformation*, Monthly Review Press, New York.

Tyler, W.G. (1981) 'Growth and export expansion in developing countries', *Journal of Development Economics*, Vol. 9.

ul Haq, M. (1973) 'Industrialisation and trade policies in the 1970s: developing country alternatives', in Streeten (1973).

UNCTAD (1964) *Towards a New Trade Policy for Development*, (Prebisch Report) United Nations.

UN Economic Commission for Latin America (1964) 'The growth and decline of import substitution in Brazil', *Economic Bulletin for Latin America*, Vol. 9, No. 1, March.

UNIDO (1983) *Industry in a Changing World*, ID/CONF.S/2, ID/304, United Nations.

UNIDO (1985) *Industry in the 1980s: Structural Change and Interdependence*, ID/331, United Nations.

Van Arkadie, B. (1964) 'Import substitution and export promotion as aids to industrialisation in East Africa', *East African Economic Review*, Vol. 1, New Series.

Warren, B. (1973) 'Imperialism and capitalist industrialisation', *New Left Review*, No. 81, September–October.

Warren, B. (1980) *Imperialism: Pioneer of Capitalism*, Verso.

Weisskoff, R. (1980) 'The growth and decline of import substitution in Brazil – revisited', *World Development*, Vol. 8, No. 9, September.

Wells, J. (1974) 'Distribution of earnings, growth and the structure of demand in Brazil during the 1960s', *World Development*, Vol. 2, No. 1, January.

Winston, G.C. (1967) 'Notes on the concept of import substitution', *Pakistan Development Review*, Vol. VII, Spring.

World Bank (1985) *World Development Report 1985*, Oxford University Press for the World Bank.

10

The transnational corporation and LDCs

10.1 Introduction

The transnational corporation (TNC)[1] has excited a great deal of interest in recent years in both developed and less developed economies as attention has increasingly been focused on the institutional framework within which goods and factors move between countries.

On the one hand, there are those who see the TNC as making possible the use of total world resources with the maximum of efficiency and the minimum of waste and whose presence is vital for the rapid growth and development of all economies, especially the LDCs. The rise of the TNC is seen as the consequence of imperfections in both goods and factor markets internationally, especially in the market for knowledge, and it is argued that TNCs,

> ... by overcoming such imperfections (e.g. non-tradability in the market for technology, trade inhibiting government economic policies, etc.), have caused greater international specialisation [and have permitted] greater exploitation of international comparative advantage. Extending from this is the presumption that [TNCs] operate, albeit unconsciously, to improve world welfare. (Hood and Young 1979, p.236)

On the other hand, there are those who see the TNC as the most important aspect of the imperialist penetration of the LDCs, heightening their dependency and deepening the process of dependent development. There is little unanimity amongst radical critics of the TNC, however. TNCs are variously alleged to develop, to underdevelop, to block or distort the development of the host LDC, depending on the specific ideological perspective adopted.

Somewhere between these two viewpoints, although closer to the first than to the second, are those economists who recognise the actual or potential conflict of interests between TNCs on the one hand and the host nation state on the other. Dunning (1981, Chapter 14) refers to the 'sovereignty, cultural and equity effects' of TNCs and argues that nation states will wish to improve their 'terms of international production' through the use of multilateral agreements and organisations, within and through which their share of the expected economic benefits of TNC involvement in their economies is clearly delineated and hopefully increased. In other words, it is argued that within a modified framework and working within an agreed set of guidelines and rules, the TNC, through its ownership of and control over technology, capital and marketing skills, can make a unique contribution to the development effort.

It is not, of course, surprising that TNCs should create controversy. Their rapid development raises many fundamental issues and poses profound problems in political economy, relating, for example, to the future of the nation state as an independent economic and political unit, to class formation and class conflict at both the national and international level and to the position and development prospects of the LDCs within the international economy. Some commentators, for example, predict the gradual demise of the nation state and the development of a truly global economy. Others see the continuation of the nation state as being vital to the interests of the TNC, providing the security and the stability necessary for secure and profitable growth. Yet others would asset the dominance of the nation state and its opposition, potential or actual, to TNCs.

Dunning (1981, Chapter 1) has referred to the 'distinctive nature' of the TNC, which differentiates it from a purely national enterprise. Unlike the multi-location domestic enterprise, the TNC owns income-generating assets in different nation states (that is, it engages in international production); unlike the national firm that exports all or part of its product, much of the TNC's trade takes place within the corporation, rather than between independent economic agents; and, unlike the national firm that exports part of its factor inputs (material or human capital), the TNC supplies such inputs as part of a 'package', and maintains control over the use that is made of them.

Large organisations engaged in international transactions are not a new phenomenon. Hymer notes that:

> Giant corporations are nothing new in international trade. They were a characteristic form of the mercantilist period when large joint-stock companies, e.g. The Hudson's Bay Company, The Royal African Company, The East India Company, to name the major English merchant firms, organized long-distance trade with America, Africa and Asia. But neither these firms, nor the large mining and plantation enterprises in the production sector, were the forerunners of the multinational corporation. (Hymer 1972, p.115)

The actual forerunners of today's TNCs did not begin to develop until the end of the nineteenth century although, according to Tugendhat (1973, Ch.1), the concept of the international manufacturing company was firmly established by 1914 (especially in the production of cars, oil, chemicals and aluminium). The growth of US TNCs was fairly rapid in the 1920s, but was slower in the 1930s, although Latin America proved to be quite attractive to foreign investors in the 1930s. With respect to the majority of LDCs, large-scale direct foreign investment, under the aegis of the TNC, is essentially a post-World War Two phenomenon. In the late nineteenth and early twentieth centuries, capital flows to the LDCs were mainly (but not exclusively) in the form of portfolio lending by private individuals to both private and public borrowers, to develop the production of foodstuffs and raw materials and to establish infrastructural and public utility facilities, although direct investment in mineral extraction was also of importance. The revival of the international capital market in the 1950s led to the rapid growth of private capital flows, mainly between the developed economies of North America and Western Europe, but there was also a substantial flow of direct investment to the LDCs, going increasingly into the emerging manufacturing sectors of these economies.

The contemporary TNC is thus distinguished from its forerunners not only but its size and the scope of its operations, but also by its structure, organisation and its view of the world economy and its role in the development of that economy. Its unique features pose special problems to LDC host economies and the TNC thus deserves special attention. In the remainder of this chapter we examine the economic characteristics of TNCs, the theory of DFI, the geographical and sectoral distribution of DFI and various aspects of the impact of the TNC on the process of growth and development – on industrial structure, linkage creation, employment creation, the balance of payments, exports of manufactured goods, transfer pricing and the emergence of TNCs from LDCs. The final section raises a number of broader issues relating to TNCs and economic development in general.

10.2   The Transnational Corporation: A Definition[2]

The transnational corporation (TNC) may be defined as an enterprise that owns or controls assets such as factories, mines, plantations and sales offices in two or more countries. On the basis of this definition, the United Nations (1979, Table 1, p.8) has estimated that in 1977 there were 10,373 firms with at least one foreign affiliate.

If the possession of a minimum number (greater than one) of affiliates or operation in a minimum number of host countries is specified, the TNC population obviously falls. In 1977, for example, there were 5,586 firms that operated in two or more host countries and there were 2,050 firms that operated in six or more host countries. The introduction of these additional criteria affects the distribution by origin of TNCs. TNCs originating in the USA, for example, account for 26.8% of all firms with one or more foreign affiliates operating in one or more host countries but

36.9% of all firms operating in six or more host countries. These data partially illustrate the dominance, by virtue of their greater size, of American TNCs. As the size of the corporation increases, the share of American TNCs in the total TNC population rises. In 1976, eight of the largest ten TNCs were of American origin.

Various measures of foreign content (relating to, for example, exports, sales, assets, earnings or employment) can also be used in defining TNCs, as can criteria relating to organisational form, motiviation and the structure of decision making or control in the TNC. Some analysts would go further and argue that the criterion for deciding whether a corporation is transnational or not is the extent to which policy is centralised and key operations integrated among affiliates.[3]

10.3   The Economic Characteristics of TNCs

Size

TNCs '... are among the most powerful economic institutions yet produced by the capitalist system' (Dunning 1981, p.3), and this power is partly a consequence of size. In 1976 there were 411 industrial firms based in developed market economies with sales of at least $1 billion, and 872 such firms with sales of $395 million or over (United Nations 1979, Table 7, p.14). The two largest TNCs, Exxon and General Motors, had annual sales in 1976 approaching $50 billion (United Nations 1978, Table IV-1, p.288). It should also be noted that there is a high degree of concentration in the TNC population, with perhaps 3–5% of TNCs accounting for the major part of direct foreign investment and total sales.

Size is a relative concept: what is ranked as a medium- or small-sized enterprise among a number of firms in various sectors or countries may well rank large in any particular sector or country. In addition, many TNCs are conglomerates and are engaged in many different activities and product lines. For the evaluation of any particular industry, the size of the relevant line may be more significant than the size of overall activity.

Ownership

The United States of America and the United Kingdom have traditionally enjoyed a dominating position as far as direct foreign investment and international production are concerned. However, as the data in Table 10.1 illustrate, that position had been eroded by the late 1970s by the increased share in the stock of global DFI accounted for by the Federal Republic of Germany and Japan, and to a lesser extent by Switzerland and Holland.

Table 10.1   Percentage Share of Developed Market Economies in Global Stock of Direct Foreign Investment, 1967–76 (%)

Country	1967	1976
USA	53.8	47.6
UK	16.6	11.2
France	5.7	4.1
Switzerland	4.8	6.5
Canada	3.5	3.9
Federal Republic of Germany	2.8	6.9
Holland	2.1	3.4
Italy	2.0	1.0
Belgium–Luxembourg	1.9	1.2
Sweden	1.6	1.7
Japan	1.4	6.7
All other developed market economies (estimate)	3.8	5.8

Source: United Nations (1978), Table III-32, p.236.

In addition to the larger number of companies and countries engaged in international production, a growing number of companies from a number of semi-industrialised LDCs (for example, India, Argentina, Hong Kong, Mexico, Singapore and South Korea) are entering international production, a development that is discussed in greater detail below.

Market Structure

TNCs most commonly operate within oligopolistic market structures (markets effectively controlled by a few sellers or buyers) and TNC behaviour can usefully be analysed within an oligopoly framework. Certain important characteristics of TNC behaviour – rapid process and product innovation, product differentiation and heavy advertising – are also characteristics of, and in turn reinforce, oligopolistic structures. In addition, the patterns of entry of TNCs into LDC markets show clear evidence of oligopolistic rivalry. Direct foreign investment in an important market by one TNC might well be seen as a rivalrous move by other firms in the industry, since their share of the market in that country, supplied through exports or a non-equity operation, might be put at risk. This perception will bring forth 'defensive' DFI by these firms, and thus DFI in individual economies by rival firms tends to be bunched together. For a discussion of the theoretical issues and an empirical study, see Yamin (1983).

Global Organisation

A unique feature of TNCs is their ability to view the world as a single economic unit and consequently to plan, manage and organise their activities on a global scale. TNCs are both products of and contributors to technological developments that have reduced the problems posed by geographical distance. For example, the widespread use of computers for data processing, collection and transmission has enabled global operations and decision making to become highly centralised. It is the parent company that determines global strategy, decides on the location of new investment, allocates export markets and research and development (R&D) programmes to various parts of the corporation and determines the prices that are charged on intra-corporate transactions (transfer prices).

Affiliates operate under the discipline and framework of a common global strategy and a common global control and, in principle at least, put the wider interest of the company as a whole before their own separate interests. The importance of intra-firm trade has continued to grow and European TNCs, like their US counterparts before them, have increasingly centralised their global operations. The United Nations (1978, p.44) has noted that:

> . . . control can become embedded within the fabric of the firm without being readily apparent to the outside observer. The more national units become conditioned to indirect, harmonized control procedures, the more difficult it becomes for them to respond unilaterally to the needs of the local economy.

Corporate Objectives

Within the capitalist system, firms are embodiments of privately owned property, organised primarily for the purpose of earning and accumulating profit. Even though there is much debate in the literature over the precise objectives that modern, large-scale corporations (both national and transnational) pursue (see Devine et al. 1979, Ch. 3), Hood and Young (1979, p.115), after an extensive review of the literature, concluded that:

> To be on safest ground it is probably wise to view [TNC] behaviour as a form of constrained profit maximisation, where financial, structural, environmental and general resource variables limit pursuit of maximum profits.[4]

TNCs will also, as far as possible, attempt to minimise the amount of tax that they pay and will also wish to minimise the risks that they face, although clearly such objectives may be mutually exclusive in many instances.

It is not always possible, however, to explain or predict the behaviour of individual affiliates along these lines. Given that the interests of any one part of the TNC are subordinate to the interests of the TNC as a whole, different affiliates may pursue various objectives, all of which may well be consistent, in the long run, with global profit maximisation (Hood and Young 1979, p.99).

To achieve the objective of global profit maximisation, TNCs have devised a variety of financial strategies and policies. Examples include a heavy reliance on local borrowing and the reinvestment of profits to finance affiliate operations; the takeover of existing operations in the LDCs, rather than the establishment of new ones; and the manipulation of transfer prices. Transfer prices are the prices that are charged on transactions that take place within the corporation (intra-corporate transactions); given that such prices are determined by the TNC itself and not by market forces, they can deviate to a considerable extent from so-called 'arms-length' or market prices (see below).

Why Do Firms Engage in International Production?

The entry of a firm into international production can take any of three forms: the production of the same goods elsewhere (horizontal extension); developing a stage in the production process that comes earlier or later than the firm's principal processing activity (vertical extension); and conglomerate diversification (Caves 1971).

A number of theories have been advanced in the attempt to explain the determinants of horizontal international production (these are well surveyed in Hood and Young (1979), Ch. 2). There is now general agreement in the literature that a necessary condition for a firm to invest directly in another country (rather than merely export to that country or license its technology to local producers) is that it must possess some advantage or asset (an ownership-specific advantage) not shared by its local competitors. Various ownership-specific advantages have been suggested as being of significance – technological advantages, the ability to differentiate products, marketing skills, superior organisational skills and management techniques – all of which have the characteristics of a public good (although public only within the firm, of course) in that the firm transferring and utilising them in a foreign market can do so at a zero or low opportunity cost.[5]

However, it is not the possession of these advantages as such that is of significance. Rather, it is the fact that certain transactions or activities can be organised and carried out at a lower cost *within* the firm (the *internalisation* of those activities) than through the market that confers on the TNC its unique advantages. Dunning (1981, Ch.2), in arguing for an eclectic, integrated approach to international economic involvement (incorporating both theories of international trade and international production), puts the point thus (p.34):

The eclectic approach would argue that it is not the possession of technology *per se* which gives an enterprise selling goods embodying that technology to foreign markets (irrespective of where they are produced) an edge over its competitors, but the advantage of internalising that technology, rather than selling it to a foreign producer for the production of those goods. It is not the orthodox type of monopoly advantages which give the enterprise an edge over its rivals – actual or potential – but the advantages which accrue through internalisation, for example, transfer price manipulation, security of supplies and markets, and control over use of intermediate goods. It is not surplus entrepreneurial resources *per se* which lead to foreign direct investment, but the ability of enterprises to combine these resources with others to take advantage of the economies of production of joint products.

To obtain a more complete explanation of international production, location-specific factors have also to be taken into account. These include relative costs of production, marketing factors, trade barriers and government policies in both the home and host economies. Clearly, the relative importance of such factors will vary according to the nature and objectives of each individual act of DFI.

Without the incentive to internalise, the firm may well prefer to sell its knowledge or license its technology, or merely export the final product. Where the rent-yielding advantage of the parent firms lies in a 'one-shot' innovation of technique or product (for example, a new method for making plate glass or the secret ingredient of a successful soft drink – Caves 1971), licensing the technology may well be the option chosen. Location-specific factors are again of importance. Host-country government policies may well preclude DFI and thus force the TNC to enter into licensing arrangements. On the other hand, the absence of the necessary skills or resources among indigenous firms in the host LDC may well make DFI unavoidable.

The discussion so far has focused on horizontal direct foreign investment. In the case of vertical direct foreign investment, the evidence from the developed economies suggests that the avoidance of oligipolistic uncertainty and the erection of barriers to the entry of new rivals are important factors underlying the investment decision (Caves 1971). For LDCs, however, it may simply be the case that no local firm, either private or state owned, has the capital, technology and expertise to exploit effectively and efficiently the country's natural resources (especially mineral resources) and thus, at the very least, a limited dependence on the vertically integrated extractive TNCs is unavoidable.[6]

An alternative explanation of DFI is based on the product-cycle hypothesis. This hypothesis, closely associated with the work of Vernon (1966, 1971, 1979), is an attempt to explain changes in locational and trading patterns over time as a product moves through its life cycle. It is argued by Vernon that, historically, US enterprises have developed and produced new products that were labour saving or designed to satisfy high-income wants. In the first stage of the product cycle, there were good reasons why production would be located in the USA: the availability of engineers and scientists with the requisite skills; close contact with prospective customers and suppliers; efficiency of communication between the research specialists themselves and the specialists and the parent company; and low price elasticity of demand for the product, reducing the importance of cost differentials at alternative locations. Foreign demand would therefore be met by exports from the USA. In its second stage, the product matures. Technology tends to become more standardised, competitors might appear and costs of production become more important. To serve overseas markets better (particularly those of Western Europe, in the original formulation of the hypothesis), the firm can either license a local producer or, more likely, establish its own production subsidiary overseas (if the marginal costs of producing in the USA for export, plus the cost of transport, are greater than the full cost of producing in a foreign subsidiary). With US subsidiary production overseas, the US increasingly becomes an importer of the product in question. In the final stage, the product becomes 'standardised', price competition becomes intensified and production might well be transferred to LDCs with lower labour costs.

Vernon recognised the specific characteristics and limitations of his hypothesis, noting that it was more applicable to firms that were expanding overseas for the first time but was less relevant to those firms with already established global networks (Vernon 1971, Ch. 3; 1979) where new products and processes could increasingly originate in any part of that global network. Vernon (1979) also recognised changes over time in the international environment, with the other developed economies 'catching up' with the USA in terms of per capita income and market characteristics. However, he still defended its application to LDCs and argued that the emergence of TNCs from LDCs was consistent with the model's predictions.

Others have been more critical. Clark (1975) argued that TNCs often transfer technology and other resources at a much earlier stage in the 'life' of products than would be predicted by the theory, and that the increasingly important practice of locating relatively labour-intensive assembly or process activities in LDCs is not consistent with the product-cycle hypothesis. He concluded that 'the product cycle theory, as it stands, is a rather unsatisfactory description of modern international techno-economic relations' (Clark 1975, p.7). Hood and Young (1979, p.83), too, urged caution in using the hypothesis to explain the expansion paths of TNCs.

10.4 Direct Foreign Investment in the LDCs

Geographical Distribution

Table 10.2 presents information on the global stock of direct foreign investment and the share of the LDCs, by destination, in that total, for selected years between the mid-1960s and the early 1980s. The data should perhaps be regarded as indicating orders of magnitude only, but they do indicate that (i) most DFI is located in developed capitalist economies and (ii) very few LDCs account for the major part of DFI located in the Third World. The OPEC countries, the tax havens and ten other LDCs (Brazil, Mexico, India, Malaysia, Argentina, Singapore, Peru, Hong Kong, the Philippines and Trinidad and Tobago) accounted for 71.2% of the total LDC stock of DFI in 1967 and 76.5% in 1975. It should be noted that the People's Republic of China is omitted from these calculations, although since 1978 it has become an increasingly important recipient of DFI (OECD 1983).

Table 10.2 Stock of Direct Foreign Investment: Worldwide and Share of LDCs, 1967–81

Year	Worldwide ($b)	Share in LDCs ($b)	Share in LDCs as % worldwide stock	OPEC countries[a] and tax havens[b] ($b)	OPEC countries[a] and tax havens[b] as % worldwide stock	as % of LDC stock
1967	105	32.8	31	11.4	10.8	34.7
1971	158	43.3	28	15.5	9.8	35.8
1975	259	68.2	26	24.5	9.5	35.9
1976	287					
1978		96)				
1979		110) variously				
1980		120) estimated				
1981		130[c]) as 25–33	22.3 (OPEC only)			

Sources: Kirkpatrick and Nixson (1981), Table 1; OECD (1982, 1983).
Notes: (a) Algeria, Ecuador, Gabon, Indonesia, Iran, Iraq, Kuwait, Libyan Arab Jamahiriya, Nigeria, Qatar, Saudi Arabia, United Arab Emirates and Venezuela.
(b) Bahamas, Barbados, Bermuda, Cayman Islands, Netherlands Antilles and Panama.
(c) OECD (1983), Table 5, p.25, gives a figure of $137b. for 1981, which includes 'unallocated amounts' and Japanese official support for private investment.

It was noted above that size is a relative concept, and even a relatively small amount of DFI will exert an influence beyond its purely quantitative significance if it is concentrated in strategic, rapidly growing, technologically advanced sectors. The TNC is often the 'market leader' in the oligopolised sectors of the host economy and, with the growth of non-equity operations, the distinction between ownership and control is becoming of increasing importance. Data relating to the stock of DFI in LDCs are thus no longer adequate indicators of the extent of TNC activities and their influence in LDCs.

Table 10.3 illustrates the geographical distribution pattern of direct investment flows from the major OECD Development Assistance Committee (DAC) countries. Geographical proximity and historical and trade relations are factors that play a major role in influencing the location of DFI, although Japanese TNC investment in Latin America is an exception to that generalisation.

The United Nations (1983, p.284) has estimated that in 1980 there were 104,000 TNC affiliates in total, of which 27,000 were located in LDCs. Data on the geographical distribution of TNC affiliates (Table 10.4) demonstrate a pattern similar to that shown by the geographical distribution of DFI. The bracketed figures in Table 10.4 show that the USA

Table 10.3 Geographical Distribution of Allocated Direct Investment Flows (Net) from Major Source Countries, 1979–81[a] (%)

Home country	LDC Region					Share of individual home countries in net DFI flow to LDCs, 1981
	Europe[c]	Africa	Latin America	Asia	Total	
France	33(34)	23(16)	39(6)	5(2)	100	7.8
Germany	21(18)	5(3)	59(7)	15(4)	100	9.2
Japan	1(4)	9(16)	29(11)	61(49)	100	16.6
UK[b]	10(13)	30(25)	36(7)	24(9)	100	8.3
USA	5(31)	9(40)	69(69)	17(36)	100	44.7

Sources: OECD (1983), Table 1, p.27; Table 2, p.18.
Notes: (a) Figures in brackets denote the home countries' share in the total DFI of the continent from the five source countries, including official support for private investment by the Japanese government.
(b) Excluding investments in the oil industry.
(c) Greece, Portugal, Spain, Yugoslavia.

Table 10.4 Distribution among LDC Regions of Foreign Affiliates of Companies from Selected Home Countries, 1980 (%)

Home country	% of total affiliates of individual home countries located in LDCs	Distribution among LDC regions				
		Latin America	Africa	West Asia	South and East Asia	Europe
France	30.5	7.7(3.1)	18.7(18.1)	1.1(6.2)	2.9(1.3)	0.1(3.2)
Germany	17.6	9.2(5.9)	3.0(4.6)	0.8(7.0)	4.4(3.2)	0.2(8.2)
Japan	58.2	13.4(3.5)	2.2(1.4)	0.8(3.0)	41.7(12.6)	– –
UK	24.2	4.7(10.1)	7.7(40.2)	0.9(26.8)	10.4(25.6)	0.5(56.4)
USA	34.7	21.4(62.2)	2.3(15.9)	0.9(36.5)	10.0(33.5)	0.1(10.9)

Sources: United Nations (1983), Table 11.8, p.34; bracketed figures from Table 11.9, p.35.
Note: The figures in brackets show the percentage of total TNC affiliates in each region accounted for by the home countries listed.

accounted for 62% of total TNC affiliates in Latin America, 37% in West Asia, and 34% in South and East Asia. The UK accounted for 40% of total TNC affiliates located in Africa and 26% of total affiliates in both West Asia and South and East Asia. Japan accounted for 13% of total TNC affiliates located in South and East Asia.

Sectoral Composition

Table 10.5 gives details of the stock of DFI in LDCs, broken down by region and industrial sector. The sectors in which DFI has traditionally played a dominant role – petroleum, and mining and smelting – still account for the major part of the total stock of DFI in LDCs, but the relative importance of these 'traditional' sectors in the overall stock of DFI has fallen, given the rapid growth of DFI in manufacturing and the services sectors characteristic of the 1960s and 1970s.

The control of sources of raw materials was initially a powerful force motivating direct foreign investment, but recent years have seen the LDC governments becoming increasingly successful in regaining control over their non-renewable natural resources, or at least obtaining a greater share of the revenue derived from their exploitation – oil is perhaps the best example of this process. The foreign ownership and exploitation of a country's basic resources is a politically explosive issue in any economy, especially a poor one which has recently acquired political independence. The TNC has become less important as a supplier of skills, technology and capital (production technology has become standardised, patents have expired, government-owned corporations have moved into this field, and so on) for the extraction and processing of raw materials, and it has thus had to develop new strategies in the light of changed economic and political conditions. The local processing of raw materials has become more important, new ownership schemes and contractual arrangements have been introduced (joint ventures, often with the TNC as a minority equity holder, management contracts, etc.) and new technologies developed, all of which demonstrate the flexibility and resourcefulness of the TNC and/or the change in the balance of economic and political power in favour of the LDC government (Warren 1973, pp.20–4). TNCs will nevertheless continue to be of great importance in petroleum and in a variety of strategic minerals – for example, iron ore, copper and bauxite.

TNC investment in the manufacturing sector can be broadly divided into two sub sections: (i) research-intensive, technologically advanced industrial activities (pharmaceuticals, chemicals, machinery and office equipment); (ii) industries where marketing power is of importance (foodstuffs, soft drinks, cigarettes, cosmetics, automobiles) and brand names, product differentiation and heavy advertising are characteristic features. This distinction cannot always be clearly made, as much research

Table 10.5 Stock of DFI in LDCs, by Region and Industrial Sector, End 1972

Sector	Africa ($b)	(%)	Latin America & Caribbean ($b)	(%)	Middle East ($b)	(%)	Asia and Oceania ($b)	(%)	Total all regions $b	% of total
Petroleum	4.1	45.0	5.3	23.5	3.6	87.8	2.4	29.6	15.4	35.0
Mining and smelting	1.5	16.5	2.2	9.7	–	–	0.6	7.4	4.3	9.8
Manufacturing	1.6	17.6	8.9	39.4	0.3	7.3	2.5	30.9	13.3	30.3
Other	1.9	20.9	6.2	27.4	0.2	4.9	2.6	32.1	10.9	24.8
Total all sectors	9.1	100.0	22.6	100.0	4.1	100.0	8.1	100.0	43.9	100.0
Region's share of total		20.7		51.5		9.3		18.4		

Source: United Nations (1978), Table III-51, p. 260.

and development expenditure (R&D) is diverted towards minor product changes (in, for example, pharmaceuticals, foodstuffs and automobiles), rather than going into basic research or the development of major new products or processes.

Throughout the 1970s, TNC investment in the services sector expanded rapidly in banking, insurance, accounting, advertising, tourism and hotels and consultancy. In addition, in the agricultural sector, so-called agribusiness TNCs are of significance for a variety of products – for example, pineapples, sugar, vegetable oils, tea, soya beans and beef. Clearly, there is overlap between the different sectors: manufacturing TNCs provide inputs for the agricultural sector (fertilisers, pesticides, etc.) and service sector TNCs provide a variety of service inputs (advertising, technical assistance, feasibility studies, legal advice, etc.) (see Feder 1977).

Why Do LDCs Want DFI?

Despite the reservations that LDCs might have about the role of foreign capital in the development process, it remains the case that competition between the LDCs for transnational involvement in their economies continues to be intense. Although no longer uncritically viewed as 'engines of development', TNCs nevertheless own, control or have access to vast resources of capital, technology and all kinds of expertise, and, of increasing importance, often provide access to export markets, all factors that are in short supply or absent in the LDCs. The main attraction of TNC direct investment, therefore, is that these resources are all part of the DFI 'package'.

This argument should, however, be qualified in two respects. Firstly, DFI began to assume a relatively less important role in the economies of the LDCs in the 1970s. For LDCs as a group, foreign trade increased much faster than DFI, but, perhaps more significantly, domestic investment increased more rapidly than DFI (United Nations 1983, p.17). Comprehensive data on rates of change of domestic investment and DFI are not readily available, but for the majority of LDCs, *in purely quantitative terms*, DFI is of only marginal importance in total capital formation (compare this with the argument in Chapter 9, Section 9.5, as to the historical importance of DFI in ISI). The inflow of DFI as a percentage of domestic investment (annual average, 1978–80) for five major recipients of DFI was as follows: Argentina, 3.0%; Brazil, 2.1%; Mexico, 3.3%; Singapore, 10.1%; Malaysia, 2.0%. With the exception of the tax havens, Liberia and Singapore, for no LDC for which data were available was the figure greater than 10%, and for the great majority of LDCs the figure was significantly less than 5% (all data from United Nations (1983), Annex Table II.4, pp.311–5).

Second, it is increasingly appreciated that the 'packaged' nature of the resource transfer makes it difficult, if not impossible, to quantify with any degree of accuracy the real cost of the individual factors being supplied in the 'package'. Emphasis is thus being placed on the 'unpackaging' of DFI (that is, separating the sources of finance, technology and expertise) or on the 'unbundling' of the actual technology, that is, the disaggregation of the individual components of the technology.

Transnational Corporations and Industrial Structure[7]

What are the effects of foreign ownership on the level of industrial concentration in LDCs? Other things being equal, the expectation is that foreign penetration rates will be highest in the most concentrated industries, which include the most technically advanced and capital-intensive activities (United Nations 1978, p.61). The available empirical evidence does not, however, allow the conclusion to be drawn that TNCs actually *cause* higher levels of concentration, although it is possible that their entry speeds up the natural process of concentration and that the weakness of local competitors (excluding state enterprises) permits them to achieve a higher degree of market dominance than they would enjoy in the developed economies.

Two contradictory hypotheses have been advanced to explain the level of industrial concentration in LDCs and the role of TNCs in influencing or determining industrial structure:

(1) The first focuses on the limited size of the domestic market in the majority of LDCs and their reliance on large-scale, capital-intensive imported technologies, which TNCs have access to and utilise in LDCs. It predicts higher levels of concentration in LDCs than in the developed economies, with the presence of foreign capital on a large scale strengthening the prediction.

(2) The second focuses on the competitive entry of TNCs into host country markets. It predicts that all the major international producers will follow one another into an important LDC market, thus producing a 'miniature replica' of that industry within the small domestic market of the LDC, leading to a lower level of concentration than would be the case without DFI.

With respect to the first hypothesis, the work of Newfarmer and Mueller (1975) on the industrial sector in Brazil and Mexico indicates a high degree of TNC penetration, with the most concentrated industries demonstrating the highest degrees of foreign domination. The second hypothesis is considered by Evans (1977) with reference to the Brazilian pharmaceutical industry. The structure of this industry appears to be consistent with the predictions of the 'miniature replica' hypothesis. The size distribution of firms was stable over time and significantly less concentrated than the American size distribution of firms (Evans 1977, p.379). Data for Mexico and Argentina, cited by Evans, also indicated more dispersed size distributions for the pharmaceutical industry than were typical for developed capitalist economies.

Lall (1979b; reprinted in Lall, 1980a) attempted to overcome what he saw as the defects of the previous studies by an analysis of how TNC entry affected market concentration within a comprehensive model of the determinants of industrial structure. Without such a model, he argued (1980a, p.65),

> . . . it is impossible to assess whether foreign entry has an influence on market structure *independently* of the industrial variables which are commonly thought to determine it, whether it is merely *associated with* structural characteristics that are inherent in different industries, or it *speeds up* the process of structural change which may occur even in its absence.

Lall's analysis suggested that the two hypotheses outlined above need not be mutually exclusive. In the short run, TNC entry may reduce concentration if it increases the number of local suppliers and if it induces competing TNCs to follow suit. In the longer run, however, TNC entry may increase concentration for two reasons: the attributes of TNCs (capital-intensive technologies, differentiated products, superior managerial and organisational skills, etc.) may raise barriers to entry for local firms; and TNC conduct may accelerate the process of concentration, via acquisition of local firms, etc.

Evidence for the latter argument is provided by Newfarmer's (1979b) study of the Brazilian electrical industry. This study suggested that the use of specific market and extra-market tactics by TNCs, which aimed at controlling competitive forces, market conditions and market development could prevent or retard the erosion of their monopolistic advantages and the deterioration of entry barriers confronting potential (especially domestic) competitors. TNC corporate behaviour 'fed back' into the market structure. In 1960 TNCs controlled approximately 66% of the assets of the 100 largest electrical firms in Brazil, but their share had grown to nearly 80% by 1976 (Newfarmer 1979b, p.108). Newfarmer estimated that takeovers accounted for over 90% of the increase in the foreign share of this industry over the period studied and he concluded (p.135):

> TNCs exhibit strong propensities towards organising and preserving various forms of market power in host economies. These tactics are often based on the advantages of global financial strength (such as in the case of cross-subsidisation or acquisitions) or perceived international and local interdependence (such as with interlocking directorates, mutual forbearance or

collusion) . . . Clearly, barriers to entry which protect the monopolistic advantage of TNCs are not solely based on superior technology, but include specific corporate practices designed to deter new entry.

On balance, the evidence would appear to lend greater support to the view that TNC involvement is likely to increase the level of industrial concentration in any given LDC. The 'miniature replica' hypothesis, although supported by some evidence, is perhaps more likely to be a short-run phenomenon; in a dynamic, longer-run context, higher levels of concentration are to be expected.

10.5 TNCs and Linkage Creation

TNCs can exert a significant influence on both the rate and characteristics of the process of growth and development through the creation of forward and backward linkages with the host economy. Forward linkages refer to the sale of the output of the TNC to domestic firms for use as inputs into their productive processes, and backward linkages refer to purchases by TNCs from domestic supplier firms.

It is usually argued that TNCs will establish few linkages with domestic firms. The highly centralised global structure of the TNC and the integrated nature of its global operations, its use of capital-intensive technologies and the nature of the final product, taken together lead many economists to argue that TNCs create a virtual 'enclave' in the host economy, integrating the 'modern', TNC-dominated sectors of the host economy with the international economy. The Chilean economist, Osvaldo Sunkel, went so far as to characterise this process as one of transnational integration and national disintegration (Sunkel 1973b; Sunkel and Fuenzalida 1979).

Langdon's study (Langdon 1975) of the Kenyan soap and detergents industry provided support for the view that TNCs create fewer linkages with domestic firms than do indigenously owned firms in the same industry. This is because TNC soap production technology offered fewer linkage possibilities than local, especially non-mechanised, soap production, but product choice was also a factor (see below). The inputs for the basic laundry soaps produced by indigenous firms were available locally, whereas TNC input requirements had no Kenyan source of supply. In addition, tie-in clauses that compel the subsidiary to buy from the parent or some other subsidiary approved by the parent were used in the industry to forestall the possibility of alternative supply sources developing. Capital equipment was also likely to be supplied by the parent company, thus preventing or retarding the development of an indigenous machine-making capacity that could supply basic, labour-intensive equipment. Where linkage possibilities did exist – in, for example, packaging and printing operations – it was more likely to be other TNC subsidiaries that were able to take advantage of these opportunities, rather than indigenous firms.

From the above discussion, it is clear that it is not only ownership as such that determines linkage possibilitilies in LDCs, but also (and perhaps more importantly) the nature of the technology utilised and the characteristics of the final product.

A general survey of the literature on TNC linkage creation in LDCs was carried out by Lall (1978). His conclusions were:

(1) With respect to import-substituting TNCs, extensive linkages had been created in the larger, semi-industrialised LDCs (India, Mexico, Brazil, Argentina), largely as a result of government pressure, but probably at an excessively high cost; in smaller or in-dustrially backward LDCs, TNCs had created relatively few linkages.

(2) With respect to export-oriented TNCs, linkage creation depended on the *type* of export activity (see Chapter 9, Section 9.8), but was least likely in the case of 'modern' industries specifically designed for export and TNC global sourcing (see Section 10.8).

Lall argued that government policy was extremely important in creating an environment that encouraged linkage creation and exerted pressure on individual firms to accelerate the development of a subcontracting net-work. Although such policies may be costly in the short run (in terms of the costs associated with 'inefficient' import-substituting industrialisation – see Chapter 9, Section 9.5 – of which linkage creation is a part), in the longer run, the costs of linkage creation may not be significant (Lall 1980b, p.224). Lall (1978, p.223) concluded that:

The extent of linkages created in particular LDCs depends upon the stage of development of indigenous industry, the availability of local skills and technology, institutions and government policies, changes in demand and technology in world markets and their political attractiveness to TNCs.

10.6 Employment Creation by TNCs

Estimates of the total numbers directly employed by TNCs globally range from 13 to 30 million. In the LDCs, TNCs employ between 2 and 4 million people, representing 0.3% of total employment and 2% of total industrial employment in the formal sector (figures quoted in UNIDO (1981), p.238).

In some LDCs (such as Brazil, Mexico, Peru, the Republic of Korea and Singapore), TNC employment represents a relatively greater proportion of total industrial employment (perhaps as high as 20% in some cases), with employment tending to be concentrated in the manufacturing sector. TNC employment is likely to be concentrated in those sectors where TNCs tend to predominate: in Mexico, for example, TNCs account for a high proportion of employment in chemicals, electrical machinery and transport equipment; in Korea, TNCs are significant employers in petroleum and electrical machinery (UNIDO 1981, Table V.I, p.239).

Indirect employment may be created by TNCs via the development of backward and forward linkages within the host LDC economy. Such indirect employment creation may be substantial in the manufacturing sector, but data are scarce. In the Republic of Korea, for example, it has been estimated that TNC investment has created 102,000 jobs through backward linkages with domestic producers (UNIDO 1981, p.239).

A further point relates to employment in the services sector of the LDC. Baer (1976) and Baer and Samuelson (1981) have highlighted the linkages between industrial modernisation and significant service sector employment, and have hypothesised that the proportion of service sector employment that represents disguised unemployment will fall over time. Baer has also maintained that the growth of capital-intensive, large-scale industrial units would be more likely to generate high rates of growth of service employment (repairs, marketing, finance, modern health and urban services) than would a labour-intensive industrial strategy (Baer 1976, p.130).

The strategy of industrialisation selected may affect the extent of TNC employment creation. Export-led industrialisation may well utilise relatively labour-intensive techniques and thus create more jobs than 'inward-looking' import-substituting industrialisation (see Chapter 9, Section 9.8). However, it is also likely to be the case that export-oriented TNCs create fewer linkages with the host economy and thus indirect employment creation is likely to be limited.

10.7   Transnational Investment and the Balance of Payments

The initial act of direct investment will usually, but not always (see below), involve a capital inflow, which will appear as a credit item in the capital account of the balance of payments. Exports by the TNC will appear as a credit item in the current account. Offsetting these credit items will be a number of debit items. The activities that the TNC engages in may be import intensive, that is, require the import of capital goods (machinery and equipment), and raw materials and intermediate goods. The TNC subsidiary is also likely to make a variety of payments to the parent company, including payments for technology (royalties, technical and managerial fees, etc.) and contributions to headquarters' overhead expenditure and research and development expenditure. In addition, if it is profitable, the TNC subsidiary will, of course, wish to remit all or part of its after-tax profits to the parent or some other part of the corporation.[8]

The act of direct investment by the TNC is not always associated with a significant capital flow. Data from Latin America, for example, indicate that American TNCs financed over 80% of their investments from local sources, either from the reinvestment of earnings or from local borrowing (or borrowing from third countries) (Cardoso 1972, p.92; see also Vaitsos 1976). For other areas of the less developed world, especially sub-Saharan Africa, the importance of domestic sources of finance is not likely to be so great, but the general point remains valid – that care must be taken when assessing the capital contribution of TNCs.

It is also relevant to note in this context that much TNC direct foreign investment involves the takeover of already existing, domestically owned enterprises (for an analysis of TNC takeovers in Brazil, and the perceived 'uneven' distribution of benefits, see Newfarmer 1979a). Clearly, it is not uncommon for TNCs to use domestic financial resources to buy out local firms. It cannot be determined *a priori* whether or not TNCs will use such resources more efficiently than domestic firms (although there is a general presumption in the literature that they will in fact do so). Nor is it known what the previous owners are likely to do with the proceeds from the sale of their enterprises, but clearly both these factors should, if possible, be taken into account in any analysis of the impact of TNCs on the host economy.

As noted above, TNC direct foreign investment is likely to be import intensive, although the extent of import intensity depends, in part at least, on the degree of linkage creation in the host economy. In some cases the local economy may not be capable of supplying the required inputs, in that it may not have the technical resources to produce the input at all or it may be unable to reach the technical or quality standards demanded by the TNC subsidiary. In other cases, tie-in clauses impose a legal obligation on the subsidiary to buy from the parent or some other part of the corporation. Vaitsos (1974, Ch. IV), when analysing technology commercialisation contracts for a number of Latin American economies (Bolivia, Ecuador and Peru), found that 67% of the contracts with relevant information had tie-in clauses. In all the countries, the pharmaceutical industry usually had the highest percentage of tie-in arrangements (Vaitsos 1974, p.45). The extent of intra-firm trade clearly determines the scope for transfer price manipulation (see below).

The balance between capital account inflows and current account outflows, both visible and invisible, will vary over time, both for individual TNC subsidiaries and with respect to the operations of all foreign direct investment located within a particular economy. Lall and Streeten (1977, Ch. 7) concluded that the net impact of their sample firms' activities on the overall balance of payments was negative in five of the countries analysed (Jamaica, India, Iran, Colombia and Malaysia), but was positive in Kenya (attributed to the importance of exports by some of the sample firms to Uganda and Tanzania). On the whole, the sample foreign firms seemed to be 'taking more out than they were putting in' (p.142). The export of manufactured goods by TNCs is discussed in Section 10.8. Much of this empirical evidence is consistent with the view that foreign capital 'decapitalises' the LDCs. In other words, by taking out more than they put in, TNCs reduce the potentially reinvestible surplus in LDCs. Econometric analysis (Bornschier 1980) has suggested that the short-term association between TNC direct foreign investment and income growth is positive and that the long-term association between cumulated DFI and income growth is negative, that is, the repatriation of income by TNCs in the longer run reduces the rate of growth of the economies thus affected.

The case for 'decapitalisation' is by no means proven, however. Hood and Young (1979, Ch. 5), after reviewing the available empirical evidence, remained agnostic as to the impact of manufacturing sector DFI on the balance of payments of the host economy. Vernon (1971, Ch. 5) argued that the 'decapitalisation' thesis is based on highly simplistic assumptions and that, once it is recognised that the presence of a TNC subsidiary has an impact on every item in the balance of payments account, the overall effect of DFI on the balance of payments crucially depends on the assumptions we make concerning the import-subsituting effect of DFI and the latter's overall impact on the industrialisation process in the LDC (Vernon 1971, pp.170-6).

Overall, therefore, it is impossible to quantify with any degree of accuracy or reliability the direct and indirect effects of the operations of TNCs on the balance of payments of host LDCs. Even if there is a large positive effect, as in the case of mineral extraction and export, other aspects of the TNCs' operations may be undesirable - for example, the rate of exploitation of a non-renewable resource may be too high, tax payments to the LDC too low, insufficient employment may be created and so on (although it must be remembered that all these various aspects of the operation of TNCs are open to negotiation). Tie-in clauses increase the import sensitivity of the economy already exacerbated by the process of ISI (see Chapter 9), and export restrictions prevent the development of new overseas markets and the earning of additional foreign exchange (see below).

The LDC government may attempt to alleviate the burden imposed on the balance of payments by profit repatriation by encouraging TNCs to reinvest a greater proportion of their profits locally. But if the rate of return on foreign capital (after tax and depreciation) is greater than the rate of growth of national income and assuming that these profits are reinvested locally, then foreign capital ownership grows at a faster rate than national income. Assuming a constant capital-output ratio, foreign capital grows at a faster rate than domestic capital and an ever-increasing proportion of the domestic capital stock will be owned by foreigners. This process is not likely to be politically acceptable and must in any case end when all capital is foreign owned. The latter is, of course, a limiting case, and is highly unlikely to be realised in practice. Nevertheless, it illustrates the serious dynamic tendencies at work. Streeten summaries the dilemma faced by LDCs:

> ... either they permit or even encourage this growth of foreign capital, in which case they are faced with growing foreign ownership of their capital stock. Or else they limit this process of alienation, in which case a part of their export earnings will be mortgaged to remitting profits and repatriating capital. It is small wonder that this ineluctable dilemma has led to ambivalence and hostility towards foreign investment. (Streeten 1972, p.213)

It could be argued, however, that too much emphasis has been placed on this aspect of TNC direct foreign investment in the past, and that this has tended to obscure the wider impact of DFI on resource mobilisation and utilisation both within the economy as a whole and within the manufacturing sector in particular.

10.8   The Export of Manufactured Goods by TNCs

A relatively small number of LDCs account for a large proportion of total exports of manufactured goods from LDCs (see Chapter 9, Section 9.7). Not a great deal is known, however, about the role of TNCs in the export of manufactured goods from these LDCs. For the early 1970s, it has been estimated (Nayyar 1978) that TNCs accounted for about 15% of total LDC manufactured goods exports, and it was predicted that their share would rise.

Not surprisingly, there were significant intercountry variations. In Singapore, for example, it was estimated that TNCs accounted for nearly 70% of manufactured exports. This was the exception, however. Estimates for other LDCs were much lower: for example, Hong Kong, 10%; India, 5%; Brazil 43%; Pakistan, 5–10%; Mexico, 25–30%; Colombia, over 30%; Taiwan, 20%; Argentina, 30%; Korea, 15% (see Nayyar 1978, Table 1, p.62). In general it appeared that TNCs in Latin America played a more important role in manufacturing for export than did TNCs in Asia, although it may well be the case that Nayyar's results underestimate the relative importance of TNC exports. Lall (1981) quoted more recent estimates: South Korea – in 1974, TNC contribution to all exports was 28%; Singapore – in 1975, 85% of exports were accounted for by foreign majority-owned enterprises and another 7% by foreign minority-owned enterprises; Brazil – in 1973, for 318 leading enterprises, which accounted for nearly two-thirds of total industrial exports, TNCs accounted for over one-half of the total; Mexico (data from Jenkins 1979) – in 1974, foreign firms were responsible for 34% of exports of manufactured goods.

TNC manufactured goods exports may be divided into three categories (Nayyar 1978):

Capital-/technology-intensive goods Included in this category are chemicals, iron and steel, light engineering goods and machinery and transport equipment. In some cases the TNCs involved were initially import-substitutors and have gradually moved into the export market, for example, the German automobile firm, Volkswagen, in Brazil.

Simple labour-intensive products These include clothing, toys, sports goods, wigs and plastic products, and a number of other non-traditional, light manufactured goods. The production of these goods is usually in the hands of indigenous entrepreneurs in such countries as Hong Kong, Taiwan and South Korea who sell to transnational buying groups, initially Japanese (the *zaibatsu*), but increasingly from the USA and UK (Hone 1974). The technologies required in the production of these goods are standardised and accessible, but they are consumer goods designed for high-income markets where design, brand names and trademarks, and advertising are all important and where the buyer guarantees market access. Foreign participation is thus an important ingredient in the export success of these economies.

Labour-intensive component manufacture and assembly (also referred to as 'footloose industries', 'export platforms' or 'worldwide sourcing') The period since the late 1960s has seen the location and development in the LDCs of specialised, relatively labour-intensive activities or processes that are a part of vertically integrated manufacturing TNCs (Helleiner 1973). TNCs identify specific, relatively labour-intensive activities within their overall manufacturing operations and transfer them to LDCs where the reduced costs of labour more than offset the transport costs incurred. This relocation of production and assembly has occurred on a large scale in electronics (semi-conductors, tuners, valves), automobile components, clothing, leather goods and, as an example of a service activity, data processing. Countries such as Hong Kong, Singapore, Taiwan, Mexico and parts of the Caribbean have been important locations for such activities and increasingly countries such as Thailand, Malaysia, the Philippines and Morocco are becoming of significance. If wage rates rise in one country, the TNC can move to a lower-wage economy because of the footloose nature of the activity concerned.

The availability of large supplies of relatively cheap labour that can be easily trained to perform semi-skilled operations is an important factor in this process of relocation. Even though labour productivity may be lower in the LDCs than in the developed economies, productivity differentials do not offset the vast differentials in wages; in any case, empirical evidence increasingly suggests that in many industries in a number of countries, productivity in the LDC may be equal to, or even higher than, productivity in the developed economy (examples are cited in Sharpston 1975). However, in addition to cheap labour, such countries must offer the TNCs political stability and labour docility (strict control over trade unions, anti-strike legislation, etc.) (Nayyer 1978, p.77).

Government policy in both the developed and less developed economies is another factor that needs to be taken into account. The tariff provisions of the industrialised economies give preferential treatment to imports that incorporate domestically produced components; that is, the tariff is applied only to the value added in the assembly or manufacturing processes undertaken overseas. In the US tariff, items 807.00 and 806.30 provide for duty-free re-entry of components that do not alter their physical identity in the assembled article, and LDC exports to the USA under this provision have increased more rapidly than total manufactured exports. Other developed economies, for example the Netherlands and the Federal Republic of Germany, have similar provisions (Finger 1975), as has the Lomé Convention between the European Economic Community and the ACP (African, Pacific and Caribbean) LDCs.

Government policy in the LDCs involves the granting of a variety of concessions to the TNCs, including tax holidays, subsidised credit and rents, direct and indirect export subsidies, freedom from import duties and exchange controls, etc. Such incentives and concessions are often very generous and are both a result of, and contribute to, the relatively weak bargaining position of the LDCs vis-à-vis the TNCs. Export processing zones are of particular importance in an increasing number of LDCs. By 1980 there were 53 such zones employing almost 1 million persons (United Nations 1983, p.155). The most important industries in these zones are those manufacturing electrical and electronic goods, textiles and wearing apparel, and TNCs are of particular significance in these industries. Export processing zones are often physically isolated from the surrounding economy, and the enclave-like nature of such developments has a more limited effect on the industrial environment of LDCs than other forms of TNC participation in their economies.

Indeed, apart from the employment and income generated, it is difficult to see what other benefits are enjoyed by the LDC. The TNC has little, if any, capital invested and is thus footloose or mobile, unskilled labour is not given any real training, technological spin-off is likely to be minimal and dependence on the TNC for inputs, markets, decisions affecting output, etc., is complete. The process confirms the position of the LDCs as suppliers of cheap labour to the developed economies.

The final issue to be considered is the relative export performance of TNCs compared to their indigenously owned counterparts. The available empirical evidence suggests that TNCs do not, in general, export a greater proportion of their output than local firms. Lall and Streeten (1977, p.135) concluded that 'transnationality does not appear to have been an important aid to exporting' and may even in certain cases inhibit exporting. TNCs are important exporters from LDCs, their supply of inputs and technology and their market access do permit the establishment of export activities that would not otherwise be possible, but they do not, in general, significantly outperform local firms in all respects.[9]

10.9   The TNC and Transfer Pricing

Transfer prices (sometimes referred to as accounting prices) are the prices that are charged on transactions that take place within the TNC. The prices that are charged on these intra-corporate transfers can clearly deviate from market prices (so-called 'arms-length' prices) because trade within the TNC may be transacted outside the sphere of market forces. Indeed, in many cases a market price may not exist for the particular good or service (the TNC being the sole owner or producer of the good or service in question).

For a variety of reasons the LDC government may wish to control the external transfer of funds by TNC subsidiaries located within its borders. The TNC, on the other hand, may wish to evade or avoid such restrictions and the parent can ensure the transfer of funds out of a country by raising the price of the inputs that it sells to its subsidiary in that country and lowering the price of what it buys from its subsidiary. Such manipulation of transfer prices – that is, the deviation of transfer prices from arms-length prices – may have a number of objectives (Lall 1973):

(1) the achievement of global profit maximisation, net of taxation, given the existence of international differentials in tax rates, import duties and export subsidies;

(2) the minimisation of exchange risks, or indeed of any other risks (the threat of nationalisation may lead a TNC to minimise its investment in a particular country);

(3) the avoidance of restrictions on profit repatriation and/or other income transfers;

(4) the avoidance of political and social pressures that might result if 'high' profits were declared by a TNC in a particular host economy

– local workers might demand higher wages, governments might be tempted to increase taxes, local shareholders (if any) might demand higher dividends, etc.

The scope and effectiveness of transfer price manipulation by TNCs vary widely from industry to industry and from one firm to another. Three sets of factors account for this uneven incidence (Lall 1979a):

(1) inter-industry variations in the trade component of TNC production;
(2) variations in the extent of intra-firm trade as a proportion of total trade by TNCs;
(3) variations in the possibilities for manipulating transfer prices.

Point 1 is self-explanatory. With respect to point 2, Lall (1979a, p.62) argued that intra-firm trade was likely to be larger in those industries that are of a 'high' technology (including large R&D requirements, high level of skills, and firm-specific products, designs, etc.), have specific marketing requirements (for example, close coordination between production and selling) and where there is risk and uncertainty attached to open market transactions. Examples of such industries include office machines, plastics, computers, instruments and transport equipment. With respect to point 3, Lall (1979a, p.63) argued that the more advanced and firm-specific was the level of technology embodied in a product, and the more discontinuous its supply, the greater was the scope for transfer pricing. Pharmaceuticals provide a major example of transfer price manipulation.

The manipulation of transfer prices in a manner detrimental to the interests of host LDCs may be extremely difficult to identify and control. As noted above, a market price will not exist where the TNC is the sole owner or producer of a good or service, and the identification of the 'correct' transfer price will pose major problems (see Lall 1979a, pp.67–8). Product differentiation also complicates matters, (Hanson 1975), and it is safe to assume that TNCs will not willingly co-operate in supplying information to LDC governments investigating their affairs. LDCs will probably not have the personnel with the abilities to deal with these problems, although this will change over time, given the possibility of increased international cooperation in these matters.

As Vaitsos (1976, p.122) has argued, 'an indispensable aid to governments . . . is the training of personnel who can understand the internal functioning of transnational enterprises, administer the policies and be able to negotiate with foreign factor suppliers'.

Offsetting these problems to a certain extent is the fact, emphasised by Lall (1979a), that not all TNCs are able to practise massive transfer price manipulation. Presumably, those that possess this potential can be identified, and attention (and perhaps legislation) directed specifically at their activities. Other authors (for example, Reuber (1973), Ch. 5; Tugendhat (1973), Ch. 10) have tried to argue that profit transfers via transfer price manipulation are not as important as has sometimes been suggested in the literature: for example, tax and customs authorities do provide some check on abuse, and affiliate management and local host-country partners may resist transfer price manipulation that is unfavourable to them.

The available empirical evidence does not lend support to these assertions. The pioneering work of Vaitsos in Latin America (Vaitsos 1974, Ch. 4) found massive over-pricing on products imported by TNC subsidiaries in the pharmaceutical industry in Colombia, Chile and Peru and in the electronics industry in Colombia and Ecuador. In the Colombian pharmaceutical industry, the weighted average overpricing of products imported by TNC subsidiaries was 155% (for local firms, the figure was 19%). Put another way, of the effective returns of the pharmaceutical TNC subsidiaries, reported profits accounted for 3.4%, royalties accounted for 14.0% and overpricing accounted for 82.6%.

Vaitsos concluded (p.50):

> In all sectors and countries that were evaluated, significant returns to foreign factors of production appeared to accrue through the profit margins of products tied into the importation of capital and/or technology.
> Foreign subsidiaries in the cases investigated apparently use transfer pricing of products as a mechanism of income remission, thus significantly under-stating their true profitability.[10]

Clearly this is a problem for all host nations, both developed and less developed. Its magnitude should not be underestimated but, on the other hand, it is something that host economies, both individually and in cooperation with one another, can attempt to do something about, and in the longer run it may well be a problem of declining importance.

10.10   TNCs and the Transfer of Tastes

The UN report on TNCs (United Nations 1978, p.40) noted that TNCs 'seek out and flourish most in foreign markets that most closely resemble the home market for which they first developed their products and processes'. Logically, it could be expected that TNCs will attempt to create, if they do not already exist, similar conditions in the more important LDC markets (Nixson and Yamin 1980). TNCs thus play a key role in the creation and moulding of consumer tastes in LDCs, and some authors have even gone so far as to refer to the creation of a 'global shopping centre' and the diffusion of an 'ideology of consumption' throughout the world (Barnett and Müller 1974, Chs. 2 and 6).

Product differentiation and innovation, heavy advertising (for a discussion of advertising in LDCs, see James and Lister 1980) and the creation of new markets are all aspects of TNC global operations and are all becoming increasingly important in LDCs. TNCs, however, are not the only sources of influence on consumption patterns in LDCs. Indigenous firms and LDC governments themselves may well introduce and encourage 'inappropriate' products and consumption patterns; Biersteker (1978, Ch. 7) points to the Nigerian government's decision to establish a colour television network as an example of the latter. Such actions by indigenous firms, however, may best be seen as a response to TNC competition, rather than as the exercise of initiative on their part (see Ch. 11, Section 11.3). Langdon (1975) argued that Kenyan firms in the soap and detergents industry had to become more like TNCs in order to survive, and this involved not only increased mechanisation but also increased product differentiation and advertising in order to promote more 'sophisticated' products.

10.11   The Profitability of TNCs in LDCs

The allegation is often made in the literature on the impact of TNCs on the process of growth and development that TNC operations in LDCs are very (perhaps excessively) profitable, and that the repatriation of these profits by TNCs drains the LDCs of a large part of their potentially reinvestible surplus.

If it were found to be the case that TNC subsidiaries in LDCs were highly profitable, either or both of the following explanations could be valid:

(1) high TNC subsidiary profitability might be the result of competent management, superior technology and the availability of inputs, both local and foreign, at low market prices; or

(2) high profitability could reflect the existence of high monopoly rents resulting from, for example, protection against foreign competition, practices that reduced domestic competition, and legal and other forms of protection against all competition (for example, patent laws) (Vaitsos 1974, Ch. 5).

In addition, the declared profits of TNCs in LDCs must be treated with great caution. The power of TNCs to manipulate transfer prices and the variety of channels that they have available to them through which they can remit funds from one country to another were noted above. There are reasons for believing that TNCs underdeclare their effective profitability in a number of LDCs, even when the tax rates are lower than in the country to which profits are remitted. Vaitsos (1974, p.68) concluded that:

In the countries in which we undertook research [Colombia, Chile, Ecuador and Peru] all foreign subsidiaries in the samples studied under-declared, sometimes considerably, the effective profitability accruing to their parent firms from their operations in such countries. Reported profits by foreign subsidiaries in Latin America are quite often much lower than those appearing in the rest of the world for affiliates of the same parents or lower than average profitability of local firms in comparable industrial activities in the host countries.

Furthermore, note must be taken of the possibility that the goal of the TNC subsidiary is not necessarily one of profit maximisation. Apparently 'unprofitable' subsidiaries may, in fact, be highly profitable for the TNC as a whole, and, to complicate matters even further, subsidiary objectives may well change over time. Data for a single year, or a limited number of years, may thus not capture the full complexity of the possibly changing relationships between the parent and any or all of its subsidiaries.

The study of Lall and Streeten (1977) examined the profitability of 53 manufacturing firms in India and 56 in Colombia, both foreign and locally owned. It was found that profitability was not greatly influenced by the origin of control or transnationality of the investment (Lall and Streeten 1977, p.122). Variations in profitability between different firms would result from a variety of factors – monopoly power, protection, managerial efficiency, financing patterns, age of enterprise – which in some cases would be associated with transnationality (monopoly power and efficiency, for example), but transnationality on its own would not be sufficient to exclude the influence of these other factors.

Reuber (1973, Ch. 4) studied 80 direct investment projects of North American, European and Japanese origin. He found planned rates of return partly depended on the type of investment that the TNC was considering. Export-oriented investment in LDCs had a planned minimum rate of return of 20% per annum with a short planning horizon (on average seven years). Market-development DFI, on the other hand, had planned rates of return of 14% per annum and a longer planning horizon (eleven–twelve years on average).

Given that these figures are likely to represent *minimum* acceptable rates of return, it is clear that TNCs expect to recover the capital that they invest in LDCs relatively quickly. Lall (1978) was rather more agnostic in his conclusions concerning TNC profitability in LDCs. He accepted that TNCs were 'fairly profitable' in LDCs and on average performed better than local firms, but he argued that this superior profit performance might reflect not greater efficiency but rather the fact that TNCs were concentrated in more profitable industries, resulting from high barriers to entry, greater risks, etc. (Lall 1978, p.233). However, TNC entry itself may well change market structures and thus the profitability of different industries.

Other things being equal, the expectation is that TNC activities in LDCs are more profitable than those of local enterprises and that TNC behaviour is dominated by the anticipation of profit. Reuber (1973, Ch. 4) argued that 'profitability is a fundamental determinant of investment' (p.109) and that 'there is little doubt that prospective profit over the life of investments has a basic influence on the level of investment' (p.133).

10.12   TNCs from LDCs

A phenomenon that dates largely, although not exclusively, from the late 1960s is the emergence of TNCs based in a selected number of LDCs. Enterprises from Hong Kong, Singapore, South Korea, India, Brazil, Mexico and Argentina are not large compared to TNCs from the developed industrialised economies, but they are nevertheless becoming increasingly significant in the manufacturing (and to a lesser extent, service) sectors of a number of LDCs. Indian firms are to be found in Sri Lanka, Iran, Kenya and Nigeria in engineering products, textiles and garments, food processing, and chemicals and petrochemicals. Indian non-manufacturing sector investment – hotels, construction, consultancies – is also growing elsewhere. Hong Kong enterprises have important investments in Indonesia, Malaysia and Singapore and are apparently about to enter the EEC (Lall 1982, p.133). Argentinian enterprises began production in Uruguay, Brazil, and Chile in the late 1920s (Diaz-Alejandro 1977). Thailand, as a 'host' nation to TNCs from LDCs, has enterprises from Hong Kong, India, Taiwan, Singapore and Malaysia located within its borders (Wells 1977; Lecraw 1977).

What 'firm-specific' advantages do such enterprises possess that enable them to go 'transnational'? Lall (1982) has suggested that TNCs from LDCs have tended to specialise in labour-intensive, standardised technologies, usually adapted and scaled down to local conditions. In Thailand, for example, Lecraw (1977) found that LDC TNCs were significantly less capital intensive than either other foreign or local firms. In addition, it appears that TNCs from LDCs are able to reduce the costs of management and engineering personnel (Wells 1977, p.141). TNCs from LDCs do not, in general, possess advantages with respect to the ability to differentiate products, but they may well possess other marketing skills – for example, the ability of firms from Hong Kong and Singapore to keep abreast of fashion, to package their products attractively, to maintain quality and to sell to high-income sophisticated markets (Lall 1982, p.130).

Lall (1982) looked in detail at the emergence of TNCs from India. He noted that the two largest industrial groups in the country – Birla and Tata – accounted for nearly 50% of total Indian foreign equity, and that all the major foreign investors were large, diversified and long-established business houses, with substantial industrial experience, and, in addition, were important exporters of manufactured goods. Their managerial, technical and financial resources were considerable and, although they were not major innovators, they nevertheless had foreign investments that were large and technologically advanced, often using capital-intensive technologies and producing sophisticated products, backed by extensive advertising and after-sales service (Lall 1982, p.139).

A feature of Indian DFI is that is uses intensively Indian plant, equipment and components, reflecting India's comparative advantage in the manufacture of a range of capital and intermediate goods and the Indian firms' experience in setting up projects and operating the technologies (Lall 1982, p.140). This, in turn, is related to India's policy with regard to technological development. India has attempted to achieve a degree of technological self-reliance not found in many other LDCs and, as Lall (1982, p.143) noted:

> While this has resulted in various inefficiencies and technological lags, it has also enabled its national enterprises to build up a very broad base of technological competence. They have acquired the 'know-why' (i.e. basic design capabilities) of many industries rather than simply the 'know-how' (production technology).... The success of many Indian enterprises ... leads us to believe that there is a strong case to be made for the protection of 'infant technological learning' rather than only the classic protection of 'infant industry' (where production know-how is mastered).[11]

The emergence of TNCs from LDCs raises a larger number of important questions that cannot at present be satisfactorily answered. Do the 'home' countries benefit from the development of their 'own' transnationals? Do 'host' countries obtain greater economic benefits from LDC TNCs than from developed economy TNCs (as Lecraw (1977) seems to suggest)? What are the implications of these developments for the alleged technological dependency of the LDCs? What are the political implications of such developments?

10.13   TNCs and the Concept of 'Dependent Development'

Theories of dependency and the concept of dependent industrial development have already been discussed in Chapter 3, Section C and Chapter 9, Section 9.9 respectively. In this section we consider briefly two further aspects of dependency – the allegation that the activities of TNCs prevent the emergence (or destroy the existence) of an entrepreneurial class dedicated to national development (the so-called national bourgeoisie) and, secondly, that TNCs prevent or retard the emergence of a domestic capital goods industry.

In those economies (mainly, but not exclusively, in Latin America) where TNCs have achieved a dominant position in the large and medium-scale industrial sector (as well as in banking, tourism, etc.), it is argued that a significant part of the domestic entrepreneurial class is transformed into what Sunkel (1973a, p.22) refers to as 'private transnational technocracies and bureaucracies' − that is, a class whose interests are tied to, and dependent on, the TNC. It is not the lack of an entrepreneurial class that retards development, but rather it is the penetration of the domestic economy by foreign interests that prevents the emergence of a social group which places priority on national ownership and control to achieve national developmental objectives.

Sunkel sees this penetration as being present at all levels and affecting all social classes and groups (of equal importance to the penetration of the productive structure are the economic and social consequences of technological transfer and the impact on cultural and ideological attitudes and values). This process incorporates into the new institutions and structures those individuals and groups most suited to fit into them, but expels others that have no place nor the ability to adapt. This is called the process of marginalisation (conditioned largely by the lack of, or difficulty of access to, a reasonable and stable income) and it affects all social classes within the LDC.

At a broader level, Sunkel in another article (1973b) has referred to the process as 'transnational integration' and 'national disintegration'. Certain groups and classes are incorporated into the new international industrial system being built largely by TNCs (referred to by Sunkel as TRANCOS − transnational conglomerates) whilst, as within the domestic economy, others are excluded. The classification of the domestic economy into integrated and segregated groups overlaps with the more traditional classification along class lines, and again we find integrated and non-integrated groups (referring in this case to integration into the new international industrial system) in all classes − entrepreneurs, the middle class and the working class.

With respect to the transfer of technology, Sunkel (and others) argue that the 'spread' effects of technology transfer (the diffusion and assimilation of technology within the host economy) will be more than offset by 'backwash' effects (forces which lead to greater concentration at the centre), thus widening the technological gap between developed and less developed countries and deepening the latters' technological dependency.

Others (e.g. Warren 1973, 1980) argue that there is a 'spin-off' effect from TNC involvement in the local economy. TNCs train local personnel who may well establish their own enterprises (often as suppliers of inputs to TNCs) on the basis of the knowledge and experience gained by employment in the TNCs. TNC technologies may become anchored and diffused throughout the LDC economy, encouraging adaptation and further development by local entrepreneurs. The public sector, too, both on its own and in conjunction with TNCs, may become a powerful entrepreneurial force. We return to these issues in Chapter 11.

A crucial element in this debate is the willingness or ability of TNCs to establish capital goods industries in LDCs. A number of reasons have been put forward to support the view that the industrialisation process in the majority of LDCs has built in a bias against the establishment of domestic capital goods industries:

(1) The limited domestic market for capital goods (arising from the fragmentation of domestic production and overdiversification, in turn leading to an absence of standardisation of equipment and materials) provides little incentive for domestic manufacture (Merhav 1969, p.133).

(2) Producers of final goods will strongly resist import substitution for their inputs in general and capital goods in particular because they know from their own experience that this may raise costs, lower quality and reduce reliability.

(3) The risks attached to the heavy investment required for the establishment of capital goods industries may be too great given the uncertainties (both economic and political) endemic in LDCs.

(4) The oligopolistic structure of the advanced capitalist economies means that a manufacturer, when deciding to invest in a new area, must take into consideration, *inter alia*, the effect of his decision on (a) his own export interests, (b) competitors' export interests, and (c) customers' export interests, if any (assuming that the new plant will not compete in the national market from which the investment originated) (Arrighi 1970, p.227). Arrighi concludes that '. . . the oligopolistic structure of the industrial centers strengthens the other factors . . . in producing . . . a sectoral pattern of foreign investment biased against the capital-goods industry'.

(5) Capital-intensive techniques and the bias against the capital goods sector reinforce one another. Capital-intensive techniques favour the use of specialised machinery and this restrains the growth of demand for capital goods that could be produced in LDCs; the lack of investment in the capital goods sector in turn prevents the development of capital goods embodying modern labour-intensive technology.

We noted in Chapter 9 that the larger, more 'developed' LDCs (Brazil, India, South Korea, Mexico) have established capital goods industries and Warren (1973) made much of the technology that has already been transferred to LDCs and the capital goods industries already established. Undoubtedly, to an increasing extent in the future, under the pressure of events and as a result of the search for profitable investment opportunities, TNCs will invest in capital goods industries, especially as the technologies required become standardised and more widely available. But unless there are very radical changes in both the geographical pattern of R&D expenditures and the objectives towards the realisation of which the expenditures are made, the most up-to-date technologies are still likely to be developed and initially utilised in the developed economies. There are no obvious reasons why TNCs should willingly surrender the monopoly they enjoy over both products and processes, although the extent to which they will be forced to compromise on this issue depends in part at least on the future course of their relationship with LDC governments. We return to these issues in Section 10.14 below and in Chapter 11, Section 11.5.

10.14 Conclusions

In this concluding section we will attempt to highlight some of the broader implications which arise from the foregoing discussion of the TNC and industrial development in LDCs.

The TNC subsidiary is a part of a wider global network, and it will always be responsive, in some degree, to the demands of the parent company's global strategy. On the other hand, the government of the host LDC within which the subsidiary is located will be pursuing its own objectives with respect to economic development in general, and industrialisation in particular, within its own country. It is highly likely, therefore, that there will be conflict between these competing sets of objectives.

The main areas of actual or potential conflict include:

(1) *The Balance of Payments* The LDC government may wish to maximise the earning, and minimise the expenditure, of foreign exchange, whereas the TNC may be reluctant to export, may establish highly import-intensive operations within the LDC, and may wish to repatriate as high a proportion of its earnings as possible (and use the manipulation of transfer prices to secure that objective).

(2) *Employment Creation* The LDC government may wish to encourage job creation, whereas the TNC may use more capital-intensive technologies than domestic firms (or at least raise the overall level of capital intensity within the manufacturing sector). TNC production may well destroy jobs in the informal or handicraft sectors of the economy, and the limited linkages established with other firms in the economy will reduce the creation of indirect employment opportunities.

(3) *Technology Transfer* The LDC government may wish to encourage the effective transfer and anchorage of useful and/or

'appropriate' technology by TNCs and stimulate the development of an indigenous technological capacity; the interests of the TNC, however, may work in the opposite direction.

These examples do not exhaust all the areas of potential or actual conflict but they demonstrate the extent of the problem and illustrate the need for the creation of a framework, at both the national and international level, within which the interests of both TNCs and LDCs can best be accommodated.

Very broadly, the impact of the TNC on the industrialisation and development of the LDC depends on three sets of factors:

(1) the global environment, both economic and political within which TNCs operate;
(2) the national environment, including systems of regulation and control and the political economy of TNC relationships with domestic capital and the state;
(3) the sectoral distribution of TNC investment.

The 'global environment' refers to the economic and institutional structures within which flows of goods and services, capital and labour take place. The developed capitalist economies have, in the postwar period, created and maintained a framework within which investment can flow freely between countries (United Nations 1983, p.94), although the more recent emergence of protectionist sentiments is also responsible for the international relocation of some production (Japanese DFI in the USA and Western Europe, for example). The TNC will undoubtedly enjoy a high degree of freedom and autonomy within the open, liberal international environment typical of the postwar period.

At the same time, however, there are under discussion and negotiation a number of both general and issue-specific instruments or codes of conduct, the basic objectives of which are to influence or control the behaviour (conduct) of TNCs. The proposed UN Code of Conduct in particular aims at ensuring 'good behaviour' on the part of TNCs so that their activities become more consistent with, and accelerate the achievement of, national development objectives.

The 'global environment' is also of importance in so far as in an expanding international economy, host countries (both developed and less developed) are more likely to attempt to improve their bargaining position vis-à-vis TNCs via regulation or control, whereas the opposite is likely to be the case in times of recession.

The importance of the latter point is reflected in the changes that have occurred in national policies with respect to DFI in recent years. The UN (1983, Chapter III) notes that a number of LDCs which established control-oriented regulatory mechanisms in the early 1970s have tended to relax their structures of control and implement their policies in a more liberal and flexible manner. Nevertheless, LDCs are becoming increasingly insistent on channelling DFI and foreign technology into priority areas and stipulating appropriate performance requirements (with respect to export obligations, the utilisation and processing of domestic raw materials, the local sourcing of supplies, the training of national person- nel, the localisation of manufacturing, the full transfer of technical know- how and the setting up of local R&D facilities). There is also an increasing awareness that the benefits occurring to the national economy from DFI, and the improvement of national bargaining strength, depend on the building up of national industrial entrepreneurial and technological capabilities. (For a fuller discussion of these issues, see Kirkpatrick *et al.* 1984, Ch. 6, Sections 6.5 and 6.7; Chapter 11, Section 11.5 below.)

We have suggested (Nixson 1983) that codes of conduct could, if properly and effectively implemented at the national level, substantially improve the bargaining position of LDCs *vis-à-vis* TNCs. The effectiveness of national action will depend, in part, on the size and strength of the in- dividual LDC, the importance of that LDC to foreign capital and the general development strategies pursued. Paradoxically, it is those LDCs with the greatest concentration of foreign capital that have the greatest potential for regulating the TNC and improving their bargining position. Whether or not this potential will be realised is discussed below.

Finally, the sectoral distribution of TNC investment is of importance. The attractiveness of the LDC to foreign capital, the characteristics of the DFI package (for example, the technology utilised, the potential for linkage creation, the employment implications, etc.), the bargaining strength of the LDC and the economic benefits that the LDC might expect to gain from the TNC, are all to a certain extent dependent upon the sector within which the DFI is located. Other things being equal, DFI in ISI (and ISI industries which eventually turn to exporting) is likely to offer important possibilities for the effective regulation of the TNC and the maximisation of its developmental impact. Export-oriented DFI, on the other hand, is likely to be highly mobile as between different LDCs, involve a limited transfer of technology and create few linkages with the local economy, although in both cases the type of technology involved and the capacity of the host economy to absorb that technology are of importance.

We are arguing, therefore, that TNCs operate within an environment determined by a combination of international and national factors. At the national level the control or regulation of TNCs is not simply a matter of technical expertise or experience (although these are clearly important fac- tors), but depends critically on the nature of the state and the complex of class forces and political relationships within the LDC, and the relation- ships that exist between TNCs and the state and various other groups or classes within the LDC.

A framework for the discussion of these issues is provided by Streeten (1971, p.242):

(1) Even if the will and the political power exist, do LDC governments have the ability to control TNCs to the extent that they consider desirable?

(2) Even if they have the political power, do they have the will?

(3) Even if they have the will and ability, do they have the political power?

It may certainly be the case that even though LDC governments cannot actually 'control' TNCs, they are increasingly able to obtain a larger share of the proceeds arising from TNC operations. The increase in the technical information about behaviour of TNCs, the pooling of information between LDCs, the standardisation and greater effectiveness of laws governing the operation of TNCs, the rationalisation of investment incentive schemes, the diversification by LDCs of their trading partners, sources of technology and of capital, the greater the number of TNCs competing to enter important LDCs and the opportunities for playing off one developed economy against another as competition for materials and markets intensifies, are all factors which indicate some shift in the balance of power in favour of LDCs.

The way Streeten frames his questions, however, implies a conflict between the TNC and the LDC nation state. Streeten recognises that the nation state is not monolithic and that different interests will align themselves in various ways with the TNC, and in this sense it is misleading to speak of the 'national interest' vis-à-vis TNCs. But Streeten does not pursue this issue. To do so involves a closer examination of the relationship between the TNC and the LDC government and the recognition that there need be no real conflict as such between the two.

What is perhaps not widely appreciated in the literature on the TNC and economic development is that the pattern or type of economic development that emerges as a result of the presence of TNCs is in large part a consequence of the various and complex relationships between foreign interests on the one hand and domestic groups or classes and the host-country government on the other hand (Kirkpatrick and Nixson 1981). For example, TNCs may well benefit from an unequal distribution of income in an LDC, but they are not, in general, the *cause* of that unequal distribution: TNCs may concentrate in the major urban centres and exacerbate regional and rural–urban inequalities, but again they are not, in general, the cause of those inequalities. The causes of such inequalities must be looked for in the totality of relationships in the LDC which determine the nature and characteristics of the development process.

Clearly, as noted above, the interests of the TNC and particular host-country governments often conflict, but it is not a simple and straightforward conflict between the TNC on the one hand and the host government as defender of the 'national interest' on the other hand. The TNC interacts with local capital and the various institutions of the state in a variety of ways, each group or class depending on the others to maintain and strengthen its own position.

From the point of view of longer-run development, therefore, the crucial issue is not the presence or absence of foreign capital or the existing weakness or subservience of domestic to foreign capital, but rather it is the strength of the state and the policies that it may be pursuing to overcome the weakness and eliminate subservience that is important. Over time, a combination of controls on foreign capital, active participation by the state in productive enterprises and the positive promotion of indigenous enterprise may well prove sufficient to create an environment within which indigenous enterprises can flourish and compete on an equal footing with TNCs in at least key sectors of the LDC economy. The impact of such policies on the wider economic and social development of the LDC cannot be predicted *a priori*, but what is clear is that the presence or absence of foreign capital does not *in itself* determine the outcome of the development process. There are various possible outcomes to the 'bargaining process' between TNCs and the state and indigenous capital in LDCs, and various forms of 'development' – 'dependent', 'national capitalist', 'socialist' – are possible.

What, then, is the contribution that TNCs can, in principle, make to the development effort? It is currently fashionable to argue that the main contributions that the TNC can make are the access that it provides to technology, foreign markets and managerial and technical skills. Given the low organisational and technical level of many LDCs, these may indeed be indispensible elements of their development process and may only be obtainable through some form of arrangement with the TNC. In many cases, only TNCs have the financial resources and technical expertise to develop new and better products which may be essential for agricultural development (for example, pesticides), exploit mineral resources and undertake large-scale construction projects. No one would deny the importance of the TNCs' *potential* contribution to the development effort.

But it is the structure of the arrangement with the TNC that is important, the way in which the vital factors are acquired, the use to which they are put, *and the price that is paid for them*. The LDC must first put its own house in order (that is, define its development objectives and establish the structures and institutions for achieving those objectives) before it can hope to approach the TNC and strike a just bargain. This is partly a matter of training and education but it is essentially a matter of political change within the LDC itself. Without this political change, new institutional forms (joint ventures) or more effective bargaining procedures will not fundamentally affect the economic position of the majority of the population of LDCs nor eradicate the conditions of poverty and inequality.

Notes

1. The term 'transnational corporation' is used to indicate that such enterprises are usually owned and controlled by the citizens of the enterprise's home country. Multinational corporations (or enterprises) on this definition will be owned, or controlled, by the citizens, or governments, of several countries. In 1974 the Group of Eminent Persons (United Nations 1974b) suggested that the definition of the TNC should be extended to include state-owned entities and cooperatives, on the grounds that such enterprises might well be profit seekers. There is as yet, however, no general agreement on this point. The 'home country' of the TNC is its country of origin; the 'host country' is the country where the direct foreign investment (DFI) is located or where the TNC otherwise conducts its operations. DFI involves the ownership of physical assets (mines, factories, plantations, sales offices, etc.) and is distinguished from portfolio investment, which involves the purchase of securities. TNCs also engage in 'non-equity operations' – the licensing of technology, management and technical agreements, the use of trademarks and brand names, etc. – which raises issues relating to the distinction between ownership and control.

2. The following sections draw heavily on Kirkpatrick *et al.* 1984, Chapter 4, Sections 4.2–4.7 and 4.9–4.15.

3. Jack Behrman, a former US Assistant Secretary of Commerce, quoted in Barnett and Müller (1974, p.40). Parry (1973) argues that there is a stereotype form of international operations towards which firms with international operations are moving (and which many, of course, have already achieved). The stereotype is defined as 'that corporate structure *where operations are in two or more countries on such a scale that growth and success depend on more than one nation, and where major decisions are made on the basis of global alternatives*' (p.1202, emphasis in original).

4. Baran and Sweezy (1968, Ch. 2) argue that the primary objectives of corporate policy are strength, rate of growth and size. These are all reducible to profitability, and the search for 'maximum' profits is the search for the greatest increase in profits which is possible in any given situation. Even if profits are not the ultimate goal, they are the means by which ultimate goals can be achieved.

5. A large part of commercialised technology is in the hands of the TNCs, but as the United Nations (1974a) report points out, basic knowledge more often originates in government-financed research and training centres, with the research expenditure of the TNC concentrated on practical development (often aimed at product differentiation) rather than basic research. The contribution of the TNC derives from its ability to combine different types of

lasting knowledge into commercially viable processes and products. Indeed, many would argue that *the* essential characteristic of the TNC is the creation, commercialisation and oligopolisation of relevant applied knowledge, and not the ownership of fixed assets or financial resources. For the argument that the opportunity cost of technology transfer is not zero, see Chapter 11, Section 11.3.

6. Japanese DFI does not fit neatly into this analytical model. It is directed mainly at the exploitation of natural resources or in manufacturing labour-intensive products in labour-abundant LDCs, exported either back to Japan or to third-country markets (see Ozawa 1979).

7. For a detailed discussion of market structures and concentration in LDCs, see Kirkpatrick *et al.* (1984), Chapter 3.

8. Barnett and Müller (1974, pp.153–4) quote figures which show that between 1960 and 1968, US TNCs took, on average, 79% of their net profits out of Latin America. Between 1965 and 1968, 52% of total profits of US TNCs in the manufacturing sector in Latin America were repatriated to the USA. In spite of this outflow, unrepatriated profits still accounted for a large share of net investment in certain sectors of Latin American industry.

9. When TNCs transfer technology to a locally owned firm, the contract often forbids the sale of goods produced using that technology outside the host country (or the countries to which sales may be made are specified). The work of Vaitsos (1974, Ch. 4, and 1975) and others in the Andean Pact group of countries indicated that such restrictions were widespread. For four of the countries (Bolivia, Colombia, Ecuador and Peru), 81% of the contracts analysed prohibited exports totally, and 86% had some restrictive clause on exports. In Chile, more than 72% of the contracts totally prohibited exports. It is of interest to note that these restrictions were more severe with respect to locally owned firms than with foreign wholly owned subsidiaries (Vaitsos 1974, p.57). These restrictive business practices (to use UN terminology) remain widespread, having been noted in, among other countries, India (see Patnaik 1972), Iran, Mexico, the Philippines, Kuwait and El Salvador.

10. Vaitsos's work has not escaped criticism. Vernon (1977, pp.154–5) argued that the results for Colombia were not typical and that the techniques of extrapolation used by Vaitsos were 'uninhibited'.

11. For Lall's later views on these issues, see Chapter 11, Section 11.5.

References

Arrighi, G. (1970) 'International corporations, labour aristocracies, and economic development in tropical Africa', in R. Rhodes (ed.), *Imperialism and Underdevelopment: A Reader*, Monthly Review Press, New York.

Baer, W. (1976) 'Technology, employment and development: empirical findings', *World Development*, Vol. 4, No. 2.

Baer, W. and Samuelson, L. (1981) 'Toward a service-oriented growth strategy', *World Development*, Vol. 9, No. 6, June.

Baran, P. (1957) *The Political Economy of Growth*, Monthly Review Press, New York.

Baran, P. and Sweezy, P. (1968) *Monopoly Capital*, Penguin Books.

Barnett, R.J. and Müller, R.E. (1974) *Global Reach: The Power of the Multinational Corporations*, Simon and Schuster.

Bierstaker, T.J. (1978) *Distortion or Development? Contending Perspectives on the Multinational Corporation*, MIT Press.

Bornschier, V. (1980) 'Multinational corporations and economic growth: a cross-national test of the decapitalisation thesis', *Journal of Development Economics*, Vol. 7.

Cardoso, F.H. (1972) 'Dependent capitalist development in Latin America', *New Left Review*, No. 74, July–August.

Caves, R.E. (1971) 'International corporations: the industrial economics of foreign investment', *Economica*, Vol. 38. Reprinted in Dunning (ed.) 1972.

Clark, N. (1975), 'The multinational corporation: the transfer of technology and dependence', *Development and Change*, Vol. 6, No. 1, January.

Devine, P.J., Lee, N., Jones, R.M. and Tyson, W.J. (1979) *An Introduction to Industrial Economics*, 3rd edn., George Allen and Unwin.

Diaz-Alejandro, C.F. (1977) 'Foreign direct investment by Latin America', in T. Agmon and C.P. Kindleberger (eds), *Multinationals from Small Countries*, MIT Press.

Dunning, J.H. (ed.) (1971) *The Multinational Enterprise*, George Allen and Unwin.

Dunning, J.H. (ed.) (1972) *International Investment*, Penguin Books.

Dunning, J.H. (ed.) (1974) *Economic Analysis and the Multinational Enterprise*, George Allen and Unwin.

Dunning, J.H. (1981) *International Production and the Multinational Enterprise*, George Allen and Unwin.

Evans, P.B. (1977) 'Direct investment and industrial concentration', *Journal of Development Studies*, Vol. 13, No. 4, July.

Feder, E. (1977) 'Capitalism's last-ditch effort to save underdeveloped agricultures: international agribusiness, the World Bank and the rural poor', *Journal of Contemporary Asia*, Vol. 7, No. 1.

Finger, J.M. (1975) 'Tariff provisions for off share assembly and the exports of developing countries', *Economic Journal*, Vol. 85, No. 338, June.

Hanson, J.S. (1975) 'Transfer pricing in the multinational corporations: a critical appraisal', *World Development*, Vol. 3, Nos. 11–12.

Helleiner, G.K. (1973), 'Manufactured exports from less developed countries and multinational firms', *Economic Journal*, Vol. 83, No. 329, March.

Helleiner, G.K. (ed.) (1976) *A World Divided: The Less Developed Countries in the International Economy*, Cambridge University Press.

Helleiner, G.K. (1975) 'Transnational enterprises in the manufacturing sector of the less developed countries', *World Development*, Vol. 3, No. 9, September.

Hone, A. (1974) 'Multinational corporations and multinational buying groups: their impact on the growth of Asia's exports of manufactures – myths and realities', *World Development*, Vol. 2, No. 2, February.

Hood, N. and Young, S. (1979) *The Economics of Multinational Enterprise*, Longman.

Hymer, S. 61972) 'The multinational corporation and the law of uneven development', in J. Bhagwati (ed.) (1972), *Economics and World Order*, Free Press. Reprinted in Radice (1975).

James, J. and Lister, S. (1980) 'Galbraith revisited: advertising in non-affluent societies', *World Development*, Vol. 8, No. 1, January.

Jenkins, R. (1979) 'The export performance of multinational corporations in Mexican industry', *Journal of Development Studies*, Vol. 15, No. 3, April.

Kirkpatrick, C.H., Lee, N., and Nixson, F.I. (1984) *Industrial Structure and Policy in Less Developed Countries*, George Allen and Unwin.

Kirkpatrick, C.H. and Nixson, F.I. (1981) 'Transnational corporations and economic development', *Journal of Modern African Studies*, Vol. 19, No. 3.

Lall, S. (1973) 'Transfer-pricing by multinational manufacturing firms', *Oxford Bulletin of Economics and Statistics*, Vol. 35, No. 3, August.

Lall, S. (1978) 'Transnationals, domestic enterprises and industrial structure in host LDCs: a survey', *Oxford Economic Papers*, Vol. 30, No. 2, July.

Lall, S. (1979a) 'Transfer pricing and developing countries: some problems of investigation', *World Development*, Vol. 7, No. 1, January.

Lall, S. (1979b) 'Multinationals and market structure in an open developing economy: the case of Malaysia', *Weltwirtschaftliches Archiv*, Vol. 115, June. Reprinted in S. Lall, *The Multinational Corporation: Nine Essays*, Macmillan.

Lall, S. (1980a) *The Multinational Corporation: Nine Essays*, Macmillan.

Lall, S. (1980b) 'Vertical inter-firm linkages in LDCs: an empirical study', *Oxford Bulletin of Economics and Statistics*, Vol. 42, No. 3, August.

Lall, S. (1981) 'Recent trends in exports of manufactures by newly-industrialising countries', in S. Lall, *Developing Countries in the International Economy: Selected Papers*, Macmillan.

Lall, S. (1982) 'The emergence of Third World multinationals: Indian joint ventures overseas', *World Development*, Vol. 10, No. 2, February.

Lall, S. and Streeten, P. (1977) *Foreign Investment, Transnationals and Developing Countries*, Macmillan.

Langdon, S. (1975) 'Multinational corporations, taste transfer and under-development: a case study from Kenya', *Review of African Political Economy*, No. 2, January–April.

Lecraw, D. (1977) 'Direct investment by firms from less developed countries', *Oxford Economic Papers*, Vol. 29, No. 3, November.

Merhav, M. (1969) *Technological Dependence, Monopoly and Growth*, Pergamon.

Nayyar, D. (1978) 'Transnational corporations and manufactured exports from poor countries', *Economic Journal*, Vol. 88, No. 349, March.

Newfarmer, R.S. (1979a) 'TNC takeovers in Brazil: the uneven distribution of benefits in the market for firms', *World Development*, Vol. 7, No. 1, January.

Newfarmer, R.S. (1979b) 'Oligopolistic tactics to control markets and the growth of TNCs in Brazil's electrical industry', *Journal of Development Studies*, Vol. 15, No. 3, April.

Newfarmer, R.S. and Mueller, W.F. (1975) *Multinational Corporations in Brazil and Mexico: Structural Sources of Economic and Non-Economic Power*, US Senate Sub-Committee on Multinational Corporations.

Nixson, F.I. (1983) 'Controlling the transnationals? Political economy and the UN code of conduct', *International Journal of the Sociology of Law*, Vol. 11, No. 1, February.

Nixson, F.I. and Yamin, M. (1980) 'The United Nations on transnational corporations: a summary and critique', *British Journal of International Studies*, Vol. 6, April.

OECD (1982) *Development Co-operation, 1982 Review*, Paris.

OECD (1983) *Investing in Developing Countries*, 5th edn, Paris.

Ozawa, T. (1979) 'International investment and industrial structure: new theoretical implications from the Japanese experience', *Oxford Economic Papers*, Vol. 31, No. 1, March.

Parry, T.G. (1973) 'The international firm and national economic policy', *Economic Journal*, Vol. 83, No. 332, December.

Patnaik, P. (1972) 'Imperialism and the growth of Indian capitalism', in R.Owen and R.B. Sutcliffe (eds) (1972), *Studies in the Theory of Imperialism*, Longman.

Radice, H. (ed.) (1975) *International Firms and Modern Imperialism*, Penguin Books.

Reuber, G.L. (1973) *Private Foreign Investment in Development*, Clarendon Press.

Sharpston, M. (1975) 'International sub-contracting', *Oxford Economic Papers*, Vol. 27, No. 1, March.

Streeten, P. (1971) 'Costs and benefits of multinational enterprises in less developed countries', in Dunning (1971).

Streeten, P. (1972) 'New approaches to direct private overseas investment in less developed countries', in P. Streeten, *The Frontiers of Development Studies*, Macmillan.

Sunkel, O. (1973a) 'The pattern of Latin American dependence', in V. Urquidi and R. Thorp (eds), *Latin America in the International Economy*, Macmillan.

Sunkel, O. (1973b) 'Transnational capitalism and national disintegration in Latin America', *Social and Economic Studies*, Vol. 22, No. 1, March.

Sunkel, O. and Fuenzalida, E.F. (1979) 'Transnationalisation and its national consequences', in J.J. Villamil (ed.), *Transnational Capitalism and National Development: New Perspectives on Dependence*, Harvester Press.

Tungendhat, C. (1973) *The Multinationals*, Penguin Books.

United Nations (1974a) *Multinational Corporations in World Development*, Praeger.

United Nations (1974b) *The Impact of Multinational Corporations on Development and on International Relations*, ST/ESA/6.

United Nations (1978) *Transnational Corporations in World Development: A Re-examination*, E/C.10/38.

United Naitons (1979) *Supplementary Material on the Issue of Defining Transnational Corporations*, E/C.10/58.

United Nations (1983) *Transnational Corporations in World Development: Third Survey*, ST/CTC/46.

UNIDO (1981) *World Industry in 1980*, United Nations.

Vaitsos, C. (1972) 'Patents revisited: their function in developing countries', *Journal of Development Studies*, Vol. 9, No. 1, October.

Vaitsos, C. (1973) 'Bargaining and the distribution of returns in the purchase of technology by developing countries', in H. Bernstein (ed.) (1973), *Underdevelopment and Development*, Penguin Books.

Vaitsos, C. (1974) *Intercountry Income Distribution and Transnational Enterprises*, Clarendon Press.

Vaitsos, C. (1975) 'The process of commercialization of technology in the Andean pact', in Radice (1975).

Vaitsos, C. (1976) 'Power, knowledge and development policy: relations between transnational enterprises and developing countries', in Helleiner (1976).

Vernon, R. (1966) 'International investment and international trade in the product cycle', *Quarterly Journal of Economics*, Vol. 80. Reprinted in Dunning (ed.) (1972).

Vernon, R. (1971) *Sovereignty at Bay: The Multinational Spread of US Enterprises*, Penguin Books.

Vernon, R. (1977) *Storm Over the Multinationals: The Real Issues*, Macmillan.

Vernon, R. (1979) 'The product cycle hypothesis in a new international environment', *Oxford Bulletin of Economics and Statistics*, Vol. 41, No. 4, November.

Warren, B. (1973) 'Imperialism and capitalist industrialisation', *New Left Review*, No. 81, September–October.

Warren, B. (1980) *Imperialism: Pioneer of Capitalism*, Verso.

Wells, L.T. (1977) 'The internationalisation of firms from developing countries', in T. Agmon and C.P. Kindleberger (eds), *Multinationals from Small Countries*, MIT Press.

Yamin, M. (1983) 'Direct foreign investment as an instrument of corporate rivalry: theory and evidence from the LDCs', in C.H. Kirkpatrick and F.I. Nixson (eds), *The Industrialisation of Less Developed Countries*, Manchester University Press.

11

Technology and industrial development

11.1 Introduction

For the purpose of this chapter, the definition of technology given by Stewart (1977, p.1) is adopted: technology encompasses the 'skills, knowledge and procedures for making, using and doing useful things' (for a discussion of alternative definitions and classifications of technology, see Dunning 1982). Technology in this sense thus includes both process technology (how something is made) and product technology (the nature and specification of what is produced) as well as managerial, organisational, financial and marketing skills, transferred through a variety of channels, including DFI, non-equity operations by TNCs (see Chapter 10) and technical training programmes.

Over the years, there have been significant shifts in the focus of the study of technology and development. In so far as development theory concerned itself with this issue, attention was initially focused on the choice of technique and in particular on the question of labour- versus capital-intensity (Section 11.2). Gradually, attention turned to the institutional framework within which techniques were transferred to, or otherwise acquired by, LDCs and questions were raised as to how techniques were actually chosen in practice (what Stewart (1977) has referred to as the 'selection mechanisms'). The problems discussed related mainly to the suitability or 'appropriateness' of technologies transferred to LDCs, largely by TNCs, and to the costs associated with such transfers (Section 11.3).

During the 1970s another shift occurred, towards the examination of technological processes and change within the LDCs themselves (Fransman 1984a, p.5). Issues relating to (i) the anchorage (that is, the implantation) and adaptation of imported technologies, (ii) their reproduction, development and assimilation within the LDC, and (iii) the various interactions between the dependence on imported technologies and the encouragement of an indigenous technological capability came to the fore. The emergence of the NICs (see Chapter 9) and the growing realisation that a number of LDCs were becoming important exporters of technology

371

(Lall 1984) also raised important issues relating to the relationships between international trade and indigenous technological change (Fransman 1984a, pp.14–21).

These are complex issues which cannot be covered fully in this chapter, but some of them are touched upon in Section 11.5.

11.2   The Theory of the Choice of Techniques[1]

The theory of the choice of techniques for LDCs arose in connection with the initiation of development planning in those countries and had the aim of suggesting criteria for the investment choices which governments would find themselves making as planning proceeded. Drawing on orthodox static economic theory, the earliest contributions in this field proposed that the LDCs should select investment projects which utilised to the full their plentiful factors (for example, labour) and economised on scarce factors (for example, capital). Thus the 'factor intensity' criterion proposed that labour-intensive techniques should be adopted, on the assumption that labour was the abundant factor.

This reasoning can be readily illustrated using simple production theory. If labour is plentiful and capital scarce, the price of labour should be low relative to that of capital, and a small amount of capital would cost the same as a large quantity of labour, as indicated by the relative price line AB in Figure 11.1. This line, which is determined by the ratio of the price of labour to the price of capital (P_l/P_k), is also known as an isocost or equal input cost line, since all combinations of capital and labour along it have the same total cost.

Given a production function for a particular product expressing output as a function of labour and capital, it is also possible to draw isoquants, such as YY, which indicate all combinations of the two inputs which can be used to produce any given level of output. The theory shows that the technique which maximises the profit from producing any desired level of output is given by the point of tangency between an isocost line and the isoquant for that level of output. For example, in Figure 11.1, given the isocost line AB, the profit maximising technique for producing Y units of the product is shown by the point of tangency u which involves combining Ol units of labour with Ok units of capital.

According to the orthodox theory, unemployment will exist if wages relative to interest rates are too 'high', resulting from 'inappropriate' minimum wage legislation and overpowerful trade unions, and/or capital is too 'cheap', resulting from overvalued exchange rates and institutionally determined real interest rates that are too low (or in some cases, even negative). Government intervention is usually blamed for creating a divergence between the market price and the social cost (the opportunity

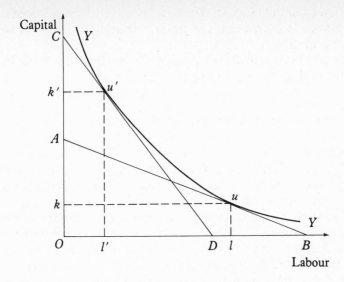

Figure 11.1

cost) of the factor of production, thus resulting in the 'distortions' that lead to the selection of 'inappropriate' capital-intensive techniques and less-than-full employment. In Figure 11.1, the isocost line CD, representing a higher relative wage, results in the selection of a more capital-intensive production technique and a lower level of employment (Ol').

An early contribution to the literature on choice of technique was the 'output–capital' criterion. This led largely to the same result as the 'factor intensity' criterion since the expectation was that if a given amount of capital was used with a greater amount of labour, there would be an increase in output. Hence if the maximum output per unit of capital was the adopted criterion, then two urgent needs of LDCs – the creation of employment and the increase in output – would both be met. Figure 11.2 illustrates this proposition.

If the available capital Ok_2 is used on a project involving a capital-intensive technology T_1, output O_1 is produced and employment Ol_1 is created. But if the labour-intensive technology T_2 is used, the same output can be produced using less capital (Ok_1) and providing more employment (Ol_2). The surplus capital could then be used to expand output by additional investment using technique T_2. Hence output O_3 and employment Ol_3 are obtained, whilst still only using the original amount of capital.

A refinement of this criterion would accept that some projects have a long gestation period and do not produce their full output very quickly.

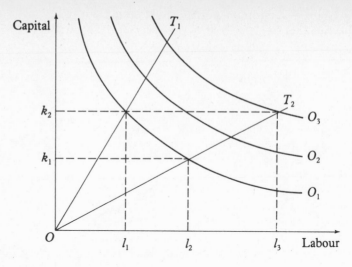

Figure 11.2

Thus the criterion could be reformulated to have as its objective the maximisation of the discounted time stream of output per unit of capital invested, taking the time stream over the lifetime of the project. It will be noted that if a high discount rate was chosen, the criterion would result in the selection of quick yielding projects, and if a low discount rate was chosen, longer lived and later yielding projects would score highly and thus be selected.

The criterion, as originally formulated, was not explicitly concerned with the social returns or benefits resulting from any given pattern of resource allocation. It was thus generalised and extended by the formulation of the social marginal product criterion (SMP) (Kahn 1953; Chenery 1953). The SMP criterion stated that the total available capital should be so deployed that the marginal unit of capital in each industry or sector should yield the same contribution to the national product. In these circumstances, the total additional output would be maximised. Chenery's (1953) version of the SMP also proposed to include with the output contribution of each project an allowance for its contribution to the balance of payments and indeed to any other objective (for example, regional equality) that the planners felt important. Chenery also proposed to deduct from the valuation of the project the cost of inputs (labour, etc.).

Several points concerning this analysis need to be made at this stage. Firstly, there are products which it might be deemed necessary (or desirable) to produce and for which only one method (technique) exists. In this case, the issue of the choice of technique does not arise. If, however, the item is not absolutely crucial to the output pattern, then a different overall capital–labour ratio can be achieved by not producing it and producing something else instead (the question of the choice of product is discussed below). In the case of other products, a range of techniques may exist, but some techniques may be old-fashioned and inefficient in the sense that they use both more labour and more capital than the others to produce the same output.[2] These techniques would presumably not be chosen for new investment purposes, unless it was felt that for social or political reasons an old-fashioned, inefficient, labour-intensive technique which generated immediate employment was desirable, even at the cost of there being less output than would otherwise be produced.

In general, the curve relating output to inputs of capital and labour (YY in Figure 11.1) will not be smooth and regular as drawn in the diagram. Figure 11.1 is drawn on the assumption of an infinite number of available techniques, so that infinitely fine trade-offs between capital and labour are possible. In reality, there would only be a small number of dots on the curve and the shape of a line drawn from one to another would not have the smooth shape of the isoquant YY. In general, however, we would expect the line to confirm that in producing a given level of output, a technique that required less capital than another would require more labour, that is, the line would in general slope downwards from left to right.

It should also be noted that the selection of projects according to these social optimisation criteria may run counter to the selection which would be implied by private profit maximisation. For example, techniques which are labour intensive will only willingly be chosen by employers if labour is cheap and capital expensive. As already noted above, it is often argued that in practice labour costs in LDCs are above the level that would be dictated by the interaction of supply and demand and that capital is artificially cheap. In selecting projects, government planners could either ignore profitability altogether in favour of the social desirability implied by the above criteria, or they could adopt a system of 'accounting prices', under which the project is evaluated not by using actual wage levels and capital costs but the levels which would be a 'true' representation of the situation so far as supply and demand for the factors are concerned. Thus labour would be accorded an accounting wage which was either very low or even zero, implying that employment of additional labour has no social cost in a labour surplus economy. Also, if additional objectives are to be considered as in Chenery's SMP criterion (balance of payments contribution, etc.), then a weight has to be applied to them in line with the planners' view of their importance, alongside the main question of the output that they generate.

However, whilst these devices may assist the planners in deciding which projects are socially desirable, they do not ensure that public development agencies or private capitalists will willingly undertake them. Various policy instruments can thus be suggested to force or induce businessmen to undertake what would otherwise be socially desirable but unprofitable projects. For example, there might be a tax on capital use and a subsidy on labour costs to bring actual costs into line with the true social opportunity costs (the accounting prices). But such policies are likely to give rise to difficult political and administrative problems (for example, politically powerful interest groups may be adversely affected by higher prices for capital and will thus resist such measures), and the literature on choice of techniques has remained much more a matter of theory than of practical application. In any case, the concept of equilibrium prices leading to optimal resource allocation depends on the assumption that income distribution is acceptable, and it may well be an objective of government policy to alter income distribution (for a discussion of this issue, see Chapter 3).

A totally different criterion from those so far discussed was proposed by Galenson and Leibenstein (1955). Instead of the aim of maximising immediate output and employment, they suggested that the aim should be growth. The creation of less employment and output now may lead to more employment and output at a future date than would otherwise have been the case. To increase current employment may actually mean sacrificing the rate of growth of both employment and output, and thus the possibility exists of a conflict between maximising current output and employment and maximising the growth rates of output and employment.

In order to ensure growth, Galenson and Leibenstein suggested that the objective should be to maximise the reinvestible surplus generated per unit of output (their suggested criterion is called the 'marginal *per capita* reinvestment quotient'). Labour-intensive techniques might generate immediate output but very little surplus since the wage bill would be large. Capital-intensive techniques should therefore be chosen because, by minimising the wage bill, they will increase the reinvestible surplus. Put another way, capital-intensive techniques generate a high output per worker and therefore, for a given wage rate, a high surplus.

Galenson and Leibenstein present figures showing the large increases in output and employment which are possible after a few years if all the surplus is reinvested, although it must be remembered that reinvestment over time may be in a technology of a different capital intensity from the initial investment and thus the rate of growth of employment may not be the same as the rate of growth of output. It is assumed that profits are the source of investment funds and that no savings take place out of wages. In other words since all wages are consumed, from the point of view of growth they are a cost. It should be noted that it is the actual wage that is relevant, not an accounting wage. It must also be assumed that wage rates do not depend on the technique chosen and that the government is unable, or unwilling, to secure the savings ratio that it desires by the use of fiscal measures or forced savings. A final point to note is that this criterion accords much more closely with the entrepreneur's pursuit of profit maximisation than do the earlier criteria discussed.

Dobb (1956–57) and Sen (1957; 1968), both of whom also propounded the surplus-maximisation criterion (in Dobb's case with an explicitly socialist regime in mind), nevertheless drew out the qualification that it is not necessarily the *most* capital-intensive technique which will maximise the surplus (as was implied by Galenson and Leibenstein). The surplus-maximising technique depends on the slope of the function relating output to inputs and on the wage rate. A high wage rate will dictate a capital-intensive technique but a low wage rate, such as may be operative in some LDCs, will mean that a relatively labour-intensive technique will maximise the surplus.

This point is illustrated by Sen thus. In Figure 11.3 the curve OQ represents total output and the wage rate is shown as the slope of the line OW (the height of OW equals the wage bill). The surplus-maximising technique is X_2 where the gap between output per unit of capital and the wage bill per unit of capital (W_2L_2) is at its maximum. The best technique from the point of view of maximising output per unit of capital and employment per unit of capital is X_3. The lower the wage rate (and hence the lower the slope of OW), the nearer does the surplus-maximising technique move to becoming one and the same as the output-maximising

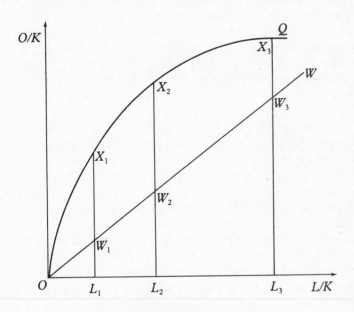

Figure 11.3

technique (in the limiting case, when the wage rate is zero, the technique maximising output and employment also maximises the reinvestible surplus). A higher wage rate will shift the point of surplus maximisation to the left (that is, towards X_1), thus increasing capital intensity.

Thus we see the conflict between the maximisation of current output and employment and the maximisation of the growth of output and employment. Labour-intensive techniques maximise output and employment in the short run but more capital-intensive techniques provide a greater surplus for reinvestment for more rapid growth (and hence higher employment) in the future. Stated thus, the choice becomes one between present and future welfare, and to quote Sutcliffe:

> ... the problem of the choice of techniques cannot in theory be solved without a clear recognition that in the first place there will be a multiplicity of goals ... some of which may conflict; nor can it be solved aside from the social rate of time preference in terms of which future alternative streams of output, consumption and employment must be ranked. (Sutcliffe 1971, pp.168–9)

Basically this is a political question concerning the goals a society sets itself and the time horizon over which those goals are to be achieved. Can the government inflict a sacrifice on the population for the sake of benefits in the future when there is such an immediate need for output and employment now? Once again, these questions remain largely in the realms of theory. In practice it may well be the case that one group has the sacrifice inflicted upon it and another group collects the eventual benefit.

However, methods have been suggested whereby the government's view of the desirable balance between present and future benefits can be taken into account in planners' calculations. Some allowance will probably have to be made for an increase in present consumption, given that it is likely to be more highly valued by society than future consumption. What is needed is an investment criterion which reflects both increases in current welfare and increases in future welfare brought about by the reinvestment of future surpluses arising from current investment. Eckstein (1957) advanced the marginal growth contribution (MGC) to meet this need. The MGC consists of (i) the present value of the project's direct contribution to consumption, and (ii) the present value of the consumption stream resulting from reinvestments associated with the project.

The choice of a discount rate is crucial here. A low discount rate which picks out projects whose benefits extend a long way into the future, that is have a high growth potential, implies that the government is prepared to sacrifice immediate benefits and is thinking a long way ahead. A high discount rate would imply that the government felt the need to generate quick results. Sen (1968, Ch. 2) has also proposed a method of discriminating between quick-yielding and growth-promoting projects. He proposes the use of a time horizon rather than a discount rate. The

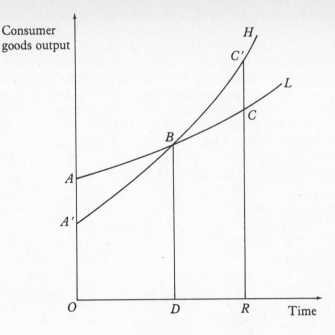

Figure 11.4

criterion can best be illustrated by reproducing Sen's diagram in Figure 11.4.

The curves H and L show the flow of real consumption over time, each representing a different technique. Technique H gives a lower immediate output but a higher rate of growth than technique L. Until D is reached, technique L produces a higher level of output than H and the gap that H has to make up is $A'AB$. At point R, the area $CC'B$ equals $A'AB$, that is, the gap in output between technique H and L is made up, and Sen calls the period OR the 'period of recovery' – 'the period of time over which the levels of aggregate consumption are the same' (Sen 1968, p.23). In selecting a technique, a comparison is made between the 'period of recovery' and the time horizon selected by the planners. If the line $C'CR$ is to the right of the time horizon, then the more labour-intensive, quick-yielding technique L will be chosen. If the line $C'CR$ is to the left of the time horizon, the capital-intensive technique H will be selected.

Before turning to a discussion of the factors that determine the choice of technique in practice, we must take a close, critical look at some assumptions made in the above analyses:

(1) It is assumed that savings depend upon the distribution of income,

that is only profits are saved while wages are consumed. But it may not be the case that wage earners do not save part of their income. They can be persuaded to save and/or the government can use direct or indirect taxes to generate a reinvestible surplus. Profit receivers may consume part of their profits, although this does not affect the selection of the surplus-maximising technique if we make the, admittedly unrealistic, assumption that profit receivers consume a constant proportion of profits, irrespective of the technique used. Of far greater significance is the repatriation of profits by TNCs. In this case, capital-intensive techniques generate a reinvestible surplus which leaves the country, and this consideration seriously undermines the arguments for increasing the share of profits in national income. (Profits arising from the use of labour-intensive techniques may also be consumed or repatriated of course; all that is being argued here is that we cannot assume that the higher reinvestible surplus associated with capital-intensive techniques will be automatically reinvested.) Critics of Galenson and Leibenstein have argued that it is best to employ fiscal and monetary measures to produce an income distribution that yields sufficient savings, rather than use the choice of techniques for this purpose. Indeed, if there are no constraints (political or economic) on the amount of income that is saved, admittedly an unlikely state of affairs, it can be argued that:

> ... the total amount of income to be saved can be determined by the planner in any way he likes, and that he can then see that this decision is executed through the machinery at his disposal.... If this is true then the link snaps between the choice of techniques and the proportion of income saved. Then technical choice may be made with the main purpose of maximising the amount of output, and the proportion of the output to be invested can be decided at a separate stage. (Sen 1969, reprinted in Meier 1976, p.438)[3]

(2) It is unrealistic to assume that the real wage rate is constant whatever technique of production is chosen. In particular, TNCs employing capital-intensive production methods are likely to pay higher wages, thus reducing the reinvestible surplus and promoting the rapid growth of consumption on the part of employed workers, rather than the rapid growth of employment (Arrighi 1970, p.246).

(3) The existence or non-existence of external economies is an important consideration. We cannot say *a priori* whether labour- or capital-intensive techniques are more likely to generate external economies (for a discussion of this point, see Sutcliffe 1971, pp.171–2) but they must not be neglected in either choice of project or technique.

(4) The availability of other factors is important – raw materials, skilled labour (discussed in greater detail below) and foreign exchange (to import capital goods required by the investment programme if the domestic

capital goods sector – assuming that one exists – is unable to supply them) are all vital. In principle, these objectives can be overcome by the use of social cost–benefit analysis which attempts to assess the social profitability of a project. This involves (i) a statement of objectives (the 'objective function'); (ii) the estimation of social measures of the unit values of project inputs and outputs (shadow prices); (iii) the selection of a decision criterion to reduce the stream of social cost and benefit flows to an index, which can be used to accept, reject or rank the project relative to others. In effect, the choice of technique literature has become merged with social cost-benefit analysis. (For a brief discussion, see Dasgupta 1974, Ch. 9.)

(5) Labour-intensive methods may require greater amounts of working capital and this will adversely affect both their absolute and relative rates of surplus (Sen 1968, Appendix C).[4]

(6) A number of other points deserve mention. As already indicated above, there may be economic and political reasons why it is considered desirable to select less efficient labour-intensive technologies which, although they involve the sacrifice of *both* current output *and* the growth of future output and employment, generate immediate employment opportunities. For example, employment creation may be used as a redistributive mechanism, unemployment is regarded as demoralising, and political dangers arise from widespread unemployment (Stewart and Streeten 1969). The creation of labour-intensive urban-based activities may well, through the need to establish physical and social infrastructure facilities (houses, schools, communal services, etc.), involve a larger outlay of capital per unit of output than capital-intensive alternatives (Baran 1957, p.286), although this will not be the case if they are located in rural areas.

It is implicit in much of the theoretical discussion summarised above that governments are both willing and able to act according to some notion of maximising social welfare and that they can, in fact, determine the technologies chosen. Some contributors to the debate (for example, Dobb) explicitly analyse the issue within the framework of a planned (socialist) economy. But it must be emphasised that it is only in the latter case that there can be any guarantee that the surplus arising from the use of capital-intensive methods of production will actually be reinvested, thus resulting in a potentially higher rate of growth of output and employment (although even centrally planned economies can waste the reinvestible surplus).

The importance of the distinction that must be made between free enterprise or 'mixed' economies and centrally planned economies is not always recognised. If the crucial assumptions upon which the arguments for capital intensity are built are not realised in practice (as is the case in the majority of LDCs), the argument for capital intensity must be treated

with caution. The issues raised by Dobb above were of real importance in
the Soviet Union during its industrialisation drive in the 1920s and 1930s.
But in the majority of LDCs other factors dominate and although these
issues are still of crucial importance to contemporary LDCs, the practical
context severely limits the significance of the theoretical propositions.
With these qualifications in mind, we may conclude this discussion by
quoting Dobb:

> The choice between more or less capital-intensive forms of investment has
> nothing to do with existing factor proportions.... It depends, not on the
> existing ratio of available labour to capital (treated as a stock), but on precisely
> the same considerations as those which determine the choice between a high
> and a low rate of investment ... namely the importance to be attached to rais-
> ing consumption in the immediate future compared with the potential increase
> of consumption in the more distant future which a particular rate of invest-
> ment or form of investment will make possible. In other words, the same
> ground which would justify a high rate of investment ... would justify also a
> high degree of capital intensity in the choice of investment forms; and vice versa.
> (Dobb 1955, p.149).

11.3   TNCs and the Transfer of Technology to LDCs

The TNC is probably the most important of the channels through which
LDCs acquire proprietary technology, and its activities in this respect
have generated a great deal of controversy. Interest has focused in particular on two aspects of TNC operations:

(1) the 'appropriateness' of the technology transferred to, and utilised
within, LDCs by TNCs to the resources and developmental objectives of the host LDCs; and

(2) the actual cost to the LDCs of the technology transferred to them
by TNCs.

The Rationale of TNC Technology Transfer

The argument concerning the 'appropriateness' of the technology
transferred to LDCs by TNCs relates to the disparity between the factor
endowments of the LDCs and the factor requirements of TNC
technologies.

Given the relatively labour-abundant/capital-scarce resource endowment of most LDCs, and assuming that the market prices of the factors of
production reflect social opportunity costs, it is argued that LDCs should
select technologies that utilise most intensively their relatively abundant
factor (labour) and economise on the scarce factor (capital) (see Section

11.2). The TNC, on the other hand, is more likely to transfer a capital-intensive technology to the LDC, a technology that has been developed and perfected in the capital-abundant/labour-scarce developed economy. Such a technology, it is argued, does not create large-scale new employment opportunities; it often creates a long-run dependence on imported equipment and associated inputs, and it prevents or slows down the effective anchorage and assimilation of the transferred technology in the host LDC.

(1)   One explanation for the apparent inconsistency between relative factor endowment and technology choice is based on the argument that in the majority of LDCs, market prices do not in fact reflect social opportunity costs. It is argued that technological choice is merely a reflection of the 'distortions' in the factor and product markets of the LDCs, and that once such 'distortions' are removed and market prices correctly reflect relative scarcities, producers, both national and transnational, will substitute between factors in the direction of greater labour intensity. This is the orthodox neoclassical view of the determination of the choice of technique (see Section 11.2).

(2)   Another explanation of the allegedly high capital intensity of TNC manufacturing operations relates to the uncompetitive environment in LDCs within which they operate. The majority of LDCs have pursued policies of import-substituting industrialisation (ISI), an important aspect of which has been the protection of domestic enterprises (both national and foreign owned) from foreign competition by a variety of protective devices. The absence of powerful competitive pressures has, it is argued, lessened the need for firms in LDCs to minimise costs and, other things being equal, has led to the selection of more capital-intensive techniques by both national and transnational firms (United Nations 1974, pp.6–7).

(3)   A third explanation relates to technical rigidity, that is, the limited substitutability of factors in the production process. This hypothesis was first advanced by Eckaus (1955), and has more recently been extended and tested by Forsyth et al. (1980). The distinction is made between:

   (i)   the basic case in which, given the state of technical knowledge, there is only one (or at most a very small number of) manufacturing process(es) that is (are) capable of producing a particular commodity;
   (ii) technical rigidities related to the specifications of the commodity to be produced (see below); and
   (iii) technical rigidities imposed by the availability of techniques; even if alternative techniques exist, LDCs may not have access to them.

(4)   A fourth set of explanations concerned with the choice of technique relates to 'behavioural' considerations. It has been argued, for example,

that it is 'engineering man', rather than 'economic man', who determines objectives and selects techniques. Engineers play an important role in the design of manufacturing plant and equipment; even if they themselves do not actually select the equipment to be used, they are still largely responsible for the range of commercially available equipment. Engineers may also have a preference for sophisticated modern equipment that gives a high-quality final product, which may not be justifiable from a purely economic point of view (Wells 1973; United Nations 1974, Ch. 1). Managers may also be 'satisficers' with respect to technological choice. That is, given that their objectives may be other than those of profit maximisation, the pressures to find a cost-minimising set of techniques will be correspondingly reduced and capital-intensive techniques therefore selected in relatively labour-abundant economies.

(5) A fifth set of factors relates to the non-homogeneity of the factors of production. It has been argued (Arrighi 1970) that capital-intensive techniques are characterised by a pattern of employment in which semi-skilled labour and high-level manpower predominate, whereas labour-intensive techniques make greater use of both skilled and unskilled labour. In most LDCs, skilled labour (in particular, supervisory personnel) is often in very short supply, and thus the need to economise on this scarce factor dictates the choice of capital-intensive technology.

Even Arrighi's qualification to the simple two-homogeneous-factor world may be an oversimplification. Robinson (1979, p.27) identified eleven inputs that could, in varying degrees, influence the choice of technology and he concluded that: 'I stress this large variety of inputs because, to an industrial economist, a discussion which fastens exclusively on [unskilled labour and capital embodied in machinery] is in the great majority of cases barren'. In addition, in many LDCs, material inputs are often expensive and difficult to obtain because of foreign exchange controls, import restrictions, etc. It will pay producers to substitute other factor inputs for such materials wherever possible, and capital-material substitution (for example, storage facilities that reduce spoilage; mechanised materials handling that reduces breakage; electronically controlled equipment to ensure mix specification, etc.) offers greater opportunities in this respect than labour-material substitution (Helleiner 1975, pp.168–9).

(6) The above explanations apply in principle to both national and transnational firms. With respect specifically to TNCs:

(i) It is factor availability at the global level that is important and not the availability of factors in any particular LDC. Given its access to international capital markets and other parts of the organisation, the TNC affiliate is unlikely to face a capital constraint and is thus not required to economise in the use of that factor.

(ii) Related to point (5), TNCs may well wish to minimise their contact with local labour, through the utilisation of capital-intensive technologies. Streeten (1972, p.234) suggested that labour in the LDC might well be 'unskilled, underfed, unhealthy, unreliable, undisciplined and perhaps hostile'. Support for this view emerged from a study of the choice of technique by manufacturing firms in Nigeria. Winston (1979) reported that the reduction of general labour problems by the choice of more capital-intensive production methods, especially in multi-shift plants, was mentioned by a number of managers. In addition to this, 'machine-paced' flows of production could be achieved by capital-intensive technologies, and the problem of theft (very costly for some industries) could be reduced.

(iii) TNCs are typically large-scale producers, and it is the scale of output that determines the efficient factor intensity (Helleiner 1975, p.168).

(iv) 'Ethnic pride' (Winston 1979) and 'good citizenship' (Helleiner 1975) are also advanced as reasons why, respectively, LDCs 'demand' capital-intensive technologies and TNCs 'bow' to such pressures.

(v) The ownership and control of technology are in many cases the most important of the ownership-specific advantages of TNCs (see Chapter 10, Section 10.3) and it would be strange indeed if TNCs did not utilise within the LDCs the product and process techniques that they themselves have developed and perfected elsewhere in the world. It is the very possession of advanced technology, combined in a profitable 'package' with organisational, financial and marketing factors, which can be applied elsewhere at little extra cost, that explains much of the transnationality of these firms. In addition, the limited domestic markets and the varying stages of development of the LDCs do not make them sufficiently attractive for TNCs to develop separate products/processes for every market within which they operate. As Lall (1978, p.238) argued:

> Minor on-the-spot adaptations may be made to suit local conditions, to meet official requirements, or to save foreign exchange, but by their very nature TNCs do not specialize in the simple labour-intensive products which can be adapted to the LDC factor endowments.

The Cost of Technology Transfer

It was argued in Chapter 10 that one of the major attractions of TNC's direct investment is that it supplies a 'package' of inputs, including technology, that are not available, or are available only in limited quantities, in the host economy. It is the very fact that technology is part of the 'package' that makes it extremely difficult, if not impossible, to estimate with any degree of accuracy the actual cost of the technology supplied to the 'buyer' of the technology, that is, the host LDC. The TNC can utilise a number of channels through which income can be remitted from an LDC, and actual payments for technology may thus pass unnoticed or be greatly underestimated. As Stewart (1977, Ch. 5) has noted, royalty payments and licence fees may cover only a small proportion of the total payment for technology, which should also include the elements of technology payments included in imports of machinery and equipment, intermediate goods imports, payments of fees and salaries to foreign personnel and the profits earned on the TNC investment (which in turn may be distorted because of the manipulation of transfer prices). It is argued by many economists that the marginal cost to the TNC of using an already developed technology is zero.[5] From the point of view of the buyer (the LDC), however, the marginal cost of replicating that technology or developing an alternative technology may be huge. Vaitsos (1973) has argued that the process of technology commercialisation is best seen as a bargaining process in which the buyer of the technology (the LDC) is in a position of structural weakness *vis-à-vis* the seller of the technology (the TNC), because the item that the buyer needs to purchase (technology) is at the same time the information that is needed in order to make a rational decision to buy. It is also alleged that the patent system and the restrictive use of trademarks, brand names, etc., are also detrimental to the interests of the LDCs (for a discussion of trademarks in the LDCs, see the special issue of *World Development*, Vol. 7, No. 7, July 1979).[6]

Keeping in mind the reservations noted above concerning the difficulty of actually measuring LDC payments for technology, some indication of the amounts involved can be given. It has been estimated (by UNCTAD, figures quoted in Stewart 1977, Ch. 5) that the direct costs to LDCs of technology transfer (in the form of patents, licences, trademarks, management and technical fees) were approximately $1.5 billion in 1968, which was the equivalent of 5% of LDC-non-oil exports and about 0.5% of their total GDP. Assuming a rate of growth of 20% per annum, it was estimated that these payments would total $9 billion by 1980. It is clear, therefore, that very large sums of money are involved in the transfer of technology to LDCs.

Is there a Choice of Technique in Practice?

Econometric estimates of factor substitutability attempt to measure the ease with which two inputs (usually capital and labour) can be substituted for one another in the production process. A low (less than one) elasticity (technical fixity or rigidity) indicates that a fall in the price of labour, for example, will induce a less than proportional increase in the use of labour in the production process. A high (greater than one) elasticity of substitution, indicates that a fall in the price of labour will be accompanied by a more than proportional increase in the use of labour, and that the relative amounts of the factors used in the productive process will be responsive to changes in relative factor prices.

There are a number of conceptual, theoretical and data problems associated with such exercises and the results, which vary widely, must be interpreted with care. In general the estimates of elasticity of substitution based on time-series data are less than unity and lower than the estimates based on cross-section data (Gaude 1975, p.41). Morawetz (1976) argues that there is some scope for factor substitutability but that it varies across industries.

In a different kind of exercise, Sutcliffe (1971, Ch. 5, p.147) surveyed US data and tentatively concluded that in some sectors of manufacturing a choice of technology could be said to exist – tobacco, lumber and wood products, leather and leather goods, rubber products and chemicals. The sectors with the least choice were electrical and other machinery, fabricated metal products, coal and petroleum products, non-metallic mineral products, primary metals, furniture and fixtures, and printing and publishing. Another group of industries (textiles, apparel, pulp and paper products and transport equipment) occupied an intermediate position. Impressionistic data from other countries suggested that foodstuffs, textile weaving, cotton spinning, clothing, woodworking, steel and wood furniture, leather goods, rubber products and bricks and roofing tiles were all technologically flexible – that is, there existed a range of alternative techniques of production embodying different factor intensities (Sutcliffe 1971, p.148).

At the risk of overgeneralisation, it is probably the case that technological choice is greatest in established, basic industries (clothing, foodstuffs, household utensils, construction activities and allied industries) with low income elasticities of demand, catering for the needs of the great mass of the population. In the case of the majority of technologically advanced, sophisticated durable consumer goods (consumed by the middle/upper-income groups in LDCs) and many intermediate goods industries (although there are exceptions – for example, iron and steel), technological choice is likely to be limited or non-existent. There is some tentative evidence which suggests that capital goods industries (producers of machinery) are among the more labour-intensive industrial branches (Pack and Todaro 1969).

Continuous technological change is likely to reduce the range of profitable alternative techniques available. When a new technology uses less capital and labour than the existing technology (to produce the same level of output), the latter becomes unambiguously 'inferior' (see note 2) and in time will cease to exist, although variations in wages and profit margins will tend to prolong its existence. Stewart (1972, p.106) argues that the 'stylised facts' of history suggest that new techniques use no more capital per unit of output and use less labour, thus making older techniques inferior. The most labour-intensive method available is likely to be the method used when the product was first introduced, although this method may have become inferior over time. The most labour-intensive efficient method is thus the earliest method which has not become inefficient (Stewart 1972, p.107). In addition, the scale of output must be taken into account. The new machine is likely to be designed for a large-scale output and thus earlier machines may remain efficient at lower output levels, but be inefficient at larger ones.

Notwithstanding the arguments relating to the nature and direction of technical progress, the available evidence clearly suggests that technological fixity is in no sense absolute. There are significant inter- and intra-industry variations in capital–labour ratios and within individual manufacturing subsectors, both TNCs and indigenous enterprises adapt in some measure to local conditions. Such adaptations are especially pronounced in ancillary or peripheral operations (transport, packing, handling and storage operations) where relative prices may play a role in determining the technique chosen. However, other considerations (quality, the appearance of the final product, etc.) may well offset factor price considerations and lead to the selection of capital-intensive, mechanised techniques even in ancillary operations.

With reference to the 'appropriateness' of TNC technologies, is there any convincing and unambiguous evidence that suggests that TNCs systematically employ more capital-intensive technologies than their indigenous counterparts in LDCs? The available evidence is surveyed in Kirkpatrick et al. (1984, Ch. 4, Section 4.8) and does not permit straightforward answers. When matched pairs of firms are compared (matched with respect to product-mix, scale of output, age of equipment, market conditions faced, etc.), it cannot be concluded that TNCs consistently select technologies with higher capital–labour ratios than indigenous forms in the same subsector or branch of industry. The evidence varies so widely that generalisation cannot be made. The conflicting results in part depend on the definitions and measures of capital and labour used, but of probable greater significance is the fact that local firms may have to become 'more like' TNCs in order to survive the competitive struggle with them (as suggested by Langdon 1975).

Helleiner has argued that:

> In particular industrial sectors, the multinational firm has often proven more responsive and adaptable in its factor and input use, especially in the ancillary activities associated with the basic production process, than local firms; and so it perhaps should with its wide range of experience upon which to draw. (Helleiner 1975, p.169)

Lall (1985, Ch. 4, p.74) too has argued that TNCs engage in considerable adaptation when transferring technologies from developed to less developed countries:

> Every new application of a technology entails considerable adaptive effort. The core process may not be significantly altered, but changes in scale, inputs, outputs, automation etc., may constitute between 10–60% of total project costs. Product ranges of TNCs in developing countries are very different from those in advanced countries, and new products are developed specifically for developing country conditions.

Given its technical knowledge, experience and flexibility, we should expect to observe some variations in TNC behaviour with respect to technology transfer and adaptation between both industries and countries. In some cases profit maximisation (or risk minimisation) will best be achieved through greater capital intensity; in other cases, relative factor prices and technological flexibility will lead to greater labour intensity, especially in ancillary operations. In yet other cases, new products or processes may well be developed for specific LDCs. It would be surprising if the TNC did not demonstrate its ability to adapt to different situations.

11.4 Choice of Product

The realisation that some commodities can be regarded as intrinsically more labour- (or capital-) intensive in production than others has led to attention being focused on the choice of product rather than the choice of technique. Once the choice of product is made, the question of technique will become irrelevant if there is only one way of producing a particular product. Variations in the product mix can thus cause variations in the overall capital–labour ratio.

Dealing first with inter-industry choices (that is, the choice between different products), the demand for different products is determined, *inter alia*, by the distribution of income (and to refer back to our discussion of the TNC, by product differentiation, advertising, etc.). We have already seen in Chapter 3 that in the majority of LDCs income distribution is highly unequal and we have argued in Chapter 9 that ISI, *ceteris paribus*, increases that inequality.

ISI increasingly produces technologically advanced goods, catering for the upper-income groups, for which only a limited technological choice may exist. In this case, choice of product, as influenced by the distribution of income, determines choice of technique – there may only be one 'best' way of producing a given product. If it is in fact the case that lower-income groups tend to purchase goods generally produced by labour-intensive techniques and upper-income groups consume goods utilising more capital-intensive techniques, it follows that a redistribution of income towards greater equality (increasing the incomes of the poor) will, through the change in the pattern of demand, lead to a change in the overall capital–labour ratio. Commodities produced by more labour-intensive methods of production (foodstuffs, clothing, basic household goods, construction materials, etc.) will be in greater demand and, other things being equal, employment opportunities in both manufacturing and agriculture will increase.

Unfortunately, as we noted in Chapter 3, Section 3.4, the real world is not as straightforward as this. The rich consume both capital-intensive goods and labour-intensive services and high-quality, handmade products, while the poor often spend their meagre incomes on heavily advertised 'non-essentials' (for example, Coca-Cola) produced by relatively capital-intensive techniques (compared, for example, to similar goods produced by local producers).

Once we take into account the intra-industry product mix, however, that is the possibility that 'more appropriate' goods are produced within each industry, the range of techniques available may well be increased. In the example given in the section on taste transfer in Chapter 10, the comparison was between locally based, labour-intensive laundry soaps and TNC subsidiary, capital-intensive detergents, both of which fulfilled the same functions but had different economic characteristics. The need for furniture can be satisfied by expensive products made of stainless steel, glass and leather or by simple wooden articles. Foodstuffs can be locally processed and unpackaged or be highly processed and overpackaged.

It is usual to classify products according to their physical attributes, but once products are so defined, and taking into account quality, the choice of technique is very limited – 'to produce identical physical products only one method may be possible' (Stewart 1972, p.111). But products can be classified according to their characteristics, that is according to the needs that they fulfil. For example, a Rolls-Royce is both a means of transport and a status symbol; thus a single product can fulfil a variety of needs. Similarly, a single need may be met by a variety of products – the need for shelter can be provided by a mud hut or a palace. Once needs are specified, alternative ways of meeting those needs can be examined and 'excess' or 'redundant' characteristics removed from existing products and/or new products more 'appropriate' to LDCs can be developed.

Obviously, the specification of needs is not straightforward. It gives rise to technical problems (the question of what constitutes a need) and raises key political questions concerning the degree of social control possible over consumption and hence, to a certain extent, over production. Although in principle there might exist a wide range of ways of meeting needs (once defined), in practice, within any given socio-economic environment, the choice may be severely limited, in part by what consumers wish to buy and are prepared to pay for.

For the present, Stewart's conclusion is worth quoting:

> The conventional distinction between choice of product and choice of technique (or choice of process) is . . . an arbitrary one. If product requirements are sufficiently finely specified, only one process may be possible. If developing countries wish to change the factor proportions employed they must first examine the product characteristics required. The development of appropriate techniques is closely tied up with the development of appropriate products. (Stewart 1972, p.114)

11.5   Technological Development

The LDCs are often described as technologically dependent economies. The concept of technological dependence is imprecise and difficult to define rigorously, but in general it refers to a situation where 'the *major source* of a country's technology comes from abroad' (Stewart 1977, p.116; emphasis in original). It originates, at least initially, in the lack of a capacity within the LDC to produce modern technology and in the limited flexibility and substitutability of domestic for foreign resources.

Stewart (1977, p.123) highlighted the following undesirable consequences of technological dependence:

(1)   the high cost of importing foreign technologies;
(2)   the loss of national control over decisions regarding technology;
(3)   the inappropriateness of the technology received; and
(4)   the lack of an effective domestic scientific and innovative capacity.

For Stewart and others, LDCs suffer from a 'double dependence' in that both the elements of technical knowledge themselves and the capacity to use that knowledge in investment and production have to be transferred.

The concept of technological dependence as applied to LDCs has increasingly come under critical scrutiny. Soete (1981, p.182) has argued that the:

> discussion on technological dependency illustrates most clearly one of the fundamental weaknesses of dependency analysis, i.e. its primarily static nature and its failure to cope with dynamic phenomena such as technical change.

Soete maintains that there are good reasons for believing that both 'the dynamic and positive effects of technical change' in LDCs and LDC technological capabilities have been underestimated. He points to the fact that over 80% of total world R&D expenditures are concentrated in six economies (USA, USSR, Japan, West Germany, France and the UK) and thus to a large degree most developed economies are in some sense technologically dependent. He concludes:

> Instead of focussing on the limits, costs and problems generally associated with

international technology transactions, one should really emphasise far more than before the enormous benefits and advantages of a continuous and massive import of technology. While the latter increases technological dependency, it also illustrates the very limited usefulness of the concept. (Soete, 1981, p.203)

The latter point clearly illustrates the problems that LDCs may face in formulating policies for the development of an indigenous technological capability. As Stewart (1977, Ch. 5) points out, in order to reduce their technological dependence, the LDCs must (i) control their technology imports to offset or modify the undesirable consequences of imported technologies, and (ii) reduce the extent of technology imports. Obviously these are not, in principle, mutually exclusive policies, but in many cases they will be, in that LDCs may find that they have to *increase* their imports of technology in order to develop their own technological capacity (that is, their ability to generate new technologies). What seems to be of importance, therefore, is not the simple fact of importing technology as such, but rather the terms and conditions under which technology is imported and the use to which that technology is put within the importing country (that is, its anchorage, adaptation, modification and diffusion within the LDC).

Stewart (1977, pp.134–5) argues that the experience of countries such as Japan and Russia suggests that a policy of controlling technology imports can succeed if it breaks 'the ties with advanced-country companies, tastes and products, which technological dependence has built up'. With respect to contemporary LDCs, increasing concern is being expressed over the control of technology imports. There is a growing awareness that the technology component is the most important part of the DFI 'package', and that the more efficient acquisition of technology should be an important objective of policies towards foreign investment and participation. There is also a growing realisation that:

> ... an indigenous technological capability is a necessary condition for the evaluation of technology to be obtained from abroad, for the effective utilisation of the transferred technology, for its adaptation to local conditions, for getting better terms for the transfer in negotiation with foreign enterprises and for the generation of 'appropriate' indigenous technologies. *In other words, indigenous technological capability is not an alternative to transfer but a necessary condition for it.* (United Nations 1983, p.67 emphasis added)

The implication of the latter point is that even if LDCs are merely to modify or adapt imported technologies (obtained via direct foreign investment, or licensing, or from any other source), they will require a fairly well-developed and sophisticated domestic technological capacity that few of them at present possess. LDCs are thus beginning to formulate technology policy strategies that include:

- identification of technological needs;
- selection of suitable technology and technology suppliers;
- strengthening the capacity of national enterprises in acquiring foreign technology;
- regulation of the terms and conditions of technology transfer arrangements;
- facilitating the absorption of imported technologies and the promotion of indigenous technological capabilities.
(United Nations 1983, p.68)

With respect to technological development, the distinction is now made between 'know-how' and 'know-why'. 'Know-how' is defined by Lall (1985, Ch. 7) as operating knowledge, that is, 'the knowledge of how to carry out manufacturing activity' (p.116), and includes the setting up of a new activity, the assimilation of imported techniques, quality control, improved plant layout and production practices, slight modifications to equipment, the use of different raw materials, etc. 'Know-why' involves 'the understanding of the nature of the underlying process and product technologies, and leads to their substantial adaptation, improvement and even replacement by new processes or products' (p.116).

Lall applies these concepts in his critique of Indian technological development. Among the more important of India's development objectives have been the priority given to the 'heavy', capital and intermediate goods sectors, the building up of a scientific/technological infrastructure and the development of self-reliance in industrial technology (Lall 1985, Ch. 10). India appears to have had the lowest relative reliance on foreign technology among the semi-industrial LDCs and licensing has been the favoured means of access to technology not available locally. A 'complex and rigid' structure of controls has been established to control technology imports and Lall argues that although India has made significant progress, the cost was often unacceptably high:

> ... India's technological strategy has had strong conflicting effects on the development of its technological capabilities. On the one hand, it has clearly led to a lot of technological effort and assimilation, and impressive growth and diversity of TE [technology exports] testifies to how far Indian enterprises have progressed with relatively small inputs of foreign technology. On the other, it has created large areas of technological backwardness. (Lall 1985, p.168)

Lall goes on to suggest that the attempt to develop an indigenous 'know-why' capability may well be detrimental to economic growth as, within the inward-looking, protectionist framework of the Indian economy, it diverts resources from technological activity which would occur in a more liberal framework and burdens the economy with outdated technologies (p.181).

He argues that 'the mastery of a certain level of know-why may not imply the capability to further develop that know-why in line with developments abroad' (p.219) and that there are 'very real limitations to know-why development in even the largest enterprises' in LDCs. Technology exports and technological development thus co-exist with growing technological backwardness. Lall concludes:

> The relationship between technology import and local technological effort is therefore a continuously varying one. At certain stages the two are substitutes, and intervention is required to bring private efforts in line with social needs. At others, they are complementary. As the economy develops, the need for intervention is correspondingly reduced. (pp.219–20)

In the light of this analysis, Lall recommends the liberalisation of policy with respect to industrialisation in general and technology imports in particular. India should be moving to more advanced technologies than its own technological capabilities can provide and these technologies can only be acquired from foreign sources.

The issue of the relationship between international trade and technological change is not simply one of free trade versus autarky (complete technological self-reliance), however. As Fransman (1984a, pp.18–19) has noted, there are significant benefits to be gained by LDCs from both the import and the export of technology, and there is some agreement on the importance of protecting and promoting learning-by-doing at least in the early stages of the development process. Countries that liberalise trade as a part of an EOI strategy may well continue to restrict the import of technology and intervene in order to encourage indigenous technological capabilities.[7] Both Brazil and South Korea have followed this course of action. Fransman concludes that technological capabilities might be enhanced under conditions of protection, but protection is neither a necessary nor a sufficient condition for this result to be achieved (p.21).

These arguments have particular significance for the establishment of a capital goods (machine-making) sector, the central role of which in the process of growth and development is now generally recognised. When the limited availability of foreign exchange restricts the import of capital goods, the expansion of the domestic capital goods sector provides the means for overcoming the problem of transforming savings into investment, thus accelerating economic growth. In addition, not only do new products and processes generally require new machines but the capital goods sector itself is a major initiator of change, and those changes transmit themselves rapidly within and across sectors. As Stewart (1977, pp.152–3) observed:

> ... innovation is likely to be concentrated in the capital goods sector ... economies without a capital goods sector are more than proportionately

weakened when it comes to innovatory activity ... lacking such sectors, underdeveloped countries have to import not only their machinery, but also their technical progress. The nature and direction of technical progress is thus determined from the outside.

Two sets of policy implications are suggested by this discussion. For those LDCs with significant capital goods sectors already established (India, Brazil, the Republic of Korea), policies need to focus on raising both static and dynamic efficiency. For those LDCs wishing to establish or encourage the development of a capital goods sector, selective and effective state intervention is necessary in order (i) to ensure the creation of external economies of scale, (ii) to protect the infant capital goods industries, and (iii) to reduce uncertainty through economic planning (Mitra 1979).

In the latter case, however, there is no guarantee of a longer-run learning process that will permit the capital goods industry eventually to attain international competitiveness. Although there is some evidence of substantial productivity gains in parts of the capital goods sector in Brazil and Argentina that were initially protected, it cannot automatically be concluded that the longer-run benefits of local production outweighed the costs. On the other hand, Fransman's (1982) study of the capital goods sector in Hong Kong suggested that some potential protection-related gains had not been realised.

In most discussions of the establishment of a capital goods sector, however, it is assumed that protection is given selectively to particular products considered important for the promotion of technological development. Ideally, this selectivity must be supplemented by a specification of the time frame for the learning process appropriate to the specific situation (UNCTAD 1985, p.153). In addition, although the protection will be for the initial development of an import-subsituting sector, the possibility of future exports should not be neglected in view of the importance of economies of scale associated with many products and the limited domestic markets of many LDCs. The possibilities for intra-LDC trade also need to be kept in mind.

11.6   Conclusions

What conclusions can be drawn from the discussion of the theoretical and real-world aspects of the choice of technique debate? Enough has been said to indicate that a straightforward answer to the question as to which techniques an LDC *should* choose cannot be expected. It is too simplistic to state merely that labour-abundant LDCs should of necessity choose labour-intensive techniques (a view uncritically advocated by too many proponents of 'intermediate technology'). The question raises fundamental political issues as to the development path to be pursued by the LDC, the nature of its goals and their realisation over time (present versus future consumption and employment, for example), and to ignore these aspects and treat the question as one of straightforward technical choice is to misunderstand the development process. Similarly, the role of the TNC and other international institutions (for example, bilateral and multilateral aid agencies) in the transfer of technology cannot be ignored. The assumption that a choice in fact exists may be incorrect in many cases, especially once we take into account the question of choice of product.

But this does not mean that the 'appropriate' techniques are not needed in LDCs. Morawetz (1974, pp.517–18) has defined appropriate technology as 'the set of techniques which makes optimum use of available resources in a given environment' and 'should be regarded as one which is suitable for particular workers producing particular products'. 'Appropriate' technologies would in general make greater use of unskilled labour, but in some cases capital-intensive methods would be more appropriate if skilled labour, rather than capital, was the main constraint.[8] In a broader sense, technologies must be 'appropriate' with respect to the wider economic and political objectives of the society in question (the value that society places on future, as compared to present, employment and consumption, for example) and also 'appropriate' with respect to scale of output, simplicity of operation, maintenance and repair and use of local inputs. The search for 'appropriate' technologies must avoid the shortcomings of the static investment criteria discussed above.

There are three possibilities of finding and implementing such technologies – they can be transferred from other countries, generated locally, or inappropriate technologies from elsewhere can be adapted to suit local needs. Morawetz sees the latter course of action as holding out the greatest hope for the future. But both this course and the second alternative are conditional on the establishment of domestic capital goods industries and the prior existence of a fair degree of technological competence in the adapting country.

Helleiner takes an optimistic view of the role of the TNC and argues that:

> Given sufficient incentives, there are good reasons for believing that multinational firms will become significant suppliers of more appropriate production technologies and products. (Helleiner 1975, p.179)

Griffin (1977), on the other hand, concludes that TNCs are not likely to be in the forefront of the development of either 'appropriate' processes or products. But even if it is made sufficiently profitable for the TNC to develop new 'appropriate' process and produce technologies and some progress is made, it is unlikely to be on a large scale and the ultimate costs to the LDC may still be unacceptably high – what is 'sufficiently profitable' for the TNC may be very expensive for the LDC!

An alternative policy is for an LDC to be more selective and purchase the components of the direct investment 'package' separately. Technology can be obtained in ways other than through direct investment by the TNC, for example, through licensing, which was used extensively by Japan, through 'turnkey' projects (the plant is built by a foreign company and then handed over to the LDC), through management contracts and fade-out or divestment agreements, etc. Complete technological independence is neither possible nor desirable for the LDCs. The complaint that the 'wrong' type of technologies are transferred by TNCs should not be read as a blanket condemnation of all modern imported technology. Once the LDC is in a position to determine for itself its development priorities, and better able to judge the value of what it is buying, the judicious use of imported technologies (in manufacturing, health, education, communications, etc.) will be of undoubted value to the development effort, and the importance of the TNC in developing and supplying these technologies must not be underestimated.

Notes

1. We are using the term 'choice of technique' narrowly to mean 'technique of production' within the manufacturing sector. But the wider implications of technological choice should not be forgotten. LDCs must choose between different 'technologies' in virtually all fields – most obviously agriculture (see Chapter 7), construction, road building, etc., but also in such fields as health and education (highly trained doctors versus medical auxiliaries; expensive urban-based schools and colleges versus mass rural education, and so on).
2. Stewart (1972, p.99) defines efficient techniques as 'those which are not inferior to any other technique among those available', inferiority in this sense meaning that it takes more of one factor, and not less of the other factor, to produce the same output as the efficient technique.
3. Thirlwall (1971, p.174) makes the point that if saving depends upon the total level of income as well as upon its distribution, 'a compromise must be reached between maximising output per head of the employed population using capital-intensive techniques and maximising output per head of the total population using less capital-intensive techniques'.
4. Sen (1968, Appendix C), is his classic discussion of the choice of technique in the cotton weaving industry in India, illustrates the complexity of the issues involved and concludes that 'The much discussed "technical superiority" of one technique over another seems to hold little water in this case, as the choice seems to be a genuine socio-economic one. It will depend ultimately on social factors (like the wage rate or the propensity to consume), political possibilities (like those of taxation), organisational considerations (like those influencing the marketing lag) and ethical factors (like the choice involving time)' (p.105).
5. Teece (1977) has argued, however, that the resources required to transfer

technology internationally are quite considerable, and that existing technology cannot be made available to all at zero social cost (see also Lall 1985).

6. Because of the characteristics of technology (it is non-exhaustible, i.e. its use by one person does not reduce its present or future availability: it cannot be 'owned' in the traditional sense of that term; it is heterogeneous, consisting of a number of different elements and it is not always certain what is meant exactly by technology importation), the patent system is in part used to create, artificially, a scarcity which results in a price system – a price is put on inventions to make them scarce, not because they are, of necessity, scarce. Vaitsos (1973, p.322) concludes that the market price mechanism cannot defend the interests of the LDCs and that they are paying too much for the technology that is actually transferred to them by TNCs.

7. Stewart (1973) makes an important point with respect to the relationship between EOI and indigeneous technological development. She maintains that although the comparative advantage of LDCs lies in the production of labour-intensive goods, as long as the developed countries are mainly responsible for technological innovation, production techniques will continually move in a capital-intensive direction, and LDCs will have to adapt both products and processes to keep up with these developments if they are to remain competitive in export markets:

> Technological dependence on the developed countries will be maintained, since without the technological transfer from the developed countries the developing countries will not be able to compete in international trade. (Stewart 1973, p.253)

8. Sutcliffe (1971, p.186) maintains that arguments for capital intensity are really arguments for *modern* techniques (which possess the characteristics that capital-intensive techniques are believed to have) – 'techniques which are first of all mechanised and possess the advantages of the influence of machine-paced operations on the productivity of labour, techniques giving a high and consistent quality of output and using easily available spare parts'.

References

Arrighi, G. (1970) 'International corporations, labour aristocracies, and economic development in tropical Africa', in R. Rhodes (ed.), *Imperialism and Underdevelopment: A Reader*, Monthly Review Press.

Baran, P. (1957) *The Political Economy of Growth*, Monthly Review Press.

Chenery, H.B. (1953) 'The application of investment criteria', *Quarterly Journal of Economics*, Vol. LXCII, No. 1, February.

Clark, N. (1975) 'The multinational corporation: the transfer of technology and dependence', *Development and Change*, Vol. 6, No. 1, January.

Cooper, C. (1972) 'Science, technology and production in the underdeveloped countries: an introduction', *Journal of Development Studies*, October. Reprinted in C. Cooper (ed.), *Science, Technology and Development*, Frank Cass.

Dasgupta, A.K. (1974) *Economic Theory and the Developing Countries*, Macmillan.

Dobb, M. (1955) *On Economic Theory and Socialism: Collected Papers*, Routledge and Kegan Paul.

Dobb, M. (1956–57) 'Second thoughts on capital intensity of investment', *Review of Economic Studies*, Vol. XXIV.

Dunning, J.H. (1982) 'Towards a taxonomy of technology transfer and possible impacts on OECD countries', in *North/South Technology Transfer: The Adjustments Ahead*, OECD.

Eckaus, R. (1955) 'The factor-proportions problem in underdeveloped areas', *American Economic Review*, Vol. 45, No. 4, September.

Eckstein, O. (1957) 'Investment criteria for economic development and the theory of inter-temporal welfare economics', *Quarterly Journal of Economics*, Vol. LXXI, No. 1, February.

Forsyth, D.J.C., McBain, N.S. and Soloman, R.F. (1980) 'Technical rigidity and appropriate technology in less developed countries', *World Development*, Vol. 8, No. 5/6, May/June.

Fransman, M. (1982) 'Learning and the capital goods sector under free trade: the case of Hong Kong', *World Development*, Vol. 10, No. 11, November.

Fransman, M. (1984a) 'Technological capability in the Third World: an overview and introduction to some of the issues raised in this book', in M. Fransman and K. King (eds), *Technological Capability in the Third World*, Macmillan.

Fransman, M. (1984b) 'Explaining the success of the Asian NICs: incentives and technology', *IDS Bulletin*, Vol. 15, No. 2.

Galenson, W. and Leibenstein, H. (1955) 'Investment criteria, productivity and economic development', *Quarterly Journal of Economics*, Vol. LXIX, No. 3, August.

Gaude, J. (1975) 'Capital–labour substitution possibilities: a review of empirical evidence', in A.S. Bhalla (ed.), *Technology and Employment in Industry: A Case Study Approach*, ILO.

Griffin, K. (1977) 'Multinational corporations and basic needs development', *Development and Change*, Vol. 8.

Helleiner, G.K. (1975) 'The role of multinational corporations in the less developed countries' trade in technology', *World Development*, Vol. 3, No. 4, April.

Kahn, A.E. (1953) 'The application of investment criteria', *Quarterly Journal of Economics*, Vol. LXVII, No. 1, February.

Kirkpatrick, C.H., Lee, N. and Nixson, F.I. (1984) *Industrial Structure and Policy in Less Developed Countries*, George Allen and Unwin.

Lall, S. (1978) 'Transnationals, domestic enterprises and industrial structure in host LDCs: a survey', *Oxford Economic Papers*, Vol. 30, No. 2, July.

Lall, S. (ed.) (1984) 'Exports of technology by newly-industrialising countries', *World Development*, Special Issue, Vol. 12, No. 5/6, May/June.

Lall, S. (1985) *Multinationals, Technology and Exports: Selected Papers*, Macmillan.

Langdon, S. (1975) 'Multinational corporations, taste transfer and under-development: a case study from Kenya', *Review of African Political Economy*, No. 2, January–April.

Meier, G.M. (ed.) (1976) *Leading Issues in Economic Development*, 3rd edn, Oxford University Press.

Mitra, J.D. (1979) 'The capital goods sector in LDCs: a case for state intervention?', *World Bank Staff Working Paper No. 343*, The World Bank.

Morawetz, D. (1974) 'Employment implications of industrialisation in developing countries: a survey', *Economic Journal*, Vol. 84, No. 335, September.

Morawetz, D. (1976) 'Elasticities of substitution in industry: what do we learn from econometric estimates?', *World Development*, Vol. 4, No. 1.

Pack, H. and Todaro, M. (1969) 'Technological transfer, labour absorption and economic development', *Oxford Economic Papers*, Vol. 21, November.

Robinson, A. (1979) 'The availability of appropriate technologies', in A. Robinson (ed.), *Appropriate Technologies for Third World Development*, Macmillan.

Sen, A.K. (1957) 'Some notes on the choice of capital intensity in development planning', *Quarterly Journal of Economics*, Vol. LXXI, No. 4, November.

Sen, A.K. (1968) *Choice of Techniques*, 3rd ed., Basil Blackwell.

Sen, A.K. (1969) 'Choice of technology: a critical survey of a class of debates', in UNIDO, *Planning for Advanced Skills and Technologies*, New York. Reprinted in Meier (1976).

Soete, L. (1981) 'Technological dependency: a critical view', in D. Seers (ed.), *Dependency Theory: A Critical Reassessment*, Frances Pinter.

Stewart, F. (1972) 'Choice of technique in developing countries', *Journal of Development Studies*, Vol. 9, No. 1, October.

Stewart, F. (1973) 'Trade and technology', in P. Streeten, *Trade Strategies for Development*, Macmillan.

Stewart, F. (1977) *Technology and Underdevelopment*, Macmillan.

Stewart, F. and Streeten, P. (1969) 'Conflicts between output and employment objectives in developing countries', *Oxford Economic Papers*, Vol. 23, No. 2, July.

Streeten, P. (1972) 'The multinational corporation and the nation state', in P. Streeten, *The Frontiers of Development Studies*, Macmillan.

Sutcliffe, R.B. (1971) *Industry and Underdevelopment*, Addison-Wesley.

Teece, D.J. (1977) 'Technology transfer by multinational firms: the resource cost of transferring technological know-how', *Economic Journal*, Vol. 87, No. 346, June.

Thirlwall, A.P. (1971) *Growth and Development*, Macmillan.

United Nations (1974) *The Acquisition of Technology from Multinational Corporations by Developing Countries*, ST/ESA/12.

United Nations (1983) *Transnational Corporations in World Development: Third Survey*, ST/CTC/46.

UNCTAD (1985) *The Capital Goods Sector in Developing Countries: Technology Issues and Policy Options*, UNCTAD/TT/78.

Vaitsos, C. (1972) 'Patents revisited: their function in developing countries', *Journal of Development Studies*, Vol. 9, No. 1, October.

Vaitsos, C. (1973) 'Bargaining and the distribution of returns in the purchase of technology by developing countries', in H. Bernstein (ed.), *Underdevelopment and Development*, Penguin Books.

Vaitsos, C. (1974) *Intercountry Income Distribution and Transnational Enterprises*, Clarendon Press.

Vaitsos, C. (1975) 'The process of commercialisation of technology in the Andean Pact', in H. Radice (ed.), *International Firms and Modern Imperialism*, Penguin Books.

Wells, L.T. (1973) 'Economic man and engineering man: choice of technology in a low wage country', *Public Policy*, Summer.

Winston, G.C. (1979) 'The appeal of inappropriate technologies: self-inflicted wages, ethnic pride and corruption', *World Development*, Vol. 7, No. 8/9, August/September.

12

Inflation and stabilisation in less developed countries

12.1 Introduction[1]

Inflation may be defined as 'a process of continuously rising prices, or equivalently, of a continuously falling value of money' (Laidler and Parkin 1975, p.741). This definition refers to the symptoms of inflation but says nothing about the causes or effects of inflation. A rise in the price of individual commodities is not, of course, inflationary if offset by falls in other prices. In addition, a once-and-for-all increase in the general price level resulting, for example, from a harvest failure, is not inflationary unless it is accompanied by responses (what structuralists would call propagation mechanisms) which produce a series of price increases continuing over time (Killick 1981b, Ch. 7). A sustained rise in the general price level means that a given sum of money will buy a smaller quantity of goods, hence the alternative definition of inflation as a continuous decline in the purchasing power of money.

Although inflation has traditionally been seen as an economic phenomenon, there is now greater awareness that the study of its causes and consequences cannot be confined to economic analysis alone: 'It pervades the political and social structures of society and may become embedded in those structures' (Hirsch and Goldthorpe 1978, p.1). *A fortiori*, the analysis of inflation in LDCs cannot be divorced from the more general problem of underdevelopment and development. Any attempt to avoid the discussion of social, political and institutional factors will merely obscure the real issues involved and will quite illegitimately reduce a complex economic and socio-political problem to a 'straightforward' technical one. As Hirschman (1981, p.177) has argued:

> It has long been obvious that the roots of inflation ... lie deep in the social and political structure in general, and in social and political conflict and conflict management in particular ... it would be difficult to find an economist who would not agree that 'underlying' social and political forces play a decisive role in causing both inflation and the success or failure of anti-inflationary policies.

In this chapter, we consider the record of inflation in LDCs (Section 12.2), the controversy over the causes of inflation in LDCs, concentrating on the early structuralist–monetarist debate (Section 12.3) and the empirical testing of alternative theories (Section 12.4), the relationship between the balance of payments and inflation in the context of the LDCs (Section 12.5), the consequences of inflation (Section 12.6) and the recent controversy concerning the role of the International Monetary Fund in LDCs (Section 12.7). A final section draws some general conclusions.

12.2   The Record of Inflation in LDCs

Table 12.1 presents data on the record of inflation for both developed and less developed countries from the mid-1960s onwards. The first point to note is that LDCs are clearly more prone to inflation than are developed, industrial economies. Over the period 1967–76, the weighted average rate of inflation of the LDCs was approximately twice that of the developed economies. From 1977 onwards, the LDC rate was approximately three times as great as that of the developed economies and in the 1980s, the gap widened even further. As the IMF (1984, p.12) noted, in the LDCs, unlike in the developed economies, inflation has not shown uniform signs of decelerating in recent years, although the estimated and projected rates for 1985 and 1986 are lower than the rates of inflation experienced in previous years. A second point relates to the varied experience of LDCs with respect to inflation. The weighted average figures in Table 12.1 show that the Western Hemisphere LDCs typically experienced rates of inflation far above those of other LDCs. Asian LDCs in particular appear to have been remarkably successful in containing inflationary pressures. The variation in individual country inflation rates explains the differences between the weighted average and median rates of inflation recorded in Table 12.1. The weighted average figures are, according to the International Monetary Fund (IMF 1984, p.12), 'dominated by the poor performance of a few large countries' and they thus tend to overstate the rise in inflation for the majority of LDCs. An examination of line three of Table 12.1 clearly shows that for LDCs the median inflation rate is significantly less than the weighted average rate. The median inflation rate peaked in 1980, declined to 10% in 1983 and is estimated to have fallen further since then. The weighted average rate also reached a peak in 1980, declined marginally in the subsequent two years, but rose quite substantially in 1983 and 1984. This disparity is attributed by the IMF to the 'quite atypical' inflationary experience of five countries – Argentina, Bolivia, Brazil, Israel and Peru – for which the composite rate of inflation accelerated from about 100% in 1981–82 to almost 260% in 1984 (IMF 1984, p.71).[2]

Table 12.1 Inflation, 1967–86 (%)[1]

	Average[2] 1967–76	1977	1978	1979	1980	1981	1982	1983	1984	1985[5]	1986[5]
Industrial countries[3]	6.7	7.5	7.6	8.0	9.2	8.7	7.2	4.9	4.1	3.9	3.7
Developing countries											
Weighted average inflation rates[4]	13.8	24.8	18.8	21.5	27.3	26.1	24.7	33.0	37.7	34.8	22.6
Median inflation rates	7.8	11.3	9.8	11.5	14.5	13.3	10.7	9.8	10.0	9.3	8.0
By region[4]											
Africa	8.5	18.8	16.9	16.7	16.6	21.4	13.4	19.0	17.8	16.1	12.7
Asia	9.4	7.8	4.0	8.0	13.1	10.6	6.2	6.6	6.9	5.5	5.4
Europe	9.0	15.1	19.8	25.9	37.9	24.0	23.8	23.2	28.0	22.4	19.0
Middle East	8.7	18.0	12.8	11.1	17.4	15.6	12.7	12.7	16.5	17.3	15.1
Western Hemisphere	24.5	49.9	41.9	46.5	54.0	58.6	65.5	100.5	119.8	113.7	59.7
By analytical criteria[4]											
Fuel exporters	9.7	18.1	12.5	11.8	15.9	16.4	18.0	25.5	20.1	15.3	12.1
Non-fuel exporters	16.2	28.0	21.4	25.7	32.2	30.6	28.0	36.9	47.1	45.0	27.9
Market borrowers	18.7	32.6	28.2	31.8	36.3	38.7	38.5	55.5	65.7	60.3	35.0
Official borrowers	9.7	17.3	13.7	19.5	22.3	28.4	17.2	21.9	15.8	13.8	13.4

Source: IMF (1985), Table 7, p.212.

Notes: (1) As measured by changes in GNP deflators for industrial countries and changes in consumer prices for developing countries.

(2) Compound annual rates of change.

(3) Averages of percentage changes in GNP deflators for individual countries weighted by the average US dollar value of their respective GNPs over the preceding three years.

(4) Except where otherwise noted, percentage changes of geometric averages of indices of consumer prices for individual countries weighted by the average US dollar value of their respective GDPs over the preceding three years. Estimates exclude China prior to 1978.

(5) Figures for 1985 are estimates; figures for 1986 are projections.

An additional feature of inflation in LDCs deserves brief mention. Fluctuations around the inflationary trend have tended to be greater in LDCs than in developed economies, with few LDCs experiencing steady inflation.

The level of inflation appears to be positively related to its variability, and there is some evidence to suggest a negative association between the extent of price instability and economic growth (Glezakos 1978). From this perspective, stabilisation of the inflation rate may be a more appropriate policy objective for LDCs than a reduction in the rate itself.

To summarise, although relatively few LDCs have experienced hyperinflation, most have, since the mid-1960s, had higher and more variable rates of inflation than those recorded in the developed industrialised economies.[3] The causes, consequences and control of inflation thus remain important issues for most LDCs.

12.3   The Causes of Inflation in LDCs: The Early Structuralist–Monetarist Debate

The Relevance of 'Orthodox' Analysis

The work of many economists on the causes of inflation in LDCs started from an explicit rejection of concepts and theories formulated within the developed, industrialised countries of the West. In particular, the Latin American 'structuralist' school of thought which emerged in the 1950s was specifically concerned with the inapplicability of the concepts of 'cost-push' and 'demand-pull'. (Arndt (1985) has traced the links between the emergence of 'structuralist thinking' in the UK and its influence on Latin American structuralism, and has outlined the evolution of the latter body of thought itself.)[4]

We noted in Chapters 2 and 4 the reservations expressed by many economists concerning the transfer of theories and concepts from one socio-economic system to another (the 'limitations of the special case'). The idea of 'misplaced aggregation' (that is, the analysis of dissimilar items in terms of a single category) was of particular use in criticising such concepts as 'employment' or the 'natural' rate of unemployment in LDCs.[5]

In addition, the use of the concepts of aggregate demand and supply, and the postulation of a ceiling to aggregate demand in real terms, which was set by aggregate supply, was open to criticism in the context of an LDC. The latter's economy was characterised by factor immobility, market imperfections and rigidities and disequilibrium between demand and supply in different sectors of the economy. Underutilisation of resources in some sectors (for example, manufacturing) coexisted with shortages in other sectors of the economy, and market imperfections and technological constraints prevented the movement of resources in response to market signals.

In these conditions, it was questionable whether 'orthodox' interpretations of inflation, in terms of aggregate demand and supply, could be applied. It could be argued that there was no overall (or global) limitation on aggregate supply. Rather, limitations were diverse and specific, and thus inflation had to be analysed taking into account the structural composition of the economy. Myrdal (1968,p.1962) rejected the idea of a single ceiling and, along with the Latin American 'structuralists', argued for an interpretation of inflation which stressed '. . . the fragmentation, the disequilibria, and the lack of balance between supplies and demands in different sectors of the economy and between different groups in the community'. In other words, inflation was seen as resulting from the existence of a number of specific bottlenecks or constraints in the economy.

The debate over the causes of inflation in LDCs arose in the mid-1950s when, as a result of chronic inflation and balance of payments problems, a number of major Latin American economies sought the assistance of the International Monetary Fund. The analysis and recommendations of the 1954 Klein-Saks Mission to Chile was challenged by the 'structuralist' school, centred around the Economic Commission for Latin America. This debate over the analysis of inflation in turn led to the emergence of the more general structuralist approach to the problems of underdevelopment. (We comment briefly in Section 12.8 below on the relevance of Latin American structuralism to other LDCs.)

The structuralist approach was juxtaposed with the orthodox 'monetarist' approach of the IMF. Each represented a certain approach to the problem of inflation in particular, and to economic development in general. In addition, the two groups were usually distinguished by differences in political ideology, structuralists being 'of the left' and monetarists 'of the right' (Felix 1961).[6] Seers (1964, p.89) delineated the two approaches in the following way:

> It is . . . not just a technical issue in economic theory. At the heart of the controversy . . . are two different ways of looking at economic development, in fact two completely different attitudes towards the nature of social change, two different sets of value judgements about the purpose of economic activity and the ends of economic policy, and two incompatible views on what is politically possible.

The Structuralist View

The structuralists argued that inflation was inevitable in an economy that was attempting to grow rapidly in the presence of structural bottlenecks or constraints, defined by Thorp (1971, p.185) as 'certain fundamental facets of the economic, institutional and socio-political structure of the country which in one way or another inhibit expansion'. Inflation in Latin America usually accompanied the transition of the LDC from an 'outward-oriented', primary export-based economy to an 'inward-oriented', domestic market-based economy, in which, as we noted in Chapter 9, ISI played a key role. The fundamental changes in the socio-economic structure that were required by economic development could not be brought about by the price mechanism operating within very imperfect market structures characterised by limited resource mobility, and thus shortages and disequilibria appeared.

The structuralist analysis was concerned with the identification and analysis of these alleged bottlenecks (the basic or structural inflationary pressures, to use Sunkel's (1960) terminology).[7] The key bottlenecks were generally taken to be (i) the inelastic supply of foodstuffs, (ii) the foreign exchange constraint and (iii) the budget constraint.

With respect to the agricultural sector bottleneck, it was argued that urbanisation and rising incomes led to a rapidly increasing demand for foodstuffs which could not be met by the agricultural sector. The supply response was poor because of the structural constraints within the sector – the domination either by large non-capitalistic *latifundia* which were not profit maximisers, or by *minifundia* operating almost at a subsistence level and hardly integrated into the market economy.[8] The inelastic supply constituted a structural inflationary factor. As Sunkel noted with respect to Chile:

> ... the stagnation of global agricultural production cannot be attributed to market, demand and/or price conditions, but must be due to factors inherent in the institutional and economic structure of the main part of the agricultural sector itself. (Sunkel 1960, p.115)

The second major bottleneck, the foreign exchange constraint, arose because the rate of growth of foreign exchange receipts was not sufficient to meet rapidly rising import demands generated by accelerated development efforts, rapid population growth and the industrialisation effort which took place in an environment of technological limitations, structural imbalances and imperfect factor mobility. Import shortages and rising import prices triggered off cumulative price rises; balance of payments difficulties eventually forced countries to devalue their currencies and this in turn added to domestic inflationary pressures, especially when the elasticity of demand for imports was very low.

The third bottleneck, identified by some structuralist writers but not others, was the lack of internal financial resources (the budget deficit). Development efforts increased the scope of necessary government involvement in the economy (especially in the provision of social and physical infrastructure facilities), but government revenue rarely expanded sufficiently rapidly to meet the growth of expenditure. Tax structures were regressive and tax collecting bureaucracies were sometimes 'antiquated, inefficient and ... corrupt' (Baer 1967, p.10). The insufficiency of revenue was usually overcome by recourse to deficit financing which had inflationary consequences.

In addition to the basic inflationary pressures, Sunkel (1960) identified exogenous inflationary pressures. These included upward movements in the prices of imported goods and services (increases in the prices of oil, fertilisers and foodstuffs, for example) and major increases in public expenditure arising out of natural disasters or political pressures. Finally, there were cumulative inflationary pressures which were induced by inflation itself. These pressures were an increasing function of the rate and extent of inflation and they included the orientation of investment (preference for safe, non-productive investments), expectations, the negative impact of inflation on productivity (including distortions introduced into the price system by price controls) and the lack of export incentives.

For the various structural constraints to give rise to price increases, which in turn led to a rapid and continuous increase in the price level, there had to exist an effective transmission or propagation mechanism which permitted the manifestation of the various inflationary pressures. If various classes or groups in society did not attempt to maintain their relative positions in the face of price increases, the chances of an inflationary spiral being generated would be reduced and the increase in prices would lead to a redistribution of income. In Chile, Sunkel (1960) argued that the propagation mechanism resulted from the inability of the political system to resolve two major struggles of economic interests, namely the distribution of income between different social classes and the distribution of productive resources between the public and the private sectors of the economy. The propagation mechanism was thus seen as:

> ... the ability of the different economic sectors and social groups continually to readjust their real income or expenditure: the wage-earning group through readjustment of salaries, wages and other benefits; private enterprise through price increases, and the public sector through an increase in nominal fiscal expenditure. (Sunkel 1960, p.111)

One of the major components of the propagation mechanism was the budget deficit which was closely related to domestic credit expansion, since public expenditure was not easily reduced and revenue not easily increased. The public-sector deficit thus represented '... the existence of a number of structural problems which preclude the realisation of a balanced-budget policy' (Sunkel 1960, p.122). To the structuralist, the increase in the supply of money was a permissive factor which allowed the inflationary spiral to manifest itself and become cumulative – it was a symptom of the structural rigidities which give rise to the inflationary pressures, rather than the cause of inflation itself. An increase in the supply of money was thus a necessary condition for the rise in the overall level of prices, but it was not a sufficient condition.

As noted above, structuralist analysis had developed in the largely stable international environment of the 1950s–early 1960s. By the early 1970s, however, inflation had become a global problem and, as Seers (1981b, p.2) noted, the 'analysis of inflation in a single nation, however big its economy, can therefore only be partial'.

Seers attempted to sketch the outline of a theory of world inflation with its roots in structuralist analysis. His basic premise was that although structural change at the global level was imperative, it had been impeded by a variety of obstacles, and the resulting price rises had been generalised by propagation mechanisms, including increases in the supply of money.

The *pressures* for structural change included rapid population growth, the political imperatives of rapid social development, the slow growth of food output, the increased dependence on imported oil and the increased dependence on imports of advanced industrial products. The *obstacles* to structural change were imperfections in labour and capital markets, inadequate transportation, the use of taxes for unproductive expenditures and bureaucratic regulations. Finally, the *mechanisms that propagated* inflation were trade unions, professional associations, etc., acting to protect real incomes; monopolies (or oligopolies) in production and services and monetary authorities that accommodated price rises.

For Seers, there were many structural reasons for world inflation and many propagating factors. Monetary expansion played an essential role in sustaining the inflationary spiral, but analysis had to focus on 'political forces that prevent the solution of structural problems and compel monetary expansion' (Seers 1981b, p.11).

The Monetarist View[9]

Monetarists saw inflation as a purely monetary phenomenon, originating in and sustained by expansionary monetary and fiscal policies (government deficit spending, expansionist credit policies and expansionary exchange operations of central banks). The control of inflation required as a necessary and sufficient condition the control of the money supply such that it grew at a rate consistent with the growth of demand for money at stable prices. Specifically, the rate of inflation would be reduced, and concomitant distortions in the economy eliminated, via the curbing of excess demand through monetary and fiscal policies, the control of wage increases and the elimination of overvalued exchange rates.

The monetary model is based on a stable demand function for real money balances. Such balances are demanded for transactions and precautionary purposes and their level is hypothesised to be a function of the level of real income and the opportunity cost of holding money instead of alternative assets which could satisfy at least the precautionary motive. It is further argued that the money supply is exogenous and can be controlled by the monetary authorities (Ayre 1982, p.68). In this model, inflation is the result of the supply of money expanding more rapidly than the demand for money. Individuals spend excess cash in order to maintain their cash balances at the desired level, and in conditions of full employment, prices will rise (see also Section 12.5 below). The empirical evidence from LDCs suggests that the demand function for money is stable, although expected price changes rather than interest rates tend to be of greater significance than in developed economies. Nevertheless, some measure of income remains the main determinant of real money holdings (Ghatak 1981, p.33).

Monetarists did not deny the existence of constraints but they argued that they were not structural or autonomous in nature. They resulted from the price and exchange-rate distortions which were generated by the inflation itself and government attempts to reduce the rate of price increase. For example, they argued that the alleged structural inelasticity of food supplies in fact resulted from the all-too-frequent administrative control of food prices, the result of attempts by governments to protect urban consumers and avoid growing pressures for wage increases. This interference in the operation of market forces had a disincentive effect on food producers, but it was a distortion induced by adminstrative controls and was not inherent in the structure of land ownership. Higher prices for some items, for example food, were necessary to induce an adequate supply, but within the context of the overall control of the money supply and the reallocation of resources through the market mechanism, higher prices for such items were offset by lower prices for others, and hence inflationary pressures were not generated. Monetarists further argued that the slow growth of exports was policy induced rather than structurally induced. Exchange rates were typically overvalued and development efforts 'inward-looking'.

Monetarists thus admitted the existence of constraints but reversed the causal relationship. The bottlenecks in the economy that retarded growth would be eliminated when inflation was brought under control. The majority of monetarists recognised the 'social priority of development' but argued that stable and sustained growth could only be achieved in an environment of monetary stability (Campos 1967). Structuralists, on the other hand, were often accused of favouring inflation as a means of accelerating growth, but in general this was not the case. They were concerned with the problem of making stability compatible with development but argued that price stability could only be achieved through economic growth, which was a long-run process. Short-run stabilisation policies, although effective in reducing the rate of inflation, imposed heavy social and economic costs and retarded the processes of structural change necessary for longer-term growth and development. In effect, structuralists preferred inflation to stagnation, it being regarded as the lesser of two evils.

The concept of 'global monetarism' is discussed in Section 12.4 below.

12.4 Empirical Evidence

Structuralism

An important investigation of one aspect of the structuralist analysis was carried out by Edel (1969) in his study of the alleged food supply bottlenecks in eight Latin American countries. He tested the propositions that (i) food supply lagged behind the required rate of growth, and (ii) that this agricultural lag was associated with inflation, balance of payments difficulties and stagnation. The adequacy of food supply was defined as that rate of autonomous growth of production (resulting from the adoption of new techniques, increases in the labour force and area of production, etc.) sufficient to satisfy demand without any change in relative prices.

Edel found that in Mexico, Brazil and Venezuela, supply outpaced or at least approximately equalled growth in food requirements. Taking into account price changes, five countries with inadequate growth rates (Chile, Colombia, Peru, Uruguay and Argentina) had increasing relative prices and thus inadequate growth could not have been a function of price deterioration. He did not find a perfect relationship between food suply and inflation but the evidence justified the conclusion that:

> ... the direction of the relationship is the one indicated by the structuralist theory that less adequate food production means more inflation, as well as relative rises in the food prices, more food imports, and slower growth in other sectors of the economy. (Edel 1969, pp.135–6)

Furthermore, the degree of price control on foodstuffs did not appear to be related systematically to agricultural performance for the countries studied, whereas there was evidence that land tenure and low productivity were related to one another.[10]

In his study of Brazil, Kahil (1973) analysed four alleged structural constraints. These were the agricultural sector bottleneck, the inadequate mobility of capital, the external sector bottleneck and the effects of rapid urbanisation (increased private- and public-sector demand for goods and services and increased costs of supplying food to the urban areas). He argued that structural weaknesses did not play a significant role in the evolution of the price level over the period studied (1946–64). The aggravation of these structural weaknesses was more an effect than a cause of inflation. Price rises were caused by large and growing public deficits, a too rapid expansion of bank credit in the early period and unnecessarily large and increasingly frequent increases in legal minimum wages at a later stage. These factors interacted in such a way that it was impossible to distinguish cause from effect, and thus the basic causes of inflation appeared to have become mere parts of the structuralist propagation mechanism.

Kahil qualified his monetarist conclusion by arguing that the factors ultimately responsible for inflation were political rather than economic. The two major policy aims of the 1950s were rapid industrialisation and the winning of the allegiance of the urban masses, at the same time serving the interests of other politically important groups (big industrialists, bankers, etc.). Inflation was thus the outcome of the attempt by the state to promote growth and development and grant privileges (albeit temporary and illusory) to mutually antagonistic groups or classes. We discuss the implications of these conclusions below.

Argy (1970) attempted to assess the contribution of structural elements to inflation using data for 22 countries for the period 1958–65. He constructed a variety of indices to test four structural hypotheses – the demand-shift hypothesis (shifts in the composition of demand, as distinct from generalised excess demand, cause upward shifts of the price level), the export instability hypothesis (fluctuations in export earnings will tend to create a long-term upward movement in the price level), the agricultural bottleneck hypothesis and the foreign exchange bottleneck (both discussed above). Two additional variables were included in some of the regressions – the government deficit rate and the rates of change in the money supply.

Argy concluded that the results for the structuralist variables were poor (except for the fact that there was a slight tendency for higher inflation in countries where food prices had risen most relative to the cost of living) but that the monetary variables performed well – 'In every case the addition of a monetary variable to structuralist variables improved substantially the results' (Argy 1970, p.83).

Argy's study clearly showed (as the author himself admitted) the difficulties involved in testing the structuralist position. It is very difficult to specify correctly and construct indicators which adequately encompass the essence of the alleged structuralist constraints. For example, to test the foreign exchange bottleneck, Argy used (i) the average annual percentage change in the terms of trade and (ii) the average import ratio (imports over gross domestic production). But neither of these measures indicate the *capacity* to import and they thus do not provide a satisfactory test of the (*ex ante*) balance of payments constraint. There is also likely to be significant multicollinearity between the independent variables used in the regression analysis.

Monetarism

Harberger's (1963) influential study of Chile covered the period 1939 to 1958, during which inflation was almost continuous and the cost of living index rose over eightfold. Within the monetarist framework, Harberger regressed the annual rate of price change in the cost of living index, upon the percentage change in the money supply during the same year and the preceding one, and upon the percentage change in real income in that year. Expected changes in the cost of holding idle balances were allowed for by introducing past changes in the rate of inflation as an additional independent variable. Wage changes were also included in the regression equation.

The results of the analysis supported the monetarist interpretation, with each of the monetary variables statistically significant and the inclusion of the wages variable failing to increase the overall explanatory power of the monetary variables. The importance of wage changes lay in their significance as 'transmitters' of inflation from one period to the next, responding to the monetary expansion of the past period.

Vogel (1974) extended the Harberger model to sixteen Latin American countries for the period 1950–69. The dependent variable was the consumer price index and the independent variables were money supply (currency plus demand deposits), real income and past changes in the rate of inflation (as a proxy for the expected cost of holding real balances). On the basis of his results, Vogel concluded that:

> The most important result of the present study . . . is that a purely monetarist model, with no structuralist variables, reveals little heterogeneity among Latin American countries, in spite of their extreme diversity. The substantial differences in rates of inflation among these countries cannot under the present model be attributed to structural differences, but must rather be attributed primarily to differences in the behaviour of the money supply. (Vogel 1974, p.113)

In reviewing other work on inflation in Latin America, Vogel noted that very different conclusions about the monetarist–structuralist controversy had been reached from essentially similar findings. He suggested that further work was needed on the determination of the money supply and that structural variables could be added to the model. Even if a purely monetarist model could adequately explain the causes of inflation, stabilisation policies might have to be more than purely monetarist in character, given that rates of inflation took up to two years to adjust to changes in the money supply and that this might be a longer period of austerity than could be tolerated politically by the majority of Latin American regimes.[11]

With respect to the analyses surveyed so far, monetarists can be criticised for treating high correlation between the monetary variables and the inflation rate as evidence of causation, and failing to offer an explanation of the underlying causal relationships that exist between structural constraints, monetary expansion and inflation. Equally, structuralist writers can be criticised on the grounds that they devoted insufficient attention to the nature of the propagation mechanism in general, and the expansion of the money supply in particular (which is necessary, other things being equal, for the manifestation of spiralling price rises). Structuralist assertions that increases in the money supply are merely permissive may tend to obscure the wider socio-economic framework within which this policy option is chosen by, or forced upon, the governments. Both structuralists and monetarists accepted the proposition that changes in the money supply occur in response to political factors, but the basic question remains as to whether these changes permit or are the actual cause of the inflationary process.

Integrating the Monetarist and Structuralist Approaches

A major criticism of structuralism has been that it lacks the theoretical underpinnings needed to compete with the monetarist hypothesis. Wachter (1976) has argued, for example, that structuralism fails to provide a formal model to explain how an increase in the relative price of food leads to an ongoing inflation; that it does not provide a theoretical justification for the assumed downward rigidity of non-food prices; that structuralists do not allow any causal role for demand-pull or expectational factors; and that the testable implications of structuralist hypotheses are not clear.

Wachter developed a reformulated structuralist model in which it is assumed food prices are more flexible than non-food prices. If prices rise in agriculture, even if there is no excess aggregate demand, inflation results in the short run, because prices in non-agricultural sectors do not fall by an equivalent amount. Once inflation becomes anticipated and expectations are validated by monetary and fiscal policy, an ongoing inflation is possible at the equilibrium-expected rate (Wachter 1976, p.136). This inflation rate cannot persist, however, without changes in government policy, specifically an increase in the rate of monetary expansion: '... for the higher inflation rate to be maintained, money must respond; but it is quite possible that the money supply is passive and does respond to higher prices' (p.136).

The monetarist (Harberger) and reformulated structuralist models are tested by Wachter with data from Argentina, Chile, Brazil and Mexico. She concludes that:

The empirical results ... support a broad model of inflation. The findings of significant coefficients with the anticipated signs for the demand-pull and expectational variables in the Harberger and Phillips-curve equations are consistent with the Latin American monetarist argument that excessive aggregate demand is responsible for inflation. However, the reformulated structuralist model is also substantially supported by the finding ... of a significant and positive coefficient for the rate of change in the relative price of food. (Wachter 1976, p.137)

Wachter also tests for the existence of a passive money supply in a two-way regression between prices and money and concludes that, at least for Brazil, Chile and Mexico, the 'structuralist hypothesis of a passive money supply cannot be rejected' (p.137). For Argentina, the results indicated that structural imbalances had an impact on the inflation rate in the short run, but that in the longer run, because the monetary authorities refused to accommodate structural inflation, the existence of structural constraints did not result in a permanently higher rate of inflation.

Bhalla's (1981) approach was to combine the basic Harberger monetarist model with structuralist variables (relative food price changes and import price changes) to form a 'hybrid reduced-form model'. The model is applied to annual time-series data for 29 LDCs covering the period 1956–75. The results indicate that the structural variables are important. The money supply variables are significant in both the Harberger model and the hybrid model, but 'for all of the countries the explanatory power of the monetarist model is considerably increased with the introduction of food supply bottlenecks and import price changes' (p.85).[12]

The major problems of so-called 'hybrid' models of inflation is that they are not adequate tests of structuralist hypotheses. To merely adapt a monetarist model by the addition of a number of proxy variables for structural factors will almost certainly increase the overall statistical 'fit' of the equation. The problem remains, however, of identifying and measuring structural constraints, relating them to the process of growth and change occurring in LDCs, especially with respect to industrialisation, and then constructing a genuinely structuralist model of inflation.

A third example of an attempt to integrate the monetarist and structuralist model is found in the analysis of the fiscal constraint bottleneck by Aghevli and Khan (1978). In this model the fiscal deficit performs the dual role of both the original force and the propagating mechanism in the inflationary process. Having accepted that government deficits perform a major destablising role, the deficit in turn is explained by the fundamental difference in the behaviour of government expenditure and revenue during an inflationary process:

Even if governments fully recognize the need to restrain expenditures during period of inflation, they find it difficult to reduce their commitments in real terms. On the other hand, in contrast to the situation in most developed countries, where nominal revenues often more than keep pace with price increases, in developing countries they lag substantially behind. The contrast arises both because of low nominal income elasticities of tax systems and long lags in tax collection in developing countries. (p.391)

An initial inflationary shock will lead to an expansion of the budget deficit which in turn leads to an expansion of the money supply. Inflation-induced fiscal deficits, explained in terms of the structural constraints on the fiscal system, thus become one of the dynamic forces sustaining inflation in LDCs. The Aghevli and Khan model is monetarist in the sense that the expansion of the money supply leads to inflation, but in contrast to the Harberger-type models, the money supply is no longer exogenous, the fiscal constraint constituting a crucial link in the inflationary process.

The Aghevli and Khan model can be criticised, however, from a structuralist perspective for presenting a somewhat superficial and mechanical explanation of the budget deficit, and of failing to identify the more fundamental determinants of government expenditure and revenue in LDCs.

12.5   Inflation and the Balance of Payments

The Monetary Approach to the Balance of Payments

The persistence of high rates of inflation in many Latin American economies during the 1950s was linked to increasing balance of payments (BOP) difficulties, and precipitated the adoption of stabilisation programmes designed to correct these macroeconomic disequilibria. Once the limits on the temporary financing of balance of payments deficits by running down reserves or borrowing had been exhausted, countries found it necessary to approach the International Monetary Fund (IMF), whose principal function is to assist member countries experiencing serious BOP disequilibria. The means by which the IMF provides support is to assure a member that it can borrow foreign exchange during a specified period of time and up to a specified amount, provided the member adheres to the terms of the borrowing. The conditions that the Fund attaches to its loans usually require the borrowing country to adopt various economic measures, designed to correct the BOP problem and reduce inflation to an acceptable level.[13]

The policy recommendations of the IMF reflected an underlying 'view' of the causes of the LDCs' macro-disequilibria. The economic theory that formed the basis for the Fund's programmes was the monetary theory of the balance of payments. The model developed by Polak (1957), at that time deputy director of the Fund's research department, established the basic conclusions of the monetary approach to the balance of payments (MABOP), and became the basis for the operations of the IMF's country programmes.

The MABOP extends the quantity theory approach to the open economy, and emphasises the role of the balance of payments in achieving an equilibrium between the demand and supply of money. The nominal demand for money is a stable function of nominal income. Real income is assumed to be fixed at the full capacity level of output, so that changes in nominal income involve changes in prices rather than output. In the open economy, the supply of money consists of the sum of domestic credit creation and international reserves. A disequilibrium between the demand and supply of money is removed by some combination of changes in prices, domestic credit creation, and/or international reserves.

The Polak version of the MABOP concentrates on the relationship between changes in reserves and changes in domestic credit creation. A number of assumptions are made in order to highlight the adjustment process. In addition to assuming a fixed exchange rate and international capital immobility, the level of exports is taken to be determined exogenously. Starting from an initial situation of monetary equilibrium, an expansion in the rate of domestic credit creation has the immediate effect of creating excess cash balances. Individuals reduce their surplus cash holdings by increased expenditure, which in the Polak model is spent entirely on imports. The current account deteriorates, reserves decline, and provided the authorities do not 'sterilise' the effect of the change in reserves on total money supply by means of compensating change in domestic credit creation, the disequilibrium is removed by a fall in the supply of money until monetary equilibrium is restored.

The policy implication of Polak's model is that BOP difficulties are caused by excess domestic credit creation: deficit countries should therefore limit their rate of domestic credit creation to a level consistent with a satisfactory BOP outcome. By emphasising the link between external balance and changes in the supply of money, Polak's model directs attention away from the role of changes in the demand for money, prices and nominal income in the adjustment process. The implication is that if excessive domestic credit creation is completely offset by changes in reserves, then the impact on prices and output is negligible.

In the 1960s, an alternative version of the MABOP was developed, which gave more attention to the role of price changes in the adjustment process (Frenkel and Johnson 1976). A distinction is drawn between internationally traded and non-traded goods. With the initial monetary equilibrium disturbed by an increase in domestic credit creation, part of the increased demand is for domestically produced goods. Since, however, the economy is assumed to be operating at or near to its full capacity output level, the result is a rise in the price of non-traded goods. This in turn diverts productive resources from the traded to the non-traded sector, reducing the supply of exports, and worsening the current account. At the same time, the increase in non-traded goods prices may lead to a rise in wages, with further upward pressure on the general price level. The policy requirement is the same as in the Polak model: to reduce the current account deficit and rate of inflation it is necessary to lower the rate of domestic credit creation (or abandon a fixed exchange rate policy).

A third variant of the MABOP, known as 'global monetarism' (Whitman 1975), offers the most direct relation between the domestic inflation rate and the balance of payments. From a global monetarist perspective, it is argued that all countries are 'coparticipants in a common process of world inflation' (Harberger 1978). The world economy had become highly integrated, and the fixed exchange rate regimes, which existed up till the early-1970s, 'operated as the international equivalent of a common (domestic) currency, linking the monetary forces operating in the various countries of the world in the same way that the possession of a common currency brings about a convergence of inflationary trends in the different regions of a nation-state' (Burton 1982, p.23). The world inflation rate is determined by the rate of growth of the world money supply and for a small open economy, with a fixed exchange rate system, the domestic rate of inflation is given exogenously by the world rate of inflation. In Harberger's (1978, p.154) words,

> ... the cause of inflation in Costa Rica or Iran or the Philippines cannot be very different from that of the 'world inflation' so long as they maintain a fixed exchange rate with the major currencies, and so long as they do not introduce dramatic new interferences with the movement of goods and services.

The Structuralist Response

The MABOP has two major implications for inflation analysis: first, the excessive domestic inflation and BOP difficulties are treated as essentially owing to domestic macro-mismanagement; and second, the process of correcting these macro-disequilibria is seen as having no effect on the level of real output in the economy. Both these propositions of the monetary approach to inflation in the open economy have been challenged by structuralists.

As we saw in Section 12.3, the early structuralist literature emphasised the role of the foreign exchange bottleneck in creating BOP difficulties and inflationary pressures. The growth in export earnings was thought to be insufficient to meet the rapidly increasing import needs associated with development, with the availability of foreign exchange acting as the effective constraint on growth. Shortfalls in 'essential' imports in turn had a deleterious effect on the level of domestic economic activity and output.

External influences on the BOP can translate into domestic inflationary pressure in a number of different ways. In the early 1970s, the LDCs were faced with a series of external 'shocks': 'unprecedented global inflation in 1973 and 1974, including the quadrupling of oil prices in 1974, was followed in 1974 and 1975 by the most severe world recession since the

Great Depression of the 1930s' (Cline and Associates 1981, p.1). Whereas previously, rapid inflation had been confined to a relatively small number of LDCs (Brazil, Argentina and Chile in particular), it became a general problem for all LDCs in 1973 and 1974. Attention thus began to be focused on the importance of 'imported inflation' in the inflationary process in LDCs, and attempts were made to identify the channels through which, or the mechanisms by which, such 'external shocks' manifested themselves within the LDCs. The major channels in principle were:

(1) a rise in the price of imported commodities (especially such important items as foodstuffs, oil and capital goods);
(2) a rise in the price of imported services, including international lending, with increases in interest rates being a significant element in imported inflation;
(3) an increase in international borrowing and consequent capital inflows into LDCs, and/or rises in export prices, not offset by rises in import prices, an accumulation of foreign exchange reserves and an increase in the domestic money supply;
(4) forced reduction in imports which caused prices to go up nationally because of supply restrictions;[14]
(5) 'forced' ISI or EOI resulting from a deteriorating current account which could not be externally financed, which raised average costs in the affected sectors and added indirectly to inflationary pressures (Griffith-Jones 1985, pp.10–11).

Bhalla (1981) attempted an empirical investigation of the importance of external inflationary pressures and concluded that the monetary channel was one of the major mechanisms for the transmission of inflation during the period 1972–75:

> External factors seem to have been to a larger extent responsible for the monetary acceleration than were domestic factors. External reserves increased (for most countries) at an unusual rate in 1972 and these increases were systematically related to money supply changes. (Bhalla 1981, p.69)

However, Bhalla argued that the behaviour of import prices was also of crucial importance, accounting for well over half of domestic inflation in 30 LDCs studied for the period 1973–74, and were largely responsible for the fall in inflation in 1975 (p.94):

> The monetarist model of inflation in the thirty developing countries examined . . . indicates that the money changes had a strong and systematic effect on the price level. Structural factors – food bottlenecks and particularly changes in import prices – were also significant. The inflation boom seems indeed to have been imported. (p.95)

Killick (1981a) takes a different view, arguing that 'it is difficult to believe that rising import prices could directly explain more than a modest part of LDC inflation' (p.10). The important point to note, however, is that whatever the relative importance of the external 'shock', its ultimate impact on the inflationary process in the LDC must in part depend on the specific structural features of the individual LDC. The susceptibility of LDCs to imported inflationary pressures depends, *inter alia*, on economic size, level and characteristics of development, degree of industrialisation, structure of trade and 'openness' of economy, availability of technical skills and infrastructure, etc. In addition, Griffith-Jones and Harvey, (1985, p.337) argue:

> ... whatever the mechanisms for transmitting external factors into higher rates of internal inflation, the consequence was frequently that those higher rates were then built into the domestic economy ... a domestic inflationary process which was started or accelerated by external forces became so institutionalised that it could only be reversed with great difficulty.

A persistent balance of payments disequilibrium may lead to devaluation of the nominal exchange rate. The immediate effect of the devaluation will be to increase the cif price of imported items, expressed in domestic currency terms. Since a significant proportion of imports consist of intermediate and capital goods, the higher import costs will increase the costs of production of locally produced final manufactures. The increase in the relative price of traded goods may also lead to corresponding increases in the prices of non-traded goods and services. Resistance on the part of organised labour to a reduction in real income may lead to increased money wages (Schydlowsky 1982).

Devaluation may also have an inflationary impact via an interest rate effect. The initial increase in prices following devaluation will reduce the real volume of bank credit. Firms are therefore forced to resort to other, informal sources of funds where the interest rate will be higher. The cost of working capital is increased, costs of production rise, and the aggregate supply curve is shifted upwards. The result is a decline in real output and increase in the price level (van Wijnbergen 1983; Buffie 1984).

There is empirical evidence to support the belief that devaluation will have inflationary repercussions. Donovan's (1981) cross-section study of a sample of countries following IMF stabilisation programmes during the 1970s found that devaluation directly increased the price level and raised the underlying rate of inflation. Over the three-year period following devaluation, annual inflation rates rose markedly, by about 5 to 7 percentage points on average. Lowinger's (1978) time-series study for Brazil, Colombia, the Philippines and South Korea during 1959–72 shows a positive, statistically significant relation between exchange-rate changes and the rate of inflation. Similar results are reported by Bautista (1982). An exception is Krueger (1978), who concludes that for the ten countries she studied, the contribution of exchange rates was small compared to other types of inflationary pressures. An explanation may be that Krueger was more concerned with the impact of a general liberalisation of the trade regime in the countries concerned. If devaluation is accompanied by a relaxation of import and exchange controls, the rents that accrued previously to those who held import and exchange licences will be reduced and the domestic market price will fall (Roemer 1986). The effect on inflation will depend, therefore, on the degree of devaluation as compared to the extent of market liberalisation.

A longer-term response to persistent BOP difficulties may be to follow a strategy of import substitution. Typically, this increases the dependence on 'essential' imports of intermediate and capital goods, thereby increasing the economy's vulnerability to 'imported inflation' which is passed on via higher costs of production to final prices.[15]

A second important structuralist criticism of the MABOP is directed towards the assumption that the process of adjusting to a BOP disequilibrium has no effect on the level of real output and employment. It is clear, however, that during the adjustment process a decline in the growth of domestic credit may be associated with a reduction in capacity utilisation and increase in unemployment, since prices are not completely flexible downwards.

Structuralists maintain that the adverse effects of monetary contraction on economic activity are likely to be severe (Bruno 1979; Taylor 1981; van Wijnbergen 1982). Khan and Knight (1985) assemble the empirical evidence on the effect of a contractionary monetary policy on the growth of output in LDCs. The results confirm that monetary contraction does tend to have a deflationary effect on real output, particularly in the short run, a 10% reduction in the growth of money or domestic credit reducing the rate of growth of output by just under one %, over one year. It has been well documented that significant declines in real output and employment have been features of recent stabilisation programmes in various Latin American economies (Diaz Alejandro 1981; Foxley 1981, 1983; Corbo and de Melo 1985). In addition, monetary contraction may also affect adversely longer-term growth through its impact on investment. A reduction in the availability of bank financing, combined with an increase in interest-rate costs, is likely to discourage private investment, thereby lowering economic growth.

12.6   The Consequences of Inflation

Inflation and Growth

Much of the discussion of the consequences of inflation in LDCs has focused on the relationship between inflation and economic growth. The early structuralist literature argued that there was a positive relation between inflation and growth, and that inflation was unavoidable if economic growth was to occur. Various rigidities and inelasticities led to the emergence of sectoral disequilibria during the growth process, and because of downward rigidity of factor prices and factor immobility, excess demand and rising relative prices in some sectors were not offset by a decline in prices in the excess supply sectors (Cardoso 1981; Canavese 1982). These 'bottlenecks' led to a build-up of inflationary pressures which had to be 'accommodated' by monetary expansion if potential economic growth was to be realised. Inflation was therefore an inevitable and unavoidable feature of rapid growth.

The case for a positive relationship between inflation and growth was strengthened by a theoretical literature that argued in favour of using inflation as an instrument to increase economic growth in LDCs. One argument for inflationary financing built on the assumption that inflation would increase the overall level of saving and investment by transferring income from wage earners as a group to profit earners as a group. If prices rose faster than wages, and if the propensity to save out of profits was higher than the propensity to save out of wages, the level of real savings and investment would increase and economic growth would be accelerated (Thirlwall 1974, Ch. 4). It must be emphasised that this process of inflationary financed saving rested on the assumption that inflation was unanticipated, and on the inability of wage earners to obtain full compensation for the reduction in their real income.

A further way in which inflation could cause an increase in the growth rate was by redistributing resources from the private to the public sector. Even if inflation was fully anticipated and adjusted for, the operation of the 'inflation tax' would transfer resources to the government.[16] Inflation thus acted as a tax on money, redistributing resources from the private sector to the government sector where they could in principle be used to finance real investment. Provided that the public sector had a higher propensity to save than the private sector, the redistributive effect of inflation would increase aggregate investment and economic growth (Mundell 1965; Aghevli 1977).

The argument that inflation will provide a positive stimulus to economic growth has not gone unchallenged. McKinnon (1973) has argued that inflation is likely to result in a lowering of the real rate of interest, creating a disequilibrium in the capital market. This will cause the supply of investment funds to fall and, as a result, private-sector investment is 'repressed' below its equilibrium level by the limited supply of loanable funds. Therefore, in so far as inflation leads to low real rates of interest and capital market disequilibrium, it retards investment and growth.

Private investment may also be depressed by inflation if the resources transferred to the government would have been used for private-sector investment in the absence of inflation. Furthermore, the increase in public-sector investment may 'crowd out' private investment if it utilises scarce resources that would otherwise be available to the private sector, or if it produces marketable output that competes with private output.[17]

If inflation is both high and variable, the composition of private-sector investment may shift towards quick-yielding financial assets, with a reduction in longer-term investment. The quality of investment in the private sector, therefore, may deteriorate as the rate and variability of inflation increase.

Finally, the argument for inflationary growth must be modified to allow for open-economy considerations (Johnson 1974, 1984). The two-gap model (see Chapters 2 and 5) shows how a developing economy's growth can be constrained by either a domestic savings or foreign exchange gap. If the latter is the effective constraint, then additional domestic savings are redundant in the sense that they cannot be used for investment, since the necessary foreign inputs of capital goods are not available. If the domestic inflation rate exceeds the general rate of world inflation, and if the exchange rate is not perfectly flexible, then inflation will lead to increased demand for imports and a reduction in export supply. The balance of trade will worsen, therefore, and the foreign exchange constraint becomes more severe.

The attempt to test empirically the relationship between inflation and growth has led to inconclusive results. The most straightforward approach has been to examine cross-country data to see if differences in GDP growth rates have had any association with differences in inflation rates. Few of these studies have produced strong statistical results in support of a positive relationship. Dorrance (1966) found some evidence of positive association at low inflation rates, but once inflation exceeded a certain level, rising prices and growth tended to be negatively associated. Similar findings are reported by Thirlwall and Barton (1971). In a later study, Thirlwall (1974) identified an inverted U-shaped relationship in his cross-section data, and suggested that the 'optimum' rate of inflation was below 10%. A more recent study by the International Monetary Fund (1982) examined 112 non-oil developing countries over the period 1969–81, and concluded that, for the most part, 'relatively low inflation rates have been associated with relatively high growth rates and that reductions, or at least relative reductions, in inflation have been associated with an improvement, or relative improvement, in growth rates' (p.134).[18]

The evidence on the relationship between investment and inflation is also inconclusive. Thirlwall's (1974) results showed a negative coefficient between inflation and the aggregate investment ratio in the developing countries. Galbis's (1979) study of cross-section data for 16 Latin American countries during 1961–73 failed to find a significant relationship between the private-sector investment ratio and inflation. When the individual countries were examined using time-series data, the results were mixed. The coefficient of the inflation variable was positive in nine countries (and statistically significant in three of them), and negative in the remaining seven.

Inflation, Distribution and Poverty

What is the likely effect of inflation on other aspects of the development process? The impact of inflation upon particular sectors or groups in the economy will depend in part upon the relative movements in prices during inflation. Inflation is seldom fully anticipated, and even when economic agents do anticipate future inflation, there are often institutional and other constraints preventing them from making the adjustments necessary to preserve their real incomes. A rise in the general rate of inflation is therefore associated with different relative price movements, depending upon the adjustment process in different factor and product markets.

The effect of price inflation on real income depends on the source of income receipts and the ability of the income group concerned to offset the effect of price increases. In the case of wages, many observers have argued that the resistance of organised labour to a reduction in real income standards creates a distributional conflict (Hirschman 1981) which intensifies the relative price oscillations (di Tella 1979), and perpetuates the inflationary process. Kaldor (1983) makes the same point, arguing that the price–wage relationship depends critically on the political strength of labour.

Even when the power of labour is reduced, however, inflation remains a problem for many (largely authoritarian) regimes. Hirschman (1981) attributes this situation both to intersectoral conflicts over distribution (between various groups within the industrial and agricultural sectors, for example) and to intrasectoral conflicts, between different groups within the industrial sector. The struggle over distribution is thus an important element in the propagation mechanism and, as Hirschman (1981, p.201) has noted: 'Inflation . . . is a remarkable invention that permits a society to exist in a situation that is intermediate between the extremes of social harmony and civil war'.

The impact of inflation on the unorganised labour force is more difficult to predict. If the prices of goods and services sold by self-employed informal urban households increase in line with the cost of their consumption purchases, real incomes may be largely unaffected. In the rural sector, landless labourers are likely to suffer a reduction in real income as the price of foodstuffs and other consumption goods increase. Rural households producing a marketed surplus of foodstuffs may gain, if food prices rise more rapidly than the general price level. Inflation may also affect the structure of the labour market, with labour shifting into the unionised and government sectors which offer the best prospects of maintaining real income levels; alternatively, if real incomes fall in the formal sector, workers may attempt to maintain their incomes by undertaking supplementary informal sector activities (Tokman 1983; Lagos and Tokman 1984).

Differences in relative price movements and in the sources of income make it difficult to assess the impact of inflation on income distribution and poverty. Household income distribution data typically record household money income by percentile group. But households with the same money income have different consumption patterns, obtain their income from different sources, and may well face different prices for the same goods. Therefore, to assess the effect of inflation on household income distribution would require detailed information on individual price movements, household income receipts, and household consumption patterns. Similar considerations arise in attempting to assess the impact on poverty levels, since there is often considerable variation in household composition within the poverty percentiles.

Given the methodological and data problems in assessing the impact of inflation on distribution and poverty, it is hardly surprising to find that the empirical evidence is scarce, difficult to interpret and not generalisable. Killick (1981a) briefly surveys a number of empirical studies and concludes that it is more likely than not that inflation will increase inequalities, with the urban poor being especially vulnerable, although the situation would obviously be different if smallholder food farmers were substantial beneficiaries of higher prices.

12.7 IMF Stabilisation Programmes and the 'New Structuralist' Critique

The increasing involvement of LDCs with the IMF during the 1970s led to the emergence of a 'new' structuralist critique of the Fund's stabilisation programmes.[19] While the focus of this critique is centred on the balance of payments policy rather than inflation control, it retains the original structuralist thesis that the characteristics of LDCs will often mean that the application of orthodox stabilisation measures has undesirable and 'perverse' effects. Rather than reinforcing the stabilisation efforts of the authorities, financial reform is likely to be associated with falling output and rising prices (Bruno 1979; Taylor 1983).

The immediate effect of an orthodox stabilisation programme will be to alter certain key relative prices, including the exchange rate, nominal interest rates, and the price of public-sector services. The 'liberalisation' of prices acts as a supply-side shock to the manufacturing sector in particular, raising firms' variable costs (imported inputs, working capital).

The combined effect of limited substitution possibilities in production and the oligopolistic structures of the modern industrial structure in many LDCs (see Kirkpatrick *et al.* 1984, Ch. 3) will be that prices are more likely to be determined on a cost-of-production basis, rather than by competitive forces. Increases in input costs are passed on, therefore, on a mark-up basis.

Inflationary pressures may also be increased via the effect of monetary reforms on the balance of payments. The potential of devaluation to exercise an upward pressure on prices has already been considered. In addition, changes in the exchange rate and domestic interest rates may result in a sudden inflow of short-term capital from abroad which, in the absence of an effective sterilisation mechanism, will increase the domestic money supply (Mathieson 1979; Diaz Alejandro 1981).

The empirical evidence on the economic consequences of Fund-supported adjustment programmes in LDCs appears to validate the structuralist argument.[20] Having reviewed various studies of pre- and post-stabilisation programme performance in the main macroeconomic variables (balance of payments, inflation, growth rate), Killick (1984, p.250) concluded that:

> The general outcome of the evidence surveyed so far is to throw doubt on the ability of Fund programmes to bring countries to BOP viability, to promote liberalisation and to reduce inflation . . . if (as we probably should) we confine ourselves to the statistically significant effects of Fund programmes, then they appear to make little difference to anything.

Cross-country studies of inflation point to a general inability of Fund programmes to bring down inflation rates. Reichmann and Stillson (1978) used quarterly data for 29 LDCs covering the period 1963–72 to compare inflation performance before and after the introduction of a programme and found that only seven countries showed a statistically significant reduction in the eight quarters following the programme. Donovan (1982) found that over the period 1971–80 the annual rate of consumer inflation rose following the adoption of stabilisation programmes in LDCs. Krueger (1978, p.229) similarly reports little success in lowering inflation in the countries studied in her project. Kirkpatrick and Onis (1985) attempt to identify a systematic pattern in the behaviour of the inflation rate in a sample of Fund programmes, by relating inflation performance to selected indicators of the economic structure of the sample economies. The success of a stabilisation programme in lowering the inflation rate is found to be (negatively) correlated with the level of urbanisation and the degree of dependence on imports of intermediate and capital good imports. These results are interpreted as confirming the structuralist hypothesis that, given the structural characteristics of a 'typical' semi-industrialised LDC, the combined effect of monetary restraint and devaluation policies is likely to be an intensification of inflationary pressures.

12.8 Conclusions: Towards a General Theory of Inflation for LDCs

Inflation is a problem endemic in most LDCs. The attempt to identify the causes of inflation still generates much controversy and the alleged 'cures' continue to impose high economic costs through reductions in output and employment.

The initial debate over the causes and consequences of inflation centred on the Latin American experience and was in part responsible for the evolution and development of the structuralist school of thought. Structuralism has exerted great influence throughout the LDCs, although almost totally ignored, until recently, in developed, industrialised economies, but the relevance of the structuralist model of inflation to individual LDCs is not always obvious and the attempt to generalise this model is not always successful.

It could be argued, for example, that the emphasis placed by structuralist writers on two or three specific bottlenecks and their presentation of a somewhat rigid and mechanical analysis of the operation of those bottlenecks is easy to refute with specific examples and presents a misleading interpretation of policy choice in LDCs. In principle, all structural constraints are in a fundamental (though restricted) sense 'policy induced' in that they are not immutable and can be removed or eased if the 'correct' policies are chosen. For example, the agricultural sector bottleneck can be broken or alleviated by land and agrarian reform; the foreign exchange constraint can be alleviated by the elimination of non-essential imports, the promotion of exports, and so on.

But within any given socio-political environment, governments are constrained with respect to the policy options that are *actually* open to them. A government consisting of, or dominated by, landed interests is, other things being equal, unlikely to pursue a policy of radical land redistribution. Politically influential middle- and upper-income groups are hardly likely to agree voluntarily to programmes that restrict the import or domestic production of durable consumer goods. The inability or unwillingness of governments to act in a manner consistent with the elimination of these constraints or bottlenecks implies that they are 'policy induced' in the sense indicated above, but that nevertheless they are the result of particular economic, political, social and institutional structures. The concept of a structural constraint cannot be divorced from the specific socio-political and historical framework within which it is operative.

From this perspective, some would argue that what is needed is a broadly based structural analysis of inflation, specific to each country, and encompassing a wide range of potential bottlenecks. Myrdal (1968, pp.1928–9), for example, argues that bottlenecks in such sectors as electricity generation, fuel, imported raw materials, transport, repair facilities and credit facilities are all important in generating inflationary pressures. The problem with such an approach (and with Seers's 'global structuralism') is that the inclusion of so many variables reduces the explanatory power of the model and provides only limited guidance to policy makers.

The debate between the different schools of thought has largely focused on the *causes* of inflation. Most structuralists would accept that an increase in the supply of money was necessary for the manifestation of an inflationary spiral but not a sufficient condition. At the same time, structuralists would argue that the control of the money supply was not a sufficient condition for the elimination of inflation. It has been argued that this is not a logically consistent perspective (Addison *et al.* 1980) and that, rather, we should speak of the proximate and fundamental causes of inflation.

> The proximate determinants of inflation are the direct causes of an inflationary situation; by the fundamental determinants of inflation are meant those factors which themselves bring about the occurrence of the proximate determinants. (Addison *et al.* 1980, p.147)

From this perspective, monetarists are mainly concerned with the issue of the proximate causes of inflation, the most important of which is argued to be monetary expansion in excess of real income growth. Structuralists, on the other hand, are concerned with the fundamental determinants, that is, those factors responsible for monetary growth itself. Put another way, monetarists view monetary growth as an exogenous variable whereas structuralists see it as endogenous (itself in need of explanation).

Most structuralist authors (for example, Seers 1981a) now attach considerable importance to monetary and fiscal policy, and countries undergoing profound structural change in particular require 'prudent short-term economic and financial management' (Griffith-Jones and Harvey 1985, p.346). Issues relating to the short- and medium-term macroeconomic management of LDCs have until recently been neglected particularly by structuralist writers, and the latter's greater recognition of the importance of these matters may well lead to a better appreciation of the monetarist perspective (although not necessarily to an acceptance of monetarist policy prescriptions!). As Seers (1981a, p.9) argued:

> ... neither structuralist nor monetarist explanations are adequate by themselves, and we need to draw on both to explain inflation. A government strong enough to suppress some of the propagating factors is a necessary but

not a sufficient condition for slowing down inflation. In particular monetary policy in itself will not eliminate inflationary pressures: it merely determines what its effects will be — price rises or social conflict, or some combination of the two.

It is perhaps too soon to look for real convergence between structuralist and monetarist perspectives, but the acceptance by the former of the importance of monetary policy, and the recognition by some economists sympathetic to the latter that 'there is an element of superficiality in monetarist explanations, which fail to examine the political circumstances which result in excess money creation' (Killick 1981a, p.16), hold out real hope for constructive dialogue between the two schools of thought and greater understanding of the causes of, and remedies for, inflation in LDCs in the future.

Notes

1. This chapter draws heavily on Kirkpatrick and Nixson (forthcoming).
2. More detailed data on both weighted average and medium rates of inflation for different groupings of LDCs are given in IMF (1985), Tables 10 and 11.
3. The data on price increase in LDCs should be treated with caution. Data are limited, and those that are available often have severe limitations. The majority of LDCs do not compile GNP deflators so that cost of living indices and/or indices of wholesale prices are frequently the only price series available. Both of these measures have serious defects. The wholesale price index is frequently heavily weighted with the price of imports and exports, which tend to be domestic equivalents of international prices rather than measures of domestic prices, while the cost of living index is usually based upon a limited sample of goods and services purchased in the major urban areas and is thus unrepresentative of the consumption patterns of the majority of the population located in smaller urban centres and rural areas. In practice, cost of living indices are usually employed as they are often the only measure available or are the least unsatisfactory of the measures of domestic price increases available.
4. Discussions of inflation theory and current controversies in the context of the advanced industrialised economies can be found in Hirsch and Goldthorpe (1978); Jackman, Mulvey and Trevithick (1982); Frisch (1983); Artis (1984).
5. Concepts such as 'employment' and 'unemployment' imply a homogeneous, mobile, adequately trained, wage-earning labour force willing and able to work and responding to incentives. But Streeten (1972, Ch. 5, p.55) argued that 'In a society of isolated communities, some of them apathetic or with religious prejudices against certain kinds of work, illiterate and unused to co-operation, the notion "Labour Force" does not make sense'.
6. However, as Hirschman (1965) noted, structuralism is a label that can be appropriated by all. Thus the current interest of the IMF in supply-side

market liberalisation policies has been labelled as 'a form of structuralism using orthodox instruments' (Foxley 1981, p.197).

7. The price increase stemming from the bottleneck is not a once-and-for-all change in relative prices, leading to a reallocation of resources and no change in the overall price level. Rather, it may trigger off an inflationary spiral: 'Price increases that, in a different institutional setting, would be confined to a few items and carry their cure with them, will in an underdeveloped country tend to spread to other items and be self-defeating' (Myrdal 1968, p.1929).

8. Balogh (1961, p.57) argued that it was not accurate to state that the owners of the latifundia and minifundia acted irrationally. Large-scale landowners were interested in the maximisation of their incomes over time, constrained by the minimisation of effort and risk (both economic and political); the small farmers and share croppers had little interest in improvement: 'Their lack of capital and access to credit at reasonable terms makes risks connected with improvement unbearably high. Should anything go wrong, even their wretched existence would be jeopardized'.

9. It is recognised that monetarism is not monolithic and that there is 'a variety of monetarist analyses and models, with differing implications for the conduct of government policy' (Burton 1982, p.31). Nevertheless, there are 'certain basic ingredients that are common to all brands of monetarism' (p.15).

10. Myrdal (1968, pp.1257–8) commented: 'Prices of agricultural products and government price policies play, of course, a vital role in determining the course of agricultural output in the West, and naturally Western economists who happen to touch on the problems of underdeveloped countries often naively assume that these countries could stimulate agricultural production by raising farm prices. Western experts who have studied the South Asian agricultural situation are more careful. Like their South Asian colleagues, they do not count much on price support as a means of raising agricultural production'.

11. This argument perhaps understates the case. Output is likely to remain depressed and unemployment high for an even longer period, thus increasing the economic and social costs of orthodox stabilisation policies. In addition, it is not certain that Vogel's regression results justified the conclusion he reached. One critic argued that monetarists would not defend the use of the same monetarist model to every Latin American country, that there were significant differences in the inflationary process in Latin America and that what was needed was a detailed comparative analysis of different groups of countries over some given time period (see Betancourt 1976). Other monetarist analyses are surveyed in Killick (1981a) and Ghatak (1981).

12. This model has also been tested with time-series data from Turkey (Onis 1983). The import price variable is important, as is the price expectations variable. The model is related to changes in the character of ISI over the period 1950–79, and performs well as a 'structuralist' explanation of inflation for the Turkish economy, as bottlenecks in the economy are aggravated by continuous and more complex ISI.

13. Misgivings about the 'conditionality' attached to the adjustment loans made

by the IMF during the 1950s gave rise to the general structuralist critique, of which the analysis of inflation was an important part.

14. Recent research into the causes of LDCs' BOP disequilibria provides support for the structuralist argument. Dell and Lawrence's (1980) detailed study of the ways in which LDCs adjusted to the oil crisis of 1974–75 found that the majority had been forced to compress 'developmental' imports below the level normally required at current levels of activity.

15. The relationship between import-subsituting industrialisation and inflation is discussed in detail in Kirkpatrick and Nixson (1976, pp.158–62); Kirkpatrick and Onis (1985).

16. The inflation tax is equivalent to the real income foregone by the private sector in maintaining its level of real cash balances constant. Since money balances must be accumulated at the same rate as the rate of inflation, the rate of tax is equal to the rate of inflation.

17. An equally plausible hypothesis is that public and private investment are complementary, and that public-sector investment in infrastructure and the provision of public goods enhances the possibilities of private investment.

18. Other empirical studies are: Glezakos 1978; Hanson 1980; Edwards 1983.

19. The IMF's involvement with LDCs during the 1970s is examined in Killick (1984); Foxley (1983) offers a critical appraisal from a structuralist perspective of the Fund's involvement with the Latin American economies.

20. There are serious difficulties in measuring performance in terms of a limited number of quantitative indicators. Ideally, one would wish to compare post-programme performance with the hypothetical no-programme results. The problems of devising appropriate performance criteria are considered in Donovan (1983).

References

Addison, J.T., Burton, J. and Torrance, T.S. (1980) 'On the causes of inflation', *The Manchester School*, Vol. XLVIII, No. 2, June.

Aghevli, B.B., (1977) 'Inflationary finance and growth', *Journal of Political Economy*, Vol. 85, No. 6, December.

Aghevli, B. and Khan, M. (1978) 'Government budget deficits and inflationary process on developing countries', *IMF Staff Papers*, Vol. 25, pp. 383–416.

Argy, V. (1970) 'Structural inflation in developing countries', *Oxford Economic Papers*, Vol. 22, No. 1, March.

Arndt, H.W. (1985) 'The origins of structuralism', *World Development*, Vol. 13, No. 2, February.

Artis, M.J. (1984) *Macroeconomics*, Clarendon Press.

Ayre, P.C.I. (1982) 'Money, inflation and growth', in S. Ghatak, *Monetary Economics in Developing Countries*, Macmillan.

Baer, W. (1967) 'The inflation controversy in Latin America: a survey', *Latin American Research Review*, Spring.

Balogh, T. (1961) 'Economic policy and the price system', *UN Economic Bulletin for Latin America*, March. Reprinted in Balogh, T. (1974) *The Economics of Poverty*, 2nd edn, Weidenfeld and Nicolson.

Bautista, R.M. (1982) 'Exchange rate variations and export competitiveness in less developed countries under generalised floating', *Journal of Development Studies*, Vol. 18, No. 3, April.

Betancourt, R.R. (1976) 'The dynamics of inflation in Latin America: comment', *American Economic Review*, Vol. 66, No. 4, September.

Bhalla, S.S. (1981) 'The transmission of inflation into developing countries', in W.R. Cline (1981).

Bruno, M. (1979) 'Stabilization and stagflation in a semi-industrialized economy', in R. Dornbusch and J.A. Frenkel (eds.), *International Economic Policy: Theory and Evidence*, The Johns Hopkins University Press.

Buffie, E. (1984) 'Financial repression, the new structuralists, and stabilization policy in semi-industrialized economies', *Journal of Development Economics*, Vol. 14, No. 3, April.

Burton, J. (1982) 'The varieties of monetarism and their policy implications', *The Three Banks Review*, No. 134, June.

Campos, R. de O. (1967) *Reflections on Latin American Development*, University of Texas Press.

Canavese, A.J. (1982) 'The structuralist explanation in the theory of inflation', *World Development*, Vol. 10, No. 7, July.

Cardoso, E.A. (1981) 'Food supply and inflation', *Journal of Development Economics*, Vol. 8, pp. 269–84.

Cline, W.R. and Associates (1981) *World Inflation and the Developing Countries*, The Brookings Institution.

Cline, W.R. and Weintraub, S. (eds) (1981) *Economic Stabilization in Developing Countries*, The Brookings Institution.

Corbo, V. and de Melo, J. (eds) (1985) 'Liberalization with stabilization in the Southern Bone of Latin America', Special Issue of *World Development*, Vol. 13, No. 8, August.

Dell, S. and Lawrence, R. (1980) *The Balance of Payments Adjustment Process in Developing Countries*, Pergamon Press.

Diaz Alejandro, C. (1981) 'Southern cone stabilization plans', in W. Cline and S. Weintraub (eds) (1981).

di Tella, G. (1979) 'Price oscillations, oligopolistic behaviour and inflation: the Argentine case', *World Development*, Vol. 7, No. 11/12, November/December.

Donovan, D.J. (1981) 'Real responses associated with exchange rate action in the upper credit tranche stabilization programs', *IMF Staff Papers*, Vol. 28, pp. 698–727.

Donovan, D. (1982) 'Macroeconomic performance and adjustment under fund-supported programs: the experience of the "seventies"', *IMF Staff Papers*, Vol. 29, pp. 171–203.

Donovan, D. (1983) 'Measuring macroeconomic performance', *Finance and Development*, Vol. 20, No. 2, June.

Dorrance, G.S. (1966) 'Inflation and growth: the statistical evidence', *IMF Staff Papers*, Vol. 13, pp. 82–101.

Edel, M. (1969) *Food Supply and Inflation in Latin America*, Praeger.

Edwards, S. (1983) 'The short-run relation between growth and inflation in Latin America: comment', *American Economic Review*, Vol. 73, No. 3, June.

Felix, D. (1961) 'An alternative view of the "monetarist" – "structuralist" controversy', in A.O. Hirschman (ed.), *Latin American Issues: Essays and Comments*, The Twentieth Century Fund, New York.

Foxley, A. (1981) 'Stabilization policies and their effects on employment and income distribution: a Latin American perspective', in W. Cline and S. Weintraub (eds) (1981).

Foxley, A. (1983) *Latin American Experiments in Neo-Conservative Economics*, University of California Press.

Frenkel, J.A. and Johnson, H.G. (eds) (1976) *The Monetary Approach to the Balance of Payments*, George Allen and Unwin.

Frisch, H. (1983) *Theories of Inflation*, Cambridge University Press.

Galbis, V. (1979) 'Money, investment and growth in Latin America, 1961–1973', *Economic Development and Cultural Change*, Vol. 27, No. 3, April.

Ghatak, S. (1981) *Monetary Economics in Developing Countries*, Macmillan.

Glezakos, C. (1978) 'Inflation and growth: a reconsideration of the evidence from the LDCs', *The Journal of Developing Areas*, Vol. 12, No. 2, January.

Griffith-Jones, S. (1985) 'Introduction', in S. Griffith-Jones and C. Harvey (eds), *World Prices and Development*, Gower.

Griffith-Jones, S. and Harvey, C. (eds) (1985) *World Prices and Development*, Gower.

Hanson, J.A. (1980) 'The short-run relation between growth and inflation in Latin America: a quasi-rational or consistent expectations approach', *American Economic Review*, Vol. 70, No. 5, December.

Harberger, A.C. (1963) 'The dynamics of inflation in Chile', in C. Christ et al., *Measurement in Economics: Studies in Mathematical Economics and Econometrics in Memory of Yehudi Grunfeld*, Stanford University Press.

Harberger, A.C. (1978) 'A primer on inflation', *Journal of Money, Credit and Banking*, Vol. 10, No. 4, November. Reprinted in Coats Jr. W.L. and Khatkhate, D.R. (eds) (1980) *Money and Monetary Policy in Less Developed Countries: A Survey of Issues and Evidence*, Pergamon Press.

Hirsch, F. and Goldthorpe, J.H. (1978) *The Political Economy of Inflation*, Martin Robertson.

Hirschman, A.O. (1965) *Journeys Toward Progress*, Anchor Books.

Hirschman, A.O. (1981) 'The social and political matrix of inflation: elaborations on the Latin American experience', in *Essays in Trespassing: Economics to Politics and Beyond*, Cambridge University Press.

International Monetary Fund (1982) *World Economic Outlook: A Survey by the Staff of the IMF*, Occasional Paper No. 9.

International Monetary Fund (1984) *Annual Report, 1984*.

International Monetary Fund (1985) *World Economic Outlook, 1985*.

Jackman, R. Mulvey, C. and Trevithick, J. (1982) *The Economics of Inflation*, 2nd edn, Martin Robertson.

Jameson, K.P. (1986) 'Latin American structuralism: a methodological perspective', *World Development*, Vol. 14, No. 2, February.

Jansen, K. (ed.) (1983) *Monetarism, Economic Crisis and the Third World*, Frank Cass.

Johnson, O.E.G. (1974) 'Credit controls as instruments of development policy in the light of economic theory', *Journal of Money, Credit and Banking*, Vol. 6, No. 1, February.

Johnson, O.E.G. (1984) 'On growth and inflation in developing countries', *IMF Staff Papers*, Vol. 31, pp. 636–60.

Johnson, S. and Salop, J. (1980) 'Distributional aspects of stabilization programs in developing countries', *IMF Staff Papers*, Vol. 27, pp. 1–23.

Kahil, R. (1973) *Inflation and Economic Development in Brazil, 1946–1963*, Clarendon Press.

Kaldor, N. (1983) 'Devaluation and adjustment in developing countries', *Finance and Development*, Vol. 20, No. 2, June.

Khan, M.S. and Knight, M.D. (1983) 'Determinants of current account balances of non-oil developing countries in the 1970s: an empirical analysis', *IMF Staff Papers*, Vol. 30, pp. 819–42.

Khan, M.S. and Knight, M.D. (1985) 'Fund-supported adjustment programmes and economic growth', *Occasional Paper* 41, International Monetary Fund.

Killick, T. (1981a) 'Inflation in developing countries: an interpretive survey', *ODI Review*, No. 1.

Killick, T. (1981b) *Policy Economics: A Textbook of Applied Economics on Developing Countries*, Heinemann.

Killick, T. (ed.) (1984) *The Quest for Economic Stabilisation*, Heinemann Educational Books.

Kirkpatrick, C. and Nixson, F. (forthcoming) 'Inflation in Less Developed Countries', in N. Gemmell (ed.), *Surveys in Development Economics*, Basil Blackwell.

Kirkpatrick, C. and Nixson, F. (1976) 'The origins of inflation in less developed countries: a selective review', in M. Parkin and G. Zis (eds), *Inflation in Open Economies*, Manchester University Press.

Kirkpatrick, C., Lee, N. and Nixson, F. (1984) *Industrial Structure and Policy in Less Developed Countries*, George Allen and Unwin.

Kirkpatrick, C. and Onis, Z. (1985) 'Industrialisation as a structural determinant of inflation performance in IMF stabilisation programmes in less developed countries', *Journal of Development Studies*, Vol. 21, No. 3, April.

Krueger, A.O. (1978) *Liberalization Attempts and Consequences*, Ballinger.

Laidler, D. and Parkin, M. (1975) 'Inflation – a survey', *Economic Journal*, Vol. 85, No. 340, December.

Lagos, R. and Tokman, V.E. (1984) 'Monetarism, employment and social stratification', *World Development*, Vol. 12, No. 1, January.

Lowinger, T.C. (1978) 'Domestic inflation and exchange rate changes: the less developed countries' case', *Weltwirtschaftliches Archiv*, Vol. 114, pp. 85–100.

McKinnon, R. (1973) *Money and Capital in Economic Development*, The Brookings Institution.

Mathieson, D.J. (1979) 'Financial reform and capital flows in a developing economy', *IMF Staff Papers*, Vol. 26.

Mundell, R. (1965) 'Growth stability and inflationary finance', *Journal of Political Economy*, Vol. 73, No. 2, April.

Myrdal, G. (1968) *Asian Drama*, Penguin Books.

Onis, Z. (1983) *Inflation, Structural Change and IMF Stabilisation Programmes in a Semi-Industrialised Economy: The Case of Turkey, 1950–1979*, PhD, University of Manchester, Mimeo.

Polak, J.J. (1957) 'Monetary analysis of income formation and payments problems', *IMF Staff Papers*, Vol. 6, pp. 1–50.

Reichmann, T.M. and Stillson, R. (1978) 'Experience with programs of balance of payments adjustment: stand-by arrangements in the higher tranches 1963–72', *IMF Staff Papers*, Vol. 25.

Roemer, M. (1986) 'Simple analytics of segmented markets: what case for liberalization?', *World Development*, Vol. 14, No. 3, March.

Schydlowsky, D.M. (1982) 'Alternative approaches to short-term economic management in developing countries', in T. Killick (ed.), *Adjustment and Financing in the Developing World: the Role of the IMF*, IMF and Overseas Development Institute.

Seers, D. (1964) 'Inflation and growth: the heart of the controversy', in W. Baer and I. Kerstenetzky (eds), *Inflation and Growth in Latin America*, Irwin.

Seers, D. (1981a) 'Inflation: the Latin American experience', *IDS Discussion Paper*, DP 168, November, Mimeo.

Seers, D. (1981b) 'Inflation: a sketch for a theory of world inflation', *IDS Discussion Paper*, DP 169, November, Mimeo.

Streeten, P. (1972) *The Frontiers of Development Studies*, Macmillan.

Sunkel, O. (1960) 'Inflation in Chile: an unorthodox approach', *International Economic Papers*, No. 10.

Taylor, L. (1981) 'IS–LM in the tropics: diagramatics of the new structuralist macro-critique', in W.R. Cline and S. Weintraub (eds), *Economic Stabilization in Developing Countries*, The Brookings Institution.

Taylor, L. (1983) *Structuralist Macroeconomics*, Harper and Row.

Thirlwall, A.P. (1974) *Inflation, Saving and Growth in Developing Economies*, Macmillan.

Thirlwall, A.P. and Barton, C.A. (1971) 'Inflation and growth: the international evidence', *Banca Nazionale del Lavoro*, No. 98, September.

Thorp, R. (1971) 'Inflation and the financing of economic development', in K. Griffin (ed.), *Financing Development in Latin America*, Macmillan.

Tokman, V.C. (1983) 'The influence of the urban informal sector on economic inequality', in F. Stewart (ed.), *Work, Income and Inequality*, Macmillan.

Van Wijnbergen, S. (1982) 'Stagflationary effects of monetary stabilisation policies : a quantitative analysis of South Korea', *Journal of Development Economics*, Vol. 10, pp. 133–69.

Van Wijnbergen, S. (1983) 'Credit policy, inflation and growth in a financially repressed economy', *Journal of Development Economics*, Vol. 13, Nos. 1–2, August–October.

Vogel, R.C. (1974) 'The dynamics of inflation in Latin America 1950–1969', *American Economic Review*, Vol. 64, March.

Wachter, S. (1976) *Latin American Inflation*, D.C. Heath and Company.

Whitman, M. (1975) 'Global monetarism and the monetary approach to the balance of payments', *Brookings Papers on Economic Activity*, 3.

Author Index

Subject Index